COMPUTER METHODS FOR CIRCUIT ANALYSIS AND DESIGN

COMPUTER METHODS FOR CIRCUIT ANALYSIS AND DESIGN

JIRI VLACH

Department of Electrical Engineering
University of Waterloo
Waterloo, Ontario, Canada

KISHORE SINGHAL

Department of Systems Design
University of Waterloo
Waterloo, Ontario, Canada

Van Nostrand Reinhold Electrical/Computer Science and Engineering Series

VNR VAN NOSTRAND REINHOLD COMPANY
New York

Library of Congress Catalog Card Number: 82-16018
ISBN: 0-442-28108-0

Manufactured in the United States of America

Published by Van Nostrand Reinhold Company Inc.
115 Fifth Avenue
New York, New York 10003

Van Nostrand Reinhold Company Limited
Molly Millars Lane
Wokingham, Berkshire RG11 2PY, England

Van Nostrand Reinhold
480 La Trobe Street
Melbourne, Victoria 3000, Australia

Macmillan of Canada
Division of Canada Publishing Corporation
164 Commander Boulevard
Agincourt, Ontario M1S 3C7, Canada

15 14 13 12 11 10 9 8 7 6 5 4

Library of Congress Cataloging in Publication Data

Vlach, Jiri.
Computer methods for circuit analysis and design.

(Van Nostrand Reinhold electrical/computer science and engineering series)
Bibliography: p.
Includes index.
1. Electronic circuits. 2. Electronic circuit design —Data processing. I. Singhal, Kishore. II. Title. III. Series.
TK7867.V58 1983 621.3815′3 82-16018
ISBN 0-442-28108-0

Van Nostrand Reinhold
Electrical/Computer Science and Engineering Series
Sanjit Mitra—Series Editor

HANDBOOK OF ELECTRONIC DESIGN AND ANALYSIS PROCEDURES USING PROGRAMMABLE CALCULATORS, by Bruce K. Murdock

COMPILER DESIGN AND CONSTRUCTION, by Arthur B. Pyster

SINUSOIDAL ANALYSIS AND MODELING OF WEAKLY NONLINEAR CIRCUITS, by Donald D. Weiner and John F. Spina

APPLIED MULTIDIMENSIONAL SYSTEMS THEORY, by N. K. Bose

MICROWAVE SEMICONDUCTOR ENGINEERING, by Joseph F. White

INTRODUCTION TO QUARTZ CRYSTAL UNIT DESIGN, by Virgil E. Bottom

DIGITAL IMAGE PROCESSING, by William B. Green

SOFTWARE TESTING TECHNIQUES, by Boris Beizer

LIGHT TRANSMISSION OPTICS, Second editon, by Dietrich Marcuse

REAL TIME COMPUTING, edited by Duncan Mellichamp

HARDWARE AND SOFTWARE CONCEPTS IN VLSI, edited by Guy Rabbat

MODELING AND IDENTIFICATION OF DYNAMIC SYSTEMS, by N. K. Sinha and B. Kuszta

COMPUTER METHODS FOR CIRCUIT ANALYSIS AND DESIGN, by Jiri Vlach and Kishore Singhal

HANDBOOK OF SOFTWARE ENGINEERING, edited by C. R. Vick and C. V. Ramamoorthy

SWITCHED CAPACITOR CIRCUITS, by Phillip E. Allen and Edgar Sanchez-Sinencio

SOFTWARE SYSTEM TESTING AND QUALITY ASSURANCE, by Boris Beizer

Preface

The general area covered by this book are appropriate portions of circuit theory and the mathematical and computational techniques required for computer aided analysis and design of electronic circuits. Details on the material can be found in the unnumbered chapter on Motivation which precedes the Table of Contents and gives the reader a clear picture of the relevance of various methods covered.

The book has 17 chapters. The first 10 concentrate on the theory and computational methods associated with linear circuits. Chapters 11, 12, and 13 cover material required for the analysis of nonlinear circuits, while Chapter 14 shows that the linear methods discussed in the earlier chapters apply to the analysis of digital and switched-capacitor networks. The remaining chapters deal with the design of both linear and nonlinear circuits. In particular, Chapter 15 is a tutorial review of recent developments in optimization theory and Chapter 16 is a review of methods for steady state analysis of periodically excited networks. The book is concluded with illustrative computer-aided design examples in Chapter 17.

About 60% of the book is suitable for a second or third undergraduate course in circuit theory. The whole book is suitable for graduate courses or as a self-study reference for scientists and engineers who seek information in this particular field. It is assumed that the reader is familiar with sophomore-level calculus, algebra, computer programming, and circuit theory, but profound knowledge is not expected and the material is reviewed before going into details. Sections requiring additional background are marked by an asterisk in the Table of Contents.

This text has been used for several years at the University of Waterloo for teaching a fourth-year undergraduate course and for graduate courses in electrical engineering. The selection of topics for a particular course depends on the instructor and the background of the students, but the following table may assist in the choice of topics for typical one-term undergraduate courses which meet for either two or three hours per week:

	Cover Sections		
Chapter	2 hours/week	3 hours/week ADD	Skip Sections or Material
1	all	all	0
2	1–6	7	sparse matrices
3	1, 2, 7	same	3–6, 8, 9
4	1, 4, 5	2, 3	two-graph formulations and their application
5	all	all	0
6	1–4, parts of 5	remaining 5	second-order derivatives
7	1, 6	2, 3 (optional)	4, 5, 7, 8, 9
8	0	0	all
9	1–4	same	0
10	0	0	all
11	1–4	same	5
12	1–3	4	5, 6
13	1, 3	same	2, 4, 5, 6
14	1–3 (optional)	same	switched capacitors
15	1–4	same	5, 6, 7
16	0	0	all
17	demonstration	same	

In graduate courses, the instructor would go through all sections without asterisk and select more difficult subjects according to the outline of his course.

The book has two sets of bibliographies. Any material specifically referred to within the text is numbered and the reference is found at the end of the chapter. General references that provide supplemental coverage are given in a special section at the end of the book. In some cases, references are given to applicable state-of-the-art computer software. Wherever relevant, simple computer codes are given for the algorithms within the various chapters. Routines suitable for instructional and production programs are given in Appendices D and E.

Appendix D gives the listing and description of a program for the *analysis* of linear networks. It has many features which are not generally available in standard packages and implements most of the material discussed in the first 10 chapters. Appendix E gives the listing and description of a sparse matrix package. The programs and the descriptions will be periodically updated and will be available, on tape, to the schools adopting the book as a text.

Larger, realistic examples given in the book were solved by the Waterloo Analysis and Design program, WATAND. It is an interactive package with advanced graphic capability and was developed at Waterloo. Many of our colleagues, present and past, have contributed to its development.

The authors would like to thank their colleagues and students for many comments and suggestions. Our thanks go especially to Professors H. K. Kesavan, S. G. Chamberlain and P. R. Bryant of the University of Waterloo, Professor N. K. Bose of the University of Pittsburgh, Professor S. K. Mitra of the University of California, and Dr. A. E. Ruehli of IBM for constructive comments on the draft of this text. Thanks are due to Martin Vlach who implemented and tested some of the algorithms and helped with the examples.

Jiri Vlach
Kishore Singhal

Motivation

A reader with a new book in his hands usually asks himself several questions. One of them—what is the book about?—is often answered by the title. If this is not sufficient, he may glance through the contents to get an idea about the material covered.

Although important, this is not the only question. Much more important is the question: Why should I read it? The answers are usually neither in the preface nor in the contents. In order to provide a better understanding, we are starting the book with this section on motivation.

Until about 20 years ago, computational methods found little use in the analysis and design of networks. In those days, a skilled designer could synthesize the simple networks he dealt with with only minimal computational effort, set it up on the bench, take measurements, make modifications, and arrive at the final version.

The situation has changed rapidly in the last few years. Integrated circuits arrived on the scene and access to computers became more and more common. Both changes came hand in hand. Integrated circuits made the fabrication of faster and cheaper computers possible and new computers, in turn, made their design easier. Recently, relatively cheap mini- and microcomputers have become so widely accessible that small companies and even individuals can afford them. It is now beyond any doubt that computational methods will become more and more important, since the means of applying them are here. Looking at the problem from another angle, technological progress has made possible the design of large functional blocks containing thousands of interconnected transistors on one chip. It is obvious that such designs cannot be carried out by experimenting on a bench. In addition to progress in computer hardware technology, four major innovations in numerical mathematics have had profound impact on all aspects of computer aided network analysis and design. The four innovations are sparse matrix methods, linear multi-step methods for the solution of sets of algebraic-differential systems, adjoint techniques for sensitivity computation, and the use of sequential quadratic programming for constrained optimization.

During the last decade, a number of programs for network analysis using one or more of these advanced features have become available. Some have high price tags, others are available for modest fees covering essentially the handling charges. These programs have certain advantages and disadvantages. On the positive side, they are quite efficient when used for the specific applications they were designed for. On the negative side is the fact that they all require large and sophisticated computers. What is even more unpleasant is the fact that they are so complicated that any changes required for other applications are usually beyond the ability of most users.

In order to write new software or make modifications to existing software when faced with new applications in the rapidly changing technical world, the designer must have a knowledge of the basic theory which computer-aided design, usually abbreviated as CAD, relies upon. To provide the reader with some idea about computer-aided analysis and design, we will go through some typical steps. The examples are not representative of the state of the art; their sole purpose is for illustration.

In the first example we describe possible steps in the design of an active filter. To start with, regions are specified where the amplitude response may or may not go. Assume that our specification calls for a fifth-order filter with equiripple amplitude characteristic in the pass-band and no transfer zeros. The pass-band should be from 0 to 1 kHz but we scale the network to the band from 0 to 1 rad/sec. Our next task is to select the network structure. This can be done in many ways using tables or specialized synthesis programs. Let us assume that the network shown in Fig. 1 will be satisfactory. At this point we consider the operational amplifiers to be ideal with infinite gain and infinite bandwidth. The designer could now specify the component values of the network; for demonstration we shall proceed somewhat differently. We will select, to some degree arbitrarily, the element values given in Table 1 as "original network" and calculate the amplitude response of such a filter, shown in Fig. 2 as curve a. The

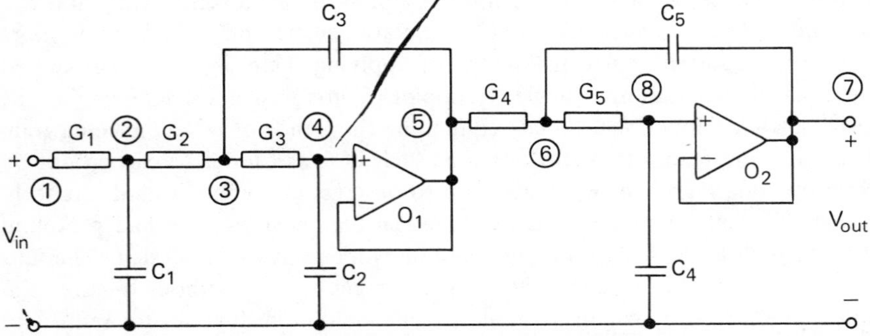

Fig. 1. A fifth-order active network with all transmission zeros at infinity.

Table 1. Original and Optimized Values for the Network in Fig. 1 and its Poles and Zeros.

	G_1	G_2	G_3	G_4	G_5	C_1	C_2	C_3	C_4	C_5
1. Original network	1	1	1	1	1	3	0.3	6	0.1	10
2. Optimized network	1.002	1.036	1.012	1.215	1.215	2.991	0.3136	5.995	0.147	9.956
3. Optimized with 741C	1.038	1.073	0.931	1.448	1.833	3.032	0.2841	5.984	0.2297	9.771

	Poles	Zeros
Network 1	-0.380679 $-0.309660 \pm j0.624956$ $-0.100000 \pm j0.994987$	all at infinity
Network 3	-24.2925 -52.6272 -0.397524 $-0.315373 \pm j0.635446$ $-0.113192 \pm j0.994867$	-5.26907 -8.99788 $0.976987 \pm j3.07642$ $0.488978 \pm j2.97666$

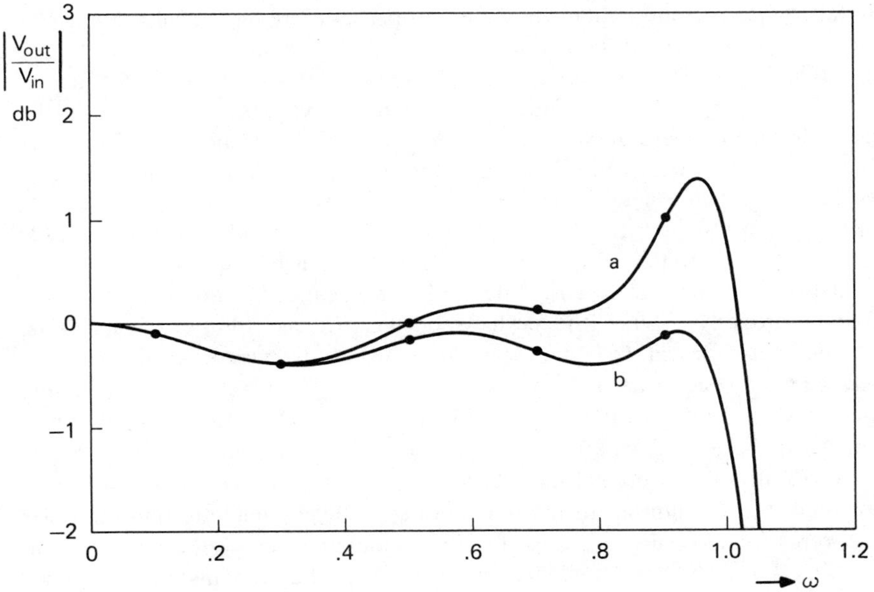

Fig. 2. Original (a) and optimized (b) response of the filter in Fig. 1. The operational amplifiers are taken as ideal.

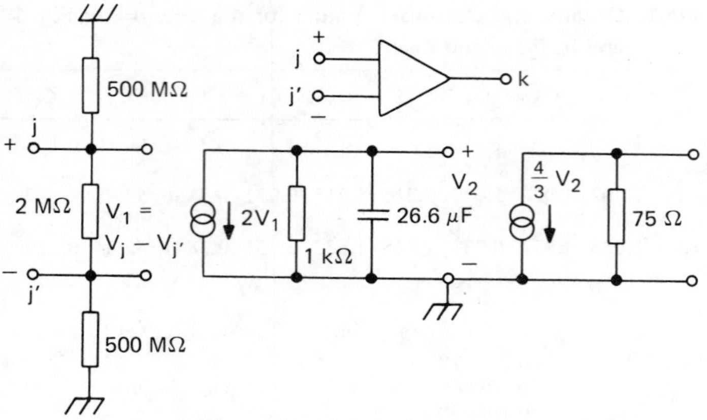

Fig. 3. Linear model of the 741C operational amplifier.

result obviously violates the requirement on equal ripples in the pass-band. At this point we decide to use computerized optimization and allow changes in all passive elements in the network. The optimization results in the element values given in Table 1 as "Optimized network." Our requirement on equal ripples is now as shown by curve b in Fig. 2, but the design is not yet over. Acutal operational amplifiers do not have infinite gain or bandwidth. In fact, they have a bandwidth of several Hz only and a gain of approximately 10^5, and this fact must be taken into account by modeling their properties more realistically. Models of various complexities can be considered; we will use the model shown in Fig. 3. It simulates the linear response of the well known 741C operational amplifier.

Once we use models for semiconductor devices, we must either work in the actual frequency band of the final filter or scale the linear model of the device. The second choice has been used and the models incorporated into the network. Its response deteriorated considerably, as shown by curve a in Fig. 4. Optimization was performed again. The final result is given by curve b in Fig. 4; the final element values are given in Table 1 as "Optimized with 741C."

At this point we have the final design but we cannot be sure whether it will operate properly. Since the device models introduce additional capacitors, the final network will, in fact, have an order higher than was originally assumed, and we must check whether the network is stable. This is done by calculating the poles and zeros of the network with the 741C model. Results for the network with both ideal and nonideal operational amplifiers are given in Table 1. All poles are in the left half-plane and we are now sure that the network will not oscillate. In addition to the required design poles, there are spurious poles and zeros which cause a change of the response. Their influence is seen in Fig. 5; a dip in the amplitude characteristic occurs at approximately 3.2 rad/sec due to spurious zeros. In the final phase of the design the network would be denormalized to the required frequency band and impedance level.

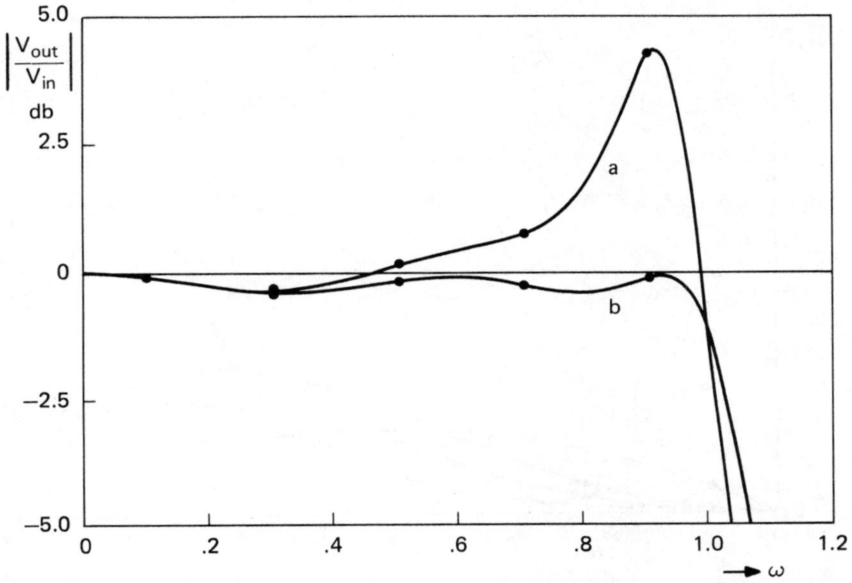

Fig. 4. (a) Response of the network in Fig. 1 with 741C operational amplifier models; (b) optimized response.

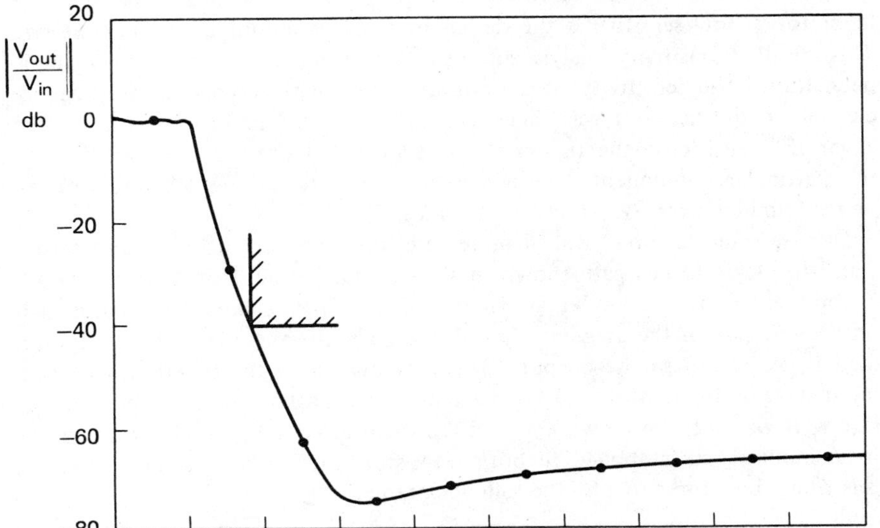

Fig. 5. Overall response of the network in Fig. 1 with 741C operational amplifiers. Note the filter specification and the spurious zeros.

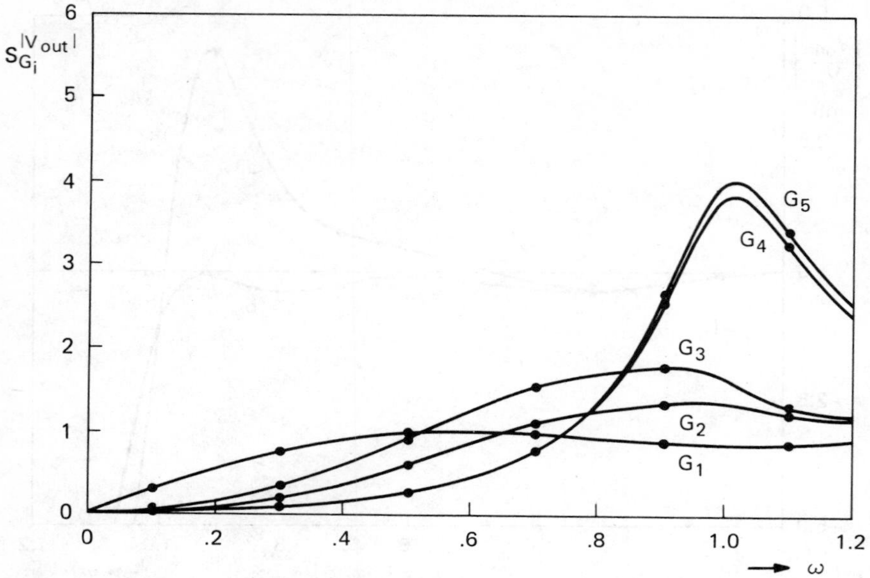

Fig. 6. Sensitivities of the absolute value of the output voltage with respect to all conductances in the network given in Fig. 1.

CAD can also provide information that is very difficult to obtain in the laboratory: how sensitive is the design to small variations in the parameters? This is called sensitivity analysis and can be performed for every element independently. The sensitivity of the output voltage with respect to every passive element in the network was calculated and is plotted in Figs. 6 and 7. The larger the sensitivity, the tighter the tolerance that needs to be specified for the particular component. In our network, we would need careful control on the conductances G_4, G_5 and capacitances C_4, C_5.

Our second example will demonstrate the analysis of the transistor-to-transistor logic (TTL) gate shown in Fig. 8. Each transistor in this network is represented by the model shown in Fig. 9. The network to be studied is on the left side of the diagram. In order to make the analysis realistic, a typical load is connected to the output. This is simulated by the two-transistor TTL input stage on the right side of the diagram. If the dotted transistor on the input side were present, the network would represent a NAND gate, giving no output if an input signal is applied to both transistors. In terms of Boolean algebra, this would be represented by the following table:

Input 1	Input 2	AND	NAND
0	0	0	1
0	1	0	1
1	0	0	1
1	1	1	0

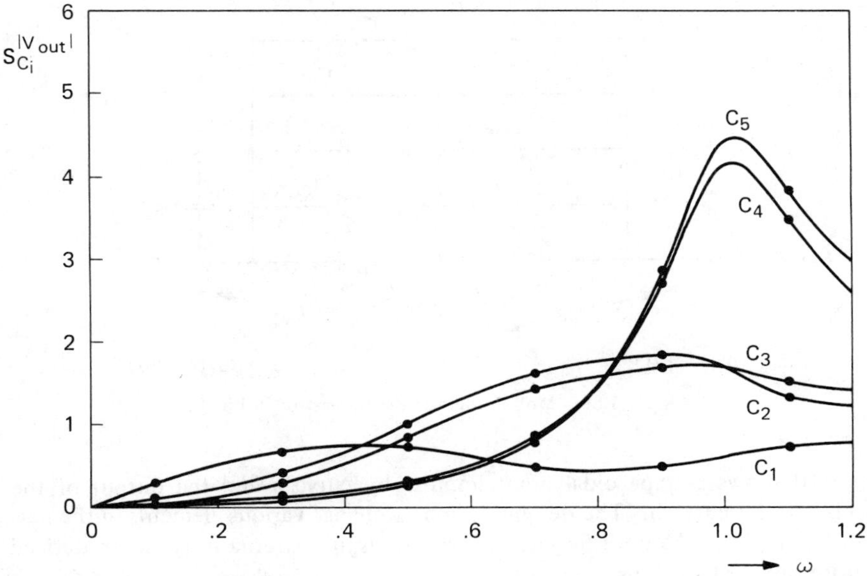

Fig. 7. Sensitivities of the absolute value of the output voltage with respect to all capacitors in the network given in Fig. 1.

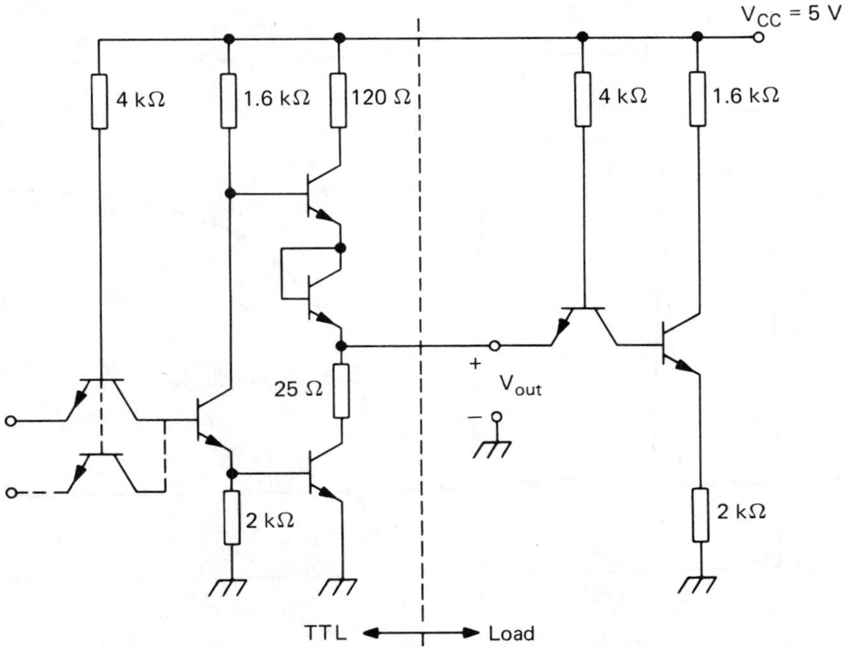

Fig. 8. Transistor-to-transistor logic (TTL) gate with its load simulated by the input stage of another TTL gate. Each transistor in the network is represented by the Ebers–Moll model shown in Fig. 9.

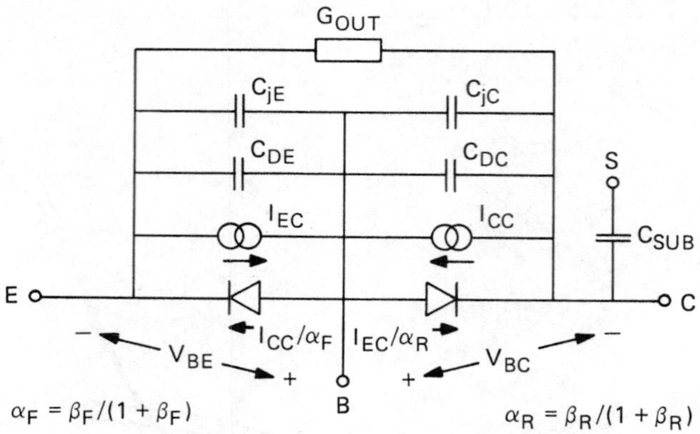

Fig. 9. Ebers–Moll model for the transistors in Fig. 8.

Fig. 10 shows a trapezoidal input impulse by curve a and the output of the TTL gate by curve b. The designer can now change various elements in the network and reanalyze until he gets the desired result. Alternatively, computerized optimization algorithms can be used.

Let us now focus attention on the various sections of the book. The first 10 chapters cover techniques applicable to linear analog network *analysis*. The rest

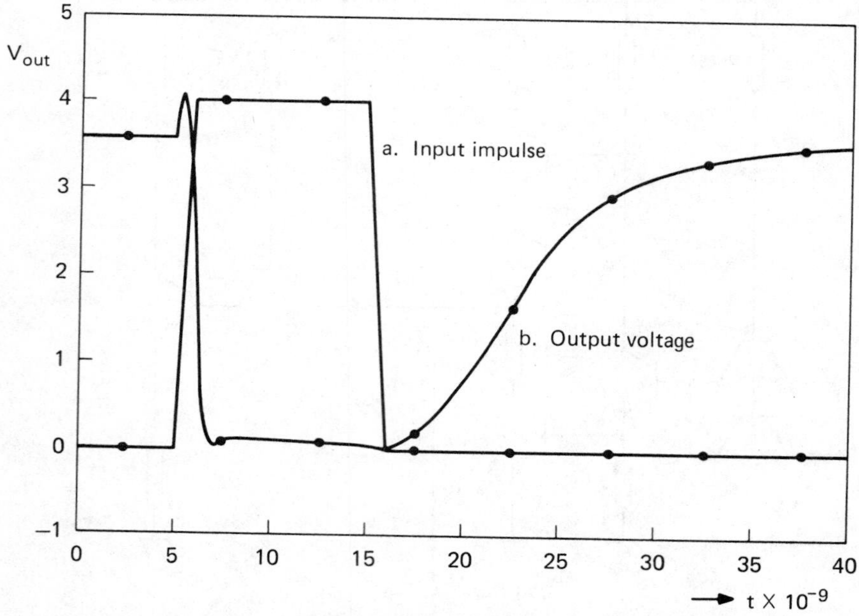

Fig. 10. Input signal and output voltage of the TTL gate shown in Fig. 8.

of the book deals with nonlinear network analysis and the *design* aspects of all types of networks. Six Appendices provide supporting material.

Since present-day networks are often quite large, involving thousands of interconnected components, special methods are required to speed up the solution. Networks with, for instance, 150 nodes are not rare; such a network would be described by at least a 150×150 matrix. Close inspection of the matrices associated with all practical networks shows that most of the entries are zeros. If we disregard this fact, the solution will cost approximately $n^3/3$ "operations" (one multiplication and one addition is usually called an operation). For a matrix of dimension $n = 150$ this would represent 1.125 million operations. Careful algorithm and software design enables one to store and operate with only the nonzeros. Practice shows that the number of operations is reduced to approximately $20n = 3000$ for our example. Such astonishing reduction in the number of operations is certainly worth considering. This topic falls under the domain of *sparse matrix solutions* and is introduced in Chapter 2.

In order to analyze a network, its structure and component values are provided to the computer. One must then set up the network equations in a form best suited for various kinds of analyses. A wide variety of formulation methods exist and are considered in Chapters 2-4. Greater emphasis is placed on formulations that lead to sparse sets of equations. Some of these methods are used in the program in Appendix D.

CAD can easily do a task that is very difficult in the laboratory: the evaluation of response variation due to small changes in network elements or due to the presence of parasitics. In a crude way, similar information could be generated through bench tests by replacing the components by other components with somewhat different values. This, of course, is not practical in integrated circuit design. Moreover, experimental study of parasitic influences is very difficult as one is unable to control their values on the breadboard. The computer can provide such information at *negligible computation cost for any number of elements* for linear networks. Another application of sensitivities appears in the generation of gradients of objective functions in optimization. *Sensitivity methods* are introduced in Chapter 5 and their computational aspects are treated in detail in Chapter 6. Most of them are coded in Appendix D. The techniques described in Chapter 6 form the foundations of linear network design and should be thoroughly understood by the reader.

Frequency domain analysis is well established but is not well suited to instability detection, particularly when parasitic components are present. We can always plot the response as a function of frequency but it may happen that a high and narrow peak is entirely missed by the set of discrete points where the analysis is performed. Such a peak would indicate the possibility of dangerous parasitic oscillations in networks containing semiconductor devices. To avoid any surprises, we can calculate the poles (and zeros, if desired), and establish conclusively whether oscillations can or cannot occur. The poles and zeros can be found as roots of polynomials or computed directly from system matrices. Suitable methods are discussed in Chapter 7.

In the study of relatively small networks, it is an established practice to derive the network function by retaining all the elements and the frequency as variables. In hand calculations this is a tedious and error-prone process and it would be nice to have a CAD method which could do the job for us. Such methods exist and are called *symbolic analysis*. We can generate the transfer function in terms of the complex frequency s, or in terms of frequency as well as the network components. The theoretical development of one such method is described in Chapters 7 and 8. This method has also been programmed, and the routines given in Appendix D can generate such functions. The relevant theory has wider applications and can be used to generate derivatives of arbitrary order of the numerator and denominator, study the influence of large changes in element values without having to resolve the problem from scratch, perform fault analysis, and so on. All these methods are discussed in Chapter 8.

When performing time domain analysis, much depends on whether the network is linear or nonlinear. For linear networks, either general methods can be used or specialized methods, valid only for linear networks, can be devised. As an introduction to general methods for time domain solution, Chapter 9 considers three simple and well known *integration formulae* and treats their properties in detail. It is also shown how they simplify for linear networks. The chapter provides the background for more powerful techniques for the solution of algebraic-differential systems covered in Chapter 13.

A specialized integration method for linear networks is given in Chapter 10. It is based on numerical inversion of the Laplace transform and has special features not available in general integration methods. For instance, Dirac impulses and their derivatives can be handled easily. Time domain sensitivity computation, generally a difficult task requiring complicated software, can be obtained in a straightforward manner and used for time domain optimization. An important aspect of numerical Laplace transform inversion is the ability to handle networks with distributed elements. Related computer routines are provided in the chapter and form part of the package in Appendix D.

The second part of the book begins with a chapter on *modeling* of various nonlinear semiconductor devices. Proper modeling is critical; after all, the simulation reliability can be only as good as the worst part of the whole simulation process, and gross misrepresentation of some elements would render the whole effort invalid. The area of device modeling requires specialization in semiconductor physics and cannot be covered fully in this book, but the problem can be approached from a practical point of view. Usually, the semiconductor specialist will cooperate with the CAD specialist and provide him with the necessary equations. Once such equations are defined, it is the task of the CAD specialist to incorporate them into his program. Chapter 11 adopts this approach; reference to physics is to a great extent avoided.

One area of modeling does fall to some extent into the domain of the CAD specialist. It is the modeling of complete semiconductor functional blocks. This process is sometimes called *macromodeling*, and although it does rely on physics, it is also based on measurements and optimization. As an example of macromodeling, Chapter 11 presents a nonlinear model of an operational amplifier.

Timing studies on many programs have shown that the evaluation of the nonlinear functions describing various semiconductor devices represents a considerable fraction of the total computer cost. Most programs also require the derivatives of the functions for the iterative solution of the nonlinear system equations. Due to the complexity of such functions this is often an error-prone task. The problems are circumvented if the CAD specialist decides to handle nonlinearities by *spline* approximations. The function values are precomputed and whenever a value, or a derivative, are required, they are provided by a relatively simple subroutine. Splines are introduced in Chapter 11 and related software is provided.

If nonlinear component models are incorporated into the network equations, their solution becomes more difficult and must rely on iteration, usually performed by the Newton–Raphson method. Details are given in Chapter 12, where it is shown that the Jacobian matrix required for the process corresponds to a linearized network for which all the formulation methods covered in Chapters 2, 3, and 4 apply directly. Once the solution for applied dc voltages has been found, the designer may be interested in the sensitivity of the dc solution with respect to the elements. This is also covered in Chapter 12 and turns out to be a very simple problem. DC analysis determines the operating point of a network. If small signals are involved, one can proceed with the linear methods covered in the first part of the book.

Time domain solutions are required when the signals are large and the network contains nonlinear elements. This is performed by *numerical integration* and Chapter 13 provides the theoretical background for integration of differential and algebraic-differential equations. The latter is more difficult and also more important, because modern formulation methods (modified nodal and tableau) lead to such systems. The theory is fairly complicated and the reader may wish to go through the simple sections first and leave the general theory for later study.

The methods covered in this book are general and are applicable to other fields as well. We do not try to cover such areas as mechanical, structural, or energy systems. Their formulation and solution methods are related to networks but the reader is probably not familiar with the background material. However, there are two rapidly developing fields of electrical engineering which are directly related to the problems covered in this book. They are *discrete systems* and *switched-capacitor networks*. Chapter 14 shows how the reader can apply the material of this book to these two fields.

In the *design process* we seek element values so as to meet given specifications. This requires a sequence of analyses, intermixed with component modifications. The modifications can be done by hand, e.g., by changing the element values and observing the result by reanalyzing the network, or they can be done automatically by means of special mathematical methods. Such methods fall under the domain of *optimization*. Details must be found in reference texts and journal articles, but the CAD designer should at least be aware of the theoretical foundations in order to be able to use them. Optimization methods seek the minimum of an *objective function*. The definition of such a function is the task of the CAD specialist. All efficient optimization algorithms require the *gradient* of the objective function. It is again the responsibility of the CAD specialist to provide it by means of sensitivity calculations, which are discussed thoroughly in this text. He must also locate appropriate minimization routines. All these problems are dealt with in Chapter 15. It is believed that the amount of theory presented is sufficient for applications in network design. Reference to reliable, state-of-the-art software is provided.

A difficult area in nonlinear network analysis is the determination of the response when the excitation is a periodic function. To observe the properties of the network, we require the *steady state* solution after all the transients have died out. This is what we would see in the laboratory. Unfortunately, to arrive at the steady state we must go through the transient process as well, and this may be computationally very expensive. Special methods have been designed to rapidly proceed through the transient state. Some of them require knowledge of sensitivities in the time domain while others arrive at the steady state solution by extrapolation techniques. These problems together with their solutions are presented in Chapter 16. The chapter is somewhat specialized and may be skipped at first reading.

The application of optimization to the design of networks is covered in Chapter 17. Here we derive the required formulae and give examples of various stages of the design process. No new material is presented; we only demonstrate what can be done with the methods considered in the book. In fact, the reader might even start with this chapter, skip all the mathematics, and see what can be accomplished. It may give him the best incentive to read the rest of the book.

Appendices accompany the book. Three of them are theoretical and cover background material or special theorems on the Laplace transform. Appendix D is the most important. It presents a FORTRAN program in which many of the methods of the book have been coded, along with a user guide and short description of the subroutines. The program can solve the following problems:

1. Frequency domain analysis and sensitivity computation of linear networks. Many ideal network elements are permitted and the user can provide values for built-in bipolar and field-effect transistor and operational amplifier models.
2. Computation of network function poles and zeros together with their sensitivity.

3. Generate symbolic functions.
4. Time domain analysis.
5. Digital network frequency domain and sensitivity analysis, pole or zero evaluation, and symbolic function generation.

Appendix E provides the code and user information on a sparse subroutine package. The package is designed for structurally symmetric matrices and it is assumed that pivoting for accuracy is not required. Though the code in this Appendix is not as sophisticated as our production codes, some parts of it execute by orders of magnitude faster than codes available in many contemporary circuit analysis programs. Finally, Appendix F provides a quick review of some advanced areas of matrix algebra.

Contents

CHAPTER 1
Fundamental Concepts

Chapter 1 summarizes material which is assumed to be known to the reader. The basic network elements, R, L, C, are defined in Section 1.1, independent sources in Section 1.2. Initial conditions on capacitors and inductors are discussed in Section 1.3, along with the definition of impedance and admittance. Ports and terminals are introduced in Section 1.4, while Section 1.5 presents dependent sources (transducers). A general matrix description is used for a port characterization of the transducers. Other ideal elementary two-ports, like the ideal transformer, gyrator, invertor, convertor, coupled coils, and ideal operational amplifier, are defined and their properties explained in Section 1.6. Transformation of sources by means of the Thévenin and Norton theorems are discussed in Section 1.7, while scaling of linear networks is treated in Section 1.8. Section 1.9 defines network functions and their poles and zeros and Section 1.10 gives time domain response by Laplace transform inversion.

1.1. BASIC NETWORK ELEMENTS

The basic network elements are linear lumped time-invariant resistors, capacitors, and inductors. A *resistor* is an element for which the current i flowing through it and the voltage v applied across it are related by *Ohm's law:*

$$v = Ri = i/G \tag{1.1.1}$$

where R is the *resistance* of the resistor, measured in ohms (Ω) and G is the *conductance*, measured in mhos (℧). The units for voltage are volts and amperes for current. The reference directions of the voltage and current are shown in Fig. 1.1.1(a).

In an i–v graph, Fig. 1.1.2, the linear time-invariant resistor is represented by a straight line passing through the origin and going through the first and third quadrants. For a short circuit, $R = 0$, the characteristic coincides with the i-axis while for an open circuit, $G = 0$, it coincides with the v-axis. Non-

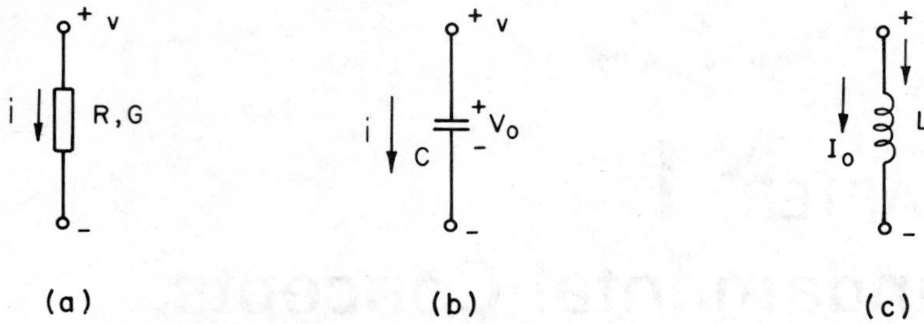

Fig. 1.1.1. Basic network elements: (a) resistor, (b) capacitor, (c) inductor.

linear resistor characteristics are also shown in Fig. 1.1.2. Curve 2 has the voltage uniquely defined for any value of i, but not vice versa. Such a resistor is *current controlled*. Curve 3 shows a characteristic for which i is uniquely defined for any voltage v, but not vice versa. Such a resistor is *voltage controlled*. The inverse function is not defined for these two curves. The horizontal line intersecting curve 2 at three points explains why i is not unique for some voltages: there are three points on this curve corresponding to the voltage v'.

A resistor is linear (possibly time-varying) only if it obeys Ohm's law, Eq. (1.1.1). Therefore, curve 4 in Fig. 1.1.2, although a straight line, does not describe a linear resistor.

A *capacitor* is an element represented as in Fig. 1.1.1(b), denoted by the letter C and its capacitance measured in farads (F). In general, the terminal characteristic may be described by

$$q = f(v) \tag{1.1.2}$$

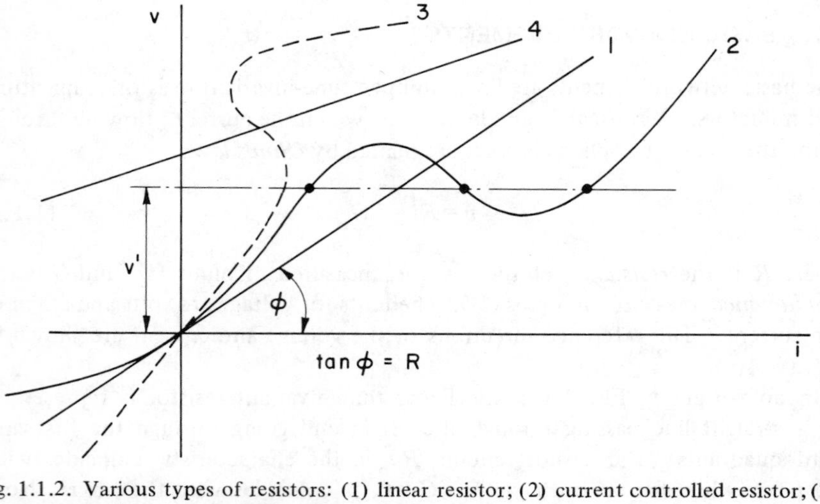

Fig. 1.1.2. Various types of resistors: (1) linear resistor; (2) current controlled resistor; (3) voltage controlled resistor; (4) nonlinear resistor.

where q denotes the charge in coulombs. If the function f is simply a multiplicative constant C, Eq. (1.1.2) reduces to

$$q = Cv \tag{1.1.3}$$

which describes a linear time-invariant capacitor. The current flowing through the capacitor is given by

$$i = \frac{dq}{dt}. \tag{1.1.4}$$

For a linear time-invariant capacitor, Eq. (1.1.4) reduces to

$$i = C\frac{dv}{dt} \tag{1.1.5}$$

with the inverse dependence expressed by

$$v(t) = V_0 + \frac{1}{C}\int_0^t i(\tau)\,d\tau \tag{1.1.6}$$

where V_0 is the voltage on the capacitor at time $t = 0$.

An *inductor* is an element represented as in Fig. 1.1.1(c). It is denoted by the symbol L, its inductance is measured in henry (H). Its terminal characteristic is described by

$$\phi = f(i) \tag{1.1.7}$$

where ϕ denotes the magnetic flux in webers. If the function f is a multiplicative constant L, then

$$\phi = Li \tag{1.1.8}$$

and the equation represents a linear time-invariant inductor. The voltage across the inductor is related to the current flowing through it by

$$v = \frac{d\phi}{dt}. \tag{1.1.9}$$

For a linear time-invariant inductor Eq. (1.1.9) is written as

$$v = L\frac{di}{dt} \tag{1.1.10}$$

with the inverse relation

$$i(t) = I_0 + \frac{1}{L}\int_0^t v(\tau)\,d\tau \tag{1.1.11}$$

where I_0 is the value of the current flowing through the inductor at time $t = 0$. Relations of the form (1.1.1), (1.1.5), or (1.1.10) define the characteristic of the component and will be termed *constitutive equations* (CE).

1.2. INDEPENDENT SOURCES

Two kinds of independent ideal sources exist which can deliver energy to a network: an independent voltage source and an independent current source.

The *independent voltage source*, Fig. 1.2.1(a), maintains a voltage e of prescribed value across its terminals no matter what current (in any direction) flows through it. Theoretically, it maintains the prescribed voltage across its terminals even if it is short-circuited. Although it is not possible to construct an ideal voltage source, we can easily model actual sources by associating resistors

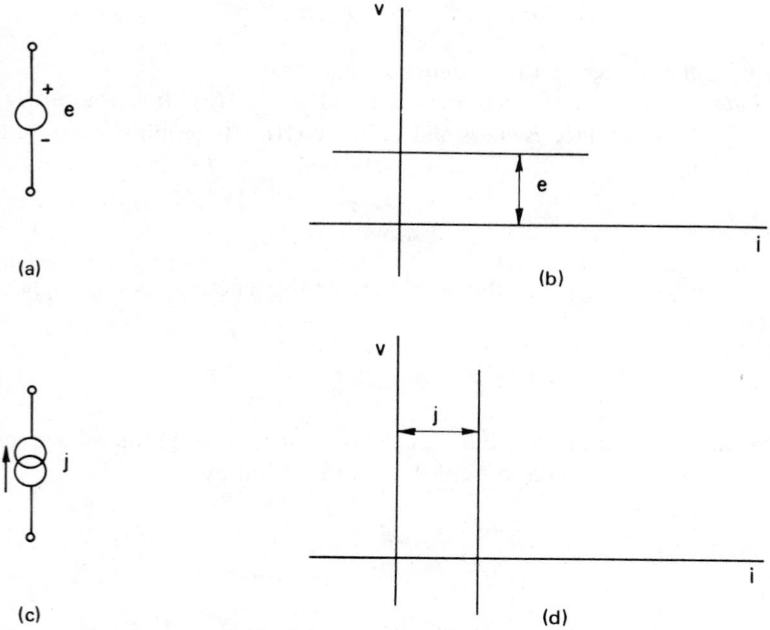

Fig. 1.2.1. Symbols and characteristics of independent sources: (a) symbol for a voltage source; (b) characteristic of a voltage source; (c) symbol for a current source; (d) characteristic of a current source.

or combinations of other elements with an ideal source. The characteristic of a voltage source in the i–v plane is shown in Fig. 1.2.1(b). Comparing with resistor characteristics, it can be seen that the independent voltage source behaves as a special nonlinear resistor. If the value of the voltage changes, the straight line moves up and down. One special case is a voltage source with voltage identically equal to zero. Then the characteristic coincides with the i-axis and any current can flow through the source, although there is no voltage generated. We conclude that an *ideal voltage source with* $e = 0$ *behaves as a short circuit.*

The *independent current source* is shown in Fig. 1.2.1(c). The voltage across it depends on the network connected to the source. The source delivers its nominal current j no matter what the actual voltage across it. Theoretically, it should deliver this current even if it is open-circuited, which is possible only if we allow infinite voltage across it. This element is an idealized one, but in combination with other elements it can be used to model actual sources. The characteristic of the current source is a vertical line in the i–v plane, as shown in Fig. 1.2.1(d). For different values of j, the line moves to the left or right. If the source delivers zero current, the characteristic coincides with the v-axis and the current is zero no matter what the applied voltage is. This is the behavior of an open circuit and we conclude that a *current source with* $j = 0$ *is equivalent to an open circuit.*

1.3. CAPACITORS AND INDUCTORS IN THE LAPLACE TRANSFORM DOMAIN

The constitutive equations for the capacitors and inductors introduced in Section 1.1 were differential relations between the voltage and current. In the case of linear time-invariant networks, these relations can be transformed into simpler algebraic equations through the use of Laplace transforms (see Appendix A). In this section we derive the constitutive equations in the transform domain, define admittance and impedance, and show that initial conditions on capacitors and inductors can be accounted for by means of equivalent independent sources. We begin by introducing some time signals and their transforms.

A unit step, $u(t)$, is a time function defined as follows:

$$u(t) = \begin{cases} 0, & \text{for} \quad t < 0 \\ 1, & \text{for} \quad t \geqslant 0. \end{cases} \tag{1.3.1}$$

Its Laplace transform is

$$F_u(s) = 1/s \tag{1.3.2}$$

where s is the complex frequency, $s = \sigma + j\omega$. Capital letters are used for functions in the Laplace transform domain.

Another important time function is the unit or Dirac impulse, $\delta(t)$, defined by the equations

$$\delta(t) = \begin{cases} 0, & \text{for} \quad t \neq 0 \\ \infty, & \text{for} \quad t = 0 \end{cases} \tag{1.3.3}$$

and the condition that the integral of the function from $t = -\infty$ to $t = \infty$ is unity. The Laplace transform of the unit impulse is

$$F_\delta(s) = 1. \tag{1.3.4}$$

Consider a general function $f(t)$ with Laplace transform $F(s)$. Symbolically:

$$\begin{aligned} \mathcal{L}[f(t)] &= F(s) \\ \mathcal{L}^{-1}[F(s)] &= f(t). \end{aligned} \tag{1.3.5}$$

The derivative of the time function is expressed in the transform domain by the formula

$$\mathcal{L}\ \frac{d}{dt} f(t) = sF(s) - f(0-) \tag{1.3.6}$$

where $f(0-)$ denotes the value of $f(t)$ when approaching the time $t = 0$ from negative values of t. Formula (1.3.6) is useful in deriving the influence of initial conditions on capacitors and inductors.

For a linear time-invariant capacitor:

$$i(t) = C\frac{dv(t)}{dt}.$$

Using (1.3.6), write

$$I = sCV - CV_0. \tag{1.3.7}$$

Similarly, for an inductor,

$$V = sLI - LI_0. \tag{1.3.8}$$

Consider first the case of zero initial conditions: (1.3.7) and (1.3.8) simplify to

$$\begin{aligned} I &= sCV \\ V &= sLI. \end{aligned} \tag{1.3.9}$$

The *admittance* of a *capacitor* and the *impedance* of an *inductor* are defined as

capacitor: $$\frac{I}{V} = sC = Y_C \tag{1.3.10}$$

inductor: $$\frac{V}{I} = sL = Z_L. \tag{1.3.11}$$

If the initial voltage on a capacitor $V_0 \neq 0$, write (1.3.7) in the form

$$CV_0 + I = sCV.$$

The voltage V is applied across the capacitor and, conceptually, two currents flow through it: one external current I, independent of the initial condition, plus one of value CV_0. This can be interpreted as a current source of value CV_0 in parallel with the capacitor. The situation is indicated in Fig. 1.3.1 in the *admittance description* part. Comparing the source due to initial conditions with (1.3.4), we see that it is an *impulse* of value CV_0.

Similar steps for the inductor lead to the representation shown for it in the *impedance description* of Fig. 1.3.1. An impulse voltage of value LI_0 appears in series with the inductor.

Equations (1.3.7) and (1.3.8) can also be written in the forms

$$V = \frac{I}{sC} + \frac{V_0}{s} \tag{1.3.12}$$

and

$$I = \frac{V}{sL} + \frac{I_0}{s}. \tag{1.3.13}$$

First, let the initial conditions be zero:

$$\begin{aligned} &\text{capacitor:} \quad V = \frac{1}{sC} I \\ &\text{inductor:} \quad I = \frac{1}{sL} V. \end{aligned} \tag{1.3.14}$$

The *impedance* of a *capacitor* and the *admittance* of an *inductor* are defined through the relations

$$\frac{V}{I} = \frac{1}{sC} = Z_C \tag{1.3.15}$$

IMPEDANCE DESCRIPTION

Capacitor:

$$Z = \frac{1}{sC} \qquad \text{(step source)} \quad \frac{V_0}{s}$$

$$V = \frac{V_0}{s} + \frac{I}{sC}$$

Inductor:

$$Z = sL \qquad \text{(impulse source)} \quad LI_0$$

$$V = sLI - LI_0$$

ADMITTANCE DESCRIPTION

Capacitor:

$$Y = sC$$

$$CV_0 \quad \text{(impulse source)}$$

$$I = sCV - CV_0$$

Inductor:

$$Y = \frac{1}{sL}$$

$$\frac{I_0}{s} \quad \text{(step source)}$$

$$I = \frac{I_0}{s} + \frac{V}{sL}$$

ELEMENT

Capacitor:

$$i(t) = C \frac{dv(t)}{dt}$$

$$v(t) = V_0 + \frac{1}{C}\int_0^t i(t)\,dt$$

Inductor:

$$v(t) = L \frac{di(t)}{dt}$$

$$i(t) = I_0 + \frac{1}{L}\int_0^t v(t)\,dt$$

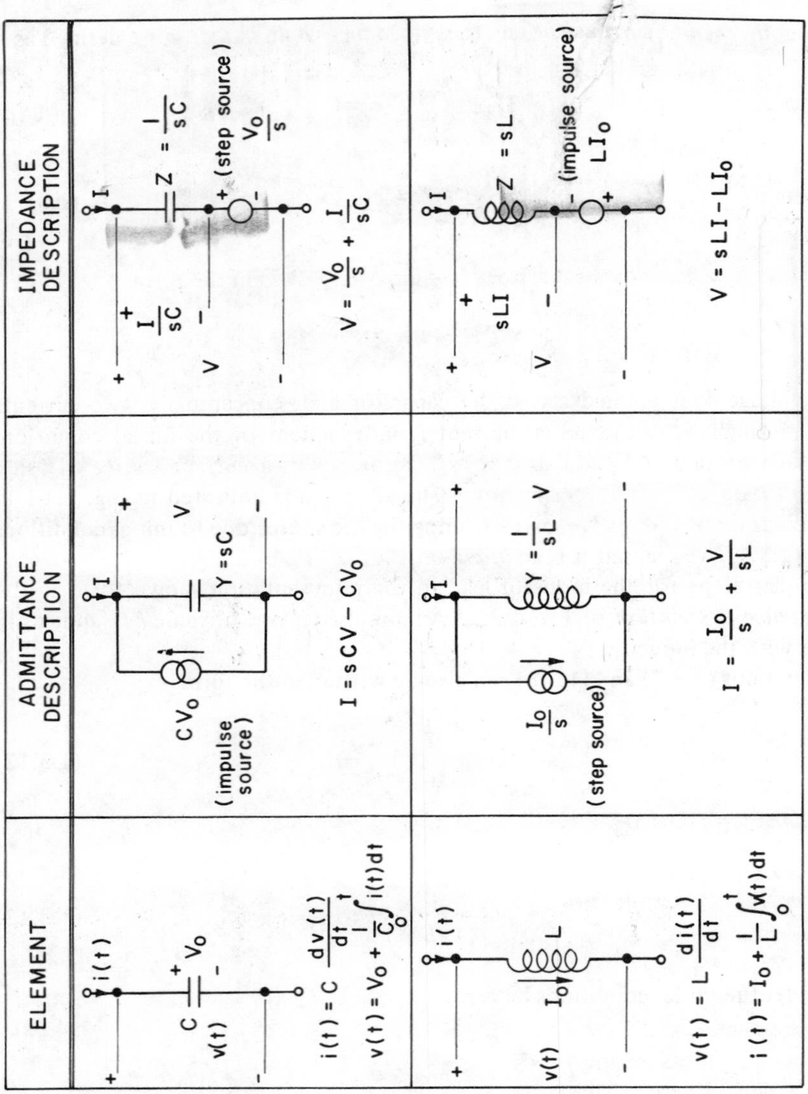

Fig. 1.3.1. Influence of initial conditions on capacitors and inductors.

and

$$\frac{I}{V} = \frac{1}{sL} = Y_L. \tag{1.3.16}$$

If the initial voltage across the capacitor $V_0 \neq 0$, (1.3.12) can be rewritten as

$$V - \frac{V_0}{s} = \frac{1}{sC} I.$$

The voltage on the left is made up of two parts: the original voltage across the capacitor, minus a step source of value V_0. This is shown in the impedance description of the capacitor in Fig. 1.3.1. Similarly, for the inductor, the admittance description calls for a step source of value I_0 in parallel with the inductor (see again Fig. 1.3.1).

For *steady state solution* of linear time-invariant networks with *sinusoidal inputs* and frequency f (in Hz), one inserts $s = 2\pi jf = j\omega$ into the equations and *disregards* any initial voltages or currents appearing in the network. In this case only the constitutive equations (1.3.10), (1.3.11), (1.3.15) and (1.3.16) are used.

Transformed variables will be used in the rest of this chapter.

1.4. DEFINITION OF PORTS AND TERMINALS

Sources or other elements are connected together either at their *terminals* or at their *ports*. A terminal is a point in the network where additional external components can be connected. If terminals are ordered in pairs, we call them ports. An n-terminal network is shown in Fig. 1.4.1(a) for $n = 6$, whereas an n-port is shown in Fig. 1.4.1(b) for $n = 4$. The definition in terms of terminals is more general, since we do not need an even number of them. At each terminal we can measure the voltage with respect to some reference node, usually marked with a zero. The current has positive orientation when it flows away from a terminal.

An important class of networks have only four terminals and two ports. In a four-terminal network, the currents and voltages will have orientations as shown in Fig. 1.4.2(a). Throughout this text, terminal quantities will have lettered subscripts, j, k, j', k' and so on, and port quantities will be denoted by numbers. If the two networks N in Fig. 1.4.2(a) and (b) are identical, then the following set of equations defines the transformation relating the two

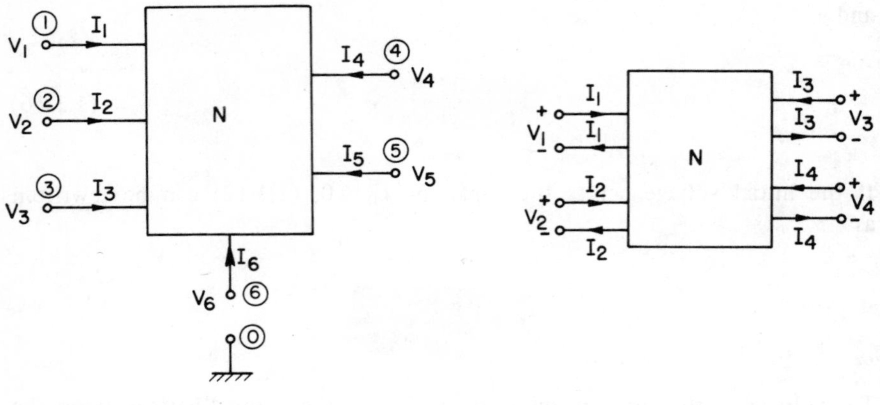

Fig. 1.4.1. Definitions of currents and voltages for *n*-ports and *n*-terminals: (a) six-terminal network; (b) four-port network.

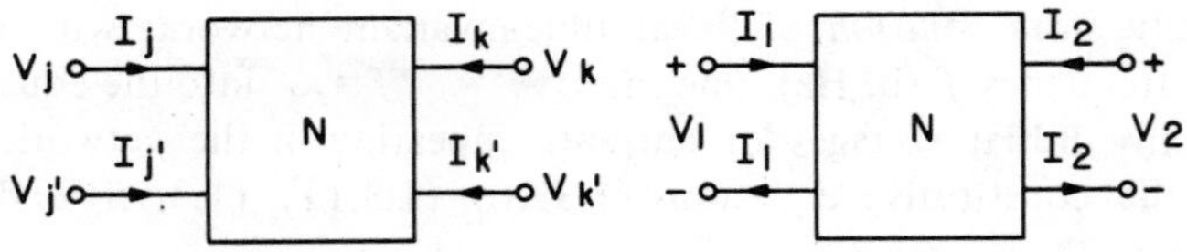

Fig. 1.4.2. Descriptions of a network *N* as: (a) four-terminal; (b) two-port.

representations:

$$
\begin{aligned}
V_j - V_{j'} &= V_1 \\
V_k - V_{k'} &= V_2 \\
I_j = -I_{j'} &= I_1 \\
I_k = -I_{k'} &= I_2 \,.
\end{aligned}
\tag{1.4.1}
$$

1.5. TRANSDUCERS (DEPENDENT SOURCES)

The first four two-port networks to be introduced are dependent sources, called *transducers* in what follows. These elements have source components which are either ideal voltage or current sources, similar to the independent sources introduced earlier. The difference is that the voltage or current values depend on either a voltage or a current at some other place in the network.

A *voltage to voltage* transducer (VVT) is shown in Fig. 1.5.1(a). Its two-port

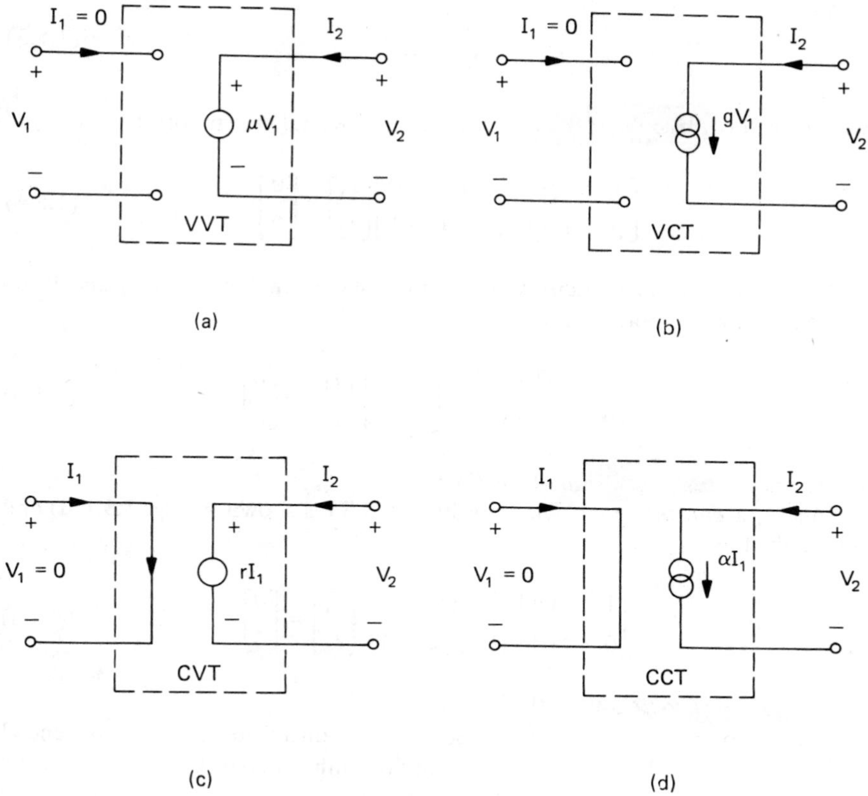

Fig. 1.5.1. Four types of transducers.

equations are

$$\begin{aligned} I_1 &= 0 \\ V_2 &= \mu V_1 \end{aligned} \tag{1.5.1}$$

where μ is the *voltage gain* of the VVT. Equations (1.5.1) can be written in the general matrix form

$$\begin{bmatrix} 0 & 0 \\ \mu & -1 \end{bmatrix} \begin{bmatrix} V_1 \\ V_2 \end{bmatrix} + \begin{bmatrix} 1 & 0 \\ 0 & 0 \end{bmatrix} \begin{bmatrix} I_1 \\ I_2 \end{bmatrix} = \begin{bmatrix} 0 \\ 0 \end{bmatrix}. \tag{1.5.2}$$

A *voltage to current* transducer (VCT) is shown in Fig. 1.5.1(b). It is described by the equations

$$I_1 = 0$$
$$I_2 = gV_1 \tag{1.5.3}$$

where g is the *transconductance* of the VCT; in general matrix form:

$$\begin{bmatrix} 0 & 0 \\ g & 0 \end{bmatrix} \begin{bmatrix} V_1 \\ V_2 \end{bmatrix} + \begin{bmatrix} 1 & 0 \\ 0 & -1 \end{bmatrix} \begin{bmatrix} I_1 \\ I_2 \end{bmatrix} = \begin{bmatrix} 0 \\ 0 \end{bmatrix}. \tag{1.5.4}$$

A *current to voltage* transducer (CVT) is shown in Fig. 1.5.1(c) and is described by the two-port equations

$$\begin{bmatrix} 1 & 0 \\ 0 & -1 \end{bmatrix} \begin{bmatrix} V_1 \\ V_2 \end{bmatrix} + \begin{bmatrix} 0 & 0 \\ r & 0 \end{bmatrix} \begin{bmatrix} I_1 \\ I_2 \end{bmatrix} = \begin{bmatrix} 0 \\ 0 \end{bmatrix} \tag{1.5.5}$$

where r is the *transresistance* of the CVT.

Finally, a *current to current* transducer (CCT) is shown in Fig. 1.5.1(d) and is described by

$$\begin{bmatrix} 1 & 0 \\ 0 & 0 \end{bmatrix} \begin{bmatrix} V_1 \\ V_2 \end{bmatrix} + \begin{bmatrix} 0 & 0 \\ \alpha & -1 \end{bmatrix} \begin{bmatrix} I_1 \\ I_2 \end{bmatrix} = \begin{bmatrix} 0 \\ 0 \end{bmatrix} \tag{1.5.6}$$

where α is the *current gain* of the CCT.

The matrix description of the transducers introduced above is entirely general and applicable to arbitrary multiport or multiterminal networks.

1.6. ELEMENTARY TWO-PORTS

The first four ideal two-ports we defined were transducers. Other ideal elements which are commonly used in the analysis of networks will now be introduced through their port descriptions.

An *ideal transformer* is defined by the equations

$$V_1 = \pm nV_2$$
$$I_1 = \mp\frac{1}{n}I_2. \tag{1.6.1}$$

Using the general matrix description introduced above,

$$\begin{bmatrix} -1 & \pm n \\ 0 & 0 \end{bmatrix} \begin{bmatrix} V_1 \\ V_2 \end{bmatrix} + \begin{bmatrix} 0 & 0 \\ \pm n & 1 \end{bmatrix} \begin{bmatrix} I_1 \\ I_2 \end{bmatrix} = \begin{bmatrix} 0 \\ 0 \end{bmatrix}. \tag{1.6.2}$$

A *gyrator* is defined as a two-port for which

$$I_1 = -g_2 V_2$$
$$I_2 = g_1 V_1 . \tag{1.6.3}$$

Its symbol is shown in Fig. 1.6.1(a). The gyrator can be represented by means of two VCTs, as follows from (1.6.3). This is shown in Fig. 1.6.1(b). If the values of the gyration constants are equal, $g_1 = g_2 = g$, the gyrator is said to be *ideal.* Equations (1.6.3) can be rewritten in the form

$$V_1 = r_2 I_2$$
$$V_2 = -r_1 I_1 \tag{1.6.4}$$

by defining $r_1 = 1/g_2$, $r_2 = 1/g_1$. These equations indicate that the gyrator can also be realized by means of two CVTs, as shown in Fig. 1.6.1(c). If the signs in (1.6.3) or (1.6.4) are reversed, the polarities of the sources in Figures 1.6.1(b) and (c) are reversed as well. Writing the general matrix form is left to the reader as an exercise.

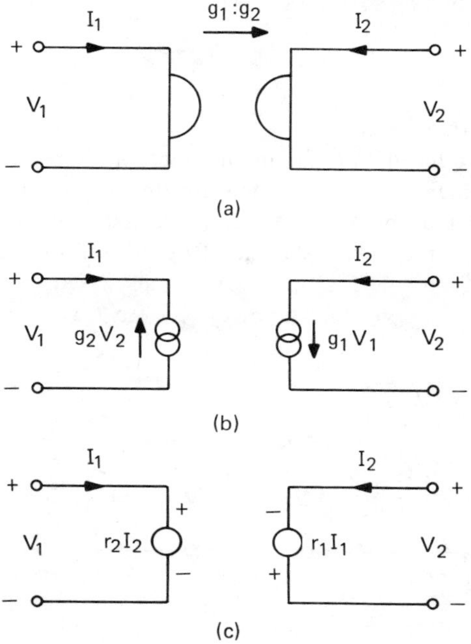

Fig. 1.6.1. Gyrator: (a) symbol; (b) realization by means of two VCTs; (c) realization by means of two CVTs.

Another elementary two-port is the *convertor*, defined by means of two-port equations

$$V_1 = k_1 V_2$$
$$I_1 = -k_2 I_2 . \tag{1.6.5}$$

Comparing with (1.6.1) we see that the ideal transformer is a special case of a convertor. If both constants have the same sign, the element is called a *positive impedance convertor*, while in the case of different signs it is called a *negative impedance convertor*.

Two mutually coupled inductors form another elementary two-port, the *transformer*. Its natural definition is

$$V_1 = sL_1 I_1 \pm sMI_2$$
$$V_2 = \pm sMI_1 + sL_2 I_2 . \tag{1.6.6}$$

The + sign of M corresponds to Fig. 1.6.2(a) with the dots on the same side, the negative sign corresponds to Fig. 1.6.2(b). The dot accompanying the specification of M expresses the relative sense of windings of the transformer. The *coefficient of coupling*, k, is defined as

$$k = M/\sqrt{L_1 L_2} \tag{1.6.7}$$

and it can be shown that $0 \leqslant k \leqslant 1$.

The elements introduced thus far in this section are realizable if we permit the use of active elements. It is convenient for the purposes of analysis to introduce two other ideal elements. Neither is realizable alone but they can be combined to simulate the ideal behavior of other useful elements. A *nullator* is an element which, by definition, does not allow current flow through it. In addition, the voltage across its terminals is zero. The element is thus de-

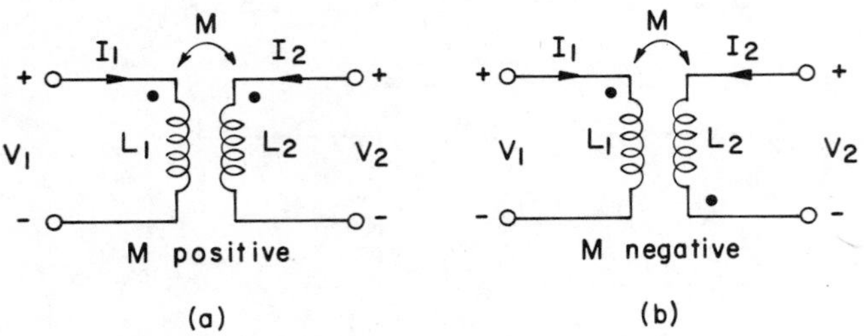

Fig. 1.6.2. Diagram of a transformer with positive or negative M.

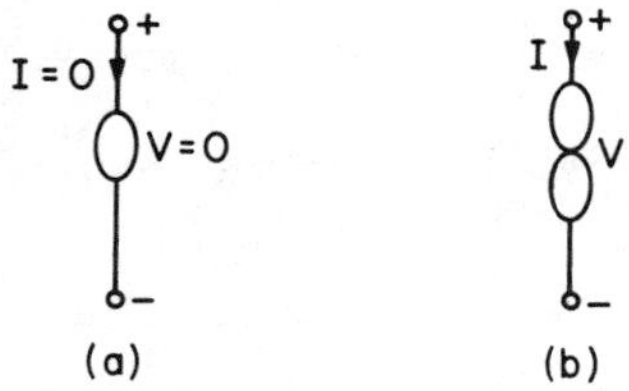

Fig. 1.6.3. Symbols for (a) Nullator and (b) Norator.

scribed by two equations:

$$V = 0; \quad I = 0. \tag{1.6.8}$$

The nullator symbol is shown in Fig. 1.6.3(a). The other element, the *norator*, has the symbol shown in Fig. 1.6.3(b). An arbitrary voltage can exist across it and simultaneously an arbitrary current can flow through it. The element has no constitutive equation. These elements are meaningful only if the number of norators is equal to the number of nullators in the network.

A two-port consisting of a nullator and a norator is sometimes called a *nullor* (see Fig. 1.6.4(a)). The nullor is equivalent to another network element called an *ideal operational amplifier* (see Fig. 1.6.4(b)). We will use the abbreviation OPAMP for the words "operational amplifier." Since the properties of the ideal OPAMP are expressed by (1.6.8) at port 1, we can write its general description as

$$\begin{bmatrix} 1 & 0 \\ 0 & 0 \end{bmatrix} \begin{bmatrix} V_1 \\ V_2 \end{bmatrix} + \begin{bmatrix} 0 & 0 \\ 1 & 0 \end{bmatrix} \begin{bmatrix} I_1 \\ I_2 \end{bmatrix} = \begin{bmatrix} 0 \\ 0 \end{bmatrix}. \tag{1.6.9}$$

Commercially available OPAMPs are devices constructed by means of transistors and diodes and usually simulate a VVT. The symbol is shown in Fig. 1.6.5(a), while its equivalent VVT representation is in Fig. 1.6.5(b). Note that the idealized representation of a commercial OPAMP will have one of the output terminals grounded, but this grounding is usually omitted on the symbol in Fig. 1.6.5(a).

If the bottom terminals of the nullor are connected together but *not neces-*

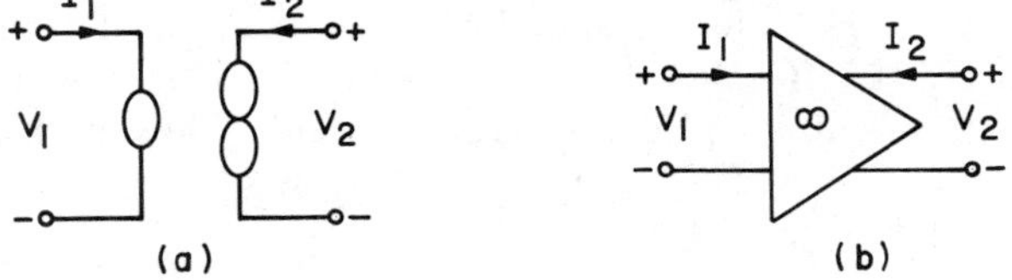

Fig. 1.6.4. Nullor: (a) modeling by means of a nullator and norator; (b) equivalent symbol.

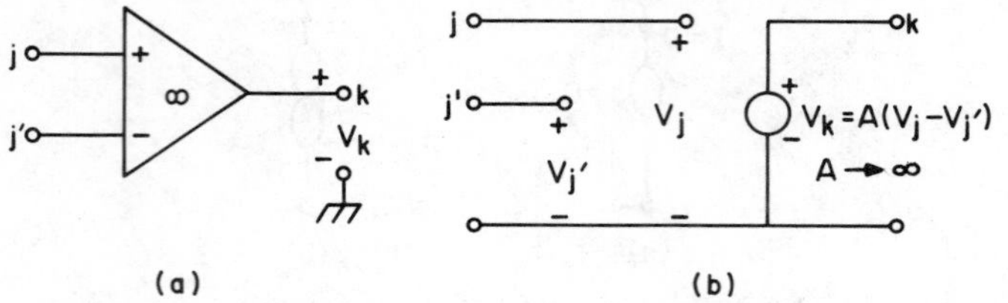

Fig. 1.6.5. Differential OPAMP: (a) symbol; (b) modeling with VVT.

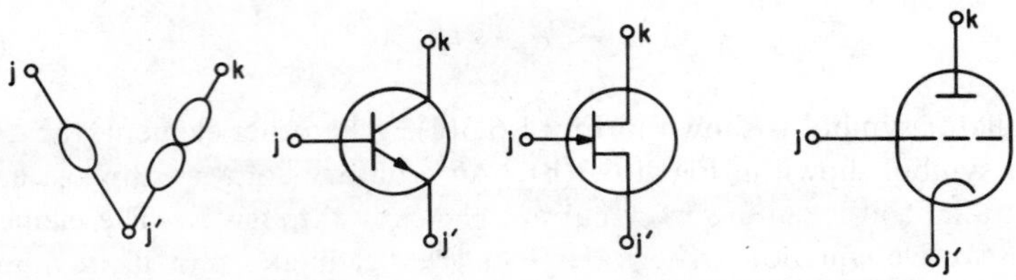

Fig. 1.6.6. Nullator–norator modeling of an ideal transistor or ideal tube.

sarily grounded, we get a device which simulates the behavior of an *ideal transistor* or a tube. Figure 1.6.6 identifies the corresponding terminals.

Nullators and norators can be used in the preliminary analysis and design phase of transistor and operational amplifier networks when the detailed non-ideal behavior of these active components is not of great interest.

1.7. THEVENIN AND NORTON TRANSFORMATIONS

The independent sources defined in Section 1.2 are ideal and not realizable using physical elements. However, they can be used to model actual, realizable sources when associated with additional ideal elements. One model for a voltage source is shown in Fig. 1.7.1(a). The resistor R_s simulates the internal resistance of the source. The voltage across the terminals A-A' is equal to the source voltage only if no current I is flowing. A model for a current source is shown in Fig. 1.7.1(b) with R_s in parallel with the ideal source.

Let us now pose the following question: What is the relationship between the value E in Fig. 1.7.1(a) and the value J in Fig. 1.7.1(b) if we wish to have the same voltage V across R_L and the same current I flowing through R_L in both networks?

For the network in Fig. 1.7.1(a) we find

$$V = \frac{ER_L}{R_s + R_L}$$

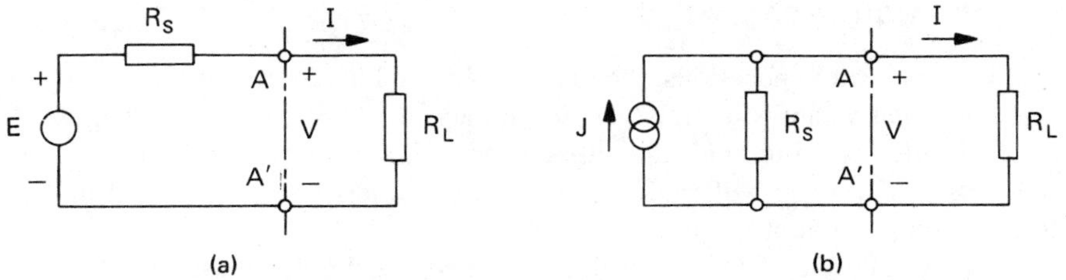

Fig. 1.7.1. Nonideal source loaded by R_L: (a) Thévenin equivalent; (b) Norton equivalent.

and for the network in Fig. 1.7.1(b)

$$J = \left(\frac{1}{R_s} + \frac{1}{R_L}\right) V.$$

Substituting the value V from the first equation into the second we arrive at

$$J = E/R_s. \tag{1.7.1}$$

Thus a voltage source in series with R_s can be transformed into a current source in parallel with R_s if the values of the sources are related by (1.7.1). The networks will be equivalent as far as the loading network is concerned, but the powers delivered by the ideal sources are different. We note that the source voltage E is equal to the open-circuit voltage at terminals A-A' when the load is removed, whereas the source current J is equal to the current flowing into a short-circuit connecting terminals A-A'. This will be true no matter how complicated the network between the source and the terminals A-A' is, even if there are many sources. If we simplify the network to the left of A-A' to the form given in Fig. 1.7.1(a), we get the so called *Thévenin equivalent* network. The network in Fig. 1.7.1(b) is called the *Norton equivalent.*

The rules described on the simple example above can be generalized for more complicated networks as follows:

1. Replace the load by either an open circuit and calculate the voltage E across the terminals A-A', or short-circuit A-A' and calculate the current J flowing into the short circuit. E will be the value of the source of the Thévenin and J that of the Norton equivalent.
2. To obtain the equivalent source resistance, short circuit all *independent voltage sources* and open-circuit all *independent current sources. Transducers in the network are left unchanged.* Apply a unit voltage source (or a unit current source) at the terminals A-A' and calculate the current I supplied by the voltage source (voltage V across the current source). Then $R_s = 1/I$ ($R_s = V$).

1.8. NETWORK SCALING

In many practical applications, the units of ohm and hertz are too small whereas farads and henrys are too large. Typical designs work in the frequency range of 10^2 to 10^8 Hz or more, with inductors measured in mH or μH and capacitors in μF or pF. This spread of values is inconvenient and leads to over- and underflows in computer applications.

For practical calculations, as well as for theoretical considerations, it is convenient to scale networks such that:

1. One (any) resistor is scaled to the value of one ohm (impedance scaling).
2. The frequency-dependent components are scaled such that some frequency of interest is reduced to 1 rad/sec (frequency scaling).

First consider impedance scaling. Let the *design* values be denoted by a subscript d, and the *scaled* values by the subscript s.

Scaling every *impedance* by a value k we get

$$R_s = R_d/k$$

$$Z_{C_s} = \frac{1}{k} \cdot \frac{1}{sC_d} = \frac{1}{s(C_d k)} = \frac{1}{sC_s} \Rightarrow C_s = kC_d$$

$$Z_{L_s} = \frac{1}{k} \cdot sL_d = s(L_d/k) = sL_s \Rightarrow L_s = \frac{L_d}{k}.$$

Frequency scaling does not change the resistors. Let the scaled frequency be designated as ω_s and the normalizing constant by ω_0:

$$\omega_s = \omega/\omega_0. \qquad (1.8.1)$$

Then the impedance of an inductor is

$$Z_L = j\omega L_d = j\frac{\omega}{\omega_0}(\omega_0 L_d) = j\omega_s L_s$$

and that of the capacitor

$$Z_C = \frac{1}{j\omega C_d} = \frac{1}{j\dfrac{\omega}{\omega_0}(\omega_0 C_d)} = \frac{1}{j\omega_s C_s}$$

Combining both impedance and frequency scalings we arrive at the formulae for all three passive elements:

Table 1.8.1. Typical Self-Consistent Units

Quantity	Standard unit	Audio unit	VHF unit	UHF unit
Voltage	volt (V)	V	V	V
Current	ampere (A)	mA	μA	mA
Resistance	ohm (Ω)	kΩ	MΩ	kΩ
Capacitance	farad (F)	μF	pF	pF
Inductance	henry (H)	H	H	μH
Frequency	hertz (Hz)	kHz	MHz	GHz
Time	second (s)	ms	μs	ns

$$R_s = \frac{R_d}{k} \quad \text{or} \quad G_s = kG_d$$

$$L_s = \frac{L_d \omega_0}{k} \tag{1.8.2}$$

$$C_s = C_d \omega_0 k.$$

Transducers are scaled as follows:

1. VVTs and CCTs remain unchanged.
2. VCT: The transconductance g is multiplied by k.
3. CVT: The transresistance r is divided by k.

Scaling is simplified if a self-consistent set of units, dependent on application, is adopted. Typical self-consistent sets of units are given in Table 1.8.1.

1.9. NETWORK FUNCTIONS, POLES AND ZEROS

Network functions are defined for networks which have no initial conditions. Using the relations $Z_C = 1/sC$, $Z_L = sL$, $Y_C = sC$, $Y_L = 1/sL$, and assuming that there is a single source, the network functions are

$$F = \begin{cases} Z_{in} = V_{in}/I_{in} & \text{(input impedance)} \\ Y_{in} = I_{in}/V_{in} & \text{(input admittance)} \\ T_V = V_{out}/V_{in} & \text{(voltage transfer function)} \\ T_I = I_{out}/I_{in} & \text{(current transfer function)} \\ Z_{TR} = V_{out}/I_{in} & \text{(transfer impedance)} \\ Y_{TR} = I_{out}/V_{in} & \text{(transfer admittance).} \end{cases} \tag{1.9.1}$$

If the network is composed of lumped elements, the functions will be rational functions in s:

$$F(s) = \frac{\sum_{i=0}^{n} a_i s^i}{\sum_{i=0}^{m} b_i s^i} = K \frac{\prod_{i=1}^{n} (s - z_i)}{\prod_{i=1}^{m} (s - p_i)} = \frac{N(s)}{D(s)}\,. \qquad (1.9.2)$$

The numerator polynomial will have n roots called *zeros*, z_i, and the denominator will have m roots called *poles*, p_i. They can be plotted in the complex plane, the zeros as small circles, the poles as crosses. Except for the multiplicative constant K in (1.9.2), such a plot fully defines the properties of the function.

EXAMPLE 1.9.1. Which network functions can be defined for the network shown in Fig. 1.9.1?

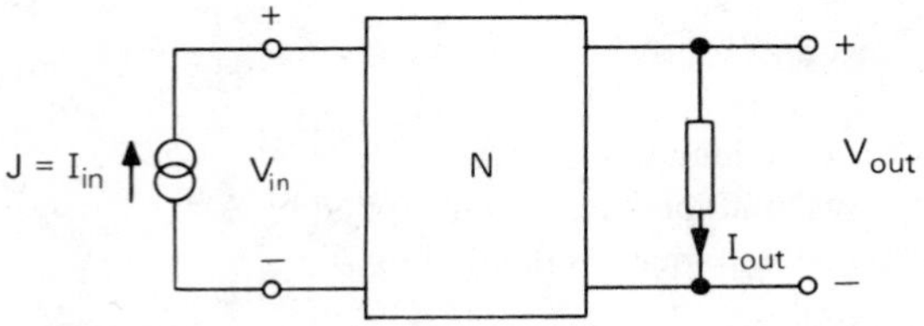

Fig. 1.9.1. Network with input current source and output voltage or current.

Because the network is excited by a current source, Z_{in}, Z_{TR}, and T_I can be obtained directly. The remaining functions can be calculated only after solving for V_{in}. The input impedance and input admittance are related by $Y_{in} = 1/Z_{in}$. Note that this is not true for the transfer impedances and admittances.

EXAMPLE 1.9.2. The transfer function of some network has been calculated as

$$F = \frac{s^2 + 9}{(s+2)^2\,(s^2 + 2s + 5)}\,.$$

What is the pole–zero plot?

The denominator polynomial $s^2 + 2s + 5$ can be written in terms of its factors. The transfer function is

$$F = \frac{s^2 + 9}{(s+2)^2\,(s + 1 + 2j)\,(s + 1 - 2j)}\,.$$

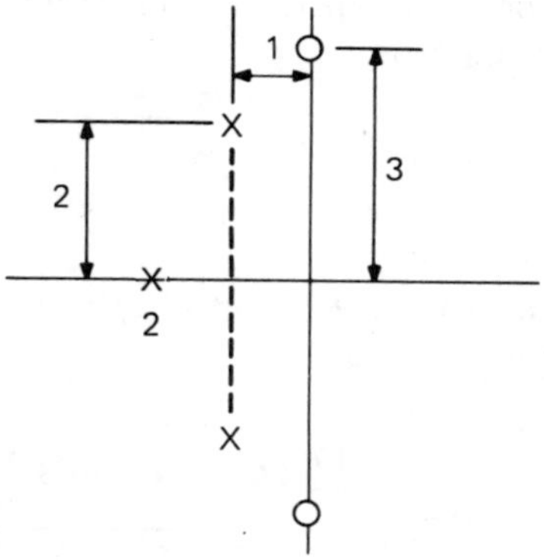

Fig. 1.9.2. Pole-zero plot with complex conjugate poles and zeros and one double real pole.

The zeros are at $\pm j3$, the network has one double pole at -2 and two complex conjugate poles $(-1 + 2j)$, $(-1 - 2j)$. The plot is shown in Fig. 1.9.2, the double pole at -2 being indicated by the number 2 at the appropriate cross.

The response of a linear network to sinusoidal input is simulated by setting $s = j\omega$ into the network function. Then

$$F(j\omega) = \text{Re}\, F(j\omega) + j\, \text{Im}\, F(j\omega) = A(\omega) + jB(\omega) \tag{1.9.3}$$

where $A(\omega)$ is an *even*, $B(\omega)$ is an *odd* function of ω. The *absolute value* of F is

$$|F(j\omega)| = \sqrt{A^2(\omega) + B^2(\omega)}\ . \tag{1.9.4}$$

The *phase angle* is

$$\phi(\omega) = \tan^{-1} \frac{B(\omega)}{A(\omega)} \tag{1.9.5}$$

and (1.9.3) can be expressed in the alternative form

$$F(j\omega) = |F(j\omega)|\, e^{j\phi(\omega)}. \tag{1.9.6}$$

When the frequency ω is considered as the independent variable, $|F(j\omega)|$ and $\phi(\omega)$ are called the *amplitude* and the *phase* characteristics of the network, respectively.

The *group delay characteristic* is defined as

$$\tau(\omega) = -\frac{d\phi(\omega)}{d\omega}\ . \tag{1.9.7}$$

Simple formulae for the characteristics can be derived if the poles and zeros are known and have the coordinates

$$\begin{aligned} z_i &= \alpha_i + j\beta_i \\ p_i &= \gamma_i + j\delta_i . \end{aligned} \tag{1.9.8}$$

Using the second expression in (1.9.2) and substituting $s = j\omega$, the amplitude characteristic is obtained in the form*

$$|F(j\omega)| = |K| \left(\frac{\prod_{i=1}^{n} [\alpha_i^2 + (\omega - \beta_i)^2]}{\prod_{i=1}^{m} [\gamma_i^2 + (\omega - \delta_i)^2]} \right)^{1/2} . \tag{1.9.9}$$

Assuming K positive, the phase characteristic (1.9.5) is expressed in the form*

$$\phi(\omega) = \sum_{i=1}^{n} \tan^{-1} \frac{\beta_i - \omega}{\alpha_i} - \sum_{i=1}^{m} \tan^{-1} \frac{\delta_i - \omega}{\gamma_i} \tag{1.9.10}$$

and differentiation with respect to ω provides the group delay

$$\tau(\omega) = \sum_{i=1}^{n} \frac{\alpha_i}{\alpha_i^2 + (\omega - \beta_i)^2} - \sum_{i=1}^{m} \frac{\gamma_i}{\gamma_i^2 + (\omega - \delta_i)^2} . \tag{1.9.11}$$

Linear networks are usually scaled from their actual operating frequencies to some computationally more advantageous frequency. If we introduce scaling by means of (1.8.1), then the shapes of $|F(j\omega_s)|$ and $\phi(\omega_s)$ remain unchanged; only the frequency scale under the curves changes. The scaling will, however, influence the shape of the group delay curve. If the frequency ω was divided by ω_0, then the scaled $\tau(\omega_s)$ will be ω_0 times larger. These results can be derived by inserting (1.8.1) into (1.9.9) through (1.9.11).

1.10. TIME DOMAIN RESPONSE

The inverse Laplace transform is a powerful tool for finding the time domain response of linear networks with or without initial conditions. The inversion of

---

*Note that if the numerator of the network function is a constant, the upper limit on the product sign in (1.9.9) and on the summation sign in (1.9.10) is smaller than the lower limit. By standard convention the value of the product is taken as unity and of the sum as zero in such cases.

the s-domain function is based on the thoery of complex variables and residue calculus. A brief review and a collection of formulae is presented in Appendix A.

In practice, the inversion is performed by first finding the poles of the function, then finding its partial fraction decomposition and finally using tables of standard inverse Laplace transforms to obtain the response. Formulae for partial fraction decomposition of functions with simple and multiple poles are derived in Appendix B and a short table of the commonly encountered transform pairs is given as well.

Experience in teaching Laplace transform theory has convinced us that the best thing to do is to restrict the number of formulae to the absolute minimum:

For a simple pole: $$\mathcal{L}^{-1}\frac{K}{s-p} = Ke^{pt} \tag{1.10.1}$$

For a multiple pole: $$\mathcal{L}^{-1}\frac{K}{(s-p)^m} = K\frac{t^{m-1}}{(m-1)!}e^{pt}. \tag{1.10.2}$$

Complex poles appear as conjugate pairs and have residues that are complex conjugates of each other. Denoting a complex pole by

$$p = c + jd \tag{1.10.3}$$

and its residue by

$$K = A + jB \tag{1.10.4}$$

the time response due to the pole pair p *and* $\bar{p}$ is

$$\mathcal{L}^{-1}\left\{\frac{A+jB}{s-c-jd} + \frac{A-jB}{s-c+jd}\right\} = 2e^{ct}(A\cos dt - B\sin dt). \tag{1.10.5}$$

Similar expressions can be derived for multiple complex poles.

EXAMPLE 1.10.1. Find the time domain response $v_2(t)$ for the network shown in Fig. 1.10.1(a).

The network is first redrawn using Fig. 1.3.1 to express the initial conditions in terms of independent sources. This is shown in Fig. 1.10.1(b). Standard nodal analysis (explained in detail in Chapter 2), leads to

$$\begin{bmatrix} 1+s & -1 \\ -1 & 1+2s \end{bmatrix}\begin{bmatrix} V_1 \\ V_2 \end{bmatrix} = \begin{bmatrix} \frac{1}{s}+2 \\ 1 \end{bmatrix}$$

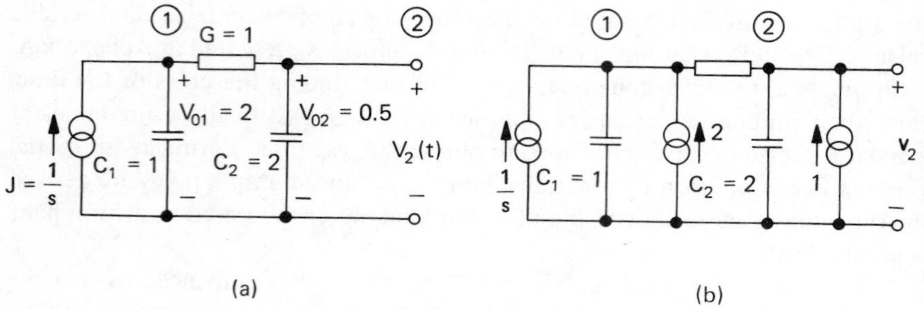

Fig. 1.10.1. Network with initial charges.

and the output voltage $V_2(s)$ is

$$V_2(s) = \frac{s^2 + 3s + 1}{2s^2(s + 3/2)}\,.$$

The decomposition is obtained using formula B.4 of Appendix B

$$V_2(s) = \frac{1}{3s^2} + \frac{7}{9s} - \frac{5}{18}\,\frac{1}{s + 3/2}\,.$$

Using formula (1.10.1) and (1.10.2), the time domain response is obtained as

$$v_2(t) = t/3 + \frac{7}{9} - \frac{5}{18}e^{-3t/2}.$$

It should be noted that finding the poles is a difficult step which requires the use of a computer for polynomials of order 3 or more. For this reason, we often wish to avoid this step and obtain the response numerically. Furthermore, Laplace transform techniques are valid only for linear time invariant networks. Chapters 9 and 13 give general methods for numerical integration, applicable to linear and nonlinear problems. Chapter 10 gives a special *numerical* Laplace transform inversion technique for linear time invariant networks which does not require the knowledge of the poles to obtain the time domain response.

PROBLEMS

P.1.1. Find the Norton and Thévenin equivalents of the networks shown in Fig. P.1.1(a) and (b).

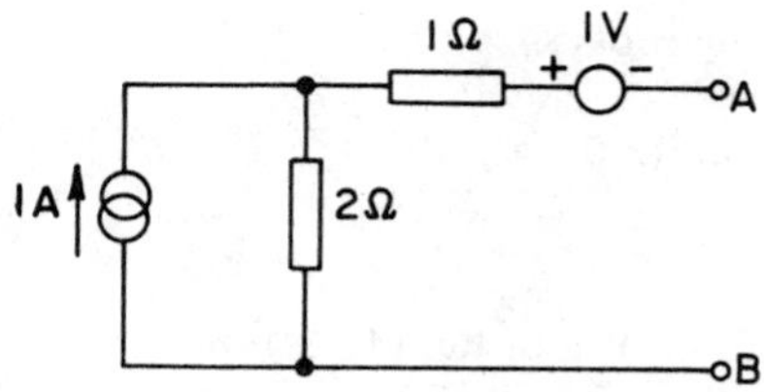

Fig. P.1.1(a)

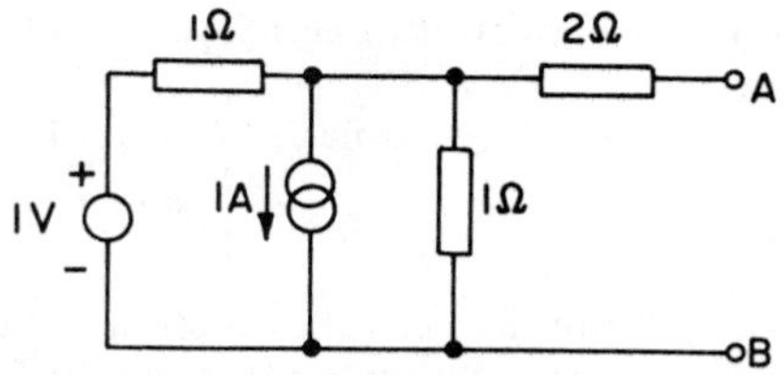

Fig. P.1.1(b)

P.1.2. For the network shown in Fig. P.1.2, find the open-circuit voltage V_{oc} and the short-circuit current I_{sc} (after connecting A–A' and B–B') and find the equivalent sources for the Norton and Thévenin transformations.

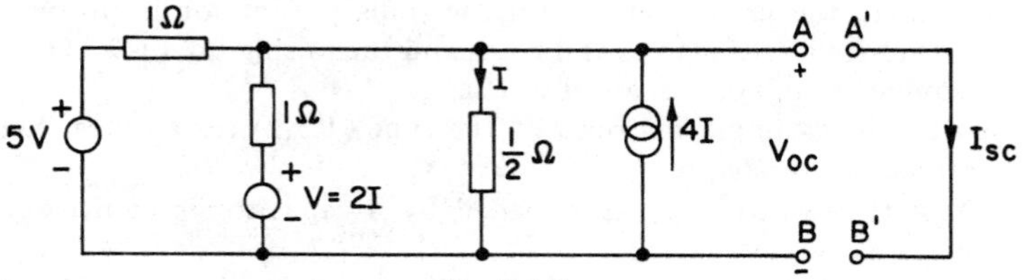

Fig. P.1.2.

P.1.3. Find both the Thévenin and Norton equivalents for the networks shown in Fig. P.1.3(a, b, c).

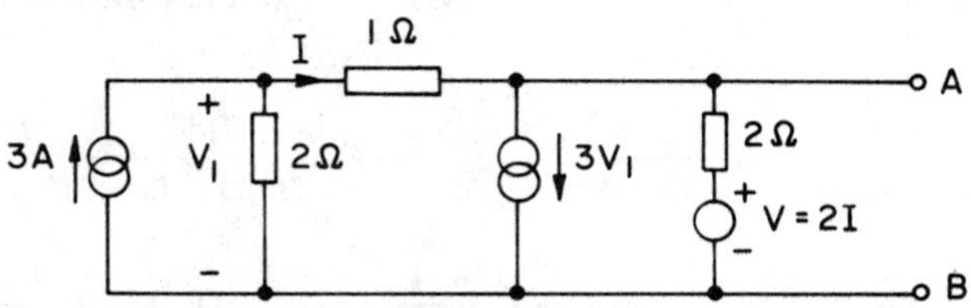

Fig. P.1.3(a)

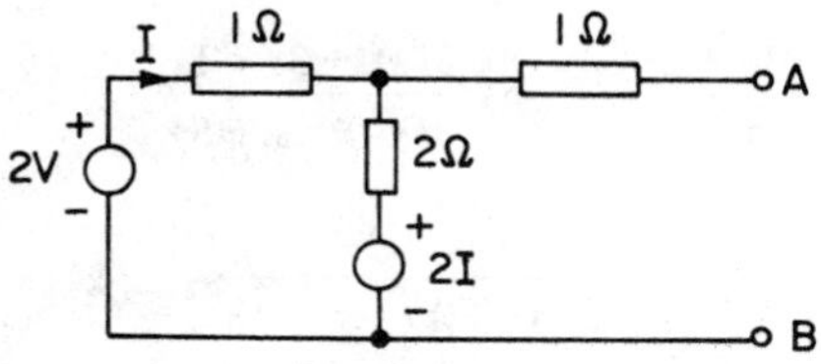

Fig. P.1.3(b)

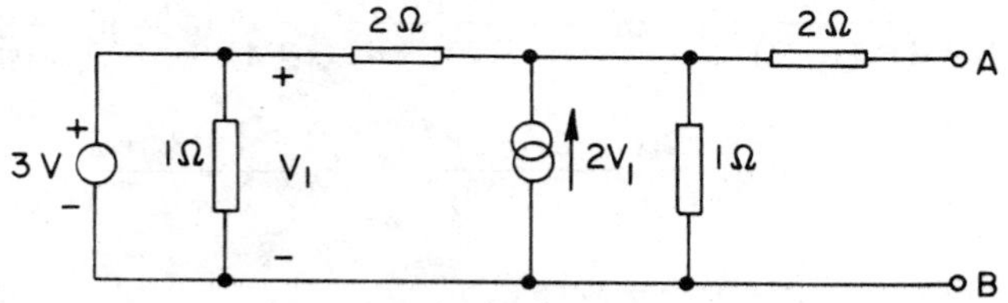

Fig. P.1.3(c)

P.1.4. A network function has the following roots:

poles: $-1; -0.5 \pm j0.5; -0.8 \pm j0.9$

zeros: $\pm j2.5; \pm j4$

Write the network function in the first form of Eq. (1.9.2)

P.1.5. Some network has the transfer function

$$F(s) = \frac{s^2 + 3}{s^2 + 2s + 2}.$$

Evaluate $|F(j\omega)|$ and $\phi(\omega)$ for $\omega = 0$, 0.5, and 1 rad/sec.

P.1.6. Calculate the group delay τ for the transfer function in problem P.1.5 by first finding the poles and zeros and then using Eq. (1.9.11). Use the frequencies $\omega = 0$, 0.5, and 1 rad/sec.

P.1.7. Write the two-port matrices of the type (1.5.2) for all ideal two-ports defined in this chapter.

P.1.8. Show that an ideal gyrator loaded by a capacitor is equivalent to an inductor.

P.1.9. Show that the input impedance of a negative impedance convertor loaded by Z_L is $-Z_L$.

P.1.10. Decompose the following rational functions into partial fractions and obtain their Laplace transform inverses. Use the formulae in Appendix A and B.

a) $\dfrac{s + 12}{s^2 + 4s}$; b) $\dfrac{s + 1}{s^2 + 4s + 13}$; c) $\dfrac{s^3 - 7s^2 + 14s - 9}{(s - 1)^2 (s - 2)^3}$

d) $\dfrac{s^4 + 3(s + 1)^3}{s^4 (s + 1)^3}$; e) $\dfrac{s^2 + 1}{(s + 1)^3 (s + 2)}$; f) $\dfrac{1}{(s + 1)^3 (s + 2)^2}$

g) $\dfrac{s^3 + 6s^2 + 11s + 5}{s^2 + 5s + 4}$; h) $\dfrac{s^2 + 3s + 1}{s(s^2 + 2s + 5)}$

i) $\dfrac{s^2 + s + 1}{(s + 1)(s + 2)^2}$; j) $\dfrac{s^3}{(s + 1)^2 (s + 2)}$; k) $\dfrac{s^2 + 3s + 5}{(s + 1)(s + 2)(s + 3)}$

l) $\dfrac{s^2 + 3s + 5}{(s + 1)^2 (s + 2)}$; m) $\dfrac{s^3 + 3s + 7}{[(s + 2)^2 + 4](s + 1)}$; n) $\dfrac{(5s^2 + 1)}{s(s^2 + 1)}$

p) $\dfrac{(3s + 2)}{s(s + 1)}$; q) $\dfrac{2(s^2 + 2s + 3)}{(s + 1)(s^2 + 1)}$; r) $\dfrac{3s^2 + 3s + 2}{s^3 + 2s^2}$

s) $\dfrac{384(s + 1)(s + 3)(s + 5)(s + 7)}{s(s + 2)(s + 4)(s + 6)(s + 8)}$

P.1.11. Calculate the Laplace transforms of the signals in Figures P.1.11 (a, b, c, d).

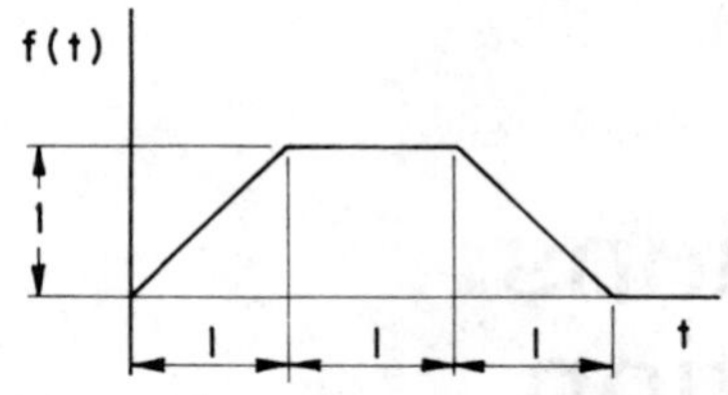

P.1.11(a)

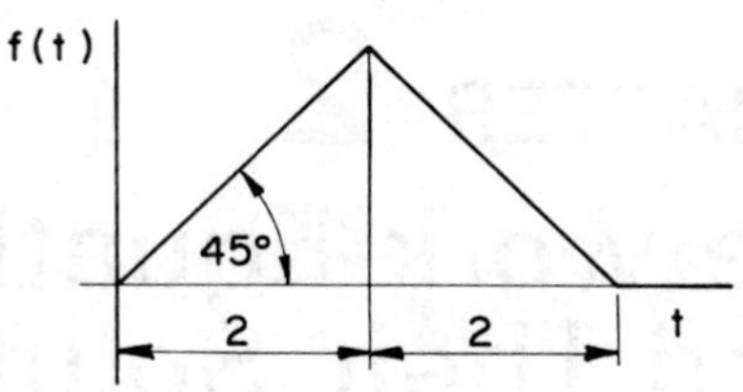

P.1.11(b)

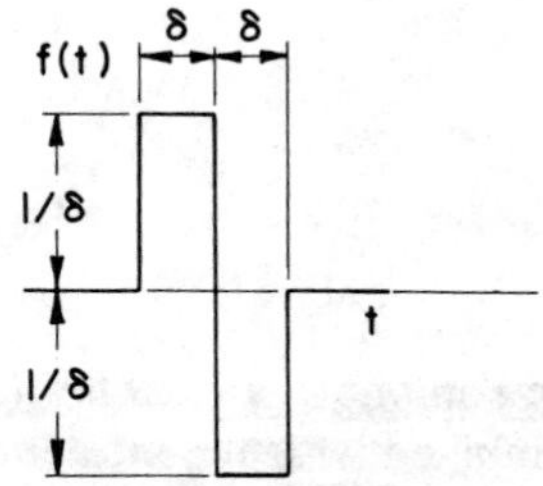

P.1.11(c)

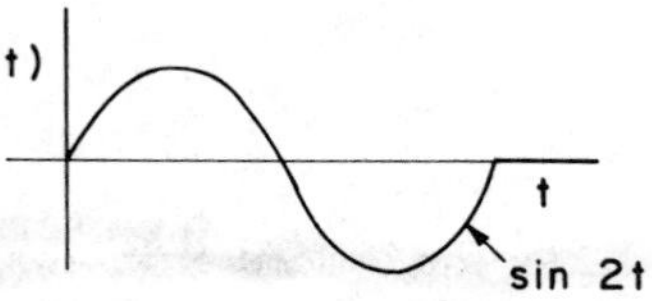

P.1.11(d)

CHAPTER 2
Network Equations and Their Solution

In this chapter the basic electric laws, namely the Kirchhoff current law (KCL) and the Kirchhoff voltage law (KVL), will be combined with the element constitutive relations to formulate network equations in the frequency domain. We will deal mainly with linear time-invariant networks that consist of R, L, C elements and independent sources. The nodal admittance and mesh impedance formulations are discussed in the first three sections. The majority of practical networks can be formulated by these methods. Emphasis is placed on the nodal formulation as it is best suited to computer applications. Both the nodal and mesh formulations lead to sets of linear algebraic equations in the case of frequency domain analysis of linear networks. The solution is carried out by ignoring initial conditions, assigning unit value to the source and replacing the Laplace transform variable by $2\pi jf$, f being the frequency of interest.

Once the network equations are formulated, sound computational algorithms are required for their solution. Gaussian elimination is explained in Section 2.4 and triangular factorization, the most important of the solution methods, in Section 2.5. Pivot selection is discussed in Section 2.6. Larger electrical circuits usually lead to sets of equations that are *sparse*. This is discussed in Section 2.7 and the substantial reduction in computational requirements resulting from judicious exploitation of sparsity are indicated. Section 2.8 provides data storage and implementation considerations for sparse matrices.

The mathematical methods and numerical techniques reviewed and introduced in this chapter are also fundamental to the solution of nonlinear algebraic equations and differential-algebraic systems. Such systems arise when the dc and time domain solution of nonlinear networks is required. These topics will be covered in later chapters.

2.1. NODAL FORMULATION

The nodal admittance formulation is based on the Kirchhoff current law which states: *The algebraic sum of currents leaving any node is zero.*

To derive properties of the nodal admittance matrix, consider the general network shown in Fig. 2.1.1. It is assumed that N contains R, L, C elements and has $n + 1$ terminals, all accessible from the outside. In addition there is a separate, $(n + 2)$nd reference node, denoted by 0 and considered as grounded. The voltages at the terminals are measured with respect to the ground node. Either voltage or current sources can be connected between any of the terminals and the reference node. Any terminal can be connected by a short-circuit to any other terminal or left as is.

The network behavior will be described by a matrix equation of the form

$$\mathbf{YV} = \mathbf{J} \tag{2.1.1}$$

or

$$\begin{bmatrix} y_{11} & y_{12} & \cdots y_{1,n+1} \\ y_{21} & y_{22} & \cdots y_{2,n+1} \\ \cdots & \cdots & \cdots \\ y_{n+1,1} & y_{n+1,2} & \cdots y_{n+1,n+1} \end{bmatrix} \begin{bmatrix} V_1 \\ V_2 \\ \vdots \\ V_{n+1} \end{bmatrix} = \begin{bmatrix} J_1 \\ J_2 \\ \vdots \\ J_{n+1} \end{bmatrix}. \tag{2.1.2}$$

Here J_i is the current flowing into the ith node from the reference node. Usually, J_i represent current sources. Voltages at the terminals will depend on the various sources and on the interconnections inside the network. To determine the y_{ij}, connect all terminals except the jth to the grounded reference node and apply a voltage source to the jth terminal. The current at any of the other terminals can then be measured. Only the jth column of the matrix

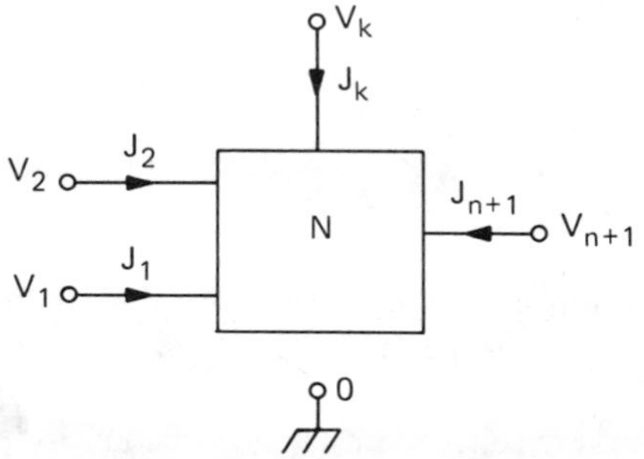

Fig. 2.1.1. Network with $n + 1$ terminals.

(2.1.2) remains, giving

$$y_{ij}V_j = J_i; \qquad i = 1, 2, \ldots, n+1 \tag{2.1.3}$$

or

$$y_{ij} = \left.\frac{J_i}{V_j}\right|_{\substack{\text{all terminals except the}\\ j\text{th grounded.}}}$$

Repeating the experiment for all other terminals will provide the entries of the matrix in (2.1.1).

An important property of the **Y** matrix is obtained by considering the sum of equations (2.1.3):

$$V_j \sum_{i=1}^{n+1} y_{ij} = \sum_{i=1}^{n+1} J_i.$$

The right side is the sum of all currents flowing out of node 0. The Kirchhoff current law requires this sum to be zero. Since a source of specified value was applied to the jth terminal, $V_j \neq 0$; the sum $\Sigma_{i=1}^{n+1}\ y_{ij}$ must be equal to zero. Letting $j = 1, 2, \ldots, n+1$, we establish that *the sum of admittances in each column of the matrix* **Y** *is equal to zero.*

Next consider the case where the voltage source is connected between the jth terminal and grounded reference node while the other terminals are left floating. This is a pathological situation since no current can flow and all the terminals of a connected network must be at the same potential V_j. Consider the first row of (2.1.2). We have

$$y_{11}V_j + y_{12}V_j + \cdots + y_{1,n+1}V_j = 0$$

or, for row i,

$$V_j \sum_{k=1}^{n+1} y_{ik} = 0.$$

Since we connected a nonzero voltage source V_j, the sum must be equal to zero and we conclude that *the sum of admittances in each row of the* **Y** *matrix is equal to zero.*

As long as the grounded reference node is not a part of the network, there is linear dependence among the rows and columns of **Y** and the determinant of the matrix is zero. This matrix is called the *indefinite nodal admittance matrix.*

In the first chapter it was shown that sources can be mutually transformed into each other by the Thévenin and Norton theorems. Assume that such transformations have been applied and that the network contains only resistors, capacitors, inductors, and current sources. We will now indicate how both the right-hand-side vector **J** and the matrix **Y** can be formed by inspection. The resulting set of equations is called the *nodal formulation.*

The method is based on the observation that the sum of currents at any node is zero (KCL). At any node, there are two sets of currents, those flowing through the passive components and those due to the independent current sources. Let us write the KCL at each node as

$$\sum\begin{pmatrix}\text{currents } \textit{leaving} \text{ the node}\\ \text{through passive components}\end{pmatrix} = \sum\begin{pmatrix}\text{currents } \textit{entering} \text{ the node}\\ \text{from independent sources}\end{pmatrix}.$$

The above relation shows directly how the right-hand-side vector is written by inspection. Now consider a general node i with some components connected to it as shown in Fig. 2.1.2. Write the KCL at this node as

$$I_C - I_G + I_L = J$$

and replace the passive element currents in terms of element admittances and node voltages:

$$sC(V_i - V_j) - G(V_k - V_i) + \frac{1}{sL}(V_i - V_l) = J \tag{2.1.4a}$$

or

$$sC(V_i - V_j) + G(V_i - V_k) + \frac{1}{sL}(V_i - V_l) = J. \tag{2.1.4b}$$

The node voltages measured with respect to the reference node have subscripts identical to the numbers on the nodes (in circles on the diagram). We do not

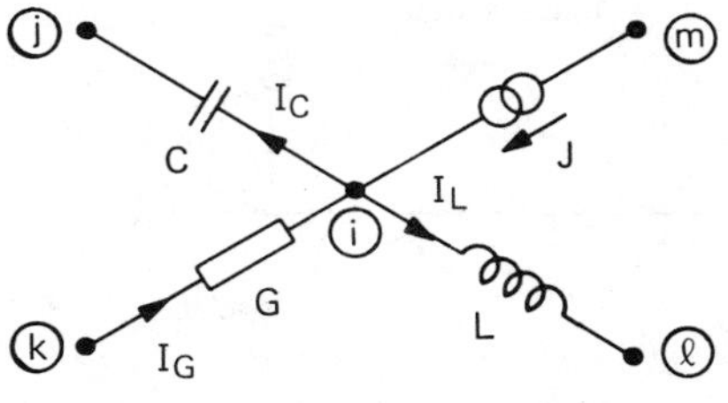

Fig. 2.1.2. A general node i in the network.

know the proper orientations for the branch currents at this stage; all we can do is assume certain orientations and then assign proper directions for the voltage across the element. This freedom in the choice of element current orientation does not change the form of the equation, as seen by comparing (2.1.4a) and (2.1.4b). The KCL for node i has as its final form

$$\left(sC + G + \frac{1}{sL}\right) V_i - sCV_j - GV_k - \frac{1}{sL} V_l = J. \tag{2.1.5}$$

EXAMPLE 2.1.1. Consider the network in Fig. 2.1.3 in which a number of sources have been applied to clearly demonstrate the way of forming **J**. Write the KCL for nodes 1 to 4 with the passive element currents given in terms of node voltages and element admittances:

$$G_1(V_1 - V_4) + (sC_4 + G_7)(V_1 - V_2) + G_6(V_1 - V_3) = J_1 - J_6 + J_4$$

$$(sC_4 + G_7)(V_2 - V_1) + \frac{1}{sL_2}(V_2 - V_4) + sC_5(V_2 - V_3) = -J_4$$

$$\frac{1}{sL_3}(V_3 - V_4) + sC_5(V_3 - V_2) + G_6(V_3 - V_1) = J_3 + J_6$$

$$G_1(V_4 - V_1) + \frac{1}{sL_2}(V_4 - V_2) + \frac{1}{sL_3}(V_4 - V_3) = -J_1 - J_3$$

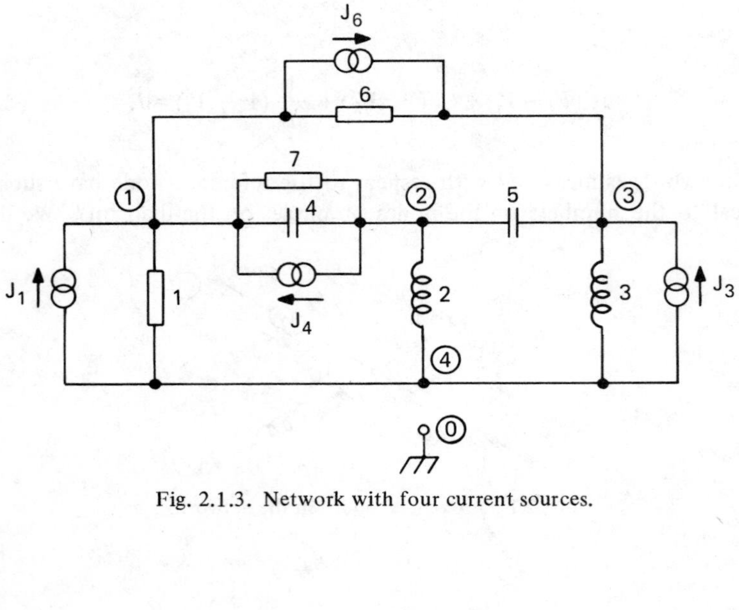

Fig. 2.1.3. Network with four current sources.

Regrouping terms we have the nodal equations

$$\begin{array}{c} \textit{node} \\ 1 \\ 2 \\ 3 \\ 4 \end{array}\begin{bmatrix} G_1+sC_4+G_6+G_7 & -sC_4-G_7 & -G_6 & -G_1 \\ -sC_4-G_7 & 1/sL_2+sC_4+sC_5+G_7 & -sC_5 & -1/sL_2 \\ -G_6 & -sC_5 & 1/sL_3+sC_5+G_6 & -1/sL_3 \\ -G_1 & -1/sL_2 & -1/sL_3 & G_1+\dfrac{1}{sL_2}+\dfrac{1}{sL_3} \end{bmatrix}$$

$$\begin{bmatrix} V_1 \\ V_2 \\ V_3 \\ V_4 \end{bmatrix} = \begin{bmatrix} J_1+J_4-J_6 \\ -J_4 \\ J_3+J_6 \\ -J_1-J_3 \end{bmatrix}.$$

The rules for forming the nodal equations by inspection can now be stated:

1. The diagonal entries of **Y** are positive and

$$y_{jj} = \sum \text{admittances connected to node } j.$$

2. The off-diagonal entries of **Y** are negative and are given by

$$y_{jk} = -\sum \text{admittances connected between nodes } j \text{ and } k$$

3. The jth entry of the right-hand-side vector **J** is

$$J_j = \sum \text{currents from independent sources entering node } j.$$

The above rules are useful when formulating network equations by hand as they enable us to write the equations on a *node-by-node* basis. For computer formulation an *element-by-element* approach is preferable, as the equations are set up in a single scan of the element list.

Consider an element with admittance y connected between nodes j and k as shown in Fig. 2.1.4. Let the current through this element be denoted by I with orientation from node j to node k. The current I will appear only in the KCL equations associated with nodes j and k, once with positive sign and once with

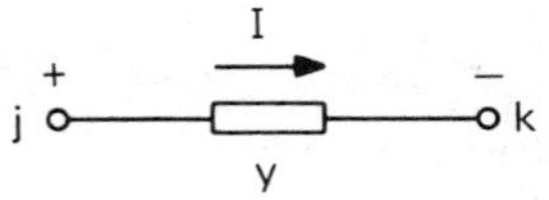

Fig. 2.1.4. An isolated element.

negative sign:

$$\text{KCL at node } j: \qquad \cdots +I \cdots = \cdots$$

$$\text{KCL at node } k: \qquad \cdots -I \cdots = \cdots$$

where $\cdots$ indicates entries due to other elements and sources. Let us now write the current I in terms of the voltage across the element, $V_j - V_k$, and the admittance y:

$$\text{KCL at node } j: \qquad \cdots +y(V_j - V_k) \cdots = \cdots$$

$$\text{KCL at node } k: \qquad \cdots -y(V_j - V_k) \cdots = \cdots$$

Separating the terms associated with the voltages,

$$\text{KCL at node } j: \qquad \cdots +yV_j \cdots -yV_k \cdots = \cdots$$

$$\text{KCL at node } k: \qquad \cdots -yV_j \cdots +yV_k \cdots = \cdots$$

We thus find that the admittance of a two-terminal element connected between nodes j and k appears only in rows and columns j and k of $\mathbf{Y}$ with plus sign at locations (j, j) and (k, k) and with a minus sign at (j, k) and (k, j). Symbolically this is written as

$$\begin{array}{c} \\ j \\ k \end{array} \begin{array}{c} \begin{array}{cc} j & k \end{array} \\ \begin{bmatrix} y & -y \\ -y & y \end{bmatrix} \end{array} \tag{2.1.6}$$

with the equivalent algebraic representation being

$$y(\mathbf{e}_j - \mathbf{e}_k)(\mathbf{e}_j - \mathbf{e}_k)^t \tag{2.1.7}$$

where superscript t denotes transpose and $\mathbf{e}_j$ is the jth unit vector with 1 at location j and zeros elsewhere. The vector $\mathbf{e}_j$ can also be viewed as the jth column of the identity matrix. In Eq. (2.1.7) we have formed the *outer product* of two vectors which gives a matrix as a result. We are now in a position to write the $\mathbf{Y}$ matrix on an element-by-element basis. Let y_i denote the admittance of element i connected between nodes j_i and k_i. Then

$$\mathbf{Y} = \sum_i y_i(\mathbf{e}_{j_i} - \mathbf{e}_{k_i})(\mathbf{e}_{j_i} - \mathbf{e}_{k_i})^t. \tag{2.1.8}$$

For the right-hand-side vector we note that an independent current source of value J connected between nodes j and k (oriented toward k) contributes to rows j and k of $\mathbf{J}$ as follows:

$$\begin{matrix} j \\ k \end{matrix} \begin{bmatrix} -J \\ J \end{bmatrix}. \tag{2.1.9}$$

Algebraically, (2.1.9) is written as $-J(\mathbf{e}_j - \mathbf{e}_k)$ and, when there are many current sources in the network, the right-hand-side vector is given as

$$\mathbf{J} = -\sum_i J_i(\mathbf{e}_{j_i} - \mathbf{e}_{k_i}). \tag{2.1.10}$$

The symbolic representations (2.1.6), (2.1.9) and the algebraic forms (2.1.8), (2.1.10) are the key to computerized equation formulation and will be extended later to other kinds of elements.

Returning to (2.1.2) we see that identifying the jth terminal of the network with the grounded reference node means that the voltage V_j becomes zero. Since the jth column of $\mathbf{Y}$ is always multiplied by V_j, the terms of this product will be equal to zero and the jth column can be deleted from the matrix. Moreover, grounding also determines the current which will flow into this terminal; it will be the negative of the sum of all the other currents flowing to the ground node (KCL, the sum of currents flowing from a node is equal to zero). Thus, there is no need to retain the jth row, since it is a linear combination of the other rows. We conclude that grounding the jth node is equivalent to deleting the jth row and column from the matrix $\mathbf{Y}$.

If at least one node of the network is connected by a short circuit to the grounded reference node, the matrix of the system becomes definite, unless some pathological situation occurs (for instance, we cannot consider as one network two unconnected structures). The resulting matrix will be called the *nodal admittance matrix*. It is usually written directly without the superfluous row and column. In terms of our symbolic representations we see that (2.1.6) or (2.1.9) will contain only a single entry if the element is connected to the ground node. No modification is required to (2.1.8) or (2.1.10) if we let $\mathbf{e}_0$ denote the null vector. The indefinite nodal matrix has limited use. From now on, $\mathbf{Y}$ will denote the nodal admittance matrix of a connected network having $n + 1$ nodes, n of these nodes ungrounded and the $(n + 1)$st, denoted by zero, connected to ground.

2.2. NODAL FORMULATION FOR NETWORKS WITH VCTs

The voltage-to-current transducer (VCT) introduced in Chapter 1 can be easily incorporated into the nodal formulation. Denote its input terminals by the letters j, j' and its output terminals by k, k', as shown in Fig. 2.2.1. Its consti-

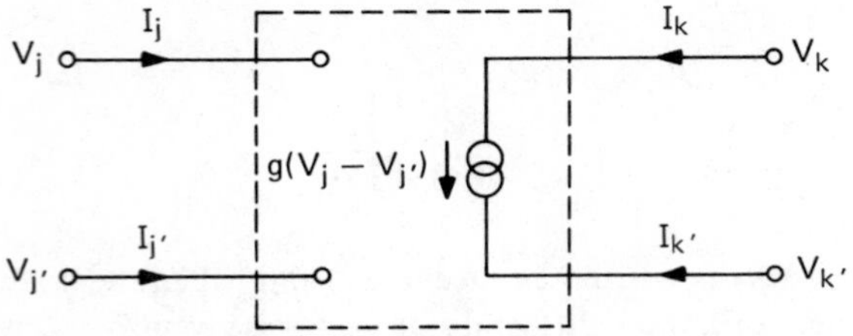

Fig. 2.2.1. VCT in terminal notation.

tutive equations in terms of the currents and voltages shown are

$$
\begin{aligned}
I_j &= 0\\
I_{j'} &= 0\\
I_k &= g(V_j - V_{j'})\\
I_{k'} &= -g(V_j - V_{j'})
\end{aligned}
$$

Proceeding as in the last section it is easy to show that the VCT transconductance g will appear in the **Y** matrix only in the positions indicated below:

$$
\begin{array}{c} \\ j \\ j' \\ k \\ k' \end{array}
\begin{array}{c} \begin{array}{cccc} j & j' & k & k' \end{array} \\
\left[\begin{array}{cccc} 0 & 0 & 0 & 0 \\ 0 & 0 & 0 & 0 \\ g & -g & 0 & 0 \\ -g & g & 0 & 0 \end{array}\right] \end{array}. \tag{2.2.1}
$$

In algebraic form the matrix is expressed as follows:

$$
g(\mathbf{e}_k - \mathbf{e}_{k'})(\mathbf{e}_j - \mathbf{e}_{j'})^t. \tag{2.2.2}
$$

EXAMPLE 2.2.1. Consider the network shown in Fig. 2.2.2. The **Y**-matrix is filled according to rule (2.1.6) for passive elements and the VCT is entered by applying rule (2.2.1) where we set $j = 2$, $j' = 0$, $k = 3$, $k' = 0$.

$$
\mathbf{Y} = \begin{bmatrix} G_1 + G_2 + G_5 & -G_2 & -G_5 \\ -G_2 & G_2 + G_3 & -G_3 \\ -G_5 & -G_3 + g & G_3 + G_4 + G_5 \end{bmatrix}.
$$

The source vector has the form $\mathbf{J} = (J, 0, 0)^t$.

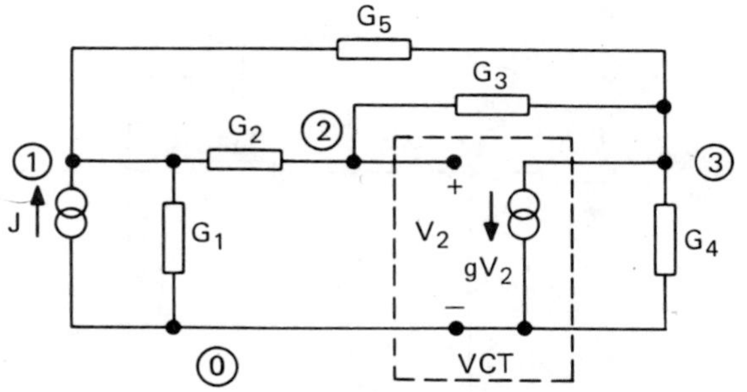

Fig. 2.2.2. Network with a VCT.

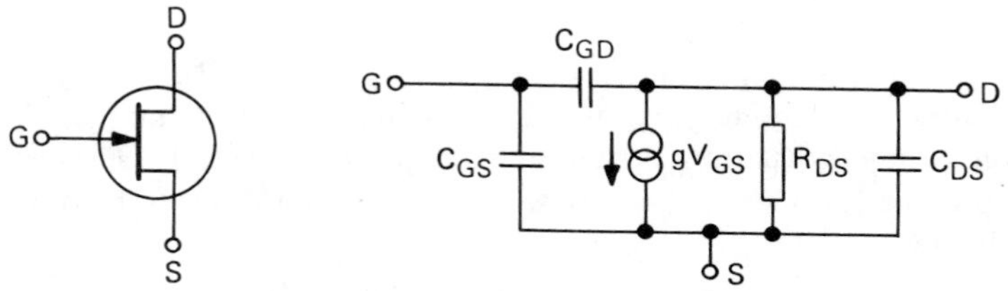

Fig. 2.2.3. Hybrid Π model for the field effect transistor.

Many practical networks can be simulated by means of VCTs. If small signals are considered, transistors or diodes can be linearized about the operating point and substituted by linear models. Figure 2.2.3 shows the usual small-signal model for a FET (field-effect transistor) and Fig. 2.2.4 that of a bipolar transistor. These are called *hybrid* Π models and are widely used. The entries created in the **Y** matrix by a FET are

$$\begin{array}{c} \\ G \\ D \\ S \end{array}\begin{array}{c} \begin{array}{ccc} G & D & S \end{array} \\ \begin{bmatrix} Y_{GD}+Y_{GS} & -Y_{GD} & -Y_{GS} \\ -Y_{GD}+g & Y_{GD}+Y_{DS} & -Y_{DS}-g \\ -Y_{GS}-g & -Y_{DS} & Y_{GS}+Y_{DS}+g \end{bmatrix} \end{array}$$

where $Y_{GD} = sC_{GD}$, $Y_{GS} = sC_{GS}$, $Y_{DS} = sC_{DS} + 1/R_{DS}$. For the bipolar transistor

$$\begin{array}{c} \\ b \\ b' \\ c \\ e \end{array}\begin{array}{c} \begin{array}{cccc} b & b' & c & e \end{array} \\ \begin{bmatrix} Y_{bb'} & -Y_{bb'} & 0 & 0 \\ -Y_{bb'} & Y_{bb'}+Y_{b'c}+Y_{b'e} & -Y_{b'c} & -Y_{b'e} \\ 0 & -Y_{b'c}+g_m & Y_{b'c}+Y_{ce} & -Y_{ce}-g_m \\ 0 & -Y_{b'e}-g_m & -Y_{ce} & Y_{b'e}+Y_{ce}+g_m \end{bmatrix} \end{array}$$

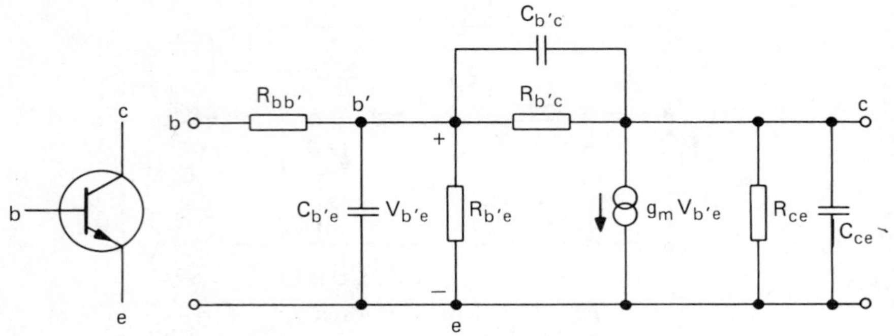

Fig. 2.2.4. Hybrid Π model for the bipolar transistor.

where $Y_{bb'} = 1/R_{bb'}$, $Y_{b'c} = sC_{b'c} + 1/R_{b'c}$, $Y_{b'e} = sC_{b'e} + 1/R_{b'e}$, $Y_{ce} = sC_{ce} + 1/R_{ce}$. Note that though transistors create nonsymmetry in the **Y** matrix, *structural* symmetry (pattern of zero-nonzero positions) is still maintained. This is an important consideration in sparse reordering algorithms, to be treated later in this chapter.

2.3. MESH FORMULATION

The mesh formulation is similar to the nodal formulation and is useful in hand calculations on simple networks. Its use in computer applications is limited because (a) it is only valid for planar networks and (b) algorithms for testing planarity and automatically generating meshes are complicated. A *planar* network is one which can be drawn on paper without any element crossing over another element. While many practical networks are planar, it is not difficult to give simple examples that are nonplanar—for instance, the network shown in Fig. 2.3.1, where each line segment denotes an element. The basis for the mesh formulation is the Kirchhoff voltage law: *the sum of voltage drops around any loop is zero.*

Consider the network shown in Fig. 2.3.2. Many different loops can be chosen which go through some of the elements and return to the point they

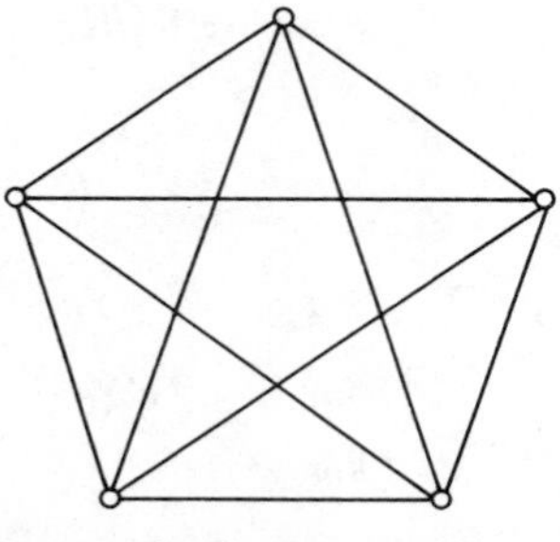

Fig. 2.3.1. A nonplanar network. Each line represents an arbitrary element.

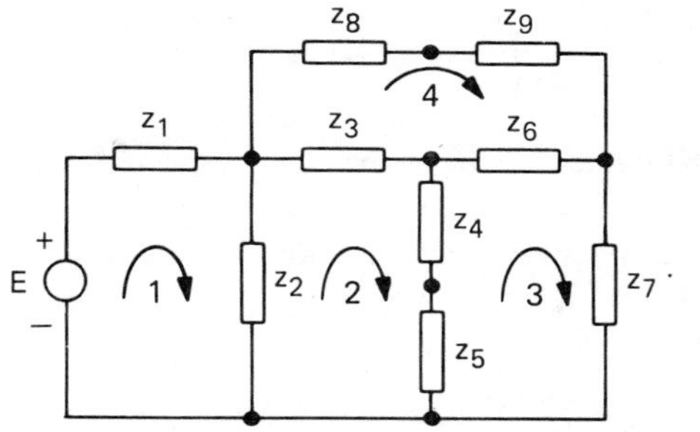

Fig. 2.3.2. Network analyzed by the mesh method.

started from. For instance, a loop could pass through the elements z_1, z_8, z_9, z_7, and the voltage source (the outer loop). Another one could go through the elements z_3, z_6, z_7, z_2, and so on. Additional loops are indicated in the figure by arrows. It is easily seen that the number of possible loops may be quite high. The important question is how many should be used in order to obtain a complete set of equations and how to choose the best set.

It will be shown in Chapter 3 that we must select $b - n$ loops, where b is the number of branches and n the number of ungrounded nodes. The independent loops may be selected in various ways. We propose the following procedure which makes the mesh formulation essentially a dual of the nodal formulation. Consider again the network shown in Fig. 2.3.2 and place one loop into each "window" formed by the elements. In a planar network this is always possible. These loops will be called ***meshes*** and are indicated by numbers 1, 2, 3, 4 in the figure. It is immaterial which orientation we assign to these meshes, but the equations are simplified if they are all either clockwise or counterclockwise. We have adopted the clockwise orientation. Associated with each mesh is a hypothetical *circulating current;* as this current passes through the elements it creates voltage drops across them. The sum of such voltages around each mesh must be zero. For the network shown we write

$$z_1 I_1 + z_2(I_1 - I_2) - E = 0$$

$$z_2(I_2 - I_1) + z_3(I_2 - I_4) + (z_4 + z_5)(I_2 - I_3) = 0$$

$$(z_4 + z_5)(I_3 - I_2) + z_6(I_3 - I_4) + z_7 I_3 = 0$$

$$z_3(I_4 - I_2) + (z_8 + z_9) I_4 + z_6(I_4 - I_3) = 0$$

Rearranging the equations we arrive at:

$$\begin{bmatrix} z_1 + z_2 & -z_2 & 0 & 0 \\ -z_2 & z_2 + z_3 + z_4 + z_5 & -z_4 - z_5 & -z_3 \\ 0 & -z_4 - z_5 & z_4 + z_5 + z_6 + z_7 & -z_6 \\ 0 & -z_3 & -z_6 & z_3 + z_6 + z_8 + z_9 \end{bmatrix} \begin{bmatrix} I_1 \\ I_2 \\ I_3 \\ I_4 \end{bmatrix} = \begin{bmatrix} E \\ 0 \\ 0 \\ 0 \end{bmatrix}$$

or

$$\mathbf{ZI} = \mathbf{E}. \tag{2.3.1}$$

Due to the special choice of the loops–the meshes–and due to the fact that the orientations of all meshes are the same, we see that the matrix **Z** and vector **E** can be written by inspection using the following simple rules:

1. The diagonal entries of **Z** are positive and

$$z_{ii} = \sum \text{impedances associated with mesh } i.$$

2. The off-diagonal entries of **Z** are negative and given by

$$z_{ij} = -\sum \text{impedances common to meshes } i \text{ and } j.$$

3. The ith entry of the right-hand-side vector **E** is

$$E_i = \sum \text{voltage rise in mesh } i \text{ due to independent sources.}$$

As in the case of the nodal formulation, a symbolic rule for entering the impedances can be stated: If the impedance z is common to meshes j and k, the value z is added to the entries (j, j), (k, k) and subtracted from the entries (j, k) and (k, j):

$$\begin{array}{c c} & \begin{array}{cc} j & k \end{array} \\ \begin{array}{c} j \\ k \end{array} & \begin{bmatrix} z & -z \\ -z & z \end{bmatrix} \end{array}. \tag{2.3.2}$$

If the element is in the jth mesh only, its impedance appears only in position (j, j), with positive sign.

The rules given above can be extended to cover current-to-voltage transducers, gyrators and transformers. Since this method is rarely used in computer applications and is not needed in subsequent chapters, we omit further details.

2.4. LINEAR EQUATIONS AND GAUSSIAN ELIMINATION

All network formulations result in a system of equations. If the network is linear, the equations are linear. Nonlinear networks lead to a system of nonlinear equations, but the solution is carried out by linearizing them about some operating point. Thus, the methods of solving systems of linear equations are basic to all problems. Solution of linear equations is carried out either by direct or iterative methods. In this text we will concentrate on direct solution methods only.

Consider the system of linear equations

$$\mathbf{Ax} = \mathbf{b} \tag{2.4.1}$$

where **A** is a constant $n \times n$ matrix, **b** is an n-vector of known constants, and **x** is an n-vector of unknowns:

$$\begin{bmatrix} a_{11} & a_{12} \cdots a_{1n} \\ a_{21} & a_{22} \cdots a_{2n} \\ \vdots & \vdots \\ a_{n1} & a_{n2} \cdots a_{nn} \end{bmatrix} \begin{bmatrix} x_1 \\ x_2 \\ \vdots \\ x_n \end{bmatrix} = \begin{bmatrix} b_1 \\ b_2 \\ \vdots \\ b_n \end{bmatrix}. \tag{2.4.2}$$

Formally, the system is solved by inverting the matrix **A**:

$$\mathbf{x} = \mathbf{A}^{-1}\mathbf{b}. \tag{2.4.3}$$

Very often, if only one "output" variable is needed, the solution is carried out by a method called *Cramer's rule*. It states that for systems of the form (2.4.1), the kth component x_k of the solution vector **x** is obtained as follows:

$$x_k = \frac{\det\,[\text{Matrix } \mathbf{A} \text{ with } k\text{th column replaced by } \mathbf{b}]}{\det \mathbf{A}}. \tag{2.4.4}$$

Cramer's rule can be used when solving small problems and is needed in theoretical considerations. However, it is computationally expensive and seldom used in computer applications. The same is true of matrix inversion.

The numerical solution of systems of linear equations is often performed by Gaussian elimination. It is one of the best known algorithms and is based on the fact that adding one equation, possibly multiplied by a constant, to another equation does not change the solution of the system.

Consider (2.4.2) but rewrite it as a set of equations and denote the components b_i of the right-hand-side vector by $a_{i,n+1}$. This simplifies further notation. The system becomes

$$\begin{aligned} a_{11}x_1 + a_{12}x_2 + \cdots + a_{1n}x_n &= a_{1,n+1} \\ a_{21}x_1 + a_{22}x_2 + \cdots + a_{2n}x_n &= a_{2,n+1} \\ \cdots\cdots\cdots\cdots\cdots\cdots & \cdots\cdots \\ a_{n1}x_1 + a_{n2}x_2 + \cdots + a_{nn}x_n &= a_{n,n+1}\,. \end{aligned} \tag{2.4.5}$$

Divide the first equation by a_{11} and write it as

$$x_1 + a_{12}^{(1)}x_2 + a_{13}^{(1)}x_3 + \cdots = a_{1,n+1}^{(1)}\,.$$

The notation means that $a_{12}^{(1)} = a_{12}/a_{11}$, etc. Multiply this equation by $-a_{21}$ and add it to the second one. The coefficients of the new second equation are

$$a_{2j}^{(1)} = a_{2j} - a_{21}a_{1j}^{(1)}; \qquad j = 1, 2, \ldots, n+1.$$

This choice of the multiplying factor secures that $a_{21}^{(1)}$ becomes zero. Similarly, for the other equations, setting

$$a_{ij}^{(1)} = a_{ij} - a_{i1} a_{1j}^{(1)}; \qquad \begin{cases} i = 2, 3, \ldots, n \\ j = 1, 2, \ldots, n+1 \end{cases}$$

makes all coefficients of the first column zero with the exception of $a_{11}^{(1)}$, which is 1. In fact, we need not calculate elements which become zero; the elements a_{i1} are left in the computer memory and the calculation proceeds from $j = 2$. As a result of the above operations, the equations will have the form

$$\begin{aligned} x_1 + a_{12}^{(1)} x_2 + a_{13}^{(1)} x_3 + \cdots + a_{1n}^{(1)} x_n &= a_{1,n+1}^{(1)} \\ a_{22}^{(1)} x_2 + a_{23}^{(1)} x_3 + \cdots + a_{2n}^{(1)} x_n &= a_{2,n+1}^{(1)} \\ \cdots\cdots\cdots\cdots\cdots\cdots\cdots\cdots &\cdots\cdots \\ a_{n2}^{(1)} x_2 + a_{n3}^{(1)} x_3 + \cdots + a_{nn}^{(1)} x_n &= a_{n,n+1}^{(1)} . \end{aligned}$$

The superscripts (in brackets) show that the values have been changed once.

In the next step we exclude the first row and column and apply the same procedure to equations 2 through n. The formulae become

$$\begin{aligned} a_{2j}^{(2)} &= a_{2j}^{(1)} / a_{22}^{(1)}; \\ a_{ij}^{(2)} &= a_{ij}^{(1)} - a_{i2}^{(1)} a_{2j}^{(2)}; \end{aligned} \qquad \begin{cases} i = 3, 4, \ldots, n \\ j = 3, 4, \ldots, n+1. \end{cases}$$

For efficiency, we omit computing $a_{i2}^{(2)} = 0$. The process will be repeated for all rows. With the initialization $a_{ij}^{(0)} = a_{ij}$, the general formula for Gaussian elimination becomes

$$\begin{aligned} a_{kj}^{(k)} &= a_{kj}^{(k-1)} / a_{kk}^{(k-1)}; \\ a_{ij}^{(k)} &= a_{ij}^{(k-1)} - a_{ik}^{(k-1)} a_{kj}^{(k)}; \end{aligned} \qquad \begin{cases} k = 1, 2, \ldots, n \\ i = k+1, \ldots, n \\ j = k+1, \ldots, n+1. \end{cases} \tag{2.4.6}$$

The resulting equations now have the form

$$\begin{aligned} x_1 + a_{12}^{(1)} x_2 + a_{13}^{(1)} x_3 + \cdots + a_{1n}^{(1)} x_n &= a_{1,n+1}^{(1)} \\ x_2 + a_{23}^{(2)} x_3 + \cdots + a_{2n}^{(2)} x_n &= a_{2,n+1}^{(2)} \\ x_3 + \cdots + a_{3n}^{(3)} x_n &= a_{3,n+1}^{(3)} \\ &\vdots \\ x_n &= a_{n,n+1}^{(n)} . \end{aligned} \tag{2.4.7}$$

The remaining steps in the solution are called *back substitution*. The last variable, x_n, is used in the $(n-1)$st equation to obtain x_{n-1}, and so on. In general, the back substitution is

$$x_i = a_{i,n+1} - \sum_{j=i+1}^{n} a_{ij}x_j; \qquad i = n-1, n-2, \ldots, 1 \tag{2.4.8}$$

where the superscripts have been dropped.

In computer jargon the cost of an algorithm is measured in terms of *operations*, each operation being the combination of a multiplication and a subtraction. It can be shown that Gaussian elimination requires $\sim n^3/3$ operations, n being the size of the matrix, while the back substitution can be performed in $\sim n^2/2$ operations.

2.5. TRIANGULAR DECOMPOSITION

In network applications, the solution of algebraic equations is best performed by the *triangular decomposition* or **LU** *factorization* technique. Algorithms for triangular factorization are closely related to Gaussian elimination, though the computations might be performed in a different sequence. The main advantage of triangular decomposition over Gaussian elimination is that it enables simple solution of systems with different right-hand-side vectors as well as *transpose systems* that are required in sensitivity computations.

Let the system of equations be given by (2.4.1) and assume that we can factor the matrix **A** as follows:

$$\mathbf{A} = \mathbf{LU} \tag{2.5.1}$$

where

$$\mathbf{L} = \begin{bmatrix} l_{11} & & & \\ l_{21} & l_{22} & & \mathbf{0} \\ l_{31} & l_{32} & l_{33} & \\ \cdots & \cdots & \cdots & \cdots \\ l_{n1} & l_{n2} & l_{n3} \cdots & l_{nn} \end{bmatrix} \tag{2.5.2}$$

and

$$\mathbf{U} = \begin{bmatrix} 1 & u_{12} & u_{13} \cdots & u_{1n} \\ & 1 & u_{23} \cdots & u_{2n} \\ & & 1 \quad \cdots & u_{3n} \\ & \mathbf{0} & & \vdots \\ & & & 1 \end{bmatrix}. \tag{2.5.3}$$

L stands for *lower triangular* and **U** for *upper triangular*. Notice the ones on the main diagonal of **U**. This means that the determinant of **A** is found as the product of the l_{ii} elements of the **L** matrix.

We will derive the algorithm for finding **L** and **U** later and assume here that the decomposition is indeed possible. The system of equations is written as follows:

$$\mathbf{LUx} = \mathbf{b}. \tag{2.5.4}$$

Define an auxiliary vector **z** as

$$\mathbf{Ux} = \mathbf{z}. \tag{2.5.5}$$

At this time, **z** cannot be calculated because **x** is unknown. However, substituting **z** into (2.5.4) we get

$$\mathbf{Lz} = \mathbf{b}. \tag{2.5.6}$$

Due to the special form of **L**, the vector **z** can be calculated very simply. Rewrite the product in the form of equations:

$$\begin{aligned}
&l_{11}z_1 &&= b_1\\
&l_{21}z_1 + l_{22}z_2 &&= b_2\\
&l_{31}z_1 + l_{32}z_2 + l_{33}z_3 &&= b_3\\
& &&\;\vdots\\
&l_{n1}z_1 + l_{n2}z_2 + \cdots + l_{nn}z_n &&= b_n.
\end{aligned}$$

Starting from the first equation we write the solution as follows:

$$\begin{aligned}
z_1 &= b_1/l_{11}\\
z_2 &= (b_2 - l_{21}z_1)/l_{22}\\
z_3 &= (b_3 - l_{31}z_1 - l_{32}z_2)/l_{33},
\end{aligned}$$

and, in general,

$$\begin{aligned}
z_1 &= b_1/l_{11}\\
z_i &= \left(b_i - \sum_{j=1}^{i-1} l_{ij}z_j\right)\Big/ l_{ii}; \qquad i = 2, 3, \ldots, n.
\end{aligned} \tag{2.5.7}$$

This is called the *forward elimination* or *substitution* process. The diagonal elements in **L** must be nonzero in order that (2.5.7) be meaningful. Now go back to (2.5.5) and solve for the unknown **x**. Write the following set of equations:

$$\begin{aligned} x_1 + u_{12}x_2 + u_{13}x_3 + \cdots + u_{1n}x_n &= z_1 \\ x_2 + u_{23}x_3 + \cdots + u_{2n}x_n &= z_2 \\ &\vdots \\ x_{n-1} + u_{n-1,n}x_n &= z_{n-1} \\ x_n &= z_n. \end{aligned}$$

Starting with the last equation and working upward we establish the following general formula:

$$\begin{aligned} x_n &= z_n \\ x_i &= z_i - \sum_{j=i+1}^{n} u_{ij}z_j; \qquad i = n-1, n-2, \ldots, 1. \end{aligned} \tag{2.5.8}$$

This process is called *back substitution*. The number of operations required for the forward and back substitutions is approximately $n^2/2$ each, a total of n^2 for the solution. A close examination of Eqs. (2.5.7) shows that b_i is used only to compute z_i and is not required later. Similarly in (2.5.8) z_i is not required after x_i has been computed. Thus the variables **b**, **z**, and **x** may share the same memory locations in a computer implementation of this scheme. Note also the equivalence in the back substitutions in Eqs. (2.5.8) and (2.4.8).

We now derive the algorithm for **LU** decomposition. Consider a 4 X 4 matrix, assume the factorization exists and take the product of **L** and **U**:

$$\begin{bmatrix} l_{11} & l_{11}u_{12} & l_{11}u_{13} & l_{11}u_{14} \\ l_{21} & l_{21}u_{12} + l_{22} & l_{21}u_{13} + l_{22}u_{23} & l_{21}u_{14} + l_{22}u_{24} \\ l_{31} & l_{31}u_{12} + l_{32} & l_{31}u_{13} + l_{32}u_{23} + l_{33} & l_{31}u_{14} + l_{32}u_{24} + l_{33}u_{34} \\ l_{41} & l_{41}u_{12} + l_{42} & l_{41}u_{13} + l_{42}u_{23} + l_{43} & l_{41}u_{14} + l_{42}u_{24} + l_{43}u_{34} + l_{44} \end{bmatrix}.$$

Let us now compare this product with the 4 X 4 matrix **A**. We see that the first column of the decomposition remains unchanged and that all $l_{i1} = a_{i1}$, $i = 1, 2, 3, 4$. We also note that the first row of the product can be used to obtain the first row of the **U** matrix by solving $l_{11}u_{1j} = a_{1j}$ for the unknown u's, $j = 2, 3, 4$. In the next step we notice that the second column contains only u_{12} and known values l_{i1} so that the $l_{i2}, i = 2, 3, 4, \ldots,$ can be calculated from

$$l_{i2} = a_{i2} - l_{i1}u_{12}; \qquad i = 2, 3, 4.$$

Since we know l_{21}, l_{22}, and u_{1j}, the second row can be used to calculate u_{2j}, $j = 3, 4$:

$$u_{2j} = (a_{2j} - l_{21}u_{1j})/l_{22}; \qquad j = 3, 4.$$

The algorithm proceeds in the same way by alternating rows and columns. At the kth step of the factorization the entries in row k of **U** and in column k of **L** are computed. To derive the algorithm formally, consider the product of **L** and **U**. We require

$$a_{ij} = \sum_{m=1}^{n} l_{im}u_{mj} = \sum_{m=1}^{\min(i,j)} l_{im}u_{mj}$$

where the upper limit on the sum is changed to reflect the zeros in **L** and **U**. Let us consider a typical entry on or below the diagonal, $i \geqslant j$, and use the index symbol k in place of j:

$$a_{ik} = \sum_{m=1}^{k} l_{im}u_{mk} = l_{ik} + \sum_{m=1}^{k-1} l_{im}u_{mk}$$

as $u_{kk} = 1$. Rewriting we get

$$l_{ik} = a_{ik} - \sum_{m=1}^{k-1} l_{im}u_{mk}; \qquad i \geqslant k. \tag{2.5.9}$$

Similarly consider a typical entry in the upper triangle, $i < j$, and use the index symbol k in place of i:

$$a_{kj} = \sum_{m=1}^{k} l_{km}u_{mj} = l_{kk}u_{kj} + \sum_{m=1}^{k-1} l_{km}u_{mj}.$$

Rearranging terms gives:

$$u_{kj} = \left(a_{kj} - \sum_{m=1}^{k-1} l_{km}u_{mj}\right)\Big/ l_{kk}; \qquad j > k. \tag{2.5.10}$$

Equations (2.5.9) and (2.5.10) constitute the *Crout algorithm* for triangular decomposition. The algorithm proceeds by setting $k = 1, 2, \ldots, n$ and using (2.5.9) and (2.5.10). Note that in these equations the required entries of **L** and

U are computed at some previous stage of the process. Further, each a_{ij} entry is required in computing only the corresponding entry of **L** or **U**, depending on whether $i \geqslant j$ or $i < j$. As the zero entries in **L** and **U** and the unit diagonal entries of **U** need not be stored, in computer implementations the matrices **L** and **U** simply overwrite **A**, with **L** occupying the lower and **U** the upper triangle of **A**, respectively. The algorithm can be summarized as follows:

1. Set $k = 1$ and go to step 3.
2. Use (2.5.9) to compute column k of **L**. If $k = n$, stop.
3. Use (2.5.10) to compute row k of **U**.
4. Set $k = k + 1$ and go to step 2.

A simple FORTRAN subroutine CROUT implementing the algorithm is shown as part of Fig. 2.5.1.

An alternative form of the algorithm is obtained if we process our 4 X 4 matrix *row-by-row*. To begin, the first row of **U** is obtained. Then l_{22} is found but computation of the rest of column 2 of **L** is delayed. Row 2 of **U** is now determined. Then the entries l_{32}, l_{33} of **L** and the 3rd row of **U** are found, and so on. In this form of the algorithm the matrix **A** can be asembled on a row-by-row basis, an advantage when dealing with large problems. The FORTRAN subroutine LUROW of Fig. 2.5.1 is a simple implementation of this version of the factorization algorithm. A dual algorithm is obtained if we proceed on a column-by-column basis.

Still another form of the algorithm is obtained by observing the entries of the matrix decomposed into its **L** and **U** factors. Write the decomposition in the form of a single matrix, as follows:

$$\begin{bmatrix} l_{11} & a_{12}/l_{11} & a_{13}/l_{11} & a_{14}/l_{11} \\ l_{21} & a_{22} - l_{21}u_{12} & (a_{23} - l_{21}u_{13})/l_{22} & (a_{24} - l_{21}u_{14})/l_{22} \\ l_{31} & a_{32} - l_{31}u_{12} & a_{33} - l_{31}u_{13} - l_{32}u_{23} & (a_{34} - l_{31}u_{14} - l_{32}u_{24})/l_{33} \\ l_{41} & a_{42} - l_{41}u_{12} & a_{43} - l_{41}u_{13} - l_{42}u_{23} & a_{44} - l_{41}u_{14} - l_{42}u_{24} - l_{43}u_{34} \end{bmatrix} \tag{2.5.11}$$

The first column and row are calculated as above. In the remaining entries we notice that the first subtraction is possible immediately in the whole matrix, since all l_{i1} and u_{1j} are known. Suppose that we perform these subtractions. By doing so, the second column becomes the final result for l_{i2}, $i = 2, 3, \ldots, n$. Similarly, in the second row all that remains to be done is divide all entries by l_{22}. These steps correspond to the steps done at the start, except that the indexing is from 2 on. Again we notice that in the remaining matrix all the second terms can be subtracted and so on. The decomposition algorithm can thus be

```
C**TEST PROGRAM FOR TRIANGULAR FACTORIZATION AND SOLUTION
      DIMENSION A(10,10), B(10)
      READ (5,*) N
      DO 20 J=1,N
         B(J) = J
         DO 10 I=1,N
   10    A(I,J) = 1.
   20 A(J,J) = N
      WRITE (6,50)
      DO 30 I=1,N
   30 WRITE (6,60) (A(I,J),J=1,N),B(I)
      CALL LUG (A,10,N)
C*TO TEST CROUT FACTORIZATION REPLACE ABOVE STATEMENT BY
C     CALL CROUT (A,10,N)
C*AND TO TEST DECOMPOSITION BY ROWS REPLACE BY
C     CALL LUROW (A,10,N)
      CALL SOLVE (A,10,N,B)
C*TO TEST TRANSPOSE SOLVER SOLVET OF CHAPTER 6 REPLACE THE ABOVE BY
C     CALL SOLVET (A,10,N,B)
      WRITE (6,70)
      DO 40 I=1,N
   40 WRITE (6,60) (A(I,J),J=1,N),B(I)
      STOP
   50 FORMAT (' MATRIX A AND RIGHT HAND SIDE VECTOR ARE')
   60 FORMAT (11F10.4)
   70 FORMAT (' FACTORED MATRIX AND SOLUTION ARE')
      END
C*********************************************************************
      SUBROUTINE LUG (A,IA,N)
C*TRIANGULAR FACTORIZATION BY GAUSSIAN TECHNIQUE
C*A IS INPUT MATRIX OF SIZE N WITH ABSOLUTE ROW DIMENSION IA IN THE
C*CALLING PROGRAMME
C*ROUTINE RETURNS LU FACTORS OF A, STORED IN A WHICH IS DESTROYED
      DIMENSION A(IA,N)
      IF (N.EQ.1) RETURN
      NM1 = N-1
      DO 10 K=1,NM1
         KP1 = K+1
         DO 10 J=KP1,N
            T = A(K,J)/A(K,K)
            A(K,J) = T
            DO 10 I=KP1,N
   10 A(I,J) = A(I,J)-T*A(I,K)
      RETURN
      END
C*********************************************************************
      SUBROUTINE SOLVE (A,IA,N,B)
C*ROUTINE SOLVES   A.X = B  WITH RESULT X RETURNED IN B WHICH IS
C*DESTROYED. ON INPUT A CONTAINS THE LU FACTORS OBTAINED FROM LUG,
C*LUROW OR CROUT. IT HAS DIMENSION N WITH THE ABSOLUTE ROW DIMENSION
C*OF A BEING IA IN THE CALLING PROGRAMME.
      DIMENSION A(IA,N), B(N)
C*FORWARD SUBSTITUTION
      B(1) = B(1)/A(1,1)
      IF (N.EQ.1) RETURN
      DO 20 I=2,N
         T = B(I)
         IM1 = I-1
         DO 10 J=1,IM1
   10    T = T-A(I,J)*B(J)
   20 B(I) = T/A(I,I)
C*BACK SUBSTITUTION
      NM1 = N-1
      DO 40 II=1,NM1
         I = N-II
         IP1 = I+1
         T = B(I)
         DO 30 J=IP1,N
   30    T = T-A(I,J)*B(J)
   40 B(I) = T
more...
```

Fig. 2.5.1. Program for triangular decomposition.

```
      RETURN
      END
C**********************************************************************
      SUBROUTINE CROUT (A,IA,N)
C*TRIANGULAR FACTORIZATION BY CROUT DECOMPOSITION
C*A IS THE INPUT MATRIX OF SIZE N WITH ABSOLUTE ROW DIMENSION
C*IA IN THE CALLING PROGRAMME.
C*ROUTINE RETURNS THE LU FACTORS OF A, STORED IN A WHICH IS DESTROYED
      DIMENSION A(IA,N)
C*PROCESS FIRST ROW
      IF (N.EQ.1) RETURN
      DO 10 J=2,N
   10 A(1,J) = A(1,J)/A(1,1)
      NM1 = N-1
      IF (N.EQ.2) GO TO 70
C*START OF MAIN LOOP
      DO 60 K=2,NM1
          KM1 = K-1
C*PROCESS COLUMN K OF L
          DO 30 I=K,N
              T = A(I,K)
              DO 20 M=1,KM1
   20         T = T-A(I,M)*A(M,K)
   30     A(I,K) = T
C*PROCESS ROW K OF U
          KP1 = K+1
          DO 50 J=KP1,N
              T = A(K,J)
              DO 40 M=1,KM1
   40         T = T-A(K,M)*A(M,J)
   50     A(K,J) = T/A(K,K)
   60 CONTINUE
C*PROCESS (N,N) ENTRY
   70 T = A(N,N)
      DO 80 M=1,NM1
   80 T = T-A(N,M)*A(M,N)
      A(N,N) = T
      RETURN
      END
C**********************************************************************
      SUBROUTINE LUROW (A,IA,N)
C*TRIANGULAR FACTORIZATION BY ROW DECOMPOSITION
C*A IS INPUT MATRIX OF SIZE N WITH ABSOLUTE ROW DIMENSION IA IN THE
C*CALLING PROGRAMME
C*ROUTINE RETURNS LU FACTORS OF A, STORED IN A WHICH IS DESTROYED
      DIMENSION A(IA,N)
      IF (N.EQ.1) RETURN
      DO 10 J=2,N
   10 A(1,J) = A(1,J)/A(1,1)
      DO 30 K=2,N
          DO 30 J=2,N
              T = A(K,J)
              MMAX = MIN0(J-1,K-1)
              DO 20 M=1,MMAX
   20         T = T-A(K,M)*A(M,J)
              IF(J.GT.K)T = T/A(K,K)
   30 A(K,J) = T
      RETURN
      END
     sample output for N=4 .....
 MATRIX A AND RIGHT HAND SIDE VECTOR ARE
    4.0000     1.0000     1.0000     1.0000      1.0000
    1.0000     4.0000     1.0000     1.0000      2.0000
    1.0000     1.0000     4.0000     1.0000      3.0000
    1.0000     1.0000     1.0000     4.0000      4.0000
 FACTORED MATRIX AND SOLUTION ARE
    4.0000     0.2500     0.2500     0.2500     -0.1429
    1.0000     3.7500     0.2000     0.2000      0.1905
    1.0000     0.7500     3.6000     0.1667      0.5238
    1.0000     0.7500     0.6000     3.5000      0.8571
```

Fig. 2.5.1. (*Continued*)

stated as follows:

$$\begin{aligned} &1.\ \text{Set } k = 1.\\ &2.\ l_{ik} = a_{ik}; \qquad i \geqslant k,\\ &3.\ u_{kj} = a_{kj}/l_{kk}; \qquad j > k\\ &4.\ a_{ij} = a_{ij} - l_{ik}u_{kj}; \qquad i, j > k\\ &5.\ \text{If } k = n, \text{ stop; else set } k = k + 1 \text{ and go to step 2.} \end{aligned} \tag{2.5.12}$$

Here the equalities should be interpreted as FORTRAN (or equivalent) assignment statements. This algorithm for **LU** decomposition is *identical* to the reduction to triangular form of a matrix by Gaussian elimination except that the zeros are not introduced into the lower triangle; it simply becomes **L**. This, then, is the Gaussian form of triangular decomposition. The FORTRAN subroutine LUG in Fig. 2.5.1 implements the algorithm.

In computer applications the Crout method or decomposition by rows (or columns) is preferred over the Gaussian technique. The reason lies in the structure of the innermost loop in the corresponding implementations (statements 20, 40, and 80 in routine CROUT; statement 20 in LUROW; and statement 10 in LUG). The CROUT and LUROW statements require one less array reference, thus saving on memory access time. Further, the innermost loop is often coded in assembly language and high-precision accumulation of the variable T is possible in CROUT and LUROW.

The important features of triangular decomposition are as follows:

1. Simple calculation of the determinant

$$\det \mathbf{A} = \prod_{i=1}^{n} l_{ii} \tag{2.5.13}$$

2. The decomposed matrices **L**, **U** can overwrite the previous values a_{ij} and be stored in the same space (there is no need to store the units on the main diagonal of **U**).
3. If only the right-hand side-vector **b** is changed, there is no need to recalculate the decomposition and only the forward and back substitutions are performed.
4. Transpose system of the form $\mathbf{A}^t\mathbf{x} = \mathbf{c}$ can be solved using the same triangular factors. This is required for sensitivity calculations and is discussed in Chapter 6.

The number of operations required for **LU** decomposition is given by

$$M = \sum_{j=1}^{n-1} [(n-j) + (n-j)^2] = \frac{n^3}{3} - \frac{n}{3}.$$

In terms of the necessary calculations, **LU** decomposition with its forward and back substitution is *equivalent* to Gaussian elimination; its advantage is in the third and fourth points mentioned above.

EXAMPLE 2.5.1. Calculate the triangular factors of the matrix

$$\begin{bmatrix} 2 & 4 & -4 & 6 \\ 1 & 4 & 2 & 1 \\ 3 & 8 & 1 & 1 \\ 2 & 5 & 0 & 5 \end{bmatrix}.$$

The matrices obtained at various stages of the decomposition using the Crout technique, the row factorization and the Gaussian method are shown below:

Crout method

2	2	-2	3
1	4	2	1
3	8	1	1
2	5	0	5

2	2	-2	3
1	2	2	-1
3	2	1	1
2	1	0	5

2	2	-2	3
1	2	2	-1
3	2	3	-2
2	1	2	5

2	2	-2	3
1	2	2	-1
3	2	3	-2
2	1	2	4

Row factorization

2	2	-2	3
1	4	2	1
3	8	1	1
2	5	0	1

2	2	-2	3
1	2	2	-1
3	8	1	1
2	5	0	5

2	2	-2	3
1	2	2	-1
3	2	3	-2
2	5	0	5

2	2	-2	3
1	2	2	-1
3	2	3	-2
2	1	2	4

Gaussian method

2	2	-2	3
1	2	4	-2
3	2	7	-8
2	1	4	-1

2	2	-2	3
1	2	2	-1
3	2	3	-6
2	1	2	0

2	2	-2	3
1	2	2	-1
3	2	3	-2
2	1	2	4

In each case the factors obtained are

$$\mathbf{L} = \begin{bmatrix} 2 & & & \\ 1 & 2 & & \\ 3 & 2 & 3 & \\ 2 & 1 & 2 & 4 \end{bmatrix}, \qquad \mathbf{U} = \begin{bmatrix} 1 & 2 & -2 & 3 \\ & 1 & 2 & -1 \\ & & 1 & -2 \\ & & & 1 \end{bmatrix}$$

although the matrices generated at intermediate stages of the decomposition are different.

Networks that consist solely of passive elements and independent sources usually lead to systems of equations with a symmetric matrix. In such cases the triangular decomposition algorithm can be modified to generate the factorization $\mathbf{A} = \mathbf{U}^t\mathbf{D}\mathbf{U}$, where $\mathbf{U}$ is unit upper triangular and $\mathbf{D}$ is diagonal. The storage requirements and computing cost are reduced nearly in half as compared with the **LU** decomposition.

2.6. PIVOTING

Partial or full pivoting are techniques which can improve the accuracy of the solution of a system of linear equations. Consider (2.4.5) with the assumption that $a_{11} = 0$. Neither Gaussian elimination nor **LU** decomposition can be used because the process requires division by a_{11}. The element by which we divide is called the *pivot* and division by a zero pivot is not permitted. If such a situation occurs, we can interchange the first equation with another equation having $a_{i1} \neq 0$ and the process becomes feasible.

Selection of the pivot may be governed by various rules and if accuracy is of prime importance, the pivot should be the element with the largest absolute value. If we select such an element from among the coefficients accompanying the variable under consideration (in the preceding discussion the coefficients accompanying x_1), we get *partial pivoting*. If we scan for the largest absolute value in the whole (remaining) matrix, then such pivoting is called *full*.

EXAMPLE 2.6.1. Consider the system

$$\begin{aligned} 0x_1 + x_2 + 3x_3 &= 3 \\ 2x_1 + 5x_2 + 8x_3 &= 2 \\ 4x_1 - 2x_2 + 10x_3 &= 1 \end{aligned}$$

and indicate partial and full pivoting.

For partial pivoting select the largest element accompanying the variable x_1.

In this case it is equivalent to interchanging the first and last equation:

$$4x_1 - 2x_2 + 10x_3 = 1$$
$$2x_1 + 5x_2 + 8x_3 = 2$$
$$0x_1 + x_2 + 3x_3 = 3$$

and elimination or decomposition could start. If we consider full pivoting, the largest element must be selected. This requires subsequent interchange of the variables x_1 and x_3 in all equations:

$$10x_3 - 2x_2 + 4x_1 = 1$$
$$8x_3 + 5x_2 + 2x_1 = 2$$
$$3x_3 + x_2 + 0x_1 = 3$$

Note that partial pivoting does not change the sequence of variables but full pivoting does. Partial pivoting is used more often, although the accuracy is somewhat less. In all cases, the element selected as the pivot must be nonzero.

It is beyond the scope of this book to give a detailed analysis of the errors occuring in the solution of linear systems. Such considerations are based on matrix norms and condition numbers. The reader can find a simple but instructive treatment of this subject in [1]. A brief explanation is also provided in Appendix F.

2.7. SPARSE MATRIX PRINCIPLES

Pivoting for highest accuracy of the solution is not the only strategy which is useful. In sparse matrices, other considerations are more important.

We recall that the number of operations necessary to solve a system of equations by Gaussian elimination or by **LU** decomposition is approximately $n^3/3$. This is valid if all operations are actually performed, even those where we multiply by or add (subtract) a zero. One can save on the number of operations by not performing these multiplications and additions (subtractions). In fact, the zeros need not even be stored, thus reducing memory requirements.

Consider the nodal formulation of a network with n ungrounded nodes and b two-terminal passive components. The matrix $\mathbf{Y}$ contains at most $n + 2b$ nonzero entries. In a typical large electrical network, the number of components range from two to four times the number of nodes. Clearly, for such networks, the total number of nonzeros in the matrix is a small fraction of n^2, the total number of entries in the matrix.

A matrix in which most of the entries are zero is called *sparse*. Sparse matrix algorithms neither store nor perform operations on zeros. Programming of these algorithms is much more complicated than the straightforward methods explained earlier but the savings in computation time and in storage can be substantial. Typically, the number of operations (and storage) grow approximately linearly with the size n, as compared to $n^3/3$ (and n^2) for dense matrices.

To motivate pivot selection strategies, we will use a simple example. Consider a matrix with two zero entries:

$$\begin{bmatrix} a_{11} & a_{12} & a_{13} \\ a_{21} & a_{22} & 0 \\ a_{31} & 0 & a_{33} \end{bmatrix}.$$

Assume that we perform **LU** decomposition. Using the explicit form (2.5.11) we get

$$\mathbf{LU} = \begin{bmatrix} l_{11} = a_{11} & u_{12} = a_{12}/l_{11} & u_{13} = a_{13}/l_{11} \\ l_{21} = a_{21} & l_{22} = a_{22} - l_{21}u_{12} & u_{23} = (0 - l_{21}u_{13})/l_{22} \\ l_{31} = a_{31} & l_{32} = 0 - l_{31}u_{12} & l_{33} = a_{33} - l_{31}u_{13} - l_{32}u_{23} \end{bmatrix}.$$

Note that in **LU** all entries are nonzero. A *fill-in* is created where the zero was changed into a nonzero. Assume next that we first pivot on the element a_{33} by placing it into the upper left corner by row and column interchange:

$$\begin{bmatrix} a_{33} & 0 & a_{31} \\ 0 & a_{22} & a_{21} \\ a_{13} & a_{12} & a_{11} \end{bmatrix}.$$

The **LU** decomposition is

$$\mathbf{LU} = \begin{bmatrix} l_{11} = a_{33} & u_{12} = 0 & u_{13} = a_{31}/l_{11} \\ l_{21} = 0 & l_{22} = a_{22} & u_{23} = a_{21}/l_{22} \\ l_{31} = a_{13} & l_{32} = a_{12} & l_{33} = a_{11} - l_{31}u_{13} - l_{32}u_{23} \end{bmatrix}.$$

We see that the zeros of the matrix have been preserved. The decomposition of the original matrix required 8 multiplications (divisions) and 5 subtractions. The modified matrix required only 4 multiplications (divisions) and 2 subtractions. This example clearly shows that *the number of operations can be reduced by proper selection of the pivot.* In sparse matrix computation, pivot selection is called *reordering.*

Having established the fact that reordering can reduce the number of operations, we will now investigate how it should be performed. There are $(n!)^2$ possible permutations of the rows and columns of a matrix of size n. Clearly, evaluating the number of fill-ins or the number of operations for each of these possibilities is not feasible. It is reasonable to simplify the search by relying on special properties of the matrix and by using locally optimal criteria for reordering. Considerable reduction in the operations is possible by using fairly simple strategies even though the pivot order obtained may not be *the* best.

Consider now the nodal admittance matrix. It has nonzero diagonal elements and its nonzero pattern is generally nearly symmetrical. Thus for reordering of equations and variables we will consider the symmetrical zero–nonzero pattern of the form $\mathbf{A} + \mathbf{A}^t$. The search for pivots can be restricted to the diagonal elements, to preserve structural symmetry, i.e., the nonzero patterns of $\mathbf{L}$ and $\mathbf{U}^t$ are the same. Even with diagonal pivoting, the number of possible permutations is still $n!$ and some local criterion must be used.

The most common pivot selection criteria that have been used in practice are as follows:

1. No reordering is performed. This is the simplest method of solving the system and corresponds to the discussion in Section 2.5. The user is responsible for a good ordering.
2. The equations are ordered according to the number of nonzero entries. Those rows having the fewest nonzero entries are numbered first. The corresponding permutations are also applied to the columns to retain symmetry.
3. The equation with the fewest nonzero entries is taken first and symbolic decomposition, in which only positions of nonzero elements and not their values are considered, is performed. The remaining matrix may have been modified by fill-ins. In the next step, the row with fewest nonzero entries in the *remaining* part of the matrix is numbered second and the process continues. This is called the *minimum degree rule.*
4. The pivot selected is the one that produces the fewest fill-ins at the current stage of processing. This is called the *minimum local fill-in criterion.*

Experiments on test matrices show that the first criterion is substantially inferior to the others. Of the remaining, the minimum local fill-in criterion usually results in a somewhat better ordering but the reordering time is somewhat higher. In most available software, the minimum degree algorithm is used.

EXAMPLE 2.7.1. Consider the 90° phase splitting network in Fig. 2.7.1, taken from [2]. It has 17 ungrounded nodes and the nodal equations contain 77 nonzero entries, as compared with 289 in the dense case. We will demonstrate the impact of various ordering techniques on the storage and computing cost for **LU** factorization on this example. Note that symmetry could be exploited to further reduce storage and computing cost.

1. The initial nonzeros are indicated by crosses in Fig. 2.7.2(a) and the fill-ins are indicated by circles. There are 68 fills with the factorization being performed without reordering, and 377 operations (multiplication-additions) are required as compared with about 1550 for the dense matrix.

2. When the rows and columns are rearranged so that equations with the fewest nonzeros are ordered first, the matrix in Fig. 2.7.2(b) is obtained. Even with this simple ordering the fill-ins are reduced to 32 and the number of operations for **LU** decomposition to 209.

3. Minimum degree ordering results in the matrix shown in Fig. 2.7.2(c). The fills are further reduced to 14, the number of operations to 147.

4. Finally, the minimum local fill-in strategy, Fig. 2.7.2(d), reduces the fills to 12 and the operation count to 141.

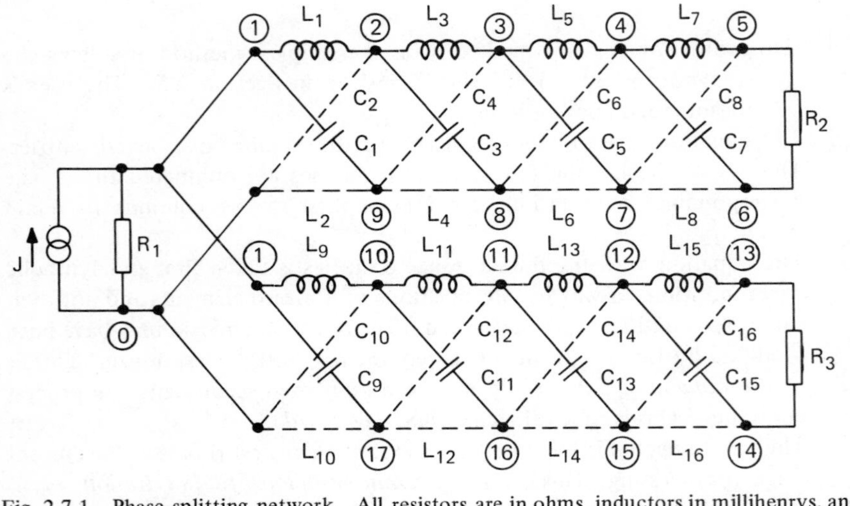

Fig. 2.7.1. Phase-splitting network. All resistors are in ohms, inductors in millihenrys, and capacitors in millifarads. Their numerical values are:

L_1, L_2, C_1, C_2:	0.102888	L_9, L_{10}, C_9, C_{10}:	0.0293307
L_3, L_4, C_3, C_4:	0.493852	$L_{11}, L_{12}, C_{11}, C_{12}$:	4.87647
L_5, L_6, C_5, C_6:	2.15717	$L_{13}, L_{14}, C_{13}, C_{14}$:	1.02583
L_7, L_8, C_7, C_8:	17.2722	$L_{15}, L_{16}, C_{15}, C_{16}$:	0.234847

$$R_1 = R_2 = R_3 = 1$$

	1	2	3	4	5	6	7	8	9	10	11	12	13	14	15	16	17
1	X	X							X	X							X
2	X	X	X					X	O	O							O
3		X	X	X			X	O	X	O							O
4			X	X	X	X	O	X	O	O							O
5				X	X	X	X	O	O	O							O
6				X	X	X	X	O	O	O							O
7			X	O	X	X	X	X	O	O							O
8		X	O	X	O	O	X	X	X	O							O
9	X	O	X	O	O	O	O	X	X	O							O
10	X	O	O	O	O	O	O	O	O	X	X					X	O
11										X	X	X			X	O	X
12											X	X	X	X	O	X	O
13												X	X	X	X	O	O
14												X	X	X	X	O	O
15											X	O	X	X	X	X	O
16										X	O	X	O	O	X	X	X
17	X	O	O	O	O	O	O	O	O	O	X	O	O	O	O	X	X

Fig. 2.7.2. Patterns of decomposed admittance matrix for the network in Fig. 2.7.1 with:
(a) No reordering, equations written in the sequence of nodes given in Fig. 2.7.1.

	2	5	6	9	10	13	14	17	1	3	4	7	8	11	12	15	16
2	X								X	X			X				
5		X	X								X	X					
6		X	X								X	X					
9				X					X	X			X				
10					X				X					X			X
13						X	X								X	X	
14						X	X								X	X	
17								X	X					X			X
1	X			X	X			X	X	O			O	O			O
3	X			X					O	X	X	X	O	O			O
4		X	X							X	X	O	X	O			O
7		X	X							X	O	X	X	O			O
8	X			X					O	O	X	X	X	O			O
11					X			X	O	O	O	O	O	X	X	X	O
12						X	X							X	X	O	X
15						X	X							X	O	X	X
16					X			X	O	O	O	O	O	O	X	X	X

Fig. 2.7.2. (b) Equations with fewest nonzeros taken first.

	2	5	6	4	7	3	8	9	1	10	17	11	16	12	13	14	15
2	X					X	X		X								
5		X	X	X	X												
6		X	X	X	X												
4		X	X	X	O	X	X										
7		X	X	O	X	X	X										
3	X			X	X	X	O	X	O								
8	X			X	X	O	X	X	O								
9						X	X	X	X								
1	X					O	O	X	X	X	X						
10									X	X	O	X	X				
17									X	O	X	X	X				
11										X	X	X	O	X			X
16										X	X	O	X	X			X
12												X	X	X	X	X	O
13														X	X	X	X
14														X	X	X	X
15												X	X	O	X	X	X

Fig. 2.7.2. (c) Minimum degree ordering.

	5	6	13	14	4	7	12	15	3	8	11	16	2	9	10	17	1
5	X	X			X	X											
6	X	X			X	X											
13			X	X			X	X									
14			X	X			X	X									
4	X	X			X	O			X	X							
7	X	X			O	X			X	X							
12			X	X			X	O			X	X					
15			X	X			O	X			X	X					
3					X	X			X	O			X	X			
8					X	X			O	X			X	X			
11							X	X			X	O			X	X	
16							X	X			O	X			X	X	
2									X	X			X	O			X
9									X	X			O	X			X
10											X	X			X	O	X
17											X	X			O	X	X
1													X	X	X	X	X

Fig. 2.7.2. (d) Minimum local fill-in ordering.

Let us next consider the forward and back substitution steps. Their computational cost can be significantly reduced if advantage is taken of the sparsity of the right-hand-side vector and of the fact that generally only a few of the components of **x** are required as outputs in the solution of **Ax** = **b**.

Take the forward substitution first. The solution of the system **Lz** = **b** was obtained *by rows* in Section 2.5. Sparsity can be used to greater advantage if we proceed by columns instead:

1. Initialize $i = 0$.
2. Set $i = i + 1$.
3. Calculate $z_i = b_i/l_{ii}$.
4. If $i = n$, the substitution is complete, else go to step 5.
5. If $z_i \neq 0$, set $b_j = b_j - z_i l_{ji}$ for $j = i + 1, i + 2, \ldots, n$ and go to step 2.

If the first few entries of **b** are zero, the corresponding entries of **z** will also be zero. If k is the index of the first nonzero entry of **b**, then in step 1 we set $i = k - 1$. Furthermore, due to the sparse nature of **L**, only a few of the entries of **b** will be changed to nonzero in step 5. In general, steps 3 and 5 need to be executed only if the value of b_i is nonzero. One symbolic forward substitution is sufficient to determine which of the z variables can be nonzero. Subsequently, only these variables are computed.

Consider next the back substitution. The system **Ux** = **z** is solved by the following algorithm:

1. Set $x_n = z_n$ and $i = n$.
2. Set $i = i - 1$.
3. Calculate $x_i = z_i - \sum_{j=i+1}^{n} u_{ij} x_j$.
4. If $i = 1$, substitution is complete, else go to Step 2.

Generally, only a few components of **x** are required as outputs. If the index of the first required component is m, then substitution is terminated at step 4 when $i = m$. Furthermore, due to the sparse nature of **U**, only a few terms of the summation in step 3 are nonzero. Thus to compute x_m, not all variables $x_{m+1}, \ldots, x_n$ may be required. One symbolic substitution is sufficient to determine which x values need actually be computed in step 3 so as to determine all the required outputs.

EXAMPLE 2.7.2. Returning to the network in Fig. 2.7.1 we note that our right-hand-side vector will contain a single nonzero in row 1 and that the voltages at nodes 5, 6, 13, and 14 are the only ones of interest.

Consider the ordering indicated in Fig. 2.7.2(b). In the forward substitution phase only the variables z_i, i = 1, 3, 4, 7, 8, 11, 12, 15, and 16 are nonzero and need to be computed. Similarly, in the back substitution, the variables x_i, i = 5, 6, 13, 14, 4, 7, 8, 11, 12, 15, and 16 need be evaluated to determine the "outputs."

2.8. SPARSE MATRIX IMPLEMENTATION

In the last section we showed that the use of sparse matrix techniques results in substantial reduction in computing cost even for relatively small problems. In this section we provide information on how these reductions can be realized in practice. For a comprehensive bibliography see [3].

A sparse matrix solver typically consists of a number of distinct segments that are executed sequentially. These consist of

1. A set of *interface* routines that insulate the user from the complicated data structures that are typical of sparse codes.
2. An *ordering* routine which renumbers the equations and variables. This routine is usually executed only once for a specified zero–nonzero structure of **A** and is often independent of actual values in the matrix.
3. A *symbolic factorization* routine which determines the zero–nonzero structure of **L** and **U**. Optionally, at this stage information required by *interpretive* codes can be created. It is even possible to directly generate *machine* code that will perform the factorization of matrices with the specified structure. This routine is executed only once for given structure of **A** and the ordering.
4. A *symbolic solution* routine which analyzes the zero–nonzero structure of the right-hand side and determines the variables that must be found in order to generate the "outputs." Optionally, at this stage information on interpretive code or the machine code for the solution phase can be generated. This routine is executed each time the structure of the right-hand side changes or one specifies new outputs.
5. A *numeric factorization* routine is invoked each time the values in **A** are modified.
6. A *numeric solution* routine is executed each time the right-hand side vector is changed.

Sparse matrix software development is a rather difficult task. Fortunately, some software that can be adapted for network solution is now available. The Yale Sparse Matrix Package [4, 5] is suitable for symmetric and nonsymmetric matrices in which the choice of pivots is restricted to the diagonal and pivoting for numerical accuracy is not required. The ME28 routines from the Harwell Library [6] are more general and are designed to operate on nonsymmetric matrices. They also include pivoting options that ensure numerical stability. A package suitable for the solution of electronic circuits in which the matrix is assumed to be structurally symmetric is given in Appendix E. While a detailed discussion of a sparse code is clearly out of place, we will provide some information on the storage and ordering of sparse matrices in the rest of this section. We will generally assume the matrix to be structurally symmetric.

A. Sparse Matrix Storage

To reduce the storage requirements of an $N \times N$ sparse matrix $\mathbf{A}$, only its nonzero entries are stored in an equivalent linear array $\mathbf{B}$. The indexing information is usually contained in two auxiliary integer vectors IB and JB where JB has the same dimension as $\mathbf{B}$ and contains the column numbers of the corresponding values in $\mathbf{B}$; thus if $B(K)$ corresponds to $A(I, J)$ then $JB(K) = J$. The row information is contained in the array IB of dimension $N + 1$ with $IB(M)$ pointing to the start of row M in arrays JB and B. As an example the 5×5 matrix

$$\mathbf{A} = \begin{array}{c} \\ 1 \\ 2 \\ 3 \\ 4 \\ 5 \end{array} \begin{array}{c} \begin{array}{ccccc} 1 & 2 & 3 & 4 & 5 \end{array} \\ \left[\begin{array}{ccccc} 3 & 7 & & & 1 \\ 4 & 8 & & 5 & \\ & 6 & 9 & & \\ & & 11 & 14 & \\ & 10 & & & 2 \end{array} \right] \end{array} \tag{2.8.1}$$

would be stored compactly as a vector of dimension 12, the number of nonzeros in $\mathbf{A}$:

$$\begin{array}{rcccccccccccc} & 1 & 2 & 3 & 4 & 5 & 6 & 7 & 8 & 9 & 10 & 11 & 12 \\ B = & [3 & 7 & 1 \,| & 4 & 8 & 5 \,| & 6 & 9 \,| & 11 & 14 \,| & 10 & 2] \\ JB = & [1 & 2 & 5 \,| & 1 & 2 & 4 \,| & 2 & 3 \,| & 3 & 4 \,| & 2 & 5] \\ IB = & [1 & 4 & 7 & 9 & 11 & 13] & & & & & & \end{array} \tag{2.8.2}$$

Note that the $N + 1$ entry of IB is one larger than the number of nonzeros in $\mathbf{A}$. With this data structure row K starts at $IB(K)$ and the number of nonzeros is found simply as $IB(K + 1) - IB(K)$. Thus in our example, if we wished to locate row 3 of $\mathbf{A}$, we have:

$IB(3) = 7$ and row 3 starts at entries 7 in B and JB;
$IB(4) - IB(3) = 2$ and row 3 contains 2 nonzeros.

These nonzeros are in columns $JB(7)$ and $JB(8)$ and have values $B(7)$, $B(8)$. Thus the nonzeros in the 3rd row of $\mathbf{A}$ are

$$A(3, 2) = 6$$

$$A(3, 3) = 9.$$

In network applications the matrices are often structurally symmetric and have nonzeros along the diagonal. The length of the indexing vector *JB* can be reduced if storage in *B* is organized as follows:

$$B = [\text{diagonal of } \mathbf{A} \mid \text{rows of } \mathbf{A} \text{ above diagonal} \mid \text{columns of } \mathbf{A} \text{ below diagonal}]\,.$$

An indexing vector of length equal to the number of nonzeros above the diagonal in **A** is now sufficient. The *row* numbers of the columns of **A** below the diagonal can be accessed from the same information. As an example, consider the following matrix:

$$\mathbf{A} = \begin{array}{c} \\ 1 \\ 2 \\ 3 \\ 4 \\ 5 \end{array} \begin{array}{c} \begin{array}{ccccc} 1 & 2 & 3 & 4 & 5 \end{array} \\ \begin{bmatrix} 3 & & & 8 & \\ & 7 & 17 & & 9 \\ & 16 & 1 & 5 & 13 \\ 10 & & 11 & 4 & 15 \\ & 6 & 12 & 14 & 2 \end{bmatrix} \end{array}. \qquad (2.8.3)$$

It would be stored as follows:

$$\begin{array}{l} \qquad\;\; 1\;\; 2\;\; 3\;\; 4\;\; 5 \;\;\; 6\;\; 7\;\; 8\;\; 9\;\; 10\;\; 11 \;\;\; 12\;\; 13\;\; 14\;\; 15\;\; 16\;\; 17 \\ B = [3\;\; 7\;\; 1\;\; 4\;\; 2 \mid 8\;\; 17\;\; 9\;\; 5\;\; 13\;\; 15 \mid 10\;\; 16\;\; 6\;\; 11\;\; 12\;\; 14] \\ IJB = [\underbrace{6\;\; 7\;\; 9\;\; 11\;\; 12}_{IB} \mid \underbrace{4\;\; 3\;\; 5\;\; 4\;\; 5\;\; 5}_{JB}] \end{array} \qquad (2.8.4)$$

where the vectors *IB* and *JB* are now combined into a single vector *IJB* for simplicity in boundary alignment with *B*. Note that *IB* now needs only *N* entries as the last row has no nonzeros above the diagonal. Typical pointers are illustrated above. Note that each entry in *JB* now serves to locate *two* nonzeros in **A**–indexing information is stored only for the upper triangle.

B. Sparse Matrix Factorization

Let us now consider the **LU** decomposition step. For illustration, consider the 3 × 3 matrix **A** with nonzeros at the positions indicated by crosses:

$$\mathbf{A} = \begin{bmatrix} \times & & \times \\ & \times & \times \\ \times & & \times \end{bmatrix}. \qquad (2.8.5)$$

Let us perform the decomposition using the Gaussian form, Eq. (2.5.12). If multiplications and additions involving zero entries are ignored, only the following arithmetic operations are required:

$$\left.\begin{aligned} A(1,3) &= A(1,3)/A(1,1) \\ A(3,3) &= A(3,3) - A(3,1) * A(1,3) \end{aligned}\right\} \text{Pivot on } (1,1) \tag{2.8.6}$$

$$A(2,3) = A(2,3)/A(2,2) \qquad \text{Pivot on } (2,2)$$

If the one-dimensional array **B** is the sparse representation of **A** with the nonzeros of **A** stored, for example, in the following entries of **B**:

$$\begin{bmatrix} 3 & & 5 \\ & 1 & 6 \\ 4 & & 2 \end{bmatrix} \tag{2.8.7}$$

then the equivalent of the code (2.8.6) is

$$\begin{aligned} B(5) &= B(5)/B(3) \\ B(2) &= B(2) - B(5) * B(4) \\ B(6) &= B(6)/B(1). \end{aligned} \tag{2.8.8}$$

In the simplest implementation of a sparse factorization code the indices of B are generated and the operations corresponding to (2.8.8) are performed each time **A** has to be factored. This approach is most economical on storage but determination of the indices involves substantial overhead which may easily exceed the computational cost associated with the arithmetic operations.

As network solutions involve many factorizations with the *same* matrix structure an *interpretive code* approach is often adopted. The indexing information is generated in a preprocessing step. It produces a sequence of operation codes and addresses which, for our example (2.8.8) may have the following form:

op code	indices
1	5 3
2	2 5 4
1	6 1

where the operation codes 1 and 2 are used for division and multiplication-subtraction, respectively. As these are the only two types of operations required in **LU** decomposition by Gaussian elimination, negative numbers can be used to still further compact the operator list. In our example, it would become

$$-5 \quad 3 \quad 2 \quad 5 \quad 4 \quad -6 \quad 1.$$

The interpretive code approach speeds up the solution, as the indexing information is generated only once for a fixed matrix structure at the expense of additional memory requirements for storing the operator list. Still further gains in speed are possible by generating a *compiled code* corresponding to (2.8.8) *directly* in machine language in the preprocessing step. The code executes rapidly because it has a *linear* structure and contains no DO, IF, GOTO, or other logic statements. A disadvantage is that the linear compiled code is often fairly long and not suitable for smaller computers.

C. Sparse Matrix Ordering

As was seen in Section 2.7, substantial reduction in computing cost and storage is possible if the equations and variables are numbered suitably. Of the four renumbering schemes considered there, the minimum degree and minimum local fill-in techniques have been used most often in practice. We will consider only the minimum fill-in algorithm under the assumption that our matrix is structurally symmetric.

A detailed set of flow charts implementing the local fill-in criterion was given by Berry [7], based on the method due to Tinney and Walker [8]. In Berry's implementation, the fill-ins produced by each pivot candidate are computed at each step and the one that produces the least number of fill-ins is taken as the next pivot. Though Berry's algorithm has been used in many analysis packages, its execution time is much higher than that of minimum degree algorithms. This is particularly so for larger problems in which the minimum fill-in criterion results in superior orderings. Wing and Huang [9] suggested that the fill information be updated rather than recomputed to save time. A subroutine based on this idea is given in Appendix E. Its execution time is comparable to that of minimum degree algorithms and is by orders of magnitude faster than Berry's algorithm. The key steps involved in fill-in information updating are best understood through a graph representation of the matrix structure.

A structurally symmetric matrix can be represented as an *associated graph* [10]. This representation is convenient when we consider reordering of the variables and equations. Each *vertex* on the associated graph corresponds to a variable and each nonzero above the diagonal contributes an *edge* to the graph. The number of edges incident on a vertex is called its *degree*. Two vertices are said to be *adjacent* to each other if they are connected by an edge. Renumbering of the vertices of the graph corresponds to a reordering of the equations and variables in the original algebraic system. In triangular decomposition by Gaussian elimination, row/column k play no further role in the process after pivot step k. At the same step any fill-ins require structural changes to the matrix. These operations are simulated on the graph model by constructing an *elimination graph*. When vertex k is renumbered, it and all edges incident on it are deleted. If vertices i and j are adjacent to k but not to each other, a fill is created at positions (i, j) and (j, i) in the matrix. This corresponds to the addition of a new edge between i and j on the graph. In the elimination graph all vertices that were adjacent to k will be adjacent to each other and form a *clique*.

EXAMPLE 2.8.1. Construct the elimination graphs corresponding to the decomposition of the matrix shown in Fig. 2.8.1.

	1	2	3	4	5	6	7	8
1	X			X		X		
2		X			X		X	
3			X	X		X		
4	X		X	X		X		X
5		X			X		X	
6	X		X	X		X		O
7		X			X		X	X
8				X		O	X	X

(a)

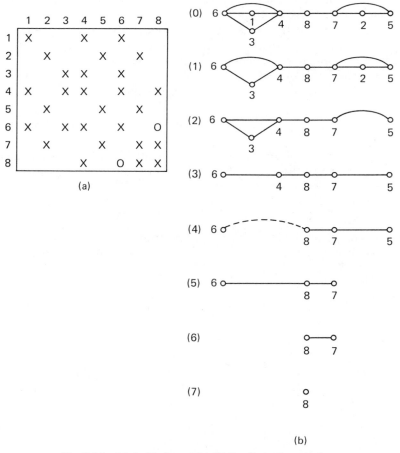

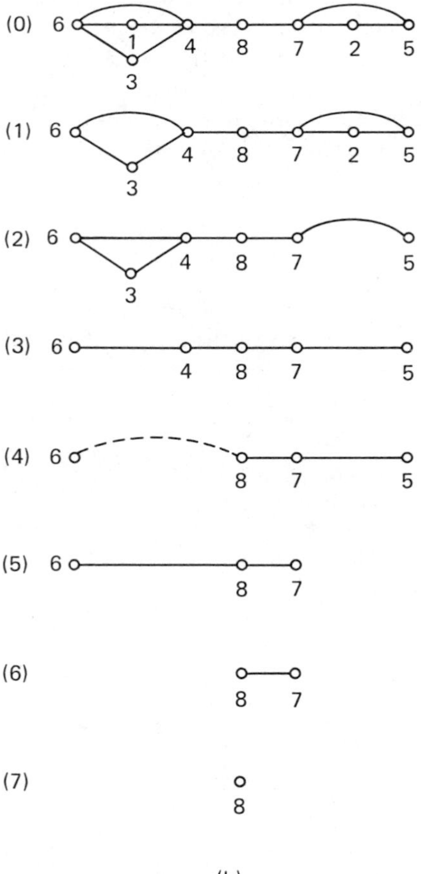

(b)

Fig. 2.8.1. (a) A simple matrix; (b) its elimination graphs.

The associated graph is shown as step 0. It has 8 vertices as we have an 8×8 matrix. Each nonzero above the diagonal contributes an edge. For example, as row 1 has entries in columns 4 and 6 above the diagonal, the graph has an edge between vertices 1 and 4 and between 1 and 6, respectively. The elimination graphs that result at each pivot step are also shown. Note that a fill occurs at step 4, as indicated by the dotted edge.

The basic minimum local fill-in algorithm with fill information updating can be stated as follows:

Step 1. Form the data structure for the associated graph of the matrix and compute the number of fills, f_i, that *would* be created *if* vertex i were eliminated first.

Step 2. Choose vertex k which creates the least fills as the one to be eliminated next. If $f_k = 0$ go to step 4.

Step 3. Scan the vertices adjacent to k and locate the fill-ins. When a fill-in is found, say at (i, j), an edge is inserted on the graph (see Fig. 2.8.2). The new edge influences fill information of other vertices in two ways:

(a) Each vertex l adjacent to *both* i and j was creating the same fill-in and we set

$$f_l \leftarrow f_l - 1.$$

(b) Subsequent elimination of vertex i will create fill-ins between vertex j and each vertex of the form m that is adjacent to i but not to j. Thus

$$f_i \leftarrow f_i + \alpha$$

where α is the number of vertices adjacent to i but not to j.
Similarly f_j is modified by vertices of the form n that are adjacent to j but not to i.

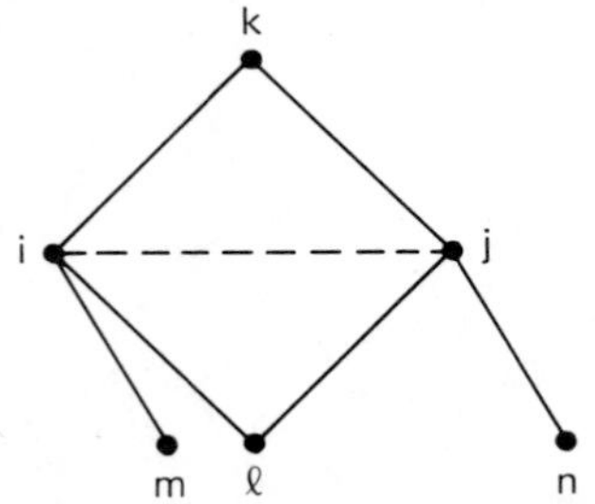

Fig. 2.8.2. Modification of fill information.

Step 4. Vertices adjacent to k can no longer create fill-in edges incident on k and their fill information is modified as follows:

$$f_i \leftarrow f_i - (d_i - d_k)$$

for each i adjacent to k, where d_i and d_k are the degrees of vertices i and k, respectively.

Step 5. Vertex k and all edges incident on it are deleted to form the next elimination graph. If it contains more than one vertex we return to step 2; else the ordering is complete.

D. Linked Storage Allocation

During the reordering phase of sparse matrix processing it is often advantageous to adopt a more general data structure for the elimination graph than was considered in (2.8.2) to represent the matrix. There are two main reasons for this:

1. The storage requirements for the adjacency set of a vertex are unpredictable, as they depend both on the new vertex number and on the fills created.
2. The data structure must permit simple *insertion* of new edges as fills occur and *deletion* of information associated with vertices that have already been numbered. The deletions save on the total memory requirements and eliminate unnecessary verification.

The simplest data structure that permits incorporation of the above features is a *linear linked list*. Each adjacency set i is stored as a list containing as many members as there are vertices adjacent to i at the current stage of the processing. The adjacency set is accessed through a *list head* which points to the first element of the list. Each element of the list consists of two storage locations; one of these is used to store the vertex number while the other is a *pointer* which stores the location of the next element of the list. The pointer of the *last element* of the list is set to some special value to indicate the end of the list. Thus a typical vertex is represented as shown in Fig. 2.8.3(a). The list is *traversed* by starting at the location stored in the list head and following the pointers till we come to the end of the list. The structure of an $N \times N$ matrix would thus be stored in N linked lists at the start of the reordering process. To enable insertions and deletions from these lists an additional *free list* is also created. The vertex information fields of the free list are not relevant and are marked by a cross. At a typical stage of the reordering the adjacency set of vertex 14 and the free list may have the forms shown in Fig. 2.8.3(b). Vertex 14 is adjacent to vertices 4, 7, 13, and 21 at this stage. Let a fill be created at

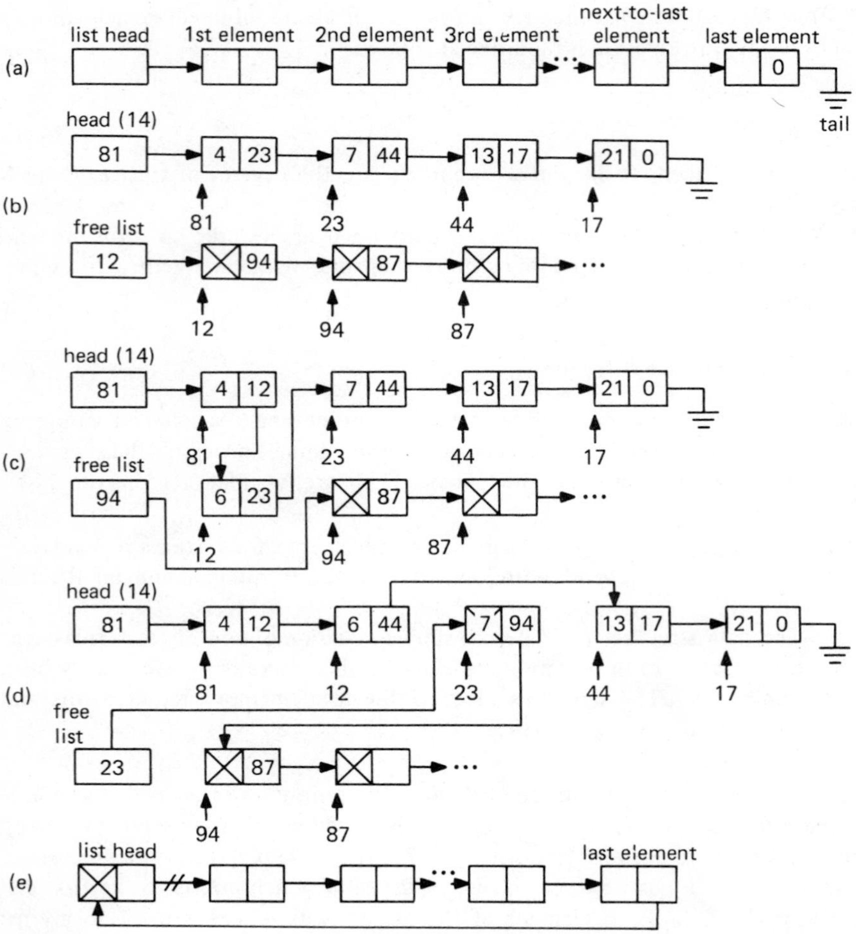

Fig. 2.8.3. Example of linked list.

location (14, 6) in our matrix. This requires that between the first and second elements of the list a new element be inserted. The first element from the free list is deleted from it and placed on the list for vertex 14, as shown in Fig. 2.8.3(c). Now consider the case when vertex 7 is numbered and will play no part in the remainder of the reordering process. Vertex 7 is now deleted from the adjacency set of 14 and placed on the free list, as shown in Fig. 2.8.3(d). In this example we have assumed that our adjacency sets were *ordered*, otherwise the inserts would be done at the beginning of the list. In actual implementations the list structure is modified slightly and made *circular* by replacing the special value in the last element of the list by the list head location (which is now a part of the list), as shown in Fig. 2.8.3(e). This enables the simple deletion of a vertex by breaking the chain of pointers as shown.

PROBLEMS

P.2.1. Write the nodal admittance matrix equation for the network in Fig. P.2.1. Attempt to do so by inspection.

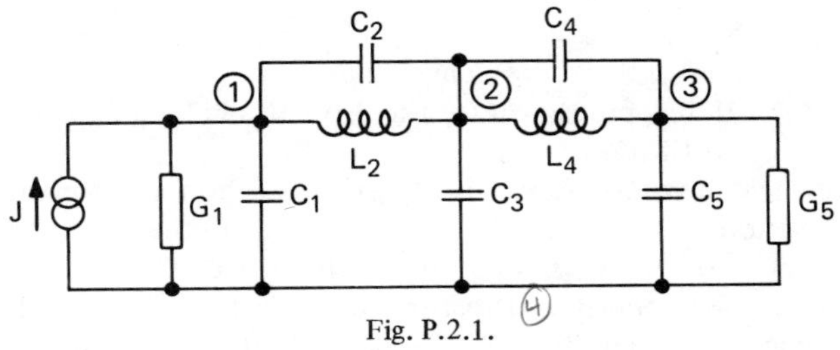

Fig. P.2.1.

P.2.2. Transform the current source into a voltage source and write the mesh matrix equation for the network in Fig. P.2.1 by inspection.

P.2.3. A gyrator can be simulated by two VCTs, as shown in Fig. 1.6.1. Use this equivalence and write the nodal matrix equation for the network in Fig. P.2.3. First transform the voltage source into a current source.

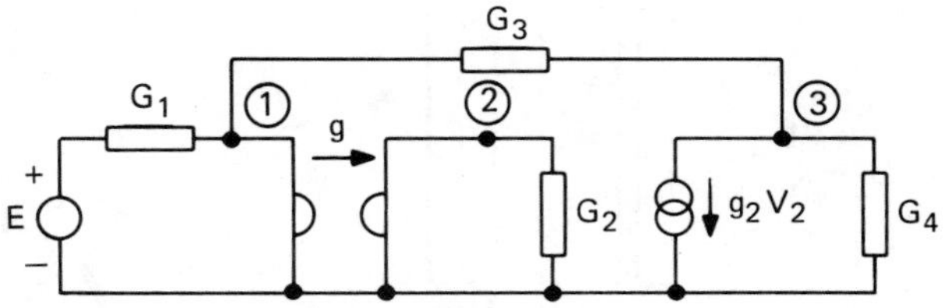

Fig. P.2.3.

P.2.4. A gyrator can be simulated by two CVTs as shown in Fig. 1.6.1. Use this equivalence and write the mesh matrix equation for the network in Fig. P.2.4.

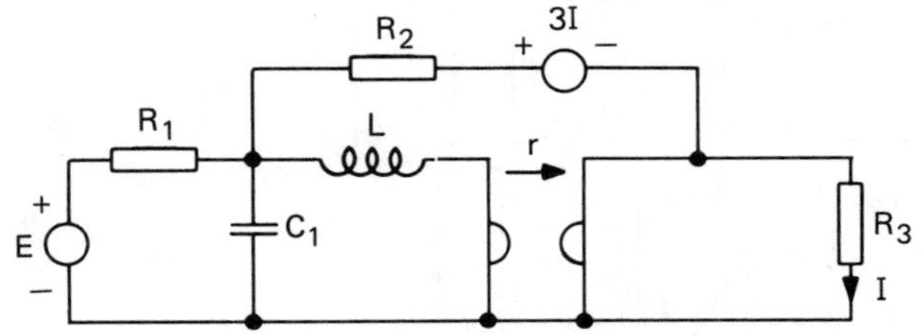

Fig. P.2.4.

P.2.5. Solve by Gaussian elimination:

(a) $\begin{bmatrix} 4 & 6 \\ 2 & 8 \end{bmatrix} \begin{bmatrix} x_1 \\ x_2 \end{bmatrix} = \begin{bmatrix} 1 \\ 0 \end{bmatrix}$ (b) $\begin{bmatrix} 2 & 4 & 6 \\ 6 & 4 & 2 \\ 1 & 8 & 4 \end{bmatrix} \begin{bmatrix} x_1 \\ x_2 \\ x_3 \end{bmatrix} = \begin{bmatrix} 4 \\ 12 \\ 13 \end{bmatrix}$

P.2.6. Apply Cramer's rule to Problems P.2.5.

P.2.7. Find the **LU** decomposition for the Problems P.2.5 and solve by forward and back substitution.

P.2.8. Solve the following systems by **LU** factorization and forward and back substitution. Note especially how the zeros in the matrix influence the decomposition and how the steps are simplified. Observe simplifications in the forward and back substitutions. These exercises will give you a feeling and first understanding for sparse matrix solutions:

(a) $$\begin{bmatrix} 1 & 0 & 0 & 2 & 1 \\ 3 & 2 & 0 & 0 & 2 \\ 0 & 1 & 1 & 0 & 0 \\ 0 & 0 & 1 & 2 & 1 \\ 0 & 0 & 1 & 1 & 1 \end{bmatrix} \begin{bmatrix} x_1 \\ x_2 \\ x_3 \\ x_4 \\ x_5 \end{bmatrix} = \begin{bmatrix} -1 \\ 3 \\ 0 \\ 0 \\ 1 \end{bmatrix}$$

(b) $$\begin{bmatrix} 2 & 4 & 0 & 2 & 0 \\ 0 & 3 & 6 & 0 & 3 \\ 1 & 2 & 1 & 2 & 0 \\ 2 & 4 & 1 & 4 & 0 \\ 0 & 1 & 2 & 2 & 3 \end{bmatrix} \begin{bmatrix} x_1 \\ x_2 \\ x_3 \\ x_4 \\ x_5 \end{bmatrix} = \begin{bmatrix} 4 \\ 0 \\ 3 \\ 6 \\ 2 \end{bmatrix}$$

(c) $$\begin{bmatrix} 11 & -10 & 0 & 0 \\ -10 & 19 & -4 & 0 \\ 0 & -4 & 39 & -20 \\ 0 & 0 & -20 & 22 \end{bmatrix} \begin{bmatrix} x_1 \\ x_2 \\ x_3 \\ x_4 \end{bmatrix} = \begin{bmatrix} 10 \\ 20 \\ -20 \\ -15 \end{bmatrix}$$

(d) $$\begin{bmatrix} 3 & -1 & -1 & 0 \\ -1 & 3 & -1 & -1 \\ -1 & -1 & 3 & -1 \\ 0 & -1 & -1 & 3 \end{bmatrix} \begin{bmatrix} x_1 \\ x_2 \\ x_3 \\ x_4 \end{bmatrix} = \begin{bmatrix} 5 \\ -10 \\ 10 \\ -5 \end{bmatrix}$$

(e) $$\begin{bmatrix} 1 & 0 & 1 & 0 \\ 2 & 2 & 2 & 4 \\ 0 & 1 & 3 & 11 \\ 1 & 0 & -1 & -5 \end{bmatrix} \begin{bmatrix} x_1 \\ x_2 \\ x_3 \\ x_4 \end{bmatrix} = \begin{bmatrix} 0 \\ 0 \\ 0 \\ 3 \end{bmatrix}$$

P.2.9. Write the zero–nonzero structure of the nodal admittance matrix for the network in Fig. P.2.9. Use first the node numbering in circles and then the numbering without circles. Apply symbolic **LU** factorization and observe the fill-ins as you proceed with the factorization. Repeat using elimination graphs.

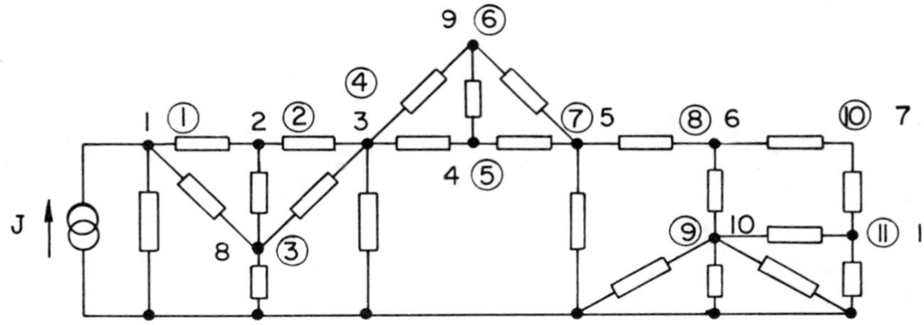

Fig. P.2.9

P.2.10. Use Fig. P.2.10 and write the nodal admittance structure for this network. How many nonzeros are created by the **LU** factorization for the node numbering indicated in the figure?

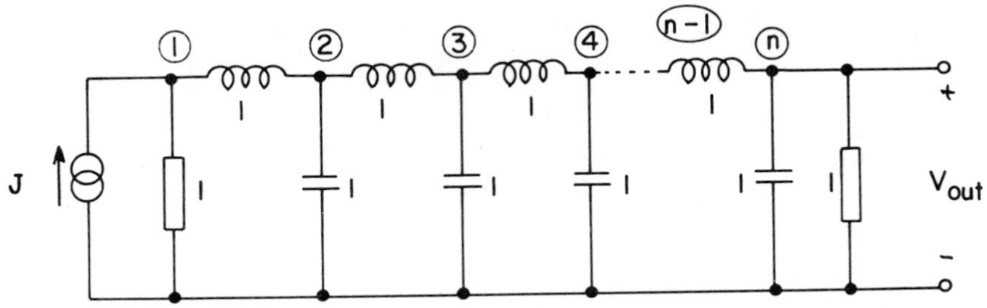

Fig. P.2.10.

P.2.11. In the small-signal simulation of transistor networks each transistor is replaced by a suitable combination of linear elements and the dc supply is considered to be at ground potential for the signal frequency. The simplest field-effect transistor model is a VCT, as shown in Fig. P.2.11(a). An amplifier is shown in Fig. P.2.11(b). Replacing the transistor by the VCT and grounding the dc source we arrive at the network in Fig. P.2.11(c). Note that the point G will be at ground potential for the signal and that the combination of 0.1 μF, 0.3 MΩ, and 1.7 MΩ can be omitted from considerations. Write the nodal formulation matrix equation by first transforming the voltage source and its 50-Ω resistor into an equivalent current source.

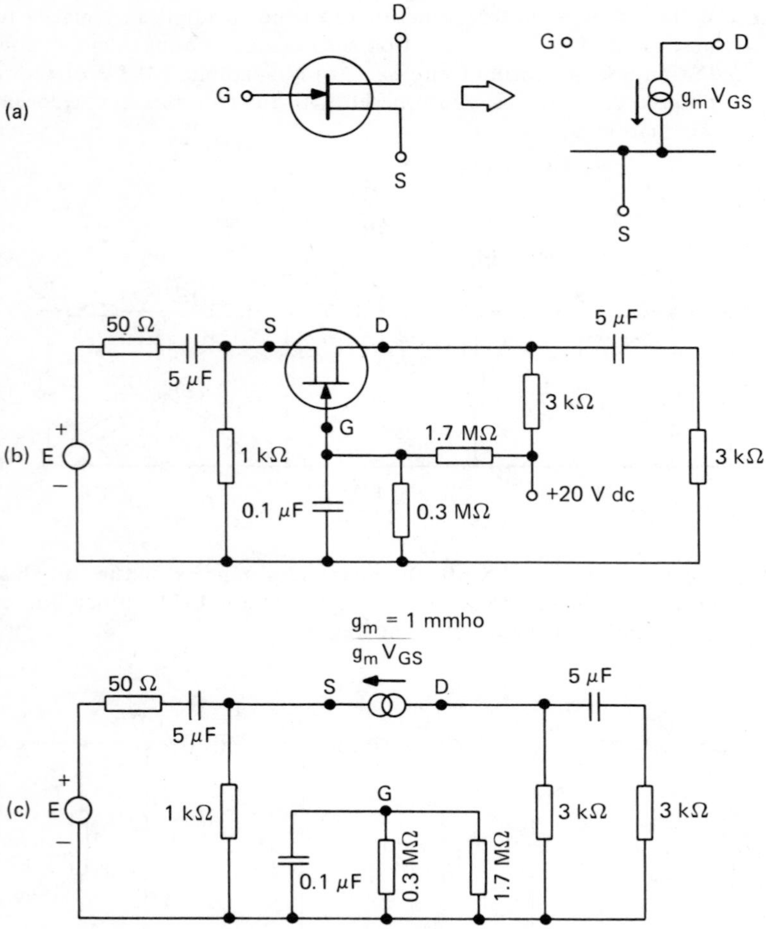

Fig. P.2.11

REFERENCES

1. G. E. Forsythe, M. A. Malcolm, and C. B. Moler: *Computer Methods for Mathematical Computations.* Prentice Hall, Englewood Cliffs, NJ, 1977.
2. J. F. Pinel and M. L. Blostein: Computer techniques for the frequency analysis of linear networks. *Proc. IEEE*, pp. 1810–1819, 1967.
3. I. S. Duff: A survey of sparse matrix research. *Proc. IEEE*, pp. 500–535, April 1977.
4. S. C. Eisenstat et al.: *Yale Sparse Matrix Package.* Parts 1 and 2. Research Reports No. 112 and 114, Yale Univ., Dep. Computer Sciences, New Haven, CT, USA.
5. S. C. Eisenstat, M. H. Schultz, and A. H. Sherman: Algorithms and data structures for sparse symmetric Gaussian elimination. *SIAM J. Scientific and Statistical Computing*, pp. 225–237, June 1981.

6. Computer Science and Systems Division, AERE Harwell, Oxfordshire, OX1 0RA, England.
7. R. D. Berry: An optimal ordering of electronic circuit equations for a sparse matrix solution. *IEEE Trans. on Circuit Theory*, pp. 40–50, January 1971.
8. W. F. Tinney and J. W. Walker: Direct solution of sparse network equations by optimally ordered triangular factorization. *Proc. IEEE*, pp. 1801–1809, 1967.
9. O. Wing and J. Huang: SCAP–A sparse matrix analysis programme. *Proc. ISCAS*, pp. 213–215, 1975.
10. S. V. Parter: The use of linear graphs in Gauss elimination. *SIAM Review*, pp. 119–130, 1961.

CHAPTER 3
Graph Theoretic Formulation of Network Equations

In the second chapter we introduced the simplest methods for formulating network equations. The two methods considered are limited in the types of ideal elements that can be included. More advanced formulation methods without restrictions on the type of circuit elements will be given in Chapter 4. They require at least an elementary knowledge of graph theory.

Graph theory is a broad, rapidly growing mathematical discipline with many applications in engineering and computer science. Our objective in this book is to develop computer methods for the formulation, analysis, and design of electrical networks. For this reason, we will restrict the presentation of graph concepts to the material suitable for this application. The motivation for the use of a graph is evident if we consider any network with two terminal components and its nodal formulation. Write the matrix equation, then replace each passive element by some other passive element of different type and write the equation again. The entries of the matrices will differ but the structures will be the same–the structure does not depend on elements, only on the interconnection. It is possible to deduce some general properties of networks by considering only the interconnections and graph theory is the tool for doing so.

In Section 3.1 graph concepts are introduced and the Kirchhoff current and voltage laws are stated. Section 3.2 introduces the incidence matrix and shows how Kirchhoff laws can be written in terms of it. Sections 1, 2 and 7 are necessary for a proper understanding of the material presented in this book. The remaining sections develop further material in graph theory and its application; they can be skipped at the first reading.

Section 3.3 introduces the concept of the tree and cotree and discusses the cutset and loopset matrices. Orthogonality relationships of these matrices are demonstrated in Section 3.4, while Section 3.5 shows that independent variables in the network are tree voltages and cotree currents.

So far, the discussion has not distinguished between sources and other elements. The way of handling independent sources is described in Section 3.6. The topological formulation of the nodal and loop equations is discussed in Sections 3.7 and 3.8. Finally, the state variable formulation is explained briefly on networks containing R, G, L, and C elements as well as both types of independent sources.

The topological relations discussed in the first six sections of this chapter are valid for linear as well as nonlinear networks. For this reason, lower case symbols for voltages and currents will be used. In the remaining sections, the network equations of linear, lumped, time invariant networks will be considered in the Laplace transform domain and upper case symbols will be used.

3.1. KVL, KCL AND ORIENTED GRAPHS

Let us replace each two-terminal element by a line segment called an *edge*. The edges will represent the interconnections or *topology* of the network. Assign distinct numbers to the nodes of the network and the same numbers to the corresponding interconnection points of the edges. The node numbers will be placed within circles to distinguish them from the numbering of the elements in the network or the edges in the graph.

Formulations of network equations are based on the fundamental laws stated first by Kirchhoff. The *Kirchhoff voltage law* (KVL) states that the sum of voltage drops around any loop is zero at any instant. The *Kirchhoff current law* (KCL) was stated in a restricted form in Chapter 2: The sum of currents flowing away from a node is zero at any moment.

The KCL can be generalized as illustrated with the help of Fig. 3.1.1. Let the network N be partitioned internally into two subnetworks N_1, N_2, joined by a number of interconnections. The sum of all currents in these connections must be zero. The connections separate the two parts or they "cut" the network. This will be true for any other set of connections in the network. We may choose only one (any) node as N_1 with the rest of the network being considered in N_2 and obtain the original version of the KCL. We restate the KCL in the following form:

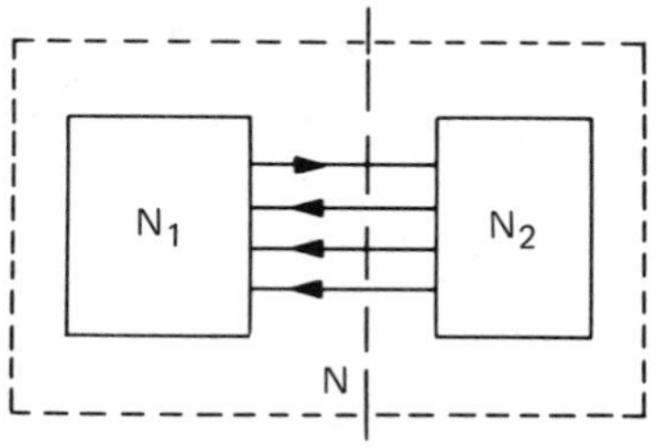

Fig. 3.1.1. Generalization of the Kirchhoff current law.

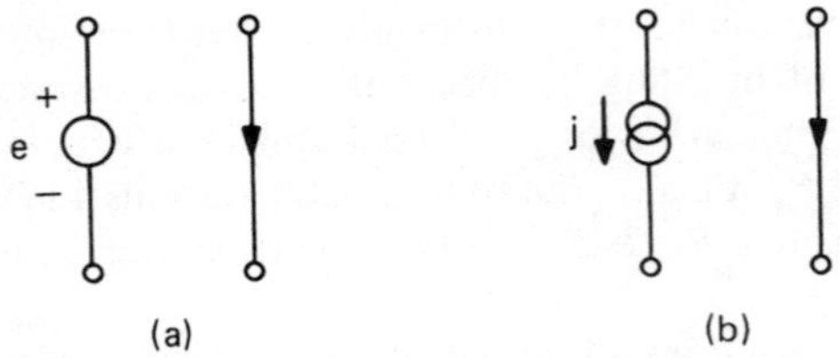

Fig. 3.1.2. Voltage and current sources and their graphs.

In any cut which separates the network into two parts, the sum of currents in the cut edges is zero.

In the graph representation of a network we replace each two-terminal element by an edge. An orientation will be associated with each edge and we can, for simplicity, assume that for nonsource branches this is the direction of the current flowing through the element. In agreement with Fig. 1.1.1, the orientation will imply that the node from which the current flows is at a higher voltage than the node to which it flows. Since the voltages in the network are not known before the solution, orientations of the graph edges are completely arbitrary for passive elements.

For current sources, the direction of the current is obvious from its symbol. For the voltage source, we will assign the *orientation of the edge as being from + to −*. The graphs for the sources are given in Fig. 3.1.2. Once all two-terminal elements have been replaced by their oriented edges, there is no reason to distinguish between the sources and other two-terminal elements; all the properties will be derived without any reference to the types of elements represented by the edges.

3.2. INCIDENCE MATRIX

Consider the simple network in Fig. 3.2.1(a) and its oriented graph in Fig. 3.2.1(b). Let us write the KCL equations with the edge orientations as indicated. A current flowing *away* from a node will be considered as *positive*. Then

$$1:\ -i_1 + i_4 + i_6 = 0$$

$$2:\ -i_2 - i_4 + i_5 = 0$$

$$3:\ -i_3 - i_5 - i_6 = 0.$$

This can be written in matrix form:

$$\mathbf{Ai} = \mathbf{0}. \tag{3.2.1}$$

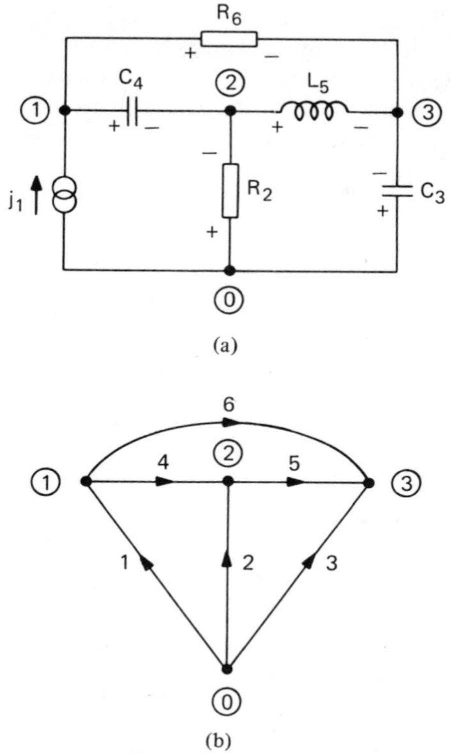

Fig. 3.2.1. A simple network and its oriented graph.

The matrix **A** is called the *incidence matrix* and, for the example,

$$\mathbf{A} = \begin{array}{c} \text{nodes} \\ \downarrow \end{array} \begin{array}{c} \\ 1 \\ 2 \\ 3 \end{array} \overset{\text{edges} \longrightarrow}{\begin{array}{cccccc} 1 & 2 & 3 & 4 & 5 & 6 \end{array}} \begin{bmatrix} -1 & 0 & 0 & 1 & 0 & 1 \\ 0 & -1 & 0 & -1 & 1 & 0 \\ 0 & 0 & -1 & 0 & -1 & -1 \end{bmatrix}. \tag{3.2.2}$$

It has n rows and b columns, n being the number of ungrounded nodes and b the number of edges in the graph. The rank of this matrix is 3, as the submatrix formed by the first three rows and columns is nonsingular. It can be proved that for a general connected network

$$\text{Rank of } \mathbf{A} = n. \tag{3.2.3}$$

The voltages in the network are also related through the incidence matrix. Denote the voltage of the ith node with respect to the reference node as $v_{n,i}$. Since in our notation the orientation of the edge coincides with the current flow through the element, the node from which the edge leaves will be at a higher potential than the node to which it points. For instance, for the fourth edge in Fig. 3.2.1(b), we will have

$$v_4 = v_{n,1} - v_{n,2}$$

which, in terms of all the nodal variables, is written as

$$v_4 = [1 \quad -1 \quad 0] \begin{bmatrix} v_{n,1} \\ v_{n,2} \\ v_{n,3} \end{bmatrix}.$$

Similarly, for the fifth edge we get the voltage relationship

$$v_5 = [0 \quad 1 \quad -1] \begin{bmatrix} v_{n,1} \\ v_{n,2} \\ v_{n,3} \end{bmatrix}$$

and so on. Writing one such equation for each edge we arrive at

$$\begin{bmatrix} v_1 \\ v_2 \\ v_3 \\ v_4 \\ v_5 \\ v_6 \end{bmatrix} = \begin{bmatrix} -1 & 0 & 0 \\ 0 & -1 & 0 \\ 0 & 0 & -1 \\ 1 & -1 & 0 \\ 0 & 1 & -1 \\ 1 & 0 & -1 \end{bmatrix} \begin{bmatrix} v_{n,1} \\ v_{n,2} \\ v_{n,3} \end{bmatrix}. \tag{3.2.4}$$

Comparing the matrix in (3.2.4) with the matrix in (3.2.2) we see that it is the transpose of $\mathbf{A}$, $\mathbf{A}^t$. The result can be summarized through the matrix equation

$$\mathbf{v} = \mathbf{A}^t \mathbf{v}_n. \tag{3.2.5}$$

Equations (3.2.1) and (3.2.5) represent the KCL and KVL relationships for a network. They will be used repeatedly in subsequent chapters.

3.3. CUTSET AND LOOPSET MATRICES

In order to derive additional properties of oriented graphs consider Fig. 3.3.1. It shows the same graph as discussed in Section 3.2, with some additional features. Recall now the generalized version of the KCL. Three more equations can be written by invoking this form of the law: The cut C_4 intersects the edges 6, 4, 2, 3; C_5 intersects the edges 6, 5, 2, 1, and cut C_6 intersects 1, 4, 5, 3. Selecting the indicated directions with respect to the cut as being positive we get

$$C_4: \quad i_2 + i_3 + i_4 + i_6 = 0$$

$$C_5: \quad -i_1 - i_2 + i_5 + i_6 = 0$$

$$C_6: \quad i_1 + i_3 - i_4 + i_5 = 0.$$

These equations can be added to the set of equations obtained in Section 3.2. The question arises which equations and how many need to be retained to form an independent set. One way of choosing them is by means of the incidence matrix. It can also be done in a systematic way by defining a tree and a cotree.

A *tree* of a connected graph is a connected subgraph containing all the nodes of the original network but no closed path. A tree of an $n + 1$ node connected network has n edges.

Any edge in the tree is called a *twig*. The remaining edges, not included in the tree, form a *cotree* and the edges of a cotree are called *chords*.

A cut with respect to a given tree edge of a graph is a cut going through *only one* twig of the tree and as many chords of the cotree as necessary to divide the graph into two separate parts. Since there are n twigs of a tree, there will be n *basic cuts*. The set of branches included in any cut is called the *cutset*.

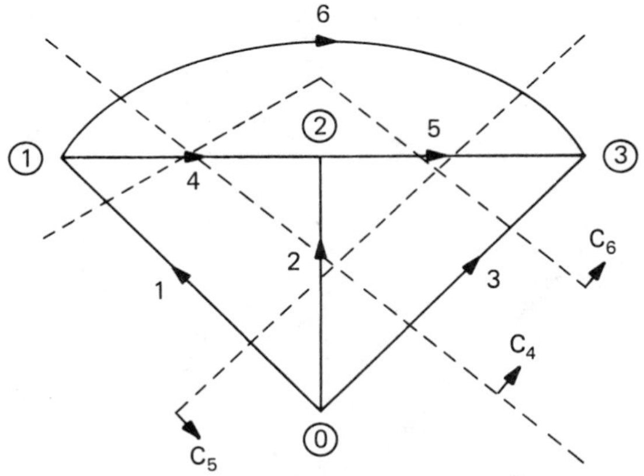

Fig. 3.3.1. Oriented graph with three additional cuts.

The numbering of the elements and of the nodes is an entirely arbitrary procedure which can in no way alter the behavior of the network. Therefore it is merely a matter of convenience how the various elements are numbered. Many considerations become quite simple, if we apply the following rule for the numbering:

1. Assign orientations to the edges.
2. Select a tree.
3. Assign consecutive integers starting from 1 to the twigs and continue numbering the chords.

Figure 3.3.2 indicates one such choice. The edges 1, 2, 3 form the tree of the graph (twigs), the edges 4, 5, 6 are the chords of the cotree.

To obtain the basic cutsets we cut one twig and as many chords as necessary to obtain two disconnected subgraphs. The cuts are indicated in the figure, numbered with subscripts corresponding to the number of the twig they cut. Each cut is assigned the same orientation as its twig. This is indicated on the figure by arrows. Then

$$i_1 - i_4 - i_6 = 0$$
$$i_2 + i_4 - i_5 = 0$$
$$i_3 + i_5 + i_6 = 0.$$

In matrix form, this is

$$\mathbf{Qi} = \mathbf{0} \tag{3.3.1}$$

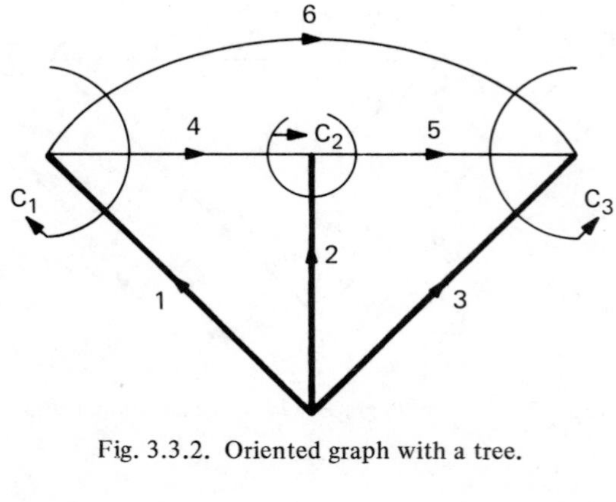

Fig. 3.3.2. Oriented graph with a tree.

where

$$\mathbf{Q} = \begin{array}{c} \text{basic} \\ \text{cuts} \\ \downarrow \end{array} \begin{array}{c} \\ 1 \\ 2 \\ 3 \end{array} \overset{\text{edges} \longrightarrow}{\begin{array}{c} \begin{array}{cccccc} 1 & 2 & 3 & 4 & 5 & 6 \end{array} \\ \left[\begin{array}{ccc|ccc} 1 & 0 & 0 & -1 & 0 & -1 \\ 0 & 1 & 0 & 1 & -1 & 0 \\ 0 & 0 & 1 & 0 & 1 & 1 \end{array}\right] \end{array}} \tag{3.3.2}$$

is called the *basic cutset matrix.*

Before making any statements about the form of the **Q** matrix, let us look at the selection of another tree and the choice of new edge directions for the same network. Consider the graph in Fig. 3.3.3 in which the tree is indicated by solid lines and where we followed the numbering suggestions given above. We get

$$\mathbf{Q} = \begin{array}{c} 1 \\ 2 \\ 3 \end{array} \begin{array}{c} \begin{array}{cccccc} 1 & 2 & 3 & 4 & 5 & 6 \end{array} \\ \left[\begin{array}{ccc|ccc} 1 & 0 & 0 & 0 & -1 & 1 \\ 0 & 1 & 0 & -1 & -1 & 1 \\ 0 & 0 & 1 & -1 & -1 & 0 \end{array}\right] \end{array}.$$

In both cases *the submatrix corresponding to the tree is a unit matrix* and is nonsingular.

The **Q** matrix can be partitioned as follows:

$$\mathbf{Q} = [\mathbf{Q}_t \quad \mathbf{Q}_c] \quad \text{or} \quad [\mathbf{1} \quad \mathbf{Q}_c] \tag{3.3.3}$$

where the subscript t stands for the tree (or twigs), the subscript c for cotree (or chords) and **1** denotes an identity matrix.

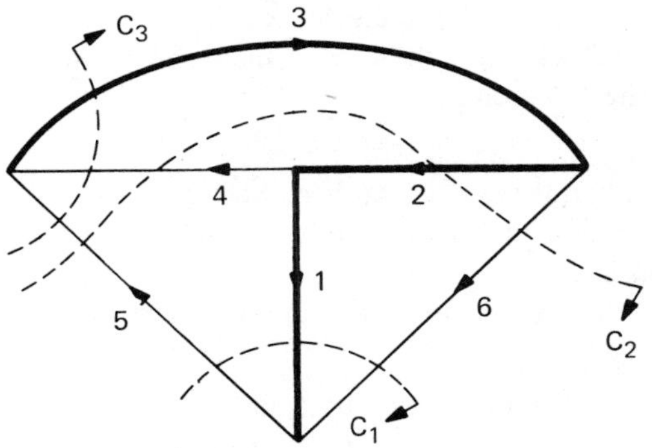

Fig. 3.3.3. Oriented graph with another tree.

The *Kirchhoff voltage law* leads to another description of the topological properties of networks. It states that the sum of voltages around any closed path is equal to zero. In our considerations we will restrict the path to be a simple loop with no crossings and no cases where the path goes two or more times through the same edge or node.

With these restrictions, we can define the following voltage loops in the graph of Fig. 3.3.2:

$$
\begin{aligned}
v_1 - v_2 + v_4 &= 0 \\
v_2 - v_3 + v_5 &= 0 \\
v_4 + v_5 - v_6 &= 0 \\
v_1 - v_3 + v_6 &= 0 \\
v_2 - v_3 - v_4 + v_6 &= 0 \\
v_1 - v_2 - v_5 + v_6 &= 0 \\
v_1 - v_3 + v_4 + v_5 &= 0
\end{aligned}
$$

and we must decide which of these equations and how many have to be retained to form an independent set. We will apply the concept of the tree and define the loops on the basis of the selected tree.

Consider one chord only and place it into its position in the subgraph formed by the tree. The chord will form, together with twigs of the tree, a loop. In the next step, take the first chord out and place another one into its proper position. This will form another loop. Doing this for all chords, we get a set of loops. Since the network has b edges and $n + 1$ nodes, the tree has n edges and there remain $b - n$ edges to form the chords of the cotree. Therefore, the number of loops formed by the above procedure will be $b - n$.

As before, the sequence in which this is done is arbitrary as are the orientations in which the loops are closed. Since there is such freedom of choice, we propose a special way of numbering which will considerably simplify the form of the resulting equations:

1. Apply all numbering steps as suggested before.
2. Take the chords in the sequence of their numbering and number the loops starting from 1.
3. Assume the direction of the loop to be the direction of its chord.

Taking Fig. 3.3.2 with the choice of arrows and numbers as shown, we get three loops:

$$v_1 - v_2 + v_4 = 0$$
$$v_2 - v_3 + v_5 = 0$$
$$v_1 - v_3 + v_6 = 0.$$

In matrix form this is

$$\mathbf{Bv} = \mathbf{0} \tag{3.3.4}$$

where **B** is called the *basic loopset matrix*. Its form is

$$\mathbf{B} = \begin{array}{c} \text{loops} \downarrow \end{array} \begin{array}{c} \\ 1 \\ 2 \\ 3 \end{array} \overset{\text{edges} \longrightarrow}{\begin{array}{c} \begin{array}{cccccc} 1 & 2 & 3 & 4 & 5 & 6 \end{array} \\ \left[\begin{array}{ccc|ccc} 1 & -1 & 0 & 1 & 0 & 0 \\ 0 & 1 & -1 & 0 & 1 & 0 \\ 1 & 0 & -1 & 0 & 0 & 1 \end{array}\right] \end{array}}. \tag{3.3.5}$$

We observe that the matrix can be partitioned as

$$\mathbf{B} = [\mathbf{B}_t \quad \mathbf{B}_c] \quad \text{or} \quad [\mathbf{B}_t \quad \mathbf{1}]. \tag{3.3.6}$$

Let us see again what happens if another tree and another choice of orientations is used for the same network, provided the recommended numbering procedure is maintained. Take the tree of Fig. 3.3.3 with the result

$$\mathbf{B} = \begin{array}{c} \text{loops} \downarrow \end{array} \begin{array}{c} \\ 1 \\ 2 \\ 3 \end{array} \overset{\text{edges} \longrightarrow}{\begin{array}{c} \begin{array}{cccccc} 1 & 2 & 3 & 4 & 5 & 6 \end{array} \\ \left[\begin{array}{ccc|ccc} 0 & 1 & 1 & 1 & 0 & 0 \\ 1 & 1 & 1 & 0 & 1 & 0 \\ -1 & -1 & 0 & 0 & 0 & 1 \end{array}\right] \end{array}}.$$

Again, **B** has a unit submatrix belonging to the chord edges. This submatrix determines the rank of **B**, which is 3 for our example, and, for a general connected network,

$$\text{Rank of } \mathbf{B} = b - n. \tag{3.3.7}$$

EXAMPLE 3.3.1. Write the **Q** and **B** matrices for the graph in Fig. 3.3.4. Use the tree formed by the first four edges:

$$
\mathbf{Q} = \left[\begin{array}{cccc|ccc} 1 & 0 & 0 & 0 & 1 & 1 & 1 \\ 0 & 1 & 0 & 0 & -1 & -1 & 0 \\ 0 & 0 & 1 & 0 & 0 & 0 & -1 \\ 0 & 0 & 0 & 1 & 0 & 1 & 1 \end{array}\right]
$$

$$
\mathbf{B} = \left[\begin{array}{cccc|ccc} -1 & 1 & 0 & 0 & 1 & 0 & 0 \\ -1 & 1 & 0 & -1 & 0 & 1 & 0 \\ -1 & 0 & 1 & -1 & 0 & 0 & 1 \end{array}\right]
$$

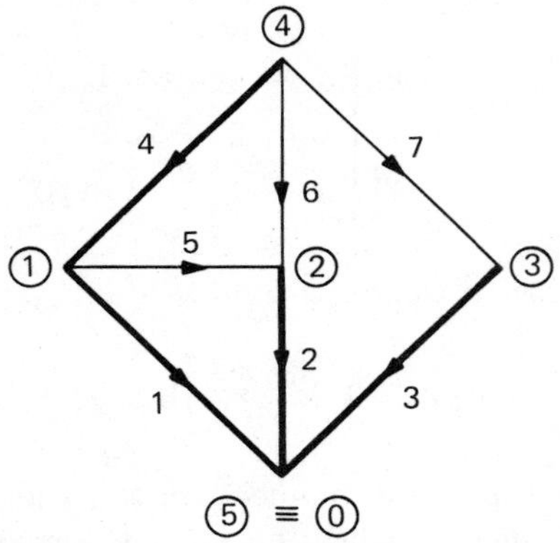

Fig. 3.3.4. A graph with a tree.

3.4. ORTHOGONALITY RELATIONS FOR THE Q AND B MATRICES

The cutset and loopset matrices are not independent and a fundamental relationship holds. The proof can be found, for instance, in [1].

Arrange the columns of the cutset and loopset matrices in the same sequence of edges; then

$$
\mathbf{BQ}^t = \mathbf{0} \tag{3.4.1}
$$

or

$$
\mathbf{QB}^t = \mathbf{0} \tag{3.4.2}
$$

We will illustrate the validity of the law by considering the matrices (3.3.2) and (3.3.5), written for the graph of Fig. 3.3.2:

$$\mathbf{QB}^t = \left[\begin{array}{ccc|ccc} 1 & 0 & 0 & -1 & 0 & -1 \\ 0 & 1 & 0 & 1 & -1 & 0 \\ 0 & 0 & 1 & 0 & 1 & 1 \end{array}\right] \left[\begin{array}{ccc} 1 & 0 & 1 \\ -1 & 1 & 0 \\ 0 & -1 & -1 \\ \hline 1 & 0 & 0 \\ 0 & 1 & 0 \\ 0 & 0 & 1 \end{array}\right] = \begin{bmatrix} 0 & 0 & 0 \\ 0 & 0 & 0 \\ 0 & 0 & 0 \end{bmatrix}.$$

Important results follow from (3.4.1) or (3.4.2). Using the partitioned forms (3.3.3) and (3.3.6)

$$\mathbf{BQ}^t = [\mathbf{B}_t \quad \mathbf{1}] \begin{bmatrix} \mathbf{1} \\ \mathbf{Q}_c^t \end{bmatrix} = \mathbf{B}_t + \mathbf{Q}_c^t = \mathbf{0}$$

or

$$\mathbf{B}_t = -\mathbf{Q}_c^t. \qquad (3.4.3)$$

Equation (3.4.3) indicates that

$$\mathbf{B} = [-\mathbf{Q}_c^t \quad \mathbf{1}] \qquad (3.4.4)$$

and

$$\mathbf{Q} = [\mathbf{1} \quad -\mathbf{B}_t^t] \qquad (3.4.5)$$

which means that either the **B** or the **Q** matrix are sufficient for applications. As an exercise, the reader may demonstrate the validity of (3.4.1) and (3.4.2) on the **Q** and **B** matrices of Example 3.3.1.

3.5. INDEPENDENT CURRENTS AND VOLTAGES

The results obtained in the last section will now be used to write the edge voltages and currents in terms of the smaller set of independent voltages and currents. Using the cutset matrix and (3.3.1),

$$\mathbf{Qi} = \mathbf{0}. \qquad (3.5.1)$$

Here **i** is the vector of edge currents. Using the partitioning

$$[\mathbf{1} \quad \mathbf{Q}_c] \begin{bmatrix} \mathbf{i}_t \\ \mathbf{i}_c \end{bmatrix} = \mathbf{i}_t + \mathbf{Q}_c \mathbf{i}_c = \mathbf{0}$$

or

$$\mathbf{i}_t = -\mathbf{Q}_c \mathbf{i}_c \tag{3.5.2}$$

the twig currents are obtained in terms of chord currents. Since all currents in the network are the union of twig and chord currents, we can write

$$\mathbf{i} = \begin{bmatrix} \mathbf{i}_t \\ \mathbf{i}_c \end{bmatrix} = \begin{bmatrix} -\mathbf{Q}_c \\ \mathbf{1} \end{bmatrix} \mathbf{i}_c = \begin{bmatrix} \mathbf{B}_t^t \\ \mathbf{1} \end{bmatrix} \mathbf{i}_c .$$

The last step followed from (3.4.3). However, the last matrix is nothing but the transpose of the matrix **B** (3.3.6) and thus

$$\mathbf{i} = \mathbf{B}^t \mathbf{i}_c . \tag{3.5.3}$$

The chord currents should be considered as independent variables. Once they are known, all the currents in the network are obtained by applying (3.5.3).

Now consider the KVL (3.3.4):

$$\mathbf{B}\mathbf{v} = \mathbf{0} \tag{3.5.4}$$

where **v** is the vector of all edge voltages. Use the partitioning

$$[\mathbf{B}_t \quad \mathbf{1}] \begin{bmatrix} \mathbf{v}_t \\ \mathbf{v}_c \end{bmatrix} = \mathbf{B}_t \mathbf{v}_t + \mathbf{v}_c = \mathbf{0}$$

from which

$$\mathbf{v}_c = -\mathbf{B}_t \mathbf{v}_t . \tag{3.5.5}$$

As in the case of the currents, all the edge voltages can be written as

$$\mathbf{v} = \begin{bmatrix} \mathbf{v}_t \\ \mathbf{v}_c \end{bmatrix} = \begin{bmatrix} \mathbf{1} \\ -\mathbf{B}_t \end{bmatrix} \mathbf{v}_t = \begin{bmatrix} \mathbf{1} \\ \mathbf{Q}_c^t \end{bmatrix} \mathbf{v}_t .$$

The last step results from the use of (3.4.3). However, the matrix on the right-hand side is nothing but $\mathbf{Q}^t$. Thus

$$\mathbf{v} = \mathbf{Q}^t \mathbf{v}_t. \tag{3.5.6}$$

We conclude that *twig voltages should be considered as independent voltages.* Once they are known, all edge voltages are obtained by applying (3.5.6).

3.6. INCORPORATING SOURCES INTO GRAPH CONSIDERATIONS

In general, a network can be excited by voltage as well as current sources. The question is: what is an advantageous way of numbering edges in such a case? Equation (3.5.3) indicates that *the chord currents are the independent variables.* The current of an independent current source cannot be a dependent variable. Thus we make sure that *all current sources are placed into the cotree.* Similarly, Eq. (3.5.6) indicates that the twig voltages are the independent variables. The voltage of the voltage source cannot be a dependent variable. Thus we must make sure that *all voltage sources are placed into the tree.*

Our preferred numbering system resulted in unit matrices in the place of $\mathbf{Q}_t$ or $\mathbf{B}_c$. In order to preserve this advantage we will:

1. Represent the voltage sources as $e_1, e_2, \ldots, e_l$ and place them into the tree branches.
2. Complete the tree by taking edges of passive elements and number them by consecutive numbers starting with one.
3. Continue numbering of the remaining edges corresponding to the passive elements.
4. Number the current sources as $j_1, j_2, \ldots, j_m$.

The orientations of the sources will be as indicated in Fig. 3.1.2, while the orientation of passive element edges are arbitrary. Whenever the sources are considered explicitly, we will consider the matrices as being *augmented* and use the subscript *a*.

EXAMPLE 3.6.1. Consider the network shown in Fig. 3.6.1. Write the $\mathbf{Q}$ matrix by using the numbering on the figure and the suggestions given above.

$$\mathbf{Q}_a = \begin{array}{c} \begin{matrix} e_1 & 1 & 2 & 3 & 4 & 5 & 6 & j_1 \end{matrix} \\ \left[\begin{array}{c|cccccc|c} 1 & 0 & 0 & 0 & -1 & 0 & 0 & 0 \\ 0 & 1 & 0 & 0 & 0 & -1 & -1 & -1 \\ 0 & 0 & 1 & 0 & 1 & 1 & 1 & 1 \\ 0 & 0 & 0 & 1 & 1 & 1 & 0 & 0 \end{array}\right] \end{array} = [\mathbf{Q}_e \quad \mathbf{Q} \quad \mathbf{Q}_j]$$

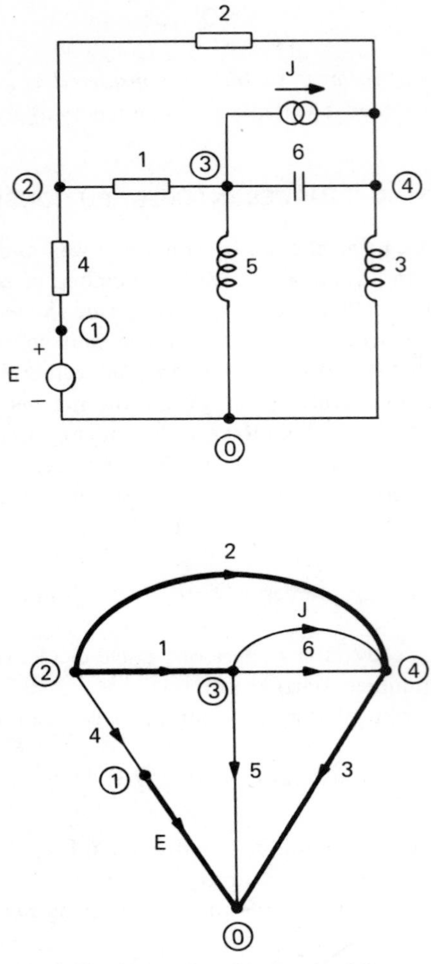

Fig. 3.6.1. Network and its graph with a tree.

3.7. TOPOLOGICAL FORMULATION OF NODAL EQUATIONS

In order to introduce the formulation for the nodal equations, we will assume that *every voltage source has been converted into an equivalent current source* by the Thévenin-Norton transformation.

In the nodal formulation, every passive element is described through the form $Y_b V_b = I_b$. All these expressions can be combined as follows:

$$\mathbf{Y}_b \mathbf{V}_b = \mathbf{I}_b. \tag{3.7.1}$$

For instance, for the network of Fig. 3.7.1(a), the constitutive equations are

$$\begin{bmatrix} G_1 & & & & & \\ & 1/sL_2 & & & & \\ & & 1/sL_3 & & & \\ & & & G_4 & & \\ & & & & sC_5 & \\ & & & & & sC_6 \end{bmatrix} \begin{bmatrix} V_1 \\ V_2 \\ V_3 \\ V_4 \\ V_5 \\ V_6 \end{bmatrix} = \begin{bmatrix} I_1 \\ I_2 \\ I_3 \\ I_4 \\ I_5 \\ I_6 \end{bmatrix}.$$

The graph for the network is shown in Fig. 3.7.1(b). To write the incidence matrix, consider first the passive elements and then the sources. Thus:

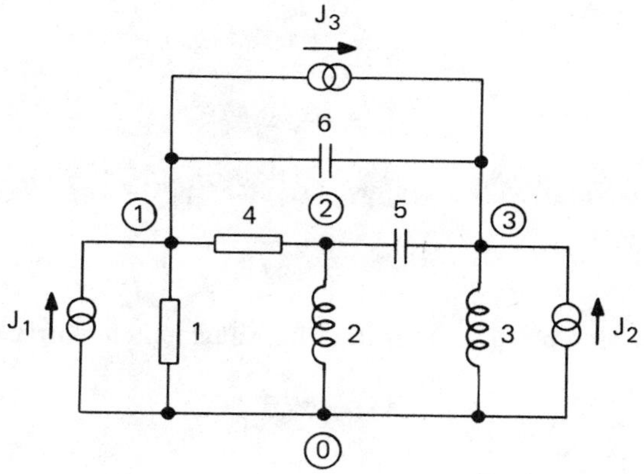

(a)

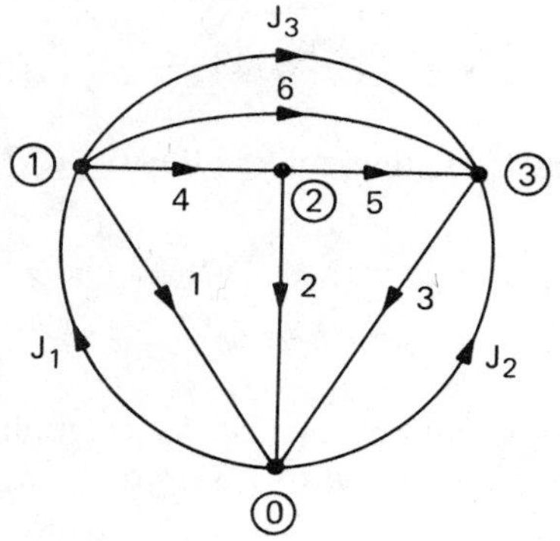

(b)

Fig. 3.7.1.

$$\mathbf{A}_a = \begin{array}{c} \\ \\ \\ \end{array}\begin{bmatrix} \overset{1}{1} & \overset{2}{0} & \overset{3}{0} & \overset{4}{1} & \overset{5}{0} & \overset{6}{1} & \vdots & \overset{J_1}{-1} & \overset{J_2}{0} & \overset{J_3}{1} \\ 0 & 1 & 0 & -1 & 1 & 0 & \vdots & 0 & 0 & 0 \\ 0 & 0 & 1 & 0 & -1 & -1 & \vdots & 0 & -1 & -1 \end{bmatrix} = [\mathbf{A} \quad \mathbf{A}_J].$$

Here $\mathbf{A}_a$ is the augmented incidence matrix. The KCL states that

$$\mathbf{A}_a\mathbf{I} = \mathbf{0}. \tag{3.7.2}$$

Partition these equations in the form

$$[\mathbf{A} \quad \mathbf{A}_J]\begin{bmatrix} \mathbf{I}_b \\ \mathbf{J}_b \end{bmatrix} = \mathbf{0} \tag{3.7.3}$$

or

$$\mathbf{A}\mathbf{I}_b = -\mathbf{A}_J\mathbf{J}_b \tag{3.7.4}$$

where $\mathbf{J}_b$ is the vector of known source currents. Substitute (3.7.1) for $\mathbf{I}_b$:

$$\mathbf{A}\mathbf{Y}_b\mathbf{V}_b = -\mathbf{A}_J\mathbf{J}_b. \tag{3.7.5}$$

The KVL is expressed by (3.2.5) for the whole augmented matrix as follows:

$$\mathbf{V} = \mathbf{A}_a^t\mathbf{V}_n. \tag{3.7.6}$$

Again partition the matrix $\mathbf{A}_a^t$:

$$\begin{bmatrix} \mathbf{V}_b \\ \mathbf{V}_J \end{bmatrix} = \begin{bmatrix} \mathbf{A}^t \\ \mathbf{A}_J^t \end{bmatrix}\mathbf{V}_n \tag{3.7.7}$$

where $\mathbf{V}_J$ are the voltages across the sources. Rewrite (3.7.7) as:

$$\mathbf{V}_b = \mathbf{A}^t\mathbf{V}_n \tag{3.7.8}$$

$$\mathbf{V}_J = \mathbf{A}_J^t\mathbf{V}_n. \tag{3.7.9}$$

The voltages across the current sources will be determined from (3.7.9) after the node voltages $\mathbf{V}_n$ are found. Insert (3.7.8) into (3.7.5):

$$\mathbf{A}\mathbf{Y}_b\mathbf{A}^t\mathbf{V}_n = -\mathbf{A}_J\mathbf{J}_b \tag{3.7.10}$$

or

$$\mathbf{Y}\mathbf{V}_n = \mathbf{J}_n. \tag{3.7.11}$$

The product

$$\mathbf{Y} = \mathbf{A}\mathbf{Y}_b\mathbf{A}^t \tag{3.7.12}$$

is the *nodal admittance matrix* discussed in Chapter 2. The right-hand side

$$\mathbf{J}_n = -\mathbf{A}_J\mathbf{J}_b \tag{3.7.13}$$

is the *nodal current source* vector of the nodal formulation.

EXAMPLE 3.7.1. Show on the example of Fig. 3.7.1 and on the graph given there that (3.7.10) is equivalent to the nodal formulation of Chapter 2.

The matrices $\mathbf{A}_a$ and $\mathbf{Y}_b$ were already written in this section. The product $\mathbf{A}\mathbf{Y}_b\mathbf{A}^t$ is

$$\mathbf{Y} = \begin{bmatrix} G_1 + G_4 + sC_6 & -G_4 & -sC_6 \\ -G_4 & G_4 + sC_5 + 1/sL_2 & -sC_5 \\ -sC_6 & -sC_5 & sC_5 + sC_6 + 1/sL_3 \end{bmatrix}.$$

For the sources the product is

$$\mathbf{J}_n = -\mathbf{A}_J\mathbf{J}_b = \begin{bmatrix} 1 & 0 & -1 \\ 0 & 0 & 0 \\ 0 & 1 & 1 \end{bmatrix} \begin{bmatrix} J_1 \\ J_2 \\ J_3 \end{bmatrix} = \begin{bmatrix} J_1 - J_3 \\ 0 \\ J_2 + J_3 \end{bmatrix}.$$

Both results agree with direct analysis.

A similar result can be obtained by using the **Q** matrix. The reader may derive the equations as an exercise. A disadvantage of using the basic cutsets is the fact that the resulting admittance matrix will often be dense, in addition to the effort required to obtain **Q**.

3.8. TOPOLOGICAL FORMULATION OF LOOP EQUATIONS

Formulation of loop equations is simple if we assume that *all current sources have been transformed into voltage sources.* In the loop formulation each passive element is described in the form $Z_bI_b = V_b$ and the expressions can be written compactly as

$$\mathbf{Z}_b \mathbf{I}_b = \mathbf{V}_b. \tag{3.8.1}$$

For instance, for the network of Fig. 3.8.1 the constitutive equations have the form

$$\begin{bmatrix} R_1 & & & & & \\ & 1/sC_2 & & & & \\ & & 1/sC_3 & & & \\ & & & sL_4 & & \\ & & & & sL_5 & \\ & & & & & 1/sC_6 \end{bmatrix} \begin{bmatrix} I_1 \\ I_2 \\ I_3 \\ I_4 \\ I_5 \\ I_6 \end{bmatrix} = \begin{bmatrix} V_1 \\ V_2 \\ V_3 \\ V_4 \\ V_5 \\ V_6 \end{bmatrix}.$$

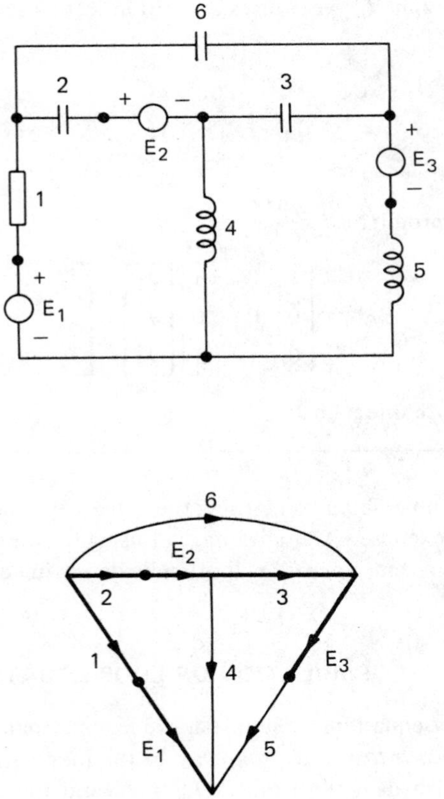

Fig. 3.8.1.

The graph of the network is shown as well. The numbering of the branches was done in agreement with Section 3.6. The $\mathbf{B}_a$ matrix is

$$\mathbf{B}_a = \begin{array}{c} \\ \left[\begin{array}{ccc|cccccc} E_1 & E_2 & E_3 & 1 & 2 & 3 & 4 & 5 & 6 \\ -1 & 1 & 0 & -1 & 1 & 0 & 1 & 0 & 0 \\ -1 & 1 & 1 & -1 & 1 & 1 & 0 & 1 & 0 \\ 0 & -1 & 0 & 0 & -1 & -1 & 0 & 0 & 1 \end{array}\right] \end{array} = [\mathbf{B}_E \quad \mathbf{B}].$$

The subscript a indicates augmentation by sources. The KVL states that

$$\mathbf{B}_a\mathbf{V} = \mathbf{0}. \tag{3.8.2}$$

Partition these equations in the form

$$[\mathbf{B}_E \quad \mathbf{B}]\begin{bmatrix}\mathbf{E}_b \\ \mathbf{V}_b\end{bmatrix} = \mathbf{0} \tag{3.8.3}$$

or

$$\mathbf{B}\mathbf{V}_b = -\mathbf{B}_E\mathbf{E}_b \tag{3.8.4}$$

where $\mathbf{E}_b$ is the vector of known source voltages. Substitute (3.8.1) for $\mathbf{V}_b$:

$$\mathbf{B}\mathbf{Z}_b\mathbf{I}_b = -\mathbf{B}_E\mathbf{E}_b. \tag{3.8.5}$$

The KCL in terms of the $\mathbf{B}$ matrix was expressed by (3.5.3):

$$\mathbf{I} = \mathbf{B}_a^t\mathbf{I}_c. \tag{3.8.6}$$

Partition this matrix equation as follows:

$$\begin{bmatrix}\mathbf{I}_E \\ \mathbf{I}_b\end{bmatrix} = \begin{bmatrix}\mathbf{B}_E^t \\ \mathbf{B}^t\end{bmatrix}\mathbf{I}_c \tag{3.8.7}$$

where $\mathbf{I}_E$ are the voltage source currents. Rewrite (3.8.7) as:

$$\mathbf{I}_E = \mathbf{B}_E^t\mathbf{I}_c \tag{3.8.8}$$

$$\mathbf{I}_b = \mathbf{B}^t\mathbf{I}_c. \tag{3.8.9}$$

Once the currents $\mathbf{I}_c$ are determined, the voltage source currents $\mathbf{I}_E$ will be found from (3.8.8). Insert (3.8.9) into (3.8.5):

$$\mathbf{B}\mathbf{Z}_b\mathbf{B}^t\mathbf{I}_c = -\mathbf{B}_E\mathbf{E}_b \tag{3.8.10}$$

or

$$\mathbf{Z}\mathbf{I}_c = \mathbf{E}_l. \tag{3.8.11}$$

The product

$$\mathbf{Z} = \mathbf{B}\mathbf{Z}_b\mathbf{B}^t \tag{3.8.12}$$

is the *impedance matrix* in the loop formulation and

$$\mathbf{E}_l = -\mathbf{B}_E\mathbf{E}_b \tag{3.8.13}$$

represents the *loop voltages* of the equation. Note that this formulation is *not* identical to the mesh formulation introduced in Chapter 2. The loops are formed here by means of chords. Its advantage, as compared with the mesh method, is the fact that it is applicable to planar as well as nonplanar networks. Its disadvantage is that the $\mathbf{Z}$ matrix is often dense.

EXAMPLE 3.8.1. Derive the matrix $\mathbf{Z}$ and the source vector $\mathbf{E}_l$ for the network of Fig. 3.8.1. Use the graph and tree given in the figure.

The product $\mathbf{B}\mathbf{Z}_b\mathbf{B}^t$ is

$$\mathbf{Z} = \begin{bmatrix} R_1 + 1/sC_2 + sL_4 & R_1 + 1/sC_2 & -1/sC_2 \\ R_1 + 1/sC_2 & R_1 + 1/sC_2 + 1/sC_3 + sL_5 & -1/sC_2 - 1/sC_3 \\ -1/sC_2 & -1/sC_2 - 1/sC_3 & 1/sC_2 + 1/sC_3 + 1/sC_6 \end{bmatrix}.$$

The source vector is

$$\mathbf{E}_l = -\mathbf{B}_E\mathbf{E}_b = \begin{bmatrix} 1 & -1 & 0 \\ 1 & -1 & -1 \\ 0 & 1 & 0 \end{bmatrix} \begin{bmatrix} E_1 \\ E_2 \\ E_3 \end{bmatrix} = \begin{bmatrix} E_1 - E_2 \\ E_1 - E_2 - E_3 \\ E_2 \end{bmatrix}.$$

3.9. STATE VARIABLE FORMULATION

In the state variable formulation all algebraic equations are eliminated and the network is described by a system of first-order differential equations. The formulation is used extensively in theoretical studies, as many theorems from mathematics are directly applicable. In the decade of the sixties, the formulation had some computational justification as well, because good computer codes for solving sets of first-order differential equations were becoming available. The disadvantage of this formulation lies in the complicated steps required to eliminate the algebraic equations and in the fact that the matrices involved are often dense. Algorithms that simultaneously handle sets of differential *and* algebraic equations are now available. Since the disadvantages of the state variable formulation far outweigh its advantages, it is no longer used in computer applications. For this reason, we will restrict our discussion to simple R, L, C, and G elements and independent sources only.

The *normal form* of the state equations in the Laplace transform domain is

$$\begin{bmatrix} sX_1 \\ sX_2 \\ \vdots \\ sX_n \end{bmatrix} = \begin{bmatrix} a_{11} & a_{12} \cdots & a_{1n} \\ a_{21} & a_{22} & a_{2n} \\ \vdots & \vdots & \vdots \\ a_{n1} & a_{n2} \cdots & a_{nn} \end{bmatrix} \begin{bmatrix} X_1 \\ X_2 \\ \vdots \\ X_n \end{bmatrix} + \begin{bmatrix} b_{11} & b_{12} \cdots & b_{1m} \\ b_{21} & b_{22} & b_{2m} \\ \vdots & \vdots & \vdots \\ b_{n1} & b_{n2} \cdots & b_{nm} \end{bmatrix} \begin{bmatrix} W_1 \\ W_2 \\ \vdots \\ W_m \end{bmatrix} \tag{3.9.1}$$

or

$$s\mathbf{X} = \mathbf{AX} + \mathbf{BW}. \tag{3.9.2}$$

The standard notation for state variable matrices is used in (3.9.2) where **A** and **B** are *not* the incidence and loopset matrices. The size of **A** is $n \times n$ (n being the number of states), the size of **B** is $n \times m$, and **W** is the vector of independent sources. The normal form of the state equations is usually accompanied by a set of output equations:

$$\mathbf{Y} = \mathbf{CX} + \mathbf{DW} \tag{3.9.3}$$

Y being here a vector of length k if there are k outputs. **C** has the dimension $k \times n$ and **D** is $k \times m$. Very often at an intermediate stage of the formulation we get an equation of the form

$$s\mathbf{M}\hat{\mathbf{X}} = \hat{\mathbf{A}}\hat{\mathbf{X}} + \hat{\mathbf{B}}\hat{\mathbf{W}} \tag{3.9.4}$$

where **M** may be a singular matrix. In this section we will indicate the methods for obtaining (3.9.4). Further processing is required to obtain (3.9.2).

Let the network be composed of resistors, capacitors and inductors. We know that the voltage across an inductor is given by $V = sLI$, whereas the current through the capacitor is given by $I = sCV$. Since (3.9.2) has $s\mathbf{X}$ on the left side, we wish to retain the voltages across the capacitors and the currents through inductors as elements of the vector $s\mathbf{X}$.

It was indicated in Section 3.5 that the twig voltages and chord currents are independent variables. Thus selecting a tree containing all capacitors while all inductors are placed into the cotree solves our problem, if such a choice is physically possible.

Further, the voltage of an independent voltage source is specified and *must* be incorporated into the tree. Similarly, the current of an independent current source is given and it *must* be taken into the cotree. In the selection of a tree (called *normal* tree), it is best to proceed with the numbering as follows:

1. Take all independent voltage sources into the tree.
2. Take as many capacitors as possible into the tree.
3. Continue taking as many resistors or conductors into the tree as possible.
4. Complete the tree by taking as many inductors as needed.
5. Number the capacitors in the cotree.
6. Number the resistors or conductors in the cotree.
7. Number the inductors in the cotree.
8. Number the independent current sources in the cotree.

To solve the problem, write the **Q**-matrix for the network graph. It will have the form $[\mathbf{1} \quad \mathbf{Q}_c]$. The KCL will have the form (3.5.2), the KVL the form (3.5.5). Writing them in one matrix equation and using (3.4.3):

$$\begin{bmatrix} \mathbf{I}_t \\ \mathbf{V}_c \end{bmatrix} = \begin{bmatrix} \mathbf{0} & -\mathbf{Q}_c \\ \mathbf{Q}_c^t & \mathbf{0} \end{bmatrix} \begin{bmatrix} \mathbf{V}_t \\ \mathbf{I}_c \end{bmatrix}. \tag{3.9.5}$$

This is the desired arrangement of variables. On the right side we have the independent twig voltages and chord currents; the dependent variables are on the left side. Equation (3.9.5) is the basis for the state variable formulation.

In the next step, constitutive equations are inserted into (3.9.5) and the matrix equation rewritten as a set of equations. Finally, only the twig capacitor voltages and chord inductor currents are retained, the other equations being eliminated. This provides a set of equations which can be written in the form (3.9.4).

The steps of the state variable formulation will be explained by means of an example.

EXAMPLE 3.9.1. Find the state variable formulation for the network shown in Fig. 3.9.1. Use the tree indicated in the figure by thicker lines.

The state variables are known: they will be twig capacitor voltages and the chord inductor current; e.g., $V_{C_2}, V_{C_3}, I_{L_6}$. The **Q** matrix is

$$\mathbf{Q} = \left[\begin{array}{ccc|cccc} 1 & 0 & 0 & 1 & 0 & 0 & 0 \\ 0 & 1 & 0 & -1 & 1 & 1 & 0 \\ 0 & 0 & 1 & 0 & -1 & -1 & 1 \end{array}\right] = [\mathbf{1} \quad \mathbf{Q}_c].$$

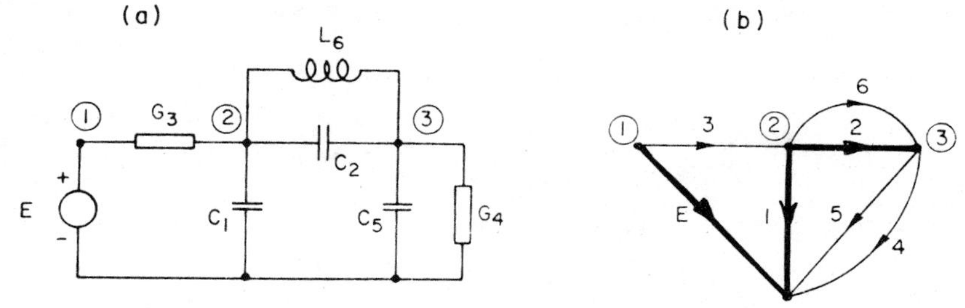

Fig. 3.9.1. Example demonstrating state variable formulation.

Equation (3.9.5) becomes

$$\begin{bmatrix} I_E \\ I_1 \\ I_2 \\ \hdashline V_3 \\ V_4 \\ V_5 \\ V_6 \end{bmatrix} = \left[\begin{array}{ccc:cccc} 0 & 0 & 0 & -1 & 0 & 0 & 0 \\ 0 & 0 & 0 & 1 & -1 & -1 & 0 \\ 0 & 0 & 0 & 0 & 1 & 1 & -1 \\ \hdashline 1 & -1 & 0 & 0 & 0 & 0 & 0 \\ 0 & 1 & -1 & 0 & 0 & 0 & 0 \\ 0 & 1 & -1 & 0 & 0 & 0 & 0 \\ 0 & 0 & 1 & 0 & 0 & 0 & 0 \end{array}\right] \begin{bmatrix} V_E \\ V_1 \\ V_2 \\ \hdashline I_3 \\ I_4 \\ I_5 \\ I_6 \end{bmatrix}.$$

This matrix equation expresses all mutual relations between the currents and voltages. The coupling is provided by the branch constitutive equations which are:

$$\begin{aligned} V_E &= E & I_4 &= G_4 V_4 \\ I_1 &= sC_1 V_1 & I_5 &= sC_5 V_5 \\ I_2 &= sC_2 V_2 & V_6 &= sL_6 I_6 . \\ I_3 &= G_3 V_3 \end{aligned}$$

Inserting the constitutive equations into the matrix equation above, we get

$$\begin{bmatrix} I_E \\ sC_1 V_1 \\ sC_2 V_2 \\ V_3 \\ V_4 \\ V_5 \\ sL_6 I_6 \end{bmatrix} = \begin{bmatrix} 0 & 0 & 0 & -1 & 0 & 0 & 0 \\ 0 & 0 & 0 & 1 & -1 & -1 & 0 \\ 0 & 0 & 0 & 0 & 1 & 1 & -1 \\ 1 & -1 & 0 & 0 & 0 & 0 & 0 \\ 0 & 1 & -1 & 0 & 0 & 0 & 0 \\ 0 & 1 & -1 & 0 & 0 & 0 & 0 \\ 0 & 0 & 1 & 0 & 0 & 0 & 0 \end{bmatrix} \begin{bmatrix} E \\ V_1 \\ V_2 \\ G_3 V_3 \\ G_4 V_4 \\ sC_5 V_5 \\ I_6 \end{bmatrix}.$$

For hand calculations, the matrix equation is rewritten as a set of equations:

$$
\begin{aligned}
I_E &= -G_3 V_3 \\
sC_1 V_1 &= G_3 V_3 - G_4 V_4 - sC_5 V_5 \\
sC_2 V_2 &= G_4 V_4 + sC_5 V_5 - I_6 \\
V_3 &= E - V_1 \\
V_4 &= V_1 - V_2 \\
V_5 &= V_1 - V_2 \\
sL_6 I_6 &= V_2 .
\end{aligned}
$$

Now eliminate all variables except V_1, V_2, I_6. The result in the form of (3.9.4) is

$$
s\begin{bmatrix} C_1 + C_5 & -C_5 & 0 \\ -C_5 & C_2 + C_5 & 0 \\ 0 & 0 & L_6 \end{bmatrix}\begin{bmatrix} V_1 \\ V_2 \\ I_6 \end{bmatrix} = \begin{bmatrix} -(G_3 + G_4) & G_4 & 0 \\ G_4 & -G_4 & -1 \\ 0 & 1 & 0 \end{bmatrix}\begin{bmatrix} V_1 \\ V_2 \\ I_6 \end{bmatrix} + \begin{bmatrix} G_3 \\ 0 \\ 0 \end{bmatrix} E.
$$

M is nonsingular and can be inverted to obtain the normal form.

PROBLEMS

P.3.1. Draw the oriented graphs for the networks shown in Fig. P.3.1. Use the convention of Fig. 3.1.2 for the sources, assign arbitrary orientations to the edges of all other elements. Write the incidence matrices **A**.

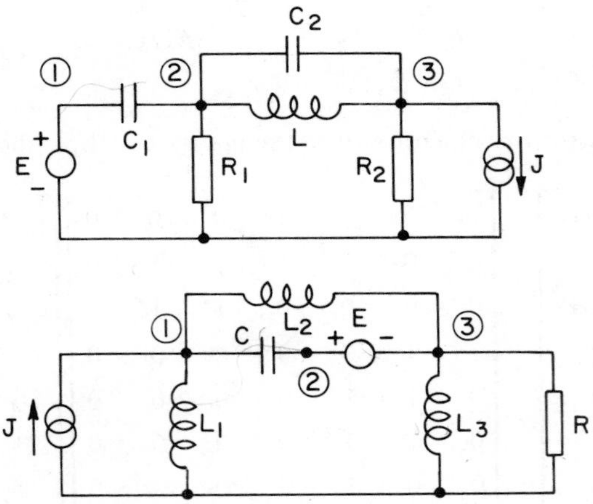

Fig. P.3.1.

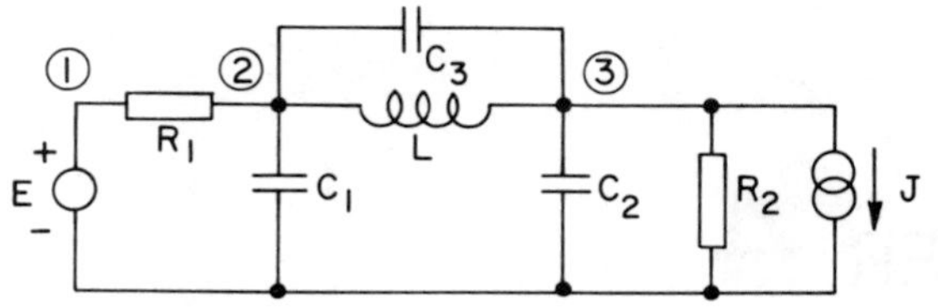

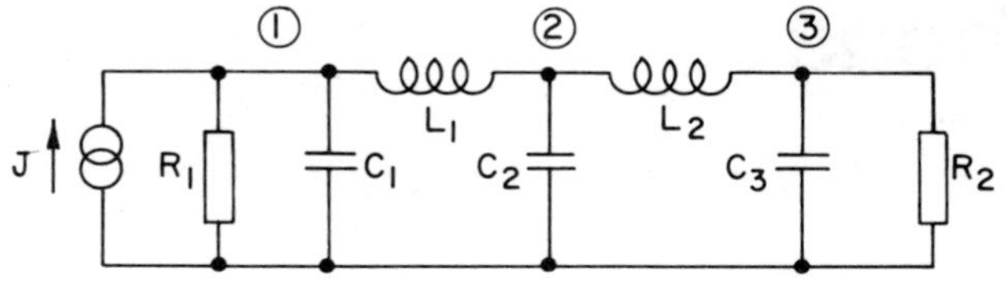

Fig. P.3.1. (*Continued*)

P.3.2. For the networks shown in Fig. P.3.1, write the **Q** and **B** matrices by using the graphs from Problem P.3.1. Select the trees.

P.3.3. Show the validity of the orthogonality relations by using the **Q** and **B** matrices derived in Problem P.3.2.

P.3.4. Transform the voltage sources in Fig. P.3.1 into equivalent current sources, draw appropriate graphs, and apply the topological formulation of nodal equations (Section 3.7) to these networks.

P.3.5. Transform the current sources in Fig. P.3.1 into equivalent voltage sources, draw appropriate graphs, and apply the topological formulation of loop equations (Section 3.8) to these networks.

P.3.6. Apply the state variable formulation to the networks in Fig. P.3.1 by using the **Q** matrices obtained in Problem P.3.2.

REFERENCE

1. W. H. Kim and H. E. Meadows, Jr.: *Modern Network Analysis.* John Wiley & Sons, New York, 1971, p. 23.

CHAPTER 4 General Formulation Methods

The formulation methods introduced in Chapter 2 are quite efficient and have been used successfully in many applications, but they cannot handle all ideal elements. To avoid the restrictions, general formulation methods are introduced in this chapter. In the Section 4.1, the tableau formulation [1] is discussed. Here all branch currents, all branch voltages, and all nodal voltages are retained as unknown variables of the problem. Thus the formulation is most general (everything is available after the solution) but leads to large system matrices.

Section 4.2 indicates that blocks of variables can be eliminated and, under special circumstances, this naturally leads to the nodal formulation. However, if we wish to retain the ability to handle all types of network elements, complete block elimination is not possible and the modified nodal formulation [2] must be used. This can be done using graphs, as discussed in Section 4.3, or without graphs, as shown in Section 4.4.

The modified nodal formulations given in Sections 4.3 and 4.4 are efficient but still retain many redundant variables. It is demonstrated in Section 4.5 that active networks can be analyzed extremely efficiently if we follow a set of special rules. The rules given there cannot be easily used for computer solutions and a systematic method must be found. The basis for eliminating redundant variables is the use of separate voltage and current graphs, discussed in Section 4.6 where they are applied to the tableau formulation. The graphs are a representation of the interconnections and as such can be replaced by tables which can be used for automated formulation. Such tabular representation is given in Section 4.7. With this background, the two-graph modified nodal formulation is developed in Section 4.8. Finally, Section 4.9 compares the various formulations introduced in this chapter, and Section 4.10 gives an example. The method explained in Section 4.4 and the two-graph modified nodal formulation of Section 4.8 are coded in the program in Appendix D.

4.1. TABLEAU FORMULATION

The formulations discussed in the last two chapters can all be derived from a general formulation called the *tableau*. In this formulation, *all* equations describing the network are collected into one large matrix equation, involving the KVL, KCL, and the constitutive equations, CE.

We will first comment on the most convenient type of tableau. For initial considerations let the network have b branches; $n+1$ nodes; R, G, L, C elements; and sources. We can express the topological properties of such a network by means of the **A**, **Q**, and **B** matrices. The last two matrices are interdependent and considerable effort is required to obtain them: a tree must be selected and the matrices brought into a proper form. It is much easier to work with the incidence matrix, and for this reason the tableau is based on it. Recall that the KCL was expressed by

$$\mathbf{A}\mathbf{I}_b = \mathbf{0} \tag{4.1.1}$$

whereas the KVL was given by

$$\mathbf{V}_b - \mathbf{A}^t\mathbf{V}_n = \mathbf{0}. \tag{4.1.2}$$

The subscript n stands for nodes, the subscript b for branches, and in applications b will be replaced by the element number. (For the fifth element 5 will be written instead of b.)

The general representation describing all possible constitutive equations has the following form:

$$\begin{matrix}\text{currents}\\ \text{voltages}\end{matrix}\quad \begin{bmatrix}\mathbf{Y}_1\\ \mathbf{K}_2\end{bmatrix}\mathbf{V}_b + \begin{bmatrix}\mathbf{K}_1\\ \mathbf{Z}_2\end{bmatrix}\mathbf{I}_b = \begin{bmatrix}\mathbf{W}_{b_1}\\ \mathbf{W}_{b_2}\end{bmatrix}$$

where $\mathbf{Y}_1$ and $\mathbf{Z}_2$ represent admittances and impedances, respectively; $\mathbf{K}_1$ and $\mathbf{K}_2$ contain dimensionless constants; and $\mathbf{W}_{b_1}$, and $\mathbf{W}_{b_2}$ include the independent current and voltage sources, as well as the influence of initial conditions on capacitors and inductors. For notational compactness, we will use the following form:

$$\mathbf{Y}_b\mathbf{V}_b + \mathbf{Z}_b\mathbf{I}_b = \mathbf{W}_b. \tag{4.1.3}$$

In all subsequent formulations, capacitors will be entered in admittance form and inductors in impedance form, to keep the variable s in the numerator. Since the Laplace transform variable s is equivalent to the differentiation operator, we will get a set of algebraic-differential equations when performing time domain

Table 4.1.1.

Element	Constitutive Equation (CE)	Value of Y_b	Value of Z_b	Value of W_b
Resistor	$V_b - R_b I_b = 0$	1	$-R_b$	0
Conductor	$G_b V_b - I_b = 0$	G_b	-1	0
Capacitor	$sC_b V_b - I_b = C_b V_0$	sC_b	-1	$C_b V_0$
Inductor	$V_b - sL_b I_b = -L_b I_0$	1	$-sL_b$	$-L_b I_0$
Voltage source	$V_b = E_b$	1	0	E_b
Current source	$I_b = J_b$	0	1	J_b

analysis. Table 4.1.1 indicates the choices of Y_b, Z_b, and W_b for various two-terminal elements.

Equations (4.1.1)-(4.1.3) can be collected, for instance, in the following sequence:

$$\mathbf{V}_b - \mathbf{A}^t \mathbf{V}_n = \mathbf{0}$$

$$\mathbf{Y}_b \mathbf{V}_b + \mathbf{Z}_b \mathbf{I}_b = \mathbf{W}_b$$

$$\mathbf{A}\mathbf{I}_b = \mathbf{0}$$

and put into one matrix equation

$$\begin{array}{c} b \\ b \\ n \end{array}\overset{\begin{array}{ccc} b & b & n \end{array}}{\begin{bmatrix} \mathbf{1} & \mathbf{0} & -\mathbf{A}^t \\ \mathbf{Y}_b & \mathbf{Z}_b & \mathbf{0} \\ \mathbf{0} & \mathbf{A} & \mathbf{0} \end{bmatrix}} \begin{bmatrix} \mathbf{V}_b \\ \mathbf{I}_b \\ \mathbf{V}_n \end{bmatrix} = \begin{bmatrix} \mathbf{0} \\ \mathbf{W}_b \\ \mathbf{0} \end{bmatrix} \tag{4.1.4}$$

or, in general,

$$\mathbf{T}\mathbf{X} = \mathbf{W}. \tag{4.1.5}$$

The arrangement indicated in (4.1.4) has square submatrices on the diagonal. In the tableau, there is no reason to distinguish between sources and passive elements, as we did in Chapter 3. The element numbering can be completely arbitrary. For theoretical considerations, one might wish to have special arrangements, depending on the purpose.

EXAMPLE 4.1.1. Write the tableau equations for the network and graph in Fig. 4.1.1.

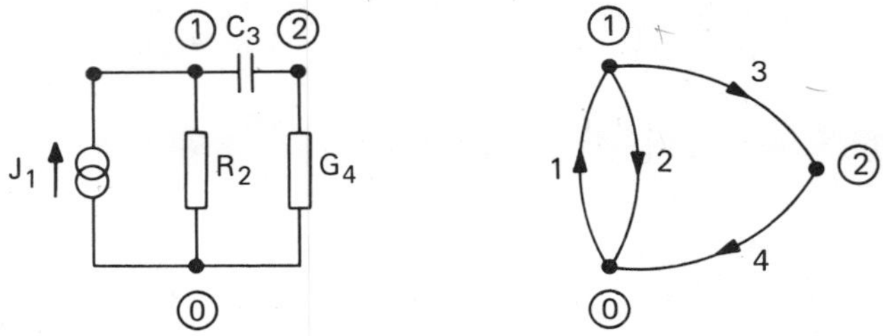

Fig. 4.1.1. Example demonstrating the tableau formulation.

The **A** matrix is

$$\mathbf{A} = \begin{array}{c} \begin{array}{cccc} 1 & 2 & 3 & 4 \end{array} \\ \begin{bmatrix} -1 & 1 & 1 & 0 \\ 0 & 0 & -1 & 1 \end{bmatrix} \end{array}.$$

In this example, both R and G elements were intentionally introduced. The tableau is

$$\left[\begin{array}{cccc|cccc|cc}
1 & & & & & & & & 1 & 0 \\
 & 1 & & & & \mathbf{0} & & & -1 & 0 \\
 & & 1 & & & & & & -1 & 1 \\
 & & & 1 & & & & & 0 & -1 \\
\hline
0 & & & & 1 & & & & & \\
 & 1 & & & & -R_2 & & & & \mathbf{0} \\
 & & sC_3 & & & & -1 & & & \\
 & & & G_4 & & & & -1 & & \\
\hline
 & \mathbf{0} & & & -1 & 1 & 1 & 0 & & \mathbf{0} \\
 & & & & 0 & 0 & -1 & 1 & &
\end{array}\right]
\left[\begin{array}{c} V_1 \\ V_2 \\ V_3 \\ V_4 \\ I_1 \\ I_2 \\ I_3 \\ I_4 \\ V_{n1} \\ V_{n2} \end{array}\right]
=
\left[\begin{array}{c} \\ \mathbf{0} \\ \\ \\ \hline J_1 \\ 0 \\ 0 \\ 0 \\ \hline \mathbf{0} \\ \\ \end{array}\right].$$

If the capacitor initially had a voltage V_0 across it, positive at node 1 and negative at node 2, the right-hand side entry of the seventh row would be $C_3 V_0$.

Until now, we have been able to handle two-terminal elements only. We do not as yet have a graph representation for the various ideal two-ports introduced in Chapter 1.

In order to generalize the tableau to any element, we will introduce first the simpler *one-graph concept* (to be distinguished from the two-graph concept introduced later). In the one-graph, each port of a two-port network is represented by an oriented line segment and two constitutive equations must

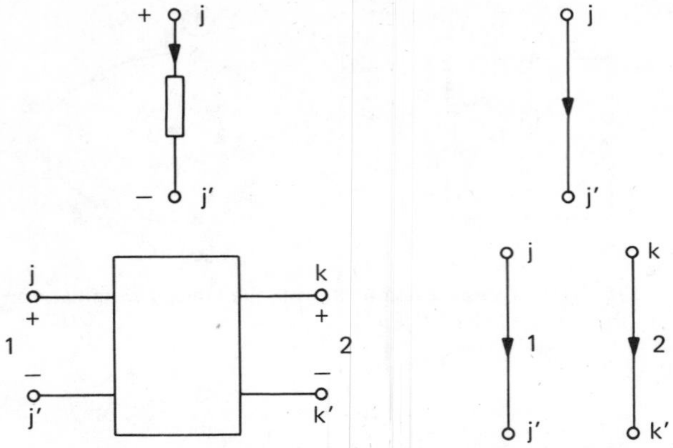

Fig. 4.1.2. One and two-port networks and their graph representations.

be given. The graph representation is shown in Fig. 4.1.2. Two numbers are associated with each two-port when numbering the edges. The constitutive equations are precisely those discussed in Chapter 1 for the two-ports; the most important ideal elements are collected in Fig. 4.1.3.

ELEMENT	SYMBOL	CONSTITUTIVE EQUATIONS
CURRENT SOURCE	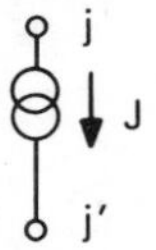	I = J
VOLTAGE SOURCE	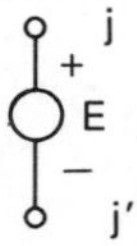	V = E
OPEN CIRCUIT		I = 0
SHORT CIRCUT		V = 0

Fig. 4.1.3. Constitutive equations of ideal elements for tableau formulation.

ELEMENT	SYMBOL	CONSTITUTIVE EQUATIONS
ADMITTANCE		$yV - I = 0$
IMPEDANCE	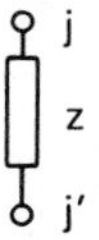	$V - zI = 0$
NULLATOR		$I = 0$ $V = 0$
NORATOR		I, V ARBITRARY (NO CONSTITUTIVE EQUATIONS)
VCT	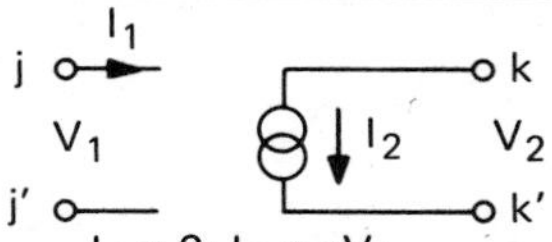 $I_1 = 0;\ I_2 = gV_1$	$\begin{bmatrix} 0 & 0 \\ g & 0 \end{bmatrix}\begin{bmatrix} V_1 \\ V_2 \end{bmatrix} + \begin{bmatrix} 1 & 0 \\ 0 & -1 \end{bmatrix}\begin{bmatrix} I_1 \\ I_2 \end{bmatrix} = \begin{bmatrix} 0 \\ 0 \end{bmatrix}$
VVT	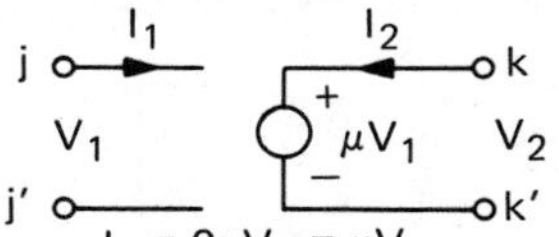 $I_1 = 0;\ V_2 = \mu V_1$	$\begin{bmatrix} 0 & 0 \\ \mu & -1 \end{bmatrix}\begin{bmatrix} V_1 \\ V_2 \end{bmatrix} + \begin{bmatrix} 1 & 0 \\ 0 & 0 \end{bmatrix}\begin{bmatrix} I_1 \\ I_2 \end{bmatrix} = \begin{bmatrix} 0 \\ 0 \end{bmatrix}$
CCT	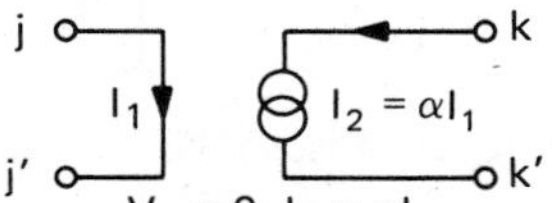 $V_1 = 0;\ I_2 = \alpha I_1$	$\begin{bmatrix} 1 & 0 \\ 0 & 0 \end{bmatrix}\begin{bmatrix} V_1 \\ V_2 \end{bmatrix} + \begin{bmatrix} 0 & 0 \\ \alpha & -1 \end{bmatrix}\begin{bmatrix} I_1 \\ I_2 \end{bmatrix} = \begin{bmatrix} 0 \\ 0 \end{bmatrix}$
CVT	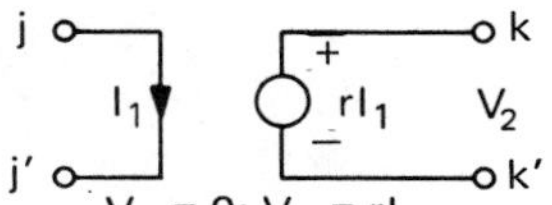 $V_1 = 0;\ V_2 = rI_1$	$\begin{bmatrix} 1 & 0 \\ 0 & -1 \end{bmatrix}\begin{bmatrix} V_1 \\ V_2 \end{bmatrix} + \begin{bmatrix} 0 & 0 \\ r & 0 \end{bmatrix}\begin{bmatrix} I_1 \\ I_2 \end{bmatrix} = \begin{bmatrix} 0 \\ 0 \end{bmatrix}$
OPAMP	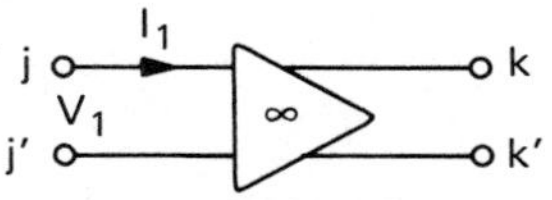 $V_1 = 0;\ I_1 = 0$	$\begin{bmatrix} 1 & 0 \\ 0 & 0 \end{bmatrix}\begin{bmatrix} V_1 \\ V_2 \end{bmatrix} + \begin{bmatrix} 0 & 0 \\ 1 & 0 \end{bmatrix}\begin{bmatrix} I_1 \\ I_2 \end{bmatrix} = \begin{bmatrix} 0 \\ 0 \end{bmatrix}$

Fig. 4.1.3. (*Continued*)

EXAMPLE 4.1.2. Write the **A** matrix and the constitutive matrices $\mathbf{Y}_b$, $\mathbf{Z}_b$ for the network and graph shown in Fig. 4.1.4.

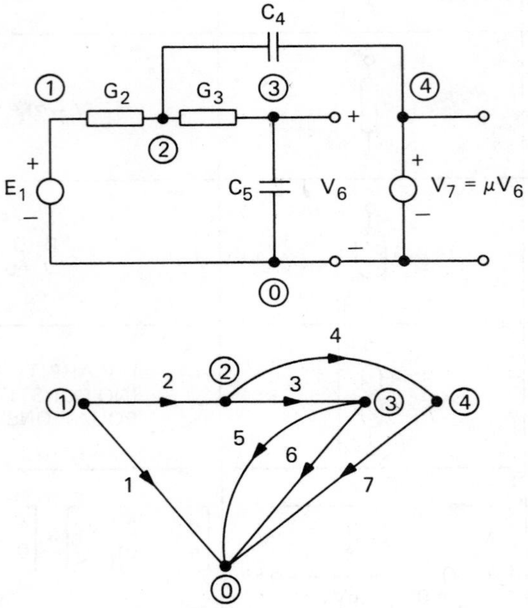

Fig. 4.1.4. Active network with a VVT and its graph.

$$\mathbf{A} = \begin{bmatrix} 1 & 1 & 0 & 0 & 0 & 0 & 0 \\ 0 & -1 & 1 & 1 & 0 & 0 & 0 \\ 0 & 0 & -1 & 0 & 1 & 1 & 0 \\ 0 & 0 & 0 & -1 & 0 & 0 & 1 \end{bmatrix}.$$

Edge 6 denotes the input, edge 7 the output of the VVT, in agreement with Fig. 4.1.2. The CE for the elements are

$$\begin{aligned} V_1 &= E_1 \\ G_2 V_2 - I_2 &= 0 \\ G_3 V_3 - I_3 &= 0 \\ sC_4 V_4 - I_4 &= 0 \\ sC_5 V_5 - I_5 &= 0 \\ I_6 &= 0 \\ \mu V_6 - V_7 &= 0. \end{aligned}$$

The last two equations describe the VVT. The CE are rewritten in the form (4.1.3):

$$\begin{bmatrix} 1 & 0 & 0 & 0 & 0 & 0 & 0 \\ 0 & G_2 & 0 & 0 & 0 & 0 & 0 \\ 0 & 0 & G_3 & 0 & 0 & 0 & 0 \\ 0 & 0 & 0 & sC_4 & 0 & 0 & 0 \\ 0 & 0 & 0 & 0 & sC_5 & 0 & 0 \\ 0 & 0 & 0 & 0 & 0 & 0 & 0 \\ 0 & 0 & 0 & 0 & 0 & \mu & -1 \end{bmatrix} \begin{bmatrix} V_1 \\ V_2 \\ V_3 \\ V_4 \\ V_5 \\ V_6 \\ V_7 \end{bmatrix} + \begin{bmatrix} 0 & 0 & 0 & 0 & 0 & 0 & 0 \\ 0 & -1 & 0 & 0 & 0 & 0 & 0 \\ 0 & 0 & -1 & 0 & 0 & 0 & 0 \\ 0 & 0 & 0 & -1 & 0 & 0 & 0 \\ 0 & 0 & 0 & 0 & -1 & 0 & 0 \\ 0 & 0 & 0 & 0 & 0 & 1 & 0 \\ 0 & 0 & 0 & 0 & 0 & 0 & 0 \end{bmatrix} \begin{bmatrix} I_1 \\ I_2 \\ I_3 \\ I_4 \\ I_5 \\ I_6 \\ I_7 \end{bmatrix} = \begin{bmatrix} E_1 \\ 0 \\ 0 \\ 0 \\ 0 \\ 0 \\ 0 \end{bmatrix} .$$

To compare various formulations, it is convenient to introduce the matrix density, defined as follows:

$$D = \frac{\text{number of nonzero entries in the matrix}}{\text{total number of all entries in the matrix}} . \tag{4.1.6}$$

For Example 4.1.2, the tableau has the size 18×18 and there are 39 nonzero entries. Thus the density becomes $D = 39/18^2 = 0.12$ or 12%.

EXAMPLE 4.1.3. The use of the operational amplifier will be demonstrated on the generalized impedance convertor shown in Fig. 4.1.5. The two OPAMPs are

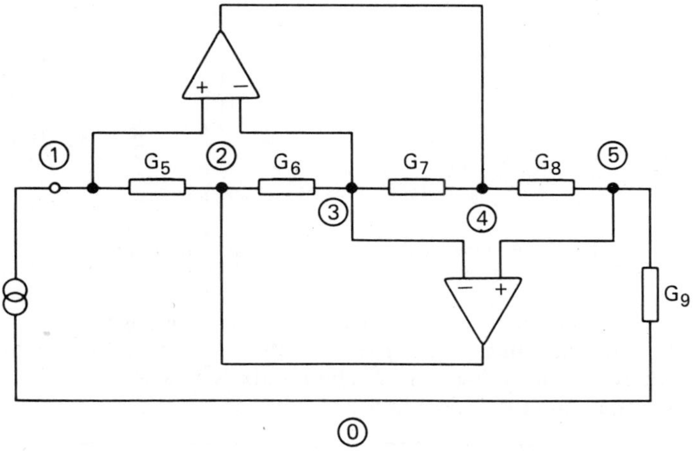

Fig. 4.1.5. Generalized impedance convertor and its graph.

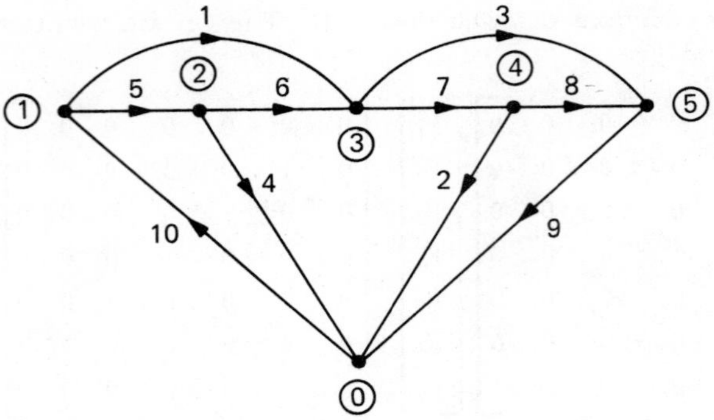

Fig. 4.1.5. (*Continued*)

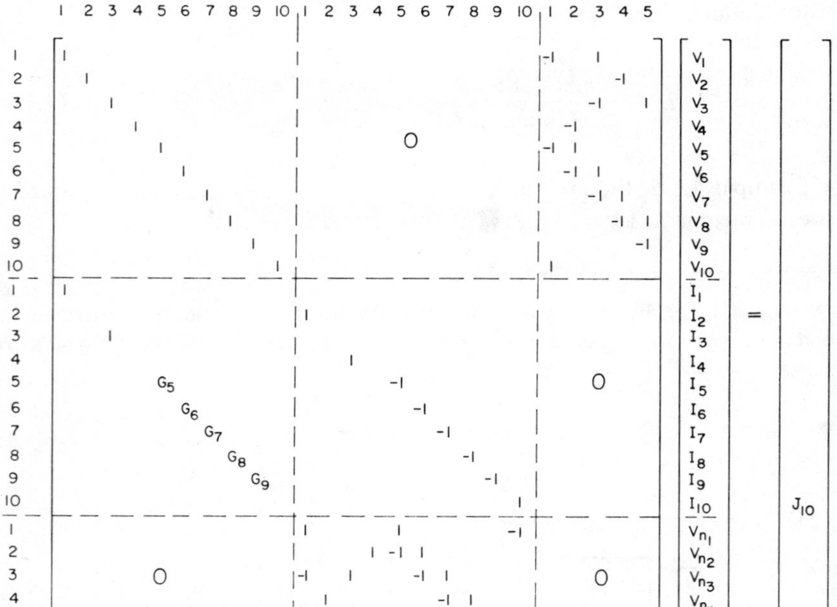

Fig. 4.1.6. One-graph tableau for the network in Fig. 4.1.5.

represented in the graph by the first four edges, the passive elements and the source by the remaining six. Write the tableau formulation for this network. The result is shown in Fig. 4.1.6. The matrix is of size 25 X 25, there are 57 nonzero entries, and the density is 9.12%.

The networks in Examples 4.1.2 and 4.1.3 will be used repeatedly in the rest of this chapter and the sizes of the matrices will be given for various formulations. The tableau discussed in this section has mainly theoretical importance. The reader should note that many ideal two-ports introduce redundant variables: for instance, the input current of the VVT or VCT, or the input branch voltage of the CVT or CCT are known to be zero but they are kept in this formulation as variables. Elimination of such variables will be the subject of Section 4.6.

The tableau formulation has another problem: the resulting matrices are always quite large and sparse matrix solvers are needed. Unfortunately, the structure of the matrix is such that coding these routines is complicated. Their treatment is beyond the scope of this book.

4.2. BLOCK ELIMINATION ON THE TABLEAU

In any network, the branch voltages are either equal to the node voltages (for grounded elements) or given by the difference of two node voltages (for elements connected between two nodes). Since this is a simple relationship and the node voltages are available after the tableau equations are solved, we can eliminate all branch voltages from the equations. Write the tableau equations again:

$$\mathbf{V}_b = \mathbf{A}^t\mathbf{V}_n$$

$$\mathbf{Y}_b\mathbf{V}_b + \mathbf{Z}_b\mathbf{I}_b = \mathbf{W}_b$$

$$\mathbf{A}\mathbf{I}_b = \mathbf{0}.$$

Substitute the first equation into the second

$$\mathbf{Y}_b\mathbf{A}^t\mathbf{V}_n + \mathbf{Z}_b\mathbf{I}_b = \mathbf{W}_b \tag{4.2.1}$$

$$\mathbf{A}\mathbf{I}_b = \mathbf{0}. \tag{4.2.2}$$

In matrix form

$$\begin{bmatrix} \mathbf{Y}_b\mathbf{A}^t & \mathbf{Z}_b \\ \mathbf{0} & \mathbf{A} \end{bmatrix} \begin{bmatrix} \mathbf{V}_n \\ \mathbf{I}_b \end{bmatrix} = \begin{bmatrix} \mathbf{W}_b \\ \mathbf{0} \end{bmatrix}. \tag{4.2.3}$$

The size of this matrix is $(b + n)$.

We can proceed even further under special circumstances. Assume that every element in the network is represented by its admittance. Then the branch current can be easily recovered either as $Y_b V_{n_j} = I_b$ or, for an ungrounded element, as $Y_b(V_{n_j} - V_{n_k}) = I_b$. In such case we can additionally eliminate the currents from Eq. (4.2.1) and (4.2.2). Let every element have the description

$$Y_b V_b - I_b = 0$$

and let only current sources be permitted:

$$I_b = J_b.$$

These two types of equations can be combined into a common matrix form:

$$\mathbf{I}_b = \mathbf{Y}_b \mathbf{V}_b + \mathbf{J}_b. \tag{4.2.4}$$

Substituting for $\mathbf{V}_b$ gives

$$\mathbf{I}_b = \mathbf{Y}_b \mathbf{A}^t \mathbf{V}_n + \mathbf{J}_b. \tag{4.2.5}$$

Inserting, finally, (4.2.5) into (4.2.2) gives

$$\mathbf{A}(\mathbf{Y}_b \mathbf{A}^t \mathbf{V}_n + \mathbf{J}_b) = \mathbf{0}$$

or

$$\mathbf{A}\mathbf{Y}_b \mathbf{A}^t \mathbf{V}_n = -\mathbf{A}\mathbf{J}_b. \tag{4.2.6}$$

This is exactly the nodal formulation discussed in Chapter 3, Eq. (3.7.10). The size of the matrix is now only $n \times n$.

It must be noted that the admittance form does not exist for many useful ideal elements: voltage source, VVT, CVT, CCT, transformer, ideal transformer, operational amplifier, norator, and nullator. Moreover, if we wish to preserve the variable s in the numerator, the inductor must be entered in its impedance form. In nonlinear networks (to be discussed later), a resistor may be a current-controlled device and its describing function may not be invertible. In all these cases, some currents must be retained in the formulation. We will present both formal and by-inspection methods for writing such formulations.

4.3. MODIFIED NODAL FORMULATION USING ONE GRAPH

This section presents the formal steps required in deriving the modified nodal formulation for all ideal elements. The idea underlying this formulation is to split the elements into groups; one group is formed by elements which have an admittance description, and the other by those which do not. Then we can eliminate all branch currents for elements having the admittance description. This will partly fill the empty block in (4.2.3) and will reduce the number of unknown currents $\mathbf{I}_b$. Every element will be represented by the graphs given in Fig. 4.1.2. Initial conditions on inductors and capacitors will be replaced by equivalent sources (see Fig. 1.3.1).

Rearrange the elements of the network so that the KCL equation can be written in the following form:

$$[\mathbf{A}_1 \quad \mathbf{A}_2 \quad \mathbf{A}_3] \begin{bmatrix} \mathbf{I}_1 \\ \mathbf{I}_2 \\ \mathbf{J} \end{bmatrix} = \mathbf{0}. \tag{4.3.1}$$

The partitions are created so that:

1. $\mathbf{I}_1$ contains branch currents of elements that have an admittance representation and which are not required as solutions.
2. $\mathbf{I}_2$ contains branch currents for elements that do not have an admittance representation. It contains, in addition, branch currents of voltage sources *and* branch currents which are required as solutions.
3. $\mathbf{J}$ contains independent current sources.

The KVL equations are partitioned the same way:

$$\begin{bmatrix} \mathbf{V}_1 \\ \mathbf{V}_2 \\ \mathbf{V}_J \end{bmatrix} = \begin{bmatrix} \mathbf{A}_1^t \\ \mathbf{A}_2^t \\ \mathbf{A}_3^t \end{bmatrix} \mathbf{V}_n. \tag{4.3.2}$$

Equation (4.3.2) in fact represents three separate matrix equations:

$$\mathbf{V}_1 = \mathbf{A}_1^t \mathbf{V}_n \tag{4.3.3}$$

$$\mathbf{V}_2 = \mathbf{A}_2^t \mathbf{V}_n \tag{4.3.4}$$

$$\mathbf{V}_J = \mathbf{A}_3^t \mathbf{V}_n. \tag{4.3.5}$$

Equation (4.3.5) is used to compute the voltages across the current sources once the $\mathbf{V}_n$ are found.

The branch relations for elements in partition 2 are

$$\mathbf{Y}_2 \mathbf{V}_2 + \mathbf{Z}_2 \mathbf{I}_2 = \mathbf{W}_2 \tag{4.3.6}$$

where the right-hand-side vector $\mathbf{W}_2$ contains nonzero entries only for the voltage sources.

The branch relations in the first partition are of the form

$$\mathbf{Y}_1\mathbf{V}_1 = \mathbf{I}_1. \tag{4.3.7}$$

Rewrite (4.3.1) in the following form:

$$\mathbf{A}_1\mathbf{I}_1 + \mathbf{A}_2\mathbf{I}_2 = -\mathbf{A}_3\mathbf{J}$$

and substitute (4.3.7) for $\mathbf{I}_1$:

$$\mathbf{A}_1\mathbf{Y}_1\mathbf{V}_1 + \mathbf{A}_2\mathbf{I}_2 = -\mathbf{A}_3\mathbf{J}.$$

Branch voltages $\mathbf{V}_1$ can be eliminated by substituting (4.3.3):

$$\mathbf{A}_1\mathbf{Y}_1\mathbf{A}_1^t\mathbf{V}_n + \mathbf{A}_2\mathbf{I}_2 = -\mathbf{A}_3\mathbf{J}. \tag{4.3.8}$$

Substituting similarly (4.3.4) into (4.3.6), obtain

$$\mathbf{Y}_2\mathbf{A}_2^t\mathbf{V}_n + \mathbf{Z}_2\mathbf{I}_2 = \mathbf{W}_2. \tag{4.3.9}$$

Equations (4.3.8) and (4.3.9) can be put into one matrix equation:

$$\begin{bmatrix} \mathbf{A}_1\mathbf{Y}_1\mathbf{A}_1^t & \mathbf{A}_2 \\ \mathbf{Y}_2\mathbf{A}_2^t & \mathbf{Z}_2 \end{bmatrix} \begin{bmatrix} \mathbf{V}_n \\ \mathbf{I}_2 \end{bmatrix} = \begin{bmatrix} -\mathbf{A}_3\mathbf{J} \\ \mathbf{W}_2 \end{bmatrix}. \tag{4.3.10}$$

Let us denote

$$\mathbf{A}_1\mathbf{Y}_1\mathbf{A}_1^t = \mathbf{Y}_{n_1} \tag{4.3.11}$$

$$-\mathbf{A}_3\mathbf{J} = \mathbf{J}_n. \tag{4.3.12}$$

Comparing with the nodal formulation (4.2.6) we see that $\mathbf{Y}_{n_1}$ is the nodal admittance matrix for the elements in partition 1 while $\mathbf{J}_n$ represents the equivalent nodal current sources. Both $\mathbf{Y}_{n_1}$ and $\mathbf{J}_n$ can be written by inspection as explained in Chapter 2. The final form of the modified nodal formulation is

	node voltages	additional currrents			
KCL	$\mathbf{Y}_{n_1}$	$\mathbf{A}_2$	$\mathbf{V}_n$	$\mathbf{J}_n$	Current sources applied to nodes
Additional equations	$\mathbf{Y}_2\mathbf{A}_2^t$	$\mathbf{Z}_2$	$\mathbf{I}_2$	$\mathbf{W}_2$	Influence of voltage sources.

$$\begin{bmatrix} \mathbf{Y}_{n_1} & \mathbf{A}_2 \\ \mathbf{Y}_2\mathbf{A}_2^t & \mathbf{Z}_2 \end{bmatrix} \begin{bmatrix} \mathbf{V}_n \\ \mathbf{I}_2 \end{bmatrix} = \begin{bmatrix} \mathbf{J}_n \\ \mathbf{W}_2 \end{bmatrix} \tag{4.3.13}$$

Once (4.3.13) has been solved, the remaining currents are obtained from (4.3.7) and the branch voltages are obtained by using (4.3.2).

Note, for future reference, that the top equations express the KCL *at the nodes.* The system (4.3.13) retains the advantages of both the nodal and the tableau methods.

EXAMPLE 4.3.1. Apply the modified nodal method to the network in Fig. 4.1.5.

The two OPAMPs are represented by the first four branches. The constitutive equations for the OPAMPs are taken from Fig. 4.1.3 and are put into one matrix equation:

$$\begin{bmatrix} 1 & 0 & 0 & 0 \\ 0 & 0 & 0 & 0 \\ 0 & 0 & 1 & 0 \\ 0 & 0 & 0 & 0 \end{bmatrix} \begin{bmatrix} V_1 \\ V_2 \\ V_3 \\ V_4 \end{bmatrix} + \begin{bmatrix} 0 & 0 & 0 & 0 \\ 1 & 0 & 0 & 0 \\ 0 & 0 & 0 & 0 \\ 0 & 0 & 1 & 0 \end{bmatrix} \begin{bmatrix} I_1 \\ I_2 \\ I_3 \\ I_4 \end{bmatrix} = \begin{bmatrix} 0 \\ 0 \\ 0 \\ 0 \end{bmatrix}.$$

The submatrix $\mathbf{A}_2$ has the following form:

$$\mathbf{A}_2 = \begin{matrix} \text{nodes} \\ \downarrow \end{matrix} \begin{matrix} \\ 1 \\ 2 \\ 3 \\ 4 \\ 5 \end{matrix} \overset{\text{edges} \longrightarrow}{\begin{matrix} 1 & 2 & 3 & 4 \\ \end{matrix}} \begin{bmatrix} 1 & 0 & 0 & 0 \\ 0 & 0 & 0 & 1 \\ -1 & 0 & 1 & 0 \\ 0 & 1 & 0 & 0 \\ 0 & 0 & -1 & 0 \end{bmatrix}$$

and the modified nodal equation is

$$\left[\begin{array}{ccccc|cccc} G_5 & -G_5 & 0 & 0 & 0 & 1 & 0 & 0 & 0 \\ -G_5 & G_5+G_6 & -G_6 & 0 & 0 & 0 & 0 & 0 & 1 \\ 0 & -G_6 & G_6+G_7 & -G_7 & 0 & -1 & 0 & 1 & 0 \\ 0 & 0 & -G_7 & G_7+G_8 & -G_8 & 0 & 1 & 0 & 0 \\ 0 & 0 & 0 & -G_8 & G_8+G_9 & 0 & 0 & -1 & 0 \\ \hline 1 & 0 & -1 & 0 & 0 & 0 & 0 & 0 & 0 \\ 0 & 0 & 0 & 0 & 0 & 1 & 0 & 0 & 0 \\ 0 & 0 & 1 & 0 & -1 & 0 & 0 & 0 & 0 \\ 0 & 0 & 0 & 0 & 0 & 0 & 0 & 1 & 0 \end{array}\right] \begin{bmatrix} V_{n_1} \\ V_{n_2} \\ V_{n_3} \\ V_{n_4} \\ V_{n_5} \\ I_1 \\ I_2 \\ I_3 \\ I_4 \end{bmatrix} = \left[\begin{array}{c} J_{10} \\ 0 \\ 0 \\ 0 \\ 0 \\ \hline 0 \\ 0 \\ 0 \\ 0 \end{array}\right].$$

The size of the matrix is 9 X 9 (as compared with the 25 X 25 tableau formulation). The number of nonzero entries is also reduced to 25. The density increased to $D = 30.9\%$.

4.4. MODIFIED NODAL FORMULATION BY INSPECTION

The formal description of the modified nodal formulation by means of one graph eliminated all branch voltages plus branch currents for elements which have an admittance description. It cannot eliminate redundant variables which are known in advance ($I_1 = 0$ for a VVT, etc.). This elimination by means of graphs is possible if we introduce separate graphs for voltages and currents. However, based on the considerations and results obtained in Section 4.3 we can introduce a method which eliminates some of the redundant variables and, in addition, does not need any graphs or incidence matrices. The result is an important practical formulation method for computer application.

Using (4.3.11), enter by inspection all elements which have the admittance description. Denote the size of the **Y** part of the matrix by $m = n$, m being initially the number of ungrounded nodes. We will increase the size of the basic matrix whenever we enter an element which does not have an admittance description. Its constitutive equation will be attached at the bottom of the set of equations (as another row of the matrix) and the current flowing into the element will be attached to the system as a new variable (additional column of the matrix).

To facilitate programming considerations, let us make some simple assumptions. Define two matrices **G** and **C** of equal sizes N (N larger than m). Define as well a vector **W** of length N for the right-hand-side vector of the system. The values of J, E, CV_0, LI_0 will be entered into this vector. All conductors and frequency-independent numbers arising in the formulation will be stored in the matrix **G**, whereas capacitor and inductor values and other values that are associated with the frequency variable will be stored in the matrix **C**. All inductors will be considered in impedance form. Once the formulation part has been completed and the matrices **G**, **C** and the vector **W** are prepared, the system matrix is obtained, for any s, by writing

$$\mathbf{T} = \mathbf{G} + s\mathbf{C}$$

and the solution may follow.

Assume that all conductances and VCTs are entered into **G** by means of the symbolic formulae discussed in Chapter 2. All capacitors are entered into the matrix **C** and the current sources are placed properly into the source vector. So far, only the upper left corners of the matrices are occupied by network entries.

Consider now, for instance, a voltage source. It is given, along with all other elements, in Fig. 4.4.1. The *nodes* are denoted by j, j' and the voltage source enforces the condition

$$V_j - V_{j'} = E.$$

This constitutive equation is in terms of *nodal voltages* and is appended to the set of previously defined equations. In addition, a current I will flow between the terminals j, j'. To unify the notation, the currents at terminals j or k will be considered to be positive; thus for the voltage source $I_j = I$, $I_{j'} = -I$. They are taken into account in the KCL as a new variable: I in the jth row and $-I$ in the j'th row. The matrix and the source vector will have the following forms:

$$\begin{array}{c} \\ j \\ j' \\ m+1 \end{array}
\begin{array}{c} \begin{array}{ccc} V_j & V_{j'} & \overset{I}{m+1} \end{array} \\ \left[\begin{array}{cc|c} & & 1 \\ & & -1 \\ \hline 1 & -1 & \end{array}\right] \end{array},
\quad
\begin{array}{c} \text{Right side} \\ \left[\begin{array}{c} \\ \\ \hline E' \end{array}\right] \end{array}.$$

The increased size is indicated by the $(m + 1)$st row and column. Should one, say the jth, node of the voltage source be grounded, the jth row and column of the **G** and **C** matrices will not exist.

For a VVT (Fig. 4.4.1) the following equations apply:

$$-\mu V_j + \mu V_{j'} + V_k - V_{k'} = 0,$$
$$I_j = I_{j'} = 0$$
$$I_k = -I_{k'} = I.$$

One row is added to the matrix, representing the constitutive equation. An additional column takes care of the unknown current I:

$$\begin{array}{c} \\ j \\ j' \\ k \\ k' \\ m+1 \end{array}
\begin{array}{c} \begin{array}{ccccc} V_j & V_{j'} & V_k & V_{k'} & I \end{array} \\ \left[\begin{array}{cccc|c} & & & & \\ & & & & \\ & & & & 1 \\ & & & & -1 \\ \hline -\mu & \mu & 1 & -1 & \end{array}\right] \end{array}.$$

The reader should have no difficulty in deriving the formulae for the remaining ideal elements. They are all collected in Fig. 4.4.1.

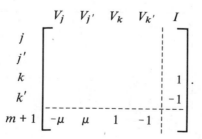

ELEMENT	SYMBOL	MATRIX	EQUATIONS
CURRENT SOURCE	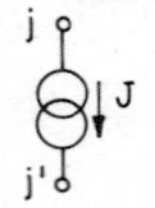	$\begin{array}{c} j \\ j' \end{array}\begin{bmatrix} -J \\ J \end{bmatrix}$ SOURCE VECTOR	$I_j = J$ $I_{j'} = -J$
VOLTAGE SOURCE	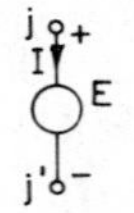	$\begin{array}{c} \\ j \\ j' \\ m+1 \end{array}\begin{array}{c} \begin{array}{ccc} V_j & V_{j'} & I \end{array} \\ \begin{bmatrix} & & 1 \\ & & -1 \\ 1 & -1 & \end{bmatrix} \end{array}$ SOURCE VECTOR $\begin{bmatrix} \\ \\ E \end{bmatrix}$	$V_j - V_{j'} = E$ $I_j = I$ $I_{j'} = -I$
OPEN CIRCUIT	j o + V j' o –	———	$V = V_j - V_{j'}$
SHORT CIRCUIT		$\begin{array}{c} \\ j \\ j' \\ m+1 \end{array}\begin{array}{c} \begin{array}{ccc} V_j & V_{j'} & I \end{array} \\ \begin{bmatrix} & & 1 \\ & & -1 \\ 1 & -1 & \end{bmatrix} \end{array}$	$V_j - V_{j'} = 0$ $I_j = I$ $I_{j'} = -I$
ADMITTANCE	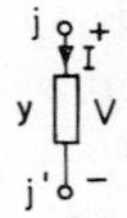	$\begin{array}{c} \\ j \\ j' \end{array}\begin{array}{c} \begin{array}{cc} V_j & V_{j'} \end{array} \\ \begin{bmatrix} y & -y \\ -y & y \end{bmatrix} \end{array}$	$I_j = y(V_j - V_{j'})$ $I_{j'} = -y(V_j - V_{j'})$
IMPEDANCE	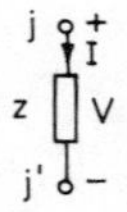	$\begin{array}{c} \\ j \\ j' \\ m+1 \end{array}\begin{array}{c} \begin{array}{ccc} V_j & V_{j'} & I \end{array} \\ \begin{bmatrix} & & 1 \\ & & -1 \\ 1 & -1 & -z \end{bmatrix} \end{array}$	$V_j - V_{j'} - zI = 0$ $I_j = -I_{j'} = I$
NULLATOR		$\begin{array}{c} \\ \\ m+1 \end{array}\begin{array}{c} \begin{array}{cc} V_j & V_{j'} \end{array} \\ \begin{bmatrix} & \\ 1 & -1 \end{bmatrix} \end{array}$	$V_j - V_{j'} = 0$ $I_j = I_{j'} = 0$
NORATOR		$\begin{array}{c} \\ j \\ j' \end{array}\begin{array}{c} \begin{array}{cc} & I \end{array} \\ \begin{bmatrix} & 1 \\ & -1 \end{bmatrix} \end{array}$	V, I ARE ARBITRARY
VCT	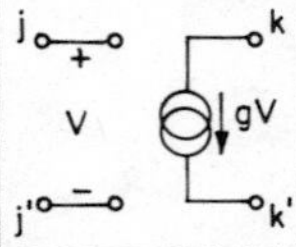	$\begin{array}{c} \\ k \\ k' \end{array}\begin{array}{c} \begin{array}{cc} V_j & V_{j'} \end{array} \\ \begin{bmatrix} g & -g \\ -g & g \end{bmatrix} \end{array}$	$I_j = 0$ $I_{j'} = 0$ $I_k = g(V_j - V_{j'})$ $I_{k'} = -g(V_j - V_{j'})$

Fig. 4.4.1. Ideal elements in the modified nodal formulation without graphs.

ELEMENT	SYMBOL	MATRIX	EQUATIONS
VVT	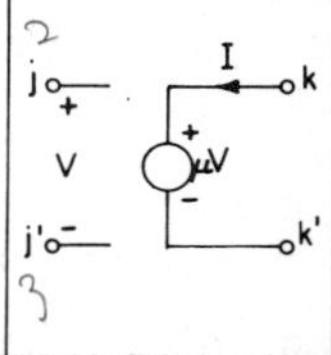	$\begin{array}{c} \\ j \\ j' \\ k \\ k' \\ m+1 \end{array}\begin{array}{ccccc} V_j & V_{j'} & V_k & V_{k'} & I \\ & & & & \\ & & & & \\ & & & & 1 \\ & & & & -1 \\ -\mu & \mu & 1 & -1 & \end{array}$	$-\mu V_j + \mu V_{j'} + V_k - V_{k'} = 0$ $I_k = I$ $I_{k'} = -I$
CCT	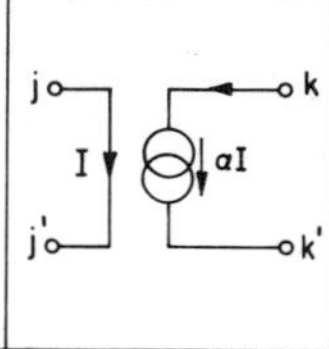	$\begin{array}{c} \\ j \\ j' \\ k \\ k' \\ m+1 \end{array}\begin{array}{ccccc} V_j & V_{j'} & V_k & V_{k'} & I \\ & & & & 1 \\ & & & & -1 \\ & & & & a \\ & & & & -a \\ 1 & -1 & & & \end{array}$	$V_j - V_{j'} = 0$ $I_j = -I_{j'} = I$ $I_k = -I_{k'} = aI$
CVT	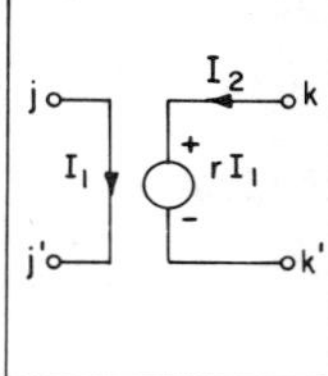	$\begin{array}{c} \\ j \\ j' \\ k \\ k' \\ m+1 \\ m+2 \end{array}\begin{array}{cccccc} V_j & V_{j'} & V_k & V_{k'} & I_1 & I_2 \\ & & & & 1 & \\ & & & & -1 & \\ & & & & & 1 \\ & & & & & -1 \\ 1 & -1 & & & & \\ & & 1 & -1 & -r & \end{array}$	$V_j - V_{j'} = 0$ $V_k - V_{k'} - rI_1 = 0$ $I_j = -I_{j'} = I_1$ $I_k = -I_{k'} = I_2$
OPERATIONAL AMPLIFIER	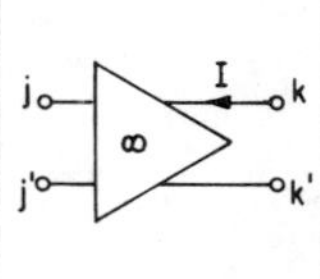	$\begin{array}{c} \\ j \\ j' \\ k \\ k' \\ m+1 \end{array}\begin{array}{ccccc} V_j & V_{j'} & V_k & V_{k'} & I \\ & & & & \\ & & & & \\ & & & & 1 \\ & & & & -1 \\ 1 & -1 & & & \end{array}$	$V_j - V_{j'} = 0$ $I_k = -I_{k'} = I$
CONVERTOR	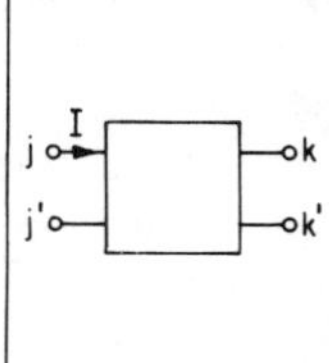	$\begin{array}{c} \\ j \\ j' \\ k \\ k' \\ m+1 \end{array}\begin{array}{ccccc} V_j & V_{j'} & V_k & V_{k'} & I \\ & & & & 1 \\ & & & & -1 \\ & & & & -K_2 \\ & & & & K_2 \\ 1 & -1 & -K_1 & K_1 & \end{array}$	$V_j - V_{j'} - K_1 V_k + K_1 V_{k'} = 0$ $I_j = -I_{j'} = I$ $I_k = -I_{k'} = -K_2 I$ FOR IDEAL TRANSFORMER $K_1 = K_2 = n$
TRANSFORMER	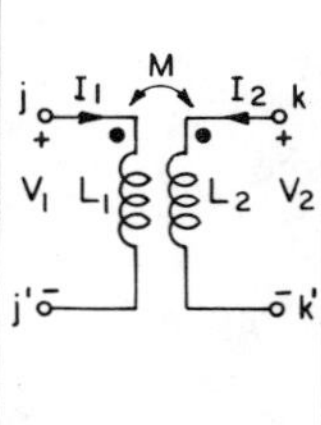	$\begin{array}{c} \\ j \\ j' \\ k \\ k' \\ m+1 \\ m+2 \end{array}\begin{array}{cccccc} V_j & V_{j'} & V_k & V_{k'} & I_1 & I_2 \\ & & & & 1 & \\ & & & & -1 & \\ & & & & & 1 \\ & & & & & -1 \\ 1 & -1 & & & -sL_1 & -sM \\ & & 1 & -1 & -sM & -sL_2 \end{array}$	$V_j - V_{j'} - sL_1 I_1 - sMI_2 = 0$ $V_k - V_{k'} - sMI_1 - sL_2 I_2 = 0$ $I_j = -I_{j'} = I_1$ $I_k = -I_{k'} = I_2$

Fig. 4.4.1. (*Continued*)

It is interesting to show that even a perfect switch can be incorporated into the formulation. Consider a conductance for which we wish to retain the current as the variable available upon the solution of the system. The constitutive equation for a conductance between nodes j, j' is

$$G(V_j - V_{j'}) - I = 0$$

and this equation is appended to the system of equations. The current is taken into account by an additional column:

$$\begin{array}{c} \\ j \\ j' \\ m+1 \end{array} \begin{array}{c} \begin{array}{ccc} j & j' & m+1 \end{array} \\ \left[\begin{array}{cc|c} & & 1 \\ & & -1 \\ \hline G & -G & -1 \end{array}\right] \end{array} .$$

For a resistor, the entries are in Fig. 4.4.1 and are repeated here:

$$\begin{array}{c} \\ j \\ j' \\ m+1 \end{array} \begin{array}{c} \begin{array}{ccc} j & j' & m+1 \end{array} \\ \left[\begin{array}{cc|c} & & 1 \\ & & -1 \\ \hline 1 & -1 & -R \end{array}\right] \end{array}$$

An open circuit requires $G = 0$ while $R = 0$ results in a short circuit. We can thus combine the above representations as follows:

$$\begin{array}{c} \\ j \\ j' \\ m+1 \end{array} \begin{array}{c} \begin{array}{ccc} j & j' & m+1 \end{array} \\ \left[\begin{array}{cc|c} & & 1 \\ & & -1 \\ \hline F & -F & F-1 \end{array}\right] \end{array} \qquad (4.4.1)$$

and select the value of F according to the following scheme:

Condition	F
Open circuit	0
Short circuit	1

If the system matrix is generated by means of (4.4.1), the switches can be opened or closed without reformulating the equations. Only the proper value for F is inserted in the matrix before the solution.

We next present two examples to demonstrate the writing of the modified nodal equations.

EXAMPLE 4.4.1. Write the modified nodal formulation for the network of Fig. 4.1.4 by inspection.

Using the node numbering in the figure, write first the nodal admittance portion for the conductors and capacitors. Then append the equation for the voltage source and finally for the VVT. Denote $I_1 = I_E$, $I_7 = I_{VVT}$.

$$
\left[\begin{array}{cccc|cc}
G_2 & -G_2 & 0 & 0 & 1 & 0 \\
-G_2 & G_2 + G_3 + sC_4 & -G_3 & -sC_4 & 0 & 0 \\
0 & -G_3 & G_3 + sC_5 & 0 & 0 & 0 \\
0 & -sC_4 & 0 & sC_4 & 0 & 1 \\
\hline
1 & 0 & 0 & 0 & 0 & 0 \\
0 & 0 & -\mu & 1 & 0 & 0
\end{array}\right]
\left[\begin{array}{c}
V_{n1} \\ V_{n2} \\ V_{n3} \\ V_{n4} \\ I_E \\ I_{VVT}
\end{array}\right]
=
\left[\begin{array}{c}
0 \\ 0 \\ 0 \\ 0 \\ \hline E_1 \\ 0
\end{array}\right].
$$

EXAMPLE 4.4.2. Write the modified nodal formulation for the network of Fig. 4.1.5.

$$
\left[\begin{array}{ccccc|cc}
G_5 & -G_5 & 0 & 0 & 0 & 0 & 0 \\
-G_5 & G_5 + G_6 & -G_6 & 0 & 0 & 0 & 1 \\
0 & -G_6 & G_6 + G_7 & -G_7 & 0 & 0 & 0 \\
0 & 0 & -G_7 & G_7 + G_8 & -G_8 & 1 & 0 \\
0 & 0 & 0 & -G_8 & G_8 + G_9 & 0 & 0 \\
\hline
1 & 0 & -1 & 0 & 0 & 0 & 0 \\
0 & 0 & 1 & 0 & -1 & 0 & 0
\end{array}\right]
\left[\begin{array}{c}
V_{n1} \\ V_{n2} \\ V_{n3} \\ V_{n4} \\ V_{n5} \\ I_{OP1} \\ I_{OP2}
\end{array}\right]
=
\left[\begin{array}{c}
J_{10} \\ 0 \\ 0 \\ 0 \\ 0 \\ \hline 0 \\ 0
\end{array}\right].
$$

For the network of Fig. 4.1.4, the original 18×18 tableau matrix was reduced to 6×6. For the example of Fig. 4.1.5, the original 25×25 tableau matrix was reduced to a 7×7 matrix without loosing any relevant information. We still calculate the current of the voltage source, the current of the source-port of the VVT and the current of the output port of the OPAMPs.

4.5. NODAL ANALYSIS OF ACTIVE NETWORKS

Active networks are, in most cases, realized by means of VVTs or by means of operational amplifiers. They are usually excited by a voltage source and their output is usually a voltage. A direct application of the nodal admittance con-

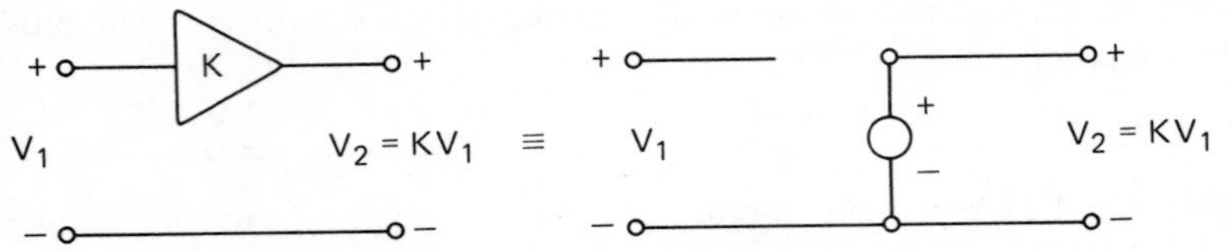

Fig. 4.5.1. Symbol for an amplifier and its VVT equivalent.

cept is not possible but considerable reduction of the system matrix size is possible if we apply some simple preprocessing steps.

The method to be presented here is intended for hand calculations and is also meant as an introduction to the formal methods presented in subsequent sections. Here we assume that *one terminal of each voltage source* is grounded, for both an independent or dependent source.

If the voltage source has one grounded terminal, the other terminal (or node) voltage is known. The output voltage of a VVT depends on some voltage elsewhere, but once that has been specified, the voltage of the source port is known as well. Moreover, as the ideal voltage source can deliver any current, we do not have to write the KCL for the node to which it is connected.

The above facts can be combined into the following rules for writing the equations of an active network:

1. Insert the known voltages into the circuit diagram.
2. Denote all resistors by their conductances $G_i = 1/R_i$.
3. Write the KCL equations for nodes *not* connected to independent or dependent voltage sources.

To illustrate the procedure, the rules will be applied to several examples. We also introduce the usual active-network symbol for the VVT, shown in Fig. 4.5.1.

EXAMPLE 4.5.1. Write the network equations for the network shown in Fig. 4.5.2.

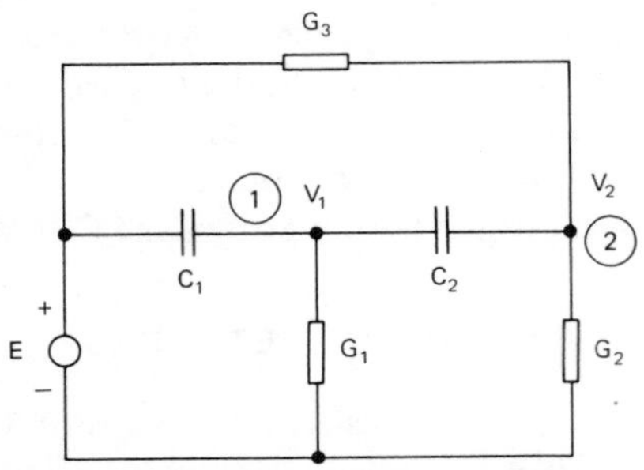

Fig. 4.5.2. Network with an independent voltage source.

The voltages are indicated in the figure. The KCL equations are written for nodes 1 and 2 only:

$$(G_1 + sC_1 + sC_2)\,V_1 - sC_2 V_2 = sC_1 E$$
$$-sC_2 V_1 + (G_2 + G_3 + sC_2)\,V_2 = G_3 E$$

It is convenient to rewrite them as a matrix equation:

$$\begin{bmatrix} G_1 + sC_1 + sC_2 & -sC_2 \\ -sC_2 & G_2 + G_3 + sC_2 \end{bmatrix} \begin{bmatrix} V_1 \\ V_2 \end{bmatrix} = \begin{bmatrix} sC_1 E \\ G_3 E \end{bmatrix}.$$

EXAMPLE 4.5.2. Apply the method to the network in Fig. 4.1.4.

Equations need be written for nodes 2 and 3 only. Denote the voltage of the fourth node as μV_3.

KCL at node 2: $(G_2 + G_3 + sC_4)\,V_2 - G_3 V_3 - sC_4 \mu V_3 = G_2 E_1$

KCL at node 3: $-G_3 V_2 + (G_3 + sC_5)\,V_3 = 0.$

In matrix form, this is:

$$\begin{bmatrix} (G_2 + G_3 + sC_4) & -(G_3 + sC_4\mu) \\ -G_3 & (G_3 + sC_5) \end{bmatrix} \begin{bmatrix} V_2 \\ V_3 \end{bmatrix} = \begin{bmatrix} G_2 E_1 \\ 0 \end{bmatrix}.$$

Analysis of networks with ideal operational amplifiers (OPAMPs) is based on the same ideas. The ideal OPAMP was introduced in Fig. 1.6.5. Its output is a voltage source, ideally with infinitely large gain, acting on the difference of the two input voltages. If an OPAMP is connected into a network with appropriate feedback, we do not observe any infinite voltages and this is possible only if *the input terminals are at the same potential.* If one of the terminals is grounded, the other must also be at zero potential. The rules stated above are supplemented by:

4. Write equal voltages at the input terminals of the OPAMP. If one of the terminals is grounded, the other one is at zero potential. Do not write the KCL equation at the output node of the OPAMP.

EXAMPLE 4.5.3. Analyze the network in Fig. 4.5.3.

Node 1 is at the same potential as the other input terminal of the OPAMP,

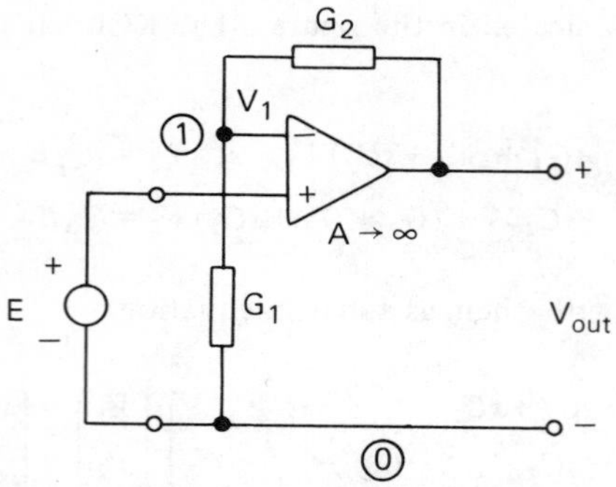

Fig. 4.5.3. OPAMP realization of a VVT with positive gain.

$V_1 = E$. KCL is written for this node only:

$$(G_1 + G_2)E - G_2 V_{out} = 0$$

$$\frac{V_{out}}{E} = 1 + \frac{G_1}{G_2}.$$

The network acts as a VVT with gain defined by the ratio of the conductances.

EXAMPLE 4.5.4. Write the equations for the network in Fig. 4.5.4 by applying the above rules.

One input terminal of each OPAMP is grounded; the voltage at the other input node must be zero. Denote the nonzero voltages by V_4, V_5, V_{out}. *Since we do not write the KCL equations at the output nodes of OPAMPs*, all we have to do is *write them for the points at ground potential.* In the figure, these nodes

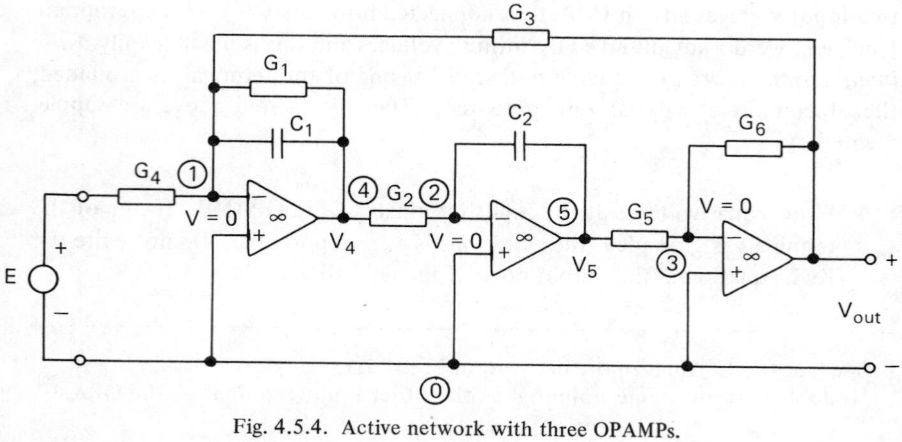

Fig. 4.5.4. Active network with three OPAMPs.

are denoted as nodes 1, 2, 3. The equations are:

$$0(G_1 + G_3 + G_4 + sC_1) - V_4(G_1 + sC_1) - V_{out}G_3 = EG_4$$
$$0(G_2 + sC_2) - V_4 G_2 - V_5 sC_2 = 0$$
$$0(G_5 + G_6) - V_5 G_5 - V_{out}G_6 = 0.$$

Here we have intentionally retained the terms multiplied by zero voltage for better understanding. Of course, these terms need not be included at all. Putting the remaining terms into a matrix equation we get

$$\begin{bmatrix} -G_1 - sC_1 & 0 & -G_3 \\ -G_2 & -sC_2 & 0 \\ 0 & -G_5 & -G_6 \end{bmatrix} \begin{bmatrix} V_4 \\ V_5 \\ V_{out} \end{bmatrix} = \begin{bmatrix} EG_4 \\ 0 \\ 0 \end{bmatrix}.$$

EXAMPLE 4.5.5. Write the necessary equations for the network shown in Fig. 4.1.5.

The two ideal OPAMPs force the voltages at nodes 1, 3, and 5 to be the same. We do not write the KCL at nodes 2, 4, where the outputs of the OPAMPs are connected. The voltages that must be retained are V_1, V_2, V_4 and the KCL are written at nodes 1, 3, 5:

$$G_5 V_1 - G_5 V_2 = J_{10}$$
$$(G_6 + G_7) V_1 - G_6 V_2 - G_7 V_4 = 0$$
$$(G_8 + G_9) V_1 - G_8 V_4 = 0$$

or, in matrix form:

$$\begin{bmatrix} G_5 & -G_5 & 0 \\ G_6 + G_7 & -G_6 & -G_7 \\ G_8 + G_9 & 0 & -G_8 \end{bmatrix} \begin{bmatrix} V_1 \\ V_2 \\ V_4 \end{bmatrix} = \begin{bmatrix} J_{10} \\ 0 \\ 0 \end{bmatrix}.$$

The networks in Examples 4.5.2 and 4.5.5 are repeatedly used throughout this chapter. The method presented in this section resulted in a 2×2 matrix for the network in Fig. 4.1.4 and 3×3 matrix for the network in Fig. 4.1.5. Their solution is trivial and suitable for hand calculation.

All examples given in this section indicate that matrix sizes can be drastically reduced if ideal elements are present and if we are willing to do additional preprocessing steps before the equations are formulated.

4.6. SEPARATE CURRENT AND VOLTAGE GRAPHS

For two-terminal elements, an edge on a single graph simultaneously represents the current through it and the voltage across it. For two-port networks, one of the variables may be zero; for instance, the input port current of a VVT. In order to handle two-ports by a single graph, we added the input current into the constitutive equations and allowed separate edges for the input and the output.

Separate voltage and current graphs offer the way to eliminate this redundancy. If the current into the port is zero, the edge is omitted on the *I*-graph but is kept on the *V*-graph.

A study of the various possibilities leads to the following set of rules for drawing the *I*- and *V*-graphs:

1. If the current in the branch *does not enter the constitutive equations* and is of no interest, its edge is collapsed on the *I*-graph.
2. If the current in the branch is zero, its edge is deleted from the *I*-graph.
3. If the voltage across the branch *does not enter the constitutive equations* and is of no interest, the edge is deleted on the *V*-graph.
4. If the voltage across the branch is zero, its edge is collapsed on the *V*-graph.

Note that the edge of a variable which enters the constitutive equations cannot be collapsed. The words "of no interest" imply that the particular variable will not be needed as the solution of the system; otherwise, the edge must be retained on the graph. For instance, one is often not interested in the current through a voltage source or the voltage across a current source.

If the rules are applied, the graphs may differ not only in structure but they may even have a different number of nodes and edges. The incidence matrix of the *I*-graph is used to write the KCL, whereas the incidence matrix of the *V*-graph is used for the KVL:

$$\begin{aligned} \mathbf{V}_b &= \mathbf{A}_v^t \mathbf{V}_n \\ \mathbf{Y}_b \mathbf{V}_b + \mathbf{Z}_b \mathbf{I}_b &= \mathbf{W}_b \\ \mathbf{A}_i \mathbf{I}_b &= \mathbf{0}. \end{aligned} \tag{4.6.1}$$

The subscripts i, v refer to the I or V-graph; $\mathbf{Y}_b$ and $\mathbf{Z}_b$ need not be square matrices any more.

The rules stated above were applied to all ideal elements and are collected in Fig. 4.6.1. It was assumed that the voltage across the current source (dependent or independent) or the current through the voltage source (dependent or independent) is of no interest. All four transducers now have only one constitutive equation; the variable whose value is known to be zero is eliminated. Two-ports which need two equations for their full description (gyrator, converter, inverter, and transformer) are represented as in the one-graph method.

Since collapsing of nodes requires renumbering, we will use the following notation:

Original nodes of the network will be denoted by numbers in circles.

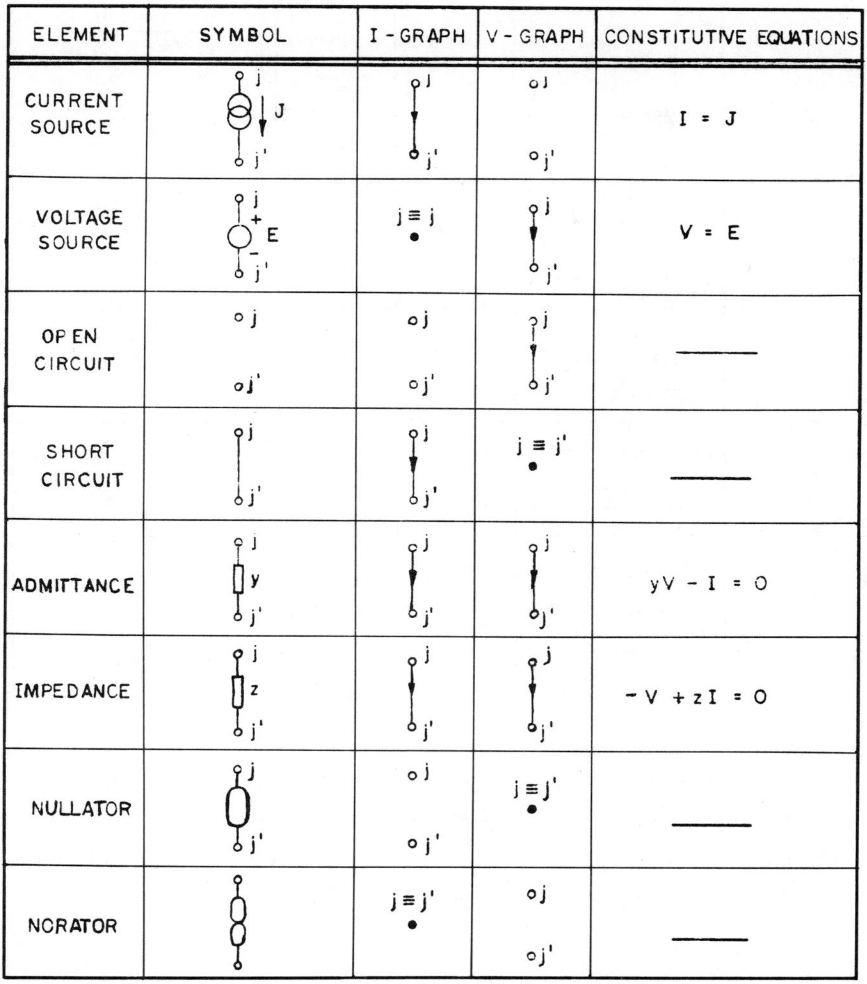

Fig. 4.6.1. Ideal elements and their two-graph representation.

ELEMENT	SYMBOL	I-GRAPH	V-GRAPH	CONSTITUTIVE EQUATIONS
VCT	j —○k V gV j'—○k'	○j ○k ○j' ○k'	○j ○k ○j' ○k'	$gV - I = 0$
VVT	j○— —○k V_1 $V_2 = \mu V_1$ j'○— —○k'	○j $k \equiv k'$ ○j'	○j ○k ○j' ○k'	$\begin{bmatrix} \mu & -1 \end{bmatrix} \begin{bmatrix} V_1 \\ V_2 \end{bmatrix} = 0$
CCT	j○— —○k I_1 $\alpha I_1 = I_2$ j'○— —○k'	○j ○k ○j' ○k'	$j \equiv j'$ ○k ○k'	$\begin{bmatrix} \alpha & -1 \end{bmatrix} \begin{bmatrix} I_1 \\ I_2 \end{bmatrix} = 0$
CVT	j○— —○k I $V = rI$ j'○— —○k'	○j $k \equiv k'$ ○j'	$j \equiv j'$ ○k ○k'	$rI - V = 0$
OPAMP	j○— I_1 I_2 —○k V_1 j'○— —○k' $V_1 = 0$; $I_1 = 0$	○j $k \equiv k'$ ○j'	$j \equiv j'$ ○k ○k'	——

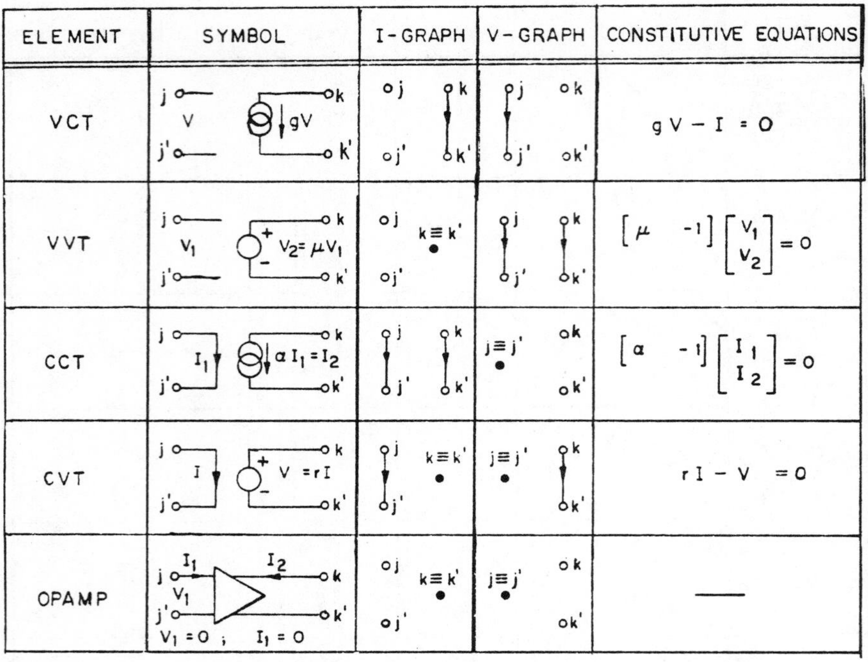

Fig. 4.6.1. (*Continued*)

Renumbered nodes of the *I*-graph will be denoted by numbers in squares. Renumbered nodes of the *V*-graph will be denoted by numbers in triangles.

The tableau matrix equation is easy to set up once we know the sizes of the various partitions. They are indicated in Eq. (4.6.2):

$$
\begin{array}{ccc}
\substack{\text{Number of}\\\text{retained}\\\text{branch}\\\text{voltages}} & \substack{\text{Number of}\\\text{retained}\\\text{branch}\\\text{currents}} & \substack{\text{Number of}\\\text{nodes on}\\V\text{-graph}}
\end{array}
$$

$$
\begin{matrix}
\substack{\text{Number of retained}\\\text{branch}\\\text{voltages}} \\ \\ \substack{\text{Number of}\\\text{constitutive}\\\text{equations}} \\ \\ \substack{\text{Number of}\\\text{nodes on}\\I\text{-graph}}
\end{matrix}
\begin{bmatrix} 1 & 0 & -A_v^t \\ Y_b & Z_b & 0 \\ 0 & A_i & 0 \end{bmatrix}
\begin{bmatrix} V_b \\ I_b \\ V_n \end{bmatrix} =
\begin{bmatrix} 0 \\ W_b \\ 0 \end{bmatrix}.
$$

$$(4.6.2)$$

EXAMPLE 4.6.1. Draw the I and V graphs for the network of Fig. 4.1.4. Write the $\mathbf{A}_i$, $\mathbf{A}_v$ matrices, determine the sizes of the submatrices in (4.6.2), and write the two-graph tableau equation.

The graphs are in Fig. 4.6.2. Collapsing of the nodes followed the instructions given in Fig. 4.6.1. The matrices are:

$$\mathbf{A}_i = \begin{array}{c} \\ \boxed{1} \\ \boxed{2} \end{array} \begin{array}{c} \begin{array}{cccc} 2 & 3 & 4 & 5 \end{array} \\ \left[\begin{array}{cccc} -1 & 1 & 1 & 0 \\ 0 & -1 & 0 & 1 \end{array}\right] \end{array}$$

$$\mathbf{A}_v = \begin{array}{c} \\ \triangle 1 \\ \triangle 2 \\ \triangle 3 \\ \triangle 4 \end{array} \begin{array}{c} \begin{array}{ccccccc} 1 & 2 & 3 & 4 & 5 & 6 & 7 \end{array} \\ \left[\begin{array}{ccccccc} 1 & 1 & 0 & 0 & 0 & 0 & 0 \\ 0 & -1 & 1 & 1 & 0 & 0 & 0 \\ 0 & 0 & -1 & 0 & 1 & 1 & 0 \\ 0 & 0 & 0 & -1 & 0 & 0 & 1 \end{array}\right] \end{array}$$

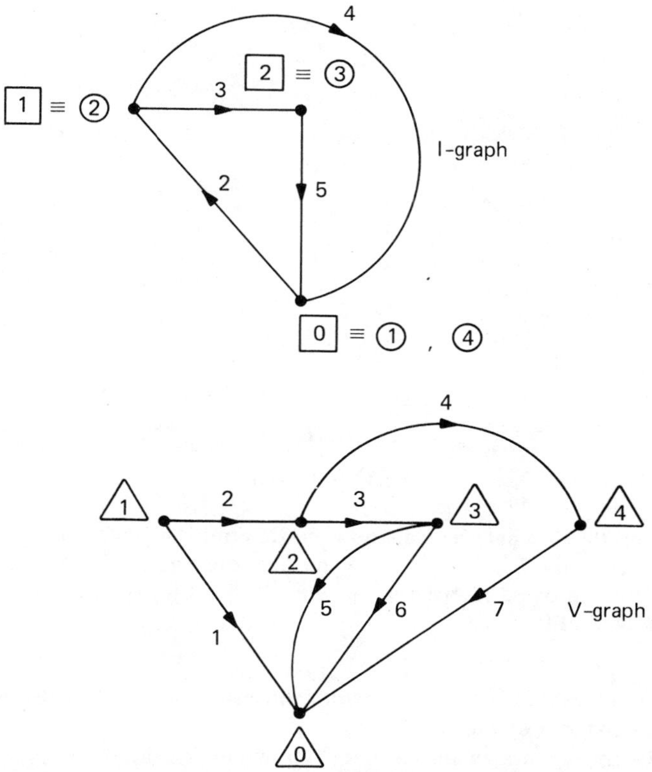

Fig. 4.6.2. Current and voltage graphs for the network in Fig. 4.1.4.

$$
\left[\begin{array}{ccccccc|cccc|cccc}
1 & & & & & & & & & & & -1 & & & \\
 & 1 & & & & & & & & & & -1 & 1 & & \\
 & & 1 & & & & & & & & & & -1 & 1 & \\
 & & & 1 & & & & & & & & & -1 & & 1 \\
 & & & & 1 & & & & & & & & & -1 & \\
 & & & & & 1 & & & & & & & & -1 & \\
 & & & & & & 1 & & & & & & & & -1 \\
\hline
1 & & & & & & & & & & & & & & \\
 & G_2 & & & & & & -1 & & & & & & & \\
 & & G_3 & & & & & & -1 & & & & & & \\
 & & & sC_4 & & & & & & -1 & & & & & \\
 & & & & sC_5 & & & & & & -1 & & & & \\
 & & & & & \mu & -1 & & & & & & & & \\
\hline
 & & & & & & & -1 & 1 & 1 & & & & & \\
 & & & & & & & & -1 & & 1 & & & &
\end{array}\right]
\left[\begin{array}{c}
V_1 \\ V_2 \\ V_3 \\ V_4 \\ V_5 \\ V_6 \\ V_7 \\ \hline I_2 \\ I_3 \\ I_4 \\ I_5 \\ \hline V_{\triangle 1} \\ V_{\triangle 2} \\ V_{\triangle 3} \\ V_{\triangle 4}
\end{array}\right]
=
\left[\begin{array}{c}
\\ \\ \\ \\ \\ \\ \\ E_1 \\ \\ \\ \\ \\ \\ \\ \\
\end{array}\right]
$$

Fig. 4.6.3. Two-graph tableau for the network in Fig. 4.1.4.

The constitutive equations are:

$$V_1 = E_1$$
$$G_2 V_2 - I_2 = 0$$
$$G_3 V_3 - I_3 = 0$$
$$sC_4 V_4 - I_4 = 0$$
$$sC_5 V_5 - I_5 = 0$$
$$\mu V_6 - V_7 = 0.$$

The sizes of the submatrices can now be determined. Horizontally they are 7 + 4 + 4, vertically 7 + 6 + 2. Once the sizes are known, it is easier to fill the constitutive equations directly one by one without preparing the matrices. The result is shown in Fig. 4.6.3.

EXAMPLE 4.6.2. Prepare the two-graph tableau formulation of the generalized impedance converter of Fig. 4.1.5.

The network is redrawn and its graphs shown in Fig. 4.6.4. The matrices are:

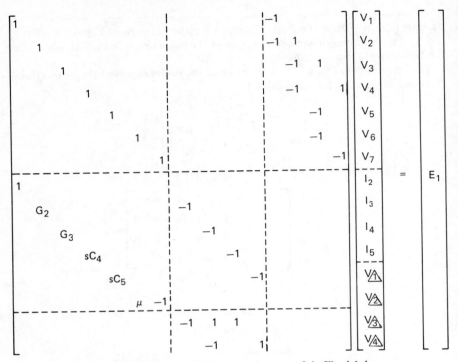

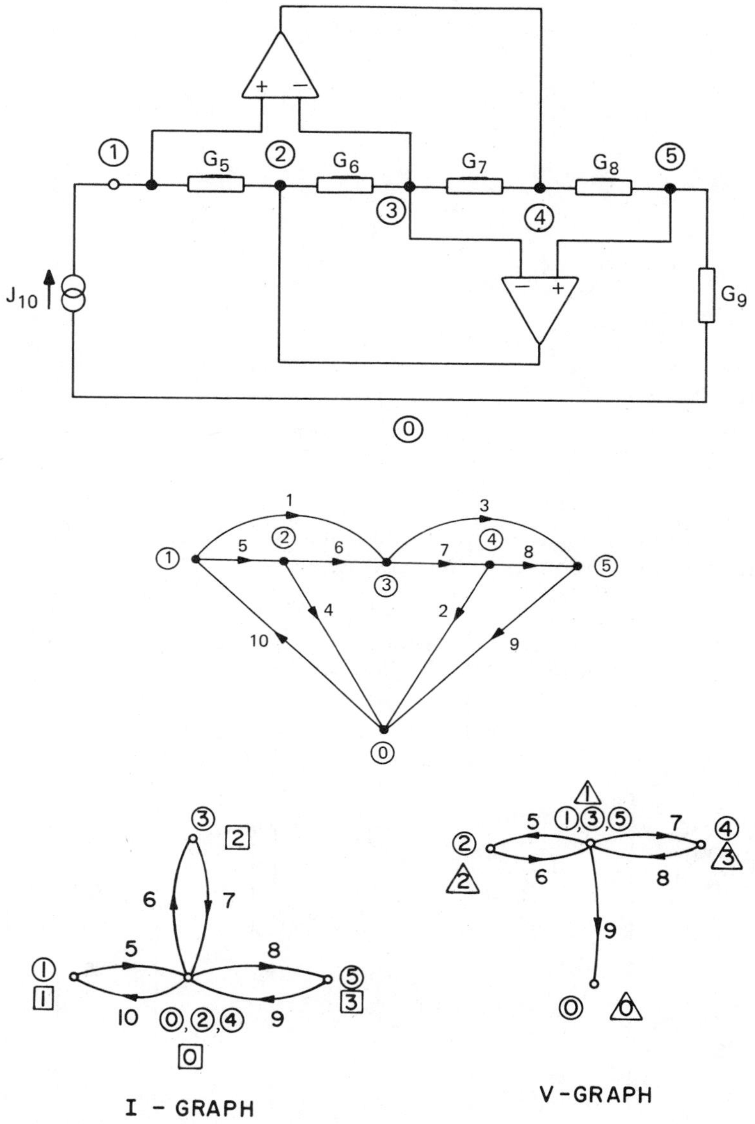

Fig. 4.6.4. Current and voltage graphs for the network of Example 4.6.2.

$$
\mathbf{A}_i = \begin{array}{c} \boxed{1} \\ \boxed{2} \\ \boxed{3} \end{array}
\overset{\begin{array}{cccccc} 5 & 6 & 7 & 8 & 9 & 10 \end{array}}{\begin{bmatrix} 1 & 0 & 0 & 0 & 0 & -1 \\ 0 & -1 & 1 & 0 & 0 & 0 \\ 0 & 0 & 0 & -1 & 1 & 0 \end{bmatrix}}
$$

$$
\mathbf{A}_v = \begin{array}{c} \triangle_1 \\ \triangle_2 \\ \triangle_3 \end{array}
\overset{\begin{array}{ccccc} 5 & 6 & 7 & 8 & 9 \end{array}}{\begin{bmatrix} 1 & -1 & 1 & -1 & 1 \\ -1 & 1 & 0 & 0 & 0 \\ 0 & 0 & -1 & 1 & 0 \end{bmatrix}}.
$$

In the two-graph method, the OPAMPs do not have any constitutive equations. The remaining ones are

$$G_i V_i - I_i = 0, \quad \text{for } i = 5, 6, 7, 8, 9$$

$$I_{10} = J_{10}$$

The sizes of the submatrices will be horizontally 5 + 6 + 3, vertically 5 + 6 + 3. The tableau formulation is shown in Fig. 4.6.5.

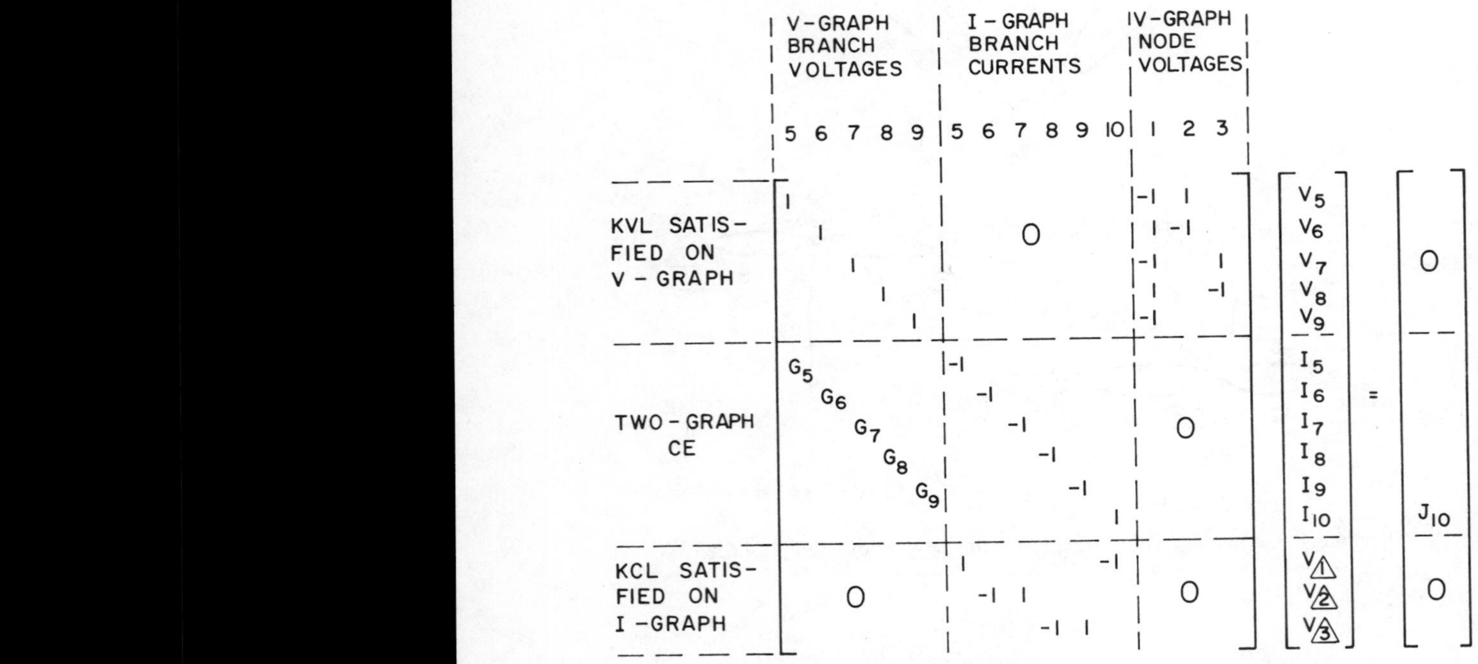

Fig. 4.6.5. Two-graph tableau for the network in Fig. 4.1.5.

4.7. REPRESENTATION OF THE GRAPHS ON THE COMPUTER

This section describes one way of representing the graphs on the computer. The topology of the network must be given to the computer in the form of a table. Such a table will contain information on the type of the element and the nodes from which and to which the element goes. The values are not needed for this explanation.

Consider the network in Fig. 4.1.4. A table of the following form will contain the necessary information:

						VVT	
Element:	E_1	G_2	G_3	C_4	C_5	Input	Output
From node:	1	1	2	2	3	3	4
To node:	0	2	3	4	0	0	0

This representation contains the required information for the one-graph method.

In the two-graph method, two new tables must be prepared, each taking into account the collapsing of the nodes due to some elements or the absence of the edges for others.

Consider first the I-graph for the preceding table. The voltage source collapses nodes zero and one. Thus 1 changes *everywhere* in the table into 0. Moreover, the VVT collapses the output node to ground. This means that 4 will change everywhere into 0. The table for the I-graph thus far would be:

Edge:	1	2	3	4	5	6	7
From node:	0	0	2	2	3	3	0
To node:	0	2	3	0	0	0	0

As there is no node 1, all the numbers are decreased by one. This amounts to the renumbering of the nodes on the I-graph:

Edge:	1	2	3	4	5	6	7
From node:	0	0	1	1	2	2	0
To node:	0	1	2	0	0	0	0

In the final step, note that there is no current associated with the voltage source or for the output of the VVT anymore and that the input current of the VVT is zero. Scan the data again and implicitly delete these edges:

Edge:	1	2	3	4	5	6	7
From node:	0	0	1	1	2	0	0
To node:	0	1	2	0	0	0	0

I-graph. (4.7.1)

The *I*-graph will have two nodes and edges 2, 3, 4, 5. Edges 1, 6, 7 will be absent (they form self-loops from 0 to 0 node). The table is in agreement with the *I*-graph in Fig. 4.6.2.

For the voltage graph, one proceeds with the same basic information. Checking the Fig. 4.6.1 we conclude that no collapsing of nodes will take place, all edges will be present; the graph is thus represented by the information in the original table and we have

Edge:	1	2	3	4	5	6	7
From node:	1	1	2	2	3	3	4
To node:	0	2	3	4	0	0	0

V-graph. (4.7.2)

4.8. MODIFIED NODAL FORMULATION USING I AND V GRAPHS

Elimination of all branch voltages and of some branch currents was considered in previous sections. The same basic approach can be applied when using the two-graph modified nodal method.

The elimination of unwanted variables is done systematically by:

1. Replacing all branch currents of elements which have admittance description by their constitutive equations. This introduces branch voltages for these elements into the KCL equations.
2. Replacing all branch voltages by the node voltages of the *V*-graph.
3. Collecting these and the remaining equations into a matrix.

The above steps are best seen on a simple example in which we eliminate the variables by using the above steps. Consider the network in Fig. 4.8.1 and its *I*- and *V*-graphs. The node numbering on the *I*-graph has been changed. There remains only one node with nonzero number. The KCL equation is:

$$\text{KCL:} \qquad -I_2 + I_3 = 0. \tag{4.8.1}$$

From the *V*-graph we have the following branch-node voltage relations:

$$\text{KVL:} \qquad \begin{aligned} V_1 &= V_{\triangle 1} \\ V_2 &= V_{\triangle 1} - V_{\triangle 2} \\ V_3 &= V_{\triangle 2} \end{aligned} \tag{4.8.2}$$

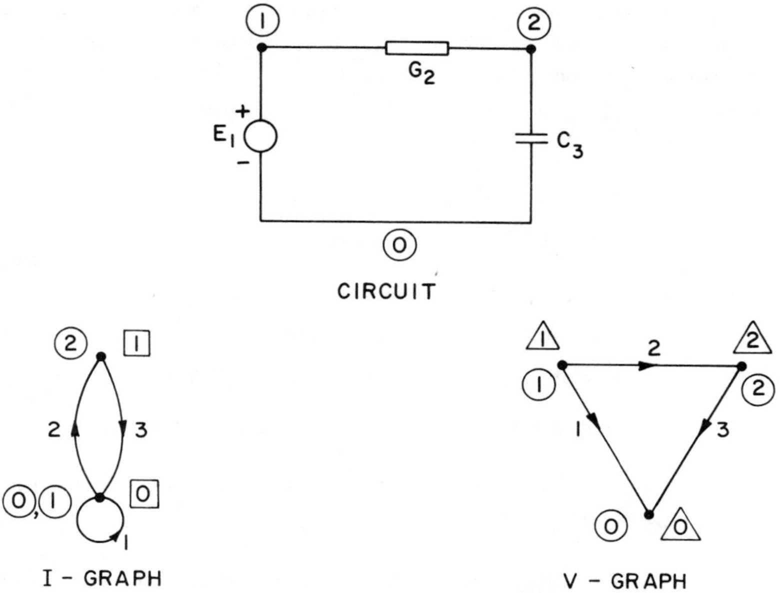

Fig. 4.8.1. Circuit demonstrating two-graph modified nodal formulation.

and the constitutive equations of the elements are

$$\text{CE:} \qquad \begin{aligned} V_1 &= E_1 \\ I_2 &= G_2 V_2 \\ I_3 &= sC_3 V_3 . \end{aligned} \tag{4.8.3}$$

Note that the current of the voltage source has been eliminated directly by the topological properties of the *I*-graph.

Substitution of the constitutive equations for the conductor and capacitor into the KCL leads to

$$-G_2 V_2 + sC_3 V_3 = 0. \tag{4.8.4}$$

Next replace all branch voltages in (4.8.4) and in $V_1 = E_1$ by the *V*-graph node voltages (4.8.2). The equations, written in matrix form, become

$$\text{KCL} \quad \left[\begin{array}{cc} -G_2 & G_2 + sC_3 \\ \hdashline 1 & 0 \end{array}\right] \begin{bmatrix} V_{\triangle 1} \\ V_{\triangle 2} \end{bmatrix} = \begin{bmatrix} 0 \\ E_1 \end{bmatrix} \tag{4.8.5}$$

The admittance portion of (4.8.5) has one row and two columns. The first row expresses the KCL relationship. The second row takes care of the constitutive equation of the voltage source whose current has been eliminated topologically.

Formally, the two-graph modified nodal formulation can be derived by partitioning appropriately the constitutive equations. Partitioning of the KCL and KVL equations must follow the same sequence. Subscripts on voltages refer to the V-graph, subscripts on currents to the I-graph, and the branch numbering on the two graphs is done independently. We have:

$$
\begin{aligned}
\mathbf{I}_1 &= \mathbf{Y}_1\mathbf{V}_1 && \text{(admittances)} \\
\mathbf{V}_2 &= \mathbf{Z}_2\mathbf{I}_2 && \text{(impedances)} \\
\mathbf{I}_3 &= \mathbf{J}_s && \text{(current sources)} \\
\mathbf{V}_3 &= \mathbf{E}_s && \text{(voltage sources)}
\end{aligned}
\tag{4.8.6}
$$

$$\mathbf{I}_4 = \boldsymbol{\alpha}\mathbf{I}_5 \quad \text{(CCTs)}, \qquad \mathbf{V}_4 = \boldsymbol{\mu}\mathbf{V}_5 \quad \text{(VVTs)}$$

$$\mathbf{Y}_6\mathbf{V}_6 + \mathbf{Z}_6\mathbf{I}_6 = \mathbf{W} \quad \text{(general multiterminal networks).}$$

Since there are six types of constitutive equations, $\mathbf{A}_i$, $\mathbf{A}_v$ must be partitioned into six submatrices. The KCL equation $\mathbf{A}_i\mathbf{I}_b = \mathbf{0}$ becomes

$$\mathbf{A}_{i_1}\mathbf{I}_1 + \mathbf{A}_{i_2}\mathbf{I}_2 + \mathbf{A}_{i_3}\mathbf{I}_3 + \mathbf{A}_{i_4}\mathbf{I}_4 + \mathbf{A}_{i_5}\mathbf{I}_5 + \mathbf{A}_{i_6}\mathbf{I}_6 = \mathbf{0}. \tag{4.8.7}$$

The KVL equation $\mathbf{V}_b = \mathbf{A}_v^t\mathbf{V}_{\triangle n}$ is rewritten as six equations:

$$\mathbf{V}_k = \mathbf{A}_{vk}^t\mathbf{V}_{\triangle n}, \qquad k = 1, 2, 3, 4, 5, 6. \tag{4.8.8}$$

Substitute for $\mathbf{I}_1$, $\mathbf{I}_3$, and $\mathbf{I}_4$ into (4.8.7) using the constitutive equations. This results in

$$\mathbf{A}_{i_1}\mathbf{Y}_1\mathbf{V}_1 + \mathbf{A}_{i_2}\mathbf{I}_2 + (\mathbf{A}_{i_4}\boldsymbol{\alpha} + \mathbf{A}_{i_5})\,\mathbf{I}_5 + \mathbf{A}_{i_6}\mathbf{I}_6 = -\mathbf{A}_{i_3}\mathbf{J}_s. \tag{4.8.9}$$

In the second step replace the branch voltage $\mathbf{V}_1$ by the first equation in (4.8.8). This results in

$$\mathbf{A}_{i_1}\mathbf{Y}_1\mathbf{A}_{v_1}^t\mathbf{V}_{\triangle n} + \mathbf{A}_{i_2}\mathbf{I}_2 + (\mathbf{A}_{i_4}\boldsymbol{\alpha} + \mathbf{A}_{i_5})\,\mathbf{I}_5 + \mathbf{A}_{i_6}\mathbf{I}_6 = -\mathbf{A}_{i_3}\mathbf{J}_s. \tag{4.8.10}$$

Use the remaining equations (4.8.8) and substitute them into the remaining constitutive equations (4.8.6). The result is

$$
\begin{aligned}
\mathbf{A}_{v2}^t\mathbf{V}_{\triangle n} &= \mathbf{Z}_2\mathbf{I}_2 \\
\mathbf{A}_{v3}^t\mathbf{V}_{\triangle n} &= \mathbf{E}_s \\
\mathbf{A}_{v4}^t\mathbf{V}_{\triangle n} &= \boldsymbol{\mu}\mathbf{A}_{v5}^t\mathbf{V}_{\triangle n} \\
\mathbf{Y}_6\mathbf{A}_{v6}^t\mathbf{V}_{\triangle n} + \mathbf{Z}_6\mathbf{I}_6 &= \mathbf{W}.
\end{aligned}
\tag{4.8.11}
$$

Equations (4.8.10) and (4.8.11) can be written in matrix form as follows:

$$\begin{Bmatrix} \text{KCL on} \\ \text{I-graph} \\ \\ \text{CE of} \\ \text{various} \\ \text{elements} \end{Bmatrix} \begin{bmatrix} \mathbf{A}_{i_1}\mathbf{Y}_1\mathbf{A}_{v_1}^t & \mathbf{A}_{i_2} & (\mathbf{A}_{i_4}\alpha + \mathbf{A}_{i_5}) & \mathbf{A}_{i_6} \\ \mathbf{A}_{v_2}^t & -\mathbf{Z}_2 & 0 & 0 \\ \mathbf{A}_{v_3}^t & 0 & 0 & 0 \\ (\mathbf{A}_{v_4}^t - \mu\mathbf{A}_{v_5}^t) & 0 & 0 & 0 \\ \mathbf{Y}_6\mathbf{A}_{v_6}^t & 0 & 0 & \mathbf{Z}_6 \end{bmatrix} \begin{bmatrix} \mathbf{V}_{\mathbf{n}} \\ \mathbf{I}_2 \\ \mathbf{I}_5 \\ \mathbf{I}_6 \end{bmatrix} = \begin{bmatrix} -\mathbf{A}_{i_3}\mathbf{J}_s \\ 0 \\ \mathbf{E}_s \\ 0 \\ \mathbf{W} \end{bmatrix}.$$

where the top columns are labeled: V-graph node voltages; Subset of branch currents on I-graph.

$$(4.8.12)$$

This is the formal expression of the formulation with two graphs. It is *not used* in this form for actual network formulation. Its properties are studied and conclusions applied below.

Equation (4.8.12) presents one important result: the portion $\mathbf{A}_{i_1}\mathbf{Y}_1\mathbf{A}_{v_1}^t$ has a form in which *the rows satisfy the KCL equations on the I-graph* whereas the *columns are expressed by nodal voltages on the V-graph.* This is the same form as in the previous type of the modified nodal formulation with the only exception that the numbers of the rows and columns are those of the nodes given on the two independent graphs. Let an admittance y have an edge going from j_i to j_i' on the I-graph. Similarly, let the edge on the V-graph go from j_v to j_v'. The symbolic formula for entering an admittance into the nodal portion has the following form:

$$\begin{array}{cc} & \begin{matrix} V\text{-graph edge pointing} \\ \begin{matrix}\text{from node} & \text{to node} \\ j_v & j_v' \end{matrix} \end{matrix} \\ I\text{-graph edge pointing} \begin{matrix} \text{from node } j_i \\ \text{to node } \quad j_i' \end{matrix} & \begin{bmatrix} y & -y \\ -y & y \end{bmatrix}. \end{array} \qquad (4.8.13)$$

If j_i or j_i' is zero, the row is omitted in the matrix. Similarly, if j_v or j_v' is zero, the column is absent from the matrix. As an example, consider the I-graph information provided by (4.7.1) and the V-graph information given by (4.7.2). The third element, G_3, has its I-graph edge pointing from node 1 to node 2 while the V-graph edge points from node 2 to node 3. Using the above schematic representation, $+G_3$ will enter into the positions $(1, 2)$ and $(2, 3)$ while $-G_3$ will be in the positions $(2, 2)$ and $(1, 3)$. All elements not having admittance description are entered into the remaining partitions. This can be done systematically and Fig. 4.8.2 collects all usually encountered ideal network elements and the way they are entered into the matrix of the two-graph modified nodal matrix *without writing the matrices* $\mathbf{A}_i, \mathbf{A}_v$. This method cannot avoid entirely the use of graphs (or their computer equivalents), but examples given below show that writing the matrix equation is as easy as in the previous cases.

ELEMENT	SYMBOL	I-GRAPH	V-GRAPH	MATRIX	EQUATIONS
CURRENT SOURCE	j, J, j′	j_I, j'_I	j_V, j'_V	$\begin{matrix} j_I \\ j'_I \end{matrix} \begin{bmatrix} -J \\ +J \end{bmatrix}$ SOURCE VECTOR	$I_{j_I} = J$ $I_{j'_I} = -J$
VOLTAGE SOURCE	j, I, +, E, −, j′	$j_I \equiv j'_I$	j_V, j'_V	$\begin{matrix} & j_V & j'_V \\ m+1 & 1 & -1 \end{matrix}$ SOURCE VECTOR $\begin{bmatrix} E \end{bmatrix}$	$V_{j_V} - V_{j'_V} = E$
OPEN CIRCUIT	j +, V, j′ −	j_I, j'_I	j_V, j'_V	———	$V = V_{j_V} - V_{j'_V}$
SHORT CIRCUIT	j, I, j′	j_I, j'_I	$j_V \equiv j'_V$	$\begin{matrix} & I \\ j_I & 1 \\ j'_I & -1 \end{matrix}$	I IS ARBITRARY
ADMITTANCE	j +, I, y, V, j′ −	j_I, j'_I	j_V, j'_V	$\begin{matrix} & j_V & j'_V \\ j_I & y & -y \\ j'_I & -y & y \end{matrix}$	$I_{j_I} = y(V_{j_V} - V_{j'_V})$ $I_{j'_I} = -y(V_{j_V} - V_{j'_V})$
IMPEDANCE	j +, I, z, V, j′ −	j_I, j'_I	j_V, j'_V	$\begin{matrix} & j_V & j'_V & I \\ j_I & & & 1 \\ j'_I & & & -1 \\ m+1 & 1 & -1 & -z \end{matrix}$	$V_{j_V} - V_{j'_V} - zI = 0$ $I_{j_I} = -I_{j'_I} = I$
NULLATOR	j, j′	j_I, j'_I	$j_V \equiv j'_V$	———	———

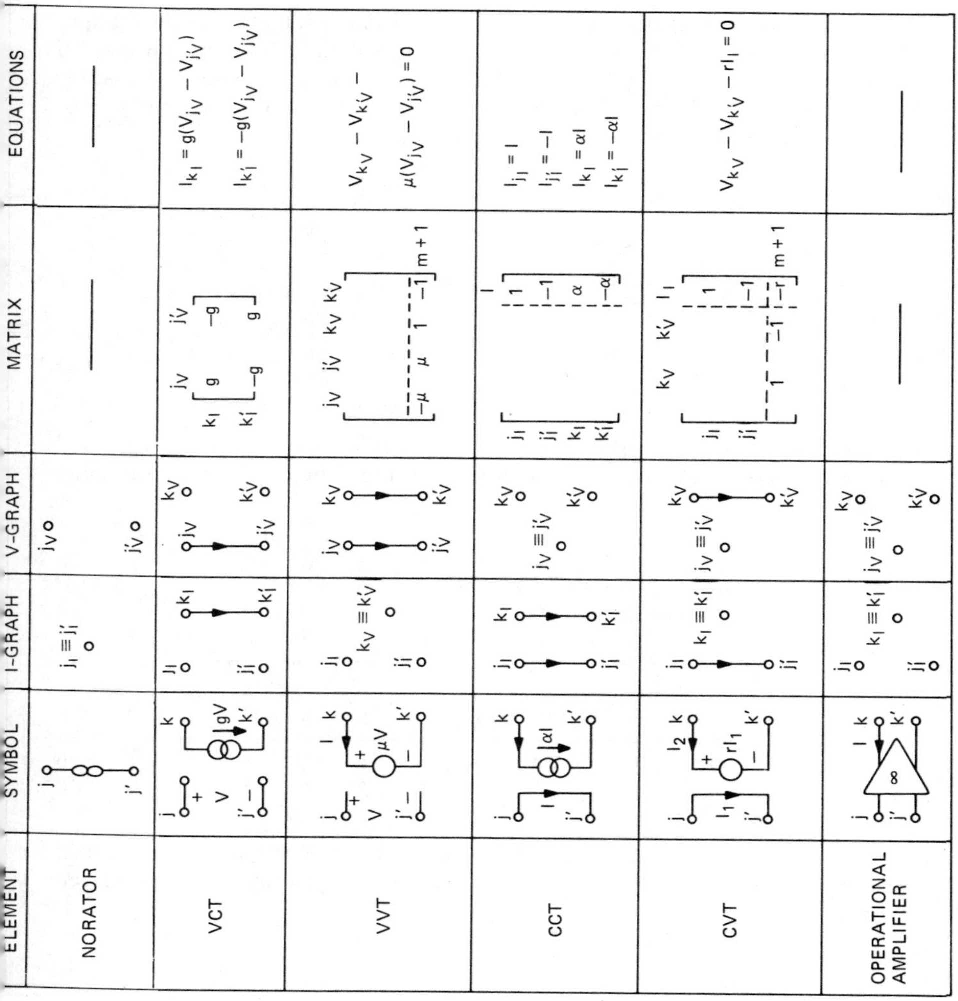
ELEMENT
SYMBOL
I-GRAPH
V-GRAPH
MATRIX
EQUATIONS
NORATOR
VCT
$I_{k_I} = g(V_{j_V} - V_{j'_V})$
$I_{k'_I} = -g(V_{j_V} - V_{j'_V})$
VVT
$V_{k_V} - V_{k'_V} - \mu(V_{j_V} - V_{j'_V}) = 0$
CCT
$I_{j_I} = I$
$I_{j'_I} = -I$
$I_{k_I} = \alpha I$
$I_{k'_I} = -\alpha I$
CVT
$V_{k_V} - V_{k'_V} - rI_I = 0$
OPERATIONAL AMPLIFIER

Fig. 4.8.2. Ideal elements in the two-graph modified nodal formulation.

EXAMPLE 4.8.1. Write the two-graph modified nodal formulation for the network of Fig. 4.1.4 without generating the matrices $\mathbf{A}_i$, $\mathbf{A}_v$. The graphs were given in Fig. 4.6.2 and their tabular equivalents are (4.7.1) and (4.7.2).

The I-graph has two ungrounded nodes while the V-graph has four. Thus the nodal portion of the formulation will be 2×4.

Element 1 does not enter the matrix since it forms a self-loop on the I-graph. The same will be true for the input and output of the VVT (edges 6 and 7). The remaining elements are filled by the schematic rule given above. Constitutive equation for the voltage source is $V_{\triangle 1} = E_1$ and for the VVT $V_{\triangle 4} - \mu V_{\triangle 3} = 0$. They are appended below the nodal portion. The result is

$$
\begin{array}{c} \\ \boxed{1} \\ \boxed{2} \\ \\ \\ \end{array}
\begin{array}{c}
\begin{array}{cccc} \triangle 1 & \triangle 2 & \triangle 3 & \triangle 4 \end{array} \\
\left[\begin{array}{cccc}
-G_2 & G_2 + G_3 + sC_4 & -G_3 & -sC_4 \\
0 & -G_3 & G_3 + sC_5 & 0 \\
\hdashline
1 & 0 & 0 & 0 \\
0 & 0 & -\mu & 1
\end{array}\right]
\end{array}
\begin{bmatrix} V_{\triangle 1} \\ V_{\triangle 2} \\ V_{\triangle 3} \\ V_{\triangle 4} \end{bmatrix}
=
\begin{bmatrix} 0 \\ 0 \\ E_1 \\ 0 \end{bmatrix}
$$

EXAMPLE 4.8.2. Consider the generalized impedance converter of Fig. 4.1.5 and its I- and V-graphs (Fig. 4.6.4). The information can be transferred into tables as follows:

I-graph:

Edge:	1	2	3	4	5	6	7	8	9	10
From j_i:	0	0	0	0	1	0	2	0	3	0
To j_i':	0	0	0	0	0	2	0	3	0	1

V-graph

Edge:	1	2	3	4	5	6	7	8	9	10
From j_v:	0	0	0	0	1	2	1	3	1	0
To j_v':	0	0	0	0	2	1	3	1	0	0

Both I- and V-graphs have 3 nodes, the matrix will be 3×3, and no additional constitutive equations will be appended. The result, filled by the scheme given above, is

$$
\begin{array}{c} \\ \\ \\ I\text{-graph nodes} \\ \\ \end{array}
\begin{array}{c} \\ \\ \boxed{1} \\ \boxed{2} \\ \boxed{3} \end{array}
\begin{array}{c}
V\text{-graph nodes} \\
\begin{array}{ccc} \triangle 1 & \triangle 2 & \triangle 3 \end{array} \\
\begin{bmatrix}
G_5 & -G_5 & 0 \\
G_6 + G_7 & -G_6 & -G_7 \\
G_8 + G_9 & 0 & -G_8
\end{bmatrix}
\end{array}
\begin{bmatrix} V_{\triangle 1} \\ V_{\triangle 2} \\ V_{\triangle 3} \end{bmatrix}
=
\begin{bmatrix} J_{10} \\ 0 \\ 0 \end{bmatrix}
$$

which is the same result as obtained in Example 4.5.5.

EXAMPLE 4.8.3. We wish to know what the idealized properties of the network in Fig. 4.8.3 are. To do so, replace the transistors by their idealized representation by means of nullators and norators. This is also done in Fig. 4.8.3, along with the *I*- and *V*-graphs. The information in the graphs can be transferred into the following tables:

I-graph:

Element:	C_a	G_b	C_c
From j_i:	1	2	2
To j_i':	0	0	0

V-graph:

Element:	C_a	G_b	C_c
From j_v:	0	2	1
To j_v':	2	0	0

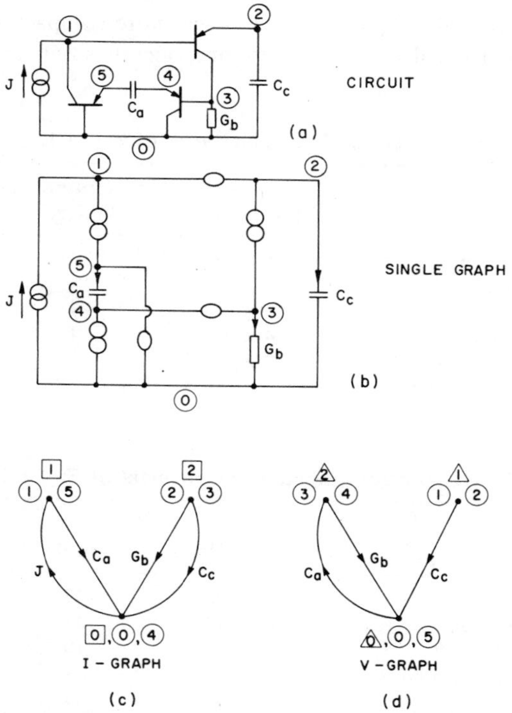

Fig. 4.8.3. (a) Transistor realization of an impedance converter; (b) idealized simulation using nullators and norators (see Fig. 1.6.6); (c, d) current and voltage graphs.

The 2 X 2 matrix equation is filled by inspection:

$$\begin{bmatrix} 0 & -sC_a \\ sC_c & G_b \end{bmatrix} \begin{bmatrix} V_{①} \\ V_{②} \end{bmatrix} = \begin{bmatrix} J \\ 0 \end{bmatrix}.$$

Solution indicates that $Z_{in} = V_1/J = G_b/s^2 C_a C_c$.

4.9. SUMMARY OF THE FORMULATION METHODS

Five methods of formulating network equations were presented in this chapter. Four of them are intended for computer use, one for hand calculation.

The methods were demonstrated repeatedly on two examples: a second order active network (Fig. 4.1.4) and a generalized impedance converter (Fig. 4.1.5). Matrix sizes and density of the matrices are compared in Tables 4.9.1 and 4.9.2.

The tableau matrices are large even for very small problems. They are always very sparse, and sparse solvers are a necessity. Unfortunately, since the matrices do not have regular structures, the renumbering and preprocessing is complicated. Modified nodal formulations are much more compact and can be solved without sparse matrix solvers even in case of moderate-size networks.

Table 4.9.1. Second-Order Active Network of Fig. 4.1.4.

	Matrix Size	Nonzero Entries	Density
One-graph tableau	18 X 18	39	12.04%
Two-graph tableau	15 X 15	33	14.67%
Modified nodal	6 X 6	15	41.67%
Two-graph modified nodal	4 X 4	9	56.25%
By hand	2 X 2	4	100%

Table 4.9.2. Generalized Impedance Converter of Fig. 4.1.5.

	Matrix Size	Nonzero Entries	Density
One-graph tableau	25 X 25	57	9.12%
Two-graph tableau	14 X 14	31	15.81%
Modified nodal	7 X 7	19	38.78%
Two-graph modified nodal	3 X 3	7	77.78%
By hand	3 X 3	7	77.78%

The two nodal formulations are recommended for problems connected with programming. The tableau equations are mainly of theoretical importance. The two-graph nodal formulation is especially advantageous for the analysis of switched capacitor networks, as demonstrated in Chapter 14.

4.10. EXAMPLE

This section will demonstrate the design of an active ninth-order Cauer-parameter low-pass filter with the following specifications: pass-band from 0 to 3470 Hz, 0.03 db ripple, stop-band starting at 3800 Hz with minimum attenuation of 50 db.

The design method will be briefly explained. First, an *LC* equivalent filter is designed. The specifications are tightened to 0.02 db in the pass-band to provide a safety margin. The filter is shown in Fig. 4.10.1, scaled to $R = 1$ and the pass-band scaled to $\omega = 1$ rad/sec. Active realization is based on impedance transformations which convert each inductor into a resistor, each resistor into a capacitor and each capacitor into an active element called a *frequency-dependent negative resistance*, FDNR (see Fig. 4.10.2). The element is realized by means of the circuit shown in Fig. 4.1.5 by replacing G_5 and G_9 by capacitances. Additional information on FDNRs and filter design using these elements can be found, for instance, in [3, 4].

The formulation method of Section 4.4 is used. Each ideal OPAMP is incorporated into the system matrix as given by Fig. 4.4.1. The pass-band response is shown in Fig. 4.10.3 and the stop-band response in Fig. 4.10.4. A slight departure from equiripple behavior is due to the rounding of element values. This filter will be optimized in Chapter 17 with linear models of nonideal OPAMPs, and the final element values will be changed.

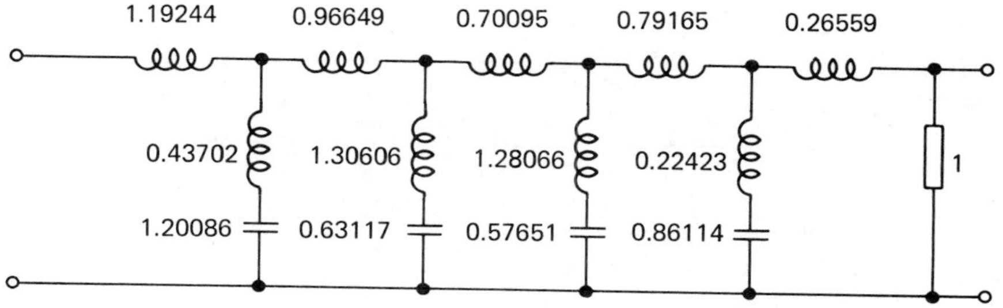

Fig. 4.10.1. Initial ninth-order Cauer-parameter low-pass filter with approximately 0.02 db in the pass-band and minimum 50 db attenuation in the stop band. The values are in F, H, and Ω and the pass-band is scaled to $\omega = 1$ rad/sec.

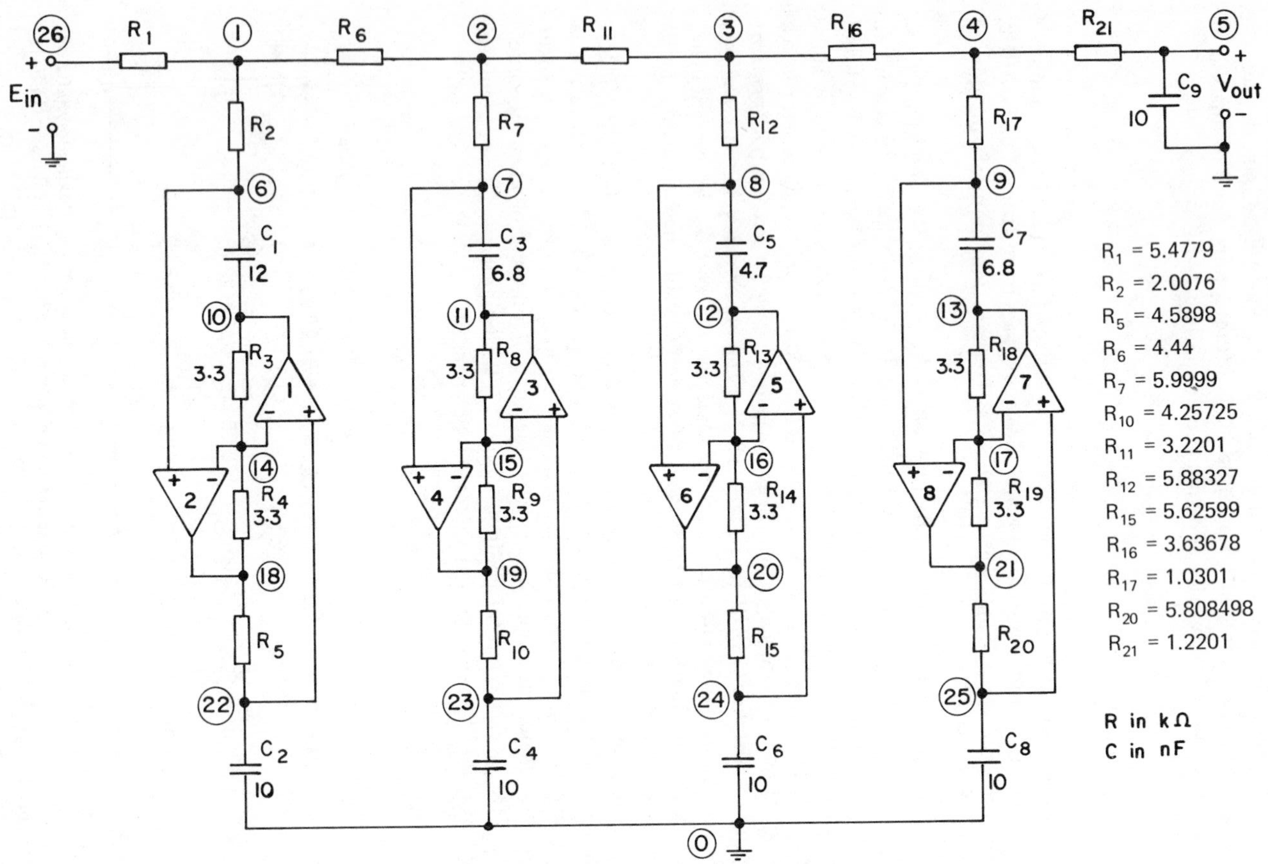

Fig. 4.10.2. Active realization of the filter shown in Fig. 4.10.1.

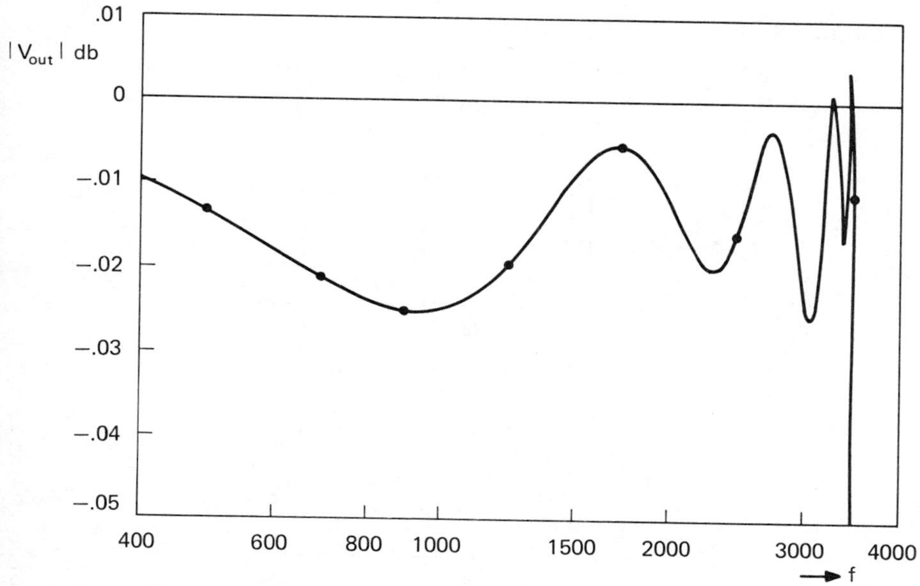

Fig. 4.10.3. Pass-band response of the filter shown in Fig. 4.10.2.

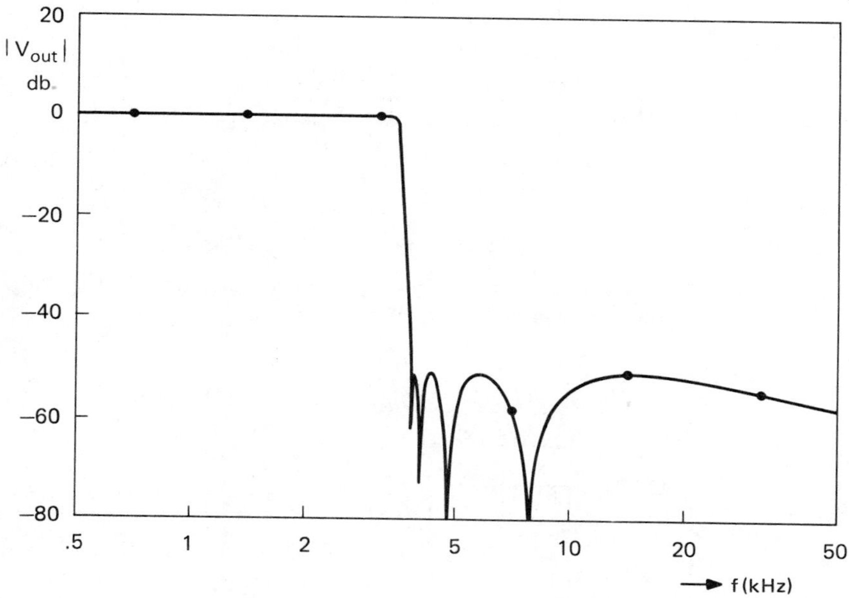

Fig. 4.10.4. Overall response of the filter in Fig. 4.10.2.

PROBLEMS

P.4.1. Write the incidence matrices for the networks shown in Fig. P.4.1 and use them in setting up the tableau matrix equations.

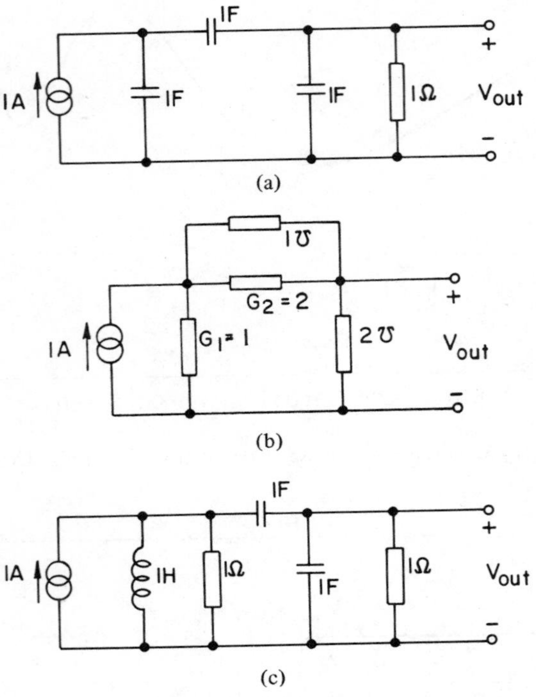

Fig. P.4.1.

P.4.2. Write the one-graph incidence matrices for the networks in Fig. P.4.2 and write their tableau matrix equations.

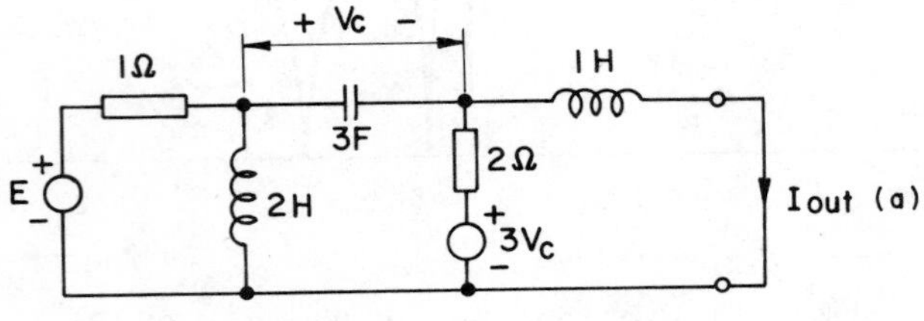

Fig. P.4.2.

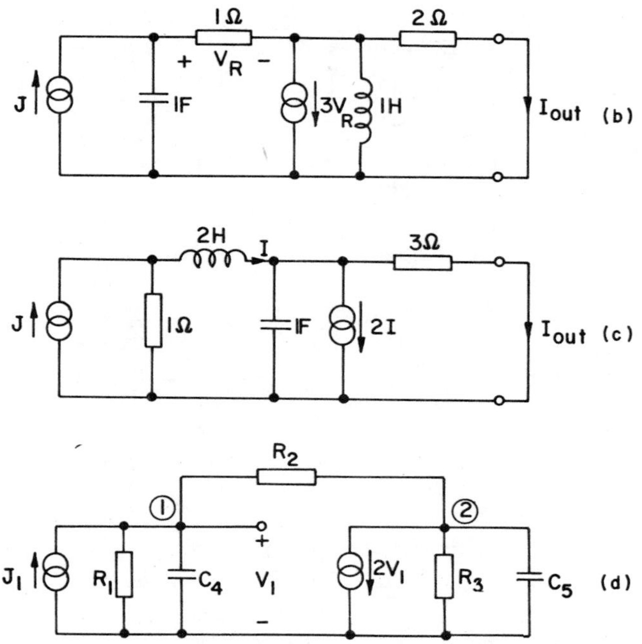

Fig. P.4.2. (*Continued*)

P.4.3. Apply the formulation of Section 4.3 to the networks shown in Fig. P.4.1.

P.4.4. Apply the modified nodal formulation without graphs to the networks shown in Fig. P.4.1.

P.4.5. Apply the modified nodal formulation without graphs to the networks shown in Fig. P.4.2.

P.4.6. Practice the modified nodal formulation without graphs on the networks shown in Fig. P.4.6. Check your results by selecting values, running the problems on the analysis program from Appendix D, and comparing the matrices.

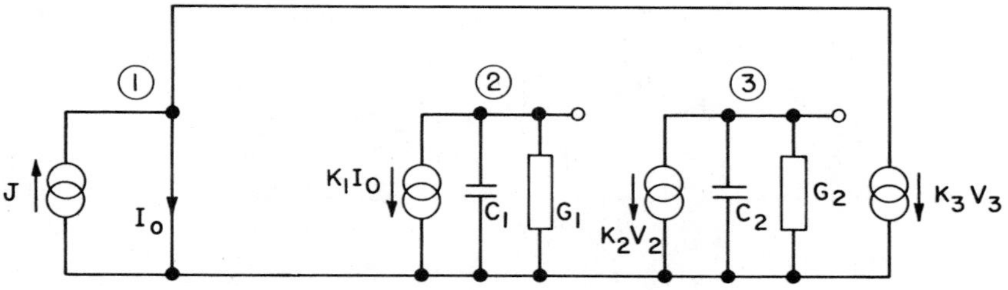

(a)

Fig. P.4.6.

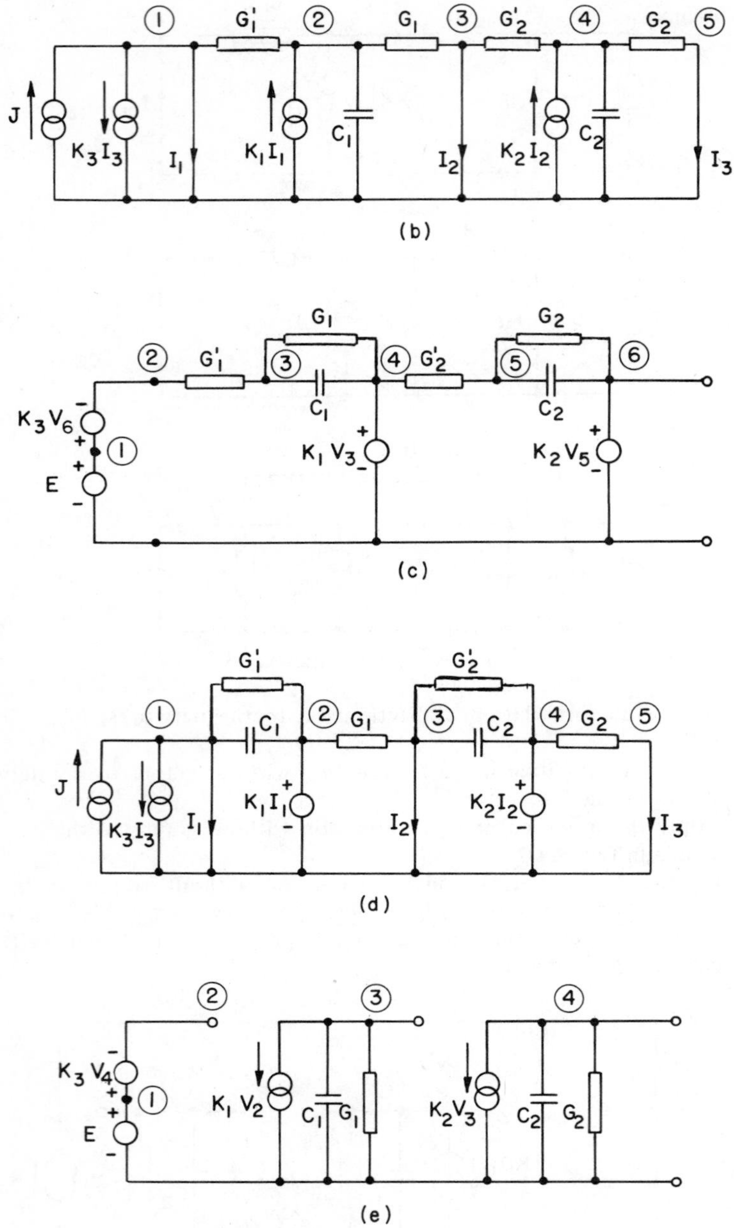

Fig. P.4.6. (*Continued*)

P.4.7. Apply the modified nodal formulation without graphs to the transformer networks shown in Fig. P.4.7.

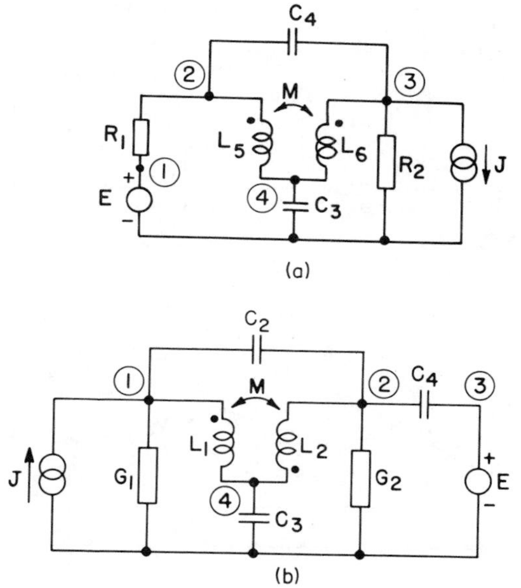

Fig. P.4.7.

P.4.8. Apply the nodal formulation of Section 4.5 to the active networks shown in Fig. P.4.8.

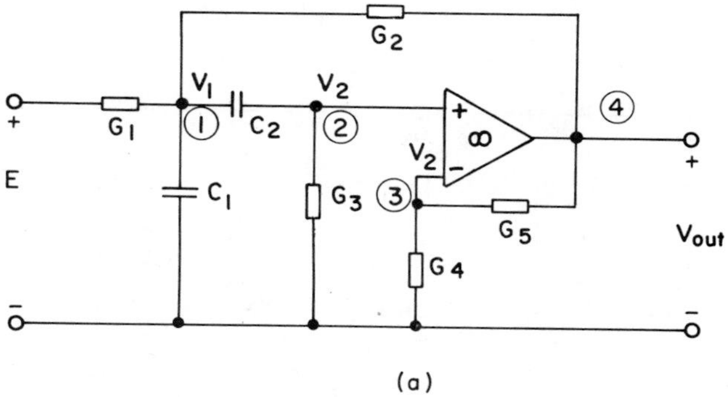

Fig. P.4.8.

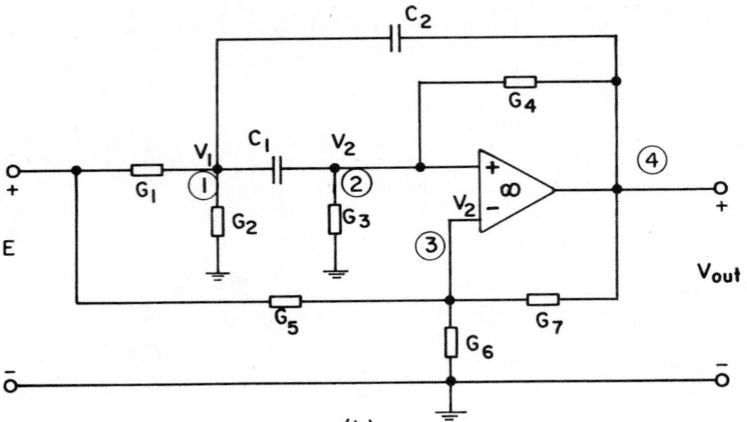

(b)

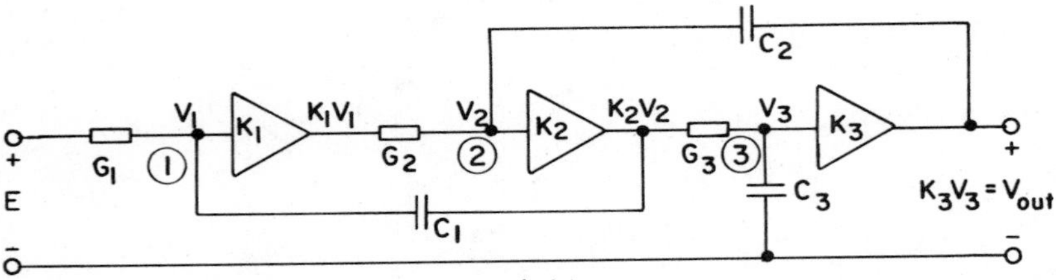

(c)

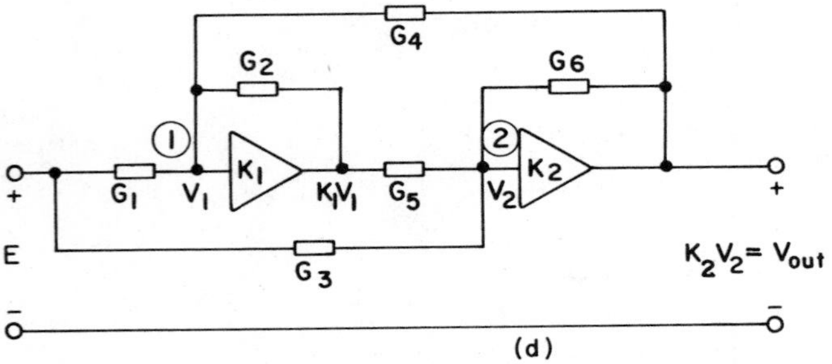

(d)

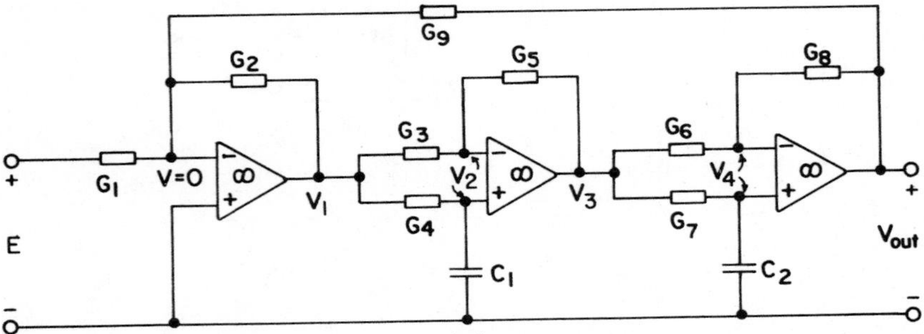

(e)

Fig. P.4.8. (*Continued*)

P.4.9. Draw separate voltage and current graphs for the networks shown in Fig. P.4.2.

P.4.10. Write the two-graph tableau formulation for the networks shown in Fig. P.4.2 by using the graphs of Problem P.4.9.

P.4.11. Write the two-graph modified nodal formulation for the networks shown in Fig. P.4.2. Check your results by selecting values, running the problems on the analysis program in Appendix D, and comparing the matrices.

P.4.12. Apply the two-graph modified nodal formulation to the networks shown in Fig. P.4.12. Check by running the program.

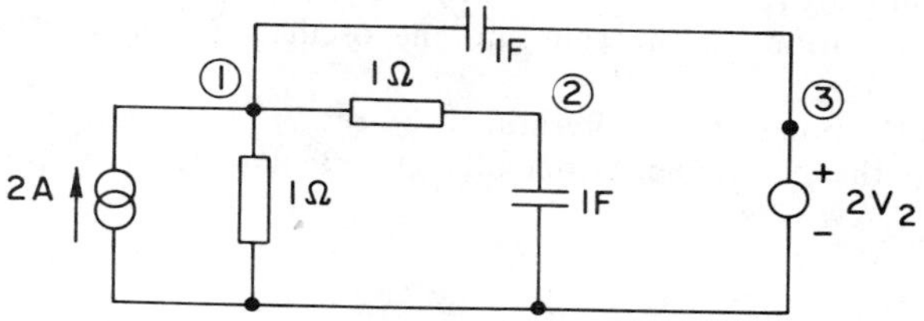

(a)

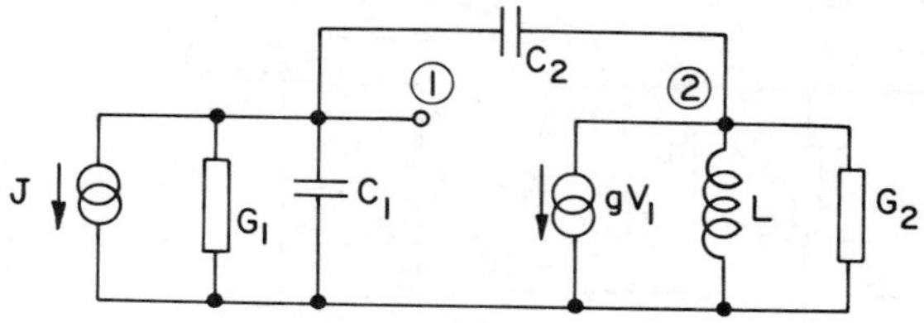

(b)

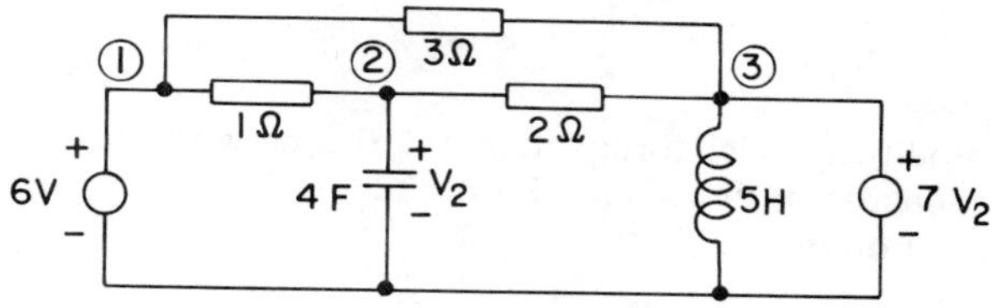

(c)

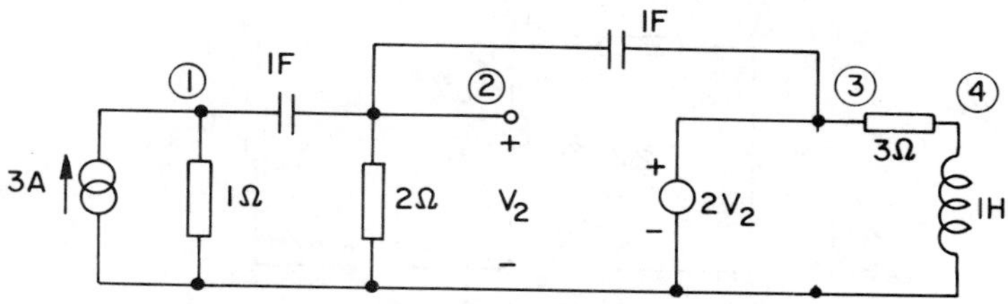

(d)

Fig. P.4.12.

P.4.13. The network shown in Fig. P.4.13 is a phase-shift oscillator provided the gain of the inverting amplifier is adjusted to $A = 29$. In such case the oscillation frequency is

$$\omega = \frac{G}{C} \frac{1}{\sqrt{6}} \text{ rad/sec.}$$

(a) Set up the system equations for this network using the formulation method of Section 4.5. Note that the right-hand-side vector will be a zero vector.
(b) Find the determinant of the system matrix, set it equal to zero, and substitute $s = j\omega$. Separating real and imaginary parts, obtain the condition on the gain and the oscillating frequency (given above).
(c) Find the poles of the determinant by retaining the variable s.
(d) Using the program in Appendix D, calculate the pole positions for $27 < A < 31$.

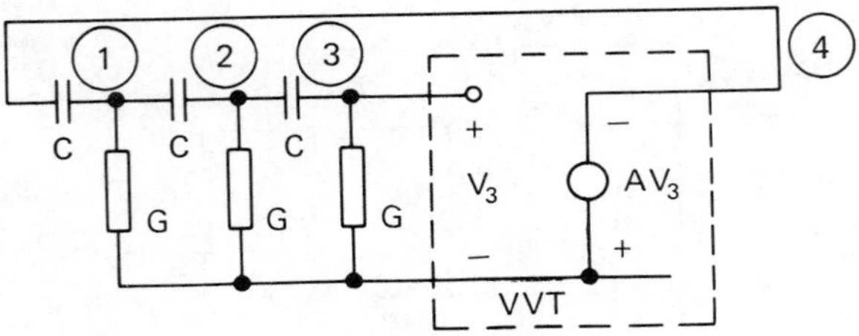

Fig. P.4.13.

P.4.14. Write the modified nodal formulation for the network in Fig. P.4.14. Enter the inductor in impedance form and use Table 4.1.1 to handle the initial conditions.

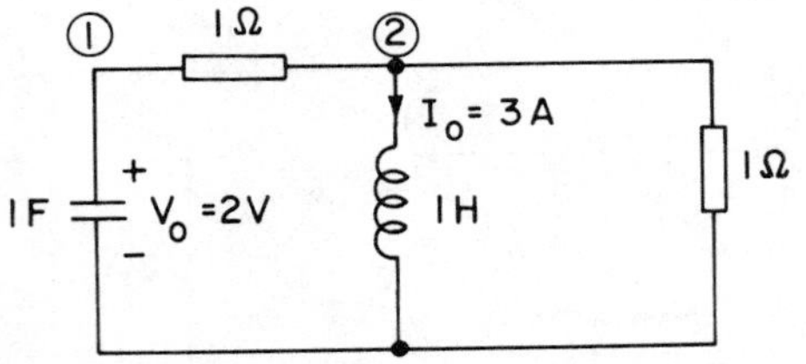

Fig. P.4.14.

REFERENCES

1. G. D. Hachtel, R. K. Brayton, and F. G. Gustavson: The sparse tableau approach to network analysis and design. *IEEE Transactions on Circuit Theory*, Vol. CT-18, pp. 101–113, January 1971.
2. C. W. Ho, A. E. Ruehli, and P. A. Brennan: The modified nodal approach to network analysis. *IEEE Transactions on Circuits and Systems*, Vol. CAS-22, pp. 504–509, June 1975.
3. L. T. Bruton: *RC-Active Circuits: Theory and Design.* Prentice-Hall, Englewood Cliffs, NJ, 1980.
4. L. P. Huelsman and P. E. Allen: *Introduction to the Theory and Design of Active Filters.* McGraw-Hill, New York, 1980.

CHAPTER 5
Sensitivities

This chapter introduces the concept of sensitivity and provides basic information by considering network functions in explicit form. Computational aspects of sensitivity evaluation will be covered in Chapter 6.

Sensitivities are mathematical measures that provide additional insight into the behavior of a physical system. There are three main reasons for their study:

1. Sensitivities help in the understanding of how variations of parameters, for instance of element values, influence the response.
2. They help in comparing the quality of various networks having the same nominal response.
3. They provide response gradients in optimization applications.

Various sensitivity definitions are introduced in Section 5.1 and applied to the most common response variables: network functions, their poles and zeros, and the Q's and ω's of the poles and zeros. The formulae derived are valid for networks of arbitrary complexity.

As a network response is usually influenced by simultaneous variations in several parameters, multiparameter sensitivity is discussed and its use demonstrated in Section 5.2.

Very often, the designer is interested in the behavior of his network in the presence of parasitic elements. Under ideal conditions, these elements have zero nominal values. Sensitivities are defined with respect to these elements and can be used to predict response variations when parasitics take on small values. Section 5.3 establishes the fact that zero-valued elements may have nonzero sensitivity. It is also shown that the ideal operational amplifier, with ideally infinite gain, can be redefined as a special type of "parasitic" so that the theory developed for zero-valued elements can be applied to it as well. Examples demonstrate the use of various sensitivity definitions.

A word of caution is in order: The sensitivities defined in this chapter are based on *first-order* approximations to network functions–they should be used with care when large parameter variations are involved. Large variations will be considered in Chapter 8.

5.1. SENSITIVITY DEFINITIONS

The simplest sensitivity is the derivative of a differentiable function F with respect to any parameter h:

$$D_h^F = \frac{\partial F}{\partial h}. \tag{5.1.1}$$

This definition is useful for computer applications but is not scale free. The most widely used definition is the normalized sensitivity

$$S_h^F = \frac{\partial \ln F}{\partial \ln h} = \frac{h}{F}\frac{\partial F}{\partial h} = \frac{h}{F} D_h^F \tag{5.1.2}$$

which forms the basis for comparing various designs. When either h or F take zero values, the definition (5.1.2) no longer provides a useful measure but two other semi-normalized sensitivities can be defined:

$$\mathsf{S}_h^F = \frac{\partial F}{\partial \ln h} = h\frac{\partial F}{\partial h} = hD_h^F \tag{5.1.3}$$

and

$$\mathcal{S}_h^F = \frac{\partial \ln F}{\partial h} = \frac{1}{F}\frac{\partial F}{\partial h} = \frac{1}{F} D_h^F. \tag{5.1.4}$$

The definition (5.1.3) finds use mainly when $F = 0$, while $\mathcal{S}_h^F$ is the natural definition when $h = 0$, i.e., is a parasitic. When both F and h are zero, (5.1.1) must be used.

In network applications the function F can be a network function, its pole or zero, the Q and ω_0 of the pole or zero, etc., while the parameters h can be component values, the frequency variable s, the operating temperature or humidity, etc.

EXAMPLE 5.1.1. Calculate $S_h^{\omega_0}$ and S_h^Q for the tuned circuit shown in Fig. 5.1.1 with h being G, C, and L.

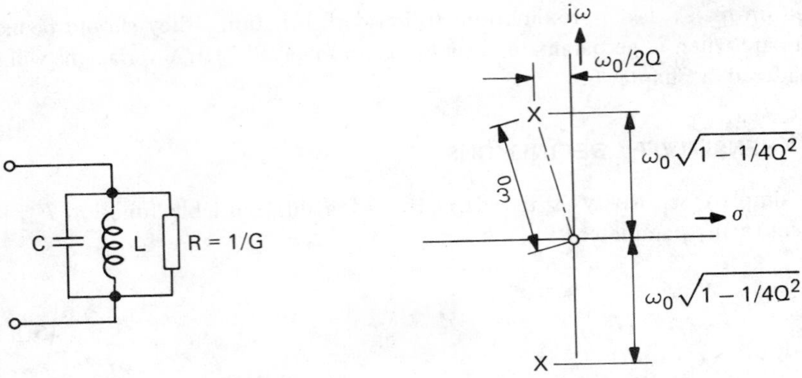

Fig. 5.1.1. Tuned circuit and the pole–zero plot of its impedance.

Write the impedance function in the following form:

$$Z = \frac{1}{C} \frac{s}{s^2 + s\dfrac{G}{C} + \dfrac{1}{LC}} = \frac{1}{C} \frac{s}{s^2 + s\dfrac{\omega_0}{Q} + \omega_0^2}.$$

Comparing terms:

$$\omega_0 = \frac{1}{\sqrt{LC}}$$

$$Q = \frac{\omega_0 C}{G} = \frac{1}{\omega_0 GL} = \frac{1}{G}\sqrt{\frac{C}{L}}.$$

To evaluate the normalized sensitivities take the logarithms of ω_0 and Q:

$$\ln \omega_0 = -\tfrac{1}{2} \ln L - \tfrac{1}{2} \ln C$$

$$\ln Q = -\ln G + \tfrac{1}{2} \ln C - \tfrac{1}{2} \ln L.$$

Using (5.1.2)

$$S_L^{\omega_0} = S_C^{\omega_0} = S_L^Q = -S_C^Q = -\tfrac{1}{2}$$

$$S_G^{\omega_0} = 0; \qquad S_G^Q = -1.$$

Note that the magnitude of every sensitivity is less than or equal to unity.

The example of the tuned circuit was used as an introduction because it is such a widely known elementary network. Moreover, its sensitivities are very low and the values derived above for S_h^Q and $S_h^{\omega_0}$ serve for comparisons with other networks. The use of sensitivities is best demonstrated by replacing the differentials by increments. Using the above example we can write, approximately,

$$S_L^Q \approx \frac{\Delta Q}{\Delta L} \cdot \frac{L}{Q}$$

or, as $S_L^Q = -\frac{1}{2}$,

$$\frac{\Delta Q}{Q} \approx -0.5 \frac{\Delta L}{L}.$$

Assume that there is a 1% *increase* in the inductor, $\Delta L/L = 0.01$. Then

$$\frac{\Delta Q}{Q} \approx -0.5 \times 0.01 = -0.005$$

and Q will *decrease* by 0.5%. Should we select $Q = 200$, then

$$\Delta Q \approx -0.005 \times 200 \approx -1$$

and we can expect the Q to change from 200 to 199.

Next, the three most frequently encountered functions in network applications will be discussed in greater detail.

A. Network Function Sensitivity

Let the network function be defined by

$$F \equiv T = N/D. \tag{5.1.5}$$

Take the logarithms and differentiate with respect to $\ln h$. The result is

$$S_h^T = S_h^N - S_h^D. \tag{5.1.6}$$

Another convenient form is obtained if the function T is written in polar form as $|T| \exp(j\phi)$, where $|T|$ is the magnitude and ϕ the phase function. Then from the relation

$$\ln T = \ln |T| + j\phi \tag{5.1.7}$$

it follows that

$$S_h^{|T|} = \text{Re}\, S_h^T \tag{5.1.8}$$

and

$$S_h^{\phi} = \frac{1}{\phi} \operatorname{Im} S_h^T \tag{5.1.9}$$

where Re and Im stand for the real and imaginary parts, respectively. The network function sensitivity obviously depends on the frequency.

B. Zero and Pole Sensitivity

One of the disadvantages of the network function sensitivity is its dependence on frequency. The sensitivity must be evaluated at a relatively dense point set to get meaningful insight into network performance. Further, the choice of the frequency set is not always apparent. In contrast, the poles and zeros provide a comparatively small set of well defined (complex) frequency points which completely determine the network response.

The sensitivity of the zero of a polynomial is best derived by recalling that the zero position is a function of the parameter. Thus, for any zero z of the polynomial P (which represents either the numerator or denominator of the network function) we can write

$$P(h, s(h))\big|_{s=z} = 0.$$

Differentiating with respect to h gives

$$\left.\frac{\partial P}{\partial h} + \frac{\partial P}{\partial s} \cdot \frac{ds}{dh}\right|_{s=z} = 0$$

or

$$\left.\frac{ds}{dh}\right|_{s=z} = \frac{dz}{dh} = -\left.\frac{\partial P/\partial h}{\partial P/\partial s}\right|_{s=z}. \tag{5.1.10}$$

This expression is valid for simple zeros; its normalized form is

$$S_h^z = \frac{h}{z}\frac{dz}{dh}. \tag{5.1.11}$$

If the coordinates of the zero are denoted by a and b:

$$z = a + jb \tag{5.1.12}$$

the sensitivity of the real and imaginary parts of the zero are given as follows:

$$S_h^a = \frac{h}{a} \operatorname{Re} \frac{dz}{dh} \tag{5.1.13}$$

$$S_h^b = \frac{h}{b} \operatorname{Im} \frac{dz}{dh}. \tag{5.1.14}$$

C. Q and ω_0 Sensitivity

Filter designers find the use of Q and ω_0 of the roots easier to work with than the roots themselves. For a pair of complex conjugate zeros, $z, \bar{z}$,

$$(s - z)(s - \bar{z}) = s^2 - (z + \bar{z})s + z\bar{z} = s^2 + \frac{\omega_0}{Q} s + \omega_0^2. \tag{5.1.15}$$

Comparing terms in (5.1.15) and using (5.1.12) we obtain relations for Q and ω_0 in terms of the root location:

$$Q = \frac{\omega_0}{-(z + \bar{z})} = \frac{-\omega_0}{2a} \tag{5.1.16}$$

$$\omega_0^2 = a^2 + b^2. \tag{5.1.17}$$

Differentiating (5.1.16) and (5.1.17) and then using (5.1.13) and (5.1.14) gives

$$S_h^Q = S_h^{\omega_0} - S_h^a \tag{5.1.18}$$

$$S_h^{\omega_0} = \frac{1}{\omega_0^2} (a^2 S_h^a + b^2 S_h^b). \tag{5.1.19}$$

In high-Q circuits $a^2 \ll b^2$ and (5.1.19) is often simplified to

$$S_h^{\omega_0} \approx S_h^b. \tag{5.1.20}$$

EXAMPLE 5.1.2. Calculate the transfer function sensitivity with respect to the amplifiers of the network shown in Fig. 5.1.2.

The transfer function is

$$T = \frac{V_{out}}{E} = \frac{G_1 G_2 A_1 A_2}{s^2 C_1 C_2 + s(C_1 G_2 + C_2 G_1 - A_1 A_2 C_1 G_2) + G_1 G_2} = \frac{N}{D}.$$

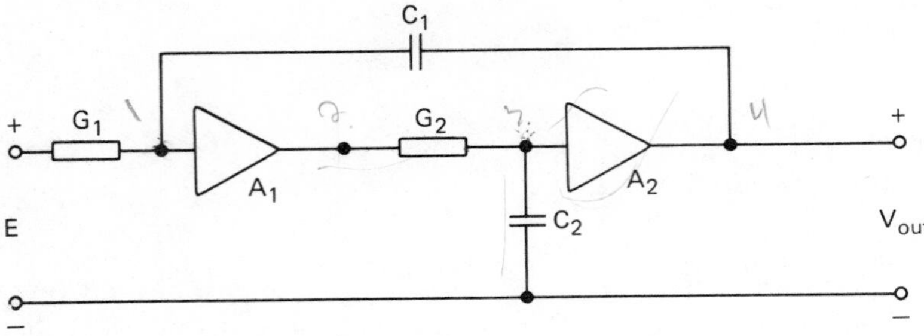

Fig. 5.1.2. Active network with two amplifiers.

The sensitivities of the numerator are $S_{A_1}^N = S_{A_2}^N = 1$. The sensitivities of the denominator are

$$S_{A_1}^D = S_{A_2}^D = \frac{-sA_1A_2C_1G_2}{D}$$

and (5.1.6) is used for the transfer function sensitivity.

EXAMPLE 5.1.3. For the network shown in Fig. 5.1.2, select $C_1 = C_2 = 1$, $G_1 = 1$, $G_2 = 2$, $A_1 = \frac{1}{2}$ and $A_2 = 1$. Use the transfer function found in Example 5.1.2 and find the pole sensitivity with respect to A_1 and A_2.

For the given values, the denominator and the poles are

$$D = s^2 + 2s + 2; \qquad p, \bar{p} = a \pm jb = -1 \pm j.$$

Consider only the pole in the upper half plane. In order to apply (5.1.10), we calculate

$$\partial D/\partial s\big|_{s=p} = 2s + 2\big|_{s=p} = 2(-1+j) + 2 = 2j$$

$$\frac{\partial D}{\partial A_1} = 2(1-j); \qquad \frac{\partial D}{\partial A_2} = (1-j).$$

Inserting this into (5.1.10) and (5.1.11) gives

$$S_{A_1}^p = S_{A_2}^p = -j/2.$$

5.2. MULTIPARAMETER SENSITIVITY

Ordinary sensitivity provides information regarding network function variation due to single parameter changes. The examples have shown that the function F

generally depends on several parameters

$$F = F(h_1, h_2, \ldots, h_m) = F(\mathbf{h}) \tag{5.2.1}$$

and it is of interest to consider variation in F when some or all the parameters change *simultaneously*. The change in F due to infinitesimally small changes in all parameters is expressed mathematically by the total differential

$$dF = \sum_{i=1}^{m} \frac{\partial F}{\partial h_i}\, dh_i. \tag{5.2.2}$$

In order to introduce normalized sensitivities into (5.2.2), divide by F and multiply and divide each term inside the summation by h_i:

$$\frac{dF}{F} = \sum \left(\frac{\partial F}{\partial h_i} \cdot \frac{h_i}{F} \right) \cdot \frac{dh_i}{h_i} = \sum S_{h_i}^{F} \frac{dh_i}{h_i}. \tag{5.2.3a}$$

Very often, increments are more instructive:

$$\frac{\Delta F}{F} \approx \sum S_{h_i}^{F} \frac{\Delta h_i}{h_i}. \tag{5.2.3b}$$

If the parameters h_i represent network elements, limits on the ratio $\Delta h_i/h_i$ are determined by the technology used in fabricating the network, but different designs may lead to different variations $\Delta F/F$ because the sensitivities may differ. In order to be able to compare various designs, we introduce *multiparameter sensitivity measures*.

In the following definitions of such measures we assume, for simplicity, that F and ΔF are real. F may be the magnitude or phase of the network function, the real part, the imaginary part, or the magnitude of a root or Q and ω_0 of the root. The perturbations $\Delta h_i/h_i$ are usually such that

$$|\Delta h_i/h_i| \leqslant t_i \tag{5.2.4}$$

where t_i is called the *tolerance* of the ith component. Discrete components have typical tolerances of a few percent while integrated circuits may have tolerances as large as few tens of percent.

Let us now consider the variation $\Delta F/F$ in the *worst case*. This occurs when the $\Delta h_i/h_i$ values are selected such that

$$\Delta h_i/h_i = \text{sign}\,(S_{h_i}^{F})\, t_i. \tag{5.2.5}$$

The variation in $\Delta F/F$ is then bounded by

$$|\Delta F/F| \leqslant \sum |S_{h_i}^F|\, t_i. \tag{5.2.6}$$

Often the tolerances are considered as being equal, e.g., $t_i = t$ for $i = 1, 2, \ldots$, and the *worst case multiparameter sensitivity* measure is defined as

$$\text{WCMS} = \sum |S_{h_i}^F| \tag{5.2.7}$$

with

$$|\Delta F/F| \leqslant t \times \text{WCMS}. \tag{5.2.8}$$

Application of the WCMS measure often leads to overly pessimistic results. One reason is that the $\Delta h_i/h_i$ sign variations among the *same type* of elements will seldom follow the relation given by (5.2.5).

Components of the same kind often have similar values of $\Delta h_i/h_i$; this is particularly true in film and integrated circuits where components *track* each other. If we split the summation in (5.2.3b) to range over a single element type, say capacitors, the normalized variation F due to equal fractional changes in the elements takes the form

$$\frac{\Delta F}{F} = \frac{\Delta h}{h} \sum S_{h_i}^F \tag{5.2.9}$$

and the *multiparameter tracking sensitivity* is defined as

$$\text{MTS}_k = \left|\sum S_{h_i}^F\right| \tag{5.2.10}$$

where the summation is over elements of type k.

If all elements of type k have tolerance t_k then the *worst case variation with tracking* is given by

$$|\Delta F/F| \leqslant \sum_k t_k \times \text{MTS}_k. \tag{5.2.11}$$

This variation will be smaller than the one given by (5.2.8).

The above multiparameter sensitivity definitions were based on the assumption that we would always be unlucky and encounter the worst possible value $\pm t_i$ in the deviations $\Delta h_i/h_i$. This is seldom the case in practice. The parameter deviations $\Delta h_i/h_i$ follow a *statistical distribution* which gives the probability of obtaining a particular value of $\Delta h_i/h_i$. Two of the commonly used distributions to model parameter deviations are the *uniform* and *normal* distributions, shown in Fig. 5.2.1. The variation $\Delta F/F$ now becomes a random variable with its

$$\text{Prob}\left(\frac{\Delta h}{h}\right) = \frac{1}{\sqrt{2\pi}\,\sigma}\exp\left[-\tfrac{1}{2}\left\{(\Delta h/h)/\sigma\right\}^2\right]$$

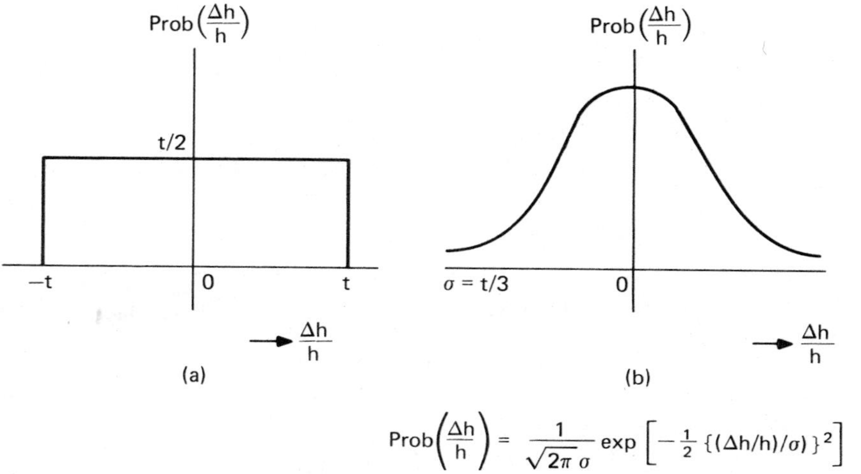

Fig. 5.2.1. Statistical distributions: (a) uniform; (b) normal.

own distribution. Under fairly general conditions, particularly when the circuit has many parameters, the distribution of $\Delta F/F$ is well approximated by a normal distribution with zero mean and variance given by

$$\sigma^2_{\Delta F/F} = \sum (S^F_{h_i})^2\, \sigma^2_{\Delta h_i/h_i} \qquad (5.2.12)$$

when the component variations are statistically independent. Here $\sigma^2_{\Delta h_i/h_i}$ is the variance of the ith component. Its value is $t_i^2/3$ for the uniform distribution and $t_i^2/9$ for the normal distribution. If equal tolerances and the same distribution are assumed for all parameters, then

$$\sigma_{\Delta F/F} = \sigma_{\Delta h/h}\left[\sum (S^F_{h_i})^2\right]^{1/2}. \qquad (5.2.13)$$

From the properties of the normal distribution it follows that the actual variation will lie in the interval $\pm\sigma_{\Delta F/F}$ 68% of the time, $\pm 2\sigma_{\Delta F/F}$ 95% of the time, and $\pm 3\sigma_{\Delta F/F}$ 99.7% of the time. Relation (5.2.13) allows us to define the *multiparameter statistical sensitivity* measure as

$$\text{MSS} = \left[\sum (S^F_{h_i})^2\right]^{1/2}. \qquad (5.2.14)$$

EXAMPLE 5.2.1. Consider the network shown in Fig. 5.1.2 and let the element values be $G_1 = G_2 = 1$ mho, $C_1 = C_2 = 1$ F and $A_1 = A_2 = \sqrt{1.9}$. These values lead to a Q of 10 and $\omega_0 = 1$. Let all elements have 1% tolerances. Illustrate the use of the various multiparameter sensitivity measures for the network Q.

(a) Consider a +1% variation in each element. The sensitivities are

$$S_{C_1}^{Q} = -S_{C_2}^{Q} = -S_{G_1}^{Q} = S_{G_2}^{Q} = 9.5; \qquad S_{A_1}^{Q} = S_{A_2}^{Q} = 19.$$

Use of the variation equation (5.2.3b) results in

$$\begin{aligned}\Delta Q/Q &= [S_{C_1}^{Q} + S_{C_2}^{Q} + S_{G_1}^{Q} + S_{G_2}^{Q} + S_{A_1}^{Q} + S_{A_2}^{Q}] \times 0.01\\ &= 0.38\end{aligned}$$

and a Q of 13.8 is predicted. Substituting actual values, we obtain $Q = 16.18$.

Although the linearized theory correctly predicted the *direction* of change (increase of Q), the 1% variation in each element was too large to get sufficiently close agreement between the linearized and exact analyses.

(b) The worst case multiparameter sensitivity measure has a value of 76, indicating Q extremes of 2.4 and 17.6. The signs of the perturbations in $(C_1, C_2, G_1, G_2, A_1, A_2)$ are $(-, +, +, -, -, -)$ to get the low value of Q and $(+, -, -, +, +, +)$ for the higher value. The exact Q values with the appropriate perturbations are 5.71 and 43.38, respectively.

(c) Let us now assume that the elements of each kind track. The multiparameter tracking sensitivities are

$$\text{MTS}_C = 0; \qquad \text{MTS}_G = 0; \qquad \text{MTS}_A = 38.$$

(d) The multiparameter statistical sensitivity (5.2.14) has a value 32.91. If the tolerances are distributed uniformly, $\sigma_{\Delta h/h} = .01/\sqrt{3}$ and $\sigma_{\Delta F/F} = 0.19$, indicating, for instance, that 95% of the time the Q would lie in the range 6.2 to 13.8.

5.3. SENSITIVITIES TO PARASITICS AND OPERATIONAL AMPLIFIERS

A *parasitic* is an element which has a nominal value of zero in an ideal circuit. Although for such a circuit the element has no influence on the network function itself, a small increment may result in a large variation. We first establish the fact that a zero-valued element has a differential sensitivity. In the calculations, all steps are performed as if the particular element existed. In the results, its zero nominal value is inserted.

EXAMPLE 5.3.1. Find the transfer function of the network shown in Fig. 5.3.1 and calculate its differential sensitivity $D_{G_2}^{Z_{TR}}$ where $G_2 = 0$ is the parasitic.

The transfer function is

$$Z_{TR} = \frac{G_2 + sC}{sC(G_1 + G_3) + G_1G_2 + G_1G_3 + G_2G_3} = \frac{N}{D}.$$

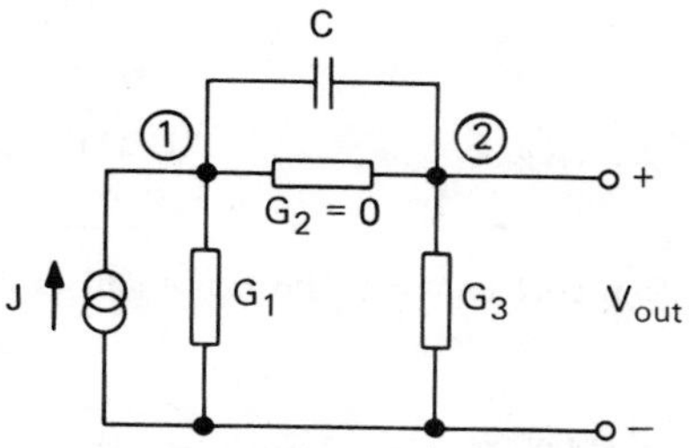

Fig. 5.3.1. Passive network with one parasitic conductance G_2.

The derivative with respect to G_2 is

$$\frac{\partial Z_{TR}}{\partial G_2} = \frac{G_1 G_3}{D^2}.$$

Inserting $G_2 = 0$ results in

$$Z_{TR} = \frac{sC}{sC(G_1 + G_3) + G_1 G_3}$$

$$\frac{\partial Z_{TR}}{\partial G_2} = \frac{G_1 G_3}{[sC(G_1 + G_3) + G_1 G_3]^2}.$$

The element has no influence on the transfer function but it has influence on the sensitivity even after inserting the nominal value $G_2 = 0$.

At this point we observe that the normalized sensitivity (5.1.2) cannot be used. It will always be zero due to the multiplication by the nominal value. We must define another normalization which will be meaningful for parasitics. To do so consider (5.2.2), divide by F, and consider small variations:

$$\frac{\Delta F}{F} \approx \sum \left(\frac{\partial F}{\partial h_i} \cdot \frac{1}{F} \right) \Delta h_i. \tag{5.3.1}$$

Some of the elements may be zero. Denote them by v_i and rewrite (5.3.1) as follows:

$$\frac{\Delta F}{F} \approx \underbrace{\sum \left(\frac{\partial F}{\partial h_i} \frac{h_i}{F} \right) \frac{\Delta h_i}{h_i}}_{\text{nonzero-valued elements}} + \underbrace{\sum \left(\frac{\partial F}{\partial v_i} \frac{1}{F} \right) \Delta v_i}_{\text{zero-valued elements}}.$$

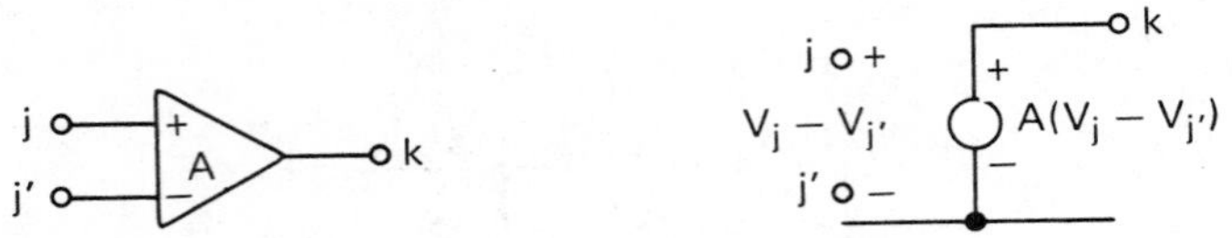

Fig. 5.3.2. Operational amplifier with gain A and its VVT equivalent.

Inserting (5.1.2) and (5.1.4) gives

$$\frac{\Delta F}{F} \approx \sum S_{h_i}^F \frac{\Delta h_i}{h_i} + \sum \mathcal{S}_{v_i}^F \Delta v_i. \tag{5.3.2}$$

Because $v_i = 0$, the increment Δv_i *represents the value of the parasitic*. For a selected fabrication technique the limits on $\Delta h_i/h_i$ are fixed. The parasitics may be present, for instance, due to the layout. Once the layout has been decided upon, Δv_i cannot be influenced either. The only way to reduce the scaled variation (5.3.2) is to provide a nominal design having small $S_{h_i}^F$ and $\mathcal{S}_{v_i}^F$.

Let us now turn to the ideal operational amplifier. We will show that it can be defined as a special "parasitic." A nonideal OPAMP is shown in Fig. 5.3.2. The voltages are related by

$$(V_j - V_{j'})A = V_k$$

or

$$V_j - V_{j'} = V_k/A.$$

Define a new variable

$$B = -1/A. \tag{5.3.3}$$

Then

$$V_j - V_{j'} + BV_k = 0. \tag{5.3.4}$$

In the limit, $B \to 0$ for an ideal OPAMP. The value B can be treated as a variable and Eq. (5.3.4) is used as the constitutive equation for the OPAMP. The input terminals of the OPAMP need not be at the same potential when $B \neq 0$.

EXAMPLE 5.3.2. Calculate the transfer function for the network in Fig. 5.3.3. Assume that the OPAMP may change and become nonideal. Obtain the transfer function sensitivity and the pole sensitivity with respect to the variable B.

The transfer function is $T = G_1/D$ with $D = B(sC + G_1 + G_2) - sC - G_2$.

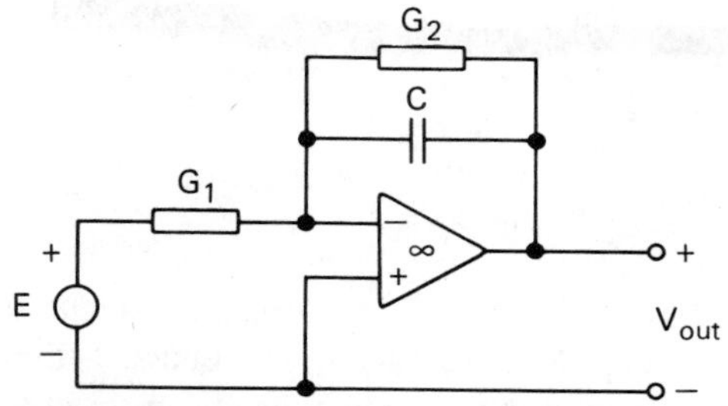

Fig. 5.3.3. Nonideal integrator with ideal OPAMP.

Differentiating with respect to the variable B gives

$$\frac{\partial T}{\partial B} = \frac{-G_1(sC + G_1 + G_2)}{D^2}$$

$$S_B^T = \frac{\partial T}{\partial B} \cdot \frac{1}{T} = \frac{-(sC + G_1 + G_2)}{D} = \frac{sC + G_1 + G_2}{sC + G_2} = 1 + \frac{G_1}{sC + G_2} .$$

To calculate the sensitivity of the pole we apply (5.1.10). The pole is obtained from the denominator for $B = 0$: $p = -G_2/C$. Differentiating the denominator D with respect to B gives

$$\frac{\partial D}{\partial B} = sC + G_1 + G_2 \Big|_{s=p} = -\frac{G_2}{C} \cdot C + G_1 + G_2 = G_1 .$$

Differentiating D with respect to s and setting $B = 0$ gives

$$\partial D/\partial s = -C.$$

The pole sensitivity is

$$\frac{\partial p}{\partial B} = -\left(\frac{G_1}{-C}\right) = \frac{G_1}{C} .$$

The semi-normalized sensitivity is

$$S_B^p = \frac{\partial p}{\partial B} \cdot \frac{1}{p} = -\frac{G_1}{G_2} .$$

Actual operational amplifiers do not have infinite gain. Their gain is a function of the frequency and is often simulated by

$$A = \frac{A_0 \omega_A}{s + \omega_A} . \qquad (5.3.5)$$

The product $A_0\omega_A$ is called the *gain-bandwidth product.* Using (5.3.3) one obtains

$$\Delta v_i = B_{\text{actual}} = -\frac{s+\omega_A}{A_0\omega_A} \approx -\frac{s}{A_0\omega_A}. \tag{5.3.6}$$

Thus the OPAMP has been transformed into an element for which we must apply the sensitivity definition (5.1.4). As discussed above, Δv_i cannot be influenced once the production technology has been selected (e.g., once a given OPAMP has been used), but we still have the freedom of selecting the elements h_i such that both $S^F_{h_i}$ as well as $S^F_{v_i}$ in (5.3.2) are minimized.

It is often convenient to have a linear OPAMP model which takes into account A_0 and ω_A. One useful model which takes care of the input admittances, output resistance, A_0, and ω_A is shown in Fig. 5.3.4. One conductance $G = \omega_A$ controls the cutoff frequency and one VCT defines the dc gain A_0 of the OPAMP.

It is necessary to stress that variations of the gain of the amplifier usually have a significant impact on the network function and we need its sensitivity to the variations of the gain. As long as the gain is finite, the normalized sensitivity S^F_A is used. If the gain approaches infinity, the definition becomes meaningless. For this reason, Moschytz [1] introduced a special sensitivity measure for ideal operational amplifiers and called it the *gain-sensitivity product*

$$\Gamma^F_A = AS^F_A = A\frac{A}{F}\frac{dF}{dA}. \tag{5.3.7}$$

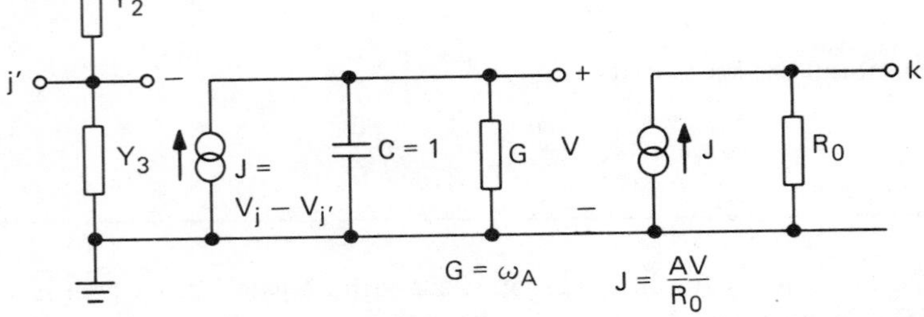

Fig. 5.3.4. Modeling a linear OPAMP with gain A_0, output resistance R_0, and cut-off frequency ω_A.

The measure is widely accepted among specialists in the active networks field. We will show that the definition is *exactly* equivalent to our definition $\mathcal{S}_B^F$ where

$$B = -1/A. \tag{5.3.8}$$

Suppose that we obtained the derivative dF/dB. Using the chain rule of differentiation

$$\frac{dF}{dA} = \frac{dF}{dB}\frac{dB}{dA}. \tag{5.3.9}$$

Differentiating (5.3.8) we obtain $dB/dA = 1/A^2$ and inserting into (5.3.9)

$$\frac{dF}{dA} = \frac{dF}{dB}\frac{1}{A^2}.$$

Finally, using (5.3.7)

$$A\frac{A}{F}\frac{dF}{dA} = \frac{1}{F}\frac{dF}{dB}$$

or

$$\Gamma_A^F = \mathcal{S}_B^F. \tag{5.3.10}$$

Although this seems to be a trivial conclusion, the CAD implications are significant. When working with $A \to \infty$, we must keep the gain A as a variable, obtain the transfer function, differentiate and then apply the limit. Only hand calculations are possible since the computer cannot handle infinity, and for larger networks this is an almost impossible task. On the other hand, $B = 0$ does not present any computational difficulties and in the next chapter we will show that the sensitivity with respect to B can be easily obtained for networks of any size.

PROBLEMS

P.5.1. Derive the transfer functions of the networks shown in Fig. P.5.1. Find the transfer function sensitivity S_h^T with respect to the capacitors and amplifiers.

P.5.2. Sensitivities S_h^Q and $S_h^{\omega_0}$ can be obtained easily in the case of second-order functions. Comparing a general polynomial

$$Us^2 + Vs + W = U\left(s^2 + \frac{V}{U}s + \frac{W}{U}\right)$$

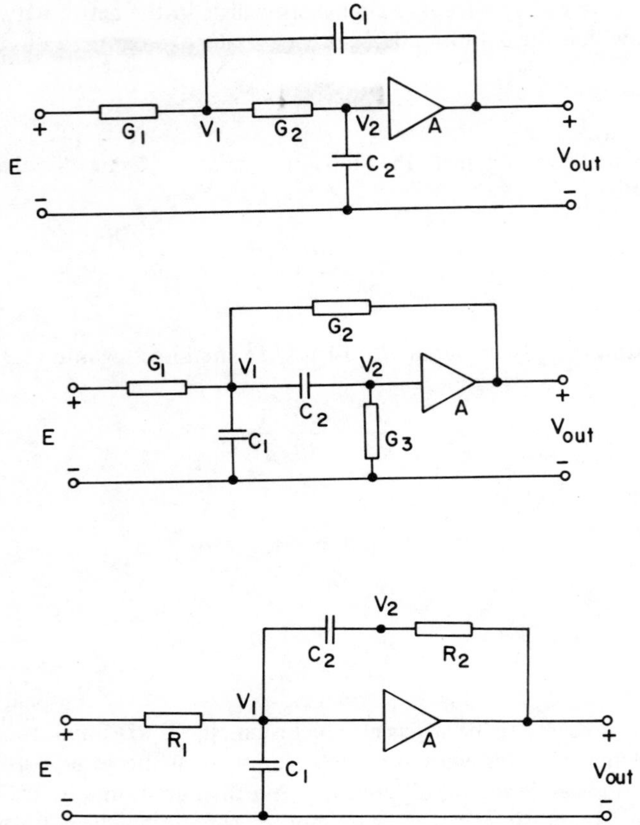

Fig. P.5.1.

with the polynomial

$$s^2 + \frac{\omega_0}{Q}s + \omega_0^2$$

we can obtain

$$S_h^{\omega_0} = -\tfrac{1}{2}S_h^U + \tfrac{1}{2}S_h^W$$
$$S_h^Q = \tfrac{1}{2}S_h^U - S_h^V + \tfrac{1}{2}S_h^W.$$

Derive these formulae and apply them to the networks shown in Fig. P.5.1.

P.5.3. For the networks shown in Fig. P.5.1, let $C_1 = C_2$. Choose values of A and G_i such that the networks realize the following transfer function:

$$T = \frac{\text{numerator}}{s^2 + 2s + 2}.$$

P.5.4. Calculate the pole sensitivity S_h^{pole} for the solutions to Problem P.5.3 by letting $h = A$.

P.5.5. Calculate the transfer functions for the networks shown in Fig. P.5.5. All these networks realize second-order functions. Also find S_h^Q, $S_h^{\omega_0}$ for h being the amplifier gains.

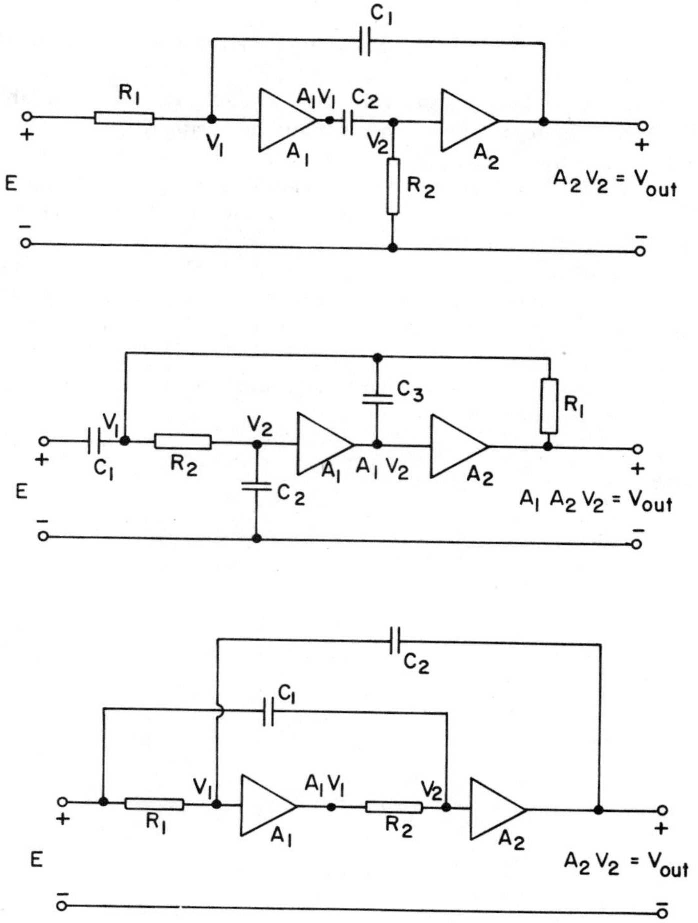

Fig. P.5.5.

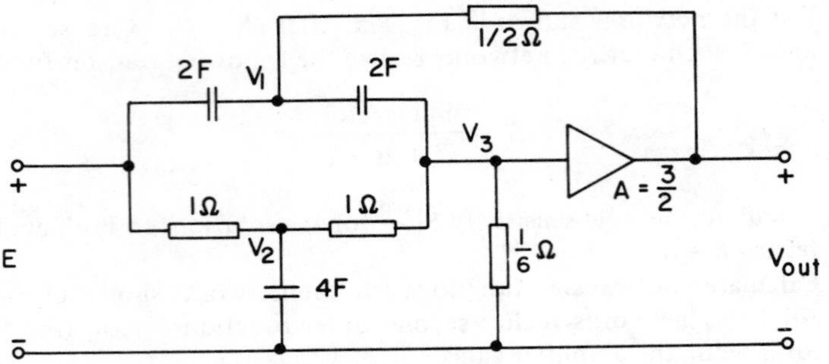

Fig. P.5.6.

P.5.6. The network shown in Fig. P.5.6 is actually a third-order network, but cancellation of terms occurs in the transfer function. Derive the transfer function by keeping the gain of the amplifier A as a variable and cancel equal factors in the numerator and denominator.

P.5.7. Find the transfer function of the network shown in Fig. P.4.8(a) (Chapter 4) by assuming that the inverted gain of the operational amplifiers, $B = -1/A$, is a variable. Find the sensitivity of the transfer function with respect to this variable, S_B^F.

P.5.8. Set $B = 0$ in the transfer function derived in Problem P.5.7, assume that $C_1 = C_2 = 1$ F and select the values of resistors such that the denominator becomes $s^2 + 2s + 2$. Find the sensitivity of Q and ω_0 with respect to B, S_B^Q, $S_B^{\omega_0}$.

P.5.9. Using the design of Problem P.5.8, find the sensitivity of the pole with respect to changes of B.

REFERENCE

1. G. S. Moschytz: *Linear Integrated Networks Design.* Van Nostrand Reinhold, New York, 1975.

CHAPTER 6
Computer Generation of Sensitivities

This chapter presents computational techniques for determining network function sensitivities in the frequency domain by operating directly on the system of linear equations. There are basically two situations: either the sensitivity of *all* system variables is computed with respect to *one* parameter or the sensitivity of *one* output with respect to *many* parameters is obtained. In practice, the second approach has greater applicability and will be considered in detail. Historically, it was developed through the use of Tellegen's theorem and was termed the *adjoint network* method [1], but the associated derivations are complicated and not valid for the two-graph formulations introduced in Chapter 4. For this reason the development in this chapter is based on general properties of linear algebraic systems. We will call it the *adjoint system* or *transpose system* method.

The theory is developed in Section 6.1. It is shown that sensitivity evaluation of a scalar output with respect to any number of parameters is obtained by the solution of the original system and a system in which the matrix is transposed and a different right-hand side used. In Section 6.2, it is shown that the close relationship between the two systems enables sharing of many computational operations. In Section 6.3, the general sensitivity formulae are viewed in terms of network applications. It is shown that they simplify considerably and that significant further reduction in computational cost is possible when the nodal, modified nodal, or tableau formulations are used. Sensitivity to parasitic elements, i.e., elements whose nominal values are zero, and to perturbation in OPAMP behavior from the ideal are considered in Section 6.4.

Section 6.5 contains subsections and examples that extend the basic ideas. Sensitivities of the amplitude and phase characteristics, of function zeros and poles, and of the quality factors and center frequencies of these zeros and poles are discussed. More general problems are handled as well: sensitivity with respect to global parameters like temperature, noise analysis, and the generation of Norton and Thévenin equivalents. Section 6.6 extends the basic theory to higher-order sensitivities, and the chapter concludes with larger examples in Section 6.7. Most of the sensitivity methods discussed in this chapter are coded in the program in Appendix D.

6.1. SENSITIVITY OF LINEAR ALGEBRAIC SYSTEMS

In this section we give the fundamental derivation for computing the sensitivity of linear algebraic systems. This is a more general problem than frequency domain sensitivity of linear networks, a topic we will return to later in this chapter.

Consider a system of linear equations in the form

$$\mathbf{TX} = \mathbf{W} \tag{6.1.1}$$

where $\mathbf{T}$ and $\mathbf{W}$ may be real or complex and depend on some parameters $\mathbf{h}$, the typical parameter being denoted by h_i, with the subscript i dropped when there is no ambiguity. The solution of (6.1.1) is written formally as follows:

$$\mathbf{X} = \mathbf{T}^{-1}\mathbf{W}. \tag{6.1.2}$$

In a brute-force evaluation of the sensitivity one could perturb the parameter by Δh, find $\Delta\mathbf{X}$ and use the relation $\partial\mathbf{X}/\partial h \approx \Delta\mathbf{X}/\Delta h$. Practical considerations rule out such a simplistic approach. First of all, the incremental values $\Delta\mathbf{X}/\Delta h$ tend to the differential sensitivity only in the limit as $\Delta h \to 0$ and a very small value for Δh in computations is precluded by roundoff errors. Secondly, sensitivity evaluation for *each* component of $\mathbf{h}$ requires the formulation and solution of (6.1.1), resulting in high computational cost. These difficulties are avoided by differentiating the system equations directly and performing some matrix manipulations as outlined in the rest of this section.

To evaluate the sensitivity of all components of the vector $\mathbf{X}$ to a *single* parameter h, we differentiate (6.1.1) with respect to h to obtain

$$\mathbf{T}\frac{\partial\mathbf{X}}{\partial h} + \frac{\partial\mathbf{T}}{\partial h}\mathbf{X} = \frac{\partial\mathbf{W}}{\partial h} \tag{6.1.3}$$

and rewrite as follows:

$$\mathbf{T}\frac{\partial\mathbf{X}}{\partial h} = -\left(\frac{\partial\mathbf{T}}{\partial h}\mathbf{X} - \frac{\partial\mathbf{W}}{\partial h}\right). \tag{6.1.4}$$

If we first solve (6.1.1) by $\mathbf{LU}$ decomposition and forward and back substitution, the vector $\mathbf{X}$ is known. Thus the product $(\partial\mathbf{T}/\partial h)\mathbf{X}$ can be formed and the right-hand side of (6.1.4) can be generated. Since the $\mathbf{LU}$ factors are already available, solution of (6.1.4) requires only one additional forward and back substitution to get $\partial \mathbf{X}/\partial h$. In network theory literature, this method has been termed the *sensitivity network* approach. We note that *it generates the sensitivity of the whole vector* $\mathbf{X}$ *with respect to a single variable element* h. If sensitivity with respect to many parameters h_i is required, (6.1.4) is solved for each h_i in turn.

The sensitivity of all components of $\mathbf{X}$ is seldom required. Frequently we have a *single output*, ϕ, which is related to $\mathbf{X}$, and we need the derivatives of ϕ with respect to many variable elements h_i. We now develop the *adjoint* or *transpose* method which tackles this problem in a computationally efficient manner. For notational simplicity the subscript i of h will not be written in the derivations.

The formal solution of (6.1.4) is

$$\frac{\partial \mathbf{X}}{\partial h} = -\mathbf{T}^{-1}\left(\frac{\partial \mathbf{T}}{\partial h}\mathbf{X} - \frac{\partial \mathbf{W}}{\partial h}\right). \tag{6.1.5}$$

Let the output of interest be a *scalar* variable $\phi(\mathbf{X})$. The case of the general function ϕ will be considered in Section 6.5(I); here we restrict $\phi(\mathbf{X})$ to be the linear combination of the components of $\mathbf{X}$:

$$\phi = \mathbf{d}^t\mathbf{X} \tag{6.1.6}$$

where $\mathbf{d}$ is a constant vector. Our objective now is to compute the sensitivity of the scalar function ϕ with respect to h. To this end differentiate (6.1.6):

$$\frac{\partial \phi}{\partial h} = \mathbf{d}^t \frac{\partial \mathbf{X}}{\partial h} \tag{6.1.7}$$

and substitute for $\partial \mathbf{X}/\partial h$ from (6.1.5):

$$\frac{\partial \phi}{\partial h} = -\mathbf{d}^t\mathbf{T}^{-1}\left(\frac{\partial \mathbf{T}}{\partial h}\mathbf{X} - \frac{\partial \mathbf{W}}{\partial h}\right). \tag{6.1.8}$$

Note that the row vector $\mathbf{d}^t\mathbf{T}^{-1}$ in (6.1.8) can be precomputed together with the solution vector $\mathbf{X}$ *before* the sensitivity calculations are carried out.

Let us define an *adjoint vector* $\mathbf{X}^a$ through the relation

$$(\mathbf{X}^a)^t = -\mathbf{d}^t\mathbf{T}^{-1}. \tag{6.1.9}$$

Postmultiply (6.1.9) by $\mathbf{T}$ and take the transpose to get $\mathbf{X}^a$ as the solution to the system:

$$\mathbf{T}^t\mathbf{X}^a = -\mathbf{d}. \tag{6.1.10}$$

Substituting (6.1.9) into (6.1.8) we get the final form:

$$\frac{\partial \phi}{\partial h} = (\mathbf{X}^a)^t \frac{\partial \mathbf{T}}{\partial h} \mathbf{X} - (\mathbf{X}^a)^t \frac{\partial \mathbf{W}}{\partial h}. \tag{6.1.11}$$

For each parameter h_i, the matrix $\partial \mathbf{T}/\partial h_i$ and the vector $\partial \mathbf{W}/\partial h_i$ will be formed and the products indicated on the right-hand side of (6.1.11) evaluated. As the vectors $\mathbf{X}$ and $\mathbf{X}^a$ are independent of the parameter index i, we see that application of (6.1.11) requires the solution of only *two* sets of algebraic equations, (6.1.1) and (6.1.10), irrespective of the number of parameters h_i. The computational procedure for the adjoint approach is summarized as follows:

Step 1. Solve the given system of equations

$$\mathbf{TX} = \mathbf{W}.$$

Step 2. Solve the adjoint system of equations defined by

$$\mathbf{T}^t\mathbf{X}^a = -\mathbf{d}.$$

Step 3. For each parameter h_i, form $\partial \mathbf{T}/\partial h_i$ and $\partial \mathbf{W}/\partial h_i$. Insert in (6.1.11) to compute $\partial \phi/\partial h_i$.

Solutions in Steps 1 and 2 can use the same triangular factors, as explained in the next section. In Step 3, advantage can be taken of any special zero–nonzero structure associated with $\partial \mathbf{T}/\partial h_i$ and $\partial \mathbf{W}/\partial h_i$, as will be clarified on examples in subsequent sections.

Application of (6.1.4) and (6.1.11) will be demonstrated on two examples.

EXAMPLE 6.1.1. Apply formula (6.1.4) to the network shown in Fig. 6.1.1 and find the sensitivity of the nodal voltages V_1, V_2 with respect to G_1.

Since any formulation can be used, let us apply the hand-calculation method

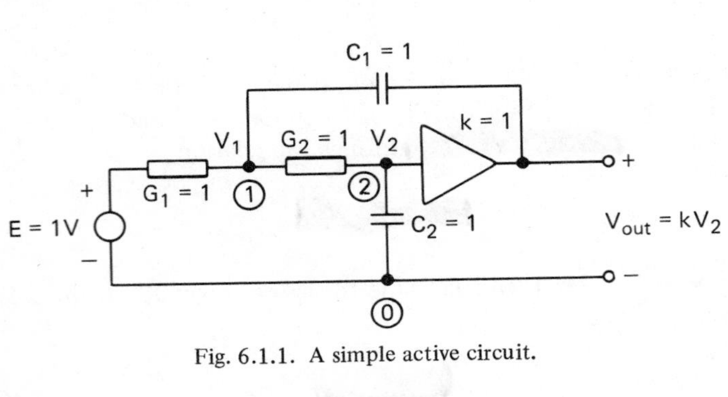

Fig. 6.1.1. A simple active circuit.

of Section 4.5. The system equations are

$$\begin{bmatrix} G_1 + G_2 + sC_1 & -sC_1K - G_2 \\ -G_2 & G_2 + sC_2 \end{bmatrix} \begin{bmatrix} V_1 \\ V_2 \end{bmatrix} = \begin{bmatrix} G_1E \\ 0 \end{bmatrix}.$$

To simplify the numerical steps, we use a real $s = 2$. The reader may repeat the steps for an actual frequency, say, $s = j2$. Inserting the values and solving gives:

$$\mathbf{X} = \begin{bmatrix} V_1 \\ V_2 \end{bmatrix} = \begin{bmatrix} \frac{1}{3} \\ \frac{1}{9} \end{bmatrix}.$$

The right-hand side of (6.1.4) is $[\frac{2}{3} \quad 0]^t$ and the solution is

$$\begin{bmatrix} \partial V_1/\partial G_1 \\ \partial V_2/\partial G_1 \end{bmatrix} = \begin{bmatrix} \frac{2}{9} \\ \frac{2}{27} \end{bmatrix}.$$

EXAMPLE 6.1.2. Apply formula (6.1.11) to the network in Fig. 6.1.1 and find the sensitivity of V_2 with respect to G_1.

The formulation and solution of the original system are the same as in Example 6.1.1:

$$\mathbf{X} = \begin{bmatrix} \frac{1}{3} \\ \frac{1}{9} \end{bmatrix}.$$

Because V_2 is the "output," $\mathbf{d} = [0 \quad 1]^t$ and (6.1.10) becomes

$$\begin{bmatrix} 4 & -1 \\ -3 & 3 \end{bmatrix} \begin{bmatrix} V_1^a \\ V_2^a \end{bmatrix} = \begin{bmatrix} 0 \\ -1 \end{bmatrix}.$$

The solution is

$$\mathbf{X}^a \equiv \begin{bmatrix} V_1^a \\ V_2^a \end{bmatrix} = \begin{bmatrix} -\frac{1}{9} \\ -\frac{4}{9} \end{bmatrix}.$$

Using formula (6.1.11), the derivative with respect to G_1 is

$$\frac{\partial V_2}{\partial G_1} = [-\tfrac{1}{9} \quad -\tfrac{4}{9}] \begin{bmatrix} 1 & 0 \\ 0 & 0 \end{bmatrix} \begin{bmatrix} \frac{1}{3} \\ \frac{1}{9} \end{bmatrix} - [-\tfrac{1}{9} \quad -\tfrac{4}{9}] \begin{bmatrix} 1 \\ 0 \end{bmatrix} = \frac{2}{27}.$$

Both terms of (6.1.11) had to be used since G_1 appears on both sides of the system equation. One would proceed similarly for the other elements.

In some applications a scalar output function must be evaluated for a number of right-hand-side vectors. Though this problem is not directly related to sensitivity computation, the adjoint system can be used to advantage. In terms of system equations, we have

$$\left.\begin{aligned} \mathbf{T}\mathbf{X}_i &= \mathbf{W}_i \\ \phi_i &= \mathbf{d}^t\mathbf{X}_i \end{aligned}\right\} \qquad i = 1, 2, \ldots, m \tag{6.1.12}$$

where $\mathbf{W}_i$ are various right-hand-side vectors and ϕ_i the corresponding outputs. The direct solution of (6.1.12) would require one factorization of $\mathbf{T}$ followed by m forward and back substitution steps. Formally the outputs are given by

$$\begin{aligned} \phi_i &= \mathbf{d}^t\mathbf{T}^{-1}\mathbf{W}_i \\ &= -(-\mathbf{d}^t\mathbf{T}^{-1})\,\mathbf{W}_i \\ &= -(\mathbf{X}^a)^t\mathbf{W}_i \end{aligned} \tag{6.1.13}$$

with $\mathbf{X}^a$ obtained as the solution of (6.1.10). Equation (6.1.13) indicates that *all* the ϕ_i can be evaluated with a *single* analysis of the adjoint system (6.1.10).

6.2. NUMERICAL SOLUTION OF THE ADJOINT SYSTEM

Assume that the original system (6.1.1) has been solved by means of triangular decomposition and we have the factors

$$\mathbf{T} = \mathbf{L}\mathbf{U}. \tag{6.2.1}$$

The adjoint system (6.1.10) uses the transpose of $\mathbf{T}$:

$$\mathbf{T}^t = \mathbf{U}^t\mathbf{L}^t. \tag{6.2.2}$$

There is no need to decompose $\mathbf{T}^t$ into its triangular factors again. All we need is to use the decomposition (6.2.1) but modify the forward and back substitution to provide the solution of the adjoint system:

$$\mathbf{U}^t\mathbf{L}^t\mathbf{X}^a = \mathbf{b} \tag{6.2.3}$$

where $\mathbf{b}$ stands for any right-hand-side vector. Solve first the auxiliary system

$$\mathbf{U}^t\mathbf{Z} = \mathbf{b}$$

and using $\mathbf{Z}$ solve

$$\mathbf{L}^t\mathbf{X}^a = \mathbf{Z}.$$

We derive the algorithm considering a decomposed 4×4 matrix. Write first

$$\begin{bmatrix} 1 & & & \\ u_{12} & 1 & & \\ u_{13} & u_{23} & 1 & \\ u_{14} & u_{24} & u_{34} & 1 \end{bmatrix} \begin{bmatrix} z_1 \\ z_2 \\ z_3 \\ z_4 \end{bmatrix} = \begin{bmatrix} b_1 \\ b_2 \\ b_3 \\ b_4 \end{bmatrix}$$

from which the algorithm

$$\begin{aligned} z_1 &= b_1 \\ z_j &= b_j - \sum_{i=1}^{j-1} u_{ij} z_i; \qquad j = 2, 3, \ldots, n \end{aligned} \tag{6.2.4}$$

is obtained. Similarly

$$\begin{bmatrix} l_{11} & l_{21} & l_{31} & l_{41} \\ & l_{22} & l_{32} & l_{42} \\ & & l_{33} & l_{43} \\ & & & l_{44} \end{bmatrix} \begin{bmatrix} x_1^a \\ x_2^a \\ x_3^a \\ x_4^a \end{bmatrix} = \begin{bmatrix} z_1 \\ z_2 \\ z_3 \\ z_4 \end{bmatrix}$$

from which we derive the algorithm

$$\begin{aligned} x_n^a &= z_n / l_{nn} \\ x_j^a &= \left(z_j - \sum_{i=j+1}^{n} l_{ij} x_i^a \right) \Big/ l_{jj}; \qquad j = n-1, n-2, \ldots, 1. \end{aligned} \tag{6.2.5}$$

In actual programming, the u_{ij} and l_{ij} are replaced by t_{ij} since the **LU** decomposition of **T** overwrites the original values. The FORTRAN-subroutine SOLVET (Fig. 6.2.1) solves systems of the form $\mathbf{A}^t\mathbf{X} = \mathbf{b}$.

6.3. ADJOINT SYSTEM METHOD APPLIED TO NETWORKS

In the last two sections we have developed the theory for finding the sensitivity of a response variable with respect to parameters when the system is described by a set of linear algebraic equations. Such is the case when we consider linear networks in the frequency domain and use any of the formulations discussed in Chapters 2-4. It was indicated previously that in terms of simplicity and computational efficiency the nodal, modified nodal, and tableau formulations are to be preferred. It turns out that these formulations are also best suited for sensitivity computations. In applying the sensitivity equation to network

```
C*********************************************************************
      SUBROUTINE SOLVET (A,IA,N,B)
C*ROUTINE SOLVES THE TRANSPOSE SYSTEM   A'.X = B   WITH THE RESULT X
C*RETURNED IN THE VECTOR B WHICH IS DESTROYED. ON INPUT A CONTAINS THE
C*LU FACTORS OBTAINED FROM ROUTINES LUG,LUROW OR CROUT OF CHAPTER 2.
C*MATRIX A HAS DIMENSION N WITH ABSOLUTE ROW DIMENSION IA IN THE
C*CALLING PROGRAMME.
      DIMENSION A(IA,N), B(N)
C*FORWARD SUBSTITUTION
      IF (N.EQ.1) GO TO 30
      DO 20 I=2,N
          T = B(I)
          IM1 = I-1
          DO 10 J=1,IM1
   10     T = T-A(J,I)*B(J)
   20 B(I) = T
C*BACK SUBSTITUTION
   30 B(N) = B(N)/A(N,N)
      IF (N.EQ.1) RETURN
      NM1 = N-1
      DO 50 II=1,NM1
          I = N-II
          IP1 = I+1
          T = B(I)
          DO 40 J=IP1,N
   40     T = T-A(J,I)*B(J)
   50 B(I) = T/A(I,I)
      RETURN
      END
```

Fig. 6.2.1. Routine for the solution of the adjoint system. For test program see Fig. 2.5.1.

problems the following features of these three formulations should be noted and used to advantage:

1. The right-hand-side vector **W** is sparse. In the case of a network excited by a single source, **W** contains only one or two nonzero entries. Advantage can be taken of this property in the forward substitution phase of solving (6.1.1).
2. The response selection vector is usually also sparse, the output often being a single node voltage, branch current, or branch voltage. In this situation **d** contains only one or two nonzero entries and advantage can be taken of this in the forward substitution phase of solving (6.1.10).
3. When finding sensitivity to a source, $\partial \mathbf{T}/\partial h$ is zero and $\partial \mathbf{W}/\partial h$ is of the form $(\mathbf{e}_i - \mathbf{e}_j)$. The sensitivity equation (6.1.11) then simplifies to

$$\begin{aligned}\frac{\partial \phi}{\partial h} &= -(\mathbf{X}^a)^t(\mathbf{e}_i - \mathbf{e}_j)\\ &= x_j^a - x_i^a.\end{aligned} \tag{6.3.1}$$

4. The parameters with respect to which the sensitivity is evaluated are often component values. In this case $\partial \mathbf{W}/\partial h$ is usually zero. Further, in the nodal and modified nodal formulations each two-terminal element or transducer generates at most 4 entries in **T**. If $\mathbf{e}_0$ denotes a null vector, these entries can always be written in the form of an outer product

$$s^\nu(\mathbf{e}_i - \mathbf{e}_j)(\mathbf{e}_k - \mathbf{e}_l)^t h \tag{6.3.2}$$

where ν is 1 for reactive elements and zero otherwise, h is an element value, and $\mathbf{e}_i$ etc., are elementary unit vectors. In the tableau formulation each element occurs in only one location and two of the subscripts in (6.3.2) take on zero values.

From (6.3.2) we see that

$$\partial\mathbf{T}/\partial h = s^{\nu}(\mathbf{e}_i - \mathbf{e}_j)(\mathbf{e}_k - \mathbf{e}_l)^t$$

and the sensitivity equation (6.1.11) takes the following form:

$$\begin{aligned}\partial\phi/\partial h &= s^{\nu}(\mathbf{X}^a)^t(\mathbf{e}_i - \mathbf{e}_j)(\mathbf{e}_k - \mathbf{e}_l)^t\mathbf{X} \\ &= s^{\nu}\{(\mathbf{X}^a)^t(\mathbf{e}_i - \mathbf{e}_j)\}\{(\mathbf{e}_k - \mathbf{e}_l)^t\mathbf{X}\} \\ &= s^{\nu}(x_i^a - x_j^a)(x_k - x_l)\end{aligned} \quad (6.3.3)$$

where braces have been used to indicate the sequence for evaluating the vector products. Equation (6.3.3) indicates that in most network problems each sensitivity is computed in at most two multiplication-subtractions once the vectors $\mathbf{X}$, $\mathbf{X}^a$ have been generated. This should be compared with the $\approx n^2$ operations required to form $(\mathbf{X}^a)^t(\partial\mathbf{T}/\partial h)\mathbf{X}$ for a general algebraic system.

5. In applying (6.1.6), (6.3.1) and (6.3.3), not all components of $\mathbf{X}$ and $\mathbf{X}^a$ may be required. This fact can be used to reduce computations in the back substitution phase of solving (6.1.1) and (6.1.10).

6.4. SENSITIVITY TO OPAMPS AND PARASITICS

Sensitivity to operational amplifier gains and to parasitic elements was discussed in Section 5.3. It required computation with the element assumed to exist in the network, differentiation with respect to it, and insertion of zero for the value after differentiation.

The adjoint system method is much simpler. In fact, it *does not require any change of the procedure* as outlined for regular elements. Let a parasitic conductance G be connected between nodes j and j'. In the one-graph modified nodal formulation, it will appear at the positions shown:

$$\begin{array}{c} \\ j \\ \\ j' \\ \\ \end{array}\begin{array}{c} \quad j \qquad\qquad j' \\ \left[\begin{array}{cccc} & \vdots & & \vdots \\ \cdots & G=0 & \cdots & -G=0\cdots \\ & \vdots & & \vdots \\ \cdots & -G=0 & \cdots & G=0\cdots \\ & \vdots & & \vdots \end{array}\right] \end{array}.$$

The zero entry does not alter the matrix and thus the **LU** decomposition and forward and back substitution for both the direct and adjoint systems do not change. In Eqs. (6.1.4) or (6.1.11) the derivatives of the entries are needed. Differentiation with respect to G will result in either +1 or −1 in the matrix shown above. The sensitivity will be $(x_j^a - x_{j'}^a)(x_j - x_{j'})$. If the element is a capacitor, differentiation with respect to it will result in s in the appropriate positions and the sensitivity will be $s(x_j^a - x_{j'}^a)(x_j - x_{j'})$. We conclude that the adjoint system method gives derivatives of the response with respect to all parasitics *without any change.*

EXAMPLE 6.4.1. Calculate the sensitivity of the output of the network shown in Fig. 6.4.1 to the parasitics. Let the frequency be $s = j$.

The nodal formulation for the network gives

$$\begin{bmatrix} G_1 + G_2 + sC_1 + sC_2 & -G_2 - sC_2 \\ -G_2 - sC_2 & G_2 + G_3 + sC_2 + sC_3 \end{bmatrix} \begin{bmatrix} V_1 \\ V_2 \end{bmatrix} = \begin{bmatrix} 1 \\ 0 \end{bmatrix}.$$

The solutions are

$$\mathbf{X} = \begin{bmatrix} V_1 \\ V_2 \end{bmatrix} = \begin{bmatrix} (3-j)/5 \\ (2+j)/5 \end{bmatrix}; \qquad \mathbf{X}^a = \begin{bmatrix} V_1^a \\ V_2^a \end{bmatrix} = \begin{bmatrix} -(2+j)/5 \\ (-3+j)/5 \end{bmatrix}.$$

The sensitivities are:

$$\frac{\partial V_{out}}{\partial C_1} = sV_1^a V_1 = \frac{1-j7}{25}$$

$$\frac{\partial V_{out}}{\partial G_2} = (V_1^a - V_2^a)(V_1 - V_2) = \frac{-3-j4}{25}$$

$$\frac{\partial V_{out}}{\partial C_3} = sV_2^a V_2 = \frac{1-j7}{25}.$$

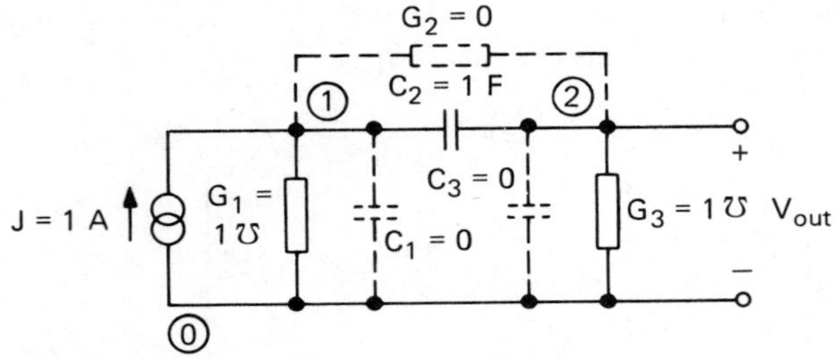

Fig. 6.4.1. Network with parasitic elements.

It was discussed in Section 5.3 that an operational amplifier can be expressed as a special "parasitic" with the inverse of the gain

$$B = -1/A \tag{6.4.1}$$

approaching zero. Although this modification seems trivial, it is crucial for computer applications: we cannot handle infinity by means of a computer but zero is a well defined value and presents no problems.

An operational amplifier and its equivalent network including input admittance, output resistance, and gain are shown in Fig. 6.4.2. The gain may be either a large real constant or a frequency-dependent function. The equation relating the voltages V_j, $V_{j'}$, V_k and the current I_k is

$$(V_j - V_{j'})A = -R_0 I_k + V_k.$$

Introducing (6.4.1)

$$V_j - V_{j'} + BV_k - R_0 B I_k = 0. \tag{6.4.2}$$

Incorporating an OPAMP into the network imposes additional restrictions on the voltages, as expressed by (6.4.2). In addition, the sum of currents at node k must be modified by incorporating the current flowing into the OPAMP. Taking this current as a new variable in the vector $\mathbf{X}$ we increase the modified nodal matrix by one row and one column. Let the size of the matrix before considering the OPAMP be of dimension $m \times m$. With the OPAMP imbedded

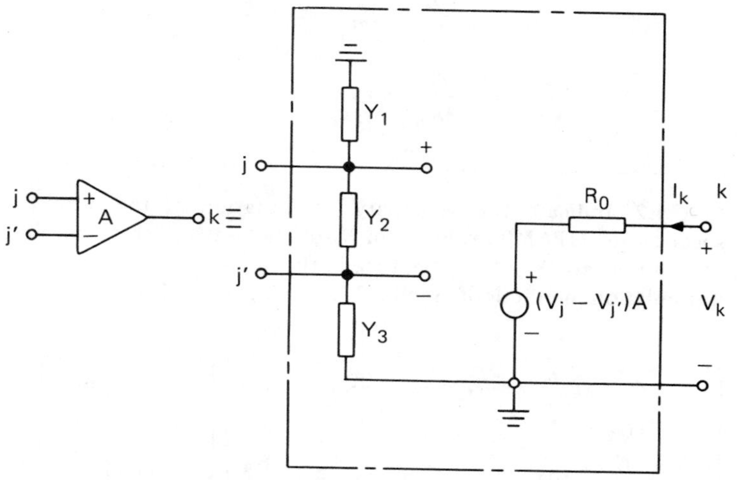

Fig. 6.4.2. Operational amplifier: symbol and equivalent network.

into the network the new matrix equation becomes

$$\begin{array}{c} \\ j \\ j' \\ k \\ m+1 \end{array}\begin{array}{c} \begin{array}{cccc} \quad j \quad & \quad j' \quad & \quad k \quad & m+1 \end{array} \\ \left[\begin{array}{ccc|c} Y_1 + Y_2 & -Y_2 & & \\ -Y_2 & Y_2 + Y_3 & & \\ & & & 1 \\ \hline 1 & -1 & B & -BR_0 \end{array}\right] \end{array}\left[\begin{array}{c} \mathbf{X}_m \\ \\ \hline I_k \end{array}\right] = \left[\begin{array}{c} \mathbf{W}_m \\ \\ \hline 0 \end{array}\right]. \tag{6.4.3}$$

The admittances Y_1, Y_2, Y_3 are added to the previous entries in the nodal admittance section. For each OPAMP, one row and column is added to the matrix. The value B is set numerically equal to zero but its *position in the matrix is recorded and B treated as a variable* during sensitivity calculations.

Assume that the system (6.4.3) has been solved and the vectors $\mathbf{X}$, $\mathbf{X}^a$ are available. Then

$$\frac{\partial \phi}{\partial B} = x^a_{m+1} x_k - R_0 x^a_{m+1} x_{m+1}$$

and

$$\frac{\partial \phi}{\partial R_0} = -B x^a_{m+1} x_{m+1}.$$

In the ideal case both B and R_0 have zero nominal values and the derivatives simplify to

$$\frac{\partial \phi}{\partial B} = x^a_{m+1} x_k$$

$$\frac{\partial \phi}{\partial R_0} = 0.$$

EXAMPLE 6.4.2. Indicate the sensitivity computation of the output voltage with respect to the OPAMP inverse gain B for the network shown in Fig. 6.4.3. Assume zero values for Y_1, Y_2, Y_3 and R_0 in the model.

The formulation method of Section 4.5, coupled with (6.4.2) for $R_0 = 0$ provides

$$\begin{bmatrix} G_1 + G_2 + sC_1 & -G_2 & 0 & -sC_1 \\ -G_2 & G_2 + sC_2 & 0 & 0 \\ 0 & 0 & G_3 + G_4 & -G_4 \\ 0 & 1 & -1 & B \end{bmatrix} \begin{bmatrix} V_1 \\ V_2 \\ V_3 \\ V_{\text{out}} \end{bmatrix} = \begin{bmatrix} G_1 E \\ 0 \\ 0 \\ 0 \end{bmatrix}.$$

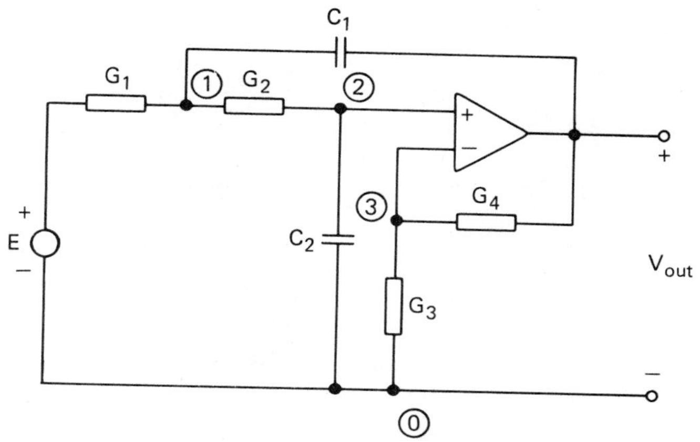

Fig. 6.4.3. Second-order active network with operational amplifier.

For the adjoint system, the vector **d** will have 1 in the fourth entry. Given the component values and the frequency of interest, the above system and the adjoint system are solved with B set to zero. The derivative of the output with respect to B is $\partial V_{out}/\partial B = V_{out}^{a} V_{out}$.

6.5 APPLICATIONS OF THE ADJOINT SYSTEM METHOD

The discussion in the previous sections concentrated on the basic understanding of the method. The output was a linear combination of the solution vector and the variables were usually element values. In this section we will present generalizations useful for many design applications. To facilitate understanding, most steps will be accompanied by an example.

For computer application we will assume that the modified nodal formulation is used and that two real matrices, **G**, **C**, are prepared such that the sum

$$\mathbf{T} = \mathbf{G} + s\mathbf{C} \tag{6.5.1}$$

represents the system matrix. The output will be denoted by ϕ and will, for the most part, be either one entry or the difference of two entries of the vector **X**.

A. Sensitivity of the Absolute Value and Phase

Write the output in the form

$$\phi = |\phi| e^{j\varphi}. \tag{6.5.2}$$

Taking natural logarithms

$$\ln \phi = \ln |\phi| + j\varphi. \tag{6.5.3}$$

Differentiating with respect to a parameter h gives

$$\frac{1}{\phi}\frac{\partial \phi}{\partial h} = \frac{1}{|\phi|}\frac{\partial |\phi|}{\partial h} + j\frac{\partial \varphi}{\partial h}.$$

This complex equation can be split into two real equations

$$\frac{\partial |\phi|}{\partial h} = |\phi| \operatorname{Re}\left(\frac{1}{\phi}\frac{\partial \phi}{\partial h}\right) \tag{6.5.4}$$

$$\frac{\partial \varphi}{\partial h} = \operatorname{Im}\left(\frac{1}{\phi}\frac{\partial \phi}{\partial h}\right) \tag{6.5.5}$$

where Re and Im denote real and imaginary parts. The sensitivity of the absolute value is given in linear units and φ is measured in radians.

Very often the absolute value is measured in decibels. To obtain the corresponding formula rewrite (6.5.3) as

$$\ln \phi = \alpha + j\varphi. \tag{6.5.6}$$

Differentiating with respect to h gives

$$\frac{1}{\phi}\frac{\partial \phi}{\partial h} = \frac{\partial \alpha}{\partial h} + j\frac{\partial \varphi}{\partial h}.$$

The sensitivity $\partial\alpha/\partial h$ is expressed in Nepers. In order to convert it to db we multiply by $20 \log_{10} e$

$$\left.\frac{\partial \alpha}{\partial h}\right|_{\text{db}} = 8.686\frac{\partial \alpha}{\partial h} = 8.686 \operatorname{Re}\left(\frac{1}{\phi}\frac{\partial \phi}{\partial h}\right). \tag{6.5.7}$$

It should be noted that computations can be simplified by absorbing the division by ϕ into the excitation of the adjoint system where the vector **d** is replaced by $(1/\phi)$ **d**.

EXAMPLE 6.5.1. In the network of Fig. 6.5.1 let V_2 be the output and L the parameter. Calculate $\partial|V_2|/\partial h$, $\partial\alpha/\partial h$, $\partial\varphi/\partial h$ for $s = j$.

The system matrix equation is

$$\left[\begin{array}{cc|c} G_1 + G_2 + sC & -G_2 & 0 \\ -G_2 - g & G_2 & 1 \\ \hline 0 & 1 & -sL \end{array}\right] \left[\begin{array}{c} V_1 \\ V_2 \\ \hline I_L \end{array}\right] = \left[\begin{array}{c} J \\ 0 \\ \hline 0 \end{array}\right].$$

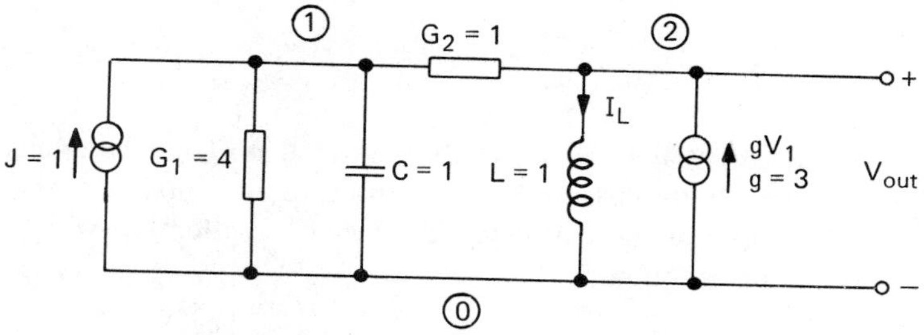

Fig. 6.5.1. Network for sensitivity calculations.

The transfer function is given for checking purposes:

$$Z_{TR} = \frac{sL(G_2 + g)}{s^2 LCG_2 + s(LG_1 G_2 - LG_2 g + C) + G_1 + G_2}\ .$$

The solution vectors are

$$\mathbf{X} \equiv \begin{bmatrix} V_1 \\ V_2 \\ I_L \end{bmatrix} = \frac{1}{20}\begin{bmatrix} 6 + 2j \\ 8 + 16j \\ 16 - 8j \end{bmatrix}; \qquad \mathbf{X}^a \equiv \begin{bmatrix} V_1^a \\ V_2^a \\ I_L^a \end{bmatrix} = \frac{1}{20}\begin{bmatrix} -8 - 16j \\ -6 - 22j \\ -22 + 6j \end{bmatrix}.$$

Then

$$\frac{\partial V_2(j)}{\partial L} = -jI_L^a I_L = (272 + 304j)/400.$$

Formulae (6.5.4), (6.5.5), and (6.5.7) can now be applied:

$$\frac{\partial |V_2|}{\partial L} = \frac{22\sqrt{320}}{400}$$

$$\left.\frac{\partial \alpha}{\partial L}\right|_{\text{db}} = 8.686 \times \frac{22}{20}$$

$$\frac{\partial \varphi}{\partial L} = -\frac{6}{20}\ .$$

The reader may wish to check the results by differentiation of the transfer function and of its absolute value.

B. Sensitivity with Respect to Frequency

In frequency domain analysis the source vector **W** is independent of ω and $\partial\mathbf{T}/\partial\omega$ becomes $j\mathbf{C}$:

$$\frac{\partial \phi}{\partial \omega} = j(\mathbf{X}^a)^t \mathbf{C}\mathbf{X}. \tag{6.5.8a}$$

In computerized equation formulation the matrix **C** may not be available explicitly, only implicitly through equivalent pointers to elements. In that case the frequency sensitivity can be calculated through its relationship with reactive element sensitivities, as follows:

$$\frac{\partial \phi}{\partial \omega} = \frac{1}{\omega}\left(\sum_{\text{capacitors}} C_i \frac{\partial \phi}{\partial C_i} + \sum_{\text{inductors}} L_i \frac{\partial \phi}{\partial L_i} \right). \tag{6.5.8b}$$

Because $\mathbf{X}^a$, $\mathbf{X}$ are generally complex, (6.5.8) will have real and imaginary components. Applying formulae (6.5.4) through (6.5.7) gives

$$\frac{\partial |\phi|}{\partial \omega} = |\phi| \operatorname{Re}\left(\frac{1}{\phi} \frac{\partial \phi}{\partial \omega}\right) \tag{6.5.9}$$

$$\left.\frac{\partial \alpha}{\partial \omega}\right|_{\text{db}} = 8.686 \operatorname{Re}\left(\frac{1}{\phi} \frac{\partial \phi}{\partial \omega}\right) \tag{6.5.10}$$

$$\frac{\partial \varphi}{\partial \omega} = \operatorname{Im}\left(\frac{1}{\phi} \frac{\partial \phi}{\partial \omega}\right). \tag{6.5.11}$$

Note that the group delay is defined as

$$\tau = -\partial \varphi / \partial \omega \tag{6.5.12}$$

and we have thus found an easy way of calculating the group delay by means of the adjoint system. The amplitude sensitivity $\partial \alpha / \partial \omega$ is useful in locating maxima and minima of the amplitude characteristic.

EXAMPLE 6.5.2. Calculate the sensitivity of the output V_2 with respect to the frequency $\omega = 1$ for the network shown in Fig. 6.5.1. Obtain simultaneously the group delay at this frequency.

The system matrix and solutions of both the direct and adjoint systems were obtained in Example 6.5.1. The matrix **C** contains nonzero entries only at locations (1, 1) and (3, 3):

$$\partial V_2 / \partial \omega = j V_1^a V_1 - j I_L^a I_L = (384 + 288j)/400.$$

Then

$$\frac{\partial |V_2|}{\partial \omega} = \frac{24\sqrt{320}}{400}$$

$$\left.\frac{\partial\alpha}{\partial\omega}\right|_{\text{db}} = 8.686 \operatorname{Re}\left(\frac{24 - j12}{20}\right) = \frac{8.686 \times 24}{20}$$

$$\tau = -\frac{\partial\varphi}{\partial\omega} = -\operatorname{Im}\left(\frac{24 - j12}{20}\right) = \frac{12}{20} \text{ sec.}$$

C. Zero Sensitivity

Let us denote the zero of the network function by z_i. The implicit function

$$\phi(s, h)\big|_{s=z_i} = 0$$

relates variations in the zero location to variations in h. Thus h may be considered as the independent variable and z_i as the dependent variable. Differentiating by the chain rule gives

$$\left.\frac{\partial\phi}{\partial s}\frac{\partial s}{\partial h}\right|_{s=z_i} + \frac{\partial\phi}{\partial h} = 0$$

and

$$\frac{\partial z_i}{\partial h} = \left.\frac{\partial s}{\partial h}\right|_{s=z_i} = \left.\frac{-\partial\phi/\partial h}{\partial\phi/\partial s}\right|_{s=z_i}$$

$$= \left.\frac{-\partial\phi/\partial h}{(\mathbf{X}^a)^t\mathbf{C}\mathbf{X}}\right|_{s=z_i} \tag{6.5.13}$$

EXAMPLE 6.5.3. Find the sensitivity of the zero of V_2 with respect to the elements C and g for the network shown in Fig. 6.5.2.

The system matrix is

$$\begin{bmatrix} G_1 + sC & -sC \\ -sC + g & sC + G_2 \end{bmatrix} \begin{bmatrix} V_1 \\ V_2 \end{bmatrix} = \begin{bmatrix} 1 \\ 0 \end{bmatrix}.$$

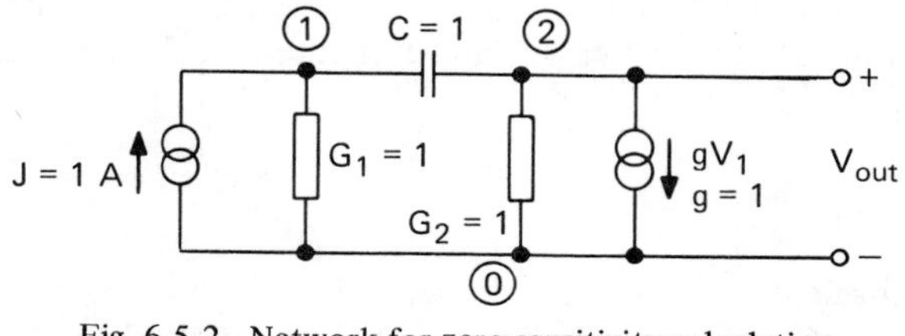

Fig. 6.5.2. Network for zero-sensitivity calculation.

The transfer function

$$Z_{TR} = \frac{sC - g}{sC(G_1 + G_2 + g) + G_1 G_2}$$

and the zero

$$z = \frac{g}{C} = 1$$

are given for reference.

Insert numerical values of the elements and $s = z = 1$. The solutions are

$$\mathbf{X} \equiv \begin{bmatrix} V_1 \\ V_2 \end{bmatrix} = \begin{bmatrix} \frac{1}{2} \\ 0 \end{bmatrix}; \qquad \mathbf{X}^a \equiv \begin{bmatrix} V_1^a \\ V_2^a \end{bmatrix} = \begin{bmatrix} 0 \\ -\frac{1}{2} \end{bmatrix}.$$

Then

$$\frac{\partial V_2}{\partial C} = s(V_1^a - V_2^a)(V_1 - V_2) = \tfrac{1}{4}$$

$$\frac{\partial V_2}{\partial g} = V_2^a V_1 = -\tfrac{1}{4}$$

$$\frac{\partial V_2}{\partial s} = C(V_1^a - V_2^a)(V_1 - V_2) = \tfrac{1}{4}.$$

Inserting into (6.5.13) gives

$$\frac{\partial z}{\partial C} = -\frac{\frac{1}{4}}{\frac{1}{4}} = -1$$

$$\frac{\partial z}{\partial g} = -\frac{-\frac{1}{4}}{\frac{1}{4}} = +1.$$

In this trivial example, differentiation of the algebraic form for the zero would have been much simpler. The reader should appreciate the fact that if the polynomial were of order higher than 3 there would be no algebraic form for the zero as a function of the elements. However, numerical results using (6.5.13) could still be obtained.

D. Pole Sensitivity

This case is equivalent to computing the sensitivity of the zero of the denominator of the network function to a parameter. Let us denote the pole by p_i and let the parameter be h. At the frequency p_i, the matrix $\mathbf{T}$ is singular and the vectors $\mathbf{X}$ and $\mathbf{X}^a$ can no longer be computed directly. To overcome this difficulty we proceed somewhat differently. Consider the factors of $\mathbf{T}$:

$$\mathbf{T} = \mathbf{L}\mathbf{U} \tag{6.5.14}$$

and differentiate with respect to the parameter

$$\frac{\partial \mathbf{T}}{\partial h} = \frac{\partial \mathbf{L}}{\partial h}\mathbf{U} + \mathbf{L}\,\frac{\partial \mathbf{U}}{\partial h}. \tag{6.5.15}$$

Pre- and postmultiply this equation by two (so far unknown) vectors $(\mathbf{X}^a)^t$ and $\mathbf{X}$, respectively, to get the scaler equation:

$$(\mathbf{X}^a)^t\,\frac{\partial \mathbf{T}}{\partial h}\mathbf{X} = (\mathbf{X}^a)^t\,\frac{\partial \mathbf{L}}{\partial h}\mathbf{U}\mathbf{X} + (\mathbf{X}^a)^t\mathbf{L}\,\frac{\partial \mathbf{U}}{\partial h}\mathbf{X}. \tag{6.5.16}$$

The vectors are now defined as the solutions of

$$\mathbf{U}\mathbf{X} = \mathbf{e}_n \tag{6.5.17a}$$

$$\mathbf{L}^t\mathbf{X}^a = l_{nn}\,\mathbf{e}_n \tag{6.5.17b}$$

where $\mathbf{e}_n$ is the nth unit vector and l_{nn} is the (n, n) entry of the matrix $\mathbf{L}$. As $\mathbf{T}$ is singular, $l_{nn} = 0$ and the right-hand side of (6.5.17b) is, in fact, a zero vector. (Partial or full pivoting may be needed to ensure this, and we will consider the influence of permutations later.) This gives us the choice of selecting x_n^a arbitrarily and we choose $x_n^a = 1$. We now show that the definitions (6.5.17) indeed provide the required sensitivity. Substitute (6.5.17) into (6.5.16), giving

$$(\mathbf{X}^a)^t\,\frac{\partial \mathbf{T}}{\partial h}\mathbf{X} = (\mathbf{X}^a)^t\,\frac{\partial \mathbf{L}}{\partial h}\,\mathbf{e}_n + l_{nn}\,\mathbf{e}_n^t\,\frac{\partial \mathbf{U}}{\partial h}\,\mathbf{X}. \tag{6.5.18}$$

Since $\mathbf{L}$ is lower triangular, the product $(\partial \mathbf{L}/\partial h)\,\mathbf{e}_n$ reduces to a vector in which all entries are zero except the last one, which is $\partial l_{nn}/\partial h$, i.e., $(\partial \mathbf{L}/\partial h)\,\mathbf{e}_n = (\partial l_{nn}/\partial h)\,\mathbf{e}_n$. This vector is premultiplied by $(\mathbf{X}^a)^t$ and only its last entry, $x_n^a = 1$, appears in the product. Moreover, $\mathbf{e}_n^t\,\partial \mathbf{U}/\partial h$ will be a zero vector, as $\mathbf{U}$ is upper triangular with $u_{nn} = 1$. These steps reduce (6.5.18) to

$$(\mathbf{X}^a)^t\,\frac{\partial \mathbf{T}}{\partial h}\mathbf{X} = \frac{\partial l_{nn}}{\partial h} \tag{6.5.19}$$

which is the basic equation for computing pole sensitivities. At this point we note that at a pole the relation $l_{nn}(s, h) = 0$ can be used in place of $\phi(s, h) = 0$, the relation required for the zero in the last subsection. Applying (6.5.13), the pole sensitivity becomes

$$\frac{\partial p_i}{\partial h} = \left. \frac{-\partial l_{nn}/\partial h}{\partial l_{nn}/\partial s} \right|_{s=p_i}$$

$$= -\frac{(\mathbf{X}^a)^t(\partial \mathbf{T}/\partial h)\,\mathbf{X}}{(\mathbf{X}^a)^t \mathbf{C}\mathbf{X}}\,. \tag{6.5.20}$$

To summarize the steps:

1. Insert $s = p_i$ into the system matrix and obtain the **LU** factors.
2. Use back substitution to find **X** from (6.5.17a).
3. Use back substitution to solve (6.5.17b) by setting $x_n^a = 1$ and finding $x_{n-1}^a, \ldots$ in turn.
4. Apply (6.5.20) to compute the pole sensitivity.

At times partial or full pivoting may be required in order that the term l_{nn} should become zero. In such cases Eqs. (6.5.14) and (6.5.19) are modified to

$$\mathbf{\Pi}_1 \mathbf{T} \mathbf{\Pi}_2 = \mathbf{LU} \tag{6.5.14$'$}$$

and

$$(\mathbf{X}^a)^t \mathbf{\Pi}_1 \frac{\partial \mathbf{T}}{\partial h} \mathbf{\Pi}_2 \mathbf{X} = \partial l_{nn}/\partial h \tag{6.5.19$'$}$$

where $\mathbf{\Pi}_1$ and $\mathbf{\Pi}_2$ are *permutation matrices.* Equation (6.5.20) is also modified in a similar way. In computing the products on the left side of (6.5.19′) note that $\mathbf{\Pi}_2 \mathbf{X}$ and $\mathbf{\Pi}_1^t \mathbf{X}^a$ are simply rearrangements of the vectors **X** and $\mathbf{X}^a$.

EXAMPLE 6.5.4. Calculate the pole sensitivity of the network shown in Fig. 6.5.1 with respect to the inductor L.

The pole coordinate can be found, for instance, from the transfer function given in Example 6.5.1, $p = -1 + 2j$. Insert this value for s into the system matrix. The **LU** factors are

$$\mathbf{LU} = \begin{bmatrix} 4+2j & 0 & 0 \\ -4 & \dfrac{1+2j}{5} & 0 \\ 0 & 1 & 0 \end{bmatrix} \begin{bmatrix} 1 & \dfrac{-4+2j}{20} & 0 \\ 0 & 1 & 1-2j \\ 0 & 0 & 1 \end{bmatrix}.$$

Use (6.5.17) to find $\mathbf{X}$ and $\mathbf{X}^a$:

$$\mathbf{X} = \begin{bmatrix} 0.5j \\ -1+2j \\ 1 \end{bmatrix}; \qquad \mathbf{X}^a = \begin{bmatrix} 2j \\ -1+2j \\ 1 \end{bmatrix}.$$

Formula (6.5.20) is now used to obtain the sensitivity:

1. Numerator of (6.5.20): $-sI_L^a I_L = 1 - 2j$.
2. Denominator of (6.5.20): $V_1^a V_1 C - I_L^a I_L L = -2$.
3. $$\frac{\partial p}{\partial L} = -\frac{1-2j}{-2} = \frac{1-2j}{2}.$$

E. Sensitivity of the Q and ω_0 of a Pole p or Zero z

Assume that the sensitivity of the pole or zero has been obtained by the above methods, and let the coordinates of a complex conjugate pair of zeros be

$$z, \bar{z} = a \pm jb. \tag{6.5.21}$$

Then

$$Q = \frac{(a^2 + b^2)^{1/2}}{-2a} \tag{6.5.22}$$

and

$$\omega_0 = (a^2 + b^2)^{1/2}. \tag{6.5.23}$$

Differentiating with respect to h gives

$$\frac{dQ}{dh} = \frac{b}{2a^2\omega_0}\left(b\frac{\partial a}{\partial h} - a\frac{\partial b}{\partial h}\right) \tag{6.5.24}$$

$$\frac{d\omega_0}{dh} = \frac{1}{\omega_0}\left(a\frac{\partial a}{\partial h} + b\frac{\partial b}{\partial h}\right). \tag{6.5.25}$$

To simplify the above expressions write the product

$$\bar{z}\frac{\partial z}{\partial h} = (a - jb)\left(\frac{\partial a}{\partial h} + j\frac{\partial b}{\partial h}\right).$$

Then

$$\mathrm{Re}\left(\bar{z}\,\frac{\partial z}{\partial h}\right) = a\,\frac{\partial a}{\partial h} + b\,\frac{\partial b}{\partial h}$$

$$\mathrm{Im}\left(\bar{z}\,\frac{\partial z}{\partial h}\right) = a\,\frac{\partial b}{\partial h} - b\,\frac{\partial a}{\partial h}\,.$$

Inserting into (6.5.24) and (6.5.25) gives

$$\frac{dQ}{dh} = \frac{-b}{2a^2\,\omega_0}\,\mathrm{Im}\left(\bar{z}\,\frac{\partial z}{\partial h}\right) \tag{6.5.26}$$

$$\frac{d\omega_0}{dh} = \frac{1}{\omega_0}\,\mathrm{Re}\left(\bar{z}\,\frac{\partial z}{\partial h}\right). \tag{6.5.27}$$

In the above expression $\partial z/\partial h$ is obtained by applying (6.5.13) for the zero and (6.5.17) and (6.5.20) for the pole.

F. Sensitivity with Respect to Temperature

Sensitivities with respect to variables which are not entries of the system matrix can be calculated by means of the chain rule for differentiation. An example of such a case is the sensitivity of the output to the temperature, e.g., $h = \tau$. Let the mth network element have its temperature dependence expressed by the general relationship

$$E_m = E_{m0}\, f_m(\tau). \tag{6.5.28}$$

Very often the function f_m is represented by the first few terms of its Taylor expansion:

$$E_m = E_{m0}(1 + r_m \tau + \cdots). \tag{6.5.29}$$

Apply the chain rule for differentiation to obtain $\partial\phi/\partial\tau$ with only element m considered:

$$\frac{\partial\phi}{\partial\tau} = \frac{\partial\phi}{\partial E_m}\,\frac{\partial E_m}{\partial\tau}\,. \tag{6.5.30}$$

Here $\partial\phi/\partial E_m$ is the sensitivity with respect to the element E_m, which stands for G, C, L, or some other entry of the matrix. The derivative $\partial E_m/\partial\tau$ is obtained from Eq. (6.5.28):

$$\frac{\partial E_m}{\partial \tau} = E_{mo} \frac{df_m(\tau)}{d\tau} .$$

Specifically, if the linear part of the relationship (6.5.29) is used, then

$$\frac{\partial E_m}{\partial \tau} = E_{mo} r_m .$$

Usually, many elements would be simultaneously influenced by the temperature and the sum over all such sensitivities must be taken:

$$\frac{\partial \phi}{\partial \tau} = \sum_{\text{elements}} E_{mo} \frac{\partial \phi}{\partial E_m} \cdot \frac{df_m(\tau)}{d\tau} . \tag{6.5.31}$$

EXAMPLE 6.5.5. Calculate the sensitivity of the output with respect to the temperature for the network in Fig. 6.4.1. Neglect the parasitics and assume that the temperature coefficient of the capacitor is negligibly small. Let $s = j$.

The system matrix is

$$\begin{bmatrix} G_1 + sC & -sC \\ -sC & G_3 + sC \end{bmatrix} \begin{bmatrix} V_1 \\ V_2 \end{bmatrix} = \begin{bmatrix} 1 \\ 0 \end{bmatrix} .$$

The problem was numerically solved in Example 6.4.1, with the result

$$\mathbf{X} = \begin{bmatrix} (3 - j)/5 \\ (2 + j)/5 \end{bmatrix} ; \qquad \mathbf{X}^a = \begin{bmatrix} (-2 - j)/5 \\ (-3 + j)/5 \end{bmatrix} .$$

Then

$$\frac{\partial V_2}{\partial G_1} = V_1^a V_1 = \frac{-7 - j}{25}$$

$$\frac{\partial V_2}{\partial G_3} = V_2^a V_2 = \frac{-7 - j}{25}$$

and

$$\frac{\partial V_2}{\partial \tau} = \frac{\partial V_2}{\partial G_1} \frac{\partial G_1}{\partial \tau} + \frac{\partial V_2}{\partial G_3} \frac{\partial G_3}{\partial \tau} .$$

Because $G_1 = G_3 = 1$, $\partial G_1/\partial \tau = \partial G_3/\partial \tau = r_m$ if the conductors have the same temperature coefficient and

$$\frac{\partial V_2}{\partial \tau} = 2r_m \frac{-7-j}{25} .$$

G. Thévenin and Norton Equivalent Circuits

In the first chapter it was indicated that the behavior of any network as viewed from a specified port could be interpreted in terms of the Norton and Thévenin equivalents. In a direct attack on the problem, two network analyses are required to generate the equivalent. The first is carried out to determine the open circuit voltage or short circuit current at the port of interest. For the second analysis, the independent current sources are removed, independent voltage sources are shorted, a unit current or voltage source applied at the port of interest, and the voltage or current calculated at this port. These operations are illustrated in Fig. 6.5.3, where the independent sources have been extracted from N and, for simplicity, only one independent source of each kind is shown.

In terms of system equations the above operations become

$$\left.\begin{aligned} \mathbf{T}\mathbf{X}_i &= \mathbf{W}_i \\ \phi_i &= \mathbf{d}^t\mathbf{X}_i \end{aligned}\right\} \quad i = 1, 2 \qquad \begin{aligned}(6.5.32)\\(6.5.33)\end{aligned}$$

where $\mathbf{W}_i$ are the two right-hand-side vectors representing sources and ϕ_i, $i = 1, 2$, are the required outputs.

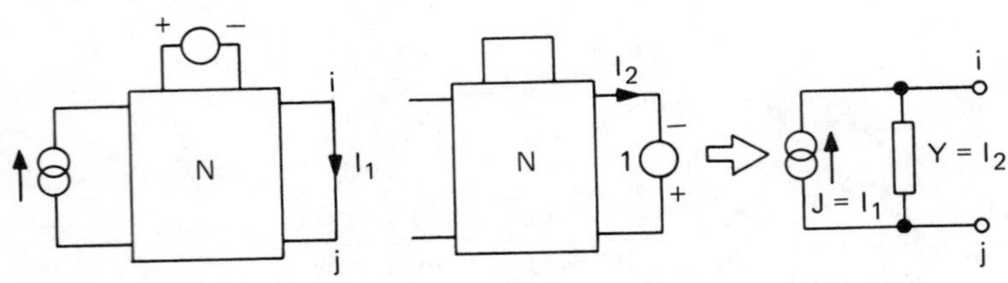

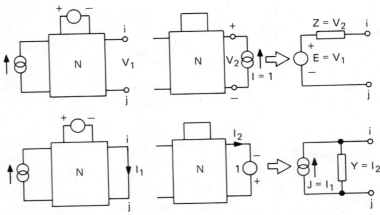

Fig. 6.5.3. Steps in determining the Thévenin and Norton equivalent circuits.

Using Eq. (6.1.13) we obtain

$$\phi_i = -(\mathbf{X}^a)^t \mathbf{W}_i. \tag{6.5.34}$$

In summary, both outputs in (6.5.33) are obtained by solving *only* the adjoint system (6.1.10) and then evaluating the vector products (6.5.34).

H. Noise Analysis

Shot noise, thermal noise, and flicker noise are the three important types of noise in electronic circuits. The first two can be modeled in terms of physical parameters, while the third requires empirical data. Noise is usually modeled by associating independent uncorrelated noise sources with resistors and semiconductor devices. The object of the analysis is to determine the contributions that the input signal and the noise sources make to the output. Noise sources differ from ordinary sources in that no phase information is available; only their magnitude is specified. This precludes the direct application of superposition and the contribution of each noise source to the output noise must be considered independently. A direct attempt at noise analysis proceeds by first analyzing the network with only independent sources present and then repeating the analysis for each noise source in turn. The total output noise amplitude is then the square root of the sum of squares of the amplitudes of the individual noise contributions. For a complicated circuit the number of noise sources may be very large, but using (6.1.13) *only one solution of the adjoint system* is needed [2].

Mathematically, our problem is formulated as solving the equations

$$\mathbf{T}\mathbf{X}_i = t_i \mathbf{W}_i, \qquad i = 0, 1, \ldots, m \tag{6.5.35}$$

with t_i indicating the value of the ith source, and then forming the output as a combination of solutions:

$$\phi_i = \mathbf{d}^t \mathbf{X}_i. \tag{6.5.36}$$

The subscript $i = 0$ represents the applied signal and there are a total of m noise sources.

The theoretical steps for deriving the procedure are exactly those discussed at the end of Section 6.1, except that there are now $m + 1$ sources. The adjoint system (6.1.10) is solved first and the ϕ_i obtained by means of (6.1.13). As each $\mathbf{W}_i$ contains at most two nonzero entries of the form ± 1, each application of (6.1.13) involves only one subtraction. The signal amplitude at the output is $|\phi_0|$ and the noise amplitude is

$$A_{\text{noise}} = \left(\sum_{i=1}^{m} |\phi_i|^2 \right)^{1/2}. \tag{6.5.37}$$

The coefficients t_i in (6.5.35) depend on the definition of the element. For instance, for a conductance

$$t_i = \sqrt{4kT\Delta f G_i}$$

multiplies an *equivalent* unit noise *current source* in parallel with G_i. Here T is the temperature in degrees kelvin, Δf is the bandwidth under consideration, and k is Boltzmann's constant.

EXAMPLE 6.5.6. Calculate the signal-to-noise ratio for the network in Fig. 6.5.4. Ignore the noise due to the VCT.

The system equation is

$$\begin{bmatrix} G_1 + G_2 & -G_2 \\ -G_2 - g & G_2 + G_3 \end{bmatrix} \begin{bmatrix} V_1 \\ V_2 \end{bmatrix} = \begin{bmatrix} J \\ 0 \end{bmatrix}$$

where $J = 2$. Numerically, the adjoint system is

$$\begin{bmatrix} 2 & -4 \\ -1 & 3 \end{bmatrix} \begin{bmatrix} V_1^a \\ V_2^a \end{bmatrix} = - \begin{bmatrix} 0 \\ 1 \end{bmatrix}$$

and its solution is

$$\begin{bmatrix} V_1^a \\ V_2^a \end{bmatrix} = \begin{bmatrix} -2 \\ -1 \end{bmatrix}.$$

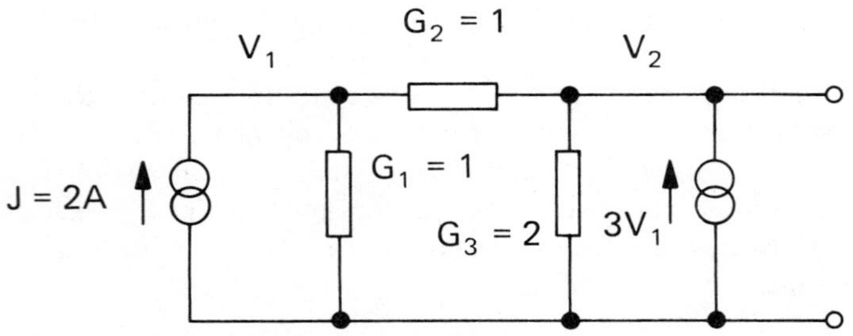

Fig. 6.5.4. Example for noise calculation.

Using (6.1.13), the signal output is

$$\phi_0 = -[-2 \quad -1] \begin{bmatrix} 2 \\ 0 \end{bmatrix} = 4.$$

The noise outputs ϕ_1, ϕ_2, ϕ_3 for G_1, G_2, G_3, respectively, are

$$\phi_1 = -[-2 \quad -1] \begin{bmatrix} 1 \\ 0 \end{bmatrix} t_1 = 2t_1$$

$$\phi_2 = -[-2 \quad -1] \begin{bmatrix} 1 \\ -1 \end{bmatrix} t_2 = t_2$$

$$\phi_3 = -[-2 \quad -1] \begin{bmatrix} 0 \\ 1 \end{bmatrix} t_3 = t_3.$$

Applying (6.5.37)

$$A_{\text{noise}} = (4t_1^2 + t_2^2 + t_3^2)^{1/2} = \sqrt{4kT\Delta f}\ (4G_1 + G_2 + G_3)^{1/2}$$
$$= \sqrt{28kT\Delta f}$$

and the signal-to-noise ratio is

$$\rho = \frac{4}{\sqrt{28kT\Delta f}}.$$

I. Sensitivity of a Generalized Output

Up to this point we have considered outputs of the form $\phi = \mathbf{d}^t\mathbf{X}$, i.e., as a linear combination of components of the solution vector. The output definition can be generalized to include scalar functions of the form

$$\psi = \phi(\mathbf{X}, \mathbf{h}) \tag{6.5.38}$$

where ϕ is a differentiable function of $\mathbf{X}$ and $\mathbf{h}$. Different symbols ψ and ϕ are used in (6.5.38) only to simplify notation in the following derivation. Differentiating ψ with respect to a component of $\mathbf{h}$ gives

$$\frac{d\psi}{dh} = \frac{\partial\phi}{\partial h} + \sum \frac{\partial\phi}{\partial x_i}\frac{dx_i}{dh} = \frac{\partial\phi}{\partial h} + \frac{\partial\phi}{\partial \mathbf{X}}\frac{\partial \mathbf{X}}{\partial h} \tag{6.5.39}$$

where $\partial\phi/\partial\mathbf{X}$ is a *row vector.* Substituting for $\partial\mathbf{X}/\partial h$ from (6.1.5)

$$\frac{d\psi}{dh} = \frac{\partial\phi}{\partial h} - \frac{\partial\phi}{\partial\mathbf{X}}\mathbf{T}^{-1}\left(\frac{\partial\mathbf{T}}{\partial h}\mathbf{X} - \frac{\partial\mathbf{W}}{\partial h}\right) \tag{6.5.40}$$

which corresponds to Eq. (6.1.8). The place of $\mathbf{d}^t$ is now taken by $\partial\phi/\partial\mathbf{X}$ and for computations the adjoint system is defined by

$$\mathbf{T}^t\mathbf{X}^a = -(\partial\phi/\partial\mathbf{X})^t. \tag{6.5.41}$$

Unlike (6.1.10) which could be solved even before (6.1.1), Eq. (6.5.41) can only be solved after (6.1.1), as the right-hand-side vector will depend on $\mathbf{X}$. The sensitivity equation (6.1.11) now takes the following form:

$$\frac{d\psi}{dh} = \frac{\partial\phi}{\partial h} + (\mathbf{X}^a)^t\frac{\partial\mathbf{T}}{\partial h}\mathbf{X} - (\mathbf{X}^a)^t\frac{\partial\mathbf{W}}{\partial h}. \tag{6.5.42}$$

EXAMPLE 6.5.7. Consider the network shown in Fig. 6.5.2 at the "frequency" $s = 2$. Calculate the sensitivity of the generalized output

$$\psi = \phi(V_1, V_2) = 7(V_1 - V_2)^2$$

with respect to g and C.

The system equations are

$$\begin{bmatrix} G_1 + sC & -sC \\ -sC + g & G_2 + sC \end{bmatrix}\begin{bmatrix} V_1 \\ V_2 \end{bmatrix} = \begin{bmatrix} 1 \\ 0 \end{bmatrix}.$$

The solution is

$$\mathbf{X} \equiv \begin{bmatrix} V_1 \\ V_2 \end{bmatrix} = \begin{bmatrix} \frac{3}{7} \\ \frac{1}{7} \end{bmatrix}$$

$$\frac{\partial\phi}{\partial V_1} = 14(V_1 - V_2) = 4$$

$$\frac{\partial\phi}{\partial V_2} = -14(V_1 - V_2) = -4.$$

The right-hand side of the adjoint system is defined by the above result:

$$\begin{bmatrix} 3 & -1 \\ -2 & 3 \end{bmatrix}\begin{bmatrix} V_1^a \\ V_2^a \end{bmatrix} = -\begin{bmatrix} 4 \\ -4 \end{bmatrix}$$

and its solution is

$$\mathbf{X}^a \equiv \begin{bmatrix} V_1^a \\ V_2^a \end{bmatrix} = \begin{bmatrix} -\frac{8}{7} \\ \frac{4}{7} \end{bmatrix}.$$

Since ψ does not depend directly on any element, $\partial\phi/\partial h = 0$ and

$$\frac{\partial \psi}{\partial g} = V_2^a V_1 = \tfrac{4}{7}\,\tfrac{3}{7} = \tfrac{12}{49}$$

$$\frac{\partial \psi}{\partial C} = s(V_1^a - V_2^a)(V_1 - V_2) = 2(-\tfrac{12}{7})(\tfrac{2}{7}) = \tfrac{-48}{49}\,.$$

6.6. HIGHER-ORDER DERIVATIVES

Obtaining higher-order derivatives is, in principle, as simple as the first-order derivatives, only more expensive computationally. We will derive relations for second-order derivatives. Differentiate (6.1.1) with respect to h_1:

$$\frac{\partial \mathbf{T}}{\partial h_1}\mathbf{X} + \mathbf{T}\frac{\partial \mathbf{X}}{\partial h_1} = \frac{\partial \mathbf{W}}{\partial h_1}\,. \tag{6.6.1}$$

Assume, for simplicity, that the sources do not depend on the parameters. This sets the right-hand side of (6.6.1) equal to zero. Differentiate again with respect to parameter h_2:

$$\frac{\partial^2 \mathbf{T}}{\partial h_1 \partial h_2}\mathbf{X} + \frac{\partial \mathbf{T}}{\partial h_1}\frac{\partial \mathbf{X}}{\partial h_2} + \frac{\partial \mathbf{T}}{\partial h_2}\frac{\partial \mathbf{X}}{\partial h_1} + \mathbf{T}\frac{\partial^2 \mathbf{X}}{\partial h_1 \partial h_2} = \mathbf{0}$$

from which

$$\frac{\partial^2 \mathbf{X}}{\partial h_1 \partial h_2} = -\mathbf{T}^{-1}\left(\frac{\partial^2 \mathbf{T}}{\partial h_1 \partial h_2}\mathbf{X} + \frac{\partial \mathbf{T}}{\partial h_1}\frac{\partial \mathbf{X}}{\partial h_2} + \frac{\partial \mathbf{T}}{\partial h_2}\frac{\partial \mathbf{X}}{\partial h_1}\right).$$

Let $\phi = \mathbf{d}^t\mathbf{X}$ be the output. Premultiplying by $\mathbf{d}^t$ gives

$$\frac{\partial^2 \phi}{\partial h_1 \partial h_2} = \mathbf{d}^t\frac{\partial^2 \mathbf{X}}{\partial h_1 \partial h_2} = -\mathbf{d}^t\mathbf{T}^{-1}\left(\frac{\partial^2 \mathbf{T}}{\partial h_1 \partial h_2}\mathbf{X} + \frac{\partial \mathbf{T}}{\partial h_1}\frac{\partial \mathbf{X}}{\partial h_2} + \frac{\partial \mathbf{T}}{\partial h_2}\frac{\partial \mathbf{X}}{\partial h_1}\right). \tag{6.6.2}$$

Introduce the same adjoint system as before, i.e., insert (6.1.10):

$$\frac{\partial^2 \phi}{\partial h_1 \partial h_2} = (\mathbf{X}^a)^t \left(\frac{\partial^2 \mathbf{T}}{\partial h_1 \partial h_2} \mathbf{X} + \frac{\partial \mathbf{T}}{\partial h_1} \frac{\partial \mathbf{X}}{\partial h_2} + \frac{\partial \mathbf{T}}{\partial h_2} \frac{\partial \mathbf{X}}{\partial h_1} \right). \tag{6.6.3}$$

Equation (6.6.3) requires the knowledge of the vectors $\partial \mathbf{X}/\partial h_1$ and $\partial \mathbf{X}/\partial h_2$. Assume that we have applied the **LU** decomposition to the matrix **T**. The desired vectors of the derivatives of **X** with respect to h_1, h_2 can be obtained in two ways. If the number of parameters with respect to which the second derivatives are required is large (larger than the dimensions of the matrix **T**), they are obtained by repeated application of the adjoint approach by considering each component of **X** as an output. In other words, we must apply n forward and back substitutions. On the other hand, if the number of parameters is small, systems of the form (6.1.4) are solved directly to generate the vectors $\partial \mathbf{X}/\partial h_i$:

$$\mathbf{T} \frac{\partial \mathbf{X}}{\partial h_i} = - \frac{\partial \mathbf{T}}{\partial h_i} \mathbf{X}.$$

The number of forward and back substitutions in this case equals the number of parameters.

Formula (6.6.3) simplifies when the parameters are element values, as $\partial^2 \mathbf{T}/\partial h_i \partial h_j$ becomes zero and $\partial \mathbf{T}/\partial h_i$ can be written as an outer product of two vectors.

EXAMPLE 6.6.1. Calculate the second derivatives $\partial^2 V_1/(\partial G \partial L)$ for the network in Fig. 6.6.1. Let $s = j$.

This simple network was selected as otherwise the explanation becomes too involved. The system matrix is

$$\begin{bmatrix} G + sC & 1 \\ 1 & -sL \end{bmatrix} \begin{bmatrix} V_1 \\ I_L \end{bmatrix} = \begin{bmatrix} 1 \\ 0 \end{bmatrix}.$$

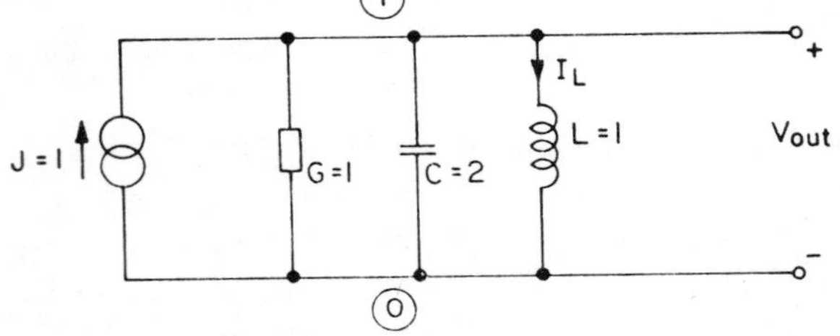

Fig. 6.6.1. Network for second-order sensitivity calculation.

The output

$$V_1 = \frac{sL}{s^2LC + sLG + 1}$$

is given for reference.

The solutions are

$$\mathbf{X} \equiv \begin{bmatrix} V_1 \\ I_L \end{bmatrix} = \begin{bmatrix} (1-j)/2 \\ (-1-j)/2 \end{bmatrix}; \qquad \mathbf{X}^a \equiv \begin{bmatrix} V^a \\ I_L^a \end{bmatrix} = \begin{bmatrix} (-1+j)/2 \\ (1+j)/2 \end{bmatrix}.$$

The derivatives $\partial\mathbf{X}/\partial G$ and $\partial\mathbf{X}/\partial L$ are obtained by solving the system

$$\mathbf{T}\frac{\partial\mathbf{X}}{\partial h} = -\frac{\partial\mathbf{T}}{\partial h}\mathbf{X}.$$

This leads to

$$\frac{\partial\mathbf{X}}{\partial G} = \begin{bmatrix} j/2 \\ \frac{1}{2} \end{bmatrix}; \qquad \frac{\partial\mathbf{X}}{\partial L} = \begin{bmatrix} -\frac{1}{2} \\ (1+2j)/2 \end{bmatrix}.$$

Applying formula (6.6.3) gives

$$\frac{\partial^2 V_1}{\partial G \partial L} = (-j)\, I_L^a \frac{\partial I_L}{\partial G} + V_1^a \frac{\partial V_1}{\partial L} = \frac{1-j}{2}.$$

The result is confirmed by differentiating the symbolic function with respect to G and L and by inserting the element values and $s = j$.

6.7. EXAMPLES

Two larger examples will be given in this section for the application of the methods discussed. The first demonstrates the calculation of group delay. For ideal transmission without distortion, the amplitude as well as the group delay responses should be constant. A Chebychev filter represents a fair approximation for the amplitude response requirements in the frequency band (0, 1) rad/sec, but its group delay generally has a large peak at the edge of the pass-band. Specifically, consider the fourth-order Chebychev filter shown in Fig. 6.7.1(a), designed for 0.5 db ripple in the pass-band. Its group delay is shown as curve a in Fig. 6.7.2. All-pass networks can add delay such that the overall delay is closer to a constant. This is called *group delay compensation*. The introduction of a compensation network, as shown in Fig. 6.7.1(b), leads to curve b in Fig.

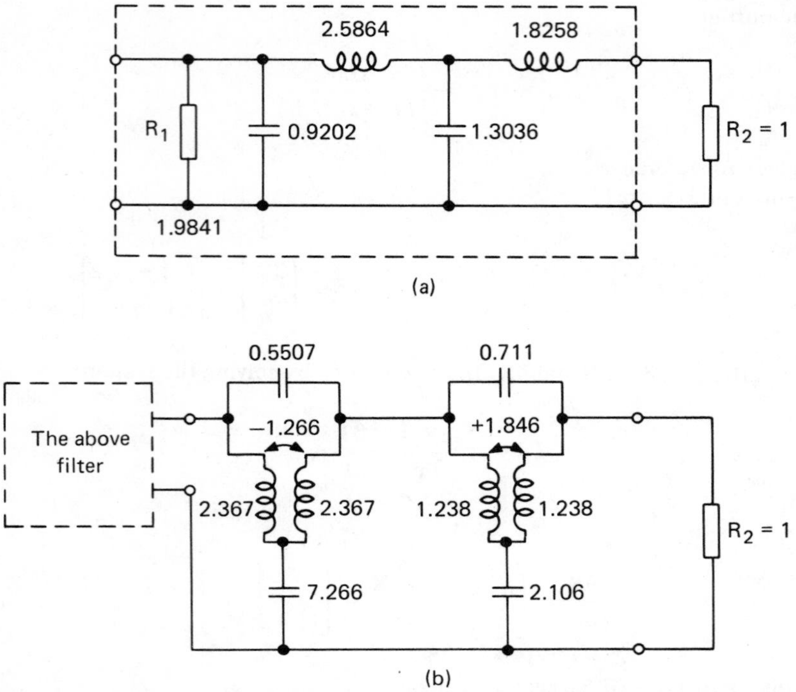

Fig. 6.7.1. Fourth-order Chebychev filter and compensation of its group delay.

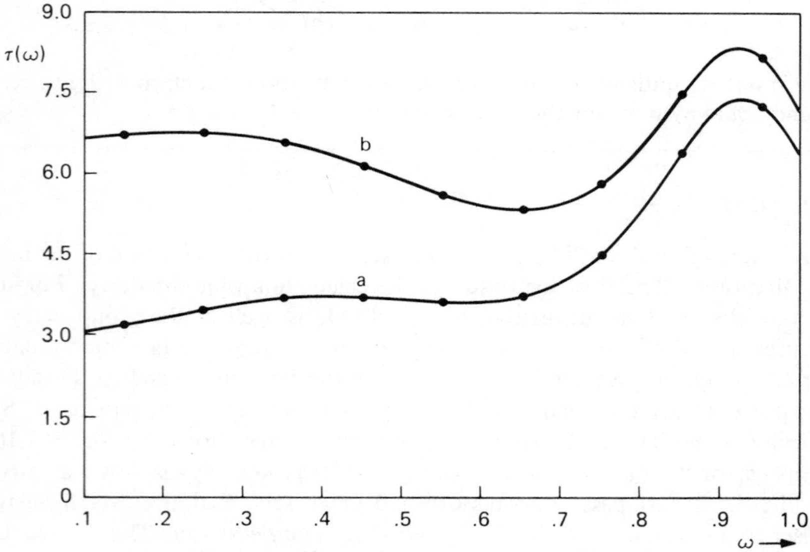

Fig. 6.7.2. Group delay responses of the filters in Fig. 6.7.1.

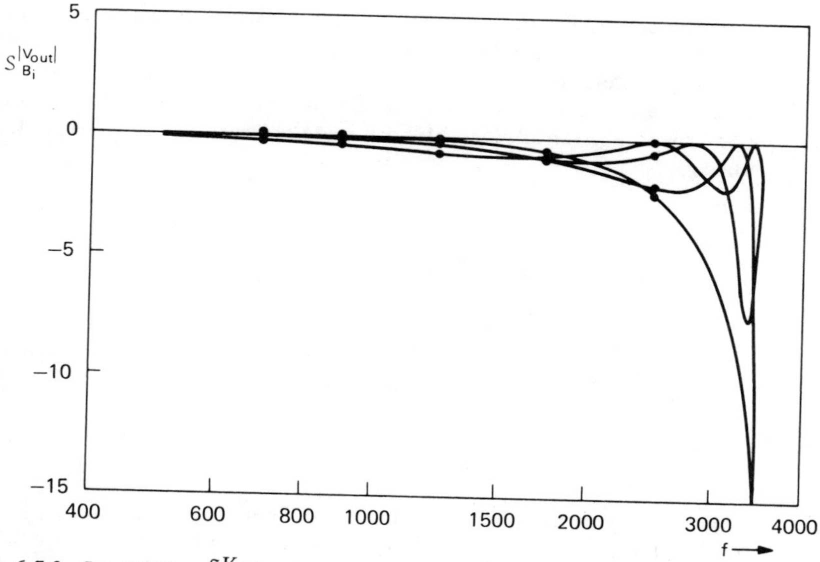

Fig. 6.7.3. Sensitivities $\mathcal{S}_{B_i}^{V_{out}}$ of the ninth-order Cauer-parameter filter shown in Fig. 4.10.2 with respect to the operational amplifiers 1, 3, 5, and 7. Curves with respect to OPAMPs 2, 4, 6, and 8 are the same as those for 1, 3, 5, and 7, respectively.

6.7.2. The performance could be further improved by optimization techniques and by addition of more all-pass sections.

The second example considers the ninth-order Cauer-parameter active filter already discussed in Section 4.10 (Fig. 4.10.2). We wish to know the $\mathcal{S}$ sensitivity of the output with respect to the operational amplifiers 1, 3, 5, and 7. The results are shown in Fig. 6.7.3. Curves with respect to OPAMPs 2, 4, 6, and 8 are the same as those for 1, 3, 5, and 7, respectively.

PROBLEMS

P.6.1. Find the sensitivity of both node voltages of the network shown in Fig. P.6.1 with respect to the conductance G_3. Use the sensitivity network method.

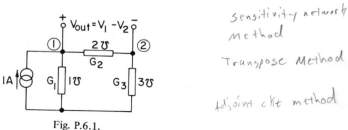

sensitivity network method

Transpose Method

Adjoint ckt method

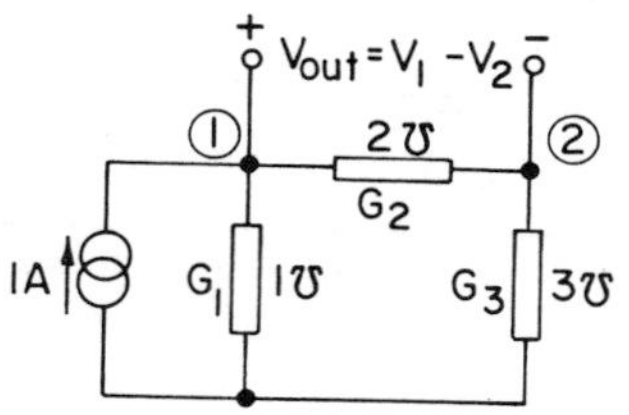

Fig. P.6.1.

P.6.2. Find the sensitivity of the output of the network shown in Fig. P.6.1 with respect to all conductances and to the current source. Use the transpose system method.

P.6.3. Apply the sensitivity network method to the network shown in Fig. P.6.3 to obtain sensitivities of both node voltages to the transconductance *g*.

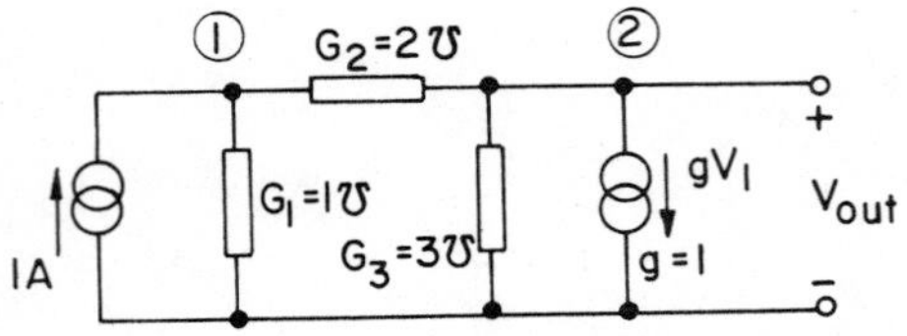

Fig. P.6.3.

P.6.4. Apply the transpose system method to the network shown in Fig. P.6.3 to find the sensitivity of the output to changes of all elements and to changes of the source.

P.6.5. Apply the transpose system method to the networks shown in Fig. P.6.5 and find the sensitivity of V_2 with respect to all elements. Let $\omega = 1$ rad/sec.

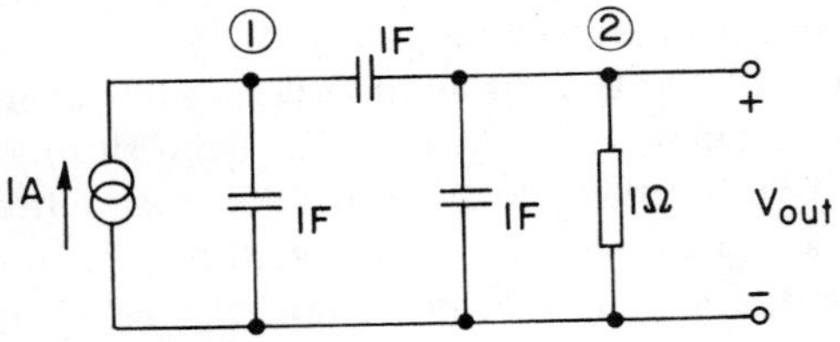

(a)

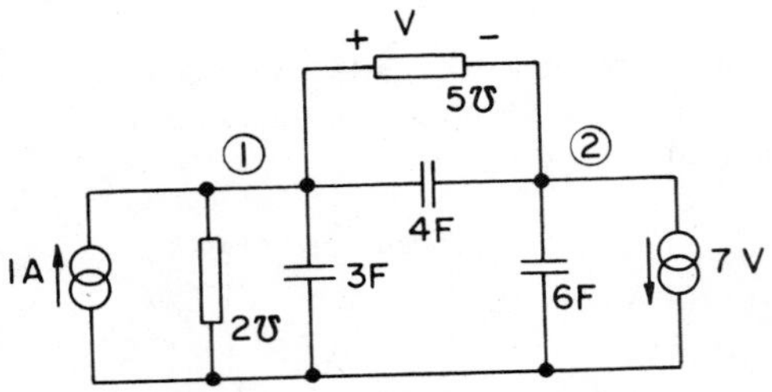

(b)

Fig. P.6.5.

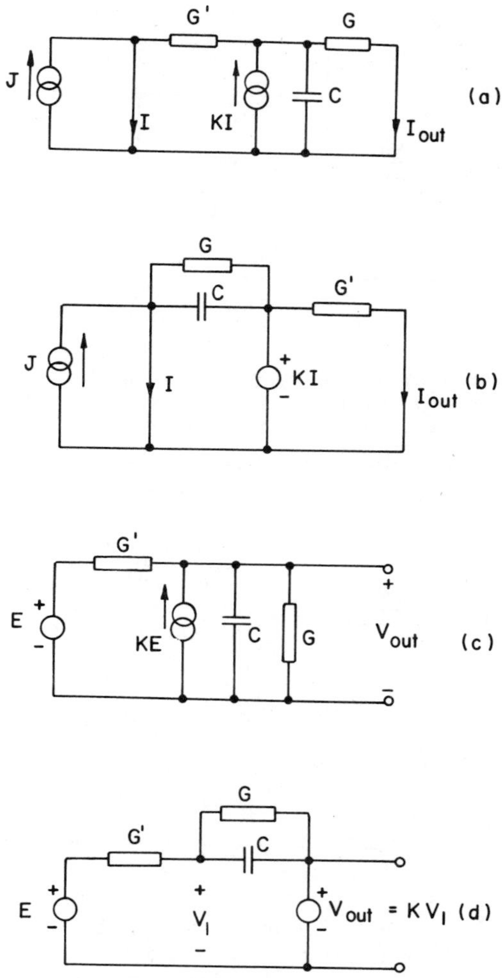

Fig. P.6.6.

P.6.6. For the networks shown in Fig. P.6.6 use formulations which result in system matrices of the least size. Applying the transpose system method, calculate the sensitivity of the output with respect to all elements. Keep the elements and the frequency s as symbols.

P.6.7. Calculate the transfer function sensitivity $S_h^{V_{out}}$ for the network shown in Fig. P.6.7, h being the inverted gain of the OPAMP, $B = -1/A$, and the parasitic capacitance. Use the method of Section 6.4.

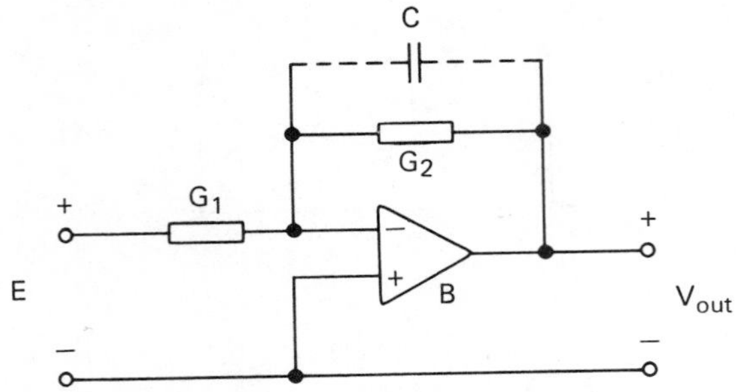

Fig. P.6.7.

P.6.8. Calculate the transfer function sensitivity $S_B^{V_{out}}$ for the network shown in Fig. P.6.8. Reduce the system matrix to 2 × 2 before proceeding with the method of Section 6.4. Check by deriving the transfer function and by differentiating with respect to B.

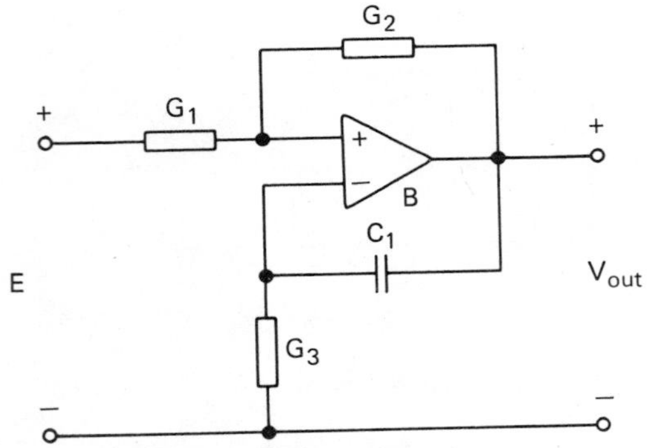

Fig. P.6.8.

P.6.9. Calculate $\partial|V_{out}|/\partial h$, $\partial\phi/\partial h$, and $\tau(\omega)$ for the network shown in Fig. P.6.5(a). Let h be the resistor. Evaluate at $s = j1$.

P.6.10. Using the method of Section 6.5(D), calculate the sensitivity $\partial(\text{pole})/\partial h$ for both poles of the network shown in Fig. P.6.10. Let h be G_1, G_2, G_3.

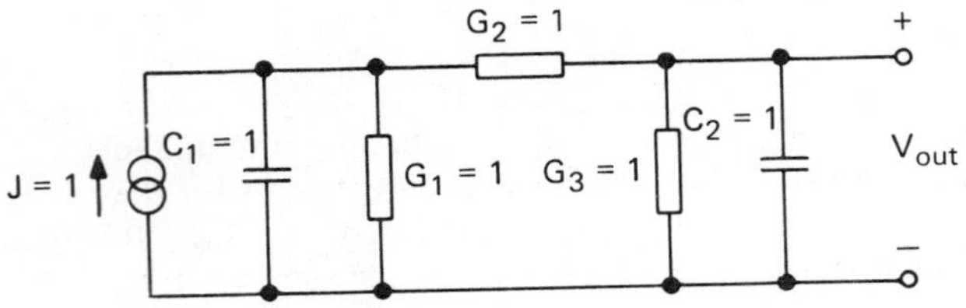

Fig. P.6.10.

P.6.11. Find the overall output sensitivity to temperature changes in the conductances of the networks shown in Figs. P.6.1 and P.6.3. Let $G_i = G_i^0(1 + 10^{-4}\tau)$.

P.6.12. For the network shown in Fig. P.6.3 find the sensitivity of the power dissipated in G_3 to changes of G_3.

P.6.13. The group delay can be computed through the solution of two related systems of equations. Show how its sensitivity to any number of parameters may be found using only two additional solutions.

REFERENCES

1. S. W. Director and R. A. Rohrer: Automated network design—the frequency domain case. *IEEE Transactions on Circuit Theory*, Vol. CT-16, pp. 330-337, August 1969. Two more papers by the same authors appeared in the same issue.
2. R. A. Rohrer, L. Nagel, R. Meyer, and L. Weber: Computationally efficient electronic circuit noise calculations. *IEEE Journal of Solid State Circuits*, Vol. SC-6, pp. 204–213, August 1971.

CHAPTER 7
Network Functions in the Frequency Domain

Network functions were introduced in Section 1.9. They are defined for linear networks which have no initial conditions. For sufficiently small signals, nonlinear networks may be linearized in a small region around the operating point and in this case the functions can be defined for networks with transistors and diodes.

In this chapter we are concerned with the numerical generation of these functions. Section 7.1 discusses basic properties of the functions and introduces two forms in which the complex frequency s is retained as the variable; in one case, the function is defined as the ratio of two polynomials of s, in the other as products of factors containing the poles and zeros. The two definitions are equivalent but require different computational procedures.

The principle for obtaining the network function as the ratio of two polynomials is discussed in Section 7.2. It is based on polynomial interpolation with an arbitrary selection of frequency points. Since there is freedom in this selection, Sections 7.3 and 7.4 show that the best interpolation possible uses complex points uniformly distributed on the unit circle. An algorithm to generate the functions is given in Section 7.5.

In order to obtain the network function in the form of poles and zeros, iterative methods must be used. Two possible ways exist. In the first, polynomial forms are created and the polynomial roots found. Methods which can do this are described in Sections 7.6 and 7.7. In the second, we proceed with the system matrix equation and find the poles and zeros directly. This can be done by the *QZ* algorithm. The theory of the *QZ* algorithm is too complex to be treated in this book. However, the software is available in standard packages and Section 7.8 provides information on its use for network problems. An example demonstrating both approaches is given in Section 7.9.

The algorithm described in Section 7.5 and calculation of zeros and poles from the system matrix by means of the *QZ* algorithm are coded in the program in Appendix D.

7.1. NETWORK FUNCTIONS, POLES AND ZEROS

Let a network be excited either by a voltage or by a current source. Its system equation is

$$\mathbf{TX} = \mathbf{W}. \tag{7.1.1}$$

The solution vector $\mathbf{X}$ may be composed of voltages and currents. Denote the source by either V_{in} or I_{in} and the output by either V_{out} or I_{out}. The network function is defined as the *ratio of the output variable to the input variable.* If the network has one input, six network functions can be defined: Z_{in}, Y_{in}, Z_{TR}, Y_{TR}, T_V and T_I, as given in Section 1.9. These functions can be defined only if *the network has no initial conditions.* If several outputs are considered, appropriate subscripts must be used.

Let us solve (7.1.1) for $\mathbf{X}$ and let the output F be a linear combination of the $\mathbf{X}$ vector:

$$F = \mathbf{d}^t\mathbf{X}. \tag{7.1.2}$$

Formally,

$$F = \mathbf{d}^t\mathbf{T}^{-1}\mathbf{W} = \mathbf{d}^t \frac{\text{adj } \mathbf{T}}{\det \mathbf{T}} \mathbf{W} \tag{7.1.3}$$

and if cancellation of terms in the numerator and denominator does not occur, we see that all network functions will have the same denominator, equal to the determinant of the system matrix $\mathbf{T}$.

Recalling that the system matrix $\mathbf{T}$ has the form

$$\mathbf{T} = \mathbf{G} + s\mathbf{C}$$

we see that the determinant of $\mathbf{T}$ and each entry of adj $\mathbf{T}$ will be polynomials in s and the immittance function F will be a rational function of s. Two equivalent forms of F will be considered in this chapter. The first is based on the representation of F as a ratio of polynomials:

$$F(s) = \frac{\sum_{i=0}^{n} a_i s^i}{\sum_{i=0}^{m} b_i s^i} \tag{7.1.4}$$

with a_i, b_i being fixed numbers. The second representation is based on the roots of the numerator and denominator of (7.1.4)

$$F(s) = K \frac{\prod_{i=1}^{n} (s - z_i)}{\prod_{i=1}^{m} (s - p_i)} \tag{7.1.5}$$

where the z_i are the *zeros* and p_i the *poles* of the particular function.

7.2. COMPUTER GENERATION OF NETWORK FUNCTIONS

The problem of generating symbolic functions with elements and the frequency s being variables will be discussed in Chapter 8. In this chapter we consider the simpler problem where all elements are assigned values and only the frequency is kept as a variable.

The network functions have the form

$$F(s) = \frac{N(s)}{D(s)} \tag{7.2.1}$$

$N(s)$ and $D(s)$ being defined either as in (7.1.4) or (7.1.5). Let us first discuss the motivation for obtaining one of these functions. Assume that the problem is to calculate the amplitude response of a network with the system equation (7.1.1). For each frequency, the matrix must be decomposed into its **LU** factors and the vector **X** found by forward and back substitution. This involves $n^3/3$ operations if sparse matrix methods are not used. If the function (7.1.4) can be obtained cheaply, then evaluation for each frequency is trivial. Another advantage of the functions (7.1.4) or (7.1.5) is the possibility of calculating the time-domain response either by exact or numerical Laplace transform inversion. Both methods are accurate and the numerical inversion will be discussed later. Time-domain solution by means of (7.1.1) is, of course, possible as well.

Methods for direct calculation of the poles and zeros will be given in Sections 7.7 and 7.8. Here we are interested in the generation of the rational form (7.1.4).

Consider the tableau or the modified nodal formulations. In both cases the frequency-dependent elements are entered in the form having s in the numerator (no terms with $1/s$ are permitted). The determinant of **T** in (7.1.1) will be a polynomial in s and the same will be true for the numerator in (7.2.1). Let us select an arbitrary value of s, s_i, insert into (7.1.1), and obtain the **LU** decomposition:

$$\mathbf{LUX} = \mathbf{W}. \tag{7.2.2}$$

The value of the determinant (denominator) is given by the product of the diagonal entries of the matrix **L**:

$$D(s_i) = \det \mathbf{T}(s_i) = \det \mathbf{L}(s_i) = \prod_{j=1}^{\text{size of } L} l_{jj}. \tag{7.2.3}$$

Solve (7.2.2) by forward and back substitution and let $\mathbf{d}^t\mathbf{X}$ represent the output of the network. One number is obtained but we know that it represents the ratio of two polynomials, evaluated at s_i:

$$F(s_i) = \frac{N(s_i)}{D(s_i)}. \tag{7.2.4}$$

Since the value of $D(s_i)$ is already known from (7.2.3), the numerator value is obtained as

$$N(s_i) = D(s_i)\, F(s_i). \tag{7.2.5}$$

This separation of the numerator and denominator was made possible by our insistence on having no term with $1/s$ in the formulation.

Let us now select additional values for s_i and repeat the above steps. As a result we will have sets of points $(s_i, N(s_i))$ and $(s_i, D(s_i))$, and we seek the coefficients of the polynomials N and D. This is a well known mathematical problem called *polynomial interpolation.* The next two sections provide the theoretical background for the best selection of points s_i.

7.3. UNIT CIRCLE POLYNOMIAL INTERPOLATION

Assume that there are $n + 1$ distinct points $(x_i, y_i = f(x_i))$, $i = 0, 1, \ldots, n$. Both x_i and y_i may be real or complex numbers. We wish to find the coefficients of the polynomial

$$P_n(x) = \sum_{j=0}^{n} a_j x^j \tag{7.3.1}$$

such that the polynomial passes through the given points.

Inserting x_i into the polynomial (7.3.1), obtain the set of equations

$$a_0 + a_1 x_i + a_2 x_i^2 + \cdots + a_n x_i^n = y_i, \qquad i = 0, 1, \ldots, n$$

with unknown a_j. Since there are $n+1$ unknown coefficients and the same number of equations, we can write the matrix equation

$$\begin{bmatrix} 1 & x_0 & x_0^2 \cdots x_0^n \\ 1 & x_1 & x_1^2 \cdots x_1^n \\ \vdots & \vdots & \vdots \qquad \vdots \\ 1 & x_n & x_n^2 \cdots x_n^n \end{bmatrix} \begin{bmatrix} a_0 \\ a_1 \\ \vdots \\ a_n \end{bmatrix} = \begin{bmatrix} y_0 \\ y_1 \\ \vdots \\ y_n \end{bmatrix} \tag{7.3.2}$$

or

$$\mathbf{Xa} = \mathbf{y}. \tag{7.3.3}$$

The solution of (7.3.3) provides the unknown coefficients.

As we have the choice of selecting the points x_i, the question arises what the choice should be in order to obtain the best possible result. It will be shown in the next section that interpolation with real x_i is numerically unstable. It will also be shown that the best choice is a set of points x_i uniformly spaced on the unit circle in the complex plane. We will derive this interpolation by introducing first a special symbol for the matrix $\mathbf{X}$ in (7.3.3)

$$\mathbf{X} = [x_i^j] \tag{7.3.4}$$

where the index i and the exponent j run from 0 to n. The points on the unit circle are

$$\begin{aligned} x_0 &= 1 \\ x_k &= \exp \frac{2k\pi\sqrt{-1}}{n+1}. \end{aligned} \tag{7.3.5}$$

As an example, Fig. 7.3.1 shows x_k for $n = 4$. Introduce the substitution

$$w = \exp \frac{2\pi\sqrt{-1}}{n+1}. \tag{7.3.6}$$

Then

$$x_k = w^k \tag{7.3.7}$$

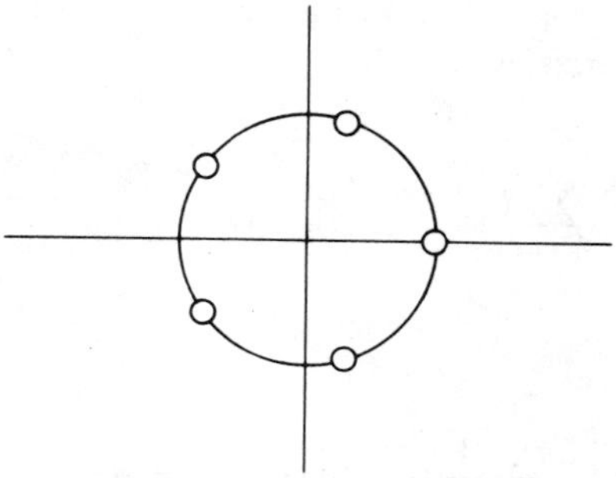

Fig. 7.3.1. Five equally spaced points on unit circle.

and

$$\mathbf{X} = [w^{ij}]. \tag{7.3.8}$$

We next show that

$$\mathbf{X}^{-1} = \frac{1}{n+1}[w^{-ij}] = \frac{1}{n+1}\mathbf{X}^*, \tag{7.3.9}$$

$\mathbf{X}^*$ denoting the transpose conjugate matrix. To do this take the product of (7.3.8) and (7.3.9). We should get

$$\frac{1}{n+1}[w^{ij}][w^{-ij}] = \mathbf{1}, \tag{7.3.10}$$

1 denoting the unit matrix. A typical term will have the following form:

$$\frac{1}{n+1}\sum_{k=0}^{n} w^{ik}w^{-kj}.$$

Let $i = j$. Then

$$\frac{1}{n+1}\sum_{k=0}^{n} w^{ik}w^{-ik} = \frac{1}{n+1}\sum_{k=0}^{n} w^0 = 1. \tag{7.3.11}$$

Now consider a term $i \neq j$:

$$\frac{1}{n+1}\sum_{k=0}^{n} w^{ik}w^{-kj} = \frac{1}{n+1}\sum_{k=0}^{n} (w^{i-j})^k.$$

The expression on the right is a geometric series. Applying the rule for the summation of such a series, we obtain

$$\frac{1}{n+1}\sum_{k=0}^{n}(w^{i-j})^k = \frac{1}{n+1}\,\frac{1-(w^{i-j})^{n+1}}{1-w^{i-j}} = 0, \qquad (7.3.12)$$

as in the numerator

$$(w^{i-j})^{n+1} = \exp\left[\frac{2\pi\sqrt{-1}}{n+1}(n+1)(i-j)\right] = \exp\left[2\pi\sqrt{-1}\,(i-j)\right] = 1.$$

Equations (7.3.11) and (7.3.12) provide the proof of (7.3.9). The solution of (7.3.2) with the points defined by (7.3.5) is

$$\mathbf{a} = \mathbf{X}^{-1}\mathbf{y} = \frac{1}{n+1}[w^{-ij}]\,\mathbf{y}$$

or

$$a_j = \frac{1}{n+1}\sum_{k=0}^{n} y_k w^{-jk}. \qquad (7.3.13)$$

The original polynomial (7.3.1), evaluated at x_k, can be written as

$$y_k = \sum_{j=0}^{n} a_j w^{jk}. \qquad (7.3.14)$$

Equations (7.3.13) and (7.3.14) represent the solution of one another. They are called the *discrete Fourier transform*, DFT. The DFT has been studied extensively. It can be programmed in a very efficient way, particularly when $n + 1 = 2^m$, m being a positive integer. It is then called the *fast Fourier transform*, FFT, and the number of operations is reduced to only $m \times (n + 1)$. Though not as simple for programming, an even more efficient and general algorithm for solving (7.3.13) and (7.3.14) is the *Winograd fast Fourier transform* [1].

7.4. CONDITION NUMBERS FOR INTERPOLATIONS

As mentioned before, real interpolation is subject to severe roundoff errors, whereas the DFT is numerically very stable. This section provides the proof of the statement. Perturbation theory of linear algebraic equations will be used because the interpolation problem is equivalent to the solution of a system of linear algebraic equations (7.3.2).

A condition number $K(\mathbf{X})$ for the matrix $\mathbf{X}$ is defined by Wilkinson [2] as

$$K(\mathbf{X}) = \sqrt{\sigma_{\max}/\sigma_{\min}} \tag{7.4.1}$$

where $\sigma_{\max}$, $\sigma_{\min}$ are the largest and smallest eigenvalues of the matrix $\mathbf{X}^*\mathbf{X}$ and $\mathbf{X}^*$ stands for the transpose conjugate of $\mathbf{X}$. The condition number depends *only* on the x-coordinates selected for the interpolation. It is a measure of the variation in $\mathbf{a}$ due to perturbations in either $\mathbf{y}$ or $\mathbf{X}$ in (7.3.2). These perturbations arise due to the truncation of $\mathbf{y}$ and $\mathbf{X}$ to a finite number of digits when using a computer. A small condition number indicates that these perturbations will not be amplified. Using (7.3.9), one has

$$\mathbf{X}^{-1}\mathbf{X} = \frac{1}{n+1}\mathbf{X}^*\mathbf{X} = \mathbf{1}$$

or

$$\mathbf{X}^*\mathbf{X} = (n+1)\mathbf{1}.$$

Clearly, all eigenvalues of $\mathbf{X}^*\mathbf{X}$ are $n + 1$ and thus

$$K(\mathbf{X}) = 1.$$

From the definition of $K(\mathbf{X})$ it is apparent that the *condition number of any other system of interpolating points cannot be less than that for equally spaced points on the unit circle*. As a matter of fact, the set of points equally spaced on the unit circle is the *only* interpolation point set that has a condition number of one.

For comparison purposes, the condition numbers corresponding to various interpolating points on the real axis have been obtained and are shown in Fig. 7.4.1. The *horizontal axis corresponds to the condition numbers for complex interpolation on the unit circle*.

Even more instructive is the impact of the condition numbers on the round-off error magnitude. Figure 7.4.2 shows the error in the coefficients of the polynomial (7.3.1) defined as

$$\epsilon = \max_k |a_k - \hat{a}_k|$$

where a_k = the specified polynomial coefficients
$\hat{a}_k$ = the coefficients obtained by interpolation.

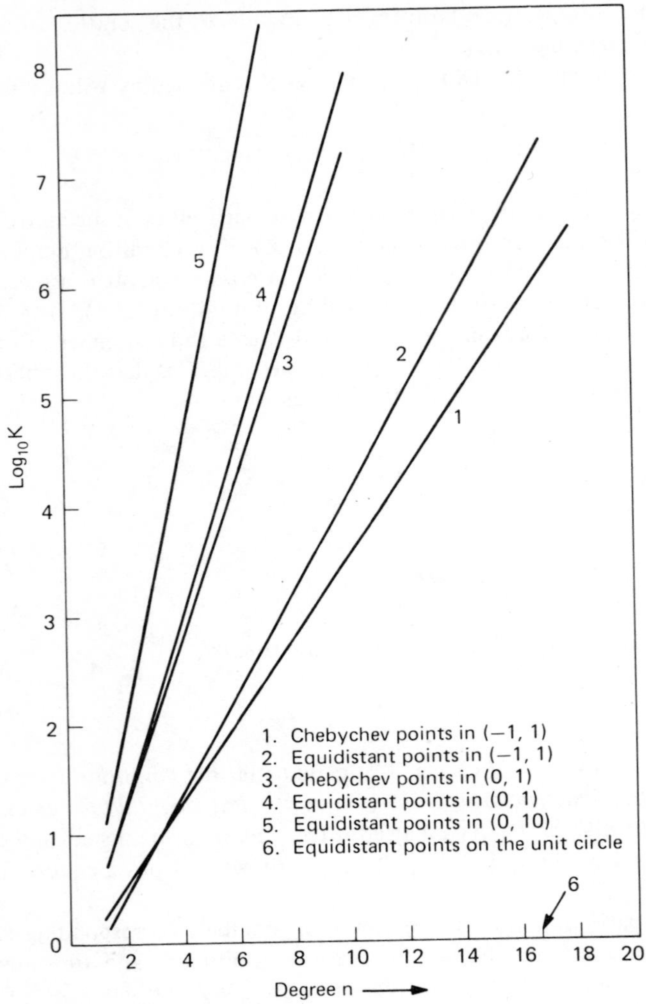

Fig. 7.4.1. Condition numbers for various interpolations.

The figure clearly indicates that real interpolation is numerically unstable whereas DFT and FFT are more accurate by many orders of magnitude. We conclude that symbolic function generation by computer must be done by interpolation on the unit circle. Complex interpolation does not represent a complication in coding, since complex evaluations are required anyway for frequency domain analysis.

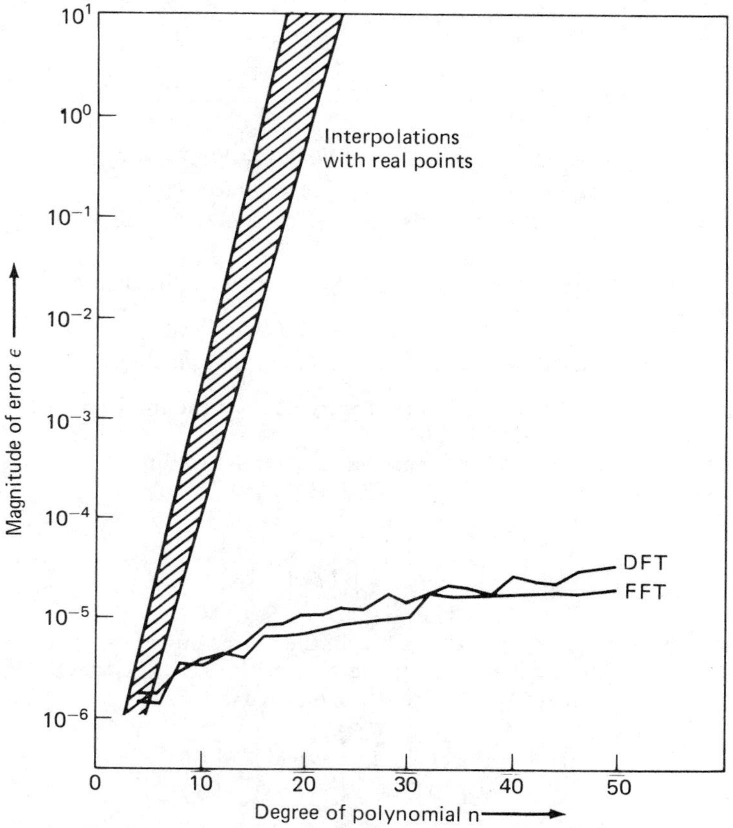

Fig. 7.4.2. Growth of error versus degree of the polynomial n. Coefficients of tested polynomials were unity and single precision arithmetic was used on an IBM/360.

7.5. ALGORITHM FOR SYMBOLIC FUNCTION GENERATION

All theoretical steps for the generation of the simplest symbolic function have now been discussed. They are collected in the following algorithm:

1. Set up the system equations $\mathbf{TX} = \mathbf{W}$ using any suitable formulation. Terms having $1/s$ are not permitted. Set unit value for the source.
2. Estimate the degree of the network function n_0. More about this estimate is given below.
3. Select points uniformly distributed on the unit circle, $s_i, i = 0, 1, \ldots, n_0$.
4. Set $i = 0$.
5. Solve $\mathbf{T}(s_i)\mathbf{X} = \mathbf{W}$ by $\mathbf{LU}$ decomposition and forward and back substitution.

6. Calculate the determinant value

$$D(s_i) = \prod l_{kk} \tag{7.5.1}$$

and store as D_i.
7. Using the selected output, calculate $N(s_i) = D_i F(s_i)$ and store as N_i.
8. If $i < n_0$, set $i = i + 1$ and go to step 5; else go to step 9.
9. Use the DFT for the points (s_i, N_i) to generate the numerator polynomial.
10. Use the DFT for the points (s_i, D_i) to generate the denominator polynomial.

EXAMPLE 7.5.1. Apply the algorithm for symbolic function generation to the network in Fig. 7.5.1 to obtain V_2/J.

There are no inductors in the network and nodal formulation can be used. The system matrix is

$$\begin{bmatrix} 1 + 3s & -3s \\ -3s & 2 + 3s \end{bmatrix} \begin{bmatrix} V_1 \\ V_2 \end{bmatrix} = \begin{bmatrix} 1 \\ 0 \end{bmatrix}.$$

There is only one capacitor in the network, the degree must be $n_0 = 1$. We need two uniformly distributed points on the unit circle: $s_0 = 1$, $s_1 = -1$. Inserting the first point and doing LU decomposition on the matrix

$$\begin{bmatrix} 4 & 0 \\ -3 & \frac{11}{4} \end{bmatrix} \begin{bmatrix} 1 & -\frac{3}{4} \\ 0 & 1 \end{bmatrix} \begin{bmatrix} V_1(s_0) \\ V_2(s_0) \end{bmatrix} = \begin{bmatrix} 1 \\ 0 \end{bmatrix}.$$

The determinant value is $D(s_0) = 4 \times \frac{11}{4} = 11$. Using forward and back substitution, obtain

$$\begin{bmatrix} V_1(s_0) \\ V_2(s_0) \end{bmatrix} = \begin{bmatrix} \frac{5}{11} \\ \frac{3}{11} \end{bmatrix}$$

and

$$V_2(s_0) = N(s_0)/D(s_0) = \frac{3}{11}.$$

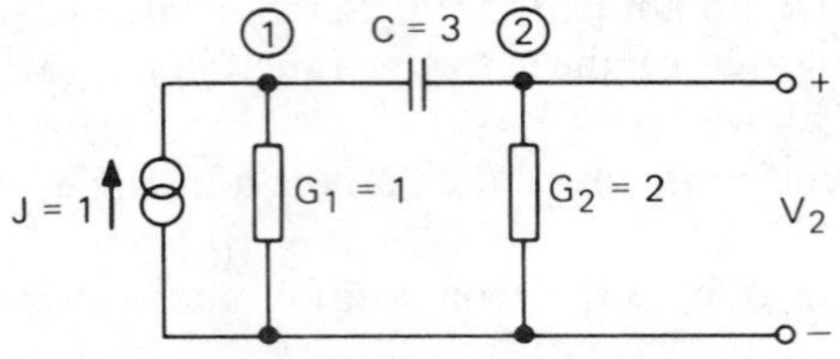

Fig. 7.5.1. Network to demonstrate symbolic function generation.

The value of the numerator is

$$N(s_0) = 11 \times \tfrac{3}{11} = 3.$$

Doing the same for $s_1 = -1$ we get the decomposition

$$\begin{bmatrix} -2 & 0 \\ 3 & \frac{7}{2} \end{bmatrix} \begin{bmatrix} 1 & -\frac{3}{2} \\ 0 & 1 \end{bmatrix} \begin{bmatrix} V_1(s_1) \\ V_2(s_1) \end{bmatrix} = \begin{bmatrix} 1 \\ 0 \end{bmatrix}.$$

The denominator is $D(s_1) = -7$; the solution is

$$\begin{bmatrix} V_1(s_1) \\ V_2(s_1) \end{bmatrix} = \begin{bmatrix} \frac{1}{7} \\ \frac{3}{7} \end{bmatrix}$$

and

$$N(s_1) = -7 \times \tfrac{3}{7} = -3.$$

The points determining the interpolation of the denominator are (1, 11) and (-1, -7). Equation (7.3.13) provides

$$b_0 = \tfrac{1}{2}(D_0 + D_1) = 2; \qquad b_1 = \tfrac{1}{2}(D_0 - D_1) = 9$$

and

$$D(s) = 9s + 2.$$

For the numerator, the points are (1, 3) and (-1, -3). The interpolating polynomial is

$$N(s) = 3s$$

and the transfer function is

$$Z_{TR} = \frac{3s}{9s + 2}.$$

The result is confirmed by direct analysis.

We still have the problem of determining in advance the degree of the network function n_0. Due to the high numerical stability of the DFT, all we do is to select a number which is *at least* equal to n_0. The superfluous terms of the resulting polynomials will be zero. If nothing is known about the network, it is safest to assume n_0 to be equal to the number of capacitors plus the number of inductors.

For simple normalized networks, it may sometimes happen that a pole coincides with one of the interpolation points on the unit circle. In this case, the determinant of **T** is zero and the system cannot be solved at this point. The simplest remedy is to increase the number of interpolating points. An alternative solution is to use a different frequency normalization for the network.

EXAMPLE 7.5.2. Find the transfer function of the Cauer-parameter filter shown in Fig. 7.5.2 using interpolation on the unit circle.

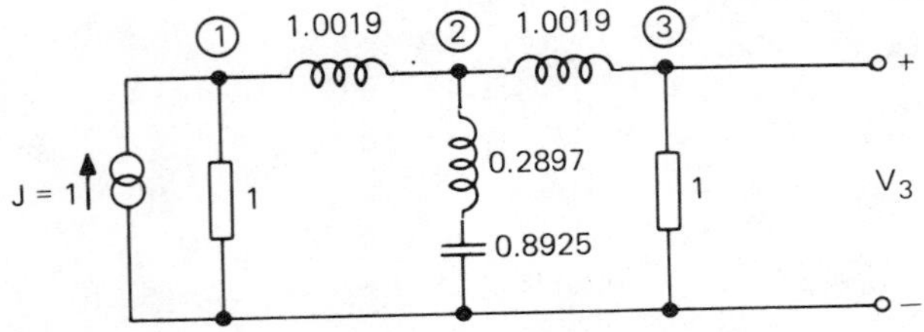

Fig. 7.5.2. A Cauer-parameter filter.

(a) Let the estimate of the degree be $n_0 = 4$, the number of inductors plus the number of capacitors. The following transfer function is obtained (using 16-decimal digit accuracy for calculation):

$$Z_{TR} = \frac{-0.124 \times 10^{-14}s^4 - 0.6217 \times 10^{-15}s^3 + 0.2586s^2 + 0.6217 \times 10^{-15}s + 1}{-0.311 \times 10^{-15}s^4 + 1.414s^3 + 2.305s^2 + 2.896s + 2}.$$

(b) Increase the estimate to $n_0 = 5$. The result is

$$Z_{TR} = \frac{-0.407 \times 10^{-15}s^5 - 0.814 \times 10^{-15}s^4 - 0.37 \times 10^{-16}s^3 + 0.2586s^2 + 0.74 \times 10^{-15}s + 1}{0.296 \times 10^{-15}s^5 - 0.740 \times 10^{-16}s^4 + 1.414s^3 + 2.305s^2 + 2.896s + 2}.$$

In both cases, the zero coefficients are clearly seen and the network function is corrected to be

$$Z_{TR} = \frac{0.2586s^2 + 1}{1.414s^3 + 2.305s^2 + 2.896s + 2}.$$

A few words of caution are in order. In higher-order networks, the coefficients of the polynomials may differ by many orders of magnitude and significant digits may be lost if the network is not scaled. The scaling can be done either directly on the system matrices or by scaling the network elements. The first point will be discussed in Section 7.9, where a larger example illustrates the problem. Scaling of network elements can be done using equations from Section 1.8. The center frequency of a band-pass filter or the band-edge of a low-pass filter should be scaled so that they become $\omega = 1$ rad/sec. Impedance levels should be reduced so that one of the resistors in the network will have the value 1 Ω.

A reader interested in the computer implementation of symbolic function generation should also incorporate the following:

1. Use the unit circle points only on and above the real axis. Contributions due to complex conjugate points are complex conjugate as well, and there is no need to solve the equations. This essentially halves the computation time.
2. Interpolation using points $(s_i, N(s_i))$ and $(s_i, D(s_i))$ can be done simultaneously by one application of the DFT. First obtain $c_i = N(s_i) + jD(s_i)$ and apply the DFT to the points c_i. The real parts in the results are coefficients of the numerator and the imaginary parts are the coefficients of the denominator.
3. The product (7.5.1) should be obtained by first taking the sum of logarithms of l_{kk} (in complex) and then finding the antilogarithm. If there is a wide spread in values of l_{kk}, this will prevent underflow and overflow.

This method is coded in the program given in Appendix D.

7.6. ROOTS OF FUNCTIONS AND POLYNOMIALS

The topics of finding roots of functions of a scalar variable and of polynomials are covered in depth in most texts on numerical analysis. Here we briefly sketch two useful methods and provide pointers to available software for a more powerful algorithm.

The best known general method for finding roots is the Newton-Raphson (N-R) iteration method, explained here with the help of Fig. 7.6.1. The sequence of iterations will be denoted by superscripts. Select an initial point x^0 and calculate $f(x^0)$ and the derivative $f'(x^0)$. Construct a tangent straight line passing through the point $(x^0, f(x^0))$

$$y - f(x^0) = f'(x^0)(x - x^0).$$

The intersection of the straight line with the horizontal axis is at the point x^1 for which $y = 0$:

$$0 - f(x^0) = f'(x^0)(x^1 - x^0)$$

or

$$x^1 = x^0 - \frac{f(x^0)}{f'(x^0)}.$$

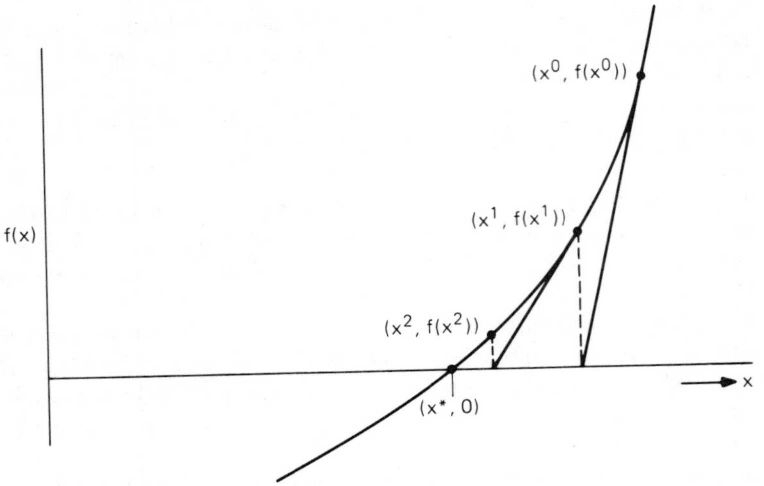

Fig. 7.6.1. Newton-Raphson iteration.

The procedure is repeated with the point $(x^1, f(x^1))$ to get x^2 and so on. In general, the Newton-Raphson method is defined by the following algorithm:

$$\begin{aligned}&1.\ \text{Set } k = 0.\\&2.\ \text{Calculate } \Delta x^k = -f(x^k)/f'(x^k).\\&3.\ \text{Calculate } x^{k+1} = x^k + \Delta x^k.\\&4.\ \text{If } |\Delta x^k| < \epsilon, \text{ stop; else set } k = k+1 \text{ and go to step 2.}\end{aligned} \tag{7.6.1}$$

The method can be used to obtain complex roots by utilizing complex arithmetic but a complex initial estimate must be given—*it cannot converge to a complex root of a real function from a real initial estimate*.

Although the Newton-Raphson method has excellent local convergence close to the root, there is no guarantee that it will converge for any arbitrary initial estimate. A method which has better global convergence properties should be used. Such a method exists for polynomials; it is called *Laguerre's method* and is defined by

$$x^{k+1} = x^k - \frac{nP_n(x^k)}{P_n'(x^k) \pm \sqrt{H^k}} \tag{7.6.2}$$

where

$$H^k = (n-1)\,[(n-1)\,\{P_n'(x^k)\}^2 - nP_n(x^k)\,P_n''(x^k)] \tag{7.6.3}$$

and P_n is the polynomial of degree n. Details can be found in Wilkinson [2]. The sign of the denominator in (7.6.2) should be chosen such that $|x^{k+1} - x^k|$ is small. The method converges for any real estimate to real roots. Such convergence cannot be proved for complex roots but good properties are retained.

Laguerre's method *can converge to a complex root from a real initial estimate* because H^k may become negative. Moreover, it is advantageous to first extract the roots with small absolute values to preserve accuracy in the deflation of the polynomial. Thus the initial estimate should start with $x^0 = 0$.

To obtain all the roots of a polynomial, one usually *deflates* the polynomial by removing the factor with the root just obtained. For polynomials with real coefficients, two complex conjugate roots are removed simultaneously by dividing $P_n(x)$ by $(x - x^k)(x - \bar{x}^k)$. Such divisions lead to errors and the deflated polynomials are increasingly less accurate. It is thus a good practice to first find all roots by deflating and subsequently correct the errors by using the roots found as initial estimates for iteration on the original polynomial.

A more recent algorithm for finding the roots of a polynomial is described in [3] and a FORTRAN code is available in [4].

7.7. ROOT REFINEMENT

Previous sections have shown that polynomial interpolation can generate the network function in rational form. Root finding routines can then be employed to compute the poles and zeros. In general, the polynomial coefficients will be in error due to roundoff errors in the evaluation of $N(s_i)$, $D(s_i)$ and in the DFT. The roots will, therefore, differ from the poles and zeros of the network. We will first obtain an estimate of the error in the roots and then outline a method to correct these errors.

Consider a polynomial in the form

$$P_{m+1}(x, \mathbf{a}) = x^{m+1} + \sum_{i=0}^{m} a_i x^i \tag{7.7.1a}$$

$$= \prod_{j=0}^{m} (x - x_j) \tag{7.7.1b}$$

and let the ith coefficient, a_i, change by a small amount. The variation in the location of the kth root can be estimated as follows:

$$\left.\frac{\partial P_{m+1}}{\partial x}\frac{\partial x}{\partial a_i}\right|_{x=x_k} + \frac{\partial P_{m+1}}{\partial a_i} = 0$$

or

$$\frac{\partial x_k}{\partial a_i} = -\frac{x_k^i}{\prod\limits_{\substack{j=0 \\ j \neq k}}^{m} (x_k - x_j)}. \tag{7.7.2}$$

If $|x_k| < 1$, the root is most sensitive to a_0; if $|x_k| > 1$, it is most sensitive to a_m. It is also seen from (7.7.2) that roots located close to one another have high sensitivity, as the denominator becomes small. Parasitic roots that have large magnitudes have large sensitivity as well.

The question naturally arises whether we can determine the roots to higher accuracy than is possible by the interpolation and root finding approach. A method that operates directly on the system matrix will be presented in the next section. Here we indicate how the poles and zeros determined from the polynomial can be refined.

Consider first the zeros of $F(s)$. Let z^0 be an approximation to a zero as obtained from the root-finding routine. If z^0 is substituted for s in the system equations (7.1.1), the matrix $\mathbf{T}$ factored, a forward and back substitution performed, and $F(z^0)$ evaluated, it may happen that its value is nonzero. The objective is to select a new value, z^1, such that $F(z^1)$ is closer to zero. The Newton-Raphson iteration can be used; it has the following form at the kth iteration:

$$z^{k+1} = z^k - \frac{F(z^k)}{(\partial F/\partial s)\big|_{s=z^k}}. \tag{7.7.3}$$

To modify our estimate, the derivative $\partial F/\partial s$ is obtained by solving the adjoint system

$$\mathbf{T}^t(z^k)\mathbf{X}^a = -\mathbf{d} \tag{7.7.4}$$

and using the theory of Chapter 6:

$$\frac{\partial F}{\partial s} = (\mathbf{X}^a)^t \frac{\partial \mathbf{T}}{\partial s}\mathbf{X} = (\mathbf{X}^a)^t \mathbf{C}\mathbf{X}. \tag{7.7.5}$$

The sequence can be terminated when $|F(z^k)| < \epsilon$, some specified small value.

Consider next the refinement of a pole starting from some approximation p^0. Let us substitute $s = p^0$ and factor the system matrix $\mathbf{T}$:

$$\mathbf{T} = \mathbf{L}\mathbf{U}. \tag{7.7.6}$$

Recall that $\mathbf{U}$ is upper triangular and has unit entries on the diagonal while $\mathbf{L}$ is lower triangular. When p is a pole, we require

$$\det \mathbf{T} = \det \mathbf{L} = \prod_{i=1}^{n} l_{ii} = 0. \tag{7.7.7}$$

From (7.7.7)

$$l_{nn} = \frac{\det \mathbf{T}}{\prod_{i=1}^{n-1} l_{ii}} = \frac{\det \mathbf{T}}{(n, n) \text{ cofactor of } \mathbf{T}}$$

and the zeros of det **T**, i.e., the system poles, are also the zeros of l_{nn}. Equation (7.7.7) can thus be replaced by

$$l_{nn} = 0. \tag{7.7.8}$$

It may be necessary to use partial pivoting to ensure that the factorization (7.7.6) can be carried out. Our objective now is to determine p by N-R iteration to satisfy (7.7.8). The advantage of using this equation rather than (7.7.7) is that the derivative of l_{nn} is much cheaper to compute than the derivative of det **T**. If we differentiate (7.7.6) with respect to s, premultiply by an arbitrary row vector $\mathbf{y}^t$, and postmultiply by another vector $\mathbf{z}$, we obtain

$$\mathbf{y}^t \frac{\partial \mathbf{T}}{\partial s} \mathbf{z} = \mathbf{y}^t \mathbf{C} \mathbf{z} = \mathbf{y}^t \frac{\partial \mathbf{L}}{\partial s} \mathbf{U} \mathbf{z} + \mathbf{y}^t \mathbf{L} \frac{\partial \mathbf{U}}{\partial s} \mathbf{z}. \tag{7.7.9}$$

Let us select the vectors **y** and **z** to satisfy the following equations:

$$\mathbf{L}^t \mathbf{y} = l_{nn} \mathbf{e}_n \tag{7.7.10a}$$

$$\mathbf{U} \mathbf{z} = \mathbf{e}_n. \tag{7.7.10b}$$

With this choice, Eq. (7.7.9) reduces to

$$\begin{aligned}
\mathbf{y}^t \mathbf{C} \mathbf{z} &= \mathbf{y}^t \frac{\partial \mathbf{L}}{\partial s} \mathbf{e}_n + l_{nn} \mathbf{e}_n^t \frac{\partial \mathbf{U}}{\partial s} \mathbf{z} \\
&= \mathbf{y}^t \left(\text{last column of } \frac{\partial \mathbf{L}}{\partial s} \right) + l_{nn} \left(\text{last row of } \frac{\partial \mathbf{U}}{\partial s} \right) \mathbf{z} \\
&= y_n \frac{\partial l_{nn}}{\partial s} \\
&= \frac{\partial l_{nn}}{\partial s}
\end{aligned} \tag{7.7.11}$$

as the last column of $\partial \mathbf{L}/\partial s$ is simply $(\partial l_{nn}/\partial s)\,\mathbf{e}_n$, the last row of $\partial \mathbf{U}/\partial s$ is zero, and the last entry of $\mathbf{y}$, y_n, is unity, as follows from (7.7.10a). Instead of (7.7.10a) we can write

$$y_n = 1 \tag{7.7.12}$$

and perform back substitution starting with y_{n-1}. The Newton-Raphson iterations can now be carried out as follows:

$$\begin{aligned} p^{k+1} &= p^k - \left.\frac{l_{nn}}{\partial l_{nn}/\partial s}\right|_{s=p^k} \\ &= p^k - \left.\frac{l_{nn}}{\mathbf{y}^t\mathbf{C}\mathbf{z}}\right|_{s=p^k}. \end{aligned} \tag{7.7.13}$$

The vectors $\mathbf{y}$ and $\mathbf{z}$ are determined from Eqs. (7.7.10) at a computational cost of one back substitution each.

A close relation exists between the material of this section to that in Sections 6.5(C, D). At convergence to the root, the auxiliary vectors $\mathbf{X}$, $\mathbf{X}^a$ or $\mathbf{y}$, $\mathbf{z}$ can also be used to compute the *sensitivity* of the root to variations in parameters.

EXAMPLE 7.7.1. Consider the network shown in Fig. 7.7.1. Its system equation is

$$\begin{bmatrix} s+2 & -(s+1) \\ -(s+1) & s+2 \end{bmatrix}\begin{bmatrix} V_1 \\ V_2 \end{bmatrix} = \begin{bmatrix} 1 \\ 0 \end{bmatrix}$$

and

$$V_2 = \frac{s+1}{2s+3}.$$

The zero is at $s = -1$ and the pole at $s = -\frac{3}{2}$.

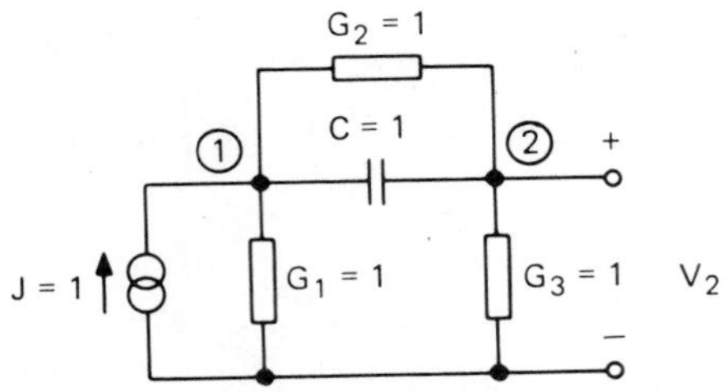

Fig. 7.7.1. Example for root refinement.

Assume the initial estimate $z^0 = -\frac{3}{4}$. The system matrix at $s = -\frac{3}{4}$ is

$$\frac{1}{4}\begin{bmatrix} 5 & -1 \\ -1 & 5 \end{bmatrix}\begin{bmatrix} V_1 \\ V_2 \end{bmatrix} = \begin{bmatrix} 1 \\ 0 \end{bmatrix},$$

the solution vector is $\mathbf{V} = [\frac{5}{6} \quad \frac{1}{6}]^t$ and $V_2 = \frac{1}{6} \neq 0$. The adjoint equations are

$$\frac{1}{4}\begin{bmatrix} 5 & -1 \\ -1 & 5 \end{bmatrix}\begin{bmatrix} V_1^a \\ V_2^a \end{bmatrix} = \begin{bmatrix} 0 \\ -1 \end{bmatrix}$$

with the solution $\mathbf{V}^a = [-\frac{1}{6} \quad -\frac{5}{6}]^t$. Using (7.7.5) one obtains

$$\left.\frac{\partial V_2}{\partial s}\right|_{s=-3/4} = -\frac{1}{36}[1 \quad 5]\begin{bmatrix} 1 & -1 \\ -1 & 1 \end{bmatrix}\begin{bmatrix} 5 \\ 1 \end{bmatrix} = \frac{4}{9},$$

Finally, using (7.7.3) one obtains

$$z^1 = z^0 - \frac{V_2(z^0)}{(\partial V_2/\partial s)|_{s=z^0}} = -\frac{3}{4} - \frac{3}{8} = -\frac{9}{8}$$

which is a better approximation to the root. Proceeding in a similar way we find $z^2 = -\frac{33}{32}$ and so on.

Let us next consider the pole at $s = -\frac{3}{2}$ and make intentionally a wrong estimate at $p^0 = -\frac{5}{4}$. The system matrix is

$$\mathbf{T}(p^0) = \begin{bmatrix} \frac{3}{4} & \frac{1}{4} \\ \frac{1}{4} & \frac{3}{4} \end{bmatrix} = \begin{bmatrix} \frac{3}{4} & 0 \\ \frac{1}{4} & \frac{2}{3} \end{bmatrix}\begin{bmatrix} 1 & \frac{1}{3} \\ 0 & 1 \end{bmatrix}.$$

The entry $l_{22} = \frac{2}{3} \neq 0$. Corresponding to (7.7.10a) we have

$$\begin{bmatrix} \frac{3}{4} & \frac{1}{4} \\ 0 & \frac{2}{3} \end{bmatrix}\begin{bmatrix} y_1 \\ y_2 \end{bmatrix} = \begin{bmatrix} 0 \\ \frac{2}{3} \end{bmatrix}$$

with the solution $\mathbf{y} = [-\frac{1}{3} \quad 1]^t$. Using similarly (7.7.10b) one obtains

$$\begin{bmatrix} 1 & \frac{1}{3} \\ 0 & 1 \end{bmatrix}\begin{bmatrix} z_1 \\ z_2 \end{bmatrix} = \begin{bmatrix} 0 \\ 1 \end{bmatrix}$$

with the solution $\mathbf{z} = [-\frac{1}{3} \quad 1]^t$. Using (7.7.11) one obtains

$$\frac{\partial l_{nn}}{\partial s} = \mathbf{y}^t\mathbf{C}\mathbf{z} = \frac{1}{9}[-1 \quad 3]\begin{bmatrix} 1 & -1 \\ -1 & 1 \end{bmatrix}\begin{bmatrix} -1 \\ 3 \end{bmatrix} = \frac{16}{9}$$

and the N–R step (7.7.13) provides

$$p^1 = -\tfrac{5}{4} - \tfrac{3}{8} = -\tfrac{13}{8}$$

which is closer to the root than p^0. Proceeding in the same way we would obtain $p^2 = -\frac{49}{32}$.

7.8. POLES AND ZEROS FROM SYSTEM EQUATIONS

In the previous sections we have outlined a method for computing the network function $F(s)$ as the ratio of two polynomials. It is reliable and efficient as long as we do not need the poles and zeros. If we do need the poles and zeros, the polynomial approach has drawbacks which were explained in Section 7.7.

Poles and zeros can be determined directly from the system equation (7.1.1) by means of the *QZ* algorithm [5]. Description of the algorithm and the underlying theory is beyond the scope of this book but the algorithm is available in subroutine packages, for instance in [6], and is extremely useful for smaller problems with system matrices less than, say, 50 × 50. This section provides relevant information for its use from a network application point of view.

We saw in (7.1.3) that the denominator of F is the determinant of $\mathbf{T} = s\mathbf{C} + \mathbf{G}$. Starting with the matrices **C** and **G**, the *QZ* algorithm finds the determinant of **T** in the following form:

$$\det\,[s\mathbf{C} + \mathbf{G}] = \prod (\alpha_i + \beta_i s) \tag{7.8.1}$$

where α_i are complex and β_i are real. Either α_i or β_i may be zero. The matrices **C** and **G** need not have any special form and both may be singular.

The denominator of the network function is now known. We next show how the numerator can be found as the determinant of another matrix, closely related to **T**. Rewrite the system equations as

$$\begin{aligned} \mathbf{TX} &= \mathbf{W} \\ F - \mathbf{d}^t\mathbf{X} &= 0 \end{aligned} \tag{7.8.2}$$

and define an additional variable $x_{n+1} = F$. Then (7.8.2) can be written compactly in the form:

$$\hat{\mathbf{T}}\hat{\mathbf{X}} = \hat{\mathbf{W}} \tag{7.8.3}$$

where

$$\hat{\mathbf{T}} = \begin{bmatrix} \mathbf{T} & \mathbf{0} \\ -\mathbf{d}^t & 1 \end{bmatrix}; \qquad \hat{\mathbf{W}} = \begin{bmatrix} \mathbf{W} \\ 0 \end{bmatrix}; \qquad \hat{\mathbf{X}} = \begin{bmatrix} \mathbf{X} \\ F \end{bmatrix}.$$

Noting that $\hat{x}_{n+1}$ is the "output" of interest, it follows from Cramer's rule that

$$F = \hat{x}_{n+1} = \frac{\det \begin{bmatrix} \mathbf{T} & \mathbf{W} \\ -\mathbf{d}^t & 0 \end{bmatrix}}{\det \begin{bmatrix} \mathbf{T} & \mathbf{0} \\ -\mathbf{d}^t & 1 \end{bmatrix}} = \frac{\det \mathbf{T}_a}{\det \mathbf{T}} \tag{7.8.4}$$

and the numerator $N(s)$ in (7.2.1) is simply the determinant of $\mathbf{T}_a$, a matrix obtained by augmenting a row and column to $\mathbf{T}$. Generally, both $\mathbf{W}$ and $\mathbf{d}$ are frequency independent and

$$N(s) = \det \mathbf{T}_a = \det (s\mathbf{C}_a + \mathbf{G}_a)$$

with

$$\mathbf{C}_a = \begin{bmatrix} \mathbf{C} & \mathbf{0} \\ \mathbf{0} & 0 \end{bmatrix}; \qquad \mathbf{G}_a = \begin{bmatrix} \mathbf{G} & \mathbf{W} \\ -\mathbf{d}^t & 0 \end{bmatrix}.$$

The network function is generated by invoking the *QZ* algorithm twice, once with matrix $\mathbf{T}$ and once with $\mathbf{T}_a$. The roots are computed to a high degree of accuracy. Some postprocessing may be required to convert the α_i, β_i coefficients produced by the algorithm into the more familiar symbolic form (7.1.5) in terms of poles and zeros. Compared with the interpolative approach, a disadvantage of the *QZ* algorithm is the need to store and process dense matrices. Possible sparsity present in $\mathbf{T}$ or $\mathbf{T}_a$ is lost when unitary transformations associated with the *QZ* algorithm are applied.

7.9. EXAMPLE

This example demonstrates that proper scaling is critical in the interpolative approach, but if applied, the method is as good as the *QZ* algorithm.

Consider the ninth-order active filter shown in Fig. 4.10.2. The problem was initially scaled by selecting a value of the variable s that makes the largest entries of $\mathbf{G}$ and $\mathbf{C}$ (see Section 4.4) about equal. The interpolative approach generated the denominator polynomial

$$D(s) = k \sum_{i=0}^{9} b_i s^i$$

with k being a normalizing constant and

$$b_0 = -2.5 \times 10^{-15} \qquad b_5 = 3.9 \times 10^{-14}$$
$$b_1 = 3.9 \times 10^{-16} \qquad b_6 = 1.2 \times 10^{-10}$$
$$b_2 = -8.3 \times 10^{-16} \qquad b_7 = 3.5 \times 10^{-7}$$
$$b_3 = -7.0 \times 10^{-16} \qquad b_8 = 5.7 \times 10^{-4}$$
$$b_4 = 2.9 \times 10^{-15} \qquad b_9 = 1.0 \times 10^{-1}.$$

Some of the coefficients are negative, which indicates that some of the roots will be in the right half plane. Since ideal operational amplifiers were used in the analysis, the network should be equivalent to the (stable) original LC network shown in Fig. 4.10.1. When the poles were determined by a root-finding routine, five of them were in the right half plane. The trouble lies in the scaling. It was shown [7] that on a computer with 16-decimal-digit accuracy, the numerical noise level in the DFT is about $\alpha \times 10^{-13}$ where $\alpha = \max_i |b_i|$, b_i being the polynomial coefficients. Hence b_0-b_5 above are completely in error. It is desirable to provide scaling such that $\max_i |b_i|$ and $\min_i |b_i|$ are as close in magnitude as possible. Details about such scaling are in [7]. If this is done, the result is

$$b_0 = 1.37 \times 10^{-2} \qquad b_5 = 1.95 \times 10^{-1}$$
$$b_1 = 4.72 \times 10^{-2} \qquad b_6 = 1.40 \times 10^{-1}$$
$$b_2 = 1.04 \times 10^{-1} \qquad b_7 = 9.06 \times 10^{-2}$$
$$b_3 = 1.65 \times 10^{-1} \qquad b_8 = 3.91 \times 10^{-2}$$
$$b_4 = 1.97 \times 10^{-1} \qquad b_9 = 1.37 \times 10^{-2}.$$

The roots computed from this polynomial are the same as those obtained from the QZ algorithm.

The roots were also found by the QZ algorithm. As the one-graph modified nodal formulation was used for this example, the system size was 35×35 for the poles. The algorithm generated 35 α_i and β_i. The β_i values were zero for $i = 1, 2, \ldots, 26$ and the corresponding α_i were real. These values contribute to the gain constant but play no role in determining the poles. The last nine α_i, β_i were nonzero and gave the following pole positions:

$$-9923 \pm j13261 \qquad -4745 \pm j19443$$
$$-459 \pm j22242 \qquad -1818 \pm j21590.$$
$$-13456$$

The process was repeated for the zeros with the dimensions of the matrices now being 36×36. All but the last 8 β_i were zero. The last 8 α_i values were imaginary resulting in the following eight finite zeros:

$$0 \pm j49576, \qquad 0 \pm j30073, \qquad 0 \pm j25354, \qquad 0 \pm j23994.$$

The interpolative approach needed three trials involving scaling, followed by root finding and root refinement. All three took only 60% of the computation time required by the *QZ* algorithm. In addition, the root sensitivities could have been obtained virtually for free at the end of the root-refinement step.

The example presented above is typical. For small networks, the *QZ* algorithm is recommended, as it is robust and does not need scaling. For large networks, the interpolative approach will require less computation time.

PROBLEMS

P.7.1. Write a subroutine which generates n complex points, equally distributed on the unit circle. Check against the subroutine COORD, given in Appendix D.

P.7.2. Write a subroutine which evaluates formula (7.3.13) using the unit circle points supplied by the routine from Problem P.7.1. Compare your result with the subroutine DFTC in Appendix D.

P.7.3. Write a subroutine which evaluates formula (7.3.14) using the unit circle points supplied by the routine from Problem P.7.1.

P.7.4. Whenever programming an iterative method, a check to limit the number of iterations must be provided in case the problem fails to converge. For instance, when programming the Newton–Raphson algorithm, at least the following is needed:

```
      EPS = a small number for stopping
      X = initial estimate on the resulting value
      ITMAX = 10 to 25, limit on iterations

      ITER = 0
1     ITER = ITER + 1
      IF(ITER.GT.ITMAX)STOP
      evaluation of f(x^k) = FX
      evaluation of f'(x^k) = DFX
      DX = -FX/DFX
      X = X + DX
      print ITER,X,DX
      IF(ABS(DX).LT.EPS)STOP
      GO TO 1
```

Complete the programming of the Newton–Raphson iteration by assuming that FX and DFX are values supplied by the user.

P.7.5. Consider the polynomial $4x^4 + 3x^3 + 2x^2 + x + 1$ which we wish to evaluate at $x = -1$. This can be done through synthetic division with detached coefficients. Write the coefficients on the first line. Next skip one line, underline, and rewrite the first term as follows:

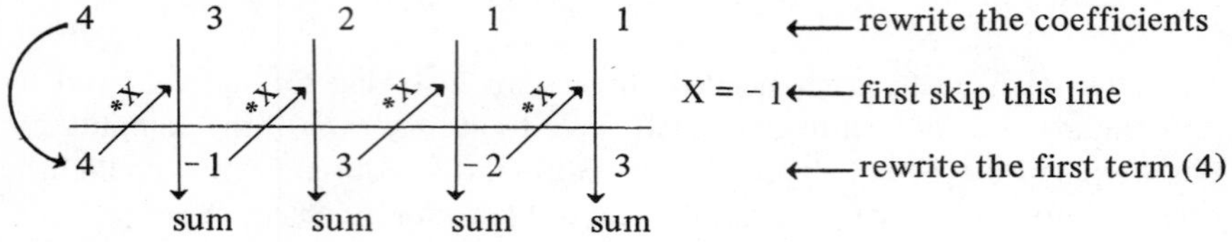

On the last line take the rewritten coefficient, multiply by the value of x at which the polynomial is to be evaluated and write on the skipped line to the right as indicated by the arrow. Take the sum of the two terms in the second column and proceed to the end. The last value is the polynomial value. The process can be continued with the following result:

rewrite	4	3	2	1	1	
		-4	1	-3	2	
	4	-1	3	-2	(3)	multiply by 0! = polynomial value for $x = -1$
rewrite		-4	5	-8		
	4	-5	8	(-10)		multiply by 1! = first polynomial derivative for $x = -1$
rewrite		-4	9			
	4	-9	(17)			multiply by 2! = second polynomial derivative for $x = -1$
rewrite		-4				
	4	(-13)				multiply by 3! = third derivative
rewrite						
	(4)					multiply by 4! = fourth derivative

For an nth order polynomial, defined as

$$P_n(x) = a_1x^n + a_2x^{n-1} + a_3x^{n-2} + \cdots + a_nx + a_{n+1}$$

the polynomial evaluation is programmed as follows:

```
      NP1 = N + 1
      DO 1 I = 2,NP1
    1 A(I) = A(I) + X * A(I - 1)
```

Using the above information, write a program which evaluates the polynomial and its first two (or more) derivatives for any given value of x. *Note:* This is the recommended way to evaluate polynomials on a computer.

P.7.6. Find at least one real root for each of the following polynomials by Newton–Raphson iteration:

(a) $x^4 + 4x^3 + 5x^2 + 4x + 2$ (one real root at -1, possibly others)
(b) $x^4 + 7x^3 + 15x^2 + 7x - 6$ (roots -2 and -3)
(c) $x^4 + 2x^3 + x^2 - 2x - 2$ (roots -1, $+1$)

P.7.7. The deflation of a polynomial, once a root has been found, is carried out by the same table as explained in Problem P.7.5. Consider the polynomial $(2x^3 + 3x^2 + 2x + 1)(x + 2) = 2x^4 + 7x^3 + 8x^2 + 5x + 2$. Using the following schematic table:

2	7	8	5	2	X = −2
	−4	−6	−4	−2	
2	3	2	1	⓪	= value of the polynomial

(2 3 2 1: coefficients of the deflated polynomial)

we get the deflated polynomial. Write a program for the deflation of a general polynomial as given in Problem P.7.5.

P.7.8. Use the Newton–Raphson algorithm to find the real root of the polynomial $2x^3 + 8x^2 + 12x + 8$. Use deflation to lower the degree of the polynomial and find the roots of the remaining quadratic polynomial by formula. (*Result:* $-2, -1 \pm j$.)

P.7.9. Using your program for the Newton–Raphson algorithm, find the nonzero roots of:

(a) $\sin x - x^3 = 0$.

(b) $x^2 - \sin \pi x = 0$.

(c) $2\sqrt{x} - \cos (\pi/2)x = 0$.

(d) $2^x - 2x^2 - 1 = 0$.

(e) $x \ln x - 1.2 = 0$.

(f) $2 - xe^x = 0$.

(g) $2x - \log_{10} x - 7 = 0$.

P.7.10. Write a subroutine for Laguerre's method, Eqs. (7.6.2) and (7.6.3). Note that for general polynomials, the programming must be done in complex.

P.7.11. Modify your program for Newton–Raphson iteration to find complex roots. Remember that a complex initial estimate must be given for such roots.

P.7.12. Use the program for network analysis, Appendix D, and check correctness of your solutions for problems from the first six chapters.

REFERENCES

1. J. H. McClellan and H. Nawab: Complex general-*N* Winograd Fourier transform algorithm (WFTA). Chapter 1.7 in the IEEE Press book *Programs for Digital Signal Processing*, 1979.
2. J. H. Wilkinson: *The Algebraic Eigenvalue Problem.* Clarendon Press, Oxford, 1965.
3. M. A. Jenkins and J. F. Traub: A three stage algorithm for real polynomials using quadratic iteration. *SIAM J. Num. Anal.*, pp. 545–566, 1970.
4. M. A. Jenkins: Algorithm 493–zeros of a real polynomial. *ACM Trans. Math. Software*, pp. 178–189, 1975.
5. C. B. Moler and G. W. Stewart: An algorithm for generalized matrix eigenvalue problems. *SIAM J. Num. Anal.*, pp. 241–256, 1973.
6. B. T. Smith, J. M. Boyle, J. Dongarra, B. S. Garbow, Y. Ikebe, V. C. Klema, and C. B. Moler: *Matrix Eigensystem Routines–EISPACK Guide.* Springer-Verlag, Heidelberg, 1976.
7. K. Singhal and J. Vlach: Generation of immittance functions in symbolic form for lumped distributed active networks. *IEEE Transactions on Circuits and Systems*, Vol. CAS-21, pp. 57–67, January 1974.

CHAPTER 8
Large Change Sensitivity and Related Topics

Chapter 8 provides the answer to the following question: Let a given network be solved for specified nominal values. Is it possible, without re-solving the whole problem, to obtain the *exact* solution if some elements are changed arbitrarily? A unified theory is given but its implications are much wider than the answer to the above question, generally termed *large change sensitivity*. We show that the differential sensitivities treated in Chapters 5 and 6 can be obtained fairly cheaply even after large changes in one or more elements. The development is then extended to show how the network functions may be generated in symbolic form in the element values.

Section 8.1 gives the theoretical development. It is based on the modification of the original system by a low-rank matrix. Assuming that m elements are subject to changes, an $(m + 1) \times (m + 1)$ matrix $\hat{\mathfrak{F}}$, by means of which all the information can be obtained, is formed. Section 8.2 shows how differential sensitivities are obtained from the $\hat{\mathfrak{F}}$ matrix after some of the elements have changed in value.

Because the changing elements can assume arbitrary values, among them zero and infinity, the theory can be used for generating fault directories needed in fault analysis of networks. This subproblem is handled in Section 8.3. A by-product of the theory developed in Section 8.1 is a method for handling zero pivots in sparse matrix solutions. The zero pivots can be modified and equations of the same type as those handled in Section 8.1 arise. Because of this similarity, *exact* solutions can be obtained even if there are several zero pivots. This theory is described in Section 8.4.

The matrix $\hat{\mathfrak{F}}$ derived in Section 8.1 contains all information necessary to obtain all derivatives of the network function numerator and denominator with respect to the variable elements. This is derived in Section 8.5, where we show that various subdeterminants of $\hat{\mathfrak{F}}$ provide the derivatives. Once they are available, it is a simple matter to generate symbolic functions in terms of network elements. Moreover, the frequency, s, can be retained as a variable as well, if we use the interpolation methods explained in Chapter 7.

All the steps and methods given in this chapter require special programming but represent considerable savings, once applied. On the other-hand, brute force methods, e.g., re-solving the network after each change, give the same results and the decision on whether or not to apply the techniques of this chapter will be based on the objectives of the software designer.

The symbolic method explained in Section 8.5 is coded in the program in Appendix D.

8.1. LARGE CHANGE SENSITIVITY

In Chapter 5 we defined sensitivity as the change in the output due to small changes in parameters. *Large change sensitivity* measures the variation in output when the parameters are subjected to variations that need not be small. In fact, the elements can take any value from zero to infinity. In this section, the basic mathematical theory is developed and the notation required is introduced [1].

Consider the network equations with the elements being assigned their nominal values

$$\mathbf{T}_0\mathbf{X}_0 = \mathbf{W} \tag{8.1.1}$$

and let the output be a linear combination of the entries of the vector $\mathbf{X}_0$:

$$F_0 = \mathbf{d}^t\mathbf{X}_0. \tag{8.1.2}$$

Formally, the solution is obtained by inverting the matrix $\mathbf{T}_0$:

$$\mathbf{X}_0 = \mathbf{T}_0^{-1}\mathbf{W} \tag{8.1.3}$$

and the output becomes

$$F_0 = \mathbf{d}^t\mathbf{T}_0^{-1}\mathbf{W}. \tag{8.1.4}$$

Denote the nominal values of the m components that are subject to large variations by $h_{10}, h_{20}, \ldots, h_{mo}$ and let them change by the amounts $\delta_1, \delta_2, \ldots, \delta_m$. The new values are

$$h_i = h_{io} + \delta_i. \tag{8.1.5}$$

For the most part we will restrict the components subject to variations to be of the type that enter the tableau or modified nodal equations in the form $h_i\mathbf{p}_i\mathbf{q}_i^t$ with

$$\begin{aligned}\mathbf{p}_i &= \mathbf{e}_{i_j} - \mathbf{e}_{i_{j'}}\\ \mathbf{q}_i &= \mathbf{e}_{i_k} - \mathbf{e}_{i_{k'}}\end{aligned} \tag{8.1.6}$$

and with $\mathbf{e}_l$ being a vector of zeros except for the lth entry, which is equal to one. The notation has already been introduced in Section 2.1. R, L, C elements, the four transducers and the inverse gain $B = -1/A$ of the operational amplifier are examples of variables that enter the equations in this way.

The equations describing the modified system are

$$\mathbf{TX} = \left(\mathbf{T}_0 + \sum_{i=1}^{m} \delta_i \mathbf{p}_i \mathbf{q}_i^t\right)\mathbf{X} = \mathbf{W} \tag{8.1.7}$$

or

$$(\mathbf{T}_0 + \mathbf{P}\boldsymbol{\delta}\mathbf{Q}^t)\mathbf{X} = \mathbf{W} \tag{8.1.8}$$

and the output is

$$F = \mathbf{d}^t\mathbf{X}. \tag{8.1.9}$$

Here $\mathbf{P}$ and $\mathbf{Q}$ are $n \times m$ matrices which contain 0 and ± 1 entries:

$$\begin{aligned}\mathbf{P} &= [\mathbf{p}_1 \quad \mathbf{p}_2 \cdots \mathbf{p}_m]\\ \mathbf{Q} &= [\mathbf{q}_1 \quad \mathbf{q}_2 \cdots \mathbf{q}_m]\end{aligned} \tag{8.1.10}$$

and $\boldsymbol{\delta}$ is a diagonal $m \times m$ matrix

$$\boldsymbol{\delta} = \text{diag}\,[\delta_i]. \tag{8.1.11}$$

The reader should consult Example 8.1.1 if he has difficulty in visualizing how the matrices are generated.

Our objective is to find the output F for specified perturbations δ_i. The variation in F due to δ_i is the *large change sensitivity*. The direct approach would be to form the new system matrix with parameter values $(h_{i0} + \delta_i)$, factor it, find $\mathbf{X}$ by forward and back substitution, and then determine F. When the number of variables subject to perturbations, m, is much smaller than the size of the system, n, an alternative technique results in substantial reduction in computational cost. To develop the technique we rewrite (8.1.8) and introduce substitutions as follows:

$$\mathbf{T}_0\mathbf{X} + \mathbf{P}\underbrace{\boldsymbol{\delta}\underbrace{\mathbf{Q}^t\mathbf{X}}_{\mathbf{y}}}_{\mathbf{z}} = \mathbf{W}.$$

This leads to a set of three equations:

$$\mathbf{T}_0\mathbf{X} + \mathbf{P}\mathbf{z} = \mathbf{W} \tag{8.1.12a}$$

$$\boldsymbol{\delta}\mathbf{y} - \mathbf{z} = \mathbf{0} \tag{8.1.12b}$$

$$-\mathbf{Q}^t\mathbf{X} + \mathbf{y} = \mathbf{0}. \tag{8.1.12c}$$

In matrix form, this is

$$\begin{bmatrix} \mathbf{T}_0 & \mathbf{0} & \mathbf{P} \\ \mathbf{0} & \boldsymbol{\delta} & -\mathbf{1} \\ -\mathbf{Q}^t & \mathbf{1} & \mathbf{0} \end{bmatrix} \begin{bmatrix} \mathbf{X} \\ \mathbf{y} \\ \mathbf{z} \end{bmatrix} = \begin{bmatrix} \mathbf{W} \\ \mathbf{0} \\ \mathbf{0} \end{bmatrix}. \tag{8.1.12}$$

The advantage of (8.1.12) is that the identity of various matrices is retained and derivations are simplified. Equations (8.1.12) could be considered as a tableau formulation of (8.1.8). Solving (8.1.12a) formally one obtains

$$\mathbf{X} = \mathbf{T}_0^{-1}\mathbf{W} - \mathbf{T}_0^{-1}\mathbf{P}\mathbf{z} \tag{8.1.13}$$

and substituting into (8.1.12b), (8.1.12c) and (8.1.9) one obtains

$$\boldsymbol{\delta}\mathbf{y} - \mathbf{z} = \mathbf{0} \tag{8.1.14a}$$

$$\mathbf{y} + \mathbf{Q}^t\mathbf{T}_0^{-1}\mathbf{P}\mathbf{z} = \mathbf{Q}^t\mathbf{T}_0^{-1}\mathbf{W} \tag{8.1.14b}$$

$$\mathbf{d}^t\mathbf{T}_0^{-1}\mathbf{P}\mathbf{z} + F = \mathbf{d}^t\mathbf{T}_0^{-1}\mathbf{W}. \tag{8.1.14c}$$

Now introduce the following notation:

$$\begin{aligned} \mathcal{F} &= \mathbf{Q}^t\mathbf{T}_0^{-1}\mathbf{P} && (m \times m \text{ matrix}) \\ \hat{\mathbf{W}} &= \mathbf{Q}^t\mathbf{T}_0^{-1}\mathbf{W} = \mathbf{Q}^t\mathbf{X}_0 && (m\text{-vector}) \\ \hat{\mathbf{d}}^t &= \mathbf{d}^t\mathbf{T}_0^{-1}\mathbf{P} && (m\text{-vector}) \\ F_0 &= \mathbf{d}^t\mathbf{T}_0^{-1}\mathbf{W}. && (\text{scalar}) \end{aligned} \tag{8.1.15}$$

Equations (8.1.14) can be written in matrix form as follows:

$$\begin{bmatrix} \boldsymbol{\delta} & -\mathbf{1} & \mathbf{0} \\ \mathbf{1} & \mathcal{F} & \mathbf{0} \\ \mathbf{0} & \hat{\mathbf{d}}^t & 1 \end{bmatrix} \begin{bmatrix} \mathbf{y} \\ \mathbf{z} \\ F \end{bmatrix} = \begin{bmatrix} \mathbf{0} \\ \hat{\mathbf{W}} \\ F_0 \end{bmatrix}. \tag{8.1.16}$$

Further reduction in system size is possible if we eliminate $\mathbf{y}$ using (8.1.14a):

$$(\boldsymbol{\delta}^{-1} + \mathcal{F})\mathbf{z} = \hat{\mathbf{W}} \tag{8.1.17a}$$

$$F = F_0 - \hat{\mathbf{d}}^t\mathbf{z}. \tag{8.1.17b}$$

From these equations it is clear that for any set of perturbations δ_i we need to solve only the set of m equations in $\mathbf{z}$ and then determine F from (8.1.17b). Even though the set of equations (8.1.17a) will normally be dense, as $m \ll n$, the solution time associated with it will be much less than the setup and solution time for (8.1.1). Note, however, that before (8.1.17) can be used, the matrix $\mathcal{F}$ and the vectors $\hat{\mathbf{W}}$ and $\hat{\mathbf{d}}$ need to be computed. This is considered next.

Denote by $\hat{\mathcal{F}}$ the augmented $(m + 1) \times (m + 1)$ matrix

$$\hat{\mathcal{F}} = \begin{bmatrix} \mathcal{F} & \hat{\mathbf{W}} \\ \hat{\mathbf{d}}^t & F_0 \end{bmatrix} \tag{8.1.18}$$

and augment the matrices $\mathbf{P}$ and $\mathbf{Q}$ by one column each to form

$$\hat{\mathbf{P}} = [\mathbf{P} \mid \mathbf{W}]$$
$$\hat{\mathbf{Q}} = [\mathbf{Q} \mid \mathbf{d}]. \tag{8.1.19}$$

Then

$$\hat{\mathcal{F}} = \hat{\mathbf{Q}}^t\mathbf{T}_0^{-1}\hat{\mathbf{P}}. \tag{8.1.20}$$

Indeed, substituting (8.1.19) into (8.1.20) and performing the multiplications gives

$$\hat{\mathcal{F}} = \begin{bmatrix} \mathbf{Q}^t \\ \hline \mathbf{d}^t \end{bmatrix} \mathbf{T}_0^{-1} [\mathbf{P} \mid \mathbf{W}] = \left[\begin{array}{c|c} \mathbf{Q}^t\mathbf{T}_0^{-1}\mathbf{P} & \mathbf{Q}^t\mathbf{T}_0^{-1}\mathbf{W} \\ \hline \mathbf{d}^t\mathbf{T}_0^{-1}\mathbf{P} & \mathbf{d}^t\mathbf{T}_0^{-1}\mathbf{W} \end{array}\right] = \left[\begin{array}{c|c} \mathcal{F} & \hat{\mathbf{W}} \\ \hline \hat{\mathbf{d}}^t & F_0 \end{array}\right].$$

The result given by (8.1.20) is of fundamental importance, because *only the original, unperturbed system is involved in the generation of* $\hat{\mathcal{F}}$. The entries of $\hat{\mathcal{F}}$ can be obtained by factoring the *original* matrix and performing $m + 1$ forward and back substitutions with the columns of $\hat{\mathbf{P}}$ serving, in turn, as right-hand-side vectors. Select any column of the matrix $\hat{\mathbf{P}}$, $\mathbf{p}_j$, and solve the system

$$\mathbf{T}_0\boldsymbol{\xi}_j = \mathbf{p}_j. \tag{8.1.21}$$

The solution vector $\boldsymbol{\xi}_j$ will represent the jth column of the product $\mathbf{T}_0^{-1}\hat{\mathbf{P}}$. Premultiplication by $\hat{\mathbf{Q}}^t$ gives the jth column of $\hat{\mathfrak{F}}$. Performing these operations on all $m + 1$ columns of the matrix $\hat{\mathbf{P}}$ provides the matrix $\hat{\mathfrak{F}}$.

EXAMPLE 8.1.1. Consider the simple network shown in Fig. 8.1.1. The nominal values for the conductances G_1, G_2, and G_3 are 1, 1, and 2 mhos respectively. All three conductances can change value. The nodal equations are

$$\begin{bmatrix} G_1 + G_2 & -G_2 \\ -G_2 & G_2 + G_3 \end{bmatrix}\begin{bmatrix} V_1 \\ V_2 \end{bmatrix} = \begin{bmatrix} 2 & -1 \\ -1 & 3 \end{bmatrix}\begin{bmatrix} V_1 \\ V_2 \end{bmatrix} = \begin{bmatrix} 1 \\ 0 \end{bmatrix}.$$

Normally, triangular decomposition would be used to solve the system but on this example inversion is simpler:

$$\mathbf{T}_0^{-1} = \frac{1}{5}\begin{bmatrix} 3 & 1 \\ 1 & 2 \end{bmatrix}.$$

The system matrix is 2 X 2, the vectors $\mathbf{e}_j$ will have the same dimension. The elements enter the matrix as follows:

$$G_1 \mathbf{e}_1 \mathbf{e}_1^t = G_1 \begin{bmatrix} 1 \\ 0 \end{bmatrix} [1 \quad 0] = \begin{bmatrix} G_1 & 0 \\ 0 & 0 \end{bmatrix}$$

$$G_2(\mathbf{e}_1 - \mathbf{e}_2)(\mathbf{e}_1 - \mathbf{e}_2)^t = G_2 \begin{bmatrix} 1 \\ -1 \end{bmatrix} [1 \quad -1] = \begin{bmatrix} G_2 & -G_2 \\ -G_2 & G_2 \end{bmatrix}$$

$$G_3 \mathbf{e}_2 \mathbf{e}_2^t = G_3 \begin{bmatrix} 0 \\ 1 \end{bmatrix} [0 \quad 1] = \begin{bmatrix} 0 & 0 \\ 0 & G_3 \end{bmatrix}.$$

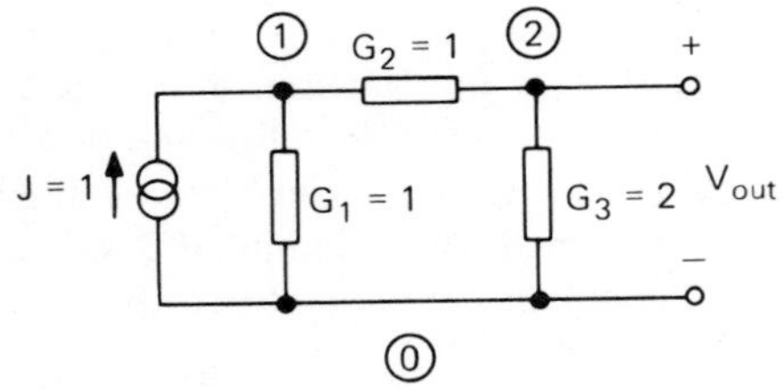

Fig. 8.1.1. Network for Example 8.1.1.

Taken together, these form

$$\underbrace{\begin{bmatrix} 1 & 1 & 0 \\ 0 & -1 & 1 \end{bmatrix}}_{\mathbf{P}} \begin{bmatrix} G_1 & & \\ & G_2 & \\ & & G_3 \end{bmatrix} \underbrace{\begin{bmatrix} 1 & 0 \\ 1 & -1 \\ 0 & 1 \end{bmatrix}}_{\mathbf{Q}^t} = \begin{bmatrix} G_1 + G_2 & -G_2 \\ -G_2 & G_2 + G_3 \end{bmatrix}.$$

We note that on this example **P** and **Q** are the same and each is identical to the incidence matrix of the network.

The matrix **P** is now augmented by $\mathbf{W} = [1 \quad 0]^t$, as follows from the original system:

$$\hat{\mathbf{P}} = \left[\begin{array}{ccc|c} 1 & 1 & 0 & 1 \\ 0 & -1 & 1 & 0 \end{array}\right].$$

The **Q** matrix is augmented by **d**. Since the output is V_2, $\mathbf{d} = [0 \quad 1]^t$ and

$$\hat{\mathbf{Q}}^t = \left[\begin{array}{cc} 1 & 0 \\ 1 & -1 \\ 0 & 1 \\ \hline 0 & 1 \end{array}\right].$$

Solve the systems $\mathbf{T}_0 \boldsymbol{\xi}_j = \mathbf{p}_j$ by taking, in turn, the columns of $\hat{\mathbf{P}}$ as the right-hand side:

$\mathbf{p}_1$: $$\boldsymbol{\xi}_1 = \frac{1}{5}\begin{bmatrix} 3 & 1 \\ 1 & 2 \end{bmatrix}\begin{bmatrix} 1 \\ 0 \end{bmatrix} = \begin{bmatrix} \frac{3}{5} \\ \frac{1}{5} \end{bmatrix}$$

$\mathbf{p}_2$: $$\boldsymbol{\xi}_2 = \frac{1}{5}\begin{bmatrix} 3 & 1 \\ 1 & 2 \end{bmatrix}\begin{bmatrix} 1 \\ -1 \end{bmatrix} = \begin{bmatrix} \frac{2}{5} \\ -\frac{1}{5} \end{bmatrix}$$

$\mathbf{p}_3$: $$\boldsymbol{\xi}_3 = \frac{1}{5}\begin{bmatrix} 3 & 1 \\ 1 & 2 \end{bmatrix}\begin{bmatrix} 0 \\ 1 \end{bmatrix} = \begin{bmatrix} \frac{1}{5} \\ \frac{2}{5} \end{bmatrix}$$

W: $$\boldsymbol{\xi}_4 = \boldsymbol{\xi}_1 \quad \text{as} \quad \mathbf{W} = \mathbf{p}_1.$$

Premultiplication of each $\boldsymbol{\xi}_i$ by $\hat{\mathbf{Q}}^t$ gives the ith column of $\hat{\mathfrak{F}}$. The matrix is

$$\hat{\mathfrak{F}} = \frac{1}{5}\left[\begin{array}{ccc|c} 3 & 2 & 1 & 3 \\ 2 & 3 & -1 & 2 \\ 1 & -1 & 2 & 1 \\ \hline 1 & -1 & 2 & 1 \end{array}\right] = \left[\begin{array}{c|c} \mathfrak{F} & \hat{\mathbf{W}} \\ \hline \hat{\mathbf{d}}^t & F_0 \end{array}\right]$$

and we identify:

$$\mathcal{F} = \frac{1}{5}\begin{bmatrix} 3 & 2 & 1 \\ 2 & 3 & -1 \\ 1 & -1 & 2 \end{bmatrix}; \qquad \hat{\mathbf{W}} = \frac{1}{5}\begin{bmatrix} 3 \\ 2 \\ 1 \end{bmatrix}; \qquad \hat{\mathbf{d}}^t = \frac{1}{5}[1 \quad -1 \quad 2]; \qquad F_0 = \frac{1}{5}.$$

Let $\delta_1 = 0.5, \delta_2 = 1, \delta_3 = -0.5$. Then

$$\boldsymbol{\delta} = \begin{bmatrix} 0.5 & & \mathbf{0} \\ & 1 & \\ \mathbf{0} & & -0.5 \end{bmatrix} \quad \text{and} \quad \boldsymbol{\delta}^{-1} = \begin{bmatrix} 2 & & \mathbf{0} \\ & 1 & \\ \mathbf{0} & & -2 \end{bmatrix}.$$

Therefore

$$(\boldsymbol{\delta}^{-1} + \mathcal{F}) = \frac{1}{5}\begin{bmatrix} 13 & 2 & 1 \\ 2 & 8 & -1 \\ 1 & -1 & -8 \end{bmatrix}$$

and (8.1.17a) is

$$\begin{bmatrix} 13 & 2 & 1 \\ 2 & 8 & -1 \\ 1 & -1 & -8 \end{bmatrix}\begin{bmatrix} z_1 \\ z_2 \\ z_3 \end{bmatrix} = \begin{bmatrix} 3 \\ 2 \\ 1 \end{bmatrix}$$

with the solution $\mathbf{z} = \frac{1}{33}[7 \quad 6 \quad -4]^t$. Finally, inserting into (8.1.17b) one obtains

$$F = F_0 - \hat{\mathbf{d}}^t\mathbf{z} = \frac{1}{5} - \frac{1}{5}\frac{1}{33}[1 \quad -1 \quad 2]\begin{bmatrix} 7 \\ 6 \\ -4 \end{bmatrix} = \frac{8}{33}.$$

By direct calculation we would obtain

$$\begin{bmatrix} 3.5 & -2 \\ -2 & 3.5 \end{bmatrix}\begin{bmatrix} V_1 \\ V_2 \end{bmatrix} = \begin{bmatrix} 1 \\ 0 \end{bmatrix}$$

and $V_2 = \frac{8}{33}$, the same result.

Later in the chapter we will need the intermediate vector **y** and also the full solution vector **X** rather than only $\mathbf{d}^t\mathbf{X}$. The vector **z** is obtained from (8.1.17a), **y** is found from (8.1.14a), and **X** is calculated from (8.1.12a) by forward and back substitution.

Let us now consider the more general case when only $m_1 < m$ of the δ_i are nonzero, i.e., only a few of the m components that *may* be subject to variations are actually changed. Equation (8.1.17a) involves $\boldsymbol{\delta}^{-1}$ and is no longer valid. In order to resolve the problem, partition the variables as $\boldsymbol{\delta}_1 \neq \mathbf{0}$ and $\boldsymbol{\delta}_2 = \mathbf{0}$ with the corresponding partitions of the vectors $\mathbf{y}$, $\mathbf{z}$, $\hat{\mathbf{W}}$, $\hat{\mathbf{d}}$ and of the matrix $\mathcal{F}$. Returning to (8.1.14a) we see that

$$\mathbf{y}_1 = \boldsymbol{\delta}_1^{-1}\mathbf{z}_1 \tag{8.1.22}$$

and

$$\mathbf{z}_2 = \mathbf{0}. \tag{8.1.23}$$

Substituting in the remaining equations gives

$$(\boldsymbol{\delta}_1^{-1} + \mathcal{F}_{11})\mathbf{z}_1 = \hat{\mathbf{W}}_1 \tag{8.1.24}$$

$$F = F_0 - \hat{\mathbf{d}}_1^t \mathbf{z}_1. \tag{8.1.25}$$

Only a system of size m_1 (number of components *actually changed*) need be solved to evaluate the output. In (8.1.24) and (8.1.25), $\mathcal{F}_{11}$, $\hat{\mathbf{W}}_1$, $\hat{\mathbf{d}}_1$ contain only rows and columns of $\mathcal{F}$, $\hat{\mathbf{W}}$, and $\hat{\mathbf{d}}$ that correspond to the $\delta_i \neq 0$ variables. The vector $\mathbf{y}_1$ is determined from (8.1.22). If the remaining portion of $\mathbf{y}$, $\mathbf{y}_2$, is needed as well, we can obtain it from the second row of (8.1.16):

$$\mathbf{y}_2 = \hat{\mathbf{W}}_2 - \mathcal{F}_{21}\mathbf{z}_1. \tag{8.1.26}$$

The full solution vector $\mathbf{X}$ is obtained by a forward and back substitution on

$$\mathbf{T}_0\mathbf{X} = \mathbf{W} - \mathbf{P}_1\mathbf{z}_1 \tag{8.1.27}$$

as follows from (8.1.12a).

We now give another example to illustrate the application.

EXAMPLE 8.1.2. Consider the network shown in Fig. 8.1.2. The conductances G_4, G_5, G_6 have nominal values of 1 mho each and are considered as fixed. The conductances G_1, G_2 and the transconductance g_3 also have nominal values of one mho each but are subject to variation. The nominal admittance matrix, denoted by $\mathbf{T}_0$, and its inverse are

$$\mathbf{T}_0 = \begin{bmatrix} 2 & -1 & 0 \\ -1 & 3 & -1 \\ 0 & 0 & 2 \end{bmatrix}; \qquad \mathbf{T}_0^{-1} = \frac{1}{10}\begin{bmatrix} 6 & 2 & 1 \\ 2 & 4 & 2 \\ 0 & 0 & 5 \end{bmatrix}; \qquad \det \mathbf{T}_0 = 10.$$

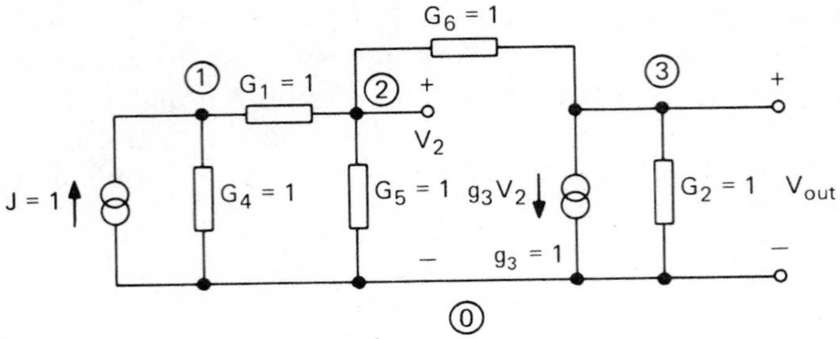

Fig. 8.1.2. Network for Example 8.1.2.

The perturbations $\delta_1, \delta_2, \delta_3$ in G_1, G_2, and g_3 modify the admittance matrix to

$$\mathbf{T} = \mathbf{T}_0 + \delta_1 \mathbf{p}_1 \mathbf{q}_1^t + \delta_2 \mathbf{p}_2 \mathbf{q}_2^t + \delta_3 \mathbf{p}_3 \mathbf{q}_3^t$$

where $\mathbf{p}_1 = \mathbf{q}_1 = \mathbf{e}_1 - \mathbf{e}_2$, $\mathbf{p}_2 = \mathbf{q}_2 = \mathbf{e}_3$, $\mathbf{p}_3 = \mathbf{e}_3$, and $\mathbf{q}_3 = \mathbf{e}_2$. The augmented matrices are formed by appending the vector $\mathbf{e}_1$ to $\mathbf{P}$ and $\mathbf{e}_3$ to $\mathbf{Q}$:

$$\hat{\mathbf{P}} = \left[\begin{array}{ccc|c} 1 & 0 & 0 & 1 \\ -1 & 0 & 0 & 0 \\ 0 & 1 & 1 & 0 \end{array}\right]; \qquad \hat{\mathbf{Q}} = \left[\begin{array}{ccc|c} 1 & 0 & 0 & 0 \\ -1 & 0 & 1 & 0 \\ 0 & 1 & 0 & 1 \end{array}\right].$$

Substituting in (8.1.20) we get

$$\hat{\mathcal{F}} = \frac{1}{10}\left[\begin{array}{ccc|c} 6 & -1 & -1 & 4 \\ 0 & 5 & 5 & 0 \\ -2 & 2 & 2 & 2 \\ \hline 0 & 5 & 5 & 0 \end{array}\right]$$

and we identify

$$\mathcal{F} = \frac{1}{10}\begin{bmatrix} 6 & -1 & -1 \\ 0 & 5 & 5 \\ -2 & 2 & 2 \end{bmatrix}; \qquad \hat{\mathbf{W}} = \frac{1}{10}\begin{bmatrix} 4 \\ 0 \\ 2 \end{bmatrix}; \qquad \hat{\mathbf{d}} = \frac{1}{10}\begin{bmatrix} 0 \\ 5 \\ 5 \end{bmatrix}; \qquad F_0 = 0.$$

Now let g_3 change to 2 while G_1 and G_2 remain at 1 mho each. In this case $m_1 = 1$ and Eq. (8.1.24) takes the following form:

$$(\delta_3^{-1} + \mathcal{F}_{33}) z_3 = \hat{W}_3$$

i.e.,

$$(1 + \tfrac{2}{10}) z_3 = \tfrac{2}{10}$$

and $z_3 = \frac{1}{6}$. The solution $F \equiv V_3$ is obtained by using (8.1.25):

$$V_3 = V_{30} - \hat{d}_3 z_3 = 0 - \frac{5}{10}\frac{1}{6} = -\frac{1}{12}.$$

From (8.1.23) z_1 and z_2 are zero. Thus $\mathbf{z} = [0 \quad 0 \quad \frac{1}{6}]^t$. From (8.1.22) we have $y_3 = \delta_3^{-1} z_3 = \frac{1}{6}$, while from (8.1.26) we have

$$\begin{bmatrix} y_1 \\ y_2 \end{bmatrix} = \frac{1}{10}\begin{bmatrix} 4 \\ 0 \end{bmatrix} - \frac{1}{10}\begin{bmatrix} -1 \\ 5 \end{bmatrix}\frac{1}{6} = \frac{1}{12}\begin{bmatrix} 5 \\ -1 \end{bmatrix}.$$

Finally from (8.1.27) the full solution of the perturbed system is obtained as follows:

$$\mathbf{T}_0\mathbf{V} = \mathbf{e}_1 - \mathbf{e}_3\frac{1}{6}$$

or

$$\mathbf{V} = \frac{1}{10}\begin{bmatrix} 6 & 2 & 1 \\ 2 & 4 & 2 \\ 0 & 0 & 5 \end{bmatrix}\begin{bmatrix} 1 \\ 0 \\ -\frac{1}{6} \end{bmatrix} = \frac{1}{12}\begin{bmatrix} 7 \\ 2 \\ -1 \end{bmatrix}.$$

The output V_3 matches the value obtained above using Eq. (8.1.25). The same solution is obtained if the system equations are modified to reflect the change in g_3.

As the results of this example will be used in later sections, we give the solution again:

$$\mathbf{X} \equiv \mathbf{V} = \frac{1}{12}\begin{bmatrix} 7 \\ 2 \\ -1 \end{bmatrix}; \qquad \mathbf{y} = \frac{1}{12}\begin{bmatrix} 5 \\ -1 \\ 2 \end{bmatrix}; \qquad \mathbf{z} = \frac{1}{12}\begin{bmatrix} 0 \\ 0 \\ 2 \end{bmatrix}.$$

8.2. DIFFERENTIAL SENSITIVITY USING THE $\hat{\mathfrak{F}}$ MATRIX

Section 8.1 showed how the solution of the modified system may be obtained without reformulating the system equations. In this section we will show that differential sensitivity of the modified system can also be obtained.

Applying the theory developed in Chapter 6, the adjoint system to (8.1.12) is given by

$$\begin{bmatrix} \mathbf{T}_0^t & \mathbf{0} & -\mathbf{Q} \\ \mathbf{0} & \boldsymbol{\delta} & \mathbf{1} \\ \mathbf{P}^t & -\mathbf{1} & \mathbf{0} \end{bmatrix}\begin{bmatrix} \mathbf{X}^a \\ \mathbf{y}^a \\ \mathbf{z}^a \end{bmatrix} = \begin{bmatrix} -\mathbf{d} \\ \mathbf{0} \\ \mathbf{0} \end{bmatrix} \tag{8.2.1}$$

where $\mathbf{y}^a$ and $\mathbf{z}^a$ are the auxiliary adjoint vectors. Using the first row of (8.2.1) we obtain

$$\mathbf{X}^a = -(\mathbf{T}_0^t)^{-1}\mathbf{d} + (\mathbf{T}_0^t)^{-1}\mathbf{Q}\mathbf{z}^a. \tag{8.2.2}$$

Similarly, using the second row we obtain

$$\mathbf{y}^a = -\boldsymbol{\delta}^{-1}\mathbf{z}^a \tag{8.2.3}$$

and inserting both into the third row we obtain

$$-\mathbf{P}^t(\mathbf{T}_0^t)^{-1}\mathbf{d} + \mathbf{P}^t(\mathbf{T}_0^t)^{-1}\mathbf{Q}\mathbf{z}^a + \boldsymbol{\delta}^{-1}\mathbf{z}^a = \mathbf{0}.$$

The notation from (8.1.15) is now introduced. It results in

$$(\boldsymbol{\delta}^{-1} + \mathcal{F}^t)\mathbf{z}^a = \hat{\mathbf{d}}. \tag{8.2.4}$$

Equation (8.2.4) represents the *adjoint system* to (8.1.17a) and could have been written directly by inspection. Assuming that (8.1.17a) has already been solved by **LU** factorization, solution of (8.2.4) represents only one forward and back substitution of the type discussed in Section 6.2. Should the full adjoint vector $\mathbf{X}^a$ be needed, it could be obtained from the first row of (8.2.1):

$$\mathbf{T}_0^t\mathbf{X}^a = -\mathbf{d} + \mathbf{Q}\mathbf{z}^a. \tag{8.2.5}$$

Again, the **LU** factors of $\mathbf{T}_0$ are already available from the solution of the original system and only one forward and back substitution is needed.

Important simplifications result when only sensitivity with respect to parameters that are subject to variation, e.g., $h_1, h_2, \ldots, h_m$, is required. In this case the relation

$$h_i = h_{io} + \delta_i$$

leads to

$$\frac{\partial F}{\partial h_i} = \frac{\partial F}{\partial \delta_i}.$$

In order to obtain the formula for $\partial F/\partial \delta_i$ denote, for the moment, the matrix in (8.1.12) by **M**. Formula (6.1.11) applies:

$$\frac{\partial F}{\partial h_i} = [(\mathbf{X}^a)^t \quad (\mathbf{y}^a)^t \quad (\mathbf{z}^a)^t] \frac{\partial \mathbf{M}}{\partial \delta_i} \begin{bmatrix} \mathbf{X} \\ \mathbf{y} \\ \mathbf{z} \end{bmatrix}.$$

Since δ_i appears in the $\boldsymbol{\delta}$ partition only, the expression can be reduced to

$$\frac{\partial F}{\partial \delta_i} = (\mathbf{y}^a)^t \frac{\partial \boldsymbol{\delta}}{\partial \delta_i} \mathbf{y}.$$

Going still further, we see that only one entry, the (i, i)th entry of $\partial \boldsymbol{\delta}/\partial \delta_i$, will be one; the rest will be zero. Therefore

$$\frac{\partial F}{\partial h_i} = y_i^a y_i \tag{8.2.6}$$

and only the vectors $\mathbf{z}$, $\mathbf{y}$ and $\mathbf{z}^a$, $\mathbf{y}^a$ are required.

As in Section 8.1, the equations must be changed when some of the δ_i variables are zero. The derivations are similar to those given in Section 8.1 and only the results corresponding to (8.1.22)–(8.1.27) are given here:

$$\mathbf{y}_1^a = -\boldsymbol{\delta}_1^{-1}\mathbf{z}_1^a \tag{8.2.7}$$

$$\mathbf{z}_2^a = \mathbf{0} \tag{8.2.8}$$

$$(\boldsymbol{\delta}_1^{-1} + \mathcal{F}_{11}^t)\mathbf{z}_1^a = \hat{\mathbf{d}}_1 \tag{8.2.9}$$

$$\mathbf{y}_2^a = -\hat{\mathbf{d}}_2 + \mathcal{F}_{12}^t\mathbf{z}_1^a \tag{8.2.10}$$

$$\mathbf{T}_0^t\mathbf{X}^a = -\mathbf{d} + \mathbf{Q}_1\mathbf{z}_1^a. \tag{8.2.11}$$

The matrix in (8.2.9) is the transpose of that in (8.1.24). At this point we can state the algorithm for sensitivity calculation by means of large change sensitivity:

1. Set up and factor $\mathbf{T}_0$ using the nominal element values.
2. Obtain the $(m+1) \times (m+1)$ matrix $\hat{\mathcal{F}}$ (8.1.20) by $m+1$ forward and back substitutions on (8.1.21), m being the number of perturbed variables. This completes the preprocessing steps.
3. If, in a given simulation, only $m_1 < m$ components have perturbations $\boldsymbol{\delta}_1$, the $m_1 \times m_1$ matrix $(\boldsymbol{\delta}_1^{-1} + \mathcal{F}_{11})$ is formed and factored. Forward and back substitutions on (8.1.24) and (8.2.9) provide the vectors $\mathbf{z}_1$, $\mathbf{z}_1^a$. The remaining components of $\mathbf{z}$ and $\mathbf{z}^a$, e.g., $\mathbf{z}_2$, $\mathbf{z}_2^a$, are zero. The output of the modified system is found from (8.1.25).
4. If only sensitivities with respect to $h_1, h_2, \ldots, h_m$ are required, the vectors $\mathbf{y}$ and $\mathbf{y}^a$ are formed from (8.1.22), (8.1.26), (8.2.7), and (8.2.10). Then

$$\frac{\partial F}{\partial h_i} = y_i^a y_i.$$

5. If sensitivities with respect to elements other than $h_1, h_2, \ldots, h_m$ are required, step 4 is skipped. Instead, the full vectors $\mathbf{X}$, $\mathbf{X}^a$ are generated from (8.1.27) and (8.2.11). This is done by forward and back substitutions using the factors of $\mathbf{T}_0$. Sensitivities are calculated using the theory of Chapter 6.

Steps 3, 4, and 5 are repeated for each set of perturbations that are to be investigated. Note that the modified system matrix $\mathbf{T}$ is *never* explicitly formulated.

EXAMPLE 8.2.1. We continue with Example 8.1.2 where we modified the transconductance g_3 to 2 mho and the solution of $\mathbf{X}$, $\mathbf{y}$, and $\mathbf{z}$ was obtained. Now consider the solution of the adjoint system.

From (8.2.9)

$$(\delta_3^{-1} + \mathcal{F}_{33})z_3^a = \hat{d}_3$$

or

$$(1 + \tfrac{2}{10})z_3^a = \tfrac{5}{10}$$

from which $z_3^a = \frac{5}{12}$ is obtained. Using (8.2.8) we find the full vector $\mathbf{z}^a = [0 \quad 0 \quad \frac{5}{12}]^t$. From (8.2.7) we have

$$y_3^a = -1 \times z_3^a = -\tfrac{5}{12}$$

and from (8.2.10) we have

$$\begin{bmatrix} y_1^a \\ y_2^a \end{bmatrix} = -\frac{1}{10}\begin{bmatrix} 0 \\ 5 \end{bmatrix} + \frac{1}{10}\begin{bmatrix} -2 \\ 2 \end{bmatrix}\left(\frac{5}{12}\right) = \frac{1}{12}\begin{bmatrix} -1 \\ -5 \end{bmatrix}.$$

The full vector is $\mathbf{y}^a = \frac{1}{12}[-1 \quad -5 \quad -5]^t$. Finally, applying (8.2.11) we obtain

$$\mathbf{T}_0^t\mathbf{V}^a = -\mathbf{e}_3 + \mathbf{e}_2 z_3^a$$

or

$$\mathbf{V}^a = \frac{1}{10}\begin{bmatrix} 6 & 2 & 0 \\ 2 & 4 & 0 \\ 1 & 2 & 5 \end{bmatrix}\begin{bmatrix} 0 \\ \frac{5}{12} \\ -1 \end{bmatrix} = \frac{1}{12}\begin{bmatrix} 1 \\ 2 \\ -5 \end{bmatrix}.$$

We are now in the position to calculate the differential sensitivities. First consider the case when only sensitivities with respect to G_1, G_2, g_3 are required. In this case only the vectors $\mathbf{y}$ and $\mathbf{y}^a$ are of use and computation of $\mathbf{V}$, $\mathbf{V}^a$ could have been bypassed. Direct application of (8.2.6) gives

$$\frac{\partial F}{\partial G_1} = -\frac{5}{144}; \qquad \frac{\partial F}{\partial G_2} = \frac{5}{144}; \qquad \frac{\partial F}{\partial g_3} = -\frac{10}{144}.$$

Now consider the case where sensitivity with respect to G_4, G_5, and G_6 are also required. Computations of $\mathbf{y}$ and $\mathbf{y}^a$ would be skipped but $\mathbf{X} \equiv \mathbf{V}$ and $\mathbf{X}^a \equiv \mathbf{V}^a$ need to be generated. From the theory in Chapter 6 we obtain

$$\frac{\partial F}{\partial G_1} = (V_1^a - V_2^a)(V_1 - V_2) = -\frac{5}{144}$$

$$\frac{\partial F}{\partial G_2} = V_3^a V_3 = \frac{5}{144}$$

$$\frac{\partial F}{\partial g_3} = V_3^a V_2 = -\frac{10}{144}$$

$$\frac{\partial F}{\partial G_4} = V_1^a V_1 = \frac{7}{144}$$

$$\frac{\partial F}{\partial G_5} = V_2^a V_2 = \frac{4}{144}$$

$$\frac{\partial F}{\partial G_6} = (V_2^a - V_3^a)(V_2 - V_3) = \frac{21}{144}.$$

8.3. FAULT ANALYSIS

A circuit may fail specifications due to variations in component values from the nominal design. This may happen at the time of manufacture or when it is in the field. *Fault analysis* is concerned with isolating the cause of the failure from a set of terminal measurements. Two forms of faults are generally considered: *drift failures*, which are due to relatively small perturbations in all the components; and *catastrophic failures*, which are due to large changes in a few components. Drift failures are usually due to aging and result in only small variations in response with consequent slow degradation in performance. Such faults are difficult to isolate and correct. On the other hand, catastrophic faults generally lead to large changes in response and are simpler to isolate. To assist the repair process, a *fault directory* is generally prepared beforehand. It establishes equivalence between response values and specific fault conditions. As the number of possible fault conditions grows very rapidly with the number of components that have failed, only one- or two-component failures are considered in practice. This is not a serious limitation, as the probability of many components failing simultaneously is fairly low.

Consider the simplest case, where the fault is due to large variation in a single element. This could be due to an incorrect element value or perhaps due to the element being either open or short circuit. In the case of a conductance of nominal value G, the fault values $G = 0$ and $G = \infty$ need to be investigated. Normally, this requirement would pose serious difficulties because neither the tableau nor the modified nodal formulations can simultaneously handle both cases and different formulations are required to simulate the two extreme fault conditions. No such difficulty is encountered when using the theory developed in Section 8.1. For an open circuit ($G \to 0$) we have $\delta = -G$, while for a short circuit ($G \to \infty$) the increment δ becomes infinitely large and its inverse $\delta^{-1} = 0$. For single faults, Eqs. (8.1.24) and (8.1.25) reduce to

$$\begin{aligned} (\delta_i^{-1} + \mathcal{F}_{ii})z &= \hat{w}_i \\ F = F_0 - \hat{d}_i z &= F_0 - \frac{\hat{d}_i \hat{w}_i}{\delta_i^{-1} + \mathcal{F}_{ii}} . \end{aligned} \tag{8.3.1}$$

Note that only the diagonal entries and the last row and column of $\hat{\mathcal{F}}$ are needed. Equation (8.3.1) represents a locus of response values as δ^{-1} changes and each element has its own locus. Comparing the measured value of F with all possible loci, the faulty component is determined and can be replaced. Should the value of the faulty component be desired, it can be obtained from (8.3.1).

EXAMPLE 8.3.1. Consider the network of Example 8.1.1 with single faults due to G_1, G_2, G_3, respectively. The output would have the following values:

$$F_1 = \frac{1}{5} - \frac{\frac{3}{5} \times \frac{1}{5}}{\delta_1^{-1} + \frac{3}{5}}$$

$$F_2 = \frac{1}{5} + \frac{\frac{2}{5} \times \frac{1}{5}}{\delta_2^{-1} + \frac{3}{5}}$$

$$F_3 = \frac{1}{5} - \frac{\frac{2}{5} \times \frac{1}{5}}{\delta_3^{-1} + \frac{2}{5}} .$$

The loci for the F_i can be plotted. The extreme fault conditions give the following values for F;

	$G = 0;\ \delta = -G$	$G = \infty;\ \delta^{-1} = 0$
F_1	$\frac{1}{2}$	0
F_2	0	$\frac{1}{3}$
F_3	1	0

8.4. ZERO PIVOTS IN SPARSE MATRIX FACTORIZATION

In the solution of sparse matrices, the equations and variables are generally pre-ordered on the basis of the sparsity pattern alone or on the basis of sparsity and numeric values at some fixed frequency. In the reordered matrix the pivots are taken along the diagonal. It may happen that we encounter a zero (or very small) value for a pivot at some other frequency. We could return to the ordering algorithm and generate a new set of node numbers but this would be fairly expensive. As such situations arise only rarely and at very few pivot steps, the problem can be resolved through the technique developed in Section 8.1. Let us denote the matrix to be factored as **A** and let the first zero pivot be encountered at step i of the factorization. We will modify the matrix by adding a unit entry to the (i, i) position of **A**. The original problem was to solve

$$\mathbf{Ax} = \mathbf{b} \tag{8.4.1}$$

which is equivalent to

$$(\mathbf{A} + \mathbf{e}_i\mathbf{e}_i^t - \mathbf{e}_i\mathbf{e}_i^t)\mathbf{x} = \mathbf{b}$$

or

$$(\mathbf{A}_1 - \mathbf{e}_i\mathbf{e}_i^t)\mathbf{x} = \mathbf{b}. \tag{8.4.2}$$

We will proceed with the factorization of $\mathbf{A}_1$ which is the modified matrix with the zero on the diagonal replaced by one. Still another zero pivot may be encountered in factoring $\mathbf{A}_1$ at pivot step j and again a unit entry is added and factorization continued with matrix

$$\mathbf{A}_2 = \mathbf{A}_1 + \mathbf{e}_j\mathbf{e}_j^t = \mathbf{A} + \mathbf{e}_i\mathbf{e}_i^t + \mathbf{e}_j\mathbf{e}_j^t.$$

The solution to our original problem is obtained by solving

$$(\mathbf{A}_2 - \mathbf{e}_i\mathbf{e}_i^t - \mathbf{e}_j\mathbf{e}_j^t)\mathbf{x} = \mathbf{b}.$$

In the general case with m such replacements we solve

$$(\mathbf{A}_m - \mathbf{P}\mathbf{P}^t)\mathbf{x} = \mathbf{b} \tag{8.4.3}$$

where

$$\mathbf{P} = [\mathbf{e}_i \quad \mathbf{e}_j \cdots \mathbf{e}_m]. \tag{8.4.4}$$

At this point we note that Eq. (8.4.3) is similar to (8.1.8) with $\mathbf{P} = \mathbf{Q}$ and $\boldsymbol{\delta} = -\mathbf{1}$. Equation (8.1.17a) is thus replaced by

$$(-\mathbf{1} + \mathfrak{F})\mathbf{z} = \hat{\mathbf{b}} \tag{8.4.5}$$

where

$$\begin{aligned} \mathfrak{F}^t &= \mathbf{P}^t(\mathbf{A}_m^{-1})^t\mathbf{P} \\ \hat{\mathbf{b}}^t &= \mathbf{b}^t(\mathbf{A}_m^{-1})^t\mathbf{P}. \end{aligned} \tag{8.4.6}$$

Note the use of the *transpose* system (8.4.6). Organizing the computations in this way saves on one forward and back substitution in the determination of $\mathfrak{F}$ and $\hat{\mathbf{b}}$. Thus we solve

$$\mathbf{A}_m^t \boldsymbol{\xi}_i = \mathbf{p}_i$$

for $i = 1, 2, \ldots, m$ in turn. Premultiplication of $\boldsymbol{\xi}_i$ by $\mathbf{P}^t$ gives the ith *row* of $\mathfrak{F}$ and premultiplication by $\mathbf{b}^t$ gives the ith entry of $\hat{\mathbf{b}}$. After the solution of the $m \times m$ system (8.4.5) has been found, the vector $\mathbf{x}$ in (8.4.1) is obtained from

$$\mathbf{A}_m\mathbf{x} = \mathbf{b} - \mathbf{P}\mathbf{z} \tag{8.4.7}$$

by forward and back substitution as follows from (8.1.12a). The matrix $(-\mathbf{1} + \mathfrak{F})$ in (8.4.5) is fairly small and dense. Partial or complete pivoting can be employed in its solution. It can be shown that if $(-\mathbf{1} + \mathfrak{F})$ is singular, then the original system matrix $\mathbf{A}$ in (8.4.1) is also singular.

EXAMPLE 8.4.1. Consider the system of equations

$$\begin{bmatrix} 0 & 1 \\ 1 & 1 \end{bmatrix} \begin{bmatrix} x_1 \\ x_2 \end{bmatrix} = \begin{bmatrix} 1 \\ 0 \end{bmatrix}$$

with the solution $\mathbf{x} = [-1 \quad 1]^t$. In the form specified, the **LU** factors cannot be determined. Let us modify the (1, 1) entry to unity. The first pivot results in a zero at position (2, 2) and again we modify to unity to complete the factorization. If $\mathbf{A}$ denotes the original matrix and $\mathbf{A}_2$ the modified matrix we have

$$\mathbf{A} = \mathbf{A}_2 - \mathbf{e}_1\mathbf{e}_1^t - \mathbf{e}_2\mathbf{e}_2^t$$

with

$$\mathbf{A}_2 = \begin{bmatrix} 1 & 1 \\ 1 & 2 \end{bmatrix}$$

Due to the form of the modification, **P** is a unit matrix. Using (8.4.6) we obtain

$$\mathfrak{F}^t = \mathbf{P}^t(\mathbf{A}_2^{-1})^t\mathbf{P} = \mathbf{A}_2^{-1} = \begin{bmatrix} 2 & -1 \\ -1 & 1 \end{bmatrix}$$

$$\hat{\mathbf{b}}^t = \mathbf{b}^t(\mathbf{A}_2^{-1})^t\mathbf{P} = \mathbf{b}^t\mathbf{A}_2^{-1} = [2 \quad -1].$$

Inserting into (8.4.5) we must solve the system

$$\left(\begin{bmatrix} -1 & 0 \\ 0 & -1 \end{bmatrix} + \begin{bmatrix} 2 & -1 \\ -1 & 1 \end{bmatrix}\right)\begin{bmatrix} z_1 \\ z_2 \end{bmatrix} = \begin{bmatrix} 2 \\ -1 \end{bmatrix}$$

and $\mathbf{z} = [1 \quad -1]^t$. The vector

$$\mathbf{b} - \mathbf{P}\mathbf{z} = \begin{bmatrix} 1 \\ 0 \end{bmatrix} - \begin{bmatrix} 1 & 0 \\ 0 & 1 \end{bmatrix}\begin{bmatrix} 1 \\ -1 \end{bmatrix} = \begin{bmatrix} 0 \\ 1 \end{bmatrix}$$

is prepared for (8.4.7); its solution is $\mathbf{x} = [-1 \quad 1]^t$, which is the exact result given above.

8.5. SYMBOLIC ANALYSIS

Explicit generation of the immittance function F in terms of the variable component deviations $\delta_1, \delta_2, \ldots, \delta_m$ is called *symbolic analysis*. The main advantage of the symbolic function is in the insight it provides. Moreover, it can find use in situations where severe numerical cancellations can lead to large round-off errors, as in crystal filters.

At any fixed frequency, the network function is bilinear in each of the variable elements

$$F(\delta_1, \delta_2, \ldots, \delta_m) = \frac{N(\delta_1, \delta_2, \ldots, \delta_m)}{D(\delta_1, \delta_2, \ldots, \delta_m)}$$

$$= \frac{a + \sum_i^m a_i\delta_i + \sum_i^m \sum_{<j}^m a_{ij}\delta_i\delta_j + \sum_i^m \sum_{<j}^m \sum_{<k}^m a_{ijk}\delta_i\delta_j\delta_k + \cdots}{b + \sum_i^m b_i\delta_i + \sum_i^m \sum_{<j}^m b_{ij}\delta_i\delta_j + \sum_i^m \sum_{<j}^m \sum_{<k}^m b_{ijk}\delta_i\delta_j\delta_k + \cdots} \tag{8.5.1}$$

For illustration, the function F with 2 variable components δ_1, δ_2 will have the form

$$F(\delta_1, \delta_2) = \frac{N(\delta_1, \delta_2)}{D(\delta_1, \delta_2)} = \frac{a + a_1\delta_1 + a_2\delta_2 + a_{12}\delta_1\delta_2}{b + b_1\delta_1 + b_2\delta_2 + b_{12}\delta_1\delta_2}. \tag{8.5.2}$$

The numerator and denominator each contain 2^m coefficients. The task in symbolic analysis is to determine the coefficients $a, a_i, a_{ij}, a_{ijk}, \ldots$ and $b, b_i, b_{ij}, b_{ijk}, \ldots$.

We first note that the coefficients of the numerator or denominator can be obtained by differentiating these multinomials with respect to the variables δ_i and taking $\boldsymbol{\delta} = \mathbf{0}$. Thus, for the illustrative example (8.5.2), we have

$$\begin{aligned} a &= N & b &= D \\ a_1 &= \partial N/\partial\delta_1 & b_1 &= \partial D/\partial\delta_1 \\ a_2 &= \partial N/\partial\delta_2 & b_2 &= \partial D/\partial\delta_2 \\ a_{12} &= \partial^2 N/(\partial\delta_1\partial\delta_2) & b_{12} &= \partial^2 D/(\partial\delta_1\partial\delta_2). \end{aligned}$$

In the following discussion we derive all properties of symbolic functions by using equations (8.1.12a, b, c) and equation (8.1.17b), put together into one matrix equation:

$$\begin{bmatrix} \mathbf{T}_0 & \mathbf{0} & \mathbf{P} & \mathbf{0} \\ \mathbf{0} & \boldsymbol{\delta} & -\mathbf{1} & \mathbf{0} \\ -\mathbf{Q}^t & \mathbf{1} & \mathbf{0} & \mathbf{0} \\ \mathbf{0} & \mathbf{0} & \hat{\mathbf{d}}^t & 1 \end{bmatrix} \begin{bmatrix} \mathbf{X} \\ \mathbf{y} \\ \mathbf{z} \\ F \end{bmatrix} = \begin{bmatrix} \mathbf{W} \\ \mathbf{0} \\ \mathbf{0} \\ F_0 \end{bmatrix}. \tag{8.5.3}$$

To simplify notation, denote the matrix in (8.5.3) by **M**. Then the denominator of the transfer function D is equal to

$$D = \det \mathbf{M}\big|_{\delta=0} = \det \mathbf{T}_0. \tag{8.5.4}$$

To obtain the numerator, use Cramer's rule and replace the last column of **M** by the right-hand side of (8.5.3):

$$N = F_0 \det \mathbf{T}_0. \tag{8.5.5}$$

In order to get the derivatives of D and N we first recall the general rule for differentiating the determinant of a matrix **B**:

$$\frac{\partial}{\partial\delta_j}(\det \mathbf{B}) = \sum_{i=1}^{n} \det \begin{bmatrix} \text{matrix } \mathbf{B} \text{ with the } i\text{th} \\ \text{column differentiated with} \\ \text{respect to } \delta_j \end{bmatrix}$$

$$= \sum_{i=1}^{n} \det \left[\mathbf{B} - \left(\mathbf{B} - \frac{\partial \mathbf{B}}{\partial\delta_j}\right)\mathbf{e}_i\mathbf{e}_i^t\right]. \tag{8.5.6}$$

Since in **M** each variable δ_j appears in only one position of the diagonal submatrix $\boldsymbol{\delta}$, the general rule (8.5.6) simplifies and only one determinant of the sum will be nonzero. Further differentiation with respect to other variations follows the same steps.

We will need derivatives of all orders of D and N, but the development is simpler if we first find the derivatives with respect to all m variables. Differentiation with respect to all the elements results in the determinant of a matrix similar to **M** with the submatrix $\boldsymbol{\delta}$ replaced by the unit matrix and all other entries of that column being zero matrices:

$$\frac{\partial^m D}{\partial\delta_1 \cdots \partial\delta_m} = \det \begin{bmatrix} \mathbf{T}_0 & \mathbf{0} & \mathbf{P} & \mathbf{0} \\ \mathbf{0} & \mathbf{1} & -\mathbf{1} & \mathbf{0} \\ -\mathbf{Q}^t & \mathbf{0} & \mathbf{0} & \mathbf{0} \\ \mathbf{0} & \mathbf{0} & \hat{\mathbf{d}}^t & 1 \end{bmatrix} = \det \mathbf{T}_0 \det (\mathbf{Q}^t \mathbf{T}_0^{-1} \mathbf{P}). \quad (8.5.7)$$

The product $\mathbf{Q}^t\mathbf{T}_0^{-1}\mathbf{P}$ was already obtained in (8.1.15) and denoted by $\mathfrak{F}$.

For the mth derivative of the numerator, replace the last column of **M** by the right-hand side of (8.5.3) and apply the rule for the differentiation of the determinant:

$$\frac{\partial^m N}{\partial\delta_1 \cdots \partial\delta_m} = \det \begin{bmatrix} \mathbf{T}_0 & \mathbf{0} & \mathbf{P} & \mathbf{W} \\ \mathbf{0} & \mathbf{1} & -\mathbf{1} & \mathbf{0} \\ -\mathbf{Q}^t & \mathbf{0} & \mathbf{0} & \mathbf{0} \\ \mathbf{0} & \mathbf{0} & \hat{\mathbf{d}}^t & F_0 \end{bmatrix} = \det \mathbf{T}_0 \det \begin{bmatrix} \mathbf{Q}^t\mathbf{T}_0^{-1}\mathbf{P} & \mathbf{Q}^t\mathbf{T}_0^{-1}\mathbf{W} \\ \hat{\mathbf{d}}^t & F_0 \end{bmatrix}.$$

The matrix on the right was also obtained before, in (8.1.18), and denoted $\hat{\mathfrak{F}}$. The size of $\hat{\mathfrak{F}}$ is $(m + 1) \times (m + 1)$ and, as will be shown below, *all derivatives of the numerator and denominator can be obtained from this matrix by retaining some rows and columns and finding the determinant.*

Turning to the lth derivative of D, $l < m$, assume that we differentiate with respect to the first l variables. The matrix **M** is partitioned appropriately and we are looking for

$$\frac{\partial^l D}{\partial\delta_1\partial\delta_2 \cdots \partial\delta_l} = \frac{\partial^l}{\partial\delta_1\partial\delta_2 \cdots \partial\delta_l} \det \left[\begin{array}{c|cc|cc|c} \mathbf{T}_0 & \mathbf{0} & \mathbf{0} & \mathbf{P}_1 & \mathbf{P}_2 & \mathbf{0} \\ \hline \mathbf{0} & \boldsymbol{\delta}_1 & \mathbf{0} & -\mathbf{1} & \mathbf{0} & \mathbf{0} \\ \mathbf{0} & \mathbf{0} & \boldsymbol{\delta}_2 & \mathbf{0} & -\mathbf{1} & \mathbf{0} \\ \hline -\mathbf{Q}_1^t & \mathbf{1} & \mathbf{0} & \mathbf{0} & \mathbf{0} & \mathbf{0} \\ -\mathbf{Q}_2^t & \mathbf{0} & \mathbf{1} & \mathbf{0} & \mathbf{0} & \mathbf{0} \\ \hline \mathbf{0} & \mathbf{0} & \mathbf{0} & \hat{\mathbf{d}}_1^t & \hat{\mathbf{d}}_2^t & 1 \end{array}\right]_{\boldsymbol{\delta}=\mathbf{0}}$$

After the differentiation with respect to $\boldsymbol{\delta}_1$ and substitution of $\boldsymbol{\delta}_2 = \mathbf{0}$ we obtain

$$\frac{\partial^l D}{\partial \delta_1 \cdots \partial \delta_l} = \det \left[\begin{array}{c|cc|cc|c} \mathbf{T}_0 & \mathbf{0} & \mathbf{0} & \mathbf{P}_1 & \mathbf{P}_2 & \mathbf{0} \\ \hline \mathbf{0} & \mathbf{1} & \mathbf{0} & -\mathbf{1} & \mathbf{0} & \mathbf{0} \\ \mathbf{0} & \mathbf{0} & \mathbf{0} & \mathbf{0} & -\mathbf{1} & \mathbf{0} \\ \hline -\mathbf{Q}_1^t & \mathbf{0} & \mathbf{0} & \mathbf{0} & \mathbf{0} & \mathbf{0} \\ -\mathbf{Q}_2^t & \mathbf{0} & \mathbf{1} & \mathbf{0} & \mathbf{0} & \mathbf{0} \\ \hline \mathbf{0} & \mathbf{0} & \mathbf{0} & \hat{\mathbf{d}}_1^t & \hat{\mathbf{d}}_2^t & 1 \end{array}\right]. \tag{8.5.8}$$

Applying Laplace expansion we obtain

$$\frac{\partial^l D}{\partial \delta_1 \cdots \partial \delta_l} = \det \begin{bmatrix} \mathbf{T}_0 & \mathbf{P}_1 \\ -\mathbf{Q}_1^t & \mathbf{0} \end{bmatrix} = \det \mathbf{T}_0 \det \begin{bmatrix} \mathbf{1} & \mathbf{T}_0^{-1}\mathbf{P}_1 \\ -\mathbf{Q}_1^t & \mathbf{0} \end{bmatrix}$$

$$= \det \mathbf{T}_0 \det (\mathbf{Q}_1^t \mathbf{T}_0^{-1} \mathbf{P}_1).$$

Denoting

$$\mathcal{F}_{11} = \mathbf{Q}_1^t \mathbf{T}_0^{-1} \mathbf{P}_1 \tag{8.5.9}$$

the lth derivative is given by

$$\frac{\partial^l D}{\partial \delta_1 \cdots \partial \delta_l} = \det \mathbf{T}_0 \det \mathcal{F}_{11}. \tag{8.5.10}$$

At this point we note that $\mathcal{F}_{11}$ is obtained from $\mathcal{F}$ by *retaining only the first l rows and columns* as follows from (8.5.9).

The lth derivative of the numerator is found by obtaining the determinant of a matrix similar to (8.5.8) with the last column replaced by the right-hand side of (8.5.3):

$$\frac{\partial^l N}{\partial \delta_1 \cdots \partial \delta_l} = \det \left[\begin{array}{c|cc|cc|c} \mathbf{T}_0 & \mathbf{0} & \mathbf{0} & \mathbf{P}_1 & \mathbf{P}_2 & \mathbf{W} \\ \hline \mathbf{0} & \mathbf{1} & \mathbf{0} & -\mathbf{1} & \mathbf{0} & \mathbf{0} \\ \mathbf{0} & \mathbf{0} & \mathbf{0} & \mathbf{0} & -\mathbf{1} & \mathbf{0} \\ \hline -\mathbf{Q}_1^t & \mathbf{0} & \mathbf{0} & \mathbf{0} & \mathbf{0} & \mathbf{0} \\ -\mathbf{Q}_2^t & \mathbf{0} & \mathbf{1} & \mathbf{0} & \mathbf{0} & \mathbf{0} \\ \hline \mathbf{0} & \mathbf{0} & \mathbf{0} & \hat{\mathbf{d}}_1^t & \hat{\mathbf{d}}_2^t & F_0 \end{array}\right] = \det \begin{bmatrix} \mathbf{T}_0 & \mathbf{P}_1 & \mathbf{W} \\ -\mathbf{Q}_1^t & \mathbf{0} & \mathbf{0} \\ \mathbf{0} & \hat{\mathbf{d}}_1^t & F_0 \end{bmatrix}$$

$$= \det \mathbf{T}_0 \det \begin{bmatrix} \mathbf{Q}_1^t \mathbf{T}_0^{-1} \mathbf{P}_1 & \mathbf{Q}_1^t \mathbf{T}_0^{-1} \mathbf{W} \\ \hat{\mathbf{d}}_1^t & F_0 \end{bmatrix}.$$

Introducing the notation

$$\hat{\mathbf{W}}_1 = \mathbf{Q}_1^t \mathbf{T}_0^{-1} \mathbf{W} \tag{8.5.11}$$

and substituting (8.5.9) we obtain

$$\frac{\partial^l N}{\partial \delta_1 \cdots \partial \delta_l} = \det \mathbf{T}_0 \det \begin{bmatrix} \mathfrak{F}_{11} & \hat{\mathbf{W}}_1 \\ \hat{\mathbf{d}}_1^t & F_0 \end{bmatrix} = \det \mathbf{T}_0 \det \hat{\mathfrak{F}}_{11}. \tag{8.5.12}$$

In addition to the rows and columns used for the denominator we must retain the entries of the last row and column of $\hat{\mathfrak{F}}$. For better understanding, let us now use a hypothetical example with 5 variable elements, in which we are looking for the derivatives with respect to the second, third, and fifth elements. For the denominator we retain the second, third, and fifth rows and columns of $\hat{\mathfrak{F}}$ and calculate the determinant of the matrix. For the numerator, the same rows and columns plus the last row and column are retained. We can thus introduce the following general notation:

$$\begin{aligned} \frac{\partial^l D}{\partial \delta_{j_1} \partial \delta_{j_2} \cdots \partial \delta_{j_l}} &= \det \mathbf{T}_0 \det \hat{\mathfrak{F}}\,(j_1, j_2, \ldots, j_l) \\ \frac{\partial^l N}{\partial \delta_{j_1} \partial \delta_{j_2} \cdots \partial \delta_{j_l}} &= \det \mathbf{T}_0 \det \hat{\mathfrak{F}}\,(j_1, j_2, \ldots, j_l, m+1) \end{aligned} \tag{8.5.13}$$

in which the subscripts $j_1, j_2, \ldots, j_l$ denote the retained rows and columns.

Let us now summarize the results. Assume that the $(m + 1) \times (m + 1)$ matrix $\hat{\mathfrak{F}}$ has been obtained:

1. Any derivative of the denominator with respect to the variable elements is obtained by retaining appropriate rows and columns of the $m \times m$ submatrix $\mathfrak{F}$, appearing in the upper left partition of $\hat{\mathfrak{F}}$, and calculating the determinant of the matrix obtained.
2. Any derivative of the numerator with respect to the variable elements is obtained by retaining the same rows and columns as for the denominator, plus the last row and column of $\hat{\mathfrak{F}}$, and calculating the determinant of the matrix obtained.

The efficient generation of the various subdeterminants of $\mathfrak{F}$ and of the symbolic function in terms of element values rather than perturbations is considered in [2]. Additional information on symbolic functions can be found in [3].

EXAMPLE 8.5.1. Consider the network in Fig. 8.1.2. Its system equation is

$$\begin{bmatrix} G_1+G_4 & -G_1 & 0 \\ -G_1 & G_1+G_5+G_6 & -G_6 \\ 0 & -G_6+g_3 & G_2+G_6 \end{bmatrix} \begin{bmatrix} V_1 \\ V_2 \\ V_3 \end{bmatrix} = \begin{bmatrix} J \\ 0 \\ 0 \end{bmatrix}.$$

The transfer function is given for reference:

$$V_3 = \frac{G_1(1-g_3)}{1+2G_1+2G_2+g_3+3G_1G_2+G_1g_3} J.$$

In terms of the variations $\delta_1, \delta_2, \delta_3$, V_3 is

$$V_3 = -\frac{\delta_3+\delta_1\delta_3}{10+6\delta_1+5\delta_2+2\delta_3+3\delta_1\delta_2+\delta_1\delta_3} J.$$

This network has already been handled in Example 8.1.2, where we obtained

$$\hat{\mathfrak{F}} = \frac{1}{10}\left[\begin{array}{ccc|c} 6 & -1 & -1 & 4 \\ 0 & 5 & 5 & 0 \\ -2 & 2 & 2 & 2 \\ \hline 0 & 5 & 5 & 0 \end{array}\right].$$

Also, we have

$$\det \mathbf{T}_0 = 10 \quad \text{and} \quad F_0 = V_3 = 0.$$

Using Eqs. (8.5.13) the coefficients of the denominator are obtained as follows:

$b = \det \mathbf{T}_0 = 10$ as follows from (8.5.4)

$b_1 = \det \mathbf{T}_0 \det \hat{\mathfrak{F}}(1) = 10 \times \frac{6}{10} = 6$ (first row and column retained)

$b_2 = \det \mathbf{T}_0 \det \hat{\mathfrak{F}}(2) = 10 \times \frac{5}{10} = 5$ (second row and column retained)

$b_3 = \det \mathbf{T}_0 \det \hat{\mathfrak{F}}(3) = 10 \times \frac{2}{10} = 2$

$$b_{12} = \det \mathbf{T}_0 \det \hat{\mathfrak{F}}(1,2) = 10 \det \begin{bmatrix} \frac{6}{10} & -\frac{1}{10} \\ 0 & \frac{5}{10} \end{bmatrix} = 3$$

(first and second row and column retained)

$$b_{13} = \det \mathbf{T}_0 \det \hat{\mathfrak{F}}(1,3) = 10 \det \begin{bmatrix} \frac{6}{10} & -\frac{1}{10} \\ -\frac{2}{10} & \frac{2}{10} \end{bmatrix} = 1$$

$b_{23} = \det \mathbf{T}_0 \det \hat{\mathfrak{F}}(2,3) = 0$

$b_{123} = \det \mathbf{T}_0 \det \hat{\mathfrak{F}}(1,2,3) = 0$

and the denominator is

$$D = 10 + 6\delta_1 + 5\delta_2 + 2\delta_3 + 3\delta_1\delta_2 + \delta_1\delta_3.$$

For the numerator we obtain

$$a = 0 \quad \text{(as follows from (8.5.5))}$$

$$a_1 = \det \mathbf{T}_0 \det \hat{\mathfrak{F}}(1,4) = 10 \det \begin{bmatrix} \frac{6}{10} & \frac{4}{10} \\ 0 & 0 \end{bmatrix} = 0$$

$$a_2 = \det \mathbf{T}_0 \det \hat{\mathfrak{F}}(2,4) = 10 \det \begin{bmatrix} 0 & 0 \\ 0 & 0 \end{bmatrix} = 0$$

$$a_3 = \det \mathbf{T}_0 \det \hat{\mathfrak{F}}(3,4) = 10 \det \begin{bmatrix} \frac{2}{10} & \frac{2}{10} \\ \frac{5}{10} & 0 \end{bmatrix} = -1$$

$$a_{13} = \det \mathbf{T}_0 \det \hat{\mathfrak{F}}(1,3,4) = 10 \det \begin{bmatrix} \frac{6}{10} & -\frac{1}{10} & \frac{4}{10} \\ -\frac{2}{10} & \frac{2}{10} & \frac{2}{10} \\ 0 & \frac{5}{10} & 0 \end{bmatrix} = -1$$

and

a_{12}, a_{23}, and a_{123} are zero.

This gives the following numerator:

$$N = -\delta_3 - \delta_1\delta_3.$$

Both results agree with direct analysis.

So far, it has been assumed that all steps have been carried out at a single frequency. The method can be extended to incorporate the frequency, s, as a variable by applying the techniques discussed in Chapter 7.

Assume that we have properly selected the number of interpolating points $(n_0 + 1)$, and generated and stored the resulting matrices $\hat{\mathfrak{F}}(s_j)$. The value of the numerator, or any derivative of the numerator or denominator, can be obtained by retaining certain rows and columns and calculating the determinant, as discussed above. This gives values of the derivatives at each s_j. The discrete Fourier transform is now used to recover the polynomials. We will indicate the steps on a simple example.

EXAMPLE 8.5.2. Consider the network in Fig. 8.5.1. The system matrix is

$$\begin{bmatrix} 1 + \delta_1 + s & -s \\ -s & 1 + \delta_2 + s \end{bmatrix} \begin{bmatrix} V_1 \\ V_2 \end{bmatrix} = \begin{bmatrix} 1 \\ 0 \end{bmatrix}.$$

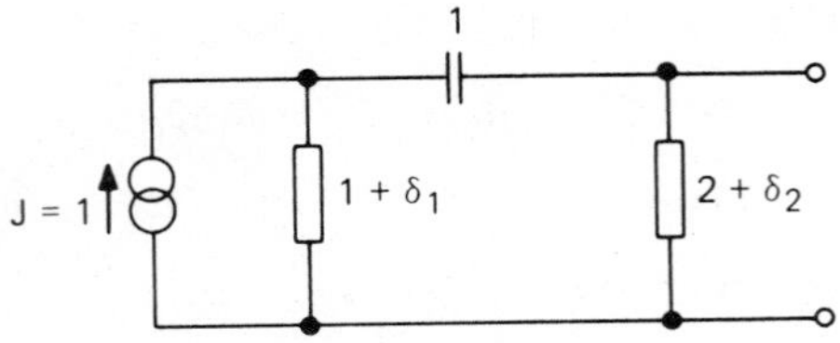

Fig. 8.5.1. Network for Example 8.5.2.

The output in terms of δ_1, δ_2 is

$$V_{out} = \frac{s}{(3s+2) + \delta_1(s+2) + \delta_2(s+1) + \delta_1\delta_2}.$$

The network is of first order, $n_0 = 1$, and only two equally spaced points on the unit circle are needed: $s_1 = 1, s_2 = -1$. Setting $\delta_1 = \delta_2 = 0$ we obtain

$$\det \mathbf{T}_0(s_1) = 5; \qquad \det \mathbf{T}_0(s_2) = -1;$$

$$\hat{\mathfrak{F}}(s_1) = \left[\begin{array}{cc|c} \frac{3}{5} & \frac{1}{5} & \frac{3}{5} \\ \frac{1}{5} & \frac{2}{5} & \frac{1}{5} \\ \hline \frac{1}{5} & \frac{2}{5} & \frac{1}{5} \end{array}\right]; \qquad \hat{\mathfrak{F}}(s_2) = \left[\begin{array}{cc|c} -1 & 1 & -1 \\ 1 & 0 & 1 \\ \hline 1 & 0 & 1 \end{array}\right]$$

Table 8.5.1. Generation of the Symbolic Function for Example 8.5.2.

	Value at $s_1 = 1$	Value at $s_2 = -1$	Interpolating points	Polynomial
$D = \det \mathbf{T}_0$	5	−1	(1, 5), (−1, −1)	$3s + 2$
$\frac{\partial D}{\partial \delta_1} = D \times \det \hat{\mathfrak{F}}(1)$	3	1	(1, 3), (−1, 1)	$s + 2$
$\frac{\partial D}{\partial \delta_2} = D \times \det \hat{\mathfrak{F}}(2)$	2	0	(1, 2), (−1, 0)	$s + 1$
$\frac{\partial^2 D}{\partial \delta_1 \partial \delta_2} = D \times \det \hat{\mathfrak{F}}(1, 2)$	1	1	(1, 1), (−1, 1)	1
$N = D \times \det \hat{\mathfrak{F}}(3)$	1	−1	(1, 1), (−1, −1)	s
$\frac{\partial N}{\partial \delta_1} = D \times \det \hat{\mathfrak{F}}(1, 3)$	0	0	(1, 0), (−1, 0)	0
$\frac{\partial N}{\partial \delta_2} = D \times \det \hat{\mathfrak{F}}(2, 3)$	0	0	(1, 0), (−1, 0)	0
$\frac{\partial^2 N}{\partial \delta_1 \partial \delta_2} = D \times \det \hat{\mathfrak{F}}(1, 2, 3)$	0	0	(1, 0), (−1, 0)	0

and Table 8.5.1 indicates the steps necessary in the generation of the full symbolic function.

Collecting the terms in the rightmost column we arrive at the same transfer function in terms of δ_i.

Symbolic functions of the type (8.5.1) are very useful in the study of small networks because they provide excellent insight. Unfortunately, the number of coefficients in (8.5.1) grows as 2^m for both the numerator and denominator and the insight is lost when $m \geqslant 5$. If the coefficients are polynomials in s, storage requirements grow unreasonably and retrieval of the information becomes cumbersome. On the other hand, all information about the network properties is contained in the matrices $\hat{\mathfrak{F}}(s_j)$ of size $(m+1) \times (m+1)$ and no problems arise in storage or retrieval for much larger m. It is therefore recommended to consider the "stack" of matrices $\hat{\mathfrak{F}}(s_j)$ (Fig. 8.5.2) as a special type of symbolic function from which all necessary information is extracted by the processing steps described above.

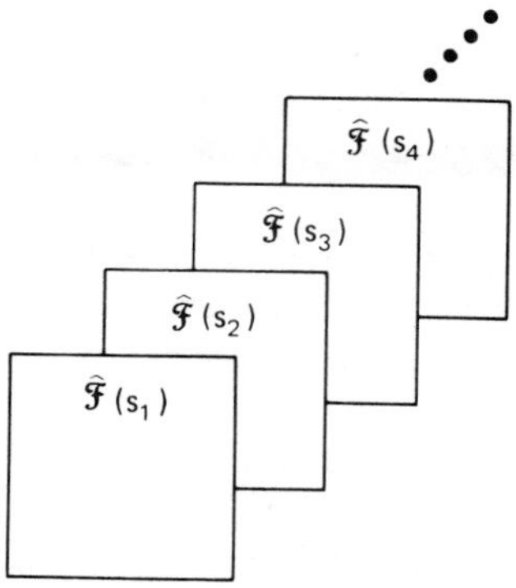

Fig. 8.5.2. Stack of matrices evaluated at several frequencies.

REFERENCES

1. K. Singhal and J. Vlach: Solution of modified systems and applications. *1981 IEEE International Symposium on Circuits and Systems*, pp. 620–623.
2. K. Singhal and J. Vlach: Symbolic analysis of analog and digital circuits. *IEEE Transactions on Circuits and Systems*, Vol. CAS-24, pp. 598–609, November 1977.
3. K. Singhal and J. Vlach: Symbolic circuit analysis. *IEE Proc.*, Vol. 128, Part G, pp. 81–86, April 1981.

CHAPTER 9
Introduction to Numerical Integration of Differential Equations

The time response of networks can be obtained by several methods, which can be broadly grouped into two categories: the linear multistep (LMS) and the Runge-Kutta (R-K) formulae. This chapter will discuss only the simplest LMS formulae: the forward Euler, backward Euler, and trapezoidal. They form the basis for the more detailed discussion in Chapter 13. Historically, R-K methods were also used extensively and reliable programs are available. Since these methods are less important for network solutions, the reader is referred to standard mathematical textbooks for more information.

Section 9.1 applies the three LMS formulae to differential equations in one variable. The concept of the predictor and corrector is established and demonstrated. It is shown that considerable simplifications may result if the equations are linear. Section 9.2 discusses the order of integration and the truncation error. Although the theory is applied only to the three formulae, the approach is general and holds in more complicated cases. Section 9.3 focuses on the stability concept and Section 9.4 applies the formulae to the solution of *linear networks.* It is demonstrated on examples that the solution is quite simple if the network is given in the normal state variable form. Since this form is rather difficult to obtain, generalization for use with any formulation is given. The formulae are useful for the solution of nonlinear equations as well, but applications and additional theoretical development are postponed to Chapter 13.

9.1. SIMPLE INTEGRATION METHODS

Let the differential equation to be integrated be

$$x' = f(x, t) \tag{9.1.1}$$

with t denoting the time. The equivalent integral equation is

$$x = x(a) + \int_a^b f(x, t)\, dt. \tag{9.1.2}$$

Let an approximate solution x_n be known at time t_n. We wish to obtain a solution x_{n+1} at the time t_{n+1} by taking a step

$$h = t_{n+1} - t_n. \tag{9.1.3}$$

If we are starting with $n = 0$, the initial value $x_0 = x(a)$ is specified. For any other n, the numerical solution x_n will generally differ from the exact solution $x(a + nh)$. Since x_0 is known, x_0' can be calculated by means of (9.1.1) and we can approximate the solution x_1 by assuming that a tangent straight line with slope x_0' connects the point x_0 with the point x_1. This is shown in Fig. 9.1.1. The formula is

$$x_0' = (x_1 - x_0)/h$$

or

$$x_1 = x_0 + hx_0'. \tag{9.1.4}$$

This relation is known as the *forward Euler formula*. As can be seen from Fig. 9.1.1, the error will be larger if h is larger.

We can also make the assumption that x_1 is determined by x_0 and the *derivative at the point* x_1. We choose the step h but x_1' cannot be calculated from (9.1.1) directly since x_1 is unknown. We may *assume* some value for x_1, for instance the value obtained by the forward Euler formula, and iterate to fulfill

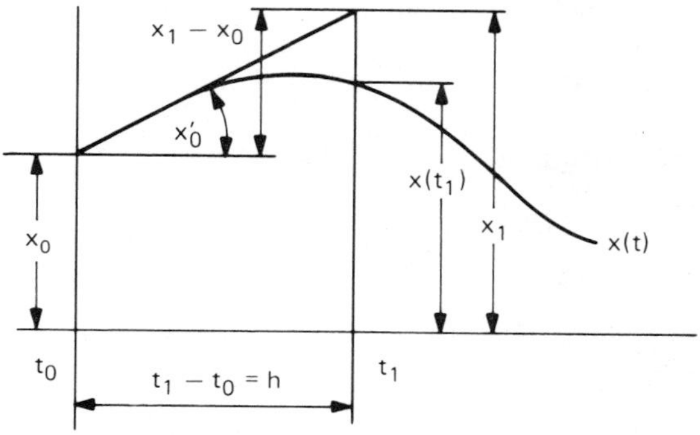

Fig. 9.1.1. Approximation of $x' = f(x, t)$ by the forward Euler formula.

$x_1' = f(x_1, h)$. From

$$x_1' = (x_1 - x_0)/h$$

we obtain

$$x_1 = x_0 + hx_1'. \tag{9.1.5}$$

This is called the *backward Euler formula.*

Still another possibility lies in weighting the derivatives at the two points. For instance, we may define

$$\frac{x_1' + x_0'}{2} = \frac{x_1 - x_0}{h}$$

where the average value of the two derivatives is used. Although x_0' can be calculated directly, x_1' and x_1 cannot and are obtained through some iterative procedure.

This formula is called the *trapezoidal rule* and is usually given in the following form:

$$x_1 = x_0 + \frac{h}{2}(x_1' + x_0'). \tag{9.1.6}$$

EXAMPLE 9.1.1. Consider the (linear) differential equation $x' = x + t^2$ and apply the forward Euler formula with the step $h = 0.025$. Let $x_0 = 1$ for $t = 0$. The exact solution of this differential equation is

$$x = 3e^t - t^2 - 2t - 2.$$

We will use the exact solution for comparison of the accuracy. Initially

$$t_0 = 0; \qquad x_0 = 1; \qquad x_0' = x_0 + t_0^2 = 1.$$

Using (9.1.4), the forward Euler formula, we obtain

$$x_1 = 1 + 0.025 \times 1 = 1.025.$$

At the next step we obtain

$$t_1 = 0.025; \qquad x_1 = 1.025; \qquad x_1' = 1.025 + 0.025^2 = 1.02565$$

and

$$x_2 = 1.025 + 0.025 \times 1.025625 = 1.05064.$$

Integration was continued by means of a computer and is shown below, where the error is defined as ϵ = (numerical result − result by formula):

t	Numerical Result	ϵ
0.000	1.0000000	0.0000000
0.025	1.0250000	−0.0003204
0.050	1.0506406	−0.0006727
0.075	1.0769691	−0.0010583
0.100	1.1040340	−0.0014788
0.125	1.1318848	−0.0019355
0.150	1.1605726	−0.0024301
0.175	1.1901494	−0.0029642
0.200	1.2206688	−0.0035395

The backward Euler and trapezoidal formulae use the derivative at the *next* point, but this point is not known yet. In oder to start the calculations an approximate value must be computed. This can be done in various ways, the simplest being the result of the previous step. Another possibility is the use of the forward Euler formula. We are thus coming to the concept of a *predictor* which predicts the value at the next point. Once such a value is available, x' can be evalued from (9.1.1) and inserted into the *corrector*, which in this chapter is either the backward Euler or trapezoidal formula. Iteration is required to correct the intial mismatch of x and x'. This iteration can be performed in various ways, the simplest one being repeated use of the corrector formula.

Although the predictors are not an absolute necessity, a better prediction will result in fewer iterations. Since predictors are very simple to use, their application is highly desirable. In addition, they can help in estimating the errors committed and in controlling the step size h. Details about step size control will be considered in Chapter 13. Here we will indicate the use of the predictor and corrector on an example.

EXAMPLE 9.1.2. Integrate the same differential equation as in Example 9.1.1 by using the forward Euler formula for prediction and the backward Euler formula for correction. Use three iterations for the corrector.

For $t_0 = 0$, $x_0 = 1$, and $h = 0.025$, the *prediction* results in

$$x_1^P = x_0 + hx_0' = 1 + 0.025 = 1.025.$$

Iteration 1:

$$x_1'^{(0)} = x_1^P + t_1^2 = 1.025 + 0.000625 = 1.025625$$

$$x_1^{(1)} = x_0 + hx_1'^{(0)} = 1.02564063.$$

Iteration 2:

$$x_1'^{(1)} = x_1^{(1)} + t_1^2 = 1.02626563$$

$$x_1^{(2)} = x_0 + hx_1'^{(1)} = 1.02565664.$$

Iteration 3:

$$x_1'^{(2)} = x_1^{(2)} + t_1^2 = 1.02628164$$

$$x_1^{(3)} = x_0 + hx_1'^{(2)} = \underline{1.02565704}.$$

The integration is continued by means of a computer and the results are shown below. The error is defined as in Example 9.1.1. The last value represents the solution at each step.

t	Numerical Result	ϵ	Corrector Iteration
0.000	1.0000000	0.0000000	
			1.0256410
			1.0256567
			1.0256570
0.025	1.0256570	0.0003367	
			1.0520036
			1.0520196
			1.0520200
0.050	1.0520200	0.0007067	
			1.0791222
			1.0791387
			1.0791391
0.075	1.0791391	0.0011117	
			1.1070483
			1.1070653
			1.1070658
0.100	1.1070658	0.0015530	

Comparison of the errors in Examples 9.1.1 and 9.1.2 shows that for the forward formula all errors are negative, whereas for the backward formula all of them are positive. Intuitively, a combination of the two should lead to a better result. Such a combination is the trapezoidal formula (9.1.6).

EXAMPLE 9.1.3. Apply the trapezoidal formula to the same differential equation as in Problem 9.1.1. Predict by means of the forward Euler formula.

The iteration results are

t	Numerical Result	ϵ	Corrector Iteration
			1.02532031
			1.02532432
0.025	1.02532437	0.00000400	1.02532437
			1.05131715
			1.05132145
0.050	1.05132150	0.00000821	1.05132150
			1.07803542
			1.07804002
0.075	1.07804008	0.00001263	1.07804008
			1.10552504
			1.10552996
0.100	1.10553002	0.00001726	1.10553002

The error is, indeed, reduced. Theoretical reasons for this fact will be given in the next section.

The three formulae used above are suitable for both linear and nonlinear differential equations. In our examples, we applied them to the linear differential equation $x' = x + t^2$ without taking advantage of the linearity.

The relationships can be simplified if the differential equations are known to be linear. We will explain this by considering a system of differential equations rather than a single equation. Let

$$\mathbf{x}' = \mathbf{A}\mathbf{x} + \mathbf{w} \tag{9.1.7}$$

where $\mathbf{A}$ is a constant matrix and $\mathbf{w}$ is a vector of functions of t which can be evaluated for any t. It is, in fact, the state variable formulation in normal form, discussed in Chapter 3. Applying the backward Euler formula to each component of $\mathbf{x}$ we obtain

$$\mathbf{x}_{n+1} = \mathbf{x}_n + h\mathbf{x}'_{n+1} \tag{9.1.8}$$

and substituting from (9.1.7) for $\mathbf{x}'_{n+1}$ we obtain

$$\mathbf{x}_{n+1} = \mathbf{x}_n + h(\mathbf{A}\mathbf{x}_{n+1} + \mathbf{w}_{n+1}).$$

Rewrite this in the following form:

$$(\mathbf{1} - h\mathbf{A})\,\mathbf{x}_{n+1} = \mathbf{x}_n + h\mathbf{w}_{n+1} \tag{9.1.9}$$

1 being a unit matrix. On the left side we have the matrix $(\mathbf{1} - h\mathbf{A})$ and on the right side a known vector. The matrix is decomposed into its triangular factors and the solution of (9.1.9) is found by forward and back substitution. The same factors are used for the next step. Note that as long as the step size h is constant, the matrix on the left side of (9.1.9) does not change and one **LU** decomposition is sufficient for all steps.

In case of the trapezoidal rule, the matrix equation becomes

$$\mathbf{x}_{n+1} = \mathbf{x}_n + \frac{h}{2}(\mathbf{A}\mathbf{x}_{n+1} + \mathbf{w}_{n+1} + \mathbf{A}\mathbf{x}_n + \mathbf{w}_n).$$

Transferring the term $\mathbf{x}_{n+1}$ to the left side we obtain the following matrix equation:

$$\left(\mathbf{1} - \frac{h}{2}\mathbf{A}\right)\mathbf{x}_{n+1} = \left(\mathbf{1} + \frac{h}{2}\mathbf{A}\right)\mathbf{x}_n + \frac{h}{2}(\mathbf{w}_{n+1} + \mathbf{w}_n) \tag{9.1.10}$$

which is solved as discussed above.

9.2. ORDER OF INTEGRATION AND TRUNCATION ERROR

The trapezoidal formula used the derivatives at the old and new points with equal weights. It is clear that different weights could be given to both the x_1 and x_1'. A generalized weighting would be

$$b_1 x_1' + b_0 x_0' = (a_1 x_1 + a_0 x_0)/h$$

or, written differently,

$$a_1 x_1 + a_0 x_0 - h(b_1 x_1' + b_0 x_0') = 0. \tag{9.2.1}$$

Further generalization can be obtained by taking more than two points x_i and x_i'; however, the discussion of this case will be postponed to Chapter 13. Special choices of a_1 and b_1 reduce (9.2.1) into the three formulae discussed in Section 9.1.

We will now derive some theoretical properties of the three formulae. Using exact values, (9.2.1) can be written for $t_1 = t_0 + h$ as follows:

$$a_1 x(t_0 + h) + a_0 x(t_0) - h[b_1 x'(t_0 + h) + b_0 x'(t_0)] = 0.$$

The functions $x(t_0 + h)$ and $x'(t_0 + h)$ can be expanded into Taylor series:

$$a_1\left[x(t_0)+\frac{h}{1!}x'(t_0)+\frac{h^2}{2!}x''(t_0)+\frac{h^3}{3!}x'''(t_0)+\cdots\right]+a_0x(t_0)$$
$$-hb_1\left[x'(t_0)+\frac{h}{1!}x''(t_0)+\frac{h^2}{2!}x'''(t_0)+\cdots\right]-hb_0x'(t_0)=0.$$

Rearranging and transferring all terms with second and higher derivatives to the right side, we obtain

$$x(t_0)[a_1+a_0]+hx'(t_0)[a_1-b_1-b_0]=-h^2x''(t_0)\left[\frac{a_1}{2!}-b_1\right]$$
$$-h^3x'''(t_0)\left[\frac{a_1}{3!}-\frac{b_1}{2!}\right]-\cdots. \qquad (9.2.2)$$

We can satisfy (9.2.2) by setting the terms in the square brackets of the various derivatives equal to zero. This leads to:

1. *For the left side:* x: $\quad a_1+a_0=0$

   x': $\quad a_1-b_1-b_0=0$

2. *For the right side:* x'': $\quad \dfrac{a_1}{2}-b_1=0$ $\qquad (9.2.3)$

   x''': $\quad \dfrac{a_1}{6}-\dfrac{b_1}{2}=0.$

The first condition on the left side is satisfied by selecting, for instance, $a_1=1$; then $a_0=-1$. The second condition on the left side can be satisfied in various ways. If we choose $b_1=0$ and $b_0=1$, we obtain the forward Euler formula. Now all free coefficients have been selected and the first term on the right side will be $c_2=-\frac{1}{2}$. Another choice is $b_0=0$, $b_1=1$. This results in the backward Euler formula and on the right side the first term is fully determined as $c_2=\frac{1}{2}$. Since in both cases the coefficients of the zeroth and first derivatives in (9.2.2) are zero, we introduce the notion of the *order of integration*, p. For the above formulae, $p=1$ and the first nonzero term on the right side represents the *truncation error*, c_{p+1}.

The third relation in (9.2.3) can be satisfied as well if we select $a_1=1, a_0=-1$, $b_0=b_1=\frac{1}{2}$. This choice increases the order of integration to $p=2$ and the truncation error becomes $c_3=-\frac{1}{12}$. Comparison with (9.1.6) shows that it is the trapezoidal formula. Recall that in Example 9.1.3 this formula gave better results than the two Euler formulae. The reason for this is the increased order of integration and smaller truncation error. The higher the value of p and the smaller the truncation error c_{p+1}, the better, in some sense, is the result obtained by the particular formula.

9.3. STABILITY OF INTEGRATION

The order of integration and the truncation error of a particular formula are not sufficient for the proper understanding of its behavior. The concept of stability of the formula is another measure of usefulness. Stability is studied on the special differential equation

$$x' = \lambda x \tag{9.3.1}$$

whose exact solution is

$$x = x(0)\, e^{\lambda t}.$$

The constant λ may be real or complex. Notice that all linear networks with lumped, time invariant elements and with simple poles respond to an impulse input signal with

$$x(t) = \sum A_i e^{\lambda_i t}$$

and thus we study the stability for one component of the response.

We will start with the forward Euler formula (9.1.4). Inserting (9.3.1) for the derivative we obtain

$$x_1 = (1 + \lambda h)\, x_0.$$

In the next step the result is used again to obtain x_2:

$$x_2 = (1 + \lambda h)\, x_1 = (1 + \lambda h)^2 x_0.$$

Proceeding n steps we obtain by successive substitutions

$$x_n = (1 + \lambda h)^n x_0.$$

Let n increase to ∞. For the result to be finite for a stable differential equation ($\text{Re}\ \lambda < 0$), we must have

$$|1 + h\lambda| \leqslant 1 \tag{9.3.2}$$

which is the condition of stability of the forward Euler formula. In (9.3.2), h is the step size (a real number) but λ may be a complex number. Let us now find the region in which condition (9.3.2) is satisfied. Introduce

$$h\lambda = q = u + jv \tag{9.3.3}$$

and insert into (9.3.2). The result is

$$|1 + u + jv| \leqslant 1$$

or

$$(1 + u)^2 + v^2 \leqslant 1.$$

This is the region inside a circle with center at $(-1, 0)$ passing through the origin (see Fig. 9.3.1). The region of stability is *inside* the circle. We interpret the result in the following way:

1. Let Re $\lambda < 0$.
2. Let h be such that the product $q = \lambda h$ is represented by a point inside the circle.
3. Under these conditions, integrating $x' = \lambda x$ by means of the forward Euler formula results in a stable solution.

For *large* $|\lambda|$, the step size must be *small* to secure stability. An example is shown in Table 9.3.1 where the forward Euler formula was used to solve $x' = -x$, $x_0 = 1$. The first column, with $h = 0.1$, has q well inside the stability region. The second column, with $h = 2$, has q on the boundary of the stability region

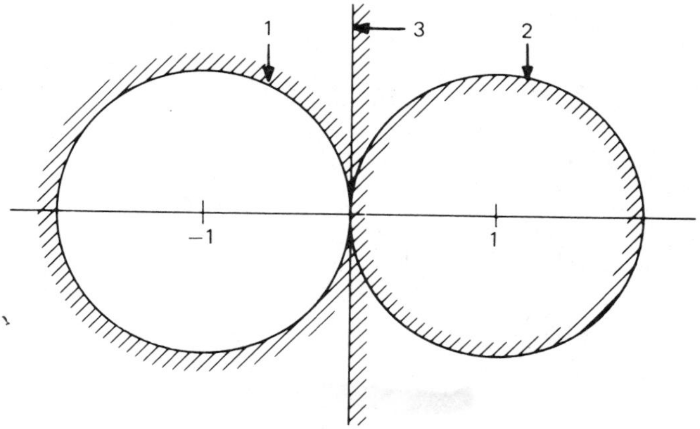

Fig. 9.3.1. Stability regions of integration formulae: (1) forward Euler, stable inside; (2) backward Euler, stable outside; (3) trapezoidal, stable in the left half plane.

Table 9.3.1. Numerical Solution of $x' = -x$ for Various h by the Forward Euler Formula.

Step k	Solution for $h = 0.1$	$h = 2$	$h = 3$
0	1	1	1
1	0.9	−1	−2
2	0.81	1	4
3	0.729	−1	−8
4	0.6561	1	16
5	0.59049	−1	−32
6	0.53144	1	64

and the solution oscillates but does not grow. The third column, with $h = 3$, is outside the stability region and the results grow and oscillate, although the exact solution is e^{-t} and decreases.

Consider next the backward Euler formula (9.1.5). Inserting (9.3.1) for x' we obtain

$$x_1 = x_0 + hx_1' = x_0 + h\lambda x_1$$

or

$$x_1 = \frac{x_0}{1 - h\lambda} = \frac{x_0}{1 - q}.$$

Proceeding to the nth step, we have

$$x_n = \left[\frac{1}{1 - q}\right]^n x_0.$$

In order to get a stable solution for $n \to \infty$ we require

$$\left|\frac{1}{1 - q}\right| \leqslant 1$$

and inserting for q from (9.3.3):

$$1 \leqslant (1 - u)^2 + v^2.$$

If we take the equality in the above relation we get a circle with center at $(1, 0)$ passing through the origin. The inequality is satisfied outside this circle, as indicated in Fig. 9.3.1. The formula is thus stable for all λ in the left half plane. If λ is in the right half plane (unstable function), the result shows instability only as long as λ is inside the unit circle. However, if λ is outside this circle in the right half plane, the formula provides a converging sequence, although the actual response grows without bound. The reader can confirm this by selecting $q = \frac{1}{2}$ (inside) and $q = 3$ (outside) the unit circle and calculating a few x_i for positive Re λ.

Now consider the trapezoidal formula (9.1.6). Inserting (9.3.1) for both x_0' and x_1':

$$x_1 = x_0 + \frac{\lambda h}{2}(x_1 + x_0)$$

or

$$x_1 = x_0 \frac{1 + \lambda h/2}{1 - \lambda h/2}.$$

For n steps we have

$$x_n = \left[\frac{2+q}{2-q}\right]^n x_0.$$

In the limiting case as $n \to \infty$ the stability requirement is

$$\left|\frac{2+q}{2-q}\right| \leqslant 1$$

or

$$\left|\frac{2+u+jv}{2-u-jv}\right| \leqslant 1.$$

Simplifying we obtain

$$4u \leqslant 0$$

which shows that the boundary of the stability region is the imaginary axis. The formula is stable for any λ with the Re $\lambda < 0$. This is shown in Fig. 9.3.1. The trapezoidal rule is thus a limiting case with order higher than the other formulae requiring x_1, x_0, x_1', x_0'. It indicates stable response for stable functions and unstable response for unstable functions. This is a valuable feature for cases where the actual behavior of the function is not known beforehand.

It should be recognized that satisfying the stability condition does not imply that the result is correct. It only means that any error in calculation does not grow in subsequent steps. The value of the error is affected by the neglected terms $\Sigma_{p+1}^{\infty} h^i c_i x^{(i)}(t_0)$, and these terms are large for large h. One way to assure *correctness* of the results for a given step size is to choose a formula with higher p. It will be shown in Chapter 13 that a higher p may result in reduced stability.

At this stage it is useful to give an informal explanation of some commonly used terms and concepts.

Formulae that directly generate the next solution, like the forward Euler formula, are called *explicit.* They are used mainly to *predict* starting values for other formulae like the backward Euler or the trapezoidal rule which, in general, require the iterative solution of a nonlinear algebraic equation at each step. Such formulae are said to be *implicit* or *corrector* formulae. Though the computing cost associated with the implicit formulae is higher, they have desirable stability properties that permit use of much larger time steps and thus, ultimately, reduce the overall computing requirements.

An integration formula is said to be *A-stable* if it leads to a bounded solution of the test differential equation (9.3.1) for any step size and any number of steps if Re $\lambda < 0$. The trapezoidal rule and the backward Euler formula have this property.

The *region of absolute stability* of a given formula is the portion of the plane $q = h\lambda$ in which the integration of the differential equation (9.3.1) with Re $\lambda < 0$ results in a bounded solution for any number of steps. For instance, the forward Euler formula is absolutely stable in the unit circle in the left half plane, see Figure 9.3.1. On the other hand, the backward Euler formula is absolutely stable in the whole left half plane.

As most networks encountered in practice operate in a stable fashion, we are generally concerned with solutions of the test equation only when Re $\lambda < 0$. There are, however, situations as in oscillator circuits where the actual system is unstable or has a periodic response. Methods whose region of stability extend into the right half plane, like the backward Euler formula, lead to numerical solutions which decay with time and are not suitable for such problems. The trapezoidal rule and other formulae, not discussed in this book, are preferable in such situations.

A *stiff system* is a system having some poles close to the origin of coordinates and some poles *very* far away from them, all in the left half plane. Such a system is stable. The solution components corresponding to the large poles generally decay rapidly. If we integrate by, say, the forward Euler formula, we must select the step size h so small that the pole which is fartherst away from the origin is brought into the stability region *regardless* of whether or not the solution component due to it is significant. On the other hand, the backward Euler formula will not present any problems, because it is stable for any h. Thus we can start with small values of h and then switch to larger values as the fast solution components decay out.

A *stiff integration formula* is a formula which can handle stiff systems without requiring very small step sizes. Such formulae will be discussed in Chapter 13. The simplest one is the backward Euler formula.

9.4. TIME DOMAIN SOLUTION OF LINEAR NETWORKS

The formulae introduced thus far can be used for the time domain solution of both linear and nonlinear networks. In this introductory chapter we will restrict their application to linear networks.

If the network equations are in the normal state variable form

$$\mathbf{x}' = \mathbf{A}\mathbf{x} + \mathbf{B}\mathbf{w}(t) \tag{9.4.1}$$

then the time domain solution poses no problem. Either (9.1.9) or (9.1.10) can be used and programming is very simple. We will demonstrate the use of (9.1.9) on a simple RC network.

EXAMPLE 9.4.1. Find the time domain response of the network in Fig. 9.4.1 to the unit step. Let the initial voltages on the capacitors be zero and let the integration step be $h = 0.05$.

For this network, we need not go through the state variable formulation by means of graphs (as in Chapter 3). Nodal formulation can be used. The nodal matrix equation is

$$\begin{bmatrix} 1+3s & -2s \\ -2s & 2+2s \end{bmatrix} \begin{bmatrix} V_1 \\ V_2 \end{bmatrix} = \begin{bmatrix} J(s) \\ 0 \end{bmatrix}.$$

Splitting the matrix into two matrices, write

$$\begin{bmatrix} 3 & -2 \\ -2 & 2 \end{bmatrix} \begin{bmatrix} sV_1 \\ sV_2 \end{bmatrix} = \begin{bmatrix} -1 & 0 \\ 0 & -2 \end{bmatrix} \begin{bmatrix} V_1 \\ V_2 \end{bmatrix} + \begin{bmatrix} J(s) \\ 0 \end{bmatrix}.$$

Inversion of the first matrix provides

$$\begin{bmatrix} sV_1 \\ sV_2 \end{bmatrix} = \begin{bmatrix} -1 & -2 \\ -1 & -3 \end{bmatrix} \begin{bmatrix} V_1 \\ V_2 \end{bmatrix} + \begin{bmatrix} J(s) \\ J(s) \end{bmatrix}$$

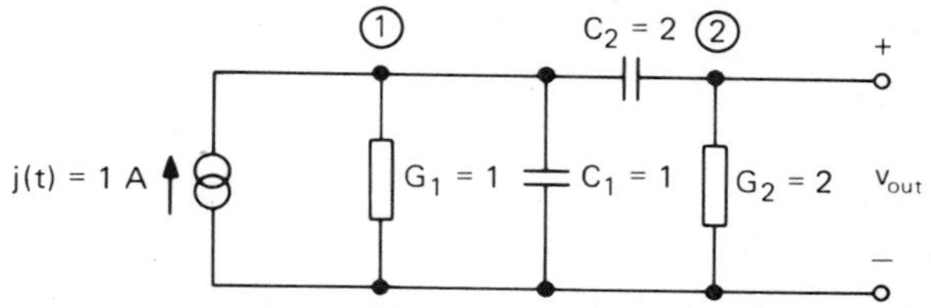

Fig. 9.4.1. Network for Example 9.4.1.

and in the time domain

$$\begin{bmatrix} v_1' \\ v_2' \end{bmatrix} = \begin{bmatrix} -1 & -2 \\ -1 & -3 \end{bmatrix} \begin{bmatrix} v_1 \\ v_2 \end{bmatrix} + \begin{bmatrix} j(t) \\ j(t) \end{bmatrix}$$

with $j(t) = 1$ for all steps, as specified in the problem.

Application of (9.1.9) requires

$$(\mathbf{1} - h\mathbf{A}) = \begin{bmatrix} 1 + h & 2h \\ h & 1 + 3h \end{bmatrix}$$

and the solution is obtained from

$$\begin{bmatrix} 1 + h & 2h \\ h & 1 + 3h \end{bmatrix} \begin{bmatrix} v_{1,i+1} \\ v_{2,i+1} \end{bmatrix} = \begin{bmatrix} v_{1,i} \\ v_{2,i} \end{bmatrix} + \begin{bmatrix} h \\ h \end{bmatrix}.$$

The response at several steps is given in the table below:

t	v_1	v_2
0.050	0.04366	0.04158
0.100	0.08195	0.07607
0.150	0.11571	0.10460
0.200	0.14562	0.12810
0.250	0.17227	0.14738
0.300	0.19615	0.16311
0.350	0.21768	0.17585

The most time-consuming part in solving Example 9.4.1 was the generation of the equivalent normal state variable form. We would like to avoid such steps and directly use the modified nodal or tableau formulation. Let the system equations in the Laplace domain be

$$(\mathbf{G} + s\mathbf{C})\,\mathbf{X} = \mathbf{W}.$$

In the time domain, this is equivalent to

$$\mathbf{G}\mathbf{x} + \mathbf{C}\mathbf{x}' = \mathbf{w}. \tag{9.4.2}$$

Rewrite in the form

$$\mathbf{C}\mathbf{x}' = \mathbf{w} - \mathbf{G}\mathbf{x} \tag{9.4.3}$$

and consider first the backward Euler formula, premultiplied by **C**:

$$\mathbf{C}\mathbf{x}_{n+1} = \mathbf{C}\mathbf{x}_n + h\mathbf{C}\mathbf{x}'_{n+1}. \tag{9.4.4}$$

Substitute (9.4.3) into (9.4.4) by using the subscripts $n + 1$ and n:

$$\mathbf{C}\mathbf{x}_{n+1} = \mathbf{C}\mathbf{x}_n + h(\mathbf{w}_{n+1} - \mathbf{G}\mathbf{x}_{n+1})$$

or

$$(\mathbf{C} + h\mathbf{G})\,\mathbf{x}_{n+1} = \mathbf{C}\mathbf{x}_n + h\mathbf{w}_{n+1}. \tag{9.4.5}$$

Formula (9.4.5) indicates that there is no need to formulate the network in terms of state variables. Once the matrices **G** and **C** are known from the modified nodal formulation, (9.4.5) is applied directly. In fact, the matrices **G** and **C** may even be singular; as long as the sum $h\mathbf{G} + \mathbf{C}$ is nonsingular, solution is possible. This will be demonstrated on an example, but first we derive a similar result for the trapezoidal rule:

$$\mathbf{C}\mathbf{x}_{n+1} = \mathbf{C}\mathbf{x}_n + \frac{h}{2}\mathbf{C}\mathbf{x}'_{n+1} + \frac{h}{2}\mathbf{C}\mathbf{x}'_n.$$

Substituting from (9.4.3) gives

$$\mathbf{C}\mathbf{x}_{n+1} = \mathbf{C}\mathbf{x}_n + \frac{h}{2}(\mathbf{w}_{n+1} - \mathbf{G}\mathbf{x}_{n+1}) + \frac{h}{2}(\mathbf{w}_n - \mathbf{G}\mathbf{x}_n).$$

Transferring terms with $\mathbf{x}_{n+1}$ to the left side we obtain

$$\left(\mathbf{C} + \frac{h}{2}\mathbf{G}\right)\mathbf{x}_{n+1} = \left(\mathbf{C} - \frac{h}{2}\mathbf{G}\right)\mathbf{x}_n + \frac{h}{2}(\mathbf{w}_{n+1} + \mathbf{w}_n). \tag{9.4.6}$$

EXAMPLE 9.4.2. Apply the backward Euler formula (9.4.5) to the time domain solution of the network in Fig. 9.4.2. Let the initial conditions be zero, the step size $h = 0.1$, and the source a unit step. Use the modified nodal formulation.

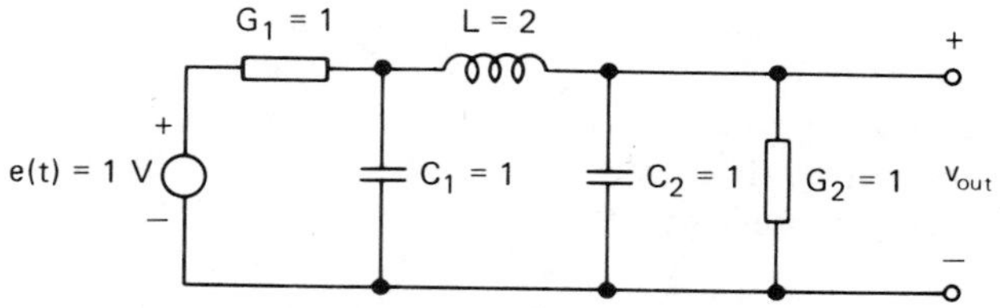

Fig. 9.4.2. Network for Example 9.4.2.

The system equation is

$$\mathbf{G}\mathbf{x} + \mathbf{C}\mathbf{x}' = \mathbf{w}$$

where

$$\mathbf{G} = \begin{bmatrix} G_1 & -G_1 & 0 & 0 & 1 \\ -G_1 & G_1 & 0 & 1 & 0 \\ 0 & 0 & G_2 & -1 & 0 \\ 0 & 1 & -1 & 0 & 0 \\ 1 & 0 & 0 & 0 & 0 \end{bmatrix}; \quad \mathbf{C} = \begin{bmatrix} 0 & 0 & 0 & 0 & 0 \\ 0 & C_1 & 0 & 0 & 0 \\ 0 & 0 & C_2 & 0 & 0 \\ 0 & 0 & 0 & -L & 0 \\ 0 & 0 & 0 & 0 & 0 \end{bmatrix};$$

$$\mathbf{w} = [0 \quad 0 \quad 0 \quad 0 \quad e(t)]^t.$$

Although $\mathbf{C}$ is clearly singular, the sum $(\mathbf{C} + h\mathbf{G})$ is nonsingular and a solution exists. The problem was run on the computer, and the first few steps are given in the table below:

Time	v_{out}
0.0	0.0
0.1	4.09500D-04
0.2	1.55650D-03
0.3	3.69602D-03
0.4	7.01808D-03
0.5	1.16553D-02
0.6	1.76897D-02

The time domain equations can also be formulated on an element-by-element basis through the use of *companion models.* Such models offer insight into the problem and aid the assembly of the equations as they reduce the time domain analysis problem to one of solving a resistive network. Consider the backward Euler formula (9.1.5), repeated here for the nth step:

$$x_{n+1} = x_n + hx'_{n+1} \tag{9.4.7}$$

and a typical capacitor in the network. The voltage across the capacitor and the current flowing through it are related by $i = C\,dv/dt$. Identify the voltage v as x, x' as $dv/dt = i/C$, and insert into (9.4.7) by using corresponding subscripts:

$$v_{n+1} = v_n + i_{n+1}\,h/C.$$

This can be rewritten as follows:

$$i_{n+1} = \frac{C}{h} v_{n+1} - \frac{C}{h} v_n. \tag{9.4.8}$$

The value $C/h = G_{eq}$ represents a conductance and the equation can be viewed in terms of the companion model shown in Fig. 9.4.3. Here v_{n+1} and i_{n+1} are the variables at step $n + 1$, whereas $(C/h)\, v_n$ represents a current source in parallel with G_{eq}.

A similar development holds for an inductor for which $v = L\, di/dt$. Identify the current i with x, $di/dt = v/L$ with x', and insert into (9.4.7) with proper subscripts:

$$i_{n+1} = i_n + \frac{h}{L} v_{n+1}$$

or

$$v_{n+1} = \frac{L}{h} i_{n+1} - \frac{L}{h} i_n \tag{9.4.9}$$

which can be interpreted as a resistive element with a voltage source in series, as shown in Fig. 9.4.3. Summarizing the above steps we see that with the backward Euler formula:

1. The network becomes a resistive network with a resistor L/h replacing each inductor and with a conductance C/h replacing each capacitor.
2. Sources that depend on the solution at the previous time step are applied in parallel with C/h and in series with L/h.

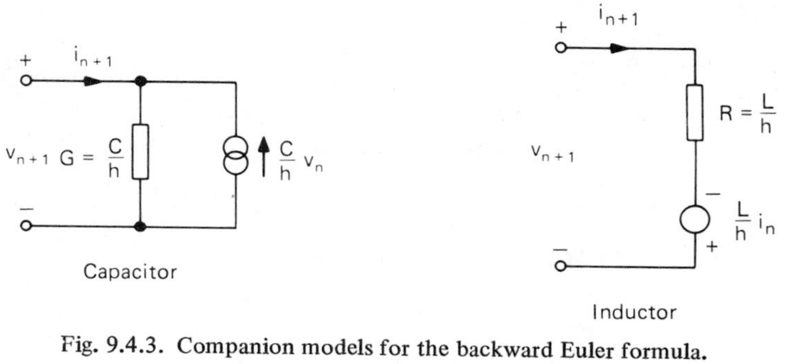

Fig. 9.4.3. Companion models for the backward Euler formula.

Similar formulae can be derived for the trapezoidal rule or for higher-order multistep formulae, to be discussed in Chapter 13. In each case, the network becomes a "resistive" network and additional sources appear in it.

EXAMPLE 9.4.3. Consider the network shown in Fig. 9.4.4 and use the companion models derived above to prepare the system of equations for time domain solution by the backward Euler formula.

$$\left[\begin{array}{cc|c} G_1+\dfrac{C_1}{h} & 0 & 1 \\ 0 & G_2+\dfrac{C_2}{h} & -1 \\ \hline 1 & -1 & -\dfrac{L}{h} \end{array}\right]\left[\begin{array}{c} v_{1,n+1} \\ v_{2,n+1} \\ \hline i_{L,n+1} \end{array}\right]=\left[\begin{array}{c} j_{n+1} \\ 0 \\ \hline 0 \end{array}\right]+\left[\begin{array}{c} \dfrac{C_1}{h}v_{1,n} \\ \dfrac{C_2}{h}v_{2,n} \\ \hline -\dfrac{L}{h}i_{L,n} \end{array}\right].$$

The reader should note that the same result is obtained by Eq. (9.4.5), if we divide that equation by h.

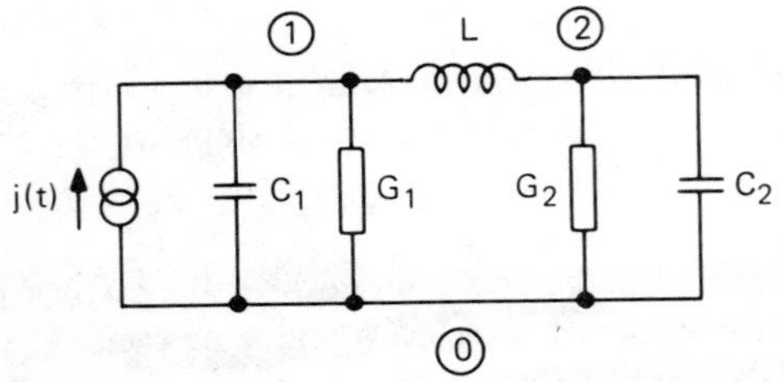

Fig. 9.4.4. Network for Example 9.4.3.

PROBLEMS

P.9.1. Several differential equations and their solutions are given. Evaluate the solutions at $t=0$ to obtain the initial condition and then integrate over several steps with $h=0.1$ using: (a) the forward Euler method; (b) the backward Euler method as corrector with the forward Euler as a predictor.

$x' = x + t^2$ solution: $x = 6e^{t-1} - t^2 - 2t - 2$

$x' = -2x$ $x = e^{-2t}$

$x' = t^2 - tx + 1$ $x = t + e^{-t^2/2}$

$x' = -xt$ $x = e^{-t^2/2}$

$$x' = \sqrt{1 - x^2} \qquad\qquad x = \sin t$$

$$x' = x - 2 \sin t \qquad\qquad x = \sin t + \cos t$$

Compare the numerical result with the exact solution.

P.9.2. Apply Eqs. (9.4.5) and (9.4.6) to the networks in Figs. P.6.3 and P.6.5 (Chapter 6). Use a step size $h = 0.1$.

P.9.3. Write a subroutine for the multiplication of an $n \times n$ matrix by a vector.

P.9.4. Write a program for the backward Euler method, Eq. (9.4.5). Test by feeding the matrices **G** and **C** by hand for any of the problems given in the previous chapters. For the solution, use the subroutines from Chapter 2. Check the results by running the program from Appendix D or compare with known exact solution, obtained by Laplace transformation.

P.9.5. Write a program for the trapezoidal method, equation (9.4.6). Test as for Problem P.9.4.

P.9.6. Using the forward and backward Euler methods, and $h = 0.1$, solve the following differential equations in the interval (0, 1):

$$x' = x \sin t - 2x^2; \qquad x(0) = 0$$

$$x' = \cos(2t + x) + 1.5(t - x); \qquad x(0) = 0$$

$$x' = 1 - \sin(t + x) + \frac{0.5x}{2 + t}; \qquad x(0) = 0$$

$$x' = -x^2 + \frac{t}{1 + t^2}; \qquad x(0) = -0.4122.$$

CHAPTER 10
Numerical Laplace Transform Inversion

The time domain solution of linear networks by means of the Laplace transform can be accomplished by first finding the appropriate transfer function in the s-domain, defining the input signal in terms of the variable s, and inverting their product. The inversion involves finding poles and residues. Accuracy may be impaired if multiple poles occur, and finding the poles is always fairly expensive. This method for inversion is taught in undergraduate courses and was briefly discussed in Section 1.10. Formulae for partial fraction expansion and inversion are collected in the Appendices A and B.

Today, various numerical methods for numerical Laplace transform inversion are available in the literature. This chapter will describe one of them which is particularly suitable for network solutions. The advantage of this approach is that if the reader has a program for frequency domain analysis of linear networks, the time domain response can be found without changes and only few additions to the program are required. The method does not require the determination of the poles and residues of the network function. It is applicable to stiff systems, to systems with multiple poles, and also to systems with distributed parameter elements. Moreover, it can be modified so that it is equivalent to an absolutely stable, very high-order integration method.

Section 10.1 gives the theoretical basis for the method, followed in Section 10.2 by a detailed analysis of the properties. Applications are discussed in Section 10.3. It is shown that the method can provide time domain sensitivities by calculating sensitivities in the frequency domain, e.g., by applying the frequency-domain methods of Chapter 6. Solutions of distributed networks are illustrated as well.

The inversion discussed in the initial portion of the chapter is achieved by a very simple formula which is very accurate for small values of time, but errors grow with time. In order to preserve the accuracy for large times, it is necessary to modify the method so as to reset the time origin after each step. This stepping is particularly easy to apply to linear networks and can be applied to network functions as well. As mentioned above, it is equivalent to very high-order absolutely stable integration. The development is described in Section 10.4, while Section 10.5 establishes the stability properties of the integration.

The stepping algorithm is used in the network analysis program given in Appendix D and other codes are incorporated in this chapter. Mathematical details may be skipped by a reader interested only in application of these techniques.

10.1. DEVELOPMENT OF THE METHOD

The development provided below was described in [1]-[2]. Consider the Laplace inversion formula

$$v(t) = \frac{1}{2\pi j} \int_{c-j\infty}^{c+j\infty} V(s)\, e^{st}\, ds. \tag{10.1.1}$$

Exact inversion is possible only if the poles of $V(s)$ are known. Since we wish to avoid root-finding procedures, we apply some approximation to the integrand in (10.1.1). This could be done on $V(s)$, but for each new problem we would have to approximate all over again. An alternate is to first remove the variable t from e^{st} by the transformation

$$z = st \tag{10.1.2}$$

and then approximate e^z. This is done numerically *only once* in the development of the method, and all further inversions use the results thus obtained.

Inserting (10.1.2) into (10.1.1) we obtain

$$v(t) = \frac{1}{2\pi jt} \int_{c'-j\infty}^{c'+j\infty} V(z/t)\, e^{z}\, dz. \tag{10.1.3}$$

Next, we approximate the function e^z by a rational function (Padé approximation)

$$R_{N,M}(z) = \frac{P_N(z)}{Q_M(z)} \tag{10.1.4}$$

where $P_N(z)$ and $Q_M(z)$ are polynomials of order N, M, respectively. The approximation formally equates a rational function to some terms of a series

$$\frac{\sum_{i=0}^{N} a_i z^i}{1+\sum_{i=1}^{M} b_i z^i} = \sum_{i=0}^{M+N} c_i z^i + \sum_{i=M+N+1}^{\infty} c_i z^i \tag{10.1.5}$$

and in our case the coefficients c_i for $i \leqslant M + N$ are the coefficients of the Taylor expansion of e^z. Therefore, the *Padé approximation* $R_{N,M}(z)$ *has the first* $M + N + 1$ *terms of its Taylor expansion equal to the Taylor expansion of* e^z. However, the expansions differ in the remaining terms.

It is not necessary to solve the system of equations arising from (10.1.5) since a closed form exists:

$$R_{N,M} = \frac{P_N(z)}{Q_M(z)} = \frac{\sum_{i=0}^{N} (M+N-i)! \binom{N}{i} z^i}{\sum_{i=0}^{M} (-1)^i (M+N-i)! \binom{M}{i} z^i}. \tag{10.1.6}$$

Several of the first approximations are shown in Table 10.1.1. The poles of all approximations are simple and, for M not differing considerably from N, all are in the right half plane. We will need this fact in the following simplified explanation of the theory; it is valid even if they are in the left half plane. Inserting (10.1.4) into (10.1.3), the approximation $\hat{v}(t)$ to $v(t)$ becomes

$$\hat{v}(t) = \frac{1}{2\pi jt} \int_{c'-j\infty}^{c'+j\infty} V(z/t)\, R_{N,M}(z)\, dz. \tag{10.1.7}$$

Now the integral (10.1.7) can be evaluated by residue calculus by closing the path of integration along an infinite arc either to the right or to the left. In

Table 10.1.1. Padé Table for the Approximation of e^z.

$M \backslash N$	0	1	2
0	$\frac{1}{1}$	$\frac{1+z}{1}$	$\frac{1+z+z^2/2}{1}$
1	$\frac{1}{1-z}$	$\frac{1+z/2}{1-z/2}$	$\frac{1+2z/3+z^2/6}{1-z/3}$
2	$\frac{1}{1-z+z^2/2}$	$\frac{1+z/3}{1-2z/3+z^2/6}$	$\frac{1+z/2+z^2/18}{1-z/2+z^2/18}$

order that the path along the infinite arc not contribute to the integral, choose M, N such that the function

$$F(z) = V(z/t)\, R_{N,M}(z) \tag{10.1.8}$$

has at least two more finite poles than zeros. Then (see Appendix C)

$$\int_C F(z)\, dz = \pm 2\pi j \sum (\text{residue at poles inside the closed path}) \tag{10.1.9}$$

where the positive sign applies when the path C is closed in the left half plane (counterclockwise), whereas the negative one applies for the other case. Important properties of the method are derived in Section 10.2 by alternately closing the paths in both half planes. For $N < M$ we have

$$R_{N,M}(z) = \sum_{i=1}^{M} \frac{K_i}{z - z_i} \tag{10.1.10}$$

where z_i are the poles of $R_{N,M}(z)$ and K_i are the corresponding residues. Closing the path of integration around the poles of $R_{N,M}(z)$ *in the right half plane* we obtain

$$\hat{v}(t) = -\frac{1}{t} \sum_{i=1}^{M} K_i V(z_i/t). \tag{10.1.11}$$

This is the basic inversion formula. Real time functions can be evaluated using only the poles z_i in the upper half plane. This reduces the computations to one-half. For M even and the bar denoting complex conjugate, we have

$$\hat{v}(t) = -\frac{1}{t} \sum_{i=1}^{M'} K_i V(z_i/t) - \frac{1}{t} \sum_{i=1}^{M'} \bar{K}_i V(\bar{z}_i/t) = -\frac{1}{t} \sum_{i=1}^{M'} 2 \operatorname{Re}\, [K_i V(z_i/t)]$$

$$= -\frac{1}{t} \sum_{i=1}^{M'} \operatorname{Re}\, [K_i' V(z_i/t)] \tag{10.1.12}$$

where $M' = M/2$ and $K_i' = 2K_i$, K_i being defined by (10.1.10). When M is odd, $M' = (M + 1)/2$ and $K_i' = K_i$ for the residue corresponding to the real pole.

The poles z_i and residues K_i' were calculated with high precision and a selection is given in Table 10.1.2. A more detailed table is given in [3]. Application of the formula (10.1.12) proceeds as follows:

Table 10.1.2. A Selection of Poles z_i and Residues K'_i for Various N, M.

		$N = M - 3$		$N = M - 2$		$N = M - 1$	
M	i	$\mathrm{Re}(z_i)$ $\mathrm{Im}(z_i)$	$\mathrm{Re}(K'_i)$ $\mathrm{Im}(K'_i)$	$\mathrm{Re}(z_i)$ $\mathrm{Im}(z_i)$	$\mathrm{Re}(K'_i)$ $\mathrm{Im}(K'_i)$	$\mathrm{Re}(z_i)$ $\mathrm{Im}(z_i)$	$\mathrm{Re}(K'_i)$ $\mathrm{Im}(K'_i)$
2	1			1.000000000000000 1.000000000000000	0.000000000000000 -2.000000000000000	2.000000000000000 1.414213562373095	2.000000000000000 -7.071067811865476
4	1	2.764346415715100 1.162323629283275	-1.486485011597801 -12.10916705674577	3.779019967010193 1.380176524272843	2.256958744418140 -39.63308700050173	4.787193103128467 1.567476416895208	26.60307999194297 -120.1434654740949
	2	1.235653584284900 3.437652493671051	1.486485011597801 3.433270826956831	2.220980032989807 4.160391445506932	-2.256958744418140 11.10883163787590	3.212806896871534 4.773087433276643	-22.60307999194297 24.94335170050046
10	1	10.82098193052256 1.517953393700372	2186.697231341063 -48581.24805840772	11.83009373916819 1.593753005885813	16286.62368050479 -139074.7115516051	12.83767707781087 1.666062584162301	73804.09376005109 -393980.9270580073
	2	10.21449035429789 4.562479433009242	-3989.181746394491 27449.17684030028	11.22085377939519 4.792964167565670	-28178.11171305163 74357.58237274176	12.22613148416215 5.012719263676865	-122553.9994117030 190817.1978146481
	3	8.932235514658323 7.637703369344925	2320.955454239880 -8164.422991702790	9.933383722175002 8.033106334266296	14629.74025233142 -19181.80818501836	10.93430343060001 8.409672996003091	57833.14454064847 -36338.37020019288
	4	6.786787372173086 10.78715258382734	-556.8837335166699 1044.522752571332	7.781146264464616 11.36889164904993	-2870.418161032078 -1674.109484084304	8.776434640082610 11.92185389830121	-9310.721692796347 3.803546061166028
	5	3.245504828348141 14.14179989064435	38.41279433021752 -29.05774606159169	4.234522494797000 14.95704378128156	132.1659412474876 17.47674798877164	5.225453367344362 15.72952904563926	237.4828037997930 282.6073846434469

Let the function $V(s)$ be given. We wish to know the time domain response at time t:

1. Select appropriate N, M and take z_i, K_i' from the Table 10.1.2.
2. Divide each z_i by t and substitute (z_i/t) for each s in $V(s)$. This provides $V(z_i/t)$.
3. Multiply each $V(z_i/t)$ by K_i' and add the products.
4. Retain only the real part and divide by $-t$.

The above steps give the approximation to $v(t)$ at the time t. Use of the formula (10.1.12) is clarified by the following example.

EXAMPLE 10.1.1. Apply the numerical inversion method to obtain the time domain approximation for the function

$$V(s) = \frac{2s + 3}{(s + 1)(s + 2)}$$

at $t = 0.1$. Select $M = 2$, $N = 0$. The exact Laplace inverse of this simple function is $v(t) = e^{-t} + e^{-2t}$.

For the numerical inversion, take from Table 10.1.2 the pole $z = 1 + j$ and the residue $K' = -2j$. For one pole, only one complex evaluation is necessary. Insert $z/t = 10 + 10j$ for each s in $V(s)$ and multiply by K':

$$K'V(z/t) = \frac{-2j(23 + 20j)}{(11 + 10j)(12 + 10j)} = \frac{40 - j46}{32 + j230} = -0.172465 - j0.19791.$$

According to (10.1.12) retain only the real part and divide by -0.1. The result is $\hat{v}(0.1) = 1.72465$. The exact response is $v(0.1) = 1.72357$.

Complex evaluations in hand calculations are difficult but programming the method for a computer is extremely easy. Figure 10.1.1 shows the program for computing the time domain response of arbitrary transforms. The user must provide his own function VS(S) in terms of the variable S. T is the starting time, TEND the end time, and DELTAT is the time increment. The data at the beginning of the program are K_i' and z_i for the case $M = 10$, $N = 8$, taken from Table 10.1.2. Because of the division by t in (10.1.12), the time function for $t = 0$ cannot be calculated by the program. This value can be obtained either by means of the initial value theorem (see Appendix A), or approximated by selecting a very small initial value of t, for instance 10^{-10}.

Application of the program will be demonstrated on networks with distributed elements. These elements are described by partial differential equations, and

```
C**SAMPLE PROGRAM FOR NUMERICAL LAPLACE TRANSFORM INVERSION
      COMPLEX*16 Z(5),KPRIME(5),VS,S
      REAL*8 T,DELTAT,TEND,VT,DREAL
      DATA Z/(11.83009373916819D0,1.593753005885813D0),(11.2208537793951
     $9D0,4.792964167565669D0),(9.933383722175002D0,8.033106334266296D0)
     $,(7.781146264464616D0,11.36889164904993D0),(4.234522494797000D0,14
     $.95704378128156D0)/,KPRIME/(16286.62368050479D0,-139074.7115516051
     $D0),(-28178.11171305162D0,74357.58237274176D0),(14629.74025233142D
     $0,-19181.80818501836D0),(-2870.418161032078D0,1674.109484084304D0)
     $,(132.1659412474876D0,17.47674798877164D0)/,MPRIME/5/
C*VS(S) IS THE FUNCTION DEFINITION IN S DOMAIN. USER SHOULD REPLACE
C*BY HIS OWN FUNCTION OR SUBROUTINE
      VS(S) = 1.D0/S
      READ (5,*) T,DELTAT,TEND
C*RESPONSE IS FOUND AT TIME = T, T+DELTAT, T+2*DELTAT,...
C*TILL T.GT.TEND
      WRITE(6,30)
10    IF (T.GT.TEND) STOP
      VT = 0.D0
      DO 20 I=1,MPRIME
20    VT = VT-DREAL(VS(Z(I)/T)*KPRIME(I))
      VT = VT/T
      WRITE (6,40) T,VT
      T = T+DELTAT
      GO TO 10
30    FORMAT (T7,'TIME',T20,'RESPONSE')
40    FORMAT (2G14.3)
      END

   sample output for T=.5, DELTAT=.5, TEND=5.   .....

       TIME            RESPONSE
      0.500            1.000
       1.00            1.000
        .                .
        .                .
       4.50            1.000
       5.00            1.000
```

Fig. 10.1.1. Program for numerical Laplace transform inversion. The function used in the example is $V(s) = 1/s$.

direct application of the numerical integration method discussed in Chapter 9 is not possible. Simple distributed elements can be described at their terminals through a chain matrix representation involving transcendental functions of s. In very simple cases, the time domain solution can be obtained as an infinite series. The numerical Laplace transform method is applicable whenever the terminal description is available in the s-domain.

Two examples will be given. The first one will establish the accuracy of the method on an RC distributed line. The next will demonstrate evaluation of the time domain response of a feedback network with an exponentially tapered line.

EXAMPLE 10.1.2. The step response of a uniform distributed RC line is given in the Laplace domain by [2]

$$\frac{V_{\text{out}}}{V_{\text{in}}} = \frac{1}{s \cosh \sqrt{sR_0 C_0}}$$

where R_0, C_0 are the total resistance and capacitance. The exact time domain response is given by the infinite series:

$$v(t) = 1 - \frac{4}{\pi} \sum_{n=0}^{\infty} \frac{(-1)^n}{2n+1} \exp\left[-\left(\frac{2n+1}{2}\pi\right)^2 \frac{t}{R_0 C_0}\right].$$

Let $\hat{v}(t)$ be the response obtained by the program of Fig. 10.1.1. The following are the results for $R_0 C_0 = 1$:

t	$\hat{v}(t)$	$v(t)$	$\epsilon = \hat{v}(t) - v(t)$
0.1	0.05069461	0.05069488	-0.27×10^{-6}
0.2	0.22768839	0.22768809	300×10^{-6}
0.3	0.39319618	0.39319935	-3.17×10^{-6}
0.4	0.52551254	0.52554060	-28×10^{-6}
...	...	...	...
1.0	0.89202296	0.89188984	-133×10^{-6}
1.4	0.95975611	0.95963681	119×10^{-6}
1.8	0.98500079	0.98500992	-9.13×10^{-6}
2.2	0.99440968	0.99456979	-160×10^{-6}

The exact response was evaluated by summing the series till the terms decreased below 10^{-12}.

EXAMPLE 10.1.3. Calculate the step response for the network shown in Fig. 10.1.2. The line is an exponentially tapered RC line having unit length and parameters $r(x) = e^x$, $c(x) = e^{-x}$. The transfer function of such a line is [4]

$$T(s) = e^{-0.5}\left[\cosh \Gamma + \frac{1}{2\Gamma} \sinh \Gamma\right]$$

where

$$\Gamma = \sqrt{s + 0.5}.$$

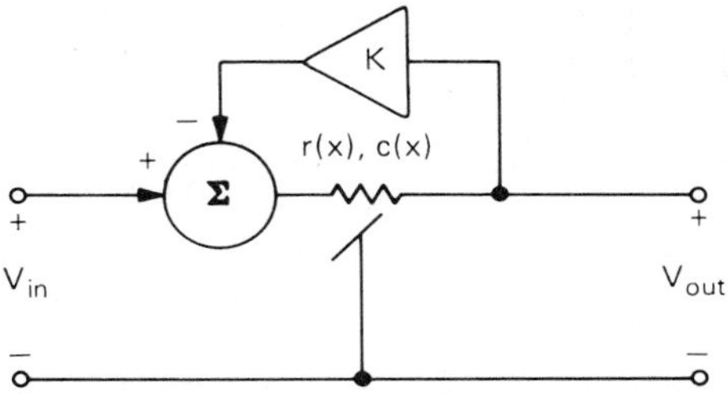

Fig. 10.1.2. Feedback network with exponentially tapered RC line.

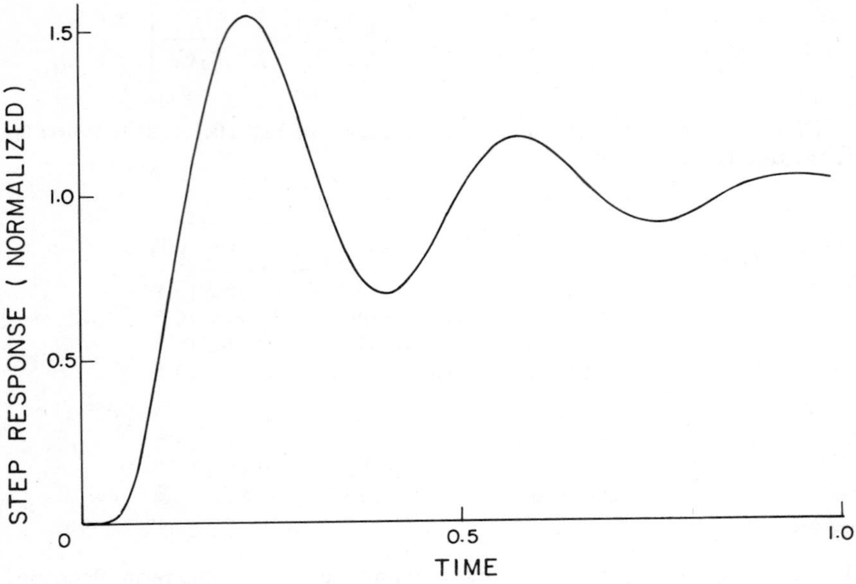

Fig. 10.1.3. Step response of the network shown in Fig. 10.1.2 for $K = 5$.

If the tapered line is used in the network of Fig. 10.1.2, the normalized step response is given by

$$V_{out} = \frac{1}{s} \frac{1 + K}{T(s) + K} .$$

The response obtained by the program of Fig. 10.1.1 is shown in Fig. 10.1.3 for $K = 5$.

The method explained in this section is suitable for the calculation of *responses to nonperiodic excitations* (impulses, steps). The error first grows with t but stabilizes and remains tolerable even for very large times. Responses to periodic excitations cannot be solved satisfactorily by the method presented above but appropriate modifications are available and will be discussed in Section 10.4.

Since the error grows with t, two questions arise:

1. How can we increase the useful time interval for a specified error?
2. How can we detect the presence of errors?

Increase of the useful time interval is achieved by selecting higher M, N. The size of the errors can be estimated by solving the same problem twice: first with a given M, N and the second time with the same M but N smaller by one. As long as the responses coincide, the results are correct. Theoretical reasons for both answers will be given in Section 10.2.

10.2. PROPERTIES OF THE METHOD

The theory given below is described in detail in [1]. The exact inverse of the function

$$V(s) = 1/s^m \tag{10.2.1}$$

is

$$v(t) = \frac{t^{m-1}}{(m-1)!} \tag{10.2.2}$$

for any $m \geqslant 1$ (see Appendix A). Insert (10.2.1) into (10.1.7):

$$\hat{v}(t) = \frac{t^{m-1}}{2\pi j} \int_{c'-j\infty}^{c'+j\infty} z^{-m} R_{N,M}(z)\, dz \tag{10.2.3}$$

and integrate by closing the path in the *left* half plane, where there is only one pole of order m at the origin. Its residue is (see Appendix B)

$$\text{Res}\,(z^{-m} R_{N,M}(z))\big|_{z=0} = \frac{1}{(m-1)!} \frac{d^{m-1}}{dz^{m-1}} R_{N,M}(z)\big|_{z=0}.$$

Since $R_{N,M}(z)$ has the first $M + N + 1$ terms of its Taylor expansion identical to those of e^z:

$$\frac{d^{m-1}}{dz^{m-1}} R_{N,M}(z)\big|_{z=0} = 1, \qquad \text{for} \quad m = 1, 2, \ldots, M + N + 1$$

and the inverse is exact:

$$\hat{v}(t) = v(t) = \frac{t^{m-1}}{(m-1)!}, \qquad \text{for} \quad m = 1, 2, \ldots, M + N + 1. \tag{10.2.4}$$

Insert next (10.1.10) into (10.2.3) and integrate by closing the path in the *right* half plane:

$$\hat{v}(t) = -t^{m-1} \sum_{i=1}^{M} K_i / z_i^m, \qquad \text{for} \quad m = 1, 2, \ldots, M + N + 1. \tag{10.2.5}$$

Comparison with (10.2.4) reveals

$$\sum_{i=1}^{M} K_i/z_i^m = -\frac{1}{(m-1)!}, \qquad \text{for} \quad m = 1, 2, \ldots, M+N+1. \tag{10.2.6}$$

We next establish a similar rule for *positive* powers of s. Our function is now $V(s) = s^m$. Choose N, M such that (10.1.8) *meets the requirements on the relative number of poles and zeros.* Now

$$\hat{v}(t) = \frac{t^{-m-1}}{2\pi j} \int_{c'-j\infty}^{c'+j\infty} z^m R_{N,M}(z)\, dz. \tag{10.2.7}$$

The function has no poles to the left of the integrating line. Closing first the path in the *left* half plane we conclude that (10.2.7) is equal to zero. Insert next for $R_{N,M}(z)$ from (10.1.10) and close the path in the *right* half plane with the result

$$\hat{v}(t) = -t^{-m-1} \sum_{i=1}^{M} K_i z_i^m, \qquad \text{for} \quad 0 \leqslant m \leqslant M - N - 2. \tag{10.2.8}$$

The inequality on the right of (10.2.8) arises from the condition on the relative number of poles and zeros. Since (10.2.8) must be satisfied for any $t > 0$ and as $\hat{v}(t) = 0$, it follows that

$$\sum_{i=1}^{M} K_i z_i^m = 0, \qquad \text{for} \quad 0 \leqslant m \leqslant M - N - 2. \tag{10.2.9}$$

Formulae (10.2.6) and (10.2.9) can be collected into one expression:

$$\sum_{i=1}^{M} K_i/z_i^m = -\frac{1}{(m-1)!}, \qquad \text{for} \quad -M+N+2 \leqslant m \leqslant M+N+1 \tag{10.2.10}$$

and used to formulate the following fundamental result of the method:

Formula (10.1.11) inverts exactly the function

$$V(s) = 1/s^m, \qquad \text{for} \quad -M+N+2 \leqslant m \leqslant M+N+1. \tag{10.2.11}$$

The inverse is

$$\hat{v}(t) = v(t) = \frac{t^{m-1}}{(m-1)!} \,. \tag{10.2.12}$$

Note that the factorial of a negative number is defined as $1/m! = 0$ for $m < 0$ and this is in agreement with our conclusions.

In the next step, introduce

$$p = M + N. \tag{10.2.13}$$

Expand $v(t)$ into a Taylor series about the origin:

$$v(t) = \sum_{i=0}^{p} \frac{d_i}{i!} t^i + \sum_{i=p+1}^{\infty} \frac{d_i}{i!} t^i \tag{10.2.14}$$

and consider only the first sum. The Laplace transform of this truncated part is

$$V_T(s) = \sum_{i=0}^{p} \frac{d_i}{s^{i+1}} \,. \tag{10.2.15}$$

Since each term of $V_T(s)$ is inverted exactly by any $R_{N,M}$ fulfilling (10.1.8), the whole function $V_T(s)$ is also inverted exactly and we can formulate the second fundamental property of the method:

Formula (10.1.11) inverts exactly the first $M + N + 1$ terms of the Taylor series of any time response.

Consequently, as long as the time function is approximated well by the initial portion of its Taylor series, the numerical inversion gives excellent results. Taking higher M, N means that a greater number of the Taylor expansion terms are matched exactly. If we solve a problem twice, once with a given M, N and the next time with the same M but N smaller by one, the difference of the two solutions will approximate the $(M + N + 1)$st term of the Taylor expansion. As long as this term is small, the inversion is likely to be accurate. The above gives the reasons for our recommendations at the end of Section 10.1.

10.3. APPLICATION

Due to the division by t in (10.1.11), the formula cannot be used for $t = 0$. For smooth functions, no problems arise, since the Taylor expansion of the response exists. The question is what happens if an impulse appears at the time $t = 0$. Will this impulse distort the results for $t > 0$?

The answer follows from the theory given in Section 10.2. The Laplace transform of an impulse is $V(s) = 1$. If we select $N = M - 2$, then

$$\hat{v}(t) = -\frac{1}{t} \sum_{i=1}^{M} K_i = 0, \qquad \text{for} \quad t > 0$$

as follows from (10.2.9) for $m = 0$. Thus the impulse at the time origin will not influence the correctness of the answer.

Let it be mentioned at this point that voltage and current transfer functions T_V and T_I can be realized if the numerator degree is equal to or is less than the denominator degree. The choice $N = M - 2$ will properly cover all realizable possibilities. For transfer impedances or admittances, Z_{TR} or Y_{TR}, the choice $N = M - 3$ will again secure the correctness of the answers for $t > 0$. The ability of the method to handle impulse sources correctly is an important and powerful property when applied to the solution of networks.

Derivatives of time responses can be obtained using the following formula:

$$\mathcal{L}[v^{(n)}(t)] = s^n V(s) - \sum_{k=1}^{n} v^{(k-1)}(0-)\, s^{n-k} \tag{10.3.1}$$

(see Appendix A). Select N, M such that $(z/t)^n V(z/t) R_{N,M}(z)$ fulfills the condition on the relative number of zeros and poles. Then all terms after the summation in (10.3.1) do not contribute to the inversion and the nth derivative is inverted as follows:

$$\hat{v}^{(n)}(t) = -\frac{1}{t} \sum_{i=1}^{M} K_i (z_i/t)^n V(z_i/t), \qquad t > 0. \tag{10.3.2}$$

Note that integration does not present difficulties, since the number of poles increases without changing the number of zeros. This tends to fulfill the condition (10.1.8) automatically.

Responses of networks are sometimes defined by such technical quantities as rise time, time delay, overshoot, or undershoot. The usual definitions are explained in Fig. 10.3.1. Using the numerical method presented here we can solve for these quantities without obtaining the full response. Assume that $v(t) = \mathcal{L}^{-1}[V(s)]$ is the step response of some network. Then

$$\hat{v}(t) = -\frac{1}{t} \sum_{i=1}^{M} K_i V(z_i/t).$$

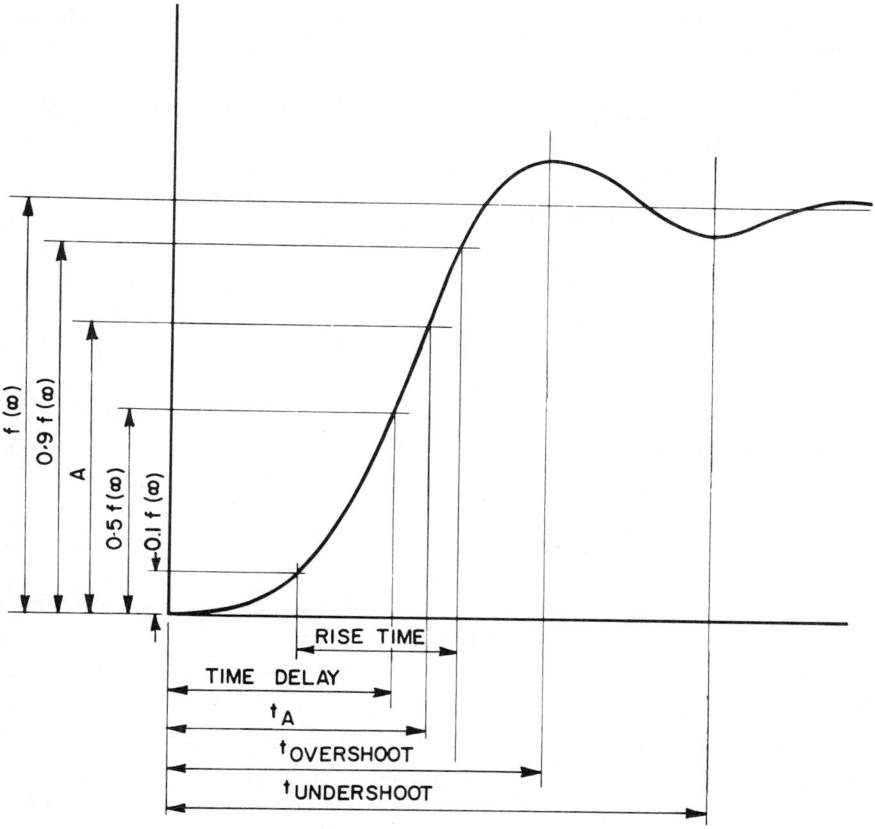

Fig. 10.3.1. Definition of various response terms.

The derivative of $v(t)$ is expressed by

$$\hat{v}'(t) = -\frac{1}{t} \sum_{i=1}^{M} K_i(z_i/t)\, V(z_i/t)$$

as follows from (10.3.2). Newton-Raphson iteration can be used to solve for the time t^* for which $\hat{v}(t^*)$ is equal to a desired value A:

$$t^{k+1} = t^k - \frac{\hat{v}(t^k) - A}{\hat{v}'(t^k)} = t^k - \frac{\sum_{i=1}^{M} K_i V(z_i/t^k) + At^k}{\sum_{i=1}^{M} K_i(z_i/t^k)\, V(z_i/t^k)}.$$

Superscript k indicates iteration. The derivative is obtained almost without additional computations, since most of the time will be spent on the evaluation of $V(z_i/t^k)$.

The method can provide *sensitivities of the time domain response by using frequency domain sensitivity methods.* Consider a network with an input $W(s)$ and transfer function $F(s)$. The output is

$$V(s) = F(s)\,W(s).$$

The time response is given by

$$\hat{v}(t) = -\frac{1}{t}\sum_{i=1}^{M} K_i F(z_i/t)\,W(z_i/t).$$

Let $F(s)$ depend on some parameter h. Then

$$\frac{\partial \hat{v}(t)}{\partial h} = -\frac{1}{t}\sum_{i=1}^{M} K_i \frac{\partial F(z_i/t)}{\partial h} W(z_i/t).$$

The sensitivity is calculated from the sum of M frequency domain sensitivities where the complex values z_i/t are used instead of the actual frequencies. The reader is referred to Chapter 6 for efficient methods based on the adjoint approach.

EXAMPLE 10.3.1. Calculate the time domain sensitivity of the output v_2 with respect to the network elements for the network shown in Fig. 10.3.2. The input is the unit step, the step size $h = 0.1$. Use the $M = 2, N = 0$ approximation for which $z = 1 + j$ and $K' = -2j$. Obtain (a) exact sensitivity expressions in the time domain, (b) frequency domain sensitivity using the adjoint method, (c) illustrate how the computer implementation or the solution progresses numerically.

(a) The system matrix is

$$\begin{bmatrix} G_1 + sC & -sC \\ -sC & G_2 + sC \end{bmatrix} \begin{bmatrix} V_1 \\ V_2 \end{bmatrix} = \begin{bmatrix} 1/s \\ 0 \end{bmatrix}.$$

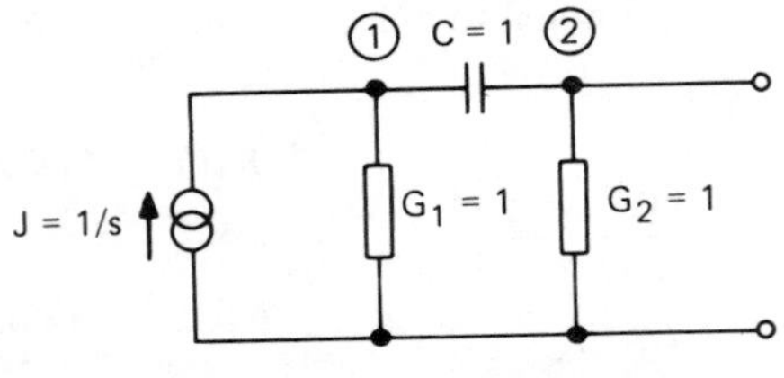

Fig. 10.3.2. Network for Example 10.3.1.

The frequency domain output is

$$V_2(s) = \frac{1}{(G_1 + G_2)\left[s + \dfrac{G_1 G_2}{C(G_1 + G_2)}\right]} .$$

The exact Laplace transform inverse is

$$v_2(t) = \frac{1}{(G_1 + G_2)} \exp\left[-\frac{G_1 G_2 t}{C(G_1 + G_2)}\right] .$$

The derivative with respect to G_1 is

$$\frac{\partial v_2(t)}{\partial G_1} = \frac{-1}{(G_1 + G_2)^2}\left[1 + \frac{G_2^2 t}{C(G_1 + G_2)}\right] \exp\left[-\frac{G_1 G_2 t}{C(G_1 + G_2)}\right] .$$

The derivative with respect to C is

$$\frac{\partial v_2(t)}{\partial C} = \frac{G_1 G_2 t}{C^2 (G_1 + G_2)^2} \exp\left[-\frac{G_1 G_2 t}{C(G_1 + G_2)}\right] .$$

The derivative with respect to G_2 is similar to that for G_1 due to the symmetry of the expression.

For the values indicated in the network and for $t = 0.1$

$$v_2(t) = \frac{1}{2} e^{-t/2} = 0.4756147123$$

$$\frac{\partial v_2(t)}{\partial G_1} = -\frac{1}{4}\left(1 + \frac{t}{2}\right) e^{-t/2} = -0.2496977239$$

$$\frac{\partial v_2(t)}{\partial C} = \frac{t}{4} e^{-t/2} = 0.0237807356.$$

(b) The steps associated with the adjoint method will be carried out first. The original system from point (a) is solved with the following result:

$$V_1(s) = \frac{G_2 + sC}{sC(G_1 + G_2) + G_1 G_2} ; \qquad V_2(s) = \frac{C}{sC(G_1 + G_2) + G_1 G_2} .$$

The adjoint system has the form

$$\begin{bmatrix} G_1 + sC & -sC \\ -sC & G_2 + sC \end{bmatrix} \begin{bmatrix} V_1^a \\ V_2^a \end{bmatrix} = \begin{bmatrix} 0 \\ -1 \end{bmatrix} .$$

The solution is

$$V_1^a = \frac{-sC}{sC(G_1 + G_2) + G_1G_2}; \qquad V_2^a(s) = \frac{-(G_1 + sC)}{sC(G_1 + G_2) + G_1G_2}.$$

Inserting the element values for the network we obtain

$$V_1(s) = \frac{s+1}{2s(s+\frac{1}{2})}; \qquad V_1^a(s) = \frac{-s}{2(s+\frac{1}{2})}$$

$$V_2(s) = \frac{1}{2(s+\frac{1}{2})}; \qquad V_2^a(s) = \frac{-(s+1)}{2(s+\frac{1}{2})}.$$

Applying the theory from Chapter 6 we obtain

$$\frac{\partial V_2(s)}{\partial G_1} = 1 \times V_1 V_1^a = \frac{-(s+1)}{4(s+\frac{1}{2})^2} \overset{\mathcal{L}^{-1}}{\Longrightarrow} -\frac{1}{4}\left(1+\frac{t}{2}\right)e^{-t/2}$$

$$\frac{\partial V_2(s)}{\partial C} = s(V_1 - V_2)(V_1^a - V_2^a) = \frac{1}{4(s+\frac{1}{2})^2} \overset{\mathcal{L}^{-1}}{\Longrightarrow} \frac{t}{4}e^{-t/2}.$$

The results give precisely the formulae derived in step (a) by direct differentiation of the time function.

(c) Numerically, the solution would proceed on the matrices by substituting $s = z/h = 10 + 10j$. The original system is

$$\begin{bmatrix} 11+10j & -(10+10j) \\ -(10+10j) & 11+10j \end{bmatrix} \begin{bmatrix} V_1 \\ V_2 \end{bmatrix} = \begin{bmatrix} \dfrac{1}{10+10j} \\ 0 \end{bmatrix}.$$

The adjoint system is

$$\begin{bmatrix} 11+10j & -(10+10j) \\ -(10+10j) & 11+10j \end{bmatrix} \begin{bmatrix} V_1^a \\ V_2^a \end{bmatrix} = \begin{bmatrix} 0 \\ -1 \end{bmatrix}.$$

Their solutions are

$$V_1 = \frac{21.05 - 22.05j}{841}; \qquad V_1^a = \frac{-410 - 10j}{841}$$

$$V_2 = \frac{21 - 20j}{841}; \qquad V_2^a = \frac{-431 + 10j}{841}.$$

The sensitivity with respect to G_1 in the time domain is obtained by applying (10.1.12):

$$\frac{\partial \hat{v}_2(t)}{\partial G_1} = -\frac{1}{0.1} \text{ Re } [(-2j)\, V_1 V_1^a] = -0.2496885962$$

Sensitivity with respect to C is

$$\frac{\partial \hat{v}_2(t)}{\partial C} = -\frac{1}{0.1} \text{ Re } [(-2j)(10 + 10j)(V_1 - V_2)(V_1^a - V_2^a)] = 0.0237529355$$

The errors are:

$$\epsilon_{G_1} = \left| \frac{\partial v_2}{\partial G_1} - \frac{\partial \hat{v}_2}{\partial G_1} \right| = 9.13 \times 10^{-6}$$

$$\epsilon_C = \left| \frac{\partial v_2}{\partial C} - \frac{\partial \hat{v}_2}{\partial C} \right| = 27.8 \times 10^{-6}$$

For smaller errors or larger h, a higher order approximation would have to be used.

10.4. STEPPING ALGORITHM FOR NETWORKS AND NETWORK FUNCTIONS

The method discussed in the previous sections of this chapter is extremely simple to apply but has the disadvantage that accuracy decreases as time increases. The question arises whether it is possible to use the method with small time intervals, where the accuracy is excellent, and reset the problem so that in the next evaluation the previous result is considered as the initial point for the new step, as in the numerical integration of differential equations. Such possibility exists for both networks [3] and rational functions [5]: the theory and application will be the subject of this section.

In lumped networks, any time can be selected as zero time by taking into account the charges on the capacitors and the fluxes through the inductors. These initial conditions "reset" the problem so that next calculation can start without any reference to previous history. Recall from Chapter 1 that the initial voltage on the capacitor can be represented as an equivalent impulse current source in parallel with the capacitor. Similarly, the initial current through the inductor can be taken care of by a voltage impulse source in series with the inductor.

Using the tableau or modified nodal formulation, let the system matrix be defined as

$$\mathbf{T}(s) = \mathbf{G} + s\mathbf{C} \tag{10.4.1}$$

with **G** containing all real entries and **C** all entries multiplied by s. The system equations are

$$\mathbf{T}_c(s)\,\mathbf{X}_c = \mathbf{W}_c(s) + \mathbf{I} \tag{10.4.2}$$

where $\mathbf{W}_c(s)$ is the Laplace transform of the sources and $\mathbf{I}$ the vector of impulse sources $C_i V_{i0}$ or $-L_i I_{i0}$, due to the initial conditions. The subscript c indicates that $\mathbf{T}_c$, $\mathbf{W}_c$, and $\mathbf{X}_c$ are complex for complex s. Denote the step size by h.

Formula (10.1.12) was written for a single equation but can be applied to vectors as well. Substituting z_i/h for s and solving will provide a vector which is equivalent to the expression $V(z_i/t)$ in (10.1.12). Repeating for other z_i and applying (10.1.12) results in the following equation:

$$\mathbf{x} = -\frac{1}{h}\sum_{i=1}^{M'} \text{Re}\,[(K_i'\mathbf{X}_{ci})] \tag{10.4.3}$$

where $\mathbf{x}$ is the solution at the time $t = h$. For the next step, the vector $\mathbf{I}$ is obtained from $\mathbf{x}$ by means of

$$\mathbf{I} = \mathbf{C}\mathbf{x}. \tag{10.4.4}$$

Calculations are simplified considerably for $M = 2, N = 0$, because only one pole $z = 1 + j$ with $K' = -2j$ is needed (see Table 10.1.2). As long as the step size h remains constant, *the matrix in (10.4.2) does not change* and one **LU** decomposition of $\mathbf{T}(z/h)$ is sufficient. The algorithm for the time domain solution of the network is:

1. Prepare the vector of initial impulse sources $\mathbf{I}(t_0)$. It is a null vector for initially relaxed networks. Select the step size h.
2. Obtain the **LU** decomposition of $\mathbf{T}(z/h) = \mathbf{T}[(1 + j)/h]$.
3. Set $k = 1$ and go to step 5.
4. Calculate $\mathbf{I}(t_{k-1}) = \mathbf{C}\mathbf{x}(t_{k-1})$.
5. Apply the forward and back substitution to obtain $\mathbf{X}_c$ from

$$\mathbf{LUX}_c = \mathbf{W}_c\left(\frac{1+j}{h}\right) + \mathbf{I}(t_{k-1}).$$

6. Calculate $\mathbf{x}(t_k) = -2\,\text{Im}\,(\mathbf{X}_c)/h$.
7. Set $k = k + 1, t_k = t_{k-1} + h$. If $t_k <$ terminal time, go to step 4, else stop.

The algorithm can be easily modified for higher M, N.

It is interesting to note that transfer functions can also be handled by the stepping algorithm if one is willing to convert them first to a "state variable" form. We will now indicate how this can be done.

Consider the transfer function $F(s)$. The response is

$$V(s) = F(s)\,W(s) = \frac{N(s)}{D(s)}\,W(s) = \frac{\sum_{i=1}^{m} a_i s^{i-1}}{s + \sum_{i=1}^{n} b_i s^{i-1}}\,W(s) \tag{10.4.5}$$

where $W(s)$ is the transform of the input signal and $V(s)$ is the transform of the output. Let us define an auxiliary system

$$X_1(s) = \frac{1}{D(s)}\,W(s) \tag{10.4.6}$$

or

$$D(s)\,X_1(s) = W(s). \tag{10.4.7}$$

The original output is given as

$$V(s) = N(s)\,X_1(s). \tag{10.4.8}$$

Equation (10.4.7) has the form

$$(s^n + b_n s^{n-1} + \cdots + b_1)\,X_1(s) = W(s). \tag{10.4.9}$$

Since multiplication by s in the transform domain corresponds to differentiation in the time domain let us introduce a set of variables $x_1, x_2, \ldots, x_n$ in the time domain such that

$$\begin{aligned} x_1' &= x_2 \\ x_2' &= x_3 \\ &\vdots \\ x_n' &= w - b_n x_n - b_{n-1} x_{n-1} - \cdots - b_1 x_1. \end{aligned} \tag{10.4.10}$$

The set (10.4.10) is equivalent to Eq. (10.4.7) with $X_1(s)$ the Laplace transform of $x_1(t)$. Equation (10.4.10) can be written as a matrix equation. Using, for the sake of simplicity, an example of order $n = 4$, we have

$$\begin{bmatrix} x_1' \\ x_2' \\ x_3' \\ x_4' \end{bmatrix} = \begin{bmatrix} 0 & 1 & 0 & 0 \\ 0 & 0 & 1 & 0 \\ 0 & 0 & 0 & 1 \\ -b_1 & -b_2 & -b_3 & -b_4 \end{bmatrix} \begin{bmatrix} x_1 \\ x_2 \\ x_3 \\ x_4 \end{bmatrix} + \begin{bmatrix} 0 \\ 0 \\ 0 \\ 1 \end{bmatrix} w. \tag{10.4.11}$$

In general we have

$$\mathbf{x}' = \mathbf{A}\mathbf{x} + \mathbf{B}w \tag{10.4.12}$$

where **A** has the form similar to (10.4.11) and **B** is a vector with all zeros except for the last which is unity. Taking the Laplace transform we get the frequency domain system

$$(s\mathbf{1} - \mathbf{A})\,\mathbf{X} = \mathbf{B}W + \mathbf{I} \tag{10.4.13}$$

where **I** is a vector of initial conditions. At the start of the algorithm $\mathbf{I} = \mathbf{0}$. Equation (10.4.13) has the form identical to (10.4.2) and the algorithm given above can be used for the solution. The output is taken only at desired instants and is obtained from the time-domain equivalent of (10.4.8)

$$\hat{v}(t) = \sum_{i=1}^{m} a_i x_i. \tag{10.4.14}$$

The above theory was programmed and the computer routine is given in Fig. 10.4.1. Because of the special form of the matrix (10.4.11), additional simplifications were incorporated [5].

EXAMPLE 10.4.1. Consider the impulse response of the function $1/(s^2 + 1)$. For this case $v(t) = \sin t$. The response was computed by direct application of (10.1.12) without stepping and also by stepping with $h = 10$, 5 and 2.5, respectively, with $M = 10$ and $N = 8$:

		Error		
t	No Stepping	$h = 10$	$h = 5$	$h = 2.5$
10	5.8*D*-5	5.8*D*-5	2.39*D*-9	4.5*D*-12
20	0.97	6.1*D*-4	1.2*D*-9	6.1*D*-12
30	0.97	1.4*D*-3	9.8*D*-8	1.2*D*-12
40	0.80	1.8*D*-3	2.0*D*-8	1.4*D*-11
50	0.25	1.6*D*-3	2.5*D*-8	3.0*D*-11

Further reduction in step size does not improve the results, as the roundoff errors dominate. Note that the order of the integration formula in this example is 18 and reducing the step size by a factor of 2 should reduce the error by a factor $2^{18} \sim 2.5 \times 10^5$. This reduction can be observed when the step size is reduced from 10 to 5. A similar reduction when using $h = 2.5$ is not observed as the round-off errors start to dominate the computation.

```
C**TIME DOMAIN RESPONSE OF TRANSFER FUNCTIONS BY NUMERICAL
C**INVERSION OF THE LAPLACE TRANSFORM
C*THIS PROGRAM WILL COMPUTE THE IMPULSE RESPONSE OF A TRANSFER
C*FUNCTION GIVEN IN THE FORM
C*        B(1) + B(2)*S + ... + B(M)*S**(M-1)
C*     -----------------------------------------
C*     A(1) + A(2)*S + ... + A(N)*S**(N-1) + S**N
C*
C*WITH N.GE.M  ,  N.LE.15  ,  AND  N.GE.2  IN THIS IMPLEMENTATION
C**THE SOLUTION IS FOUND TILL TIME TEND WITH AN INTERNAL STEP OF
C**DELT AND WITH OUTPUT PRODUCED EVERY KK*DELT TIME UNITS
C*
      IMPLICIT REAL*8 (A-H,O-Z)
      COMPLEX*16 Z(5),KP(5),SK,RES(5),PK(5),QI(15,5),P,RESK,PP,XN
      REAL*8 A(16),B(15),X(15),XT(15)
      DATA Z/(11.83009373916819D0,1.593753005885813D0),(11.2208537793951
     $9D0,4.792964167565669D0),(9.933383722175002D0,8.033106334266296D0)
     $,(7.781146264464616D0,11.36889164904993D0),(4.234522494797D0,14.
     $95704378128156D0)/,KP/(16286.62368050479D0,-139074.7115516051D0),(
     $-28178.11171305162D0,74357.58237274176D0),(14629.74025233142D0,-
     $19181.80818501836D0),(-2870.418161032078D0,1674.109484084304D0),
     $(132.1659412474876D0,17.47674798877164D0)/
      READ (5,*) N,M,(A(I),I=1,N),(B(I),I=1,M),DELT,TEND,KK
      NP1 = N+1
      A(NP1) = 1.D0
      WRITE (6,90) (B(I),I=1,M)
      WRITE (6,100) (A(I),I=1,NP1)
      WRITE (6,110) DELT,KK
C*INITIALIZE STATE VECTOR
      DO 10 I=1,N
         X(I) = 0.D0
   10 XT(I) = 0.D0
      NN = N-1
C*COMPUTE LU FACTORIZATION AT THE 5 PRESELECTED FREQUENCIES
      DO 30 K=1,5
         SK = Z(K)/DELT
         RES(K) = KP(K)/DELT
         PK(K) = 1.D0/SK
         QI(1,K) = A(1)
         DO 20 J=2,N
   20    QI(J,K) = A(J)+QI(J-1,K)*PK(K)
   30 QI(N,K) = 1.D0/(QI(N,K)+SK)
      T = 0.D0
C*TIME DOMAIN COMPUTATION STARTS HERE
   40 IF (T.GT.TEND) STOP
      DO 70 L=1,KK
         DO 60 K=1,5
            P = PK(K)
            RESK = RES(K)
            PP = (-1.D0,0.D0)
            DO 50 J=1,NN
   50       PP = PP+QI(J,K)*X(J)
            XN = (X(N)-P*PP)*QI(N,K)
            XT(N) = XT(N)-DREAL(RESK*XN)
            DO 60 I=1,NN
               XN = (X(N-I)+XN)*P
   60    XT(N-I) = XT(N-I)-DREAL(XN*RESK)
         DO 70 I=1,N
            X(I) = XT(I)
   70 XT(I) = 0.D0
C*X NOW CONTAINS NEW STATE VECTOR
      RESPON = 0.D0
      DO 80 I=1,M
   80 RESPON = RESPON+B(I)*X(I)
C*RESPONSE COMPUTED FROM STATE VECTOR AT OUTPUT POINTS
      T = T+KK*DELT
C*THE FOLLOWING STATEMENT CALCULATES ERROR IN RESPONSE FOR SAMPLE TEST
C*PROBLEM
      ERR=DSIN(T)-RESPON
more...
```

Fig. 10.4.1. Stepping algorithm for transfer function.

```
      WRITE (6,120) T,RESPON,ERR
      GO TO 40
C
   90 FORMAT ('1'///' NUMERATOR COEFFECIENTS'/(5G15.5))
  100 FORMAT (' DENOMINATOR COEFFECIENTS'/(5G15.5))
  110 FORMAT (' DELTA=',G15.5,'     OUTPUT EVERY',I3,' STEPS'///T8,'TIME',
     $8X,'RESPONSE')
  120 FORMAT (3G15.3)
      END

2 2 1. 0. 0. 1. 1. 50. 2       ... sample input

                Sample output follows ...

 NUMERATOR COEFFECIENTS
    0.00000          1.0000
 DENOMINATOR COEFFECIENTS
     1.0000          0.00000          1.0000
 DELTA=        1.0000          OUTPUT EVERY   2 STEPS


       TIME            RESPONSE          error for sample input
       2.00             0.909              0.271D-11
       4.00            -0.757             -0.515D-11
       6.00            -0.279             -0.118D-10
        .                 .                  .
        .                 .                  .
       48.0            -0.768             -0.139D-10
       50.0            -0.262             -0.924D-10
```

Fig. 10.4.1. *cont.*

EXAMPLE 10.4.2. Calculate the impulse response of the transfer function

$$F(s) = \frac{1}{(s+1)^5} = \frac{1}{s^5 + 5s^4 + 10s^3 + 10s^2 + 5s + 1}$$

for which

$$v(t) = (t^4 e^{-t})/24.$$

Computer routines that employ partial fraction expansion to evaluate the time function often have difficulty in the case of multiple roots. To capture the shape of the response, the maximum step size that should be employed is about $h = 0.25$. For such a value of h the error in the response stays below 10^{-12}. Even for a step size as large as 5, the error remains below 10^{-10}, although in this case only the tail of the response is obtained.

The stepping algorithm is similar to methods for the integration of differential equations, only here the evaluations are done at complex points. Because of the similarity, several theoretical answers must be established before we can be convinced that the method is useful and reliable. In particular, do local errors propagate or do they die out as we proceed with the calculations? This question is answered in the next section by deriving the stability properties as was done in Chapter 9 for the Euler and trapezoidal formulae.

10.5. STABILITY PROPERTIES

The stability of numerical integration methods is studied on the following test differential equation

$$x' = \lambda x \tag{10.5.1}$$

where λ is either a real or complex constant. Apply the Laplace transformation (Appendix A, Eq. A.7):

$$sX - x_0 = \lambda X \tag{10.5.2}$$

or

$$X = \frac{x_0}{s - \lambda}.$$

Use the inversion formula (10.1.11) with a step $t = h$:

$$x_1 = -\frac{1}{h} \sum_{i=1}^{M} K_i \frac{x_0}{z_i/h - \lambda} = x_0 \sum_{i=1}^{M} \frac{K_i}{\lambda h - z_i}. \tag{10.5.3}$$

Introducing the substitution

$$z = u + jv = \lambda h, \tag{10.5.4}$$

$$x_1 = x_0 \sum_{i=1}^{M} \frac{K_i}{z - z_i},$$

and taking n steps we obtain

$$x_n = x_0 \left(\sum_{i=1}^{M} \frac{K_i}{z - z_i} \right)^n. \tag{10.5.5}$$

To make (10.5.5) stable for arbitrarily large n, we require

$$\left| \sum_{i=1}^{M} \frac{K_i}{z - z_i} \right| \leqslant 1. \tag{10.5.6}$$

Comparing (10.5.6) with (10.1.10) we conclude that the stability region is given by the Padé approximation of e^z:

$$|R_{N,M}(z)| \leqslant 1. \tag{10.5.7}$$

The stability curves are plotted for $N = M - 1$ in Fig. 10.5.1, *the stable region being outside of the curves.* Similar curves are obtained for $N = M - 2$. They indicate that if Re λ is negative (stable differential equation), the integration will *always* be stable.

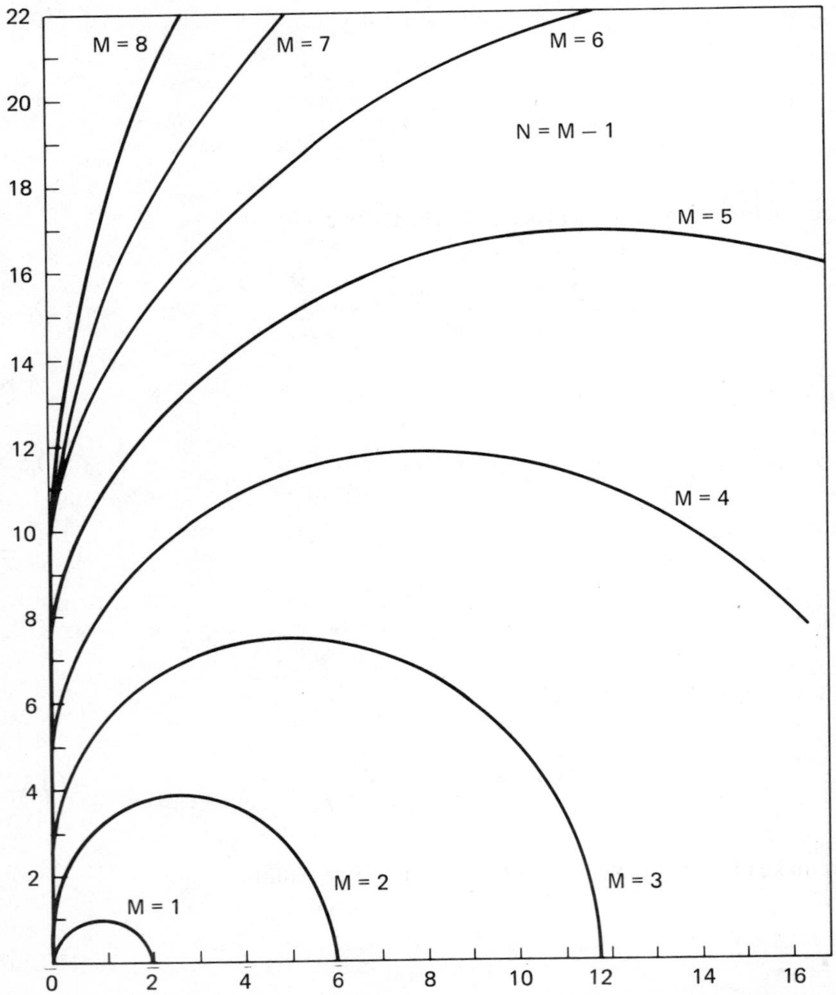

Fig. 10.5.1. Stability boundaries for $N = M - 1$. The curves are symmetric about the real axis. Solutions are stable outside the curves.

It is worth comparing the results with other methods. For $M = 1$, $N = 0$, $R_{0,1}(z) = 1/(1 - z)$ so that $K = -1$ and $z = -1$. The boundary is expressed by $|1/(1 - z)| = 1$. This is a unit circle touching the imaginary axis with center at $(1, 0)$. The order of integration is $p = 1$ and the case is *identical* to the backward Euler formula. Only real numbers are involved. The case $M = 2, N = 0$ has $K' = -2j$, $z = 1 + j$ and only one complex evaluation is needed. The order of integration is $p = 2$. For $M = 2$, $N = 1$, again only one complex function evaluation is necessary but the order of integration is now $p = 3$ and the integration is stable for any stable function.

The excellent stability properties of the method will be demonstrated by an example which uses the program in Fig. 10.4.1.

EXAMPLE 10.5.1. Consider the "stiff" function

$$F(s) = \frac{999}{(s+1)(s+1000)} = \frac{999}{s^2 + 1001s + 1000}$$

for which the impulse response is

$$f(t) = e^{-t} - e^{-1000t}.$$

A step size of the order 10^{-4} is required to observe the initial fast transient. After $t = 5 \times 10^{-3}$, the step size can be increased to about 0.1. The resulting error is of order 10^{-11} throughout. In many cases, the initial fast transient is due to parasitic effects and is of no interest to the analyst. The use of a step size $h = 0.1$ from the start still gave an error of 10^{-11} in the dominant response, although the initial fast transient was not observed.

REFERENCES

1. K. Singhal and J. Vlach: Computation of time domain response by numerical inversion of the Laplace transform. *Journal of the Franklin Institute*, Vol. 299, No. 2, pp. 109–126, February 1975.
2. J. Vlach: Numerical method for transient responses of linear networks with lumped, distributed or mixed parameters. *Journal of the Franklin Institute*, Vol. 288, No. 2, pp. 99–113, August 1969.
3. K. Singhal, J. Vlach, and M. Nakhla: Absolutely stable, high order method for time domain solution of networks. *Archiv für Elektronik und Uebertragungstechnik (Electronics and Communication)*, Vol. 30, pp. 157–166, 1976.
4. K. Singhal and J. Vlach: Approximation of nonuniform *RC*-distributed networks for frequency and time domain computations. *IEEE Transactions on Circuit Theory*, Vol. CT-19, pp. 347–354, July 1972.
5. K. Singhal and J. Vlach: Method for computing time response of systems described by transfer functions. *Journal of the Franklin Institute*, Vol. 311, pp. 123–130, 1981.

CHAPTER 11
Modeling

In the context of this book, modeling is the process by which we represent the electrical properties of a semiconductor device or a group of interconnected devices by means of mathematical equations, circuit representations or tables. Complex devices and large scale systems are characterized by *macromodels* which reflect their terminal behavior. Modeling at both levels, device and terminal, is equally important. Device level models are used for accurate analysis and design of smaller networks. Eventually, if these networks represent typical building blocks in larger systems, macromodeling is used to simplify the representation and speed up the analysis.

Modeling of electronic devices requires a thorough understanding of semiconductor physics and specialization in this area. Since it is impossible to provide detailed information on the few pages devoted to the subject, we have decided to describe the models on a strictly mathematical basis, without any reference to the underlying physics. Very often, the specialist in computer aided design will obtain device information from the device specialist and will only be faced with the task of implementing these models. A somewhat different situation occurs in macromodeling, where computer aided design itself can be used to obtain suitable terminal representations for such building blocks as operational amplifiers, logic gates, etc. Alternatively, the macromodel can be constructed from measured data or on the basis of manufacturer specifications.

This chapter discusses models for the most commonly encountered semiconductor devices: diodes, field-effect transistors, and bipolar transistors. In addition, the macromodeling of an operational amplifier is described.

Physical device models usually involve many complicated equations. Typical timing studies have shown that the major part of the computational effort in network analysis is spent in evaluating these complicated relationships. Further, most analysis methods also require derivatives of the model equations—a cumbersome and error-prone task for the designer. For these reasons, increasing use is being made of approximations to the model equations; a section on cubic splines provides the reader with an introduction to this powerful mathematical tool.

11.1. DIODE MODELS

The semiconductor diode is the most common nonlinear element. Its terminal behavior is described by the equation

$$I = I_s\left[\exp\left(\frac{qV}{kT}\right) - 1\right] \tag{11.1.1}$$

and its symbol is shown in Fig. 11.1.1. In (11.1.1), $q = 1.6022 \times 10^{-19}$ C is the electronic charge, $k = 1.3806 \times 10^{-23}$ J/°K is the Boltzmann's constant, T is the temperature in degrees kelvin (273.16°K = 0°C), and V is the voltage across the diode. At 17°C ≈ 290°K, the constant $V_T \equiv kT/q \approx 25$ mV. When the polarity of V is as shown, the diode is in the *conducting* region. I_s is a constant which depends on the physical properties of the diode and is usually in the range 10^{-6}–10^{-9} A. For $V < -3V_T$ (≈ -75 mV), $I \approx -I_s$. The value I_s is usually referred to as the *saturation current*. If the diode is forward biased with $V > 4V_T$ (over 100 mV), Eq. (11.1.1) may be approximated by $I = I_s \exp(qV/kT)$.

When a constant voltage V_0 is applied to the diode, a constant current I_0 flows through it. The pair of values (V_0, I_0) is called the *operating point* of the diode:

$$I_0 = I_s[\exp(V_0/V_T) - 1]. \tag{11.1.2}$$

A small incremental voltage may be superimposed on V_0. The corresponding small variation in I is found by differentiating (11.1.1):

$$\left.\frac{dI}{dV}\right|_{V=V_0} = g(V_0) = (I_s/V_T)\exp(V_0/V_T). \tag{11.1.3}$$

Figure 11.1.2 indicates the situation. The value

$$g(V_0) = \left.\frac{dI}{dV}\right|_{V=V_0}$$

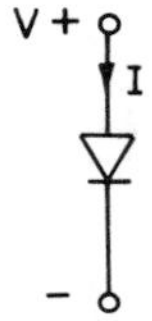

Fig. 11.1.1. Symbol of a diode.

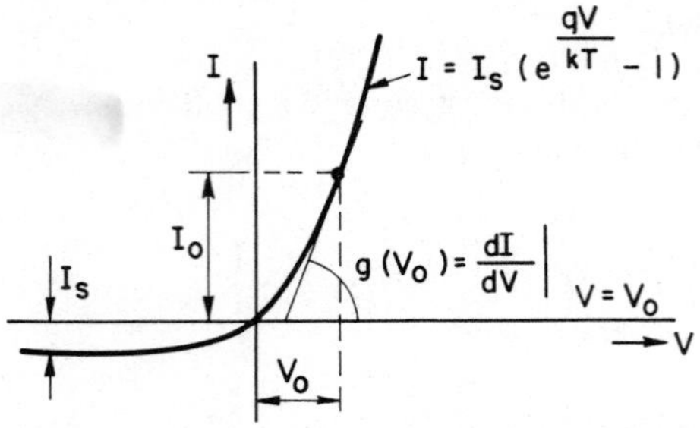

Fig. 11.1.2. *V–I* characteristic of the diode.

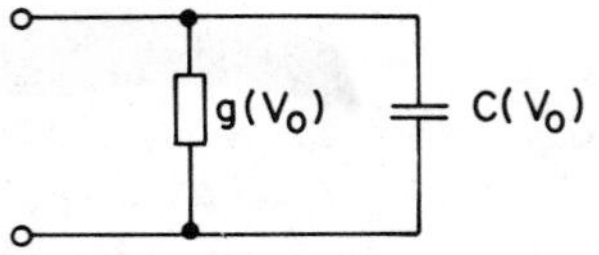

Fig. 11.1.3. Medium-frequency incremental model for the diode.

is the slope of the curve at V_0. It has the dimension of a conductance and is called the *dynamic conductance* of the diode. It relates *increments* of the current to the *increments* of the voltage.

As we go to higher frequencies, additional physical effects come into play and the diode may no longer be treated as a simple resistor. Charges stored in the semiconductor material will change the small-signal equivalent network into a parallel combination of a resistor and a capacitor as shown in Fig. 11.1.3. The value of the capacitance is, in general, a function of the voltage across the diode.

In some applications, the simple model does not express the properties sufficiently accurately and other modifications are required. One model with a constant resistor R, representing the bulk resistance, is shown in Fig. 11.1.4. In this model the capacitance across the diode is split into two components: C_j is the depletion capacitance while C_D is the diffusion capacitance. The

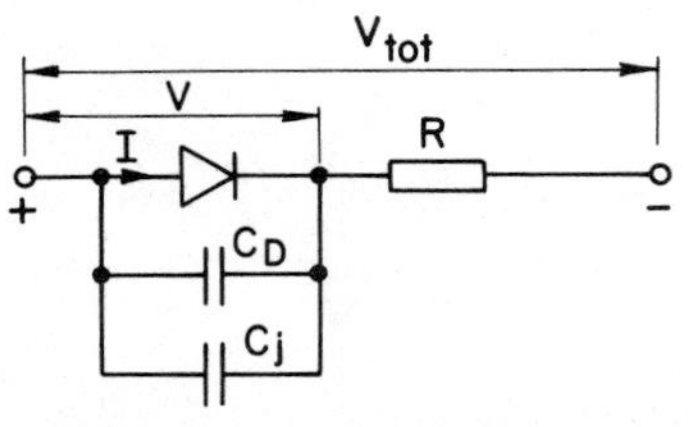

Fig. 11.1.4. More general model of the diode including bulk resistance *R*.

capacitance C_j is a function of the voltage across the diode and is given by

$$C_j = \begin{cases} \dfrac{C_{jo}}{\left(1 - \dfrac{V}{\phi}\right)^{\gamma}}, & \text{for} \quad V \leqslant \phi - Z \qquad (11.1.4a) \\ K_1 V + K_2, & \text{for} \quad V > \phi - Z \qquad (11.1.4b) \end{cases}$$

where

$$K_1 = \left.\frac{dC_j}{dV}\right|_{V=\phi-Z}$$

$$K_2 = -K_1(\phi - Z) + C_j\Big|_{V=\phi-Z}.$$

Here ϕ depends on the material (~0.8 V for silicon, ~0.4 V for germanium) and γ is typically between $\frac{1}{2}$ and $\frac{1}{3}$. C_{jo} is usually a few pF. The reason for the above modeling can be seen from Fig. 11.1.5, where the measured curve representing C_j is shown by curve 1. Equation (11.1.4a) simulates the response well up to a given point but beyond that it grows to infinity for $V = \phi$. To better represent the actual value, the curve is replaced by a tangent line at a selected point $V = \phi - Z$, where Z is a value between 0.05 and 0.5. This simplification does not take into account the drop in the value of C_j but is usually satisfactory for most applications. Alternatively, the curve could be represented by cubic splines, discussed later in this chapter.

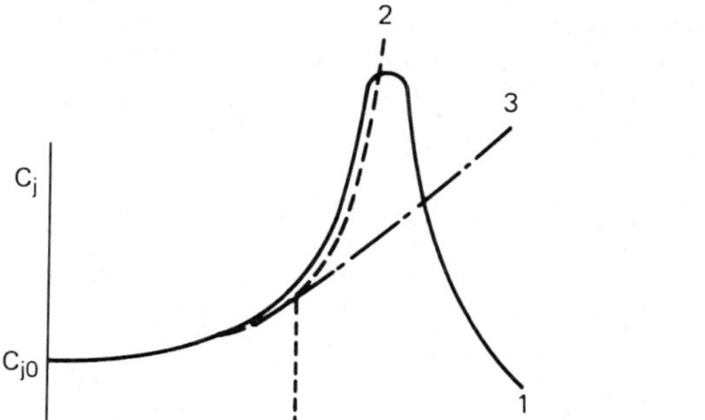

Fig. 11.1.5. Modeling of C_j. Curve 1 is the measured value of $C_j(V)$. Curve 2 is the simulation by (11.1.4a), curve 3 is the tangent line to C_j at $V = \phi - Z$.

The diffusion capacitance is modeled by

$$C_D = \begin{cases} \tau \dfrac{dI}{dV}, & V > 0 \\ 0, & V \leqslant 0 \end{cases} \tag{11.1.5}$$

where dI/dV is the derivative of (11.1.1) and τ is a constant determined from measurements. C_D is usually fairly large compared to C_j and may have values in the range 50–1000 pF.

In computer applications *linearized models* of the diode are required. Consider again (11.1.1) and (11.1.3). Their sum is

$$I + dI = I_s[\exp(V/V_T) - 1] + \frac{I_s}{V_T}\exp(V/V_T)\,dV$$

or, using increments,

$$\begin{aligned} I + \Delta I &= I_s[\exp(V/V_T) - 1] + \frac{I_s}{V_T}\exp(V/V_T)\,\Delta V \\ &= J_{\text{eq}} + Y_{\text{eq}}\Delta V. \end{aligned} \tag{11.1.6}$$

This equation can be represented by the equivalent network in Fig. 11.1.6 as a conductance in parallel with a source. Since the ideal diode is nothing but a nonlinear resistor, *the same figure illustrates linearization of any nonlinear conductance.* For a linear conductance, the equivalent source J_{eq} has value zero.

In summary, the large-signal nonlinearity can be replaced locally by an equivalent incremental conductance *and* an equivalent source J_{eq}. This is true when the dc bias sources are included. If the signals are small, the operating point is first determined and only the incremental model of Fig. 11.1.3 is used.

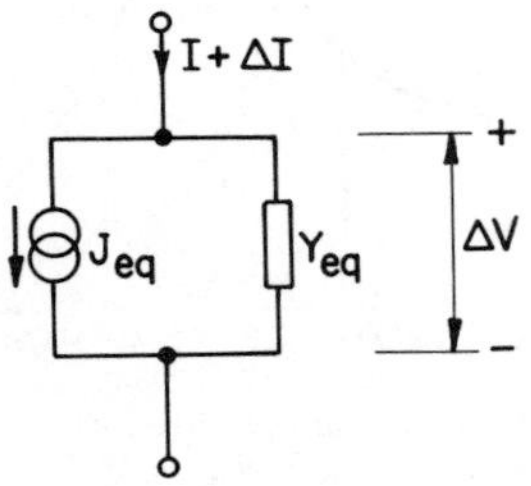

Fig. 11.1.6. Incremental model for a diode.

11.2. FIELD EFFECT TRANSISTOR MODELS

Transistors are devices whose properties can, in general, be described by sets of equations of the following form:

$$\begin{aligned} I_1 &= f_1(V_{13}, V_{23}) \\ I_2 &= f_2(V_{13}, V_{23}). \end{aligned} \tag{11.2.1}$$

They relate to the general three-terminal network shown in Fig. 11.2.1.

Field effect transistors (FETs) are devices for which the first function f_1 is zero. Their terminals are called *gate*, *drain*, and *source* and are denoted by the letters G, D, and S, respectively. While detailed modeling requires inclusion of the substrate as a terminal, this will not be considered in the following simple analysis. Equations (11.2.1) thus reduce to

$$\begin{aligned} I_G &= 0 \\ I_D &= f(V_{GS}, V_{DS}). \end{aligned} \tag{11.2.2}$$

In this section we give descriptions of two types of FETs. The first ones, JFET and MESFET (for junction field effect transistors and FET with metal-semiconductor barrier), have the symbols shown in Fig. 11.2.2. The drain-to-source current, I_D, is expressed, for an n-channel device, by

$$\frac{I_D}{I_0} = -3\frac{V_{DS}}{V_0} - 2\left[\left(\frac{V_{GS} - V_{DS} + V_b}{V_0}\right)^{3/2} - \left(\frac{V_{GS} + V_b}{V_0}\right)^{3/2}\right] \tag{11.2.3}$$

in the linear region defined by $V_{DS} \leqslant V_{GS} - V_0 + V_b$, and by

$$\frac{I_D}{I_0} = -1 + 3\,\frac{V_{GS} - V_{DS} + V_b}{V_0} - 2\left(\frac{V_{GS} - V_{DS} + V_b}{V_0}\right)^{3/2} \tag{11.2.4}$$

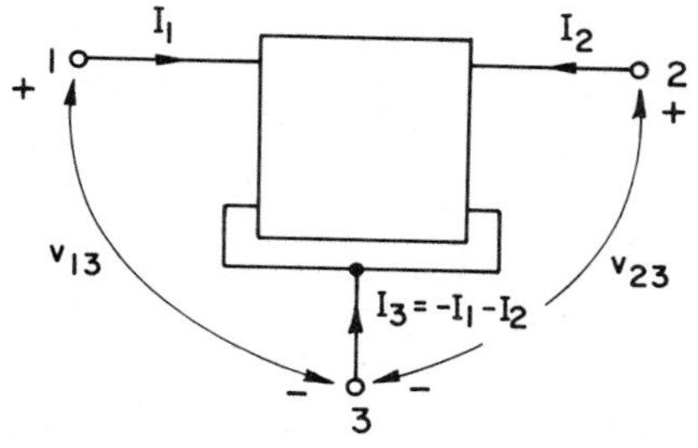

Fig. 11.2.1. A three-terminal device obtained from the two-port description.

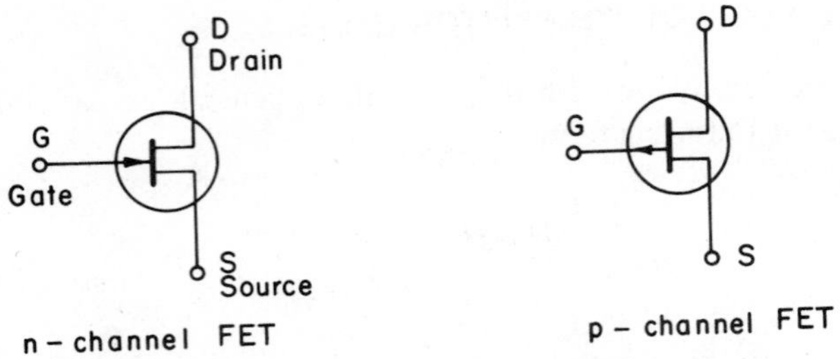

Fig. 11.2.2. Symbols for field effect transistors (FET).

in the saturation region where $V_{DS} > V_{GS} - V_0 + V_b$. Here

I_0 = the drain current for $V_{GS} + V_b = 0$ and $V_{DS} = -V_0$
V_0 = the gate-channel potential required to produce pinch-off, typically 4 V
V_b = the built-in potential, usually about 0.7 V; negative for n-channel and positive for p-channel FET, respectively
V_{GS}, V_{DS} = the gate-source and drain-source voltages, respectively.

For the n-channel device, all voltages are positive, for the p-channel device they are negative.

In the saturation region, the capacitance C_{GS} has the following form:

$$C_{GS} = C_0 \frac{2\left[1 + \left(\frac{V_{GS} + V_b}{V_0}\right)^{1/2}\right]}{\left[1 + 2\left(\frac{V_{GS} + V_b}{V_0}\right)^{1/2}\right]^2} \tag{11.2.5}$$

where C_0 is one-half of the total gate-source capacitance for $V_{GS} + V_b = 0$ and $V_{DS} = -V_0$. Expression (11.2.5) can be used for the linear region with the understanding that the actual values will be somewhat smaller. Finally, the

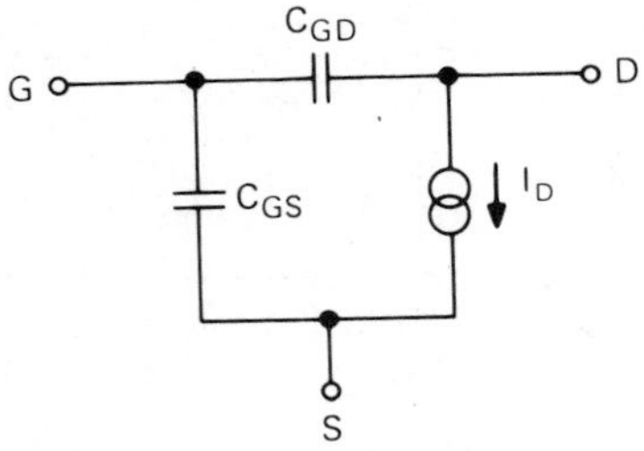

Fig. 11.2.3. Large-signal JFET model.

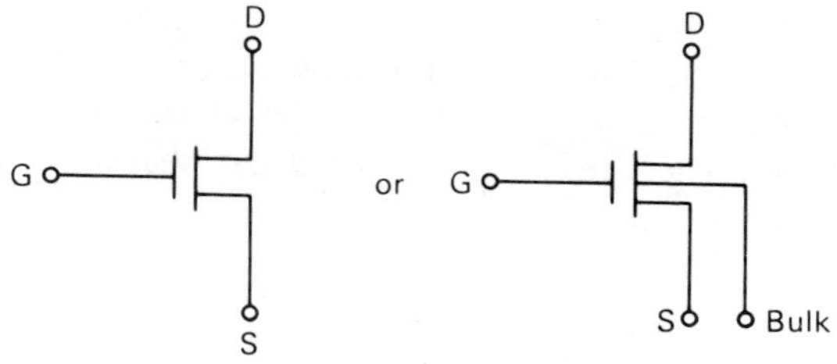

Fig. 11.2.4. Symbols for MOSFET or IGFET.

capacitance C_{GD} is usually about 50 times smaller than C_{GS} and is usually swamped by the extrinsic capacitance. The values and voltages given above refer to Fig. 11.2.3.

The other types of FETs are MOSFETs (for metal-oxide semiconductor) or IGFETs (for insulated gate). Their symbols are given in Fig. 11.2.4 and the equivalent network is shown in Fig. 11.2.5. Here

$$I_{BD'} = I_{SD'}[\exp(V_{BD'}/V_T) - 1]$$

$$I_{BS'} = I_{SS'}[\exp(V_{BS'}/V_T) - 1]$$

$$I_D = \beta\left[(V_{GS'} - V_\tau)\,V_{DS'} - \frac{V_{DS'}^2}{2}\right], \quad \text{for } V_{DS'} \leqslant V_{GS'} - V_\tau \qquad (11.2.6)$$

$$I_D = \frac{\beta}{2}[V_{GS'} - V_\tau]^2, \quad \text{for } V_{DS'} > V_{GS'} - V_\tau$$

with β = the amplification factor
V_τ = the threshold voltage.

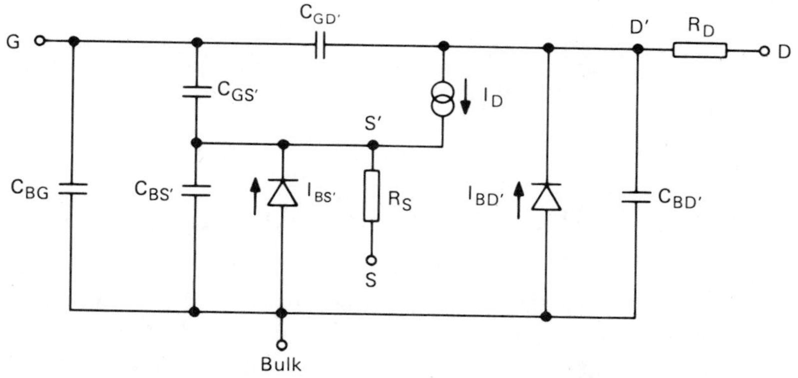

Fig. 11.2.5. Equivalent network for an *n*-channel MOSFET or IGFET.

Typically, V_T is between 0 and 1.5 V and is constant for a given technology. It can be measured by short-circuiting the gate and drain and by applying voltage $V_{GS} = V_T$ such that $I_{SD} = 0.1\ \mu A$. The above equations are valid for long-channel transistors. The capacitances can be assumed as fixed, defined by geometry and technology,

$$C = \frac{\epsilon_0 \epsilon_R A}{t_{\text{oxide}}} \tag{11.2.7}$$

where A = the area
ϵ_R = dielectric constant
ϵ_0 = permittivity of free space
t_{oxide} = the thickness of the oxide.

For more details, the reader is referred to the literature, for instance [1]-[4].

The operating point of a FET is established by applying dc voltages to the device. This results in the currents

$$I_G = 0$$
$$I_{D_0} = f(V_{GS_0}, V_{DS_0})$$

and small signals may be superimposed over the dc operating voltages, resulting in small variations of the current I_D. Expanding I_D into a Taylor series and retaining only the linear terms

$$dI_D = \frac{\partial f}{\partial V_{GS}}\, dV_{GS} + \frac{\partial f}{\partial V_{DS}}\, dV_{DS}. \tag{11.2.8}$$

If V_{DS} is kept constant, the second term of the expansion vanishes and

$$\frac{\partial I_D}{\partial V_{GS}} = \frac{\partial f}{\partial V_{GS}} = g_m(V_{GS_0}, V_{DS_0}) = g_m. \tag{11.2.9}$$

On the other hand, if V_{GS} is kept constant

$$\frac{\partial I_D}{\partial V_{DS}} = \frac{\partial f}{\partial V_{DS}} = G_{DS}(V_{GS_0}, V_{DS_0}) = G_{DS}. \tag{11.2.10}$$

The constant g_m has the dimension of a conductance but I_D is influenced by a voltage applied at the terminals *G–S*. Thus g_m represents the *transconductance* of a VCT whereas G_{DS} is a conductance connected between the terminals *D–S*.

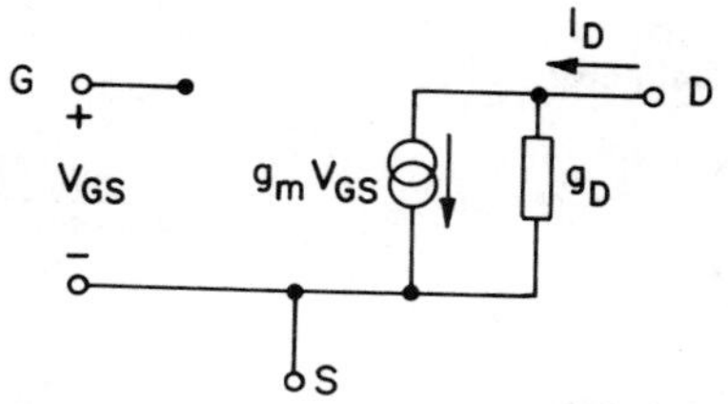

Fig. 11.2.6. Small-signal low-frequency model for a field effect transistor.

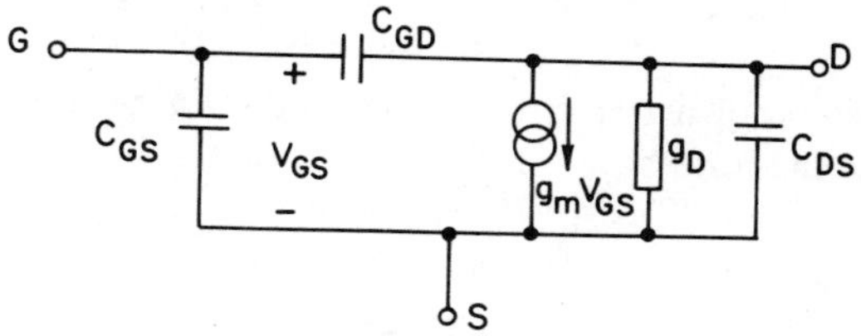

Fig. 11.2.7. Small-signal medium-frequency simplified model for a field effect transistor.

Equation (11.2.8) can be modeled by the linear network shown in Fig. 11.2.6. This is the simplest small-signal FET model. At higher frequencies, the capacitances must be taken into consideration, evaluated at the operating point. Thus a more realistic small-signal FET model will have the form of Fig. 11.2.7. Typical values are given in the following table:

	JFET	MOSFET
g_m	0.1–10 mA/V	0.1–30 mA/V
R_{DS}	0.1–1 MΩ	0.1–4 MΩ
C_{DS}	0.1–1 pF	0.1–1 pF
C_{GS}	1–10 pF	1–10 pF
C_{GD}	1–10 pF	1–10 pF

11.3. BIPOLAR TRANSISTOR MODELS

The simplest description of bipolar transistors has the same form as (11.2.1) but the terminals are called *base*, *emitter*, and *collector* and the symbols are shown in Fig. 11.3.1. For low frequencies

$$
\begin{aligned}
I_C &= f_1(V_{BC}, V_{BE}) \\
I_E &= f_2(V_{BC}, V_{BE}).
\end{aligned}
\tag{11.3.1}
$$

The voltages refer to Fig. 11.3.2 for a *pnp* transistor.

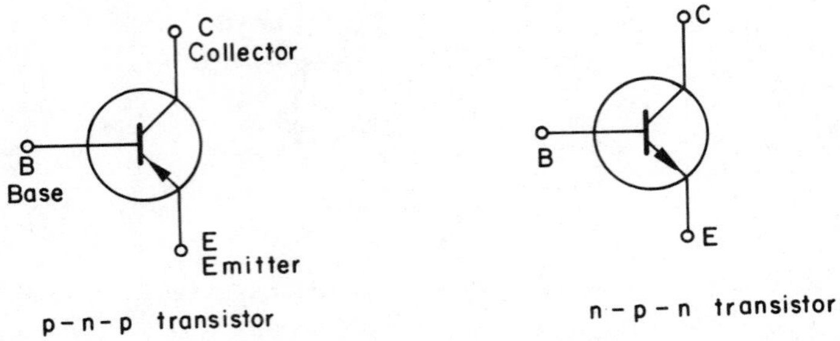

Fig. 11.3.1. Symbols for bipolar transistors.

One of the best known transistor models is the *Ebers-Moll* model in which Eqs. (11.3.1) take the form

$$
\begin{aligned}
I_C &= \alpha_F I_F - I_R \\
I_E &= -I_F + \alpha_R I_R
\end{aligned}
\tag{11.3.2}
$$

with

$$
\begin{aligned}
I_F &= I_{ES}\,[\exp\,(V_{BE}/V_T) - 1] \\
I_R &= I_{CS}\,[\exp\,(V_{BC}/V_T) - 1]
\end{aligned}
\tag{11.3.3}
$$

where I_{ES}, I_{CS} are the base-emitter and base-collector saturation currents,
V_{BE}, V_{BC} are the base-emitter and base-collector voltages,
α_F, α_R are the large-signal forward and reverse current gains of the transistor in the common base configuration

and

$$
V_T = \frac{kT}{q} = \frac{(\text{Boltzmann's constant}) \times (\text{junction temperature in } ^\circ\text{K})}{\text{electronic charge}}.
$$

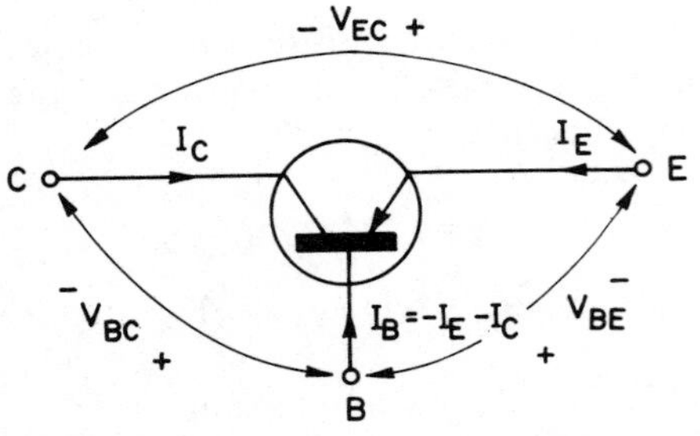

Fig. 11.3.2. A bipolar (*pnp*) transistor considered as a three-terminal device.

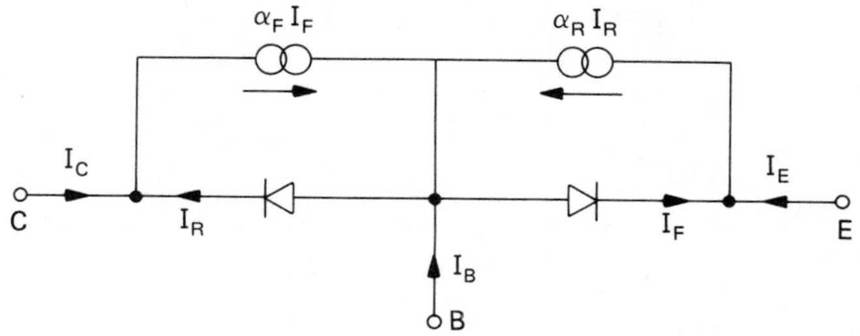

Fig. 11.3.3. Injection version of the Ebers–Moll model.

Equations (11.3.2) represent the *injection* version of the Ebers-Moll model; the corresponding equivalent circuit is shown in Fig. 11.3.3.

The constants α_F, α_R and the saturation currents I_{ES}, I_{CS} are not independent. The physical properties of the transistor require

$$\alpha_F I_{ES} = \alpha_R I_{CS} \equiv I_S. \tag{11.3.4}$$

Using I_S it is possible not only to modify equations (11.3.2) into a form better suited to computer applications but also to reduce the number of constants from four to three:

$$\begin{aligned} I_C &= I_{CC} - I_{EC}/\alpha_R \\ I_E &= -I_{CC}/\alpha_F + I_{EC} \end{aligned} \tag{11.3.5}$$

where

$$I_{CC} = I_S\,[\exp\,(V_{BE}/V_T) - 1] = \text{reference collector source current}$$

and

$$I_{EC} = I_S\,[\exp\,(V_{BC}/V_T) - 1] = \text{reference emitter source current.}$$

Equations (11.35) represent the *transport* version of the Ebers-Moll model; its equivalent circuit is shown in Fig. 11.3.4.

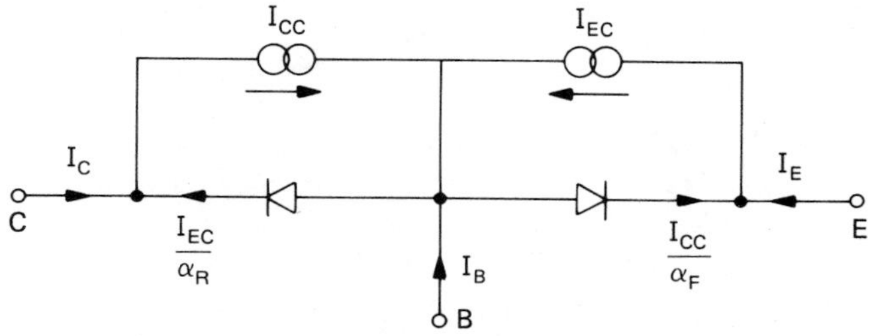

Fig. 11.3.4. Transport version of the Ebers–Moll model.

Still another model can be derived if we introduce

$$\alpha_F = \frac{\beta_F}{1 + \beta_F}; \qquad \alpha_R = \frac{\beta_R}{1 + \beta_R} \tag{11.3.6}$$

where β_F, β_R are the *forward and reverse current gains* in the common emitter configuration, respectively. Inserting into (11.3.5) we obtain

$$\begin{aligned} I_C &= (I_{CC} - I_{EC}) - \frac{I_{EC}}{\beta_R} \\ I_E &= -\frac{I_{CC}}{\beta_F} - (I_{CC} - I_{EC}) \end{aligned} \tag{11.3.7}$$

Introducing the notation

$$I_{CT} = I_{CC} - I_{EC} \tag{11.3.8}$$

the equations can be modeled as shown in Fig. 11.3.5 with only one current source. This model is called the *nonlinear hybrid* Π model.

The above models are valid only for low frequencies because they do not take into account the charges stored in the semiconductor material. Additional components are needed at higher frequencies and also for a more precise prediction of the dc behavior.

A model often used for high frequencies is shown in Fig. 11.3.6. It has three additional components r'_C, r'_E and r'_B that represent bulk resistances and four nonlinear capacitors. The low frequency models given above can be considered as connected to the points B', C', E'.

Usually, the resistors are taken as being constant. Here

r'_C = collector resistance, typically from several ohms to several hundred ohms
r'_E = emitter resistance, typically 1 ohm and often neglected

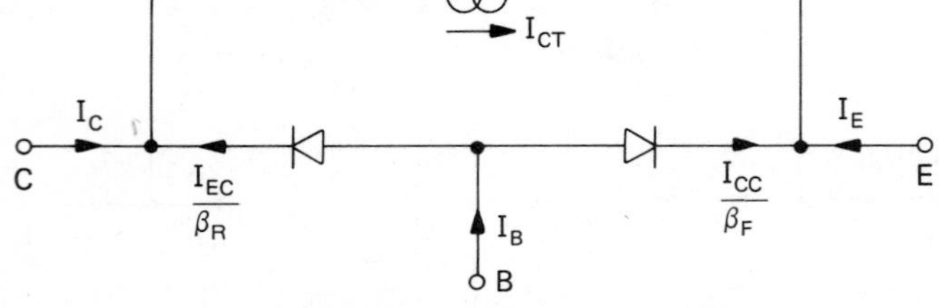

Fig. 11.3.5. Hybrid π nonlinear Ebers–Moll model.

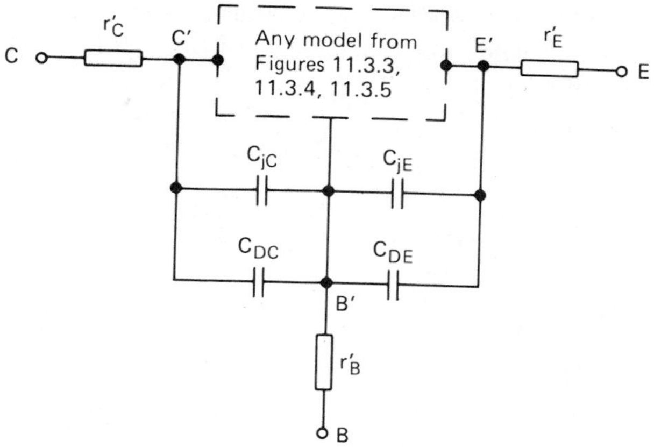

Fig. 11.3.6. More general Ebers–Moll model.

r_B' = base resistance, typically about 10 ohms for microwave transistors and up to several kΩ for low frequency devices.

The junction capacitances are functions of voltages and are modeled by equations similar to those introduced for the diode in Section 11.1. Thus, for instance, the collector-junction capacitance is given by

$$C_{jC} = \begin{cases} \dfrac{C_{jCo}}{\left(1 - \dfrac{V_{BC}}{\phi_C}\right)^{\gamma_C}}, & \text{for } V_{BC} \leqslant \phi_C - Z_C \qquad (11.3.9a) \\ K_1 V_{BC} + K_2, & \text{for } V_{BC} > \phi_C - Z_C \qquad (11.3.9b) \end{cases}$$

where

$$K_1 = \left.\frac{dC_{jC}}{dV_{BC}}\right|_{V_{BC}=\phi_C - Z_C} \qquad (11.3.9c)$$

$$K_2 = -K_1(\phi_C - Z_C) + C_{jC}\Big|_{V_{BC}=\phi_C - Z_C} \qquad (11.3.9d)$$

with Z_C typically in the range 0.05–0.5, $\phi_C = 0.8$, and $\gamma_C = 0.5$. If the resistors r_B' and r_C' are taken into consideration, the voltage V_{BC} in these equations is replaced by $V_{B'C'}$. The same type of equations hold for the junction emitter capacitance; all we have to do is replace the letter C by E. The constants are different and the typical values are $\phi_E = 0.6$ and $\gamma_E = \frac{1}{3}$.

The emitter diffusion capacitance is determined from measurements. Let f_t be the frequency at which the small-signal current gain β_F decreases to one. Let I_{CF} be the current at this point. Then

$$C_{DE} = \begin{cases} \tau_F g_E, & \text{if} \quad V_{BE} > 0 \\ 0, & \text{if} \quad V_{BE} \leqslant 0 \end{cases} \tag{11.3.10}$$

where

$$\tau_F = \begin{cases} \dfrac{1}{2\pi f_t}, & \text{if} \quad I_{CF} \approx 0 \\ \dfrac{1}{2\pi f_t} - \dfrac{V_T}{I_{CF}} \left[C_{jE} + C_{jC} \left(1 + \dfrac{I_{CF}}{V_T} r_C' \right) \right], & \text{if} \quad I_{CF} \neq 0 \end{cases} \tag{11.3.11}$$

and

$$g_E = \frac{\partial I_{CC}}{\partial V_{BE}} = \frac{I_S}{V_T} \exp\,(V_{BE}/V_T) = (I_{CC} + I_S)/V_T. \tag{11.3.12}$$

If τ_F obtained from (11.3.11) becomes negative, it is set to zero.

Finally, the collector diffusion capacitance is given by

$$C_{DE} = \begin{cases} \tau_R g_C, & \text{if} \quad V_{BC} > 0 \\ 0, & \text{if} \quad V_{BC} \leqslant 0 \end{cases} \tag{11.3.13}$$

where

$$\tau_R = \begin{cases} 0, & \text{if} \quad \beta_R = 0 \\ \dfrac{\tau_{SAT}}{\beta_R} \left(1 + \beta_R - \dfrac{\beta_F \beta_R}{1 + \beta_F} \right) - \dfrac{\beta_F (1 + \beta_R)}{\beta_R (1 + \beta_F)} \tau_F, & \text{otherwise} \end{cases} \tag{11.3.14}$$

and

$$g_C = (I_{EC} + I_S)/V_T. \tag{11.3.15}$$

More complex models (Gummel-Poon) exist as well, but their description is beyond the scope of this book. The reader is referred to [5] where he can find an excellent description, theoretical results, and suggestions for the measurement of the various parameters.

When the transistor is operated with small signals superimposed over the dc operating voltages and currents, it is advantageous to use V_{BE} and V_{CE} as independent variables and I_B, I_C as dependent variables. This "common emitter" equivalent of (11.3.1) is described by

$$\begin{aligned} I_B &= g_1(V_{BE}, V_{CE}) \\ I_C &= g_2(V_{BE}, V_{CE}). \end{aligned} \tag{11.3.16}$$

An operating point is established by applying constant V_{BE_0}, V_{CE_0}:

$$\begin{aligned} I_{B_0} &= g_1(V_{BE_0}, V_{CE_0}) \\ I_{C_0} &= g_2(V_{BE_0}, V_{CE_0}). \end{aligned} \tag{11.3.17}$$

Small variations superimposed on the operating point are obtained by expanding (11.3.16) into a Taylor series. Retaining only the linear terms one has

$$\begin{aligned} dI_B &= \frac{\partial g_1}{\partial V_{BE}} dV_{BE} + \frac{\partial g_1}{\partial V_{CE}} dV_{CE} \\ dI_C &= \frac{\partial g_2}{\partial V_{BE}} dV_{BE} + \frac{\partial g_2}{\partial V_{CE}} dV_{CE}. \end{aligned} \tag{11.3.18}$$

Since we are interested in the increments only, we can replace the derivatives by short-circuit small-signal admittances:

$$\begin{aligned} I_B &= y_{11} V_{BE} + y_{12} V_{CE} \\ I_C &= y_{21} V_{BE} + y_{22} V_{CE}. \end{aligned} \tag{11.3.19}$$

These equations can be represented by the equivalent network of Fig. 11.3.7.

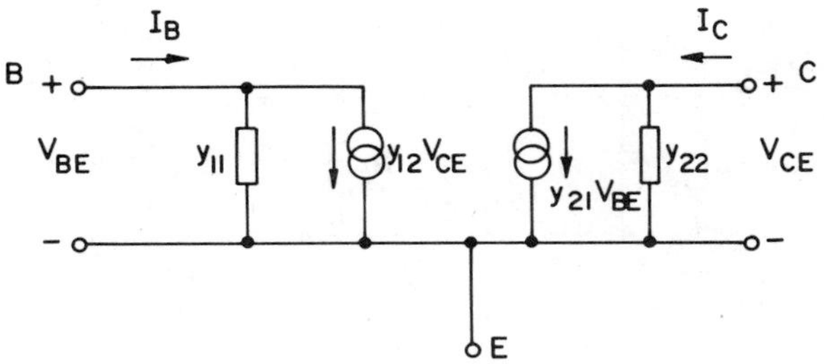

Fig. 11.3.7. Representation of a two-port short-circuit admittance matrix by a network with two VCTs.

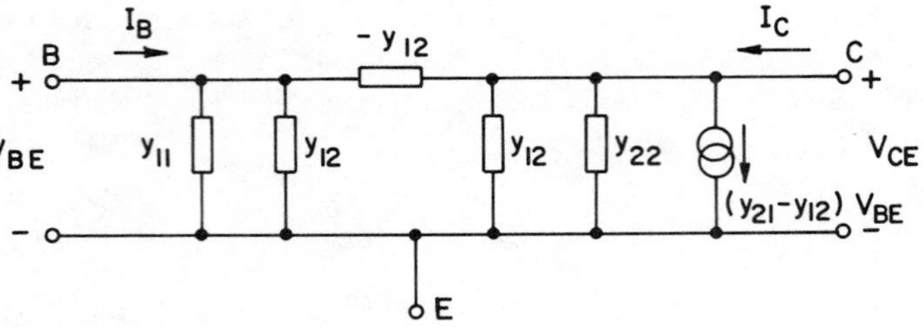

Fig. 11.3.8. Representation of a two-port short-circuit admittance matrix by a network with one VCT.

Two voltage-to-current transducers account for the transfer admittances. Because for the transistor $|y_{21}| > |y_{12}|$, we can rewrite (11.3.19) in the form

$$I_B = y_{11}V_{BE} + y_{12}V_{CE}$$

$$I_C = y_{12}V_{BE} + y_{22}V_{CE} + (y_{21} - y_{12})\, V_{BE}.$$

The term in the brackets represents a VCT at the right-hand-side terminals and the rest describes a passive two-port. The equivalent network is shown in Fig. 11.3.8. The model is called the *hybrid* π model. For higher frequencies, capacitors cannot be neglected and a more general model would have the form shown in Fig. 11.3.9. Typical values of the elements are in the following ranges:

$$R_{BB'} = 25\text{–}200\ \Omega \qquad R_\mu = 10^6\text{–}10^7\ \Omega$$

$$R_\pi = 150\text{–}1000\ \Omega \qquad R_0 = 2 \times 10^4\text{–}10^6\ \Omega$$

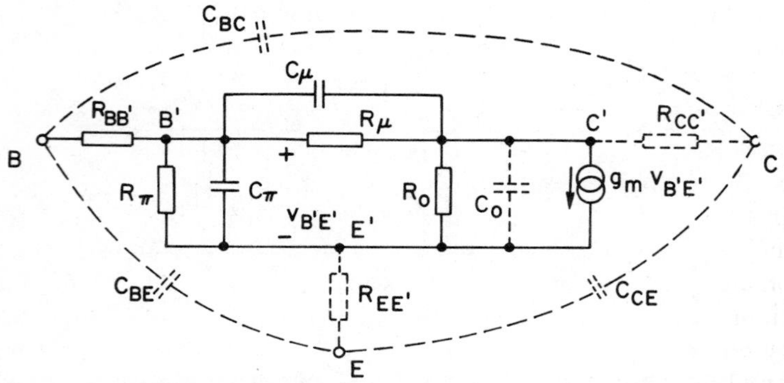

Fig. 11.3.9. Small-signal hybrid π model of the bipolar transistor.

$$C_\pi = 10\text{-}200 \text{ pF} \qquad C_\mu = 0.2\text{-}6 \text{ pF}$$

$$C_0 = 0.1\text{-}1 \text{ pF} \qquad g_m = 0.02\text{-}0.2 \text{ mmho.}$$

$R_{EE'}$ and $R_{CC'}$ are usually small and neglected. The capacitors C_{BE}, C_{CE}, and C_{BC} are stray capacitors and may have values from 0.4 to 2 pF.

The main advantage of the hybrid π model is the presence of the VCT and thus the simple nodal formulation can handle small-signal analysis of transistor networks. The modified nodal formulation must be used for the Ebers-Moll model.

11.4. MACROMODELS

The models described thus far dealt with single semiconductor elements. In most applications these elements are interconnected to perform specific overall functions. Examples of functional blocks are operational amplifiers, gates, modulators, demodulators, and so on. Although functional blocks could, in principle, be analyzed at the device level, this is not desirable in practice. A typical operational amplifier contains 20–30 transistors in addition to resistors and capacitors. Use of the eleven-component Ebers-Moll transistor model in Fig. 11.3.6 would lead to at least 220 components in the operational amplifier representation. Since we want to analyze circuits with many operational amplifiers, we would be faced with a large analysis problem. Another difficulty with this approach is that the designer seldom has access to the internal structure of the amplifier and to the parameter values for the transistors. It is thus preferable, when analyzing networks with standard functional blocks, to use *macromodels*. Macromodels characterize the terminal behavior of the functional block with sufficient accuracy for the task at hand. The macromodel may be developed on the basis of physical properties of the devices, measured data, manufacturer specifications, or a combination thereof. It may take the form of a simple equivalent circuit, a set of equations or simply a table of values. As an example of macromodeling we consider an operational amplifier. Macromodels of other functional blocks can be found in the literature, usually in the *IEEE Transactions on Electron Devices* and the *IEEE Journal of Solid State Circuits*.

A linear model for the OPAMP was introduced in Chapter 5. It includes finite input and output resistances and finite gain with a single-pole roll-off. Depending on the application and the desired accuracy, other aspects of OPAMP behavior must be considered. These include bias voltages and currents, finite common mode rejection, slew rate limitations, gain dependence on higher poles, finite output voltage swing, noise source models, etc. In our macromodel we only consider higher-order poles, limited output voltage swing, and finite slew rate. Other models are found in [8–10].

A. Gain Characteristics

The operational amplifier gain is frequency dependent and a typical Bode plot of the amplitude response is shown in Fig. 11.4.1. Each break point on the characteristics represents a negative real pole and can be modeled by the network section shown in Fig. 11.4.2 with transfer function

$$\frac{V_{ok}}{V_{ik}} = \frac{g_{mk}R_k}{1 + sC_kR_k}. \tag{11.4.1}$$

The dc gain of the section is $g_{mk}R_k$ and the pole it represents is located at $-1/R_kC_k$. The sections are coupled to each other through VCTs that provide isolation. The number of sections depends on how many poles need to be

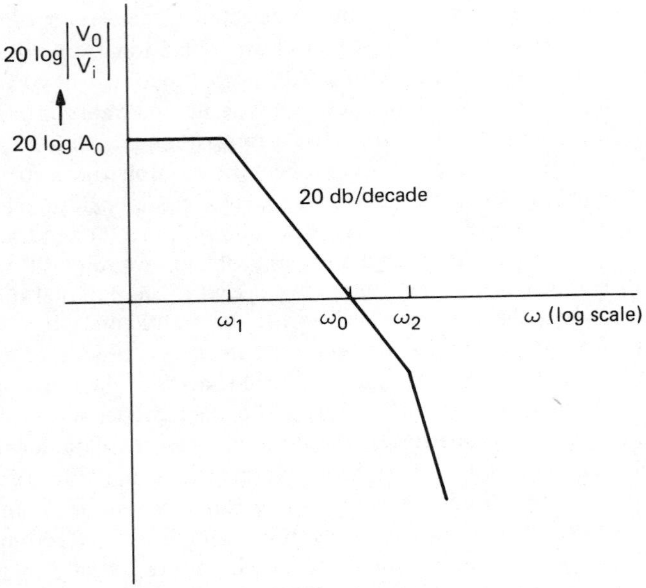

Fig. 11.4.1. Bode plot for an OPAMP.

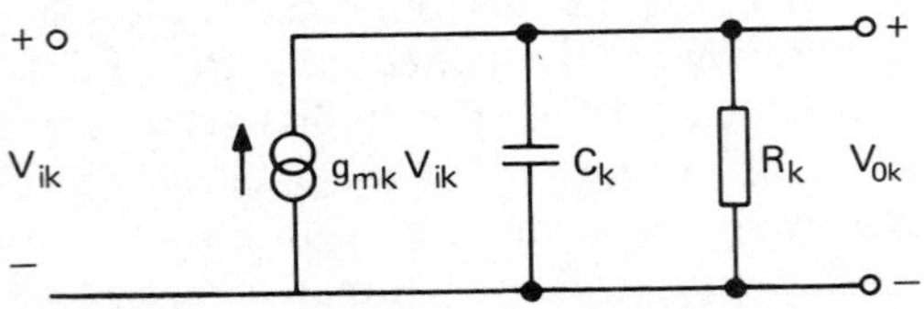

Fig. 11.4.2. The kth pole simulation stage.

represented. Though theoretically the individual R_k and C_k can have any values, numerical conditioning is improved if similar values as in the remainder of the circuit are chosen in the macromodel. Similarly, the dc gain A_0 should be distributed over the stages.

B. Finite Output Swing

The output voltage swing is restricted by the dc supply level and, in the simplest case, we would have

$$|V_0| \leqslant V_{0\,\max}. \tag{11.4.2}$$

This behavior may be characterized by placing a nonlinear resistor at the output with the V-I response as shown in Fig. 11.4.3. This resistor acts as an open circuit for $|V_0| < V_{0\,\max}$ and as a large conductance for V_0 outside this range.

C. Slew Rate Limiting

The slew rate S_r is the "maximum time rate of change of the output voltage" that can be attained by the operational amplifier and is an important parameter in high-speed circuits. Slew rate limitations arise because the transistors inside the OPAMP are unable to provide sufficient current to rapidly charge capacitive loads. The slew rate also depends on the external circuitry connected to the OPAMP. Usually, the *worst case* occurs when the OPAMP is connected as a unity gain amplifier. Slew rate is modeled by the network section shown in Fig. 11.4.4. It contains a *nonlinear* VCT which provides a maximum current of magnitude I_m to the capacitor. The capacitor voltage change is thus limited by

$$\left|\frac{dv_C}{dt}\right| = \frac{1}{C}\,|i_C| \leqslant \frac{I_m}{C}. \tag{11.4.3}$$

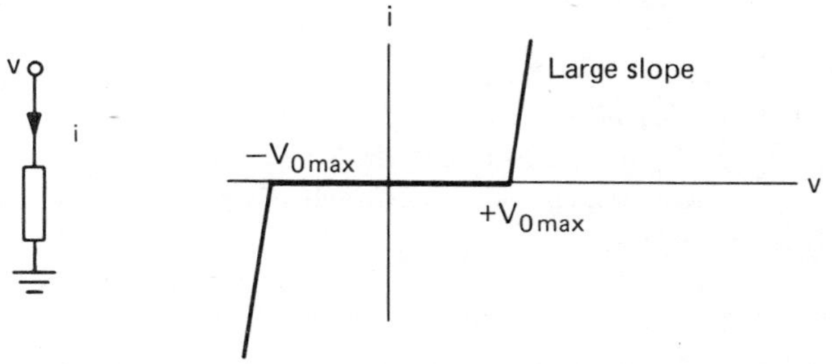

Fig. 11.4.3. Nonlinear output resistor to simulate output limiting.

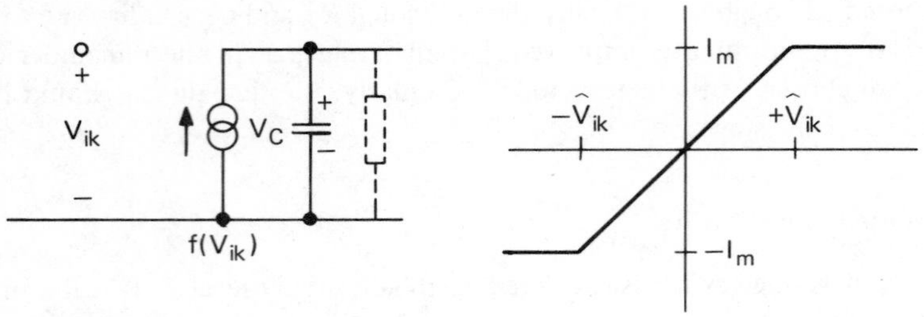

Fig. 11.4.4. Nonlinear transconductance simulating slew rate limiting.

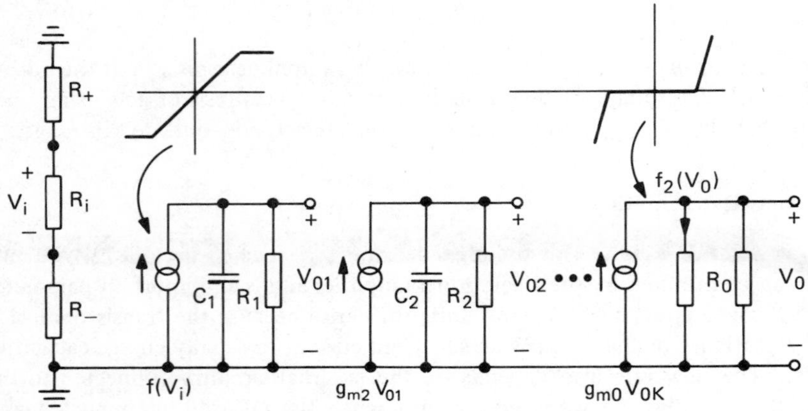

Fig. 11.4.5. OPAMP model simulating several poles, output limiting and slew rate limiting.

It follows that if I_m/C is selected equal to S_r the slew rate constraint would be satisfied. The dotted resistor in Fig. 11.4.4 provides a dc path for discharging the capacitor. Comparing with Fig. 11.4.2 we note that the slew rate limiting section can also be used to represent a pole stage. In this case $\hat{V}_{ik}$ in Fig. 11.4.4 is selected as

$$\hat{V}_{ik} = I_m/g_{mk}. \tag{11.4.4}$$

Incorporating the modifications indicated above into the linear model from Chapter 5 we arrive at the macromodel shown in Fig. 11.4.5. The parameter values of this model can usually be determined from data provided on manufacturer specification sheets.

EXAMPLE 11.4.1. Find a macromodel for the popular μA741 OPAMP with the following prescribed parameters (these are typical values from manufacturers specification sheet):

Open loop gain $A_0 = 2 \times 10^5$
Input resistance $R_i = 2\ \text{M}\Omega$
$R_+, R_- = 2000\ \text{M}\Omega$
Output resistance $R_0 = 75\ \Omega$
Peak output voltage $V_{0\,max} = 10$ V
Maximum slew rate $S_r = 0.5\ \text{V}/\mu\text{s} = 5 \times 10^5$ V/sec
Dominant pole frequency $\omega_1 = 10\pi$ rad/sec
2nd pole frequency $\omega_2 = 4\pi \times 10^6$ rad/sec.

In Fig. 11.4.5 the parameters R_i, R_+, R_-, and R_0 are directly given. Let us choose (arbitrarily)

$$R_1 = 100\ \text{k}\Omega$$

$$R_2 = 100\ \Omega.$$

The specifications on ω_1 and ω_2 enable determination of the two capacitors C_1 and C_2 as follows:

$$C_1 = 1/(\omega_1 R_1) = 0.318\ \mu\text{F}$$

$$C_2 = 1/(\omega_2 R_2) = 0.796\ \text{nF}.$$

The dc gain condition is

$$g_{m_1} R_1 g_{m_2} R_2 g_{m_0} R_0 = 2 \times 10^5$$

where g_{m_1} is the slope of the function f_1 in the linear region. With the resistors specified, the transconductances are selected as

$$g_{m_1} = g_{m_2} = 100\ \text{mmho}$$

$$g_{m_0} = 26.7\ \text{mmho}.$$

This leaves only the nonlinearities to be determined.

The output nonlinearity f_2 has a $V_{0\,max}$ of 10 V and the slope outside the range $|V_0| < V_{0\,max}$ is selected as 100 mho. The slew rate condition requires

$$I_m = C_1 S_r = 159\ \text{mA}$$

and

$$\hat{V}_i = I_m / g_{m_1} = 1.59\ \text{V}.$$

11.5. APPROXIMATE DEVICE MODELS

In the computer analysis and design of nonlinear electronic circuits increasing use is made of approximations to model device characteristics. These approximations are constructed from measured data when the functional form of the nonlinearity is not known. When the functional form is known, approximations are used to speed up computations and avoid a common error–incorrect derivatives supplied by users of CAD packages. Two of the commonly used approximations are piecewise linearization and cubic splines. Both are applicable to functions of several variables but our discussion will be restricted to one independent variable.

A *piecewise linear approximation* is obtained by joining adjacent data points by straight line segments as shown in Fig. 11.5.1. The points at which the line segments join are called *knots* and are placed so as to keep the error between the approximation and the exact function small. The evaluation of the approximation for given x is rapid and simple. As we shall show in the next chapter, this approximation is particularly useful for dc analysis when use is made of a variant of Newton's algorithm for the solution of nonlinear equations.

A major disadvantage of the piecewise linear approach is the fact that though the approximation is continuous at the knots, the derivatives are discontinuous. Another disadvantage is that often many knots are required to adequately describe the characteristics.

These disadvantages are overcome by *spline* fitting techniques where the characteristic is approximated by separate low-order polynomials between adjacent knots and continuity of the approximation and a few of its derivatives is ensured. The most popular spline approximation is the *cubic spline*, where each polynomial is a cubic and continuous first and second derivatives are maintained at the knots.

Consider n given data points $(x_1, y_1), (x_2, y_2), \ldots, (x_n, y_n)$ in Fig. 11.5.2. Our objective is to construct $n - 1$ polynomials $P_1(x), P_2(x), \ldots, P_{n-1}(x)$, each of degree 3:

$$P_i(x) = a_i + b_i(x - x_i) + c_i(x - x_i)^2 + d_i(x - x_i)^3 ; \qquad x_i \leqslant x \leqslant x_{i+1} \tag{11.5.1}$$

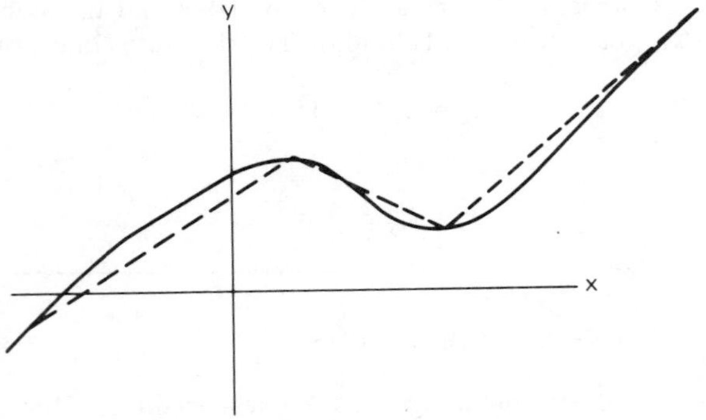

Fig. 11.5.1. Piecewise linearization of a curve.

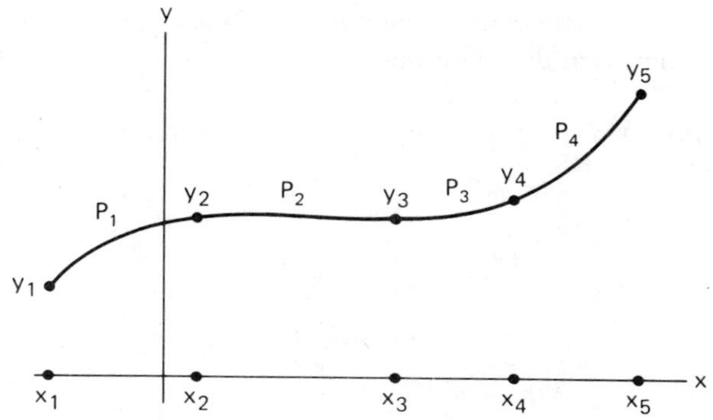

Fig. 11.5.2. Function points and spline polynomials P_i for $n = 5$.

such that

(a) the approximations pass through the given data points:

$$\begin{aligned} P_i(x_i) &= y_i \\ P_i(x_{i+1}) &= y_{i+1} \end{aligned} \qquad i = 1, 2, \ldots, n-1 \tag{11.5.2}$$

(b) the first derivatives are continuous at the internal knots:

$$P_i'(x_{i+1}) = P_{i+1}'(x_{i+1}); \qquad i = 1, 2, \ldots, n-2 \tag{11.5.3}$$

(c) the second derivatives are continuous at the internal knots:

$$P_i''(x_{i+1}) = P_{i+1}''(x_{i+1}); \qquad i = 1, 2, \ldots, n-2. \tag{11.5.4}$$

The number of unknown constants in (11.5.1) is $4n - 4$ while Eqs. (11.5.2)-(11.5.4) provide a total of $4n - 6$ constraints. To enable a solution of (11.5.1), two additional constraints are required. These may be specified in many ways and lead to different spline approximations. Often the *natural* boundary conditions which make the second derivatives zero at the terminal knots are used:

$$P_1''(x_1) = 0 \tag{11.5.5a}$$

$$P_{n-1}''(x_n) = 0. \tag{11.5.5b}$$

The $4n - 4$ equations could now be solved for the unknowns in (11.5.1).

A little foresight enables us to simplify our task. Let us, for the moment, write the polynomials in the following form:

$$P_i(x) = \bar{z}y_i + zy_{i+1} + h_i[(e_i - f_i)z\bar{z}^2 - (e_{i+1} - f_i)z^2\bar{z}] \qquad (11.5.6a)$$

where

$$h_i = x_{i+1} - x_i \qquad (11.5.6b)$$

$$z = (x - x_i)/h_i \qquad (11.5.6c)$$

$$\bar{z} = 1 - z \qquad (11.5.6d)$$

$$f_i = (y_{i+1} - y_i)/h_i \qquad (11.5.6e)$$

and the e_i are n unknown constants.

With this representation of the spline $z = 0, \bar{z} = 1$ at $x = x_i$ and $z = 1, \bar{z} = 0$ at x_{i+1}. Substitution of these relations in (11.5.6a) shows that the $2n - 2$ constraints (11.5.2) are automatically satisfied. The first and second derivatives of (11.5.6a) are

$$P_i'(x) = f_i + [(e_i - f_i)\bar{z}(\bar{z} - 2z) - (e_{i+1} - f_i)z(2\bar{z} - z)] \qquad (11.5.7)$$

and

$$P_i''(x) = \frac{2}{h_i}[(e_i - f_i)(z - 2\bar{z}) - (e_{i+1} - f_i)(\bar{z} - 2z)] \qquad (11.5.8)$$

where the chain rule was used together with the relations

$$dz/dx = 1/h_i; \qquad d\bar{z}/dx = -1/h_i. \qquad (11.5.9)$$

At the internal knots (11.5.7) gives

$$P_i'(x_{i+1}) = P_i'(z = 1, \bar{z} = 0) = e_{i+1} \qquad (11.5.10a)$$

$$P_{i+1}'(x_{i+1}) = P_{i+1}'(z = 0, \bar{z} = 1) = e_{i+1} \qquad (11.5.10b)$$

and we see that the $n - 2$ constraints (11.5.3) are also satisfied automatically by our representation (11.5.6). This leaves us with the n constraints (11.5.4) and (11.5.5) which will be used to determine the e_i. The conditions (11.5.4) lead to the following set of equations:

$$\frac{1}{h_i}[e_i + 2e_{i+1} - 3f_i] = \frac{1}{h_{i+1}}[-2e_{i+1} - e_{i+2} + 3f_{i+1}]$$

or

$$g_i e_i + 2(g_i + g_{i+1})e_{i+1} + g_{i+1}e_{i+2} = 3(g_i f_i + g_{i+1}f_{i+1}); \qquad i = 1, 2, \ldots, n-2 \tag{11.5.11}$$

where

$$g_i = 1/h_i. \tag{11.5.12}$$

The remaining conditions (11.5.5) give

$$2g_1 e_1 + g_1 e_2 = 3g_1 f_1 \tag{11.5.13a}$$

and

$$g_{n-1}e_{n-1} + 2g_{n-1}e_n = 3g_{n-1}f_{n-1}. \tag{11.5.13b}$$

Taken together, (11.5.11) and (11.5.13) may be written in the form of a symmetric tri-diagonal matrix equation which is positive definite and generally well conditioned. It can be solved easily for the unknown constants e_i:

$$\begin{bmatrix} 2g_1 & g_1 & & & & \\ g_1 & 2(g_1+g_2) & g_2 & & & \\ & g_2 & 2(g_2+g_3) & \ddots & & \\ & & g_3 & \ddots & \ddots & \\ & & & \ddots & \ddots & g_{n-1} \\ & & & & g_{n-1} & 2g_{n-1} \end{bmatrix} \begin{bmatrix} e_1 \\ e_2 \\ e_3 \\ \vdots \\ e_{n-1} \\ e_n \end{bmatrix} = 3 \begin{bmatrix} g_1 f_1 \\ g_1 f_1 + g_2 f_2 \\ g_2 f_2 + g_3 f_3 \\ \vdots \\ g_{n-2}f_{n-2} + g_{n-1}f_{n-1} \\ g_{n-1}f_{n-1} \end{bmatrix} \tag{11.5.14}$$

When the spline must be evaluated at many values of x, as is the case for network applications, the representation (11.5.1) is preferred over (11.5.6a). Equating values of the polynomial and its three derivatives at the knots obtained from the two representations gives

$$\left.\begin{aligned} a_i &= y_i \\ b_i &= e_i \\ c_i &= g_i[3f_i - 2e_i - e_{i+1}] \\ d_i &= g_i^2[-2f_i + e_i + e_{i+1}] \end{aligned}\right\} \quad i = 1, 2, \ldots, n-1. \tag{11.5.15}$$

In Fig. 11.5.3 we give two subroutines, SPLINE and SPEVAL. SPLINE computes the coefficients in (11.5.15) from given data (x_i, y_i). SPEVAL finds the operating interval through binary search and evaluates the approximation and its first derivative. The sample test program constructs an approximation

```
      PROGRAMME FOR CUBIC SPLINES
      DIMENSION X(11), Y(11), B(11), C(11), D(11)
      N = 11
      P = 2.*3.14159/(N-1)
      DO 10 I=1,N
         X(I) = (I-1)*P
   10 Y(I) = SIN(X(I))
      CALL SPLINE (X,Y,N,B,C,D)
      U = 1.
      CALL SPEVAL (X,Y,B,C,D,N,U,V,W)
      WRITE (6,20) U,V,SIN(U),W,COS(U)
      STOP
C
   20 FORMAT (5G14.4)
      END
C**********************************************************************
      SUBROUTINE SPLINE (X,Y,N,B,C,D)
C*ROUTINE COMPUTES THE NATURAL SPLINE POLYNOMIAL COEFFICIENTS GIVEN THE
C*N DATA POINTS X(I),Y(I),I=1,2,...,N. IT IS ASSUMED THAT X(I).LT.X(I+1)
C*THE SPLINE IS DEFINED IN THE I TH INTERVAL AS
C*         Y(I) + B(I)*Z + C(I)*Z**2 + D(I)*Z**3
C*WITH     Z = X-X(I)
      DIMENSION X(N), Y(N), B(N), C(N), D(N)
C*SET UP TRIDIAGONAL MATRIX EQUATION
C*B CONTAINS RHS, C THE SUPER DIAGONAL AND D THE DIAGONAL
      B(1) = 0
      D(1) = 0
      NM1 = N-1
      DO 10 I=1,NM1
         J = I+1
         C(I) = 1./(X(J)-X(I))
         B(J) = 3.*(Y(J)-Y(I))*C(I)*C(I)
         D(J) = 2.*C(I)
         B(I) = B(I)+B(J)
   10 D(I) = D(I)+D(J)
C*FORWARD SUBSTITUTION
      DO 20 I=2,N
         J = I-1
         P = C(J)/D(J)
         D(I) = D(I)-C(J)*P
   20 B(I) = B(I)-B(J)*P
C*BACK SUBSTITUTION
      B(N) = B(N)/D(N)
      DO 30 I=1,NM1
         J = N-I
   30 B(J) = (B(J)-C(J)*B(J+1))/D(J)
C*B NOW CONTAINS THE CONSTANTS B(I)
C*EVALUATE THE CONSTANTS C(I), D(I) OF THE SPLINE POLYNOMIAL
      DO 40 I=1,NM1
         J = I+1
         FI = (Y(J)-Y(I))*C(I)
         D(I) = (-2.*FI+B(J)+B(I))*C(I)*C(I)
   40 C(I) = (3.*FI-B(J)-2.*B(I))*C(I)
      RETURN
      END
C**********************************************************************
      SUBROUTINE SPEVAL (X,Y,B,C,D,N,U,V,W)
C*THIS ROUTINE COMPUTES THE CUBIC SPLINE V AND ITS DERIVATIVE
C*W FOR GIVEN ABSCISSA U. THE SPLINE IS DEFINED
C*AS      V = Y(I) + B(I)*Z + C(I)*Z**2 + D(I)*Z**3
C*WHERE I IS SUCH THAT  X(I).LE.U.LT.X(I+1)
C*        I = 1 IF U.LT.X(1)  ;   I = N-1 IF U.GT.X(N-1)
C*        AND    Z = U-X(I)
C*X,Y ARE THE DATA POINTS AND B,C,D THE ARRAYS GENERATED BY SPLINE
      DIMENSION X(N), Y(N), B(N), C(N), D(N)
C*USE BINARY SEARCH TO FIND THE OPERATING INTERVAL. SEARCH CAN BE
C*IMPROVED IF INTERVAL ON LAST CALL IS STORED AND CHECKED FIRST.
      I = 1
      J = N
more...
```

Fig. 11.5.3. Subroutines SPLINE and SPEVAL.

```
10 IF (J.LE.I+1) GO TO 50
   K = (I+J)/2
   IF (U-X(K)) 20,40,30
20 J = K
   GO TO 10
30 I = K
   GO TO 10
40 I = K
50 Z = U-X(I)
C*COMPUTE SPLINE AND ITS DERIVATIVE BY SYNTHETIC DIVISION
   W = Z*D(I)
   V = C(I)+W
   W = V+W
   V = B(I)+Z*V
   W = V+W*Z
   V = Y(I)+Z*V
   RETURN
   END

   Sample output .....

  1.000         0.8411          0.8415          0.5413          0.5403
```

Fig. 11.5.3. *cont.*

to cos x in the range zero to 2π using 11 points and then evaluates the approximation at $x = 1$. The values obtained from the spline are 0.8411 and 0.5413, compared with actual values of 0.8415 and 0.5403 for the function and the derivative, respectively. Additional information on splines can be found in [11, 12].

PROBLEMS

P.11.1. Consider the network shown in Fig. P.11.1 in which the transistor model is that of Fig. 11.3.9. The values are $R_{BB'} = 100\ \Omega$, $R_\pi = 250\ \Omega$, $C_\pi = 200$ pF, $g_m = 0.2$ mho and $R_0 = 10^5\ \Omega$; all other components are neglected. Write the system matrices **G** and **C** and obtain the frequency response of the network. Use either the program from Appendix D or your own program, into which you feed the matrices **G** and **C** manually.

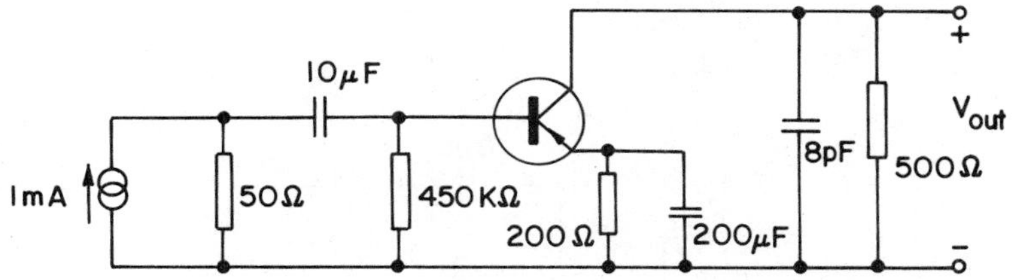

Fig. P.11.1.

P.11.2. Analyze the network shown in Fig. P.11.1 as above, but use the equivalent transistor model with $R_{BB'} = 25\ \Omega$, $R_\pi = 50\ \Omega$, $C_\pi = 0.3$ pF, $R_\mu = 200$ kΩ, $C_\mu = 0.2$ pF, $g_m = 3$ mho, $R_0 = 500$ kΩ, $C_0 = 0.3$ pF, $R_{CC'} = 10\ \Omega$, $R_{EE'} = 10\ \Omega$, $C_{BC} = C_{CE} = C_{BE} = 1$ pF.

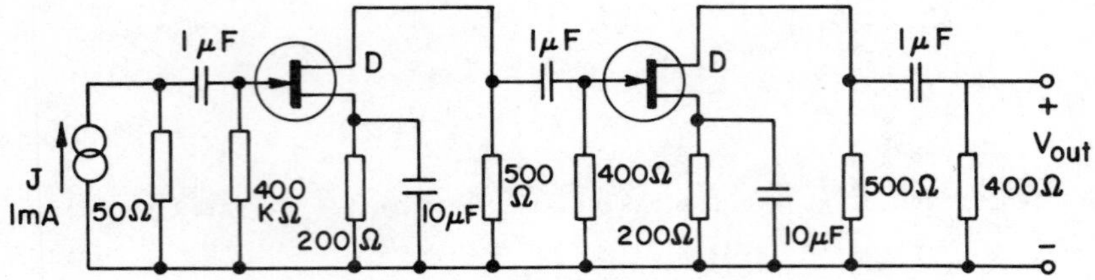

Fig. P.11.3.

P.11.3. A cascade FET amplifier is shown in Fig. P.11.3. Use the simplified model of Fig. 11.2.7 with the values $g_m = 5 \times 10^{-3}$ mho, $g_D = 10^5$ mho, $C_{GS} = 2$ pF, $C_{GD} = 2$ pF; neglect C_{DS}. Analyze as in Problem P.11.1.

P.11.4. A two-stage feedback amplifier with bipolar transistors is shown in Fig.

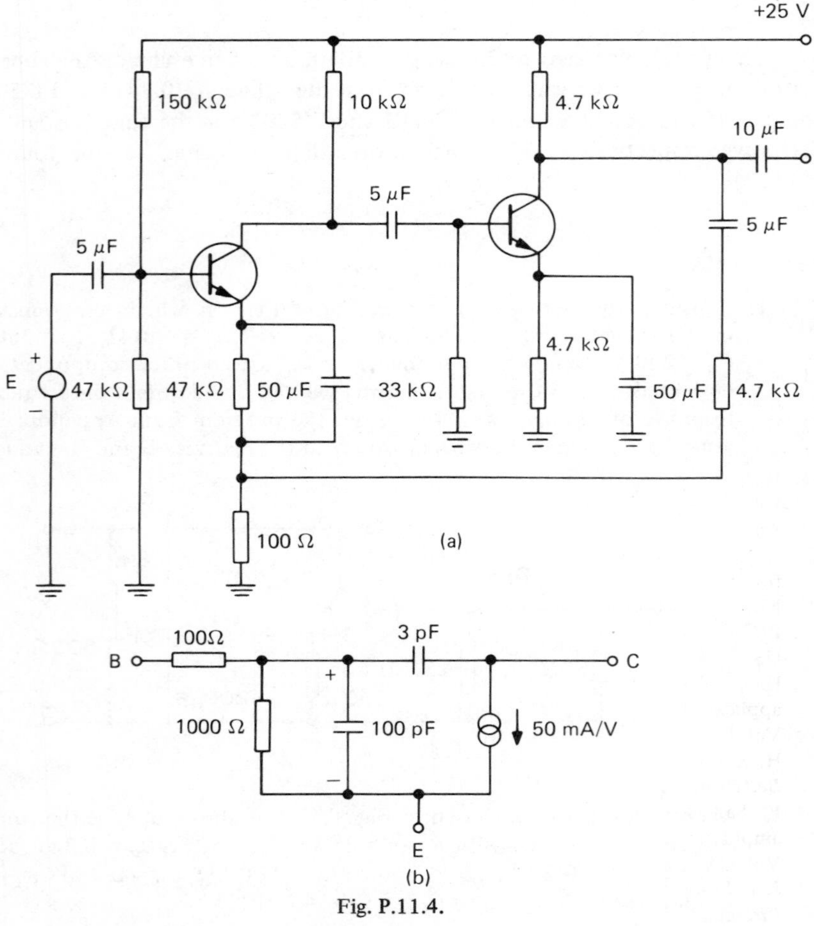

Fig. P.11.4.

P.11.4(a). Replace each transistor by the hybrid π model given in Fig. P.11.4(b) and consider the dc source to be at ground potential for the signal frequency. Calculate the frequency response of the amplifier by using the analysis program in Appendix D.

P.11.5. Analyze the two-stage amplifier in Fig. P.11.5 by the program in Appendix D. Use the same hybrid π model as in Problem P.11.4.

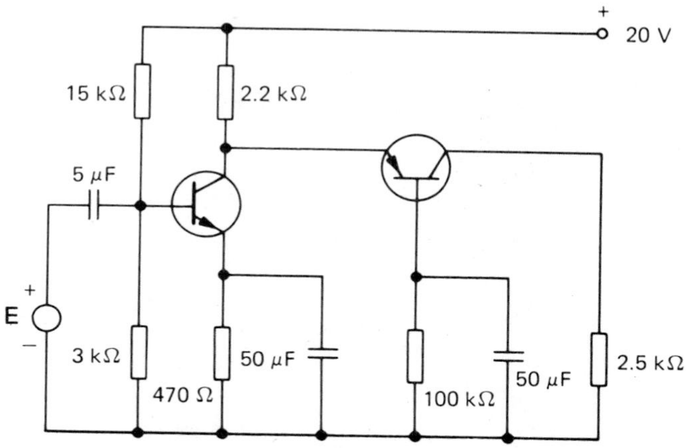

Fig. P.11.5.

REFERENCES

1. A. G. Milnes: *Semiconductor Devices and Integrated Electronics*. Van Nostrand Reinhold Co., New York, 1980.
2. H. C. Poon, L. D. Yau, and R. C. Johnston: D.C. model for short channel IGFET's. *Abstracts of International Solid State Circuits Conference*, 1973.
3. R. M. Swanson and J. D. Meindl: Ion-implanted complementary MOS transistors in low voltage circuits. *IEEE Journal of Solid State Circuits*, Vol. SC-7, No. 2, pp. 146–153, April 1972.
4. G. Merckel, J. Borel, and N. Z. Cupcea: An accurate large-signal MOS transistor model for use in computer aided design. *IEEE Transactions on Electron Devices*, Vol. ED-19, No. 5, pp. 681–690, May 1972.
5. I. Getreu: *Modeling the Bipolar Transistor*. Tektronix, Inc., Beaverton, Oregon 97077, USA, 1976.
6. H. C. Poon: Modeling of bipolar transistor using integral charge-control model with application to third-order distortion studies. *IEEE Transactions on Electron Devices*, Vol. ED-19, pp. 719–731, June 1972.
7. H. K. Gummel and H. C. Poon: An integral charge control model of bipolar transistors. *Bell System Technical Journal*, pp. 927–951, May–June 1970.
8. E. Sanchez-Sinencio and M. L. Majewski: A nonlinear macromodel of operational amplifiers in the frequency domain. *IEEE Transactions on Circuits and Systems*, Vol. CAS-26, pp. 395–402, June 1979.
9. J. E. Solomon: The monolithic op. amp.: A tutorial study. *IEEE Journal of Solid State Circuits*, Vol. SC-9, pp. 314–332, December 1974.

10. G. R. Boyle, B. M. Cohn, D. O. Pederson, and J. E. Solomon: Macromodeling of integrated circuit operational amplifiers. *IEEE Journal of Solid State Circuits*, Vol. SC-9, pp. 353–363, December 1974.
11. J. Ahlberg, E. Nilson, and J. Walsh: *The Theory of Splines and Their Applications.* Academic Press, New York, 1967.
12. C. de Boor: *A Practical Guide to Splines.* Springer-Verlag, New York, 1978.

CHAPTER 12
DC Solution of Networks

CHAPTER 12. DC SOLUTION OF NETWORKS

Finding the "operating point" or "dc solution" of a network is usually the first step in the analysis of nonlinear networks. It involves determining node voltages for given values of dc sources and is equivalent to the solution of nonlinear algebraic systems of equations. The problems associated with solutions of network equations are discussed in this chapter.

Section 12.1 introduces the Newton-Raphson algorithm for several variables. Because the procedure is well known, only the algorithmic steps are discussed and the reader is referred to mathematical books for more detailed information. Application to the nodal formulation is given in Section 12.2. The steps are derived for the case where the incidence matrix is known but the result shows that the Jacobian matrix can be constructed directly by inspection without resorting to topological matrices. A similar development is indicated for the tableau and modified nodal formulations in Section 12.3.

Models of active devices usually involve exponential functions. These functions may cause numerical problems and a special method to avoid them is given in Section 12.4. Once the dc solution has been obtained, the designer may be interested in the sensitivity of the solution to network parameters. The formulation and solution of this problem is given in Section 12.5.

In many cases, the nonlinear functions involved in diode and transistor models are not available in functional form but rather in the form of tables. For this case, it is possible to apply piecewise linearization between the specified points and take advantage of the linearity. An algorithm operating on piecewise linearized systems was proposed by Katzenelson [1] and we give its basic principles in Section 12.6.

12.1. THE NEWTON-RAPHSON ALGORITHM

The Newton-Raphson (N-R) algorithm was introduced earlier as one of the methods for finding the roots of polynomials. It is well known, widely used, and has quadratic convergence if the initial estimate is close to the solution. The detailed theory is available in books on numerical analysis and the reader is referred to these sources for the theoretical background. We will concentrate on its application to network solutions. In the scalar case the N–R iteration to solve $f(x) = 0$ is given by

$$x^{k+1} = x^k + \Delta x^k = x^k - f(x^k)/f'(x^k). \tag{12.1.1}$$

The iteration number will be denoted by the superscripts.

For some networks, it may be possible to eliminate some of the variables and reduce the problem to a single equation. As an introduction to the dc solution of nonlinear networks, we will first take a simple example.

EXAMPLE 12.1.1. Figure 12.1.1. shows a nonlinear network with one diode. Let the problem be scaled such that the saturation current $I_s = 1$ A. The diode equation is

$$i_D = e^{40 v_D} - 1.$$

Find the dc solution for 1 A dc current supplied by the current source.

The nodal formulation leads to two equations

$$3v_1 - 2v_2 = 1$$
$$-2v_1 + 2v_2 + (e^{40 v_2} - 1) = 0.$$

Since v_1 appears linearly, it can be eliminated and the set reduced to one equation. From the first equation obtain $v_1 = \frac{1}{3} + \frac{2}{3} v_2$ and insert into the second

$$f(v_2) = \tfrac{2}{3} v_2 + e^{40 v_2} - \tfrac{5}{3} = 0.$$

To apply (12.1.1) find the derivative

$$f'(v_2) = \tfrac{2}{3} + 40 e^{40 v_2}.$$

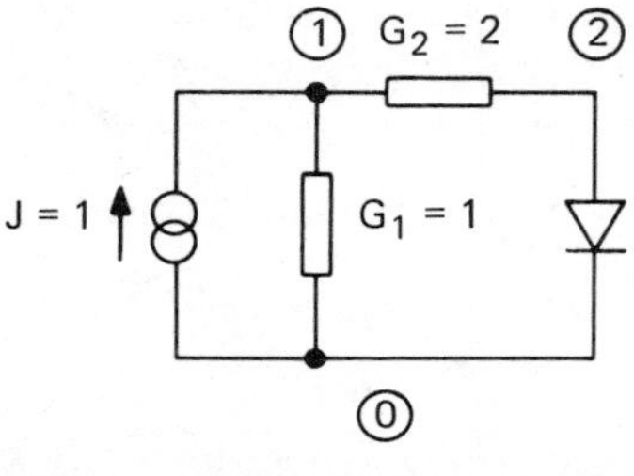

Fig. 12.1.1. Network for Example 12.1.1.

To start the iteration, assume that the initial voltage is $v_2^0 = 0.1$ V. The iteration proceeds as indicated below:

k	v_2^k	Δv_2^{k-1}
1	0.75740D – 01	–0.24260D – 01
2	0.52712D – 01	–0.23029D – 01
3	0.32705D – 01	–0.20007D – 01
4	0.18883D – 01	–0.13822D – 01
5	0.13356D – 01	–0.55267D – 02
6	0.12654D – 01	–0.70199D – 03
7	0.12644D – 01	–0.99424D – 05
8	0.12644D – 01	–0.19579D – 08

The final voltages are $v_2 = 1.264388 \times 10^{-2}$ and $v_1 = 3.4176258 \times 10^{-1}$ V.

A small change in the network of Fig. 12.1.1, namely replacement of the first conductance by another diode, will lead to two nonlinear equations and elimination of v_1 will not be possible. A method for the solution of systems of nonlinear equations is needed.

Consider the system of n nonlinear equations f_i in n variables x_i:

$$\begin{aligned} f_1(x_1, x_2, \ldots, x_n) &= 0 \\ f_2(x_1, x_2, \ldots, x_n) &= 0 \\ &\vdots \\ f_n(x_1, x_2, \ldots, x_n) &= 0. \end{aligned} \tag{12.1.2}$$

Denote the vector of variables by $\mathbf{x}$ and the vector of functions by $\mathbf{f}$. Then (12.1.2) has a compact form

$$\mathbf{f}(\mathbf{x}) = \mathbf{0}. \tag{12.1.3}$$

Assume that the system has a solution; denote it by $\mathbf{x}^*$ and expand each function in a Taylor series about $\mathbf{x}$:

$$\begin{aligned} f_1(\mathbf{x}^*) &= f_1(\mathbf{x}) + \frac{\partial f_1}{\partial x_1}(x_1^* - x_1) + \frac{\partial f_1}{\partial x_2}(x_2^* - x_2) + \cdots + \frac{\partial f_1}{\partial x_n}(x_n^* - x_n) + \cdots \\ f_2(\mathbf{x}^*) &= f_2(\mathbf{x}) + \frac{\partial f_2}{\partial x_1}(x_1^* - x_1) + \frac{\partial f_2}{\partial x_2}(x_2^* - x_2) + \cdots + \frac{\partial f_2}{\partial x_n}(x_n^* - x_n) + \cdots \\ &\vdots \\ f_n(\mathbf{x}^*) &= f_n(\mathbf{x}) + \frac{\partial f_n}{\partial x_1}(x_1^* - x_1) + \frac{\partial f_n}{\partial x_2}(x_2^* - x_2) + \cdots + \frac{\partial f_n}{\partial x_n}(x_n^* - x_n) + \cdots . \end{aligned}$$

Assuming that $\mathbf{x}$ is close to $\mathbf{x}^*$ higher order terms may be neglected and the system may be written in linearized form:

$$\mathbf{f}(\mathbf{x}^*) \approx \mathbf{f}(\mathbf{x}) + \mathbf{M}(\mathbf{x}^* - \mathbf{x}) \tag{12.1.4}$$

where

$$\mathbf{M}\big|_{\mathbf{x}} = \begin{bmatrix} \frac{\partial f_1}{\partial x_1} & \frac{\partial f_1}{\partial x_2} & \cdots & \frac{\partial f_1}{\partial x_n} \\ \frac{\partial f_2}{\partial x_1} & \frac{\partial f_2}{\partial x_2} & \cdots & \frac{\partial f_2}{\partial x_n} \\ \vdots & \vdots & & \\ \frac{\partial f_n}{\partial x_1} & \frac{\partial f_n}{\partial x_2} & \cdots & \frac{\partial f_n}{\partial x_n} \end{bmatrix}_{|\mathbf{x}} \tag{12.1.5}$$

is the Jacobian matrix of the function $\mathbf{f}$. If we set (12.1.4) equal to zero and solve, the result will not be the vector $\mathbf{x}^*$ (because the higher-order terms have been neglected) but some new value for $\mathbf{x}$. Using superscripts to indicate iteration sequence we have

$$\mathbf{f}(\mathbf{x}^k) + \mathbf{M}(\mathbf{x}^{k+1} - \mathbf{x}^k) = \mathbf{0}. \tag{12.1.6}$$

Formally, the solution of (12.1.6) is obtained by writing

$$\mathbf{x}^{k+1} = \mathbf{x}^k - \mathbf{M}^{-1}\mathbf{f}(\mathbf{x}^k). \tag{12.1.7}$$

In practice, the Jacobian matrix is not inverted. Instead, define

$$\Delta\mathbf{x}^k = \mathbf{x}^{k+1} - \mathbf{x}^k. \tag{12.1.8}$$

Then

$$\mathbf{M}\Delta\mathbf{x}^k = -\mathbf{f}(\mathbf{x}^k) \tag{12.1.9}$$

is solved by **LU** factorization and the new $\mathbf{x}^{k+1}$ is obtained from

$$\mathbf{x}^{k+1} = \mathbf{x}^k + \Delta\mathbf{x}^k. \tag{12.1.10}$$

Formulae (12.1.9) and (12.1.10) represent the Newton–Raphson algorithm for systems of equations, and in the following discussion (12.1.9) will be referred to as the *Newton-Raphson equation.* The algorithm has fast convergence (quadratic close to the solution). Its disadvantage is the need to evaluate the Jacobian matrix.

The purpose of the N-R iteration is to reduce the error norm so that

$$\|\mathbf{f}(\mathbf{x}^{k+1})\| \leqslant \|\mathbf{f}(\mathbf{x}^{k})\|. \tag{12.1.11}$$

Since this may not result automatically at each step, a modification of the form

$$\mathbf{x}^{k+1} = \mathbf{x}^{k} + t^{k}\Delta\mathbf{x}^{k} \tag{12.1.12}$$

is sometimes used. The parameter t^k is selected such that (12.1.11) is satisfied. Usually $0 < t^k \leqslant 1$.

EXAMPLE 12.1.2. Apply the N-R algorithm to the solution of the two-diode network shown in Fig. 12.1.2. Let each diode be represented by $i_D = e^{40v_D} - 1$ and let the initial estimates for the voltages be $v_1^0 = v_2^0 = 0.1$.

Nodal formulation leads to the equations

$$i_{D1} + G(v_1 - v_2) = j$$
$$G(-v_1 + v_2) + i_{D2} = 0.$$

Inserting numerical values we obtain

$$f_1(v_1, v_2) = e^{40v_1} + v_1 - v_2 - 2 = 0$$
$$f_2(v_1, v_2) = -v_1 + v_2 + e^{40v_2} - 1 = 0.$$

The Jacobian is

$$\mathbf{M} = \begin{bmatrix} 40e^{40v_1} + 1 & -1 \\ -1 & 40e^{40v_2} + 1 \end{bmatrix}.$$

Evaluation at the initial estimates provides

$$f_1 = 52.59815$$
$$f_2 = 53.59815.$$

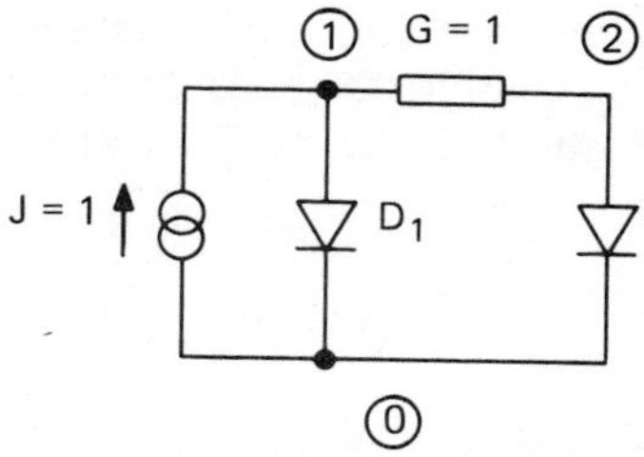

Fig. 12.1.2 Network for Example 12.1.2.

The Jacobian becomes

$$\mathbf{M} = \begin{bmatrix} 2184.926 & -1 \\ -1 & 2184.926 \end{bmatrix}.$$

Solution of (12.1.9) is

$$\Delta v_1^0 = -0.0240844$$
$$\Delta v_2^0 = -0.0245419$$

and application of (12.1.10) provides the first approximation to $\mathbf{v}$:

$$v_1^1 = 0.0759156$$
$$v_2^1 = 0.07545810.$$

The problem was run on the computer and the iteration is given below:

k	Δv_1^k	Δv_2^k	v_1^{k+1}	v_2^{k+1}
0	−0.02408	−0.02454	0.07592	0.07546
1	−0.02260	−0.02378	0.05331	0.05168
2	−0.01909	−0.02182	0.03423	0.02986
3	−0.01234	−0.01736	0.02188	0.01250
4	−0.00432	−0.00962	0.01757	0.00289
5	−0.00044	−0.00236	0.01712	0.00053
6	−0.00001	−0.00012	0.01712	0.00041
7	−0.00000	−0.00000	0.01712	0.00041

The solution is $v_1 = 0.01712$, $v_2 = 0.00041$. Although the initial estimate was quite poor, the algorithm converged in 7 iterations.

12.2. NODAL FORMULATION

For dc solution, all inductors are short-circuited and all capacitors are removed from the network. The steps involved in the solution of Example 12.1.2 will now be formalized. We first consider the nodal formulation which requires that all resistors be voltage controlled: the nonlinearities must have constitutive equations of the form

$$i_b = g(v_b). \tag{12.2.1}$$

The subscript b will denote branch voltages and currents. For nodes, the subscript n will be used. In addition, all sources in the network will be current sources. Then, using the theory of Chapter 3,

KVL: $$\mathbf{v}_b = \mathbf{A}^t\mathbf{v}_n \tag{12.2.2}$$

KCL: $$\mathbf{A}\mathbf{i}_b = -\mathbf{A}_J\mathbf{j}_b = \mathbf{j}_n \tag{12.2.3}$$

where $\mathbf{A}_J$ is the incidence matrix of the independent sources and $\mathbf{j}_n$ denotes equivalent nodal current sources.

Substituting the constitutive relations (12.2.1) into the KCL

$$\mathbf{A}\mathbf{g}(\mathbf{v}_b) = \mathbf{j}_n. \tag{12.2.4}$$

Substituting for $\mathbf{v}_b$ from (12.2.2) one obtains

$$\mathbf{A}\mathbf{g}(\mathbf{A}^t\mathbf{v}_n) = \mathbf{j}_n. \tag{12.2.5}$$

This is the generalized form of the nodal equations for a nonlinear network. To solve it by means of the N–R algorithm, transfer $\mathbf{j}_n$ to the left side to form

$$\mathbf{f}(\mathbf{v}_n) \equiv \mathbf{A}\mathbf{g}(\mathbf{A}^t\mathbf{v}_n) - \mathbf{j}_n = \mathbf{0}. \tag{12.2.6}$$

The Jacobian is obtained by applying the chain rule for differentiation:

$$\mathbf{M} = \frac{\partial \mathbf{f}}{\partial \mathbf{v}_n} = \mathbf{A}\frac{\partial \mathbf{g}}{\partial \mathbf{v}_b}\frac{\partial \mathbf{v}_b}{\partial \mathbf{v}_n}. \tag{12.2.7}$$

Here $\partial\mathbf{g}/\partial\mathbf{v}_b$ is a matrix which will be denoted by $\mathbf{G}_b$. Differentiation of (12.2.2) with respect to $\mathbf{v}_n$ provides

$$\partial\mathbf{v}_b/\partial\mathbf{v}_n = \mathbf{A}^t$$

and (12.2.7) reduces to

$$\mathbf{M} = \mathbf{A}\mathbf{G}_b\mathbf{A}^t.$$

Note that linear conductors are defined by $i_b = Gv_b$ and $\partial i_b/\partial v_b = G$, the value of the conductance. Assuming an initial guess $\mathbf{v}_n^0$, the N–R algorithm takes the following form:

1. Set $k = 0$ and calculate $\mathbf{j}_n = -\mathbf{A}_J\mathbf{j}_b$.
2. Calculate the branch voltages $\mathbf{v}_b^k = \mathbf{A}^t\mathbf{v}_n^k$.
3. Calculate the branch currents $\mathbf{i}_b^k = \mathbf{g}(\mathbf{v}_b^k)$.
4. Calculate the matrix $\mathbf{G}_b^k = \partial\mathbf{g}(\mathbf{v}_b)/\partial\mathbf{v}_b$. For linear conductors, the entries are the values of their conductances.

5. Calculate $\mathbf{M} = \mathbf{A}\mathbf{G}_b^k\mathbf{A}^t$.
6. Calculate $\mathbf{f}(\mathbf{v}_n^k) = \mathbf{A}\mathbf{i}_b^k - \mathbf{j}_n$.
7. Solve the N-R equation $\mathbf{M}\Delta\mathbf{v}_n^k = -\mathbf{f}(\mathbf{v}_n^k)$.
8. Obtain $\mathbf{v}_n^{k+1} = \mathbf{v}_n^k + \Delta\mathbf{v}_n^k$.
9. If convergence has not been achieved, set $k = k + 1$ and go to step 2.

EXAMPLE 12.2.1. Apply the N-R algorithm to the network shown in Fig. 12.1.1. Let the vector of initial nodal voltages be estimated as $\mathbf{v}_n^0 = [0.3 \quad 0.02]^t$. The dc current source is 1 A and the diode equation is $i_D = e^{40v_D} - 1$.

The matrix **A** follows from the graph in Fig. 12.2.1:

$$\mathbf{A}_a = [\mathbf{A} \mid \mathbf{A}_J] = \left[\begin{array}{ccc|c} -1 & 1 & 0 & -1 \\ 0 & -1 & 1 & 0 \end{array}\right].$$

The vector of the independent source is

$$\mathbf{j}_n = -\mathbf{A}_J\mathbf{j}_b = \begin{bmatrix} 1 \\ 0 \end{bmatrix}$$

and the branch voltages are

$$\mathbf{v}_b^0 = \mathbf{A}^t\mathbf{v}_n^0 = \begin{bmatrix} -1 & 0 \\ 1 & -1 \\ 0 & 1 \end{bmatrix} \begin{bmatrix} 0.3 \\ 0.02 \end{bmatrix} = \begin{bmatrix} -0.3 \\ 0.28 \\ 0.02 \end{bmatrix}.$$

The branch currents are

$$\mathbf{i}_b = \begin{bmatrix} G_1 v_{b1} \\ G_2 v_{b2} \\ e^{40v_{b3}} - 1 \end{bmatrix} = \begin{bmatrix} -0.3 \\ 0.56 \\ 1.22554093 \end{bmatrix}.$$

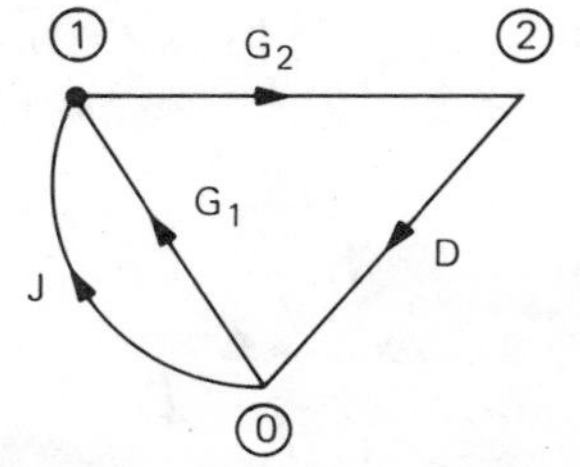

Fig. 12.2.1. Oriented graph for the network of Fig. 12.1.1.

The matrix of derivatives with respect to the branch voltages is

$$\mathbf{G}_b = \begin{bmatrix} G_1 & & \\ & G_2 & \\ & & 40e^{40v_{b3}} \end{bmatrix} = \begin{bmatrix} 1 & & \\ & 2 & \\ & & 89.02163712 \end{bmatrix}.$$

The Jacobian matrix $\mathbf{M}$ is equivalent to the linearized nodal admittance matrix:

$$\mathbf{M} = \mathbf{A}\mathbf{G}_b\mathbf{A}^t = \begin{bmatrix} 3 & -2 \\ -2 & 91.02163712 \end{bmatrix}.$$

The vector $\mathbf{f}(\mathbf{v}_n)$ is obtained as follows:

$$\mathbf{f}(\mathbf{v}_n) = \begin{bmatrix} -1 & 1 & 0 \\ 0 & -1 & 1 \end{bmatrix} \begin{bmatrix} -0.3 \\ 0.56 \\ 1.22554093 \end{bmatrix} - \begin{bmatrix} 1 \\ 0 \end{bmatrix} = \begin{bmatrix} -0.14 \\ 0.66554093 \end{bmatrix}.$$

The Newton–Raphson equation is

$$\begin{bmatrix} 3 & -2 \\ -2 & 91.02163712 \end{bmatrix} \begin{bmatrix} \Delta v_{n1}^0 \\ \Delta v_{n2}^0 \end{bmatrix} = - \begin{bmatrix} -0.14 \\ 0.66554093 \end{bmatrix}.$$

Its solution is

$$\begin{bmatrix} \Delta v_{n1}^0 \\ \Delta v_{n2}^0 \end{bmatrix} = \begin{bmatrix} 0.04241336145 \\ -0.00637995784 \end{bmatrix}.$$

Finally, the new nodal voltages (using the full correction $t^0 = 1$) are

$$\begin{bmatrix} v_{n1}^1 \\ v_{n2}^1 \end{bmatrix} = \begin{bmatrix} 0.3424133614 \\ 0.01362004216 \end{bmatrix}.$$

The iteration was run on the computer with the following result:

k	Δv_{n1}^{k-1}	Δv_{n2}^{k-1}	v_{n1}^{k}	v_{n2}^{k}
1	0.04241	−0.00638	0.34241	0.01362
2	−0.00064	−0.00096	0.34178	0.01266
3	−0.00001	−0.00002	0.34176	0.01264
4	−0.00000	−0.00000	0.34176	0.01264

The problem of this example is the same as in Example 12.1.1. The initial estimate was different and convergence faster; the result is exactly the same.

The above derivations required the use of the incidence matrix to generate the equations necessary for the N–R iteration. We now give an alternative method which enables the direct construction of the Jacobian matrix and the right-hand-side vector of (12.1.9) on an element-by-element basis.

Consider a nonlinear conductance connected between nodes k and l with node k assumed to be at higher potential. Let the constitutive equation be

$$i_b = g(v_b). \tag{12.2.10}$$

In the nodal formulation, each equation results from the application of the KCL to a node. The current i_b will appear only in the equations associated with nodes k and l. Substituting the constitutive equation (12.2.10) for i_b with v_b replaced by the nodal voltages $v_k - v_l$:

$$\begin{aligned} &\text{Equation at node } k: \quad \cdots + g(v_k - v_l) \cdots = 0 \\ &\text{Equation at node } l: \quad \cdots - g(v_k - v_l) \cdots = 0. \end{aligned} \tag{12.2.11}$$

In order to solve the nonlinear system (12.2.11), the Jacobian is formed. Each row of the Jacobian is obtained by partial differentiation of the corresponding equation with respect to the various variables. Differentiation will result in

$$\begin{array}{ll} \text{variable} \longrightarrow & \quad v_k \qquad\qquad\qquad\quad v_l \\ \begin{array}{l} \text{row } k \\ \\ \text{row } l \end{array} & \begin{bmatrix} \cdots & \partial g/\partial v_b & \cdots & -\partial g/\partial v_b & \cdots \\ & & & & \\ \cdots & -\partial g/\partial v_b & \cdots & \partial g/\partial v_b & \cdots \end{bmatrix}. \end{array}$$

The Jacobian matrix has *exactly* the same form as the nodal conductance matrix. Linear conductances remain in the matrix unchanged. In place of nonlinear conductances the derivatives of their constitutive equations, $\partial g/\partial v_b$, evaluated at the voltages of the iteration appear. The Jacobian structure is fixed, enabling the use of sparse-matrix methods for larger networks. The *steps involving topological matrices need not be followed at all* and the direct formulation method discussed in Chapter 2 can be applied.

The function $\mathbf{f}$ appearing on the right-hand side of the N–R equation (12.1.9) is the value of the left-hand side of (12.2.11) evaluated at the node voltages of the iteration. Its kth entry is the sum of all currents leaving node k, be it from linear, nonlinear, or source branches. For a diode, this is shown schematically in Fig. 12.2.2.

12.3. TABLEAU AND MODIFIED NODAL FORMULATION

The one-graph tableau will be used for explanation; the modified nodal and two-graph formulations follow the same development.

$$\begin{array}{c} \\ k \\ \ell \end{array}\begin{array}{c} \begin{array}{cc} k & \ell \end{array} \\ \begin{bmatrix} \partial h/\partial v & -\partial h/\partial v \\ -\partial h/\partial v & \partial h/\partial v \end{bmatrix} \end{array} \qquad \begin{bmatrix} h(v) \\ -h(v) \end{bmatrix}\begin{array}{c} k \\ \ell \end{array}$$

Jacobian Right-hand side

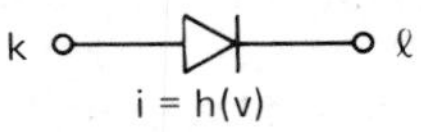

Fig. 12.2.2. A diode and its entries in the Jacobian and right-hand side of (12.1.9).

Let the tableau equations be in the following form:

$$\begin{aligned} \mathbf{v}_b - \mathbf{A}^t\mathbf{v}_n &= \mathbf{0} \\ \mathbf{p}(\mathbf{v}_b, \mathbf{i}_b) &= \mathbf{w} \\ \mathbf{A}\mathbf{i}_b &= \mathbf{0}. \end{aligned} \tag{12.3.1}$$

The set $\mathbf{p}(\mathbf{v}_b, \mathbf{i}_b) = \mathbf{w}$ represents the constitutive equations in implicit form; some terms in it may be linear. Form the equivalent of (12.2.6) by writing

$$\mathbf{f}(\mathbf{x}) \equiv \begin{bmatrix} \mathbf{v}_b - \mathbf{A}^t\mathbf{v}_n \\ \mathbf{p}(\mathbf{v}_b, \mathbf{i}_b) - \mathbf{w} \\ \mathbf{A}\mathbf{i}_b \end{bmatrix} = \mathbf{0} \tag{12.3.2}$$

where $\mathbf{x}^t = [\mathbf{v}_b^t \quad \mathbf{i}_b^t \quad \mathbf{v}_n^t]$.

The Jacobian matrix at the kth iteration will be

$$\mathbf{M} = \begin{bmatrix} \mathbf{1} & \mathbf{0} & -\mathbf{A}^t \\ \mathbf{G}^k & \mathbf{R}^k & \mathbf{0} \\ \mathbf{0} & \mathbf{A} & \mathbf{0} \end{bmatrix} \tag{12.3.3}$$

where

$$\mathbf{G}^k = \left.\frac{\partial \mathbf{p}}{\partial \mathbf{v}_b}\right|_{\mathbf{x}^k}; \qquad \mathbf{R}^k = \left.\frac{\partial \mathbf{p}}{\partial \mathbf{i}_b}\right|_{\mathbf{x}^k}. \tag{12.3.4}$$

The N-R equation is

$$\mathbf{M}^k \Delta\mathbf{x}^k = -\mathbf{f}(\mathbf{x}^k) \tag{12.3.5}$$

where

$$\Delta \mathbf{x}^k = \begin{bmatrix} \Delta \mathbf{v}_b \\ \Delta \mathbf{i}_b \\ \Delta \mathbf{v}_n \end{bmatrix}. \tag{12.3.6}$$

The structure of the Jacobian is fixed and has the form of the tableau equations of linear networks. Solution of (12.3.5) provides $\Delta \mathbf{x}^k$ and

$$\mathbf{x}^{k+1} = \mathbf{x}^k + t^k \Delta \mathbf{x}^k. \tag{12.3.7}$$

12.4. CONVERGENCE IN DIODE-TRANSISTOR NETWORKS

In the dc solution of networks with diodes and bipolar transistors we may run into convergence and numerical problems involving overflows when the N–R iteration is used. This is explained with the help of Fig. 12.4.1 in which the diode is represented by a function $i = I_s(e^{40v} - 1)$. Assume that at the kth iteration the point (v^k, i^k) has been generated and that the algorithm predicts a new point v^* with the corresponding new value i^* on the *linearized* characteristic. In a standard procedure, the function value would be calculated which is equivalent to projecting a vertical line through v^* upward onto the curve. Since the exponential function grows extremely rapidly for positive values of v, this may involve an overflow.

One possible remedy to the situation is to use the point i^* and move onto the curve *horizontally* instead of vertically. Inversion of the diode characteristic

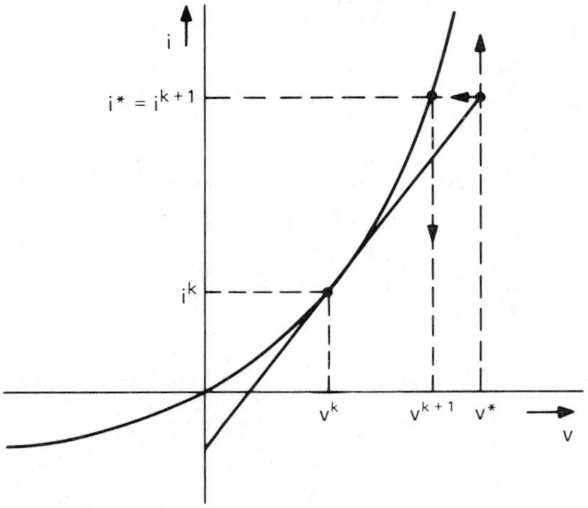

Fig. 12.4.1. Overflow problem in diodes.

will provide the new voltage $v^{k+1} = 0.025 \ln (1 + i^*/I_s)$. The horizontal projection may be programmed for all voltages $v^* > 0.7$, the normal vertical projection for $v^* < 0.7$ (this corresponds to $e^{40 \times 0.7} = 1.4463 \times 10^{12}$, safely below the overflow of computers). Another heuristic rule would be to apply the horizontal projection when $v^* - v^k > 0$ and the vertical projection otherwise. Various computer programs have different techniques for accomodating the highly nonlinear exponential characteristic; see, for instance, [5].

Another source of difficulty arises when the diode is negatively biased. The N-R iteration requires the derivative, $i' = I_s 40 e^{40v}$. Division by a small number may again cause overflow. To avoid this situation for negative v, we can substitute the characteristic by a tangent straight line at, for instance, $v = -0.3$ to -0.5.

12.5. DC SENSITIVITY

Once the dc operating point $\mathbf{x}^0$ has been found, the sensitivity of the solution to changes in element values can be found quite simply. Write the system of dc equations as

$$\mathbf{f}(\mathbf{x}^0, \mathbf{h}, \mathbf{w}) = \mathbf{0}. \tag{12.5.1}$$

Here $\mathbf{x}^0$ is the vector of the voltages and currents, $\mathbf{h}$ is the vector of parameters, and $\mathbf{w}$ represents dc sources which are assumed to be independent of $\mathbf{h}$ for simplicity.

As in Chapter 6, there are two ways of obtaining sensitivity. In the first approach the sensitivity of the whole vector $\mathbf{x}^0$ is found with respect to *one* parameter at a time. Differentiate (12.5.1) with respect to one h_i

$$\frac{\partial \mathbf{f}}{\partial h_i} + \left.\frac{\partial \mathbf{f}}{\partial \mathbf{x}}\right|_{\mathbf{x}^0} \frac{\partial \mathbf{x}^0}{\partial h_i} = \mathbf{0}$$

or

$$\mathbf{M}\frac{\partial \mathbf{x}^0}{\partial h_i} = -\frac{\partial \mathbf{f}}{\partial h_i} \tag{12.5.2}$$

where $\mathbf{M} = (\partial \mathbf{f}/\partial \mathbf{x})_{|\mathbf{x}^0}$ is the Jacobian matrix about the operating point. It is available (in factored form) at convergence of the N-R algorithm and (12.5.2) is solved using these factors. For *each* h_i, a new right-hand side must be generated and the solution is obtained by forward and back substitution.

In the second method, sensitivity of some scalar function

$$\psi = \phi(\mathbf{x}^0, \mathbf{h}) \tag{12.5.3}$$

is needed. Often, this function is only a single voltage or the difference of two voltages. Differentiating (12.5.3) with respect to h_i gives

$$\frac{\partial \psi}{\partial h_i} = \frac{\partial \phi}{\partial h_i} + \left.\frac{\partial \phi}{\partial \mathbf{x}}\right|_{\mathbf{x}^0} \frac{\partial \mathbf{x}^0}{\partial h_i}. \tag{12.5.4}$$

Here $\partial \phi / \partial \mathbf{x}$ is a *row vector* evaluated at the dc solution $\mathbf{x}^0$. Formal solution of (12.5.2) provides

$$\frac{\partial \mathbf{x}^0}{\partial h_i} = -\mathbf{M}^{-1} \frac{\partial \mathbf{f}}{\partial h_i}.$$

Inserting into (12.5.4):

$$\frac{\partial \psi}{\partial h_i} = \frac{\partial \phi}{\partial h_i} - \left.\frac{\partial \phi}{\partial \mathbf{x}}\right|_{\mathbf{x}^0} \mathbf{M}^{-1} \frac{\partial \mathbf{f}}{\partial h_i}. \tag{12.5.5}$$

In this equation, it is convenient to define

$$-\left.\frac{\partial \phi}{\partial \mathbf{x}}\right|_{\mathbf{x}^0} \mathbf{M}^{-1} = (\mathbf{x}^a)^t$$

or

$$\mathbf{M}^t \mathbf{x}^a = -\left(\left.\frac{\partial \phi}{\partial \mathbf{x}}\right|_{\mathbf{x}^0}\right)^t. \tag{12.5.6}$$

Solving for the unknown vector $\mathbf{x}^a$ and inserting its transpose into (12.5.5) gives

$$\frac{\partial \psi}{\partial h_i} = \frac{\partial \phi}{\partial h_i} + (\mathbf{x}^a)^t \frac{\partial \mathbf{f}}{\partial h_i} \tag{12.5.7}$$

and sensitivities to all the elements are found using the same $\mathbf{x}^a$.

Both methods will be illustrated on examples.

EXAMPLE 12.5.1. Find the sensitivity of the nodal voltages to changes in the conductance G_2 in the network in Fig. 12.1.1. Use the result obtained in Example 12.1.1 for the dc voltages.

The equations for the network are

$$\mathbf{f}(\mathbf{x}, \mathbf{h}, \mathbf{w}) \equiv \begin{bmatrix} (G_1 + G_2) v_1 - G_2 v_2 - 1 \\ -G_2 v_1 + G_2 v_2 + e^{40 v_2} - 1 \end{bmatrix} = \begin{bmatrix} 0 \\ 0 \end{bmatrix}.$$

The Jacobian is

$$\mathbf{M} = \begin{bmatrix} G_1 + G_2 & -G_2 \\ -G_2 & G_2 + 40e^{40v_2} \end{bmatrix}.$$

The result from Example 12.1.1 is

$$\mathbf{x}^0 = \begin{bmatrix} v_1 \\ v_2 \end{bmatrix} = \begin{bmatrix} 0.34176258 \\ 0.01264388 \end{bmatrix}.$$

At the solution, the Jacobian is

$$\mathbf{M} = \begin{bmatrix} 3 & -2 \\ -2 & 68.32949392 \end{bmatrix}$$

and

$$\frac{\partial \mathbf{f}}{\partial G_2} = \begin{bmatrix} v_1 - v_2 \\ -v_1 + v_2 \end{bmatrix} = \begin{bmatrix} 0.3291187 \\ -0.3291187 \end{bmatrix}.$$

Using (12.5.2), the sensitivity of the nodal voltages is obtained as the solution of

$$\begin{bmatrix} 3 & -2 \\ -2 & 68.32949392 \end{bmatrix} \begin{bmatrix} \partial v_1/\partial G_2 \\ \partial v_2/\partial G_2 \end{bmatrix} = - \begin{bmatrix} 0.3291187 \\ -0.3291187 \end{bmatrix}.$$

The result is

$$\begin{bmatrix} \partial v_1/\partial G_2 \\ \partial v_2/\partial G_2 \end{bmatrix} = \begin{bmatrix} -0.1086146 \\ 0.0016375 \end{bmatrix}.$$

EXAMPLE 12.5.2. Find the sensitivity of the dc current through G_2 in Fig. 12.1.1 to changes in G_2.

In this problem we define

$$i_{G_2} = \psi = \phi(\mathbf{x}^0, h) = G_2(v_1 - v_2).$$

Then

$$\left.\frac{\partial \phi}{\partial \mathbf{x}}\right|_{\mathbf{x}^0} = [G_2 \quad -G_2] = [2 \quad -2].$$

In the next step we have to solve (12.5.6). The Jacobian matrix from the previous example is transposed (in this case the matrix is symmetric and the transpose is equal to the original matrix). We solve

$$\begin{bmatrix} 3 & -2 \\ -2 & 68.32949392 \end{bmatrix} \begin{bmatrix} v_1^a \\ v_2^a \end{bmatrix} = - \begin{bmatrix} 2 \\ -2 \end{bmatrix}.$$

The result is

$$\begin{bmatrix} v_1^a \\ v_2^a \end{bmatrix} = \begin{bmatrix} -0.66003279 \\ 0.0099508 \end{bmatrix}.$$

To apply (12.5.7) we need

$$\frac{\partial \phi}{\partial G_2} = v_1 - v_2 = 0.3291187$$

where v_1, v_2 are taken from Example 12.5.1, and

$$\frac{\partial \mathrm{f}}{\partial G_2} = \begin{bmatrix} v_1 - v_2 \\ -v_1 + v_2 \end{bmatrix} = \begin{bmatrix} 0.3291187 \\ -0.3291187 \end{bmatrix}.$$

Inserting into (12.5.7) we obtain

$$\frac{\partial i_{G2}}{\partial G_2} = v_1 - v_2 + [v_1^a \quad v_2^a] \begin{bmatrix} v_1 - v_2 \\ -v_1 + v_2 \end{bmatrix}$$

$$= (v_1 - v_2)(1 + v_1^a - v_2^a) = 0.10861457.$$

12.6. PIECEWISE LINEARIZATION

In many cases, the equations describing the nonlinearities are not known in functional form and only tables of measured values are given. In other cases, the functions may be known but are very complicated and it is convenient to replace the nonlinearities by piecewise linear segments. In either case, the nonlinear network is replaced by a piecewise linear network with a corresponding simplification of the problem. The algorithm described below is due to Katzenelson. The tableau will be used for its explanations and an example, based on the nodal formulation, will clarify the steps.

In the tableau formulation, the nonlinear elements may be either voltage or current controlled. Both are represented by their piecewise linear approximation and are shown in Fig. 12.6.1. Note that in the lth segment having the slope G_l (for the voltage-controlled case), or R_l (for the current-controlled case) there is an additional source i_l^0 or v_l^0 having a value indicated in the figures. The

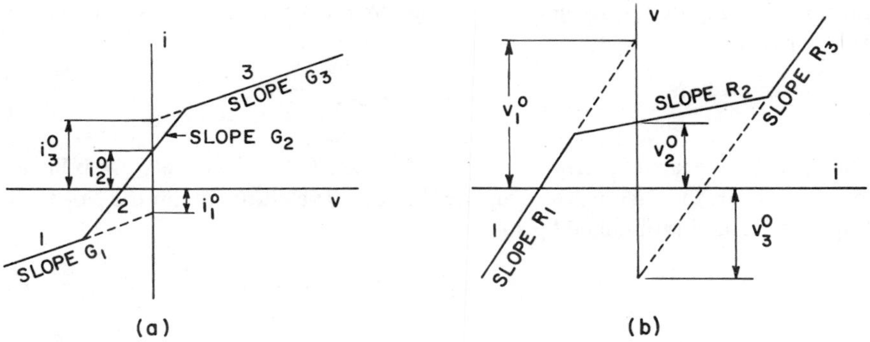

Fig. 12.6.1. Piecewise linear resistors: (a) voltage controlled; (b) current controlled.

equations for the elements in the lth segment are

$$\begin{aligned} v &= v_l^0 + R_l i \\ i &= i_l^0 + G_l v \end{aligned} \tag{12.6.1}$$

and, in general,

$$\mathbf{G}_l \mathbf{v}_b + \mathbf{R}_l \mathbf{i}_b = \mathbf{w}_l. \tag{12.6.2}$$

The tableau equations can be written as follows:

$$\begin{bmatrix} \mathbf{1} & \mathbf{0} & -\mathbf{A}^t \\ \mathbf{G}_l & \mathbf{R}_l & \mathbf{0} \\ \mathbf{0} & \mathbf{A} & \mathbf{0} \end{bmatrix} \begin{bmatrix} \mathbf{v}_b \\ \mathbf{i}_b \\ \mathbf{v}_n \end{bmatrix} = \begin{bmatrix} \mathbf{0} \\ \mathbf{w}_l \\ \mathbf{0} \end{bmatrix} + \begin{bmatrix} \mathbf{0} \\ \mathbf{w} \\ \mathbf{0} \end{bmatrix} \tag{12.6.3}$$

or in compact form

$$\mathbf{T}_l \mathbf{x}_l = \mathbf{w}_l + \mathbf{w}. \tag{12.6.4}$$

The subscript l denotes the *region* in which the network operates. The right-hand-side vectors denote the equivalent sources due to linearization and the independent sources; they are written separately for clarity. The dc solution can be found by solving the tableau equation (12.6.4). Since at the beginning the regions are unknown, we select the node voltages arbitrarily. The branch voltages $\mathbf{v}_b$ are then known and corresponding values of $\mathbf{i}_b$ are determined from the characteristics. Branch currents of current-controlled elements may be specified arbitrarily. This represents the starting value of the vector $\mathbf{x}^0$. Equation (12.6.3) is not satisfied at the beginning and we must apply some iterative process of corrections. Assume that we are at the kth iteration. We can define an error vector

$$\mathbf{f}^k = \mathbf{T}_l^k \mathbf{x}^k - \mathbf{w}_l^k - \mathbf{w}. \tag{12.6.5}$$

The solution is reached when we reduce $\mathbf{f}^k$ to zero. Since the network is linear in each region, the Jacobian is simply $\mathbf{M}^k = \mathbf{T}^k$. The correction in the Newton-Raphson method is obtained by solving

$$\mathbf{T}_l^k \, \Delta\mathbf{x}^k = -\mathbf{f}^k \tag{12.6.6}$$

and the new solution is

$$\hat{\mathbf{x}}^{k+1} = \mathbf{x}^k + \Delta\mathbf{x}^k \tag{12.6.7}$$

provided none of the elements crossed to a new region. If this is true, $\hat{\mathbf{x}}^{k+1}$ is the desired final solution.

If at least one element crossed into a new region, the full step is not taken and the formula

$$\mathbf{x}^{k+1} = \mathbf{x}^k + t^k \Delta\mathbf{x}^k \tag{12.6.8}$$

is used. Katzenelson proposed that t^k be selected such that the operating point on *only one element* goes to the boundary of its present region. To find the appropriate value of t^k calculate, for each element i that changes its operating region,

$$t_i^k = \frac{x_{li} - x_i^k}{\Delta x_i}, \qquad \text{if } \Delta x_i > 0 \tag{12.6.9}$$

$$t_i^k = \frac{x_i^k - x_{(l-1)i}}{\Delta x_i}, \qquad \text{if } \Delta x_i < 0 \tag{12.6.10}$$

where x_{li} and $x_{(l-1)i}$ are the boundary points. Note that we assume that the regions are numbered from left to right, as indicated in Fig. 12.6.2. The step size reduction coefficient is

$$t^k = \min_i \, (t_i^k) \tag{12.6.11}$$

and (12.6.8) is used. This results in only one element changing its operating region. If two or more elements change their operating regions simultaneously (corner problem), rules exist for handling the situation. Experience on practical

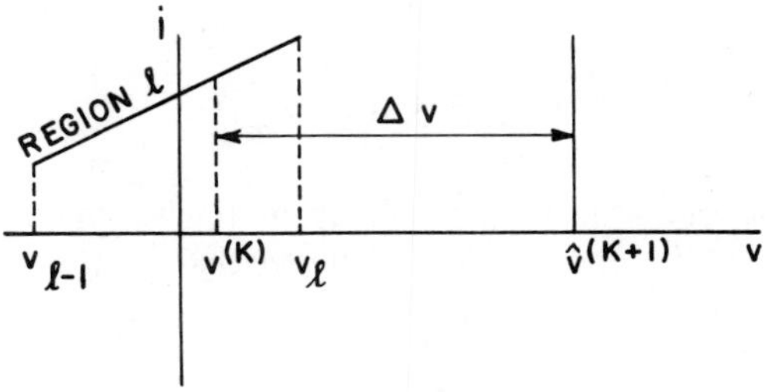

Fig. 12.6.2. Obtaining the step-reducing coefficient t^k.

problems has shown that if one disregards the corner problem entirely, the algorithm corrects itself in subsequent iterations.

We could go back to (12.6.5) and repeat the process, but considerable simplification follows from the fact that the piecewise linear characteristics are continuous. Since at the kth step we are at the boundary of two regions, two equations are simultaneously valid:

$$\mathbf{f}^{k+1} = \mathbf{T}_l^{k+1}\mathbf{x}^{k+1} - \mathbf{w}_l^{k+1} - \mathbf{w} \tag{12.6.12}$$

$$= \mathbf{T}_l^{k}\mathbf{x}^{k+1} - \mathbf{w}_l^{k} - \mathbf{w}. \tag{12.6.13}$$

Substituting for $\mathbf{x}^{k+1}$ from (12.6.8), rearranging the terms, and taking (12.6.5) and (12.6.6) into consideration we have

$$\begin{aligned}\mathbf{f}^{k+1} &= (\mathbf{T}_l^k\mathbf{x}^k - \mathbf{w}_l^k - \mathbf{w}) + t^k\mathbf{T}_l^k\Delta\mathbf{x}^k \\ &= \mathbf{f}^k - t^k\mathbf{f}^k \\ &= (1 - t^k)\,\mathbf{f}^k.\end{aligned} \tag{12.6.14}$$

Let us summarize the steps of Katzenelson's algorithm:

1. Assign arbitrary node voltages $\mathbf{v}_n$ and find the branch voltages and currents v_b, i_b of linear elements and of the voltage controlled piecewise linear elements. Select arbitrary regions for all piecewise linear current controlled elements and in these regions select corresponding values v_b, i_b.
2. Calculate

$$\mathbf{f}^0 = \mathbf{T}_l^0\mathbf{x}^0 - \mathbf{w}_l^0 - \mathbf{w}.$$

Set $k = 0$.

3. Solve

$$\mathbf{T}_l^k\Delta\mathbf{x}^k = -\mathbf{f}^k.$$

4. Find

$$\hat{\mathbf{x}}^{k+1} = \mathbf{x}^k + \Delta \mathbf{x}^k.$$

Check if the operating region of any piecewise linear element changes. If not, stop; $\hat{\mathbf{x}}^{k+1}$ is the solution. Otherwise go to step 5.

5. Discard the result $\hat{\mathbf{x}}^{k+1}$. Calculate

$$t_i^k = \frac{x_{li} - x_i^k}{\Delta x_i}, \qquad \text{if } \Delta x_i > 0$$

$$t_i^k = \frac{x_i^k - x_{(l-1)i}}{\Delta x_i}, \qquad \text{if } \Delta x_i < 0$$

for all piecewise linear elements that cross regions.

6. Select

$$t^k = \min_i \, (t_i^k).$$

7. Calculate

$$\mathbf{x}^{k+1} = \mathbf{x}^k + t^k \Delta \mathbf{x}^k.$$

8. Calculate

$$\mathbf{f}^{k+1} = (1 - t^k)\, \mathbf{f}^k.$$

9. Update the value of the element which crossed into the new region. Set $k = k + 1$ and go to 3.

Although the algorithm presented in this section deals with functions of a single variable, such restriction is not basic and methods are available for handling multivariate functions. The details are beyond the scope of this text; additional information can be found in [2-4].

EXAMPLE 12.6.1. Consider the network in Fig. 12.6.3 with its nonlinearities described by the characteristics shown. Apply Katzenelson's algorithm by using the nodal formulation for the network. Let the initial nodal voltages be $v_{n1} = v_{n2} = -3$.

Denote the branch voltages by v_i. The voltages are $v_1 = v_3 = -3$, $v_2 = 0$. In the regions shown in the figure, $G_1 = 2$, $G_2 = 1$, $G_3 = 2$. This initial state of the network is shown in the figure. Applying the steps of the algorithm:

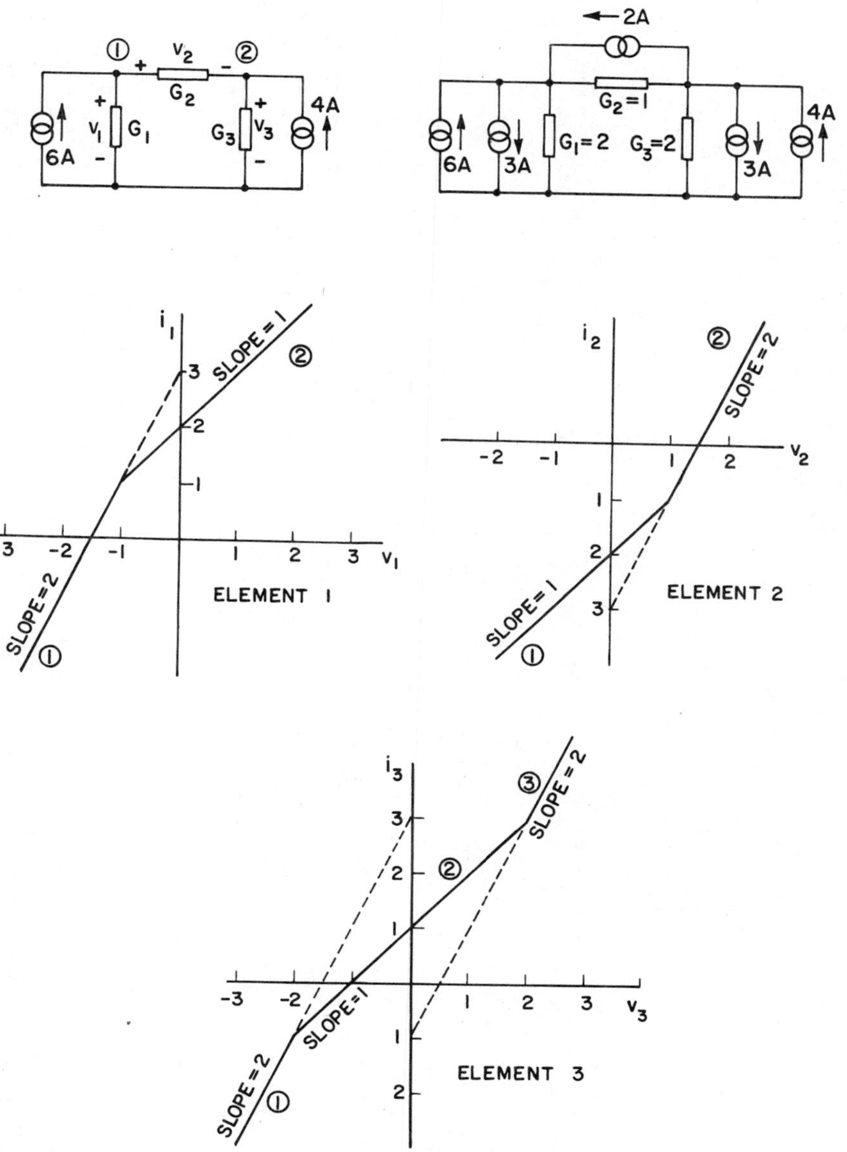

Fig. 12.6.3. Piecewise linear network and its initial equivalent with additional sources resulting from the piecewise linear resistors.

Step 2:

$$\mathbf{f}^0 = \begin{bmatrix} 3 & -1 \\ -1 & 3 \end{bmatrix} \begin{bmatrix} -3 \\ -3 \end{bmatrix} - \begin{bmatrix} -1 \\ -5 \end{bmatrix} - \begin{bmatrix} 6 \\ 4 \end{bmatrix} = \begin{bmatrix} -11 \\ -5 \end{bmatrix}.$$

Step 3:

$$\begin{bmatrix} 3 & -1 \\ -1 & 3 \end{bmatrix} \begin{bmatrix} \Delta v_{n1}^0 \\ \Delta v_{n2}^0 \end{bmatrix} = \begin{bmatrix} 11 \\ 5 \end{bmatrix}.$$

The solution is

$$\begin{bmatrix} \Delta v_{n1}^0 \\ \Delta v_{n2}^0 \end{bmatrix} = \begin{bmatrix} \frac{19}{4} \\ \frac{13}{4} \end{bmatrix}.$$

Step 4:

$$\begin{bmatrix} \hat{v}_{n1}^1 \\ \hat{v}_{n2}^1 \end{bmatrix} = \begin{bmatrix} -3 \\ -3 \end{bmatrix} + \begin{bmatrix} \frac{19}{4} \\ \frac{13}{4} \end{bmatrix} = \begin{bmatrix} \frac{7}{4} \\ \frac{1}{4} \end{bmatrix}.$$

For the elements we have

$$\begin{bmatrix} \hat{v}_1^1 \\ \hat{v}_2^1 \\ \hat{v}_3^1 \end{bmatrix} = \begin{bmatrix} \frac{7}{4} \\ \frac{6}{4} \\ \frac{1}{4} \end{bmatrix}; \quad \begin{bmatrix} \Delta v_1^0 \\ \Delta v_2^0 \\ \Delta v_3^0 \end{bmatrix} = \begin{bmatrix} \frac{19}{4} \\ \frac{6}{4} \\ \frac{13}{4} \end{bmatrix}.$$

All the increments are positive and all elements cross into new regions. The full step is not possible so discard $\hat{\mathbf{v}}^1$ and calculate the step-reduction coefficients using Fig. 12.6.2.

Step 5:

$$t_1^0 = \frac{-1 - (-3)}{\frac{19}{4}} = \frac{8}{19}$$

$$t_2^0 = \frac{1 - 0}{\frac{6}{4}} = \frac{4}{6}$$

$$t_3^0 = \frac{-2 - (-3)}{\frac{13}{4}} = \frac{4}{13}.$$

Step 6:

$$t^0 = \min_i \; (t_i^0) = \tfrac{4}{13}.$$

Step 7:

$$\begin{bmatrix} v_{n1}^1 \\ v_{n2}^1 \end{bmatrix} = \begin{bmatrix} -3 \\ -3 \end{bmatrix} + \frac{4}{13}\begin{bmatrix} \frac{19}{4} \\ \frac{13}{4} \end{bmatrix} = \begin{bmatrix} -\frac{20}{13} \\ -\frac{26}{13} \end{bmatrix}.$$

and the element voltages are

$$\begin{bmatrix} v_1^1 \\ v_2^1 \\ v_3^1 \end{bmatrix} = \begin{bmatrix} -\frac{20}{13} \\ \frac{6}{13} \\ -\frac{26}{13} \end{bmatrix}.$$

Step 8:

$$\mathbf{f}^1 = (1 - \tfrac{4}{13}) \begin{bmatrix} -11 \\ -5 \end{bmatrix} = \begin{bmatrix} -\frac{99}{13} \\ -\frac{45}{13} \end{bmatrix}.$$

Step 9: We are now in a new region in which $G_1 = 2$, $G_2 = 1$ (remain unchanged) and $G_3 = 1$; the new nodal admittance matrix

$$\begin{bmatrix} 3 & -1 \\ -1 & 2 \end{bmatrix}$$

is used when returning to step 3.

This completes one iteration. The solution of the problem is

$$\mathbf{v} = \begin{bmatrix} 4 \\ 1.5 \\ 2.5 \end{bmatrix}.$$

PROBLEMS

P.12.1. Write a program for the solution of a system of nonlinear equations. Declare a matrix **M** for the Jacobian and a vector **f** for the function. They should be supplied by user-defined subroutines JACOB and FUNCT. For the solution of (12.1.9) either write your own routines or use those from Chapter 2. Also use the information provided in Problem P.7.4.

P.12.2. Solve the system

$$3x_1 - 2x_2^2 - 5x_2 + 15 = 0$$
$$2x_1^2 - 3x_1 + x_2^2 + 2x_2 - 7 = 0$$

either by hand or by using the program from Problem P.12.1. Let the initial estimate be $x_1 = x_2 = 1.5$. (*Result*: $x_1 = 1$, $x_2 = 2$.)

P.12.3. Solve the system

$$x_1^2 + 2x_2 - x_3 + 6 = 0$$
$$x_1x_2 + x_3^2 - 7 = 0$$
$$x_1 + x_2^2 + x_3 - 8 = 0$$

by using various initial estimates and observe convergence. (*Result*: $x_1 = 1, x_2 = -2, x_3 = 3$.)

P.12.4. Solve the following nonlinear systems by the program from Problem P.12.1:

(a) $x_1^2 + 2x_2 - 5 = 0$

$3x_1^2 + 2x_2^2 - 11 = 0$ (*Result:* $x_1 = 1, x_2 = 2$)

(b) $x_1^2 + 2x_1x_2 - 2x_2^2 + 3 = 0$

$x_1 + 2x_2 + 2x_1^2 + x_1x_2 - 9 = 0$ (*Result:* $x_1 = 1, x_2 = 2$)

(c) $x_1 + x_1^2 - 2x_2 + x_2x_3 - 3 = 0$

$x_1 + x_2 + x_3^2 + x_2x_3 = 0$ (*Result:* $x_1 = x_3 = 1, x_2 = -1$)

$2x_1 + x_2 - x_3 + x_1x_2 + 1 = 0$

(d) $\sin(x_1 + x_2) - 1.1x_1 - 0.2 = 0$

$x_1^2 + x_2^2 - 1 = 0$

(e) $2x_1^2 - x_1x_2 - 5x_1 + 1 = 0$

$x_1 + 3\log_{10} x_1 - x_2^2 = 0$

(f) $\sin x_1 - x_2 - 1.32 = 0$

$\cos x_2 - x_1 + 0.85 = 0$

(g) $2x_1^2 - x_1x_2 - x_2^2 + 2x_1 - 2x_2 + 6 = 0$

$x_2 - x_1 - 1 = 0$

(h) $x_1 - \log_{10} \dfrac{x_2}{x_3} - 1 = 0$

$2x_1^2 + x_2 - x_3^2 - 0.4 = 0$

$\dfrac{x_1x_2}{20} - x_3 + 2 = 0$

P.12.5. Consider the network shown in Fig. 12.6.3 but let the G_i be nonlinear conductances defined by $i = v^2$. Find the dc solution and the sensitivity of v_1 to changes in all elements.

P.12.6. In the network in Fig. P.12.6 let the transconductance be nonlinear

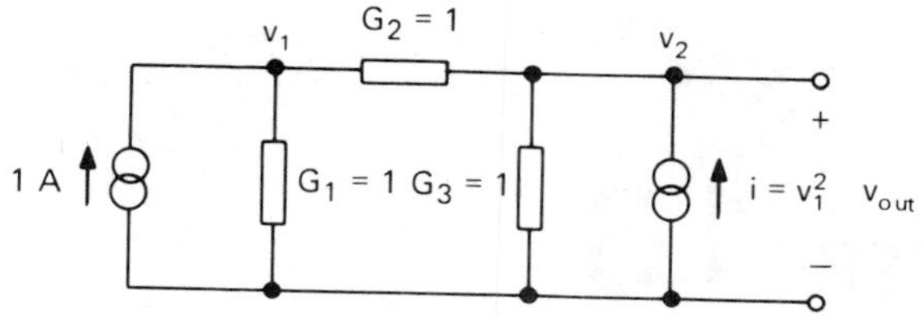

Fig. P.12.6.

and governed by the relationship $i = v^2$. Find the dc solution and dc sensitivity with respect to all elements.

REFERENCES

1. J. Katzenelson: An algorithm for solving nonlinear resistive networks. *Bell Syst. Tech. J.*, Vol. 44, pp. 1605–1620, October 1965.
2. M. J. Chien and E. S. Kuh: Solving nonlinear resistive networks using piecewise-linear analysis and simplical subdivision. *IEEE Trans. on Circuits and Systems*, Vol. CAS-24, pp. 305–317, June 1977.
3. T. Fujisawa and E. S. Kuh: Piecewise linear theory of nonlinear networks. *SIAM J. Appl. Math.*, Vol. 22, pp. 307–328, March 1972.
4. M. E. Zaghloul and P. R. Bryant: Error bounds on solutions of nonlinear networks when using approximate element characteristics. *IEEE Trans. on Circuits and Systems*, Vol. CAS-27, pp. 20–29, January 1980.
5. C. W. Ho, D. A. Zein, A. Ruehli, and P. A. Brennan: An algorithm for dc solutions in an experimental general purpose interactive circuit design program. *IEEE Trans. on Circuits and Systems*, Vol. CAS-24, pp. 416–422, August 1977.

CHAPTER 13
Numerical Integration of Differential and Algebraic-Differential Equations

Before proceeding to the time domain solution of nonlinear networks we first discuss the principles of higher-order linear multistep formulae (LMS) for the numerical integration of differential equations. The simplest ones of this class, the forward Euler, backward Euler and the trapezoidal formula, were introduced in Chapter 9.

In Section 13.1 we give a unified method for deriving LMS formulae for equal time steps. In order to find the solution at a time point, use is made of information about past solution and derivative values. Different formulae result, depending on which of these values and derivatives are used. The solution is assumed to be approximated by a polynomial in the neighborhood of the current time point. Using interpolation, the coefficients of this approximating polynomial are determined by a technique similar to the adjoint approach of Chapter 6. Depending on whether or not the solution at the current time point is used in the interpolation, two distinct classes–explicit predictors and implicit correctors–are obtained. A number of such formulae are derived in the examples.

In Section 13.2, we investigate the stability, order of integration, and truncation error of higher-order LMS formulae. Such a study is necessary to select results which have practical utility from among all those that can be derived by the technique of Section 13.1. Section 13.3 reviews properties of some well known formulae and points out that Gear's backward differentiation formulae (BDF) are among the best for *stiff* problems. Section 13.4 indicates how the formulae are used on systems of differential equations.

The situation becomes more complicated when we get to the time domain solution of networks. First of all, the recommended formulation methods result in sets of *algebraic-differential* instead of only differential equations. Moreover, to speed up the solution, it is necessary to change the integration step size or order to adapt to the behavior of the system. The BDF formulae are still among the best for this purpose, but methods for step size and order control must be used. This is introduced in Section 13.5.

Having selected the method of integration, special attention has to be paid to the formulation of network equations. If nonlinear capacitors or inductors are involved, it is useful to introduce the charges and fluxes as additional system variables. Such a modification has the advantage that all differential equations in the system become linear and all nonlinearities are transformed into algebraic equations. This type of formulation and its solution by application of the BDF formulae and the Newton-Raphson iteration is summarized in Section 13.6, which concludes the chapter.

13.1. DERIVATION OF LMS FORMULAE

All linear multistep formulae for integrating differential equations are based on the principle of matching a number of known values and derivatives by means of an interpolating polynomial. This section develops a unified theory for such matching. It is assumed that the step size, h, is constant and an arbitrary selection of solutions and/or derivatives obtained at previous steps can be used. In order to decide whether the resulting formula is useful in practice, additional theory is required. These theoretical aspects are discussed in the next section.

Consider the situation where the values $x_n, x_{n+1}, \ldots, x_{n+k-1}$ and the derivatives $x'_n, x'_{n+1}, \ldots, x'_{n+k-1}$ are known at time instants $t_n, t_{n+1}, \ldots, t_{n+k-1}$. The values x_{n+k} and x'_{n+k} are considered as unknown or x_{n+k} may be *assumed* to be known. The first case leads to formulae which are called *predictors*, the second one provides *correctors*.

It is advantageous to define the approximating polynomial with respect to a time origin at t_{n+k}, as considerable simplifications follow. In addition, further simplifications follow if the step size is normalized to unit value. This leads to the representation of the mth degree interpolation polynomial in the from

$$x_m(t) = \sum_{i=0}^{m} d_i \left(\frac{t_{n+k} - t}{h}\right)^i = \sum_{i=0}^{m} d_i \tau^i. \tag{13.1.1}$$

Its derivative is

$$x'_m(t) = -\frac{1}{h} \sum_{i=1}^{m} i d_i \left(\frac{t_{n+k} - t}{h}\right)^{i-1} = -\frac{1}{h} \sum_{i=1}^{m} i d_i \tau^{i-1} \tag{13.1.2}$$

where we introduced

$$\tau = \frac{t_{n+k} - t}{h}. \tag{13.1.3}$$

At the time of interest, t_{n+k}, where $\tau = 0$, we obtain

$$x_{n+k} = d_0 \tag{13.1.4}$$

and

$$x'_{n+k} = -\frac{1}{h} d_1. \tag{13.1.5}$$

In order to find the coefficients d_i, assume that some past values and derivatives are available. A total of $(m + 1)$ independent conditions are required to find the d_i. These conditions may be made up entirely of past values, past derivatives or a combination thereof. At the various points we have

$$x_{n+k-j} = \sum_{i=0}^{m} d_i \left(\frac{t_{n+k} - t_{n+k-j}}{h} \right)^i, \qquad j = 1, 2, \ldots \tag{13.1.6}$$

$$-hx'_{n+k-j} = \sum_{i=1}^{m} id_i \left(\frac{t_{n+k} - t_{n+k-j}}{h} \right)^{i-1}, \qquad j = 1, 2, \ldots. \tag{13.1.7}$$

Since we assume that the intervals are equal:

$$t_{n+k} - t_{n+k-j} = jh \tag{13.1.8}$$

and the expressions simplify to

$$x_{n+k-j} = \sum_{i=0}^{m} d_i j^i \tag{13.1.9}$$

$$-hx'_{n+k-j} = \sum_{i=1}^{m} id_i j^{i-1}. \tag{13.1.10}$$

A. Predictors

Let us now assume that we are using k past values and derivatives and wish to derive a predictor formula for x_{n+k}. We can fit a polynomial of degree $2k - 1 = m$ using this information. The equations are

$$
\begin{aligned}
d_0^P + d_1^P + \cdots + d_m^P &= x_{n+k-1}\\
d_0^P + 2d_1^P + 4d_2^P + \cdots + 2^m d_m^P &= x_{n+k-2}\\
d_0^P + 3d_1^P + 3^2 d_2^P + \cdots + 3^m d_m^P &= x_{n+k-3}\\
&\vdots\\
d_1^P + 2d_2^P + \cdots + m d_m^P &= -hx'_{n+k-1}\\
d_1^P + 2\times 2d_2^P + \cdots + m2^{m-1} d_m^P &= -hx'_{n+k-2}\\
d_1^P + 2\times 3d_2^P + \cdots + m3^{m-1} d_m^P &= -hx'_{n+k-3}
\end{aligned}
$$

In the matrix form this is

$$
\begin{bmatrix}
1 & 1 & 1 & 1 & \cdots & 1\\
1 & 2 & 2^2 & 2^3 & \cdots & 2^m\\
1 & 3 & 3^2 & 3^3 & \cdots & 3^m\\
\hline
0 & 1 & 2 & 3 & \cdots & m\\
0 & 1 & 2\times 2 & 3\times 2^2 & \cdots & m2^{m-1}\\
0 & 1 & 2\times 3 & 3\times 3^2 & \cdots & m3^{m-1}
\end{bmatrix}
\begin{bmatrix} \\ \mathbf{d}^P \\ \\ \end{bmatrix}
=
\begin{bmatrix} \mathbf{x} \\ \hline -h\mathbf{x}' \end{bmatrix}
\qquad (13.1.11)
$$

or

$$\mathbf{V}^P \mathbf{d}^P = \mathbf{z}^P \qquad (13.1.12)$$

where the superscript P stands for *Predictor*. Formally, the solution is

$$\mathbf{d}^P = (\mathbf{V}^P)^{-1}\mathbf{z}^P. \qquad (13.1.13)$$

The vector $\mathbf{d}^P$ changes at each time step as the right-hand-side vector changes. Note however that the full vector of coefficients $\mathbf{d}^P$ is not needed for our purpose: all we need is the value $x_{n+k} = d_0^P$. Rather than solving (13.1.11) we proceed as in Chapter 6. Define the vector

$$\mathbf{e}_0^t = [1 \quad 0 \quad 0 \quad 0 \quad \cdots \quad 0]. \qquad (13.1.14)$$

Premultiplying (13.1.13) by $\mathbf{e}_0^t$ provides

$$x_{n+k} = d_0^P = \mathbf{e}_0^t\,\mathbf{d}^P = \mathbf{e}_0^t(\mathbf{V}^P)^{-1}\mathbf{z}^P. \qquad (13.1.15)$$

Define in this equation an auxiliary vector $\boldsymbol{\phi}^P$ as

$$(\boldsymbol{\phi}^P)^t = \mathbf{e}_0^t(\mathbf{V}^P)^{-1}$$

which can be rewritten as

$$(\mathbf{V}^P)^t \boldsymbol{\phi}^P = \mathbf{e}_0. \tag{13.1.16}$$

Entries of the vector $\boldsymbol{\phi}^P$ are written in partitioned form as follows:

$$\boldsymbol{\phi}^P = [a_1^P \;\; a_2^P \;\; \cdots \;\; a_k^P \;\vdots\; b_1^P \;\; b_2^P \;\; \cdots \;\; b_k^P]^t. \tag{13.1.17}$$

For future reference we write (13.1.16) using three coefficients a_i^P, b_i^P:

$$\begin{bmatrix} 1 & 1 & 1 & 0 & 0 & 0 \\ 1 & 2 & 3 & 1 & 1 & 1 \\ 1 & 2^2 & 3^2 & 2 & 2\times 2 & 2\times 3 \\ 1 & 2^3 & 3^3 & 3 & 3\times 2^2 & 3\times 3^2 \\ 1 & 2^4 & 3^4 & 4 & 4\times 2^3 & 4\times 3^3 \\ 1 & 2^5 & 3^5 & 5 & 5\times 2^4 & 5\times 3^4 \end{bmatrix} \begin{bmatrix} a_1^P \\ a_2^P \\ a_3^P \\ b_1^P \\ b_2^P \\ b_3^P \end{bmatrix} = \begin{bmatrix} 1 \\ 0 \\ 0 \\ 0 \\ 0 \\ 0 \end{bmatrix}. \tag{13.1.18}$$

Solve (13.1.16) and insert into (13.1.15) to obtain

$$x_{n+k} = (\boldsymbol{\phi}^P)^t \mathbf{z}^P. \tag{13.1.19}$$

Using the entries of $\boldsymbol{\phi}^P$ and $\mathbf{z}^P$, the predictor formula becomes

$$x_{n+k} = \sum_{j=1}^{k} a_j^P x_{n+k-j} - h \sum_{j=1}^{k} b_j^P x'_{n+k-j}. \tag{13.1.20}$$

In other words, instead of solving (13.1.12) we solve (13.1.16) and the solution vector contains the coefficients of the formula (13.1.20). An important consequence is that the vector $\boldsymbol{\phi}^P$ depends *only* on the *selection* of which previous x_i and x'_i are used but not on their values.

EXAMPLE 13.1.1. Find the formula for calculating x_{n+k} using x_{n+k-1} and x'_{n+k-1}.

As two conditions are specified, a first-order approximating polynomial

$$x_1(\tau) = d_0^P + d_1^P \tau$$

is used. Matching conditions at t_{n+k-1} we obtain

$$\begin{aligned} x_{n+k-1} &= d_0^P + d_1^P \\ -hx'_{n+k-1} &= d_1^P. \end{aligned}$$

In matrix form this is

$$\begin{bmatrix} 1 & 1 \\ 0 & 1 \end{bmatrix} \begin{bmatrix} d_0^P \\ d_1^P \end{bmatrix} = \begin{bmatrix} x_{n+k-1} \\ -hx'_{n+k-1} \end{bmatrix} .$$

The corresponding transpose system (13.1.16) is

$$\begin{bmatrix} 1 & 0 \\ 1 & 1 \end{bmatrix} \begin{bmatrix} a_1^P \\ b_1^P \end{bmatrix} = \begin{bmatrix} 1 \\ 0 \end{bmatrix} .$$

The solution is

$$(\phi^P)^t = [a_1^P \quad b_1^P] = [1 \quad -1]$$

and, following (13.1.20),

$$x_{n+k} = x_{n+k-1} + hx'_{n+k-1}$$

which is the forward Euler formula derived in Chapter 9.

EXAMPLE 13.1.2. Calculate the formula which predicts x_{n+k} from known values x_{n+k-1} and known derivatives x'_{n+k-1}, x'_{n+k-2}.

The polynomial must be of second order. The equations, written in matrix form, are

$$\begin{bmatrix} 1 & 1 & 1 \\ 0 & 1 & 2 \\ 0 & 1 & 4 \end{bmatrix} \begin{bmatrix} d_0^P \\ d_1^P \\ d_2^P \end{bmatrix} = \begin{bmatrix} x_{n+k-1} \\ -hx'_{n+k-1} \\ -hx'_{n+k-2} \end{bmatrix} .$$

The right-hand side of the transpose system is $[1 \quad 0 \quad 0]^t$, the solution is

$$(\phi^P)^t = [a_1^P \quad b_1^P \quad b_2^P] = [1 \quad -\tfrac{3}{2} \quad \tfrac{1}{2}]$$

and

$$x_{n+k} = x_{n+k-1} + \frac{h}{2}(3x'_{n+k-1} - x'_{n+k-2}).$$

This formula is known as the *Adams–Bashforth second-order predictor*.

The formulae derived above are used in finding the value of x_{n+k} from known previous values and derivatives x_i, x'_i, respectively. The result provides x_{n+k} *explicitly*; the derivative x'_{n+k} is *not involved.*

B. Correctors

The requirements on the formula can be changed and we can look for x'_{n+k} from previous known values x_i, previous known derivatives x'_i, *and* from x_{n+k} which is *assumed* to be known. The system of equations becomes

$$
\begin{aligned}
d_0^C &= x_{n+k}\\
d_0^C + d_1^C + d_2^C + \cdots + d_m^C &= x_{n+k-1}\\
d_0^C + 2d_1^C + 4d_2^C + \cdots + 2^m d_m^C &= x_{n+k-2}\\
&\vdots\\
d_1^C + 2d_2^C + 3d_3^C + \cdots + md_m^C &= -hx'_{n+k-1}\\
d_1^C + 2\times 2d_2^C + 3\times 2^2 d_3^C + \cdots + m2^{m-1}d_m^C &= -hx'_{n+k-2}\\
d_1^C + 2\times 3d_2^C + 3\times 3^2 d_3^C + \cdots + m3^{m-1}d_m^C &= -hx'_{n+k-3}.
\end{aligned}
$$

In matrix form this is

$$
\begin{bmatrix}
1 & 0 & 0 & 0 & \cdots & 0\\
1 & 1 & 1 & 1 & \cdots & 1\\
1 & 2 & 4 & 8 & \cdots & 2^m\\
\hdashline
0 & 1 & 2 & 3 & \cdots & m\\
0 & 1 & 2\times 2 & 3\times 2^2 & \cdots & m2^{m-1}\\
0 & 1 & 2\times 3 & 3\times 3^2 & \cdots & m3^{m-1}
\end{bmatrix}
\begin{bmatrix} \\ \mathbf{d}^C \\ \\ \end{bmatrix}
=
\begin{bmatrix} \mathbf{x} \\ \hdashline -h\mathbf{x}' \end{bmatrix}
\qquad (13.1.21)
$$

or

$$\mathbf{V}^C \mathbf{d}^C = \mathbf{z}^C. \qquad (13.1.22)$$

The superscript C stands for *Corrector.* Formally the solution is

$$\mathbf{d}^C = (\mathbf{V}^C)^{-1}\mathbf{z}^C. \qquad (13.1.23)$$

The full vector $\mathbf{d}^C$ is not needed for our purpose; all we need is the value $-hx'_{n+k} = d_1^C$, as follows from (13.1.5). To avoid solving (13.1.22) for each new $\mathbf{z}^C$, define the vector

$$\mathbf{e}_1^t = [0 \quad 1 \quad 0 \quad 0 \quad \cdots \quad 0]. \qquad (13.1.24)$$

Premultiplying (13.1.23) by $\mathbf{e}_1^t$:

$$-hx'_{n+k} = d_1^C = \mathbf{e}_1^t \mathbf{d}^C = \mathbf{e}_1^t (\mathbf{V}^C)^{-1}\mathbf{z}^C. \qquad (13.1.25)$$

Define

$$(\phi^C)^t = \mathbf{e}_1^t(\mathbf{V}^C)^{-1}$$

which can be rewritten as

$$(\mathbf{V}^C)^t\phi^C = \mathbf{e}_1. \tag{13.1.26}$$

The entries of the vector ϕ^C are

$$(\phi^C)^t = [a_0^C \quad a_1^C \quad \cdots \quad a_k^C \;\vdots\; b_1^C \quad b_2^C \quad \cdots \quad b_k^C]. \tag{13.1.27}$$

For future reference, write (13.1.26) when two past values and three past derivatives are used:

$$\begin{bmatrix} 1 & 1 & 1 & 0 & 0 & 0 \\ 0 & 1 & 2 & 1 & 1 & 1 \\ 0 & 1 & 2^2 & 2 & 2\times 2 & 2\times 3 \\ 0 & 1 & 2^3 & 3 & 3\times 2^2 & 3\times 3^2 \\ 0 & 1 & 2^4 & 4 & 4\times 2^3 & 4\times 3^3 \\ 0 & 1 & 2^5 & 5 & 5\times 2^4 & 5\times 3^4 \end{bmatrix} \begin{bmatrix} a_0^C \\ a_1^C \\ a_2^C \\ b_1^C \\ b_2^C \\ b_3^C \end{bmatrix} = \begin{bmatrix} 0 \\ 1 \\ 0 \\ 0 \\ 0 \\ 0 \end{bmatrix}. \tag{13.1.28}$$

Solve (13.1.26) and insert into (13.1.25) to obtain

$$-hx'_{n+k} = (\phi^C)^t\mathbf{z}^C. \tag{13.1.29}$$

Using the entries of ϕ^C and $\mathbf{z}^C$, the corrector formula becomes

$$-hx'_{n+k} = \sum_{j=0}^{k} a_j^C x_{n+k-j} - h\sum_{j=1}^{k} b_j^C x'_{n+k-j}. \tag{13.1.30}$$

As in the case of the predictors, instead of solving (13.1.22) we solve (13.1.26) and the resulting vector contains the coefficients of (13.1.30). For convenience, the formula can be further modified:

$$x'_{n+k} = -\frac{1}{h}\left\{\sum_{j=0}^{k} a_j^C x_{n+k-j} - h\sum_{j=1}^{k} b_j^C x'_{n+k-j}\right\}. \tag{13.1.31}$$

Since both x_{n+k} and x'_{n+k} are unknown, the corrector formulae are implicit and are usually solved by iteration.

EXAMPLE 13.1.3. Obtain a corrector that uses x_{n+k-1} and x'_{n+k-1}.

With an assumed value for x_{n+k} we can fit a quadratic polynomial. Equating values gives

$$\begin{bmatrix} 1 & 0 & 0 \\ 1 & 1 & 1 \\ 0 & 1 & 2 \end{bmatrix} \begin{bmatrix} d_0^C \\ d_1^C \\ d_2^C \end{bmatrix} = \begin{bmatrix} x_{n+k} \\ x_{n+k-1} \\ -hx'_{n+k-1} \end{bmatrix}.$$

The right-hand side of the transpose system is $[0 \quad 1 \quad 0]^t$ and the solution is

$$(\phi^C)^t = [a_0^C \quad a_1^C \quad b_1^C] = [-2 \quad 2 \quad -1].$$

Our formula thus becomes

$$x'_{n+k} = -\frac{1}{h}(-2x_{n+k} + 2x_{n+k-1} + hx'_{n+k-1}).$$

Rearranging terms we get the trapezoidal formula:

$$x_{n+k} = x_{n+k-1} + \frac{h}{2}(x'_{n+k-1} + x'_{n+k}).$$

An important class of formulae called *backward differentiation* use no past derivatives in either the predictor or the corrector. The derivation of the relevant formulae is demonstrated in the next example.

EXAMPLE 13.1.4. Derive the backward differentiation predictor by using known values x_{n+k-1}, x_{n+k-2}, x_{n+k-3}. Then assume that x_{n+k} is available and derive the formula for the corrector *of the same order* which uses x_{n+k}, x_{n+k-1}, and x_{n+k-2}.

In both cases, a second order polynomial is needed. For the predictor we write in matrix form

$$\begin{bmatrix} 1 & 1 & 1 \\ 1 & 2 & 4 \\ 1 & 3 & 9 \end{bmatrix} \begin{bmatrix} d_0^P \\ d_1^P \\ d_2^P \end{bmatrix} = \begin{bmatrix} x_{n+k-1} \\ x_{n+k-2} \\ x_{n+k-3} \end{bmatrix}.$$

The right-hand side of the transpose system is $[1 \quad 0 \quad 0]^t$, the solution is

$$(\phi^P)^t = [a_1^P \quad a_2^P \quad a_3^P] = [3 \quad -3 \quad 1]$$

and the predictor formula is

$$x_{n+k} = 3x_{n+k-1} - 3x_{n+k-2} + x_{n+k-3}.$$

For the corrector, the equations change to

$$\begin{bmatrix} 1 & 0 & 0 \\ 1 & 1 & 1 \\ 1 & 2 & 4 \end{bmatrix} \begin{bmatrix} d_0^C \\ d_1^C \\ d_2^C \end{bmatrix} = \begin{bmatrix} x_{n+k} \\ x_{n+k-1} \\ x_{n+k-2} \end{bmatrix}.$$

The right-hand side of the transpose system is $[0 \quad 1 \quad 0]^t$, the solution is

$$(\phi^C)^t = [a_0^C \quad a_1^C \quad a_2^C] = [-\tfrac{3}{2} \quad 2 \quad -\tfrac{1}{2}]$$

and the corrector formula becomes

$$x'_{n+k} = -\frac{1}{h}\left(-\frac{3}{2}x_{n+k} + 2x_{n+k-1} - \frac{1}{2}x_{n+k-2}\right).$$

13.2. THEORY OF LMS FORMULAE

Section 13.1 provided a unified method for obtaining any predictor or corrector from known previous values or derivatives. The predictors generally have the form given by (13.1.20), the correctors are usually expressed in the form (13.1.31). For theoretical analysis, it is convenient to define one common form for both:

$$\sum_{i=0}^{k} \alpha_i x_{n+k-i} - h\sum_{i=0}^{k} \beta_i x'_{n+k-i} = 0. \tag{13.2.1}$$

Some constants in (13.2.1) may be zero. Depending on the choice we have:

1. Explicit predictor formulae for *either* α_0 or β_0 zero.
2. Implicit corrector formulae for *both* α_0, β_0 nonzero.
3. Backward differentiation (BDF) for $\beta_1 = \beta_2 = \cdots = \beta_k = 0$.

The derivations of the last section show that we can find many different formulae. Since not all of them are practical, we need to find out which of them are suitable for a network analysis program.

The theory of LMS formulae provides the answer by:

1. Studying the stability properties by means of the test equation $x' = \lambda x$.
2. Determining the order of approximation p.
3. Calculating the local truncation error constant c^*_{p+1}.

We will start by studying the stability conditions. Inserting $x' = \lambda x$ into (13.2.1):

$$\sum_{i=0}^{k} (\alpha_i - h\lambda\beta_i)\, x_{n+k-i} = 0. \tag{13.2.2}$$

Since the test equation has the known solution

$$x(t) = x(0)\, e^{\lambda t}$$

we anticipate that the solution of (13.2.2) will have a similar form

$$x_{n+k-i} = x(0)\, e^{\lambda h(n+k-i)} = x(0)\, e^{q(n+k-i)} \tag{13.2.3}$$

where $q = \lambda h$. Insert this anticipated solution into (13.2.2):

$$x(0)\, e^{qn} \left\{ \sum_{i=0}^{k} \alpha_i e^{q(k-i)} - q \sum_{i=0}^{k} \beta_i e^{q(k-i)} \right\} = 0. \tag{13.2.4}$$

The multiplicative factor can be removed. Introducing a new variable

$$z = e^q \tag{13.2.5}$$

we simplify (13.2.4) to

$$\sum_{i=0}^{k} \alpha_i z^{k-i} - q \sum_{i=0}^{k} \beta_i z^{k-i} = 0. \tag{13.2.6}$$

It is usual to introduce new notations for the polynomials in z:

$$\rho(z) = \sum_{i=0}^{k} \alpha_i z^{k-i}; \qquad \sigma(z) = \sum_{i=0}^{k} \beta_i z^{k-i}. \tag{13.2.7}$$

This simplifies (13.2.6) to

$$\rho(z) - q\sigma(z) = 0. \tag{13.2.8}$$

It is a polynomial equation of degree k in the variable z and must have k roots which we designate as z_i. Assume that all of them are simple. Then

$$\rho(z) - q\sigma(z) = \gamma(z - z_1)(z - z_2)(z - z_3) \cdots (z - z_k). \tag{13.2.9}$$

Insert the jth root into (13.2.3); at the $(n + k - i)$th step we have

$$(x_{n+k-i})_j = x(0)\, z_j^{n+k-i}.$$

Now assume that we take a large number of steps, $n \to \infty$. To obtain a stable solution, we require

$$|z_j| \leqslant 1. \tag{13.2.10}$$

This condition must be fulfilled for each root in (13.2.9), which means that *all roots* must be inside or on the unit circle (multiple roots must be inside the unit circle). Let us now make several simplifications. If the step size is so small that $h \to 0$, (13.2.8) reduces to

$$\rho(z) = 0 \tag{13.2.11}$$

and the zeros of $\rho(z)$ must be inside or on the unit circle to secure stability. This condition must be met by any LMS formula. Since the assumption was $h \to 0$, such stability is called *zero stability*. In a similar way, we may take an extremely large step, $h \to \infty$, and still require a stable solution. Very large h makes the second term dominant, which is equivalent to the simplification

$$\sigma(z) = 0 \tag{13.2.12}$$

and all roots of $\sigma(z)$ would have to be inside or on the unit circle to secure stability. Such stability is called A_∞ *stability*.

Stability properties can be studied fairly simply by *assuming that the root is on the unit circle.* This means that $z = e^{j\phi}$. Inserting into (13.2.8) gives

$$q = \frac{\rho(e^{j\phi})}{\sigma(e^{j\phi})}$$

The resulting value q will be a point on the stability boundary. The choice $z = \pm 1$ ($\phi = 0°$ or $180°$) will provide the intersection of the boundary with the real axis of the q-plane. It is thus fairly easy to establish in which half plane, left or right, the stability boundary closes. Let the calculation proceed by selecting points on the unit circle going counterclockwise. The inside of the unit circle is to the left. In the q-plane, the inside of the stability boundary will be to the left of the curve, in the direction given by the sequence of calculated points. This is sketched in Fig. 13.2.1.

The order and the error constant of the formula can be derived similarly as indicated in Chapter 9. Rewrite (13.2.1) in terms of exact values in the follow-

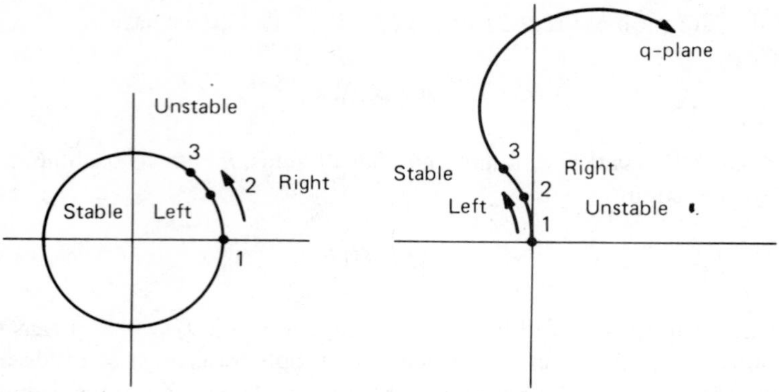

Fig. 13.2.1. A sketch indicating determination of the stable and unstable regions in the q-plane.

ing form:

$$\sum_{i=0}^{k} \alpha_i x(t_{n+k} - ih) - h \sum_{i=0}^{k} \beta_i x'(t_{n+k} - ih) \tag{13.2.13}$$

and expand each function into the Taylor series about t_{n+k}. The formulae are:

$$x(t_{n+k} - ih) = x(t_{n+k}) - \frac{ih}{1!} x'(t_{n+k}) + \frac{(ih)^2}{2!} x''(t_{n+k}) + \cdots$$

$$x'(t_{n+k} - ih) = x'(t_{n+k}) - \frac{ih}{1!} x''(t_{n+k}) + \frac{(ih)^2}{2!} x'''(t_{n+k}) + \cdots . \tag{13.2.14}$$

If (13.2.14) are inserted into (13.2.13) for all i, the coefficients associated with the various derivatives can be collected and the result rewritten in the form

$$C_0 x(t_{n+k}) + hC_1 x'(t_{n+k}) + h^2 C_2 x''(t_{n+k}) + \cdots + h^m C_m x^{(m)}(t_{n+k}) + \cdots . \tag{13.2.15}$$

Simple algebra leads to

$$C_0 = \alpha_0 + \alpha_1 + \alpha_2 + \cdots + \alpha_k$$

$$C_1 = -\left\{\frac{1}{1!}(\alpha_1 + 2\alpha_2 + \cdots + k\alpha_k) + \frac{1}{0!}(\beta_0 + \beta_1 + \cdots + \beta_k)\right\}$$

$$C_2 = \frac{1}{2!}(\alpha_1 + 2^2\alpha_2 + \cdots + k^2\alpha_k) + \frac{1}{1!}(\beta_1 + 2\beta_2 + \cdots + k\beta_k)$$

$$C_3 = -\left\{\frac{1}{3!}(\alpha_1 + 2^3\alpha_2 + \cdots + k^3\alpha_k) + \frac{1}{2!}(\beta_1 + 2^2\beta_2 + \cdots + k^2\beta_k)\right\}$$

$$\vdots$$

$$C_m = (-1)^m\left\{\frac{1}{m!}(\alpha_1 + 2^m\alpha_2 + 3^m\alpha_3 + \cdots + k^m\alpha_k) + \frac{1}{(m-1)!}(\beta_1 + 2^{m-1}\beta_2 + 3^{m-1}\beta_3 + \cdots + k^{m-1}\beta_k)\right\}. \tag{13.2.16}$$

For the pth-order formula, the coefficients up to C_p must be equal to zero. Comparing (13.2.13) and (13.2.15) we see that

$$\sum_{i=0}^{k}\alpha_i x(t_{n+k} - ih) - h\sum_{i=0}^{k}\beta_i x'(t_{n+k} - ih) = h^{p+1}C_{p+1}x^{(p+1)}(t_{n+k}) + \cdots. \tag{13.2.17}$$

Considering (13.2.1) again, we see that its validity remains unchanged if the equation is multiplied by any nonzero constant: some type of normalization is needed. Various possibilities exist. We took $a_0^P = -\alpha_0 = 1$ for the predictors and $b_0 = -\beta_0 = 1$ for the correctors. Sometimes, the normalization

$$\text{norm} = \sum_{i=0}^{k}\beta_i$$

is used. With any type of normalization, the truncation error c_{p+1}^* becomes

$$c_{p+1}^* = C_{p+1}/\text{norm}. \tag{13.2.18}$$

It remains to be shown that the formulae derived by the methods of Section 13.1 indeed fulfill the condition that the coefficients $C_0, C_1, \ldots, C_p$ in (13.2.16) be zero. To be specific, we will go up to α_3 and β_3 and write (13.2.16) as a matrix equation with zero right-hand side:

$$\begin{bmatrix} 1 & 1 & 1 & 1 & 0 & 0 & 0 & 0 \\ 0 & 1 & 2 & 3 & 1 & 1 & 1 & 1 \\ 0 & 1 & 2^2 & 3^2 & 0 & 2\times 1 & 2\times 2 & 2\times 3 \\ 0 & 1 & 2^3 & 3^3 & 0 & 3\times 1^2 & 3\times 2^2 & 3\times 3^2 \\ 0 & 1 & 2^4 & 3^4 & 0 & 4\times 1^3 & 4\times 2^3 & 4\times 3^3 \\ 0 & 1 & 2^5 & 3^5 & 0 & 5\times 1^4 & 5\times 2^4 & 5\times 3^4 \\ 0 & 1 & 2^6 & 3^6 & 0 & 6\times 1^5 & 6\times 2^5 & 6\times 3^5 \\ 0 & 1 & 2^7 & 3^7 & 0 & 7\times 1^6 & 7\times 2^6 & 7\times 3^6 \end{bmatrix} \begin{bmatrix} \alpha_0 \\ \alpha_1 \\ \alpha_2 \\ \alpha_3 \\ \beta_0 \\ \beta_1 \\ \beta_2 \\ \beta_3 \end{bmatrix} = \begin{bmatrix} 0 \\ 0 \\ 0 \\ 0 \\ 0 \\ 0 \\ 0 \\ 0 \end{bmatrix}. \tag{13.2.19}$$

In Section 13.1 we defined the predictors such that $a_0 = -\alpha_0 = 1$ and $b_0 = \beta_0 = 0$. This means that column 1 can be transferred to the right side and column 5 deleted. To make the matrix a square one, delete also the last two rows of (13.2.19). The result becomes precisely the matrix equation (13.1.18) used for the derivation of the predictors.

Proceeding similarly for the correctors we note that our selection was $b_0 = -\beta_0 = 1$. Thus the fifth column can be transferred to the right side. Assume also that we select $\alpha_3 = 0$, which means that the fourth column of (13.2.19) can be deleted. To make the matrix a square one, delete the last two rows as well. The result is precisely the matrix equation given by (13.1.28). Thus our numerical method for defining predictors or correctors is in agreement with the theory described above and the truncation constant can be obtained by using (13.2.16).

13.3. PROPERTIES OF LMS FORMULAE

This section will discuss briefly two widely used families of formulae. The first family is the Adams-Bashforth predictors and Adams-Moulton correctors. One Adams-Moulton formula was derived in Example 13.1.2. They all use one previous solution x_{n+k-1} and a number of derivatives x'_{n+k-i}. Table 13.3.1 gives the first three predictors and correctors.

In applications, the predictor is used only once at each step, to predict a new value. The stability properties of the predictors are thus not all that important. Nevertheless, we show the stability regions for both the predictors and correctors in Fig. 13.3.1. The predictors are denoted by P, correctors by C, and the number indicates the order.

All stability regions for the predictors close in the left half plane and the size of the stability region decreases with the order. The stable region is *inside* the curves. The first-order corrector is absolutely stable *outside* the curve $C1$ and comparing with Chapter 9 we see that it is the backward Euler formula. The second-order corrector has the stability boundary identical to the imaginary axis of the q-plane. It is the well known trapezoidal formula. The third-order corrector closes in the left half plane and the region of stability is *inside* the curve.

The stability boundaries for higher-order Adams-Moulton correctors close in the left half plane. This is disappointing since it forces us to reduce the step size. Ideally, one would like to have formulae which are stable whenever the differential equation is stable. This type of stability, called ***absolute***, is the property of the backward Euler and trapezoidal formulae. Unfortunately, as was proved by Dahlquist [1], absolutely stable linear multistep formulae are restricted to orders $p = 1$ and 2. Further, Dahlquist showed that the trapezoidal rule has the lowest possible truncation error for an absolutely stable formula.

Gear [2] studied the stability problem and derived the second family of LMS formulae to be discussed in this section. He suggested that a formula having the stability region as sketched in Fig. 13.3.2 is better suited for practical problems. His argument, expressed in terms of networks, goes as follows: Whenever a network has desired as well as parasitic elements, there will be some desired poles in the region close to $q = 0$ and some parasitic poles that are far from the origin, as sketched in Fig. 13.3.2. All poles contribute to the response with components of the form $x' = \lambda x$ and must be located inside the region of stability. If a formula with the stability region of Fig. 13.3.2 is applied to a *stiff* problem, stability of the solution can be secured even for larger step sizes. Parasitic poles that have large magnitude and lie close to the imaginary axis require the formula to be A_∞ stable.

The requirement can be satisfied by selecting $\beta_1 = \beta_2 = \cdots = \beta_k = 0$. Formulae of this type are called ***backward differentiation***, BDF, and were already intro-

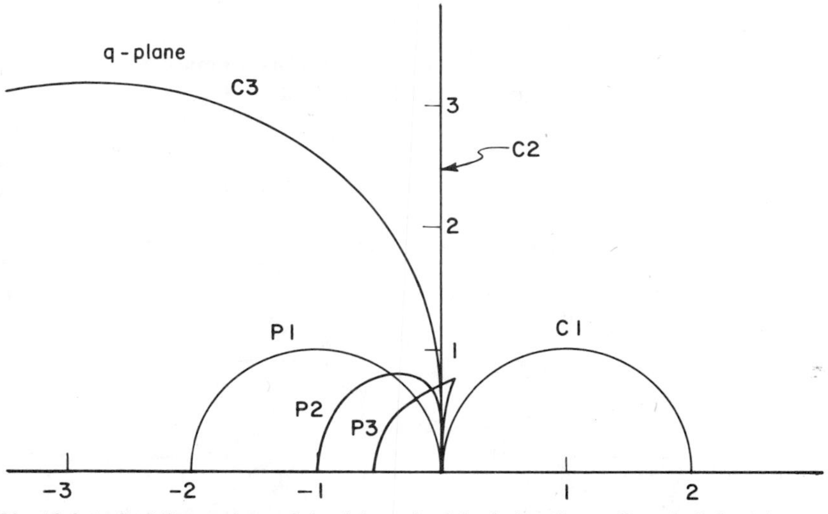

Fig. 13.3.1. Stability regions of the Adams–Bashforth (predictor, P) and of the Adams–Moulton (corrector, C) formulae. The numbers correspond to k in Table 13.3.1.

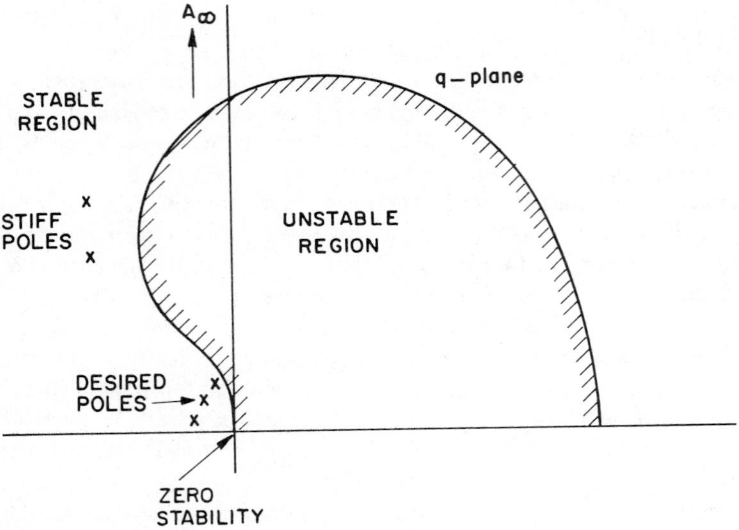

Fig. 13.3.2. Desired shape of the stability region and positions of desired and stiff poles.

duced in Example 13.1.4. They are always A_∞ stable because the roots of (13.2.12) are all inside the unit circle, at the origin. Using the notation introduced in Section 13.1, the BDF predictors have the form

$$x_{n+k} = \sum_{j=1}^{k} a_j^P x_{n+k-j} \tag{13.3.1}$$

Table 13.3.1. The First Three Adams-Bashforth Predictors and Adams-Moulton Correctors.

$$x_{n+k} = x_{n+k-1} + h \sum_{j=1}^{k} \gamma_j x'_{n+k-j+1}$$

	k	γ_1	γ_2	γ_3	γ_4	Truncation Error
predictor	1	0	1	–	–	$\frac{1}{2}h^2x^{(2)}$
corrector		1	–	–	–	$-\frac{1}{2}h^2x^{(2)}$
predictor	2	0	$\frac{3}{2}$	$-\frac{1}{2}$	–	$\frac{5}{12}h^3x^{(3)}$
corrector		$\frac{1}{2}$	$\frac{1}{2}$	–	–	$-\frac{1}{12}h^3x^{(3)}$
predictor	3	0	$\frac{23}{12}$	$-\frac{16}{12}$	$\frac{5}{12}$	$\frac{9}{24}h^4x^{(4)}$
corrector		$\frac{5}{12}$	$\frac{8}{12}$	$-\frac{1}{12}$	–	$-\frac{1}{24}h^4x^{(4)}$

and the correctors are

$$x'_{n+k} = -\frac{1}{h}\sum_{j=0}^{k-1} a_j^C x_{n+k-j}. \tag{13.3.2}$$

They are collected in Table 13.3.2. The stability boundaries of the correctors are shown in Fig. 13.3.3, the stable region being outside the curves. The highest-order formula which is useful is of order 6, because for higher orders the boundaries protruding into the left half plane start crossing the negative real axis and each other. The BDF formulae have their most important application in the solution of algebraic-differential equations.

Table 13.3.2. Backward Differentiation Formulae (BDF).

BDF Predictors

$$x_{n+k} = \sum_{j=1}^{k} a_j^P x_{n+k-j}$$

Order k	a_1^P	a_2^P	a_3^P	a_4^P	a_5^P	a_6^P	a_7^P
1	2	−1	–	–	–	–	–
2	3	−3	1	–	–	–	–
3	4	−6	4	−1	–	–	–
4	5	−10	10	−5	1	–	–
5	6	−15	20	−15	6	1	–
6	7	−21	35	−35	21	−7	1

BDF Correctors

$$x'_{n+k} = -\frac{1}{h}\sum_{j=0}^{k-1} a_j^C x_{n+k-j}$$

Order k	a_0^C	a_1^C	a_2^C	a_3^C	a_4^C	a_5^C	a_6^C
1	−1	1	–	–	–	–	–
2	$-\frac{3}{2}$	2	$-\frac{1}{2}$	–	–	–	–
3	$-\frac{11}{6}$	3	$-\frac{3}{2}$	$\frac{1}{3}$	–	–	–
4	$-\frac{25}{12}$	4	−3	$\frac{4}{3}$	$-\frac{1}{4}$	–	–
5	$-\frac{137}{60}$	5	−5	$\frac{10}{3}$	$-\frac{5}{4}$	$\frac{1}{5}$	–
6	$-\frac{147}{60}$	6	$-\frac{15}{2}$	$\frac{20}{3}$	$-\frac{15}{4}$	$\frac{6}{5}$	$-\frac{1}{6}$

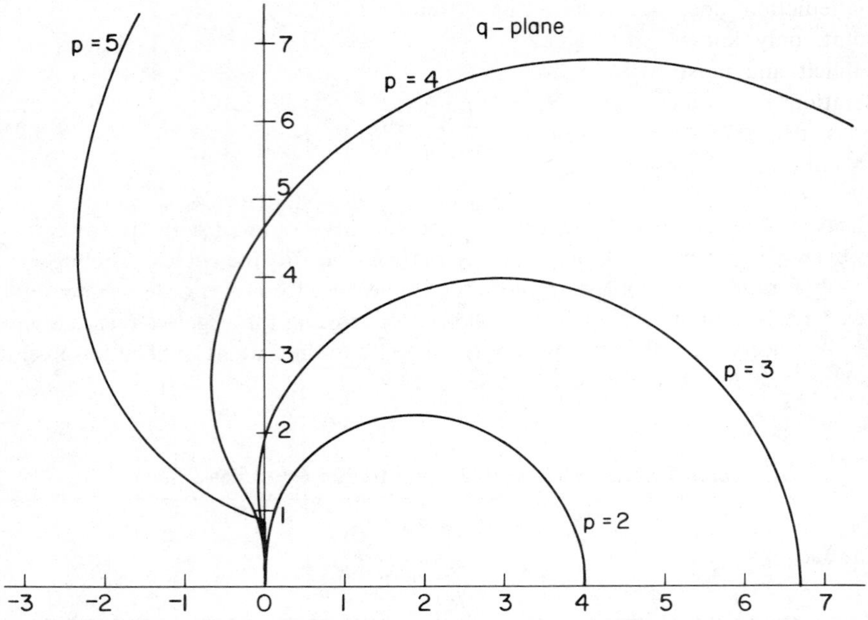

Fig. 13.3.3. Stability regions of Gear's corrector formulae. The curves close in the right half plane and the stable region is outside the curves.

13.4. SYSTEMS OF DIFFERENTIAL EQUATIONS

Let the system of differential equations be

$$\mathbf{x}' = \mathbf{f}(\mathbf{x}, t) \tag{13.4.1}$$

and assume that the vectors $\mathbf{x}_n, \mathbf{x}_{n+1}, \ldots, \mathbf{x}_{n+k-1}, \mathbf{x}'_n, \mathbf{x}'_{n+1}, \ldots, \mathbf{x}'_{n+k-1}$ are known. The vector predictor and corrector formulae are:

Predictor:

$$\mathbf{x}_{n+k} = \sum_{j=1}^{k} a_j^P \mathbf{x}_{n+k-j} - h \sum_{j=1}^{k} b_j^P \mathbf{x}'_{n+k-j} \tag{13.4.2}$$

Corrector:

$$\mathbf{x}'_{n+k} = -\frac{1}{h}\left\{\sum_{j=0}^{k} a_j^C \mathbf{x}_{n+k-j} - h \sum_{j=1}^{k} b_j^C \mathbf{x}'_{n+k-j}\right\}. \tag{13.4.3}$$

Prediction does not involve the differential equation at the current time point, only known past values and derivatives. The corrector equations are implicit and must be solved iteratively. The starting value for the corrector iterations is generally taken as $\mathbf{x}_{n+k}^P$, the predicted value. In network applications, the corrector equation is generally solved by Newton-Raphson iteration. Substitute (13.4.3) into (13.4.1) and rewrite as

$$\boldsymbol{\epsilon}(\mathbf{x}_{n+k}, t_{n+k}) \equiv a_0^C \mathbf{x}_{n+k} + \sum_{j=1}^{k} a_j^C \mathbf{x}_{n+k-j} - h \sum_{j=1}^{k} b_j^C \mathbf{x}'_{n+k-j} + h\mathbf{f}(\mathbf{x}_{n+k}, t_{n+k}) = \mathbf{0}. \quad (13.4.4)$$

In a given step the summations are known and can be collected into one vector $\mathbf{r}$. Thus (13.4.4) is written as follows:

$$\boldsymbol{\epsilon}(\mathbf{x}_{n+k}, t_{n+k}) \equiv a_0^C \mathbf{x}_{n+k} + \mathbf{r} + h\mathbf{f}(\mathbf{x}_{n+k}, t_{n+k}) = \mathbf{0}. \quad (13.4.5)$$

The Jacobian of (13.4.5) is

$$\frac{\partial \boldsymbol{\epsilon}}{\partial \mathbf{x}_{n+k}} = \mathbf{M} = a_0^C \mathbf{1} + h \frac{\partial \mathbf{f}(\mathbf{x}_{n+k}, t_{n+k})}{\partial \mathbf{x}_{n+k}} \quad (13.4.6)$$

and $\mathbf{1}$ denotes the unit matrix. Then the Newton-Raphson iteration proceeds as follows:

$$\mathbf{M}^i \Delta \mathbf{x}_{n+k}^i = -\boldsymbol{\epsilon}^i \quad (13.4.7)$$

$$\mathbf{x}_{n+k}^{i+1} = \mathbf{x}_{n+k}^i + \Delta \mathbf{x}_{n+k}^i \quad (13.4.8)$$

where superscript indicates iteration number. Since all multistep formulae are covered by the expressions involving $\mathbf{r}$, the following example will use the simplest corrector, the backward Euler formula.

EXAMPLE 13.4.1. Solve the network in Fig. 13.4.1. Use the forward Euler predictor and backward Euler corrector. The nonlinearity is defined by the relationship $i = v^2$, initial conditions are zero, and $j(t)$ is a unit step. The step size is $h = 0.2$.

The equations describing the network are

$$\begin{bmatrix} 1 & -1 \\ -1 & 2 \end{bmatrix} \begin{bmatrix} dv_1/dt \\ dv_2/dt \end{bmatrix} = \begin{bmatrix} -v_1 + j(t) \\ -v_2^2 \end{bmatrix}.$$

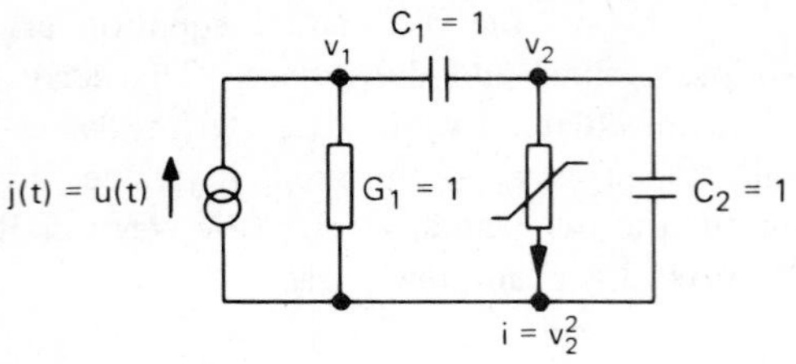

Fig. 13.4.1. Network for Example 13.4.1.

Inverting the matrix and setting $j(t) = u(t)$ gives

$$\mathbf{f}(\mathbf{v}, t) = \begin{bmatrix} dv_1/dt \\ dv_2/dt \end{bmatrix} = \begin{bmatrix} -2v_1 + 2 - v_2^2 \\ -v_1 + 1 - v_2^2 \end{bmatrix} .$$

For the given initial conditions $\mathbf{f}^0 = [2 \quad 1]^t$ and the Euler formula provides

$$\begin{bmatrix} v_1^P \\ v_2^P \end{bmatrix} = \begin{bmatrix} 0 \\ 0 \end{bmatrix} + h \begin{bmatrix} 2 \\ 1 \end{bmatrix} = \begin{bmatrix} 2h \\ h \end{bmatrix} .$$

For the Newton–Raphson iteration, define (13.4.4):

$$\boldsymbol{\epsilon}(\mathbf{v}_{n+1}, t_{n+1}) \equiv - \begin{bmatrix} v_{1,n+1} - v_{1,n} - h(-2v_{1,n+1} + 2 - v_{2,n+1}^2) \\ v_{2,n+1} - v_{2,n} - h(-v_{1,n+1} + 1 - v_{2,n+1}^2) \end{bmatrix} = \mathbf{0}.$$

The Jacobian is

$$\mathbf{M} = - \begin{bmatrix} 1 & 0 \\ 0 & 1 \end{bmatrix} + h \begin{bmatrix} -2 & -2v_{2,n+1} \\ -1 & -2v_{2,n+1} \end{bmatrix} .$$

Several steps are given below. In each step, the last value represents the solution. The Newton–Raphson algorithm needed only three iterations to reduce the correction below 10^{-6}:

	v_1	v_2	Δv_1	Δv_2
Step 1	0.28342	0.14011	–0.1166*D*-00	–0.5989*D*-01
	0.28293	0.13952	–0.4890*D*-03	–0.5868*D*-03
	0.28293	0.13952	–0.4694*D*-07	–0.5633*D*-07
Step 2	0.48086	0.23301	–0.3551*D*-01	–0.4603*D*-01
	0.48008	0.23268	–0.2803*D*-03	–0.3363*D*-03
	0.48008	0.23268	–0.1496*D*-07	–0.1796*D*-07
Step 3	0.61656	0.29248	–0.6065*D*-01	–0.3336*D*-01
	0.61642	0.29230	–0.1445*D*-03	–0.1734*D*-03
	0.61642	0.29230	–0.3902*D*-07	–0.4682*D*-07

13.5. BACKWARD DIFFERENTIATION WITH VARIABLE STEP AND ORDER

We now turn our attention to the application of the BDF formulae for situations where the step size or order may change from step to step to better adapt to the local behavior of the solution. As before, let there be k known previous solutions $x_n, x_{n+1}, \ldots, x_{n+k-1}$ at $t_n, t_{n+1}, \ldots, t_{n+k-1}$. The predictor uses these values and its order is $(k - 1)$. Once the predicted value x_{n+k} has been obtained, the corrector formula uses the new value and discards the value x_n. Because of the step size variation, h will denote *only* the current step

$$h = t_{n+k} - t_{n+k-1}. \tag{13.5.1}$$

The situation is sketched in Fig. 13.5.1 along with some results to be given below.

A polynomial passing through the known points is given as before by

$$x_{k-1}(t) = \sum_{i=0}^{k-1} d_i \left(\frac{t_{n+k} - t}{h}\right)^i = \sum_{i=0}^{k-1} d_i \tau^i. \tag{13.5.2}$$

For the general point x_{n+k-j} at t_{n+k-j} we introduce the notation

$$\tau_j = \frac{t_{n+k} - t_{n+k-j}}{h}. \tag{13.5.3}$$

Then

$$x_{n+k-j} = \sum_{i=0}^{k-1} d_i \tau_j^i. \tag{13.5.4}$$

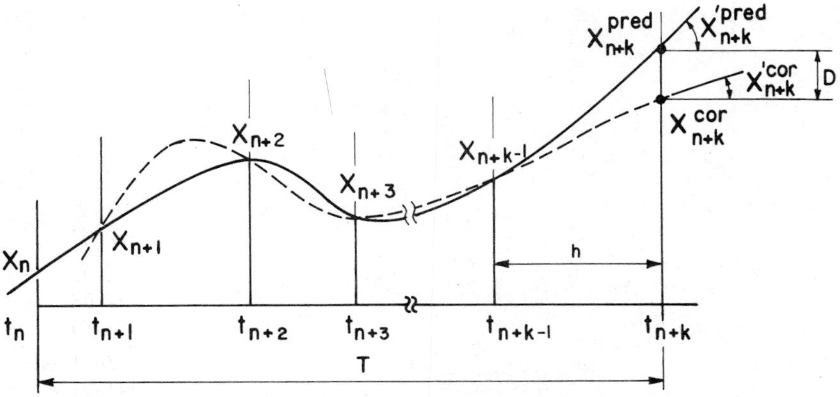

Fig. 13.5.1. Error estimate for a multistep formula with unequal steps. The values D, T, and h refer to Eq. (13.5.13).

Since $\tau_0 = 0$ for $t = t_{n+k}$, the function and derivative values at this time are

$$x_{n+k} = d_0 \tag{13.5.5}$$

$$x'_{n+k} = -\frac{1}{h} d_1. \tag{13.5.6}$$

Following the same development as in Section 13.1, the predictor using points $x_n, x_{n+1}, \ldots, x_{n+k-1}$ has order $(k - 1)$ and is defined by the following matrix equation:

$$\begin{bmatrix} 1 & 1 & 1 & \cdots & 1 \\ 1 & \tau_2 & \tau_2^2 & \cdots & \tau_2^{k-1} \\ \vdots & \vdots & \vdots & & \vdots \\ 1 & \tau_k & \tau_k^2 & \cdots & \tau_k^{k-1} \end{bmatrix} \begin{bmatrix} d_0^P \\ d_1^P \\ \vdots \\ d_{k-1}^P \end{bmatrix} = \begin{bmatrix} x_{n+k-1} \\ x_{n+k-2} \\ \vdots \\ x_n \end{bmatrix} \tag{13.5.7}$$

or

$$\mathbf{V}^P \mathbf{d}^P = \mathbf{z}^P. \tag{13.5.8}$$

Solving the transpose system (13.1.16) instead, we arrive at

$$x_{n+k} = d_0 = \sum_{j=1}^{k} a_j^P x_{n+k-j}. \tag{13.5.9}$$

For the corrector, assume that x_{n+k} is known. The set of equations for a polynomial of the same order as the predictor will be

$$\begin{bmatrix} 1 & 0 & 0 & \cdots & 0 \\ 1 & 1 & 1 & \cdots & 1 \\ \vdots & \vdots & \vdots & & \vdots \\ 1 & \tau_{k-1} & \tau_{k-1}^2 & \cdots & \tau_{k-1}^{k-1} \end{bmatrix} \begin{bmatrix} d_0^C \\ d_1^C \\ \vdots \\ d_{k-1}^C \end{bmatrix} = \begin{bmatrix} x_{n+k} \\ x_{n+k-1} \\ \vdots \\ x_{n+1} \end{bmatrix} \tag{13.5.10}$$

or

$$\mathbf{V}^C \mathbf{d}^C = \mathbf{z}^C. \tag{13.5.11}$$

Solving the transpose system (13.1.26) instead, we obtain

$$x'_{n+k} = -\frac{1}{h} \sum_{j=0}^{k-1} a_j^C x_{n+k-j}. \tag{13.5.12}$$

The matrices $\mathbf{V}^P$ and $\mathbf{V}^C$ may change at each step.

Adjustment of step size requires an estimate of the error committed by a given BDF formula and a given step size. Various formulae are given in the literature. Brayton [3, 4] compared them and concluded that the correct formula is

$$E = \frac{h(x_{n+k}^C - x_{n+k}^P)}{a_0^C(t_{n+k} - t_n)} = \frac{hD}{a_0^C T}. \tag{13.5.13}$$

Here x_{n+k}^C is the result obtained by the corrector when the iterations have converged, x_{n+k}^P is the result obtained by the predictor of the same order and a_0^C is the first coefficient in (13.5.12). The quantities h, D, and T are shown in Fig. 13.5.1 for easy visualization. It is seen that the predictor not only speeds up the N-R iteration by providing a good initial estimate for the corrector but serves in the expression for error control as well.

The choice of the next step size is based on various considerations, one of them given here. The user usually knows the total time span over which he needs his results and also knows the error he will tolerate at the end. Define the error allowed per unit time as

$$\epsilon = \frac{\text{permitted error at } t_{\text{end}}}{t_{\text{end}}}. \tag{13.5.14}$$

The value ϵ is used at each step to monitor the error. Assume that a step has been completed with a given h_{old} and an estimated error E_{old}. Use of (13.5.14) anticipates

$$E_{\text{new}} \approx h_{\text{new}}\,\epsilon. \tag{13.5.15}$$

Since the approximation was of order $k - 1$, the first nonzero coefficient of the Taylor expansion (see (13.2.15)) in both the old and new step will be of the following form:

$$E_{\text{old}} \approx h_{\text{old}}^k C_k x^{(k)}(\theta)/k!$$

$$E_{\text{new}} \approx h_{\text{new}}^k C_k x^{(k)}(\theta)/k!$$

where θ is some intermediate time point. Assuming that the kth derivative of x varies slowly, their ratio provides

$$E_{\text{new}} \approx \frac{h_{\text{new}}^k}{h_{\text{old}}^k} E_{\text{old}}.$$

Comparing with (13.5.15) we see that

$$\epsilon h_{\text{new}} \approx \frac{h_{\text{new}}^k}{h_{\text{old}}^k} E_{\text{old}} \tag{13.5.16}$$

from which the estimate of h_{new} could be calculated for a scalar equation. Since we generally have a system of equations, define

$$\eta = \frac{h_{\text{new}}}{h_{\text{old}}} \tag{13.5.17}$$

and use it in (13.5.16) to get

$$\eta_j = \left| \frac{\epsilon h_{\text{old}}}{E_{\text{old},\, j}} \right|^{1/(k-1)}. \tag{13.5.18}$$

Calculate η_j for *each* variable to be controlled in the system and select the *smallest* η. The new step size for the system follows from (13.5.17):

$$h_{\text{new}} = h_{\text{old}} (\min \eta_j). \tag{13.5.19}$$

For the decision about the *order* of the approximation, one must have E_{k-1}, E_k, E_{k+1}, find the appropriate η in each case, and select the order which provides the *largest* h_{new}. Since full evaluation of all three cases is too costly, the estimates E_{k-1} and E_{k+1} can be found by using x_{n+k}^C, obtained at the end of corrector iteration of the order currently used, and predictor values of orders lower and higher by one, respectively. The decision about the change of the order can be made either at each step or after several steps.

The iteration starts from given initial conditions using the zeroth-order predictor, $x_1^P = x_0$. The error E_1 can thus be evaluated after the first step and the above description applies for all k.

Actual implementation of a variable-step-size, variable-order routine will depend on the complexity and efficiency which is required. If the whole range of BDF formulae has to be considered, then it is advisable to use *divided differences* instead of the method explained here. Considerable savings in computation and improved accuracy are secured, but the problem requires extensive additional studies on the part of the reader [5]. In some cases [6], only the first and second order BDF formulae are used. There are three reasons for such a decision. First, the problem simplifies considerably. Second, although stability theory is not available for variable step sizes, it is argued that a formula having excellent stability properties in the case of equal steps will retain many of these properties even in the case of unequal steps. Methods for detecting unstable behavior and adjusting the algorithm accordingly are available [7]. Finally, the storage overhead is significantly reduced. Formulae derived by means of (13.5.1) through (13.5.12) are collected in Table 13.5.1 for orders up to 2.

Table 13.5.1. Explicit Formulae for Predictors and Correctors Up to Order 2.

Order $k-1$	k	Predictor	Corrector
0	1	$x_{n+1} = x_n$	$x'_{n+1} = 0$
1	2	$a_1^P = \tau_2/(\tau_2 - 1)$ $a_2^P = -1/(\tau_2 - 1)$ $x_{n+2} = a_1^P x_{n+1} + a_2^P x_n$	$a_0^C = -1$ $a_1^C = 1$ $x'_{n+2} = -\frac{1}{h}(a_0^C x_{n+2} + a_1^C x_{n+1})$
2	3	$D^P = (\tau_3 - \tau_2)(1 + \tau_2\tau_3 - \tau_2 - \tau_3)$ $a_1^P = \tau_2\tau_3(\tau_3 - \tau_2)/D^P$ $a_2^P = \tau_3(1 - \tau_3)/D^P$ $a_3^P = \tau_2(\tau_2 - 1)/D^P$ $x_{n+3} = a_1^P x_{n+2} + a_2^P x_{n+1} + a_3^P x_n$	$D^C = \tau_2(\tau_2 - 1)$ $a_0^C = (1 - \tau_2^2)/D^C$ $a_1^C = \tau_2^2/D^C$ $a_2^C = -1/D^C$ $x'_{n+3} = -\frac{1}{h}(a_0^C x_{n+3} + a_1^C x_{n+2} + a_2^C x_{n+1})$

13.6 TABLEAU AND MODIFIED NODAL FORMULATIONS OF NONLINEAR NETWORKS

Nonlinear elements are incorporated into the tableau and modified nodal formulations quite simply. There is no change in the topological equations as the KVL and KCL are independent of the branch relations. Linear elements are incorporated as before and have linear constitutive equations. Nonlinear elements will, in general, be in implicit form. For resistive branches,

$$p(v_R, i_R) = w_R. \tag{13.6.1}$$

Nonlinear capacitors and inductors are best incorporated by introducing their charges and fluxes as additional variables, because this makes the differential relationships linear. For capacitive branches,

$$\begin{aligned} C(v_C, q_C) &= 0 \\ i_C &= \frac{d}{dt} q_C \end{aligned} \tag{13.6.2}$$

and for inductive branches,

$$\begin{aligned} L(i_L, \phi_L) &= 0 \\ v_L &= \frac{d}{dt} \phi_L. \end{aligned} \tag{13.6.3}$$

Often, the nonlinearities may be expressed in explicit forms. For resistors

$$\begin{aligned} i_R &= g(v_R) \\ v_R &= r(i_R) \end{aligned} \tag{13.6.4}$$

and similarly for the first equations of the inductive and capacitive branches. Note that the charges and fluxes of nonlinear elements must be taken into the vector of unknowns. Introduction of these variables allows us to write both the tableau or modified nodal formulations in the following form:

$$\mathbf{f}(\mathbf{x}', \mathbf{x}, \mathbf{w}, t) \equiv \mathbf{E}\mathbf{x}' + \mathbf{G}\mathbf{x} + \mathbf{p}(\mathbf{x}) - \mathbf{w} = \mathbf{0} \tag{13.6.5}$$

where **E** and **G** are now constant matrices and all nonlinearities are collected in $\mathbf{p}(\mathbf{x})$.

Solution of (13.6.5) by means of the BDF formulae and the Newton-Raphson algorithm needs the function vector

$$\mathbf{f}_{n+k} \equiv \mathbf{f}(\mathbf{x}'_{n+k}, \mathbf{x}_{n+k}, \mathbf{w}_{n+k}, t_{n+k}) = \mathbf{E}\mathbf{x}'_{n+k} + \mathbf{G}\mathbf{x}_{n+k} + \mathbf{p}(\mathbf{x}_{n+k}) - \mathbf{w}_{n+k} \tag{13.6.6}$$

and the Jacobian

$$\mathbf{M}_{n+k} = \frac{\partial \mathbf{f}_{n+k}}{\partial \mathbf{x}_{n+k}} = \mathbf{E}\frac{\partial \mathbf{x}'_{n+k}}{\partial \mathbf{x}_{n+k}} + \mathbf{G} + \frac{\partial \mathbf{p}(\mathbf{x}_{n+k})}{\partial \mathbf{x}_{n+k}}. \tag{13.6.7}$$

Since from (13.5.12) we have for each x'_{n+k}

$$x'_{n+k} = -\frac{1}{h}\sum_{j=0}^{k-1} a_j^C x_{n+k-j} \tag{13.6.8}$$

we get

$$\frac{\partial \mathbf{x}'_{n+k}}{\partial \mathbf{x}_{n+k}} = -\frac{1}{h} a_0^C \mathbf{1} \tag{13.6.9}$$

and the Jacobian (13.6.7) becomes

$$\mathbf{M}_{n+k} = -\frac{a_0^C}{h}\mathbf{E} + \mathbf{G} + \frac{\partial \mathbf{p}(\mathbf{x}_{n+k})}{\partial \mathbf{x}_{n+k}}. \tag{13.6.10}$$

Additional comments on the form of the Jacobian will be given later in this section. Since all equations have now been derived, the algorithm for the integration of nonlinear algebraic differential equations can be given. The steps apply for any order, including the start from initial conditions.

Let the k previous solutions at times $t_n, t_{n+1}, \ldots, t_{n+k-1}$ be denoted as the vectors $\mathbf{x}_n, \mathbf{x}_{n+1}, \ldots, \mathbf{x}_{n+k-1}$.

1. Select the step size h using (13.5.19) and calculate the coefficients a_j^P and a_j^C used in Eqns. (13.5.9) and (13.5.12).
2. Predict x_{n+k}^P using (13.5.9) for each variable. Form the vector $\mathbf{x}_{n+k}^P$.
3. Calculate x'_{n+k} using (13.5.12) for every equation containing x' and form the vector $\mathbf{x}'_{n+k}$.
4. Calculate the function vector (13.6.6).
5. Calculate the Jacobian (13.6.10).
6. Apply the Newton-Raphson algorithm. This will require repeated use of steps 3, 4, 5.
7. Calculate the error (13.5.13) for every equation. If the error is too large, reject the solution, reduce h and go to step 2.
8. The step has been completed. Set $n = n + 1$, denote the previous step as h_{old} and the error vector as $\mathbf{E}_{\text{old}}$.
9. Calculate η_j from (13.5.18) and find the smallest entry.
10. If the decision on the order is not pending at this step, calculate $h_{\text{new}} = h_{\text{old}}(\min \eta_j)$ and go to step 2. Else go to step 11.
11. Determine the error vectors $\mathbf{E}_{k-1}$ and $\mathbf{E}_{k+1}$. Find the corresponding $\min \eta_j$ and use the order that gives the largest $\min \eta_j$. Compute the step size h_{new} and go to step 2.

The following discussion will comment on the form of the Jacobian (13.6.10). It will be best understood if we start by considering a linear network in the modified nodal formulation. In such case the function $\mathbf{p}(\mathbf{x}) \equiv \mathbf{0}$ and $\mathbf{E}$ becomes identical to the matrix $\mathbf{C}$ while $\mathbf{G}$ will be the same as discussed in Chapter 4. Thus any linear conductance appears in the Jacobian in the same position as in the linear admittance formulation. A nonlinear conductor will be described by (13.6.4) and the derivative $G_n = \partial g(v)/\partial v$ will enter the Jacobian in the same way as a linear conductor of value G_n would enter the admittance matrix.

A nonlinear capacitor (inductor) will be represented by two equations and the charge q (flux ϕ) will become an additional unknown. This differs from the linear formulation where the charges and fluxes are generally not considered. However, if we decided to handle linear capacitors and inductors by introducing their charges and fluxes, the form of the Jacobian would again be identical to the form of the matrix in the linear formulation.

In summary, the Jacobian will have identical structure to the linear case. It will, in general, be sparse, and sparse matrix methods can be employed in solving the Newton-Raphson iterations. Wherever s appeared in the linear formulation, its equivalent $-a_0^C/h$ will multiply the appropriate value of the element.

EXAMPLE 13.6.1. Write the modified nodal equations and the Jacobian matrix for the network shown in Fig. 13.6.1. The capacitors C_1, C_2 and conductance G_1 are linear. The current through the diode is given by $i_D = e^{kv_D} - 1$ and the nonlinear capacitor is governed by the charge relationship $q = C_3(1 + v^2)$.

The equations are

$$\mathbf{f}(v_1, v_2, q, t) \equiv \begin{bmatrix} G_1 v_1 + C_1 v_1' + q' - j \\ e^{kv_2} - 1 + C_2 v_2' - q' \\ C_3[1 + (v_1 - v_2)^2] - q \end{bmatrix} = \begin{bmatrix} 0 \\ 0 \\ 0 \end{bmatrix}.$$

The Jacobian is written directly:

$$\mathbf{M} = \begin{bmatrix} \left[G_1 + C_1 \dfrac{dv_1'}{dv_1}\right] & 0 & \dfrac{dq'}{dq} \\ 0 & \left[ke^{kv_2} + C_2 \dfrac{dv_2'}{dv_2}\right] & -\dfrac{dq'}{dq} \\ 2C_3(v_1 - v_2) & -2C_3(v_1 - v_2) & -1 \end{bmatrix}.$$

The reader may wish to identify the matrices $\mathbf{E}$, $\mathbf{G}$ and $\partial\mathbf{p}(\mathbf{x})/\partial\mathbf{x}$ in the formal expression (13.6.10). They are

$$\mathbf{E} = \begin{bmatrix} C_1 & 0 & 1 \\ 0 & C_2 & -1 \\ 0 & 0 & 0 \end{bmatrix}; \qquad \mathbf{G} = \begin{bmatrix} G_1 & 0 & 0 \\ 0 & 0 & 0 \\ 0 & 0 & -1 \end{bmatrix}$$

$$\frac{\partial\mathbf{p}(\mathbf{x})}{\partial\mathbf{x}} = \begin{bmatrix} 0 & 0 & 0 \\ 0 & ke^{kv_2} & 0 \\ 2C_3(v_1 - v_2) & -2C_3(v_1 - v_2) & 0 \end{bmatrix}.$$

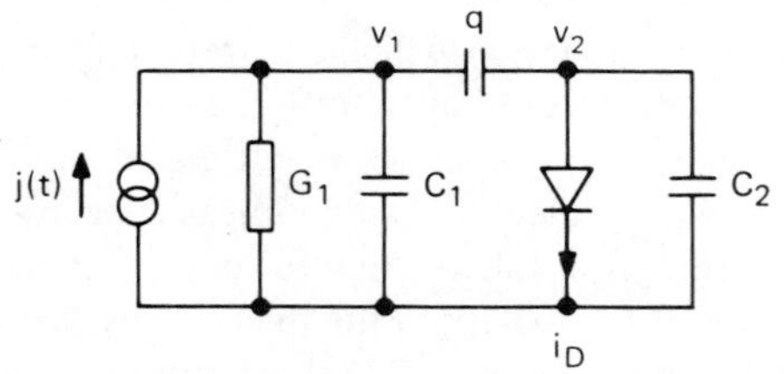

Fig. 13.6.1. Newtork for Example 13.6.1.

PROBLEMS

P.13.1. Solve Problems P.9.6 using second-order Gear's predictor and corrector. In order to proceed, find the solution at $t = 0.1$ by reducing the step to 0.05, take two steps by the Euler forward-backward combination and then proceed with the specified step $h = 0.1$.

P.13.2. Apply the Adams–Bashforth and Adams–Moulton formulae as in Problem P.13.1.

P.13.3. Solve the following systems by the forward and backward Euler formulae at the first two steps, then proceed with the second-order Gear's formulae:

(a) $x_1' = -tx_2;$ $\quad x_1(0) = 1$

$x_2' = x_1/t;$ $\quad x_2(0) = 0$

(b) $x_1' = (x_2 - x_1)\,t;$ $\quad x_1(0) = 1$

$x_2' = (x_2 + x_1)\,t;$ $\quad x_2(0) = 1$

(c) $x_1' = x_2 + x_3;$ $\quad x_1(0) = -1$

$x_2' = x_1 + x_3;$ $\quad x_2(0) = 1$

$x_3' = x_1 - x_2;$ $\quad x_3(0) = 0$

(d) $x_1' = x_2 - 2x_3;$ $\quad x_1(0) = 1$

$x_2' = x_3 - x_1;$ $\quad x_2(0) = 1$

$x_3' = 2x_1 - x_2;$ $\quad x_3(0) = 1$

(e) $x_1' = x_1 - x_2 + x_3;$ $\quad x_1(0) = 1$

$x_2' = x_1 + 2.25\,x_2 - x_3;$ $\quad x_2(0) = 1$

$x_3' = -x_1 + x_2 + x_3;$ $\quad x_3(0) = 1$

P.13.4. Higher-order differential equations can always be reduced to systems of first-order differential equations. For instance, the second-order differential equation

$$x'' + tx' + x^2 - 1 = 0$$

can be redefined by setting $x' = z$ into the system

$$x' = z$$

$$z' = 1 - tz - x^2.$$

Apply this method to the following higher-order differential equations. Use the Euler first-order formulae, step size $h = 0.1$ and interval (0, 1).

(a) $x'' = 1 + (1 - t)\sin^2 x - \frac{3}{2}t$ $\qquad x(0) = 0, \quad x'(0) = 0.5$

(b) $x'' = \dfrac{t}{1 + t} + \cos x - t$ $\qquad x(0) = 0, \quad x'(0) = 0.5$

(c) $x'' = -\dfrac{2x}{t} - x$ $\qquad x(0) = 1, \quad x'(0) = 0$

REFERENCES

1. G. Dahlquist: A special stability problem for linear multistep methods. *BIT*, Vol. 3, pp. 27–43, 1963.
2. C. W. Gear: *Numerical Initial Value Problems in Ordinary Differential Equations*. Prentice-Hall, Englewood Cliffs, NJ, 1971.
3. R. K. Brayton: Error estimates for the variable-step backward differentiation methods. IBM Research Report RC 6205 (#26655), September 1976.
4. R. K. Brayton, F. G. Gustavson, and G. D. Hachtel: A new efficient algorithm for solving differential-algebraic systems using implicit backward differentiation formulas. *Proc. IEEE*, Vol. 60, No. 1, pp. 98–108, January 1972.
5. W. M. G. van Bokhoven: Linear implicit differentiation formulas of variable step and order. *IEEE Trans. on Circuits and Systems*, Vol. CAS-22, No. 2, pp. 109–115, February 1975.
6. D. A. Zein, C. W. Ho, and A. J. Gruodis: A new interactive circuit design program in APL. *1980 International Symposium on Circuits and Systems*, pp. 913–917.
7. S. Skelboe: The control of order and steplength for backward differentiation methods. *BIT*, pp. 91–107, 1977.

CHAPTER 14
Digital and Switched-Capacitor Networks

The purpose of this chapter is to show that the mathematical and computational methods covered earlier in this book are applicable to other kinds of circuits than those already considered. In particular, we look at digital and switched-capacitor networks.

Digital networks operate on sampled signals and can, in fact, be viewed as special purpose computers which provide storage elements, delays, and multiplications. Digital networks are superior to analog networks in low-frequency applications, such as oil exploration or seismic research, where signals well below one Hz may occur and where real time application does not present problems. In audio frequency regions, analog and digital systems may compete and much depends on technological progress. The first three sections of this chapter show that once the reader is familiar with the principles and terminology, he will be able to apply all the linear-network computational methods of this book without any change to digital networks.

Switched-capacitor networks are an entirely new and highly promising development and have the potential of taking over many applications in the audio and intermediate frequency regions. For a long time, analog networks suffered from the disadvantage that present day MOS technology cannot easily produce resistors. This, in turn, prevented integration of analog networks. Switched-capacitor networks simulate resistors by rapidly switching capacitors. Since capacitors and transistors are easy to manufacture on a chip, integration of analog systems became possible. It is now very likely that these networks will take over most of the applications which require integration and in some cases will be useful even without integration. Theoretical treatment of these networks is considerably more difficult than the treatment of analog networks but

Sections 14.4–14.11 show that most of the methods discussed in this book are still applicable once the formulation difficulties have been overcome.

Analysis of digital networks is coded in Appendix D.

14.1. DISCRETE SIGNALS

Discrete signals are usually represented as a sequence of values occurring at regular intervals. For instance, the step sequence, $u(n)$, is defined as follows:

$$u(n) = \begin{cases} 1, & \text{for} \quad n \geqslant 0 \\ 0, & \text{for} \quad n < 0 \end{cases} \tag{14.1.1}$$

and is shown in Fig. 14.1.1(a). This corresponds to the unit step in analog signals. A delta sequence is defined by

$$\delta(n) = \begin{cases} 1, & \text{for} \quad n = 0 \\ 0, & \text{for} \quad n \neq 0 \end{cases} \tag{14.1.2}$$

and is shown in Fig. 14.1.1(b). It is a single value occurring at $n = 0$, and corresponds to the Dirac impulse of the analog domain. If this signal is shifted by k units of the sequence, then

$$\delta(n - k) = \begin{cases} 1, & \text{for} \quad n = k \\ 0, & \text{for} \quad n \neq k. \end{cases} \tag{14.1.3}$$

A sequence of impulses having heights $x(k)$ can be written in the form

$$x(n) = \sum_{k=-\infty}^{+\infty} x(k)\, \delta(n - k). \tag{14.1.4}$$

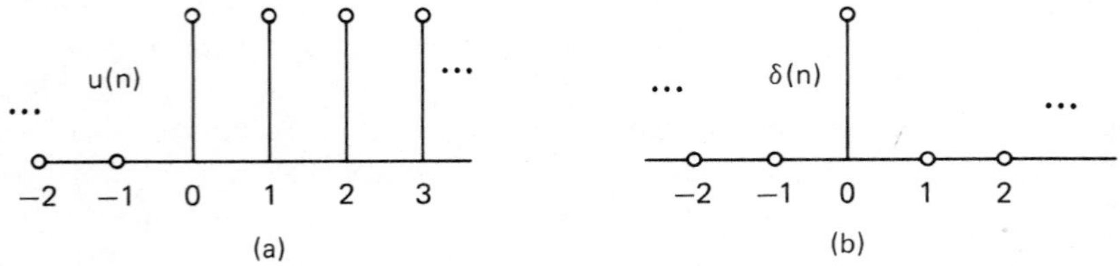

Fig. 14.1.1. Step and Dirac sequences.

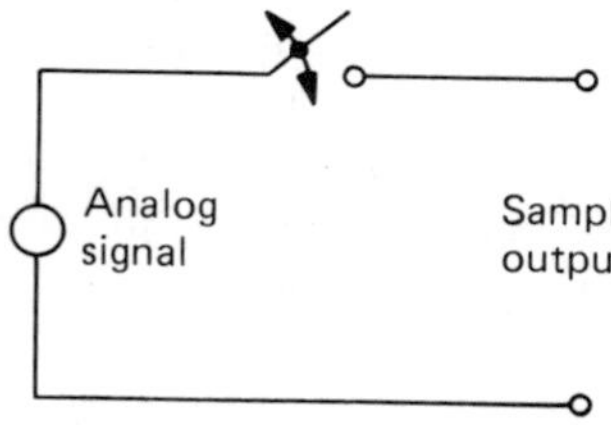

Fig. 14.1.2. Generation of a sampled signal. The switch closes periodically for very short times.

This signal can be generated from an analog signal by periodically closing a switch, as shown in Fig. 14.1.2. The switch is open for all times except for $t = k$.

Consider a linear time invariant system which operates on the discrete signal sequence. This is schematically shown in Fig. 14.1.3, where $\mathcal{H}$ represents an operator. The output sequence will be

$$y(n) = \mathcal{H}\,[w(n)] = \mathcal{H}\left[\sum w(k)\,\delta(n-k)\right].$$

If $\mathcal{H}$ is assumed to be a linear operator, then

$$y(n) = \sum w(k)\,\mathcal{H}\,[\delta(n-k)]\,.$$

Further, if we assume shift invariance, then

$$h(n-k) = \mathcal{H}\,[\delta(n-k)]$$

where $h(n)$ is the impulse response of the network to the sequence $\delta(n)$. Thus, finally,

$$y(n) = \sum w(k)\,h(n-k). \tag{14.1.5}$$

In the following discussion, we will only deal with linear shift invariant systems.

Substituting $k = n - m$ in (14.1.5) we get $\Sigma_{n=-\infty}^{+\infty}\ w(n-m)\,h(m)$. Replacing the index m by another index k cannot change the equation; thus

$$y(n) = \sum_{k=-\infty}^{+\infty} w(k)\,h(n-k) = \sum_{k=-\infty}^{+\infty} w(n-k)\,h(k). \tag{14.1.6}$$

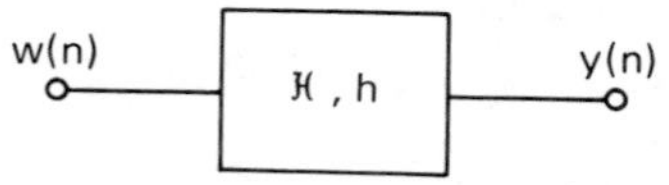

Fig. 14.1.3. Symbol for a digital network, its input and output.

This expression is the discrete equivalent of the *convolution theorem* in analog systems.

The output of the network shown schematically in Fig. 14.1.3 may be a combination of previous inputs or previous inputs and outputs. In general, a linear system will be described by the *difference equation*

$$\sum a_k y(n-k) - \sum b_k w(n-k) = 0 \qquad (14.1.7)$$

which resembles the equation for linear multistep formulae we dealt with in Chapter 13. In order to solve the equation, we must know the initial conditions. If the output at a step depends only on the present and past m inputs and past outputs, then the system is *causal* and Eq. (14.1.7) can be rewritten at the nth time step as follows:

$$a_0 y(n) = -\sum_{k=1}^{n} a_k y(n-k) + \sum_{k=0}^{m} b_k w(n-k).$$

The constant a_0 is usually assumed to be equal to one. If the system output depends on inputs only, e.g., all $a_k = 0$ for $k = 1, 2, \ldots, n$, then it is called a *finite impulse response* system; otherwise it is called an *infinite impulse response* system.

EXAMPLE 14.1.1. Calculate the responses of systems described by:

(a) $y(n) = w(n) + w(n-1) + w(n-2)$ for $w(n) = u(n)$ = step sequence

(b) $y(n) = w(n) + 0.6y(n-1)$ for $w(n) = \delta(n)$ = impulse sequence

let $y(-1) = 0$

Solution:

(a) $y(0) = w(0) = 1$

$y(1) = w(1) + w(0) = 2$

$y(2) = w(2) + w(1) + w(0) = 3$

$y(3) = w(3) + w(2) + w(1) = 3$

$\vdots$

$y(n) = w(n) + w(n-1) + w(n-2) = 3, \quad \text{for } n \geqslant 2.$

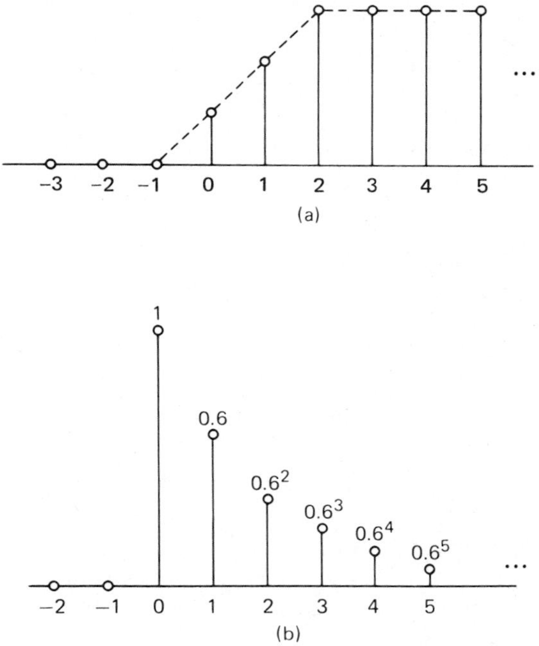

Fig. 14.1.4. Responses of the difference equations in Example 14.1.1.

The response is shown in Fig. 14.1.4(a).

(b) $y(0) = w(0) = 1$

$$y(1) = w(1) + 0.6y(0) = 0 + 0.6 = 0.6$$

$$y(2) = w(2) + 0.6y(1) = 0 + 0.6^2 = 0.6^2$$

$$y(3) = 0 + 0.6y(2) = 0.6^3$$

$$\vdots$$

$$y(n) = 0.6^n, \quad \text{for } n \geqslant 0.$$

The response is shown in Fig. 14.1.4(b).

One of the more important signals is the *sinusoid*. It can be visualized as the real projection of a vector rotating with constant angular velocity. If the signal is sampled at a constant rate higher than the angular frequency, we get the situation indicated in Fig. 14.1.5. The frequency of rotation of the vector is given

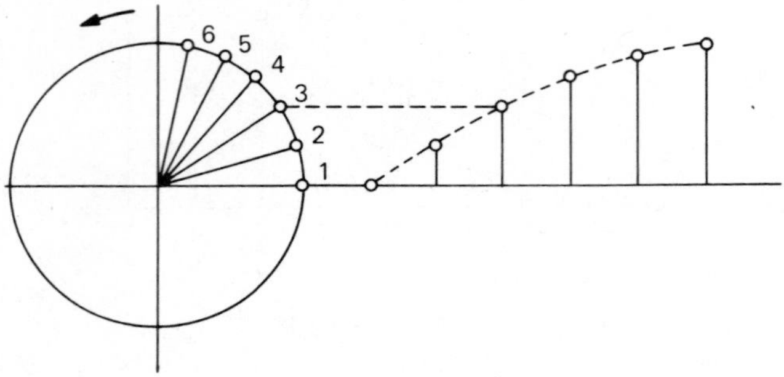

Fig. 14.1.5. Sampled sinusoid.

by $\omega = 2\pi f$ rad/sec. The signal can be considered as the real part of the *phasor*:

$$w(t) = e^{j\omega t}.$$

Sampling at every T time units, this can be written as

$$w(nT) = e^{j\omega nT}. \tag{14.1.8}$$

Let us now insert this signal into (14.1.6). The output will be

$$y(nT) = \sum_{k=-\infty}^{+\infty} h(kT)\, e^{j\omega T(n-k)} = e^{j\omega nT} \sum_{k=-\infty}^{+\infty} h(kT)\, e^{-j\omega kT}$$

or

$$y(nT) = w(nT) \sum_{k=-\infty}^{+\infty} h(kT)\, e^{-j\omega kT}. \tag{14.1.9}$$

At this point we can define the *frequency domain transfer function* of the system:

$$H(e^{j\omega T}) = \sum_{k=-\infty}^{+\infty} h(kT)\, e^{-j\omega kT}. \tag{14.1.10}$$

The expression is usually normalized by setting $T = 1$. We can now see that $H(e^{j\omega})$ is a periodic function in ω since $e^{j\omega} = e^{j(\omega + 2m\pi)}$, m being an arbitrary integer. Periodic functions can be analyzed by means of *Fourier series*, which gives

$$H(e^{j\omega}) = \sum_{k=-\infty}^{\infty} h(k)\, e^{-j\omega k}$$
$$h(k) = \frac{1}{2\pi}\int_{-\pi}^{\pi} H(e^{j\omega})\, e^{j\omega k}\, d\omega. \qquad (14.1.11)$$

In fact, every periodic signal itself can be decomposed into a series. If we have a periodic sequence $w(k)$, then it can be expressed as follows:

$$W(e^{j\omega}) = \sum_{k=-\infty}^{\infty} w(k)\, e^{-j\omega k}$$
$$w(k) = \frac{1}{2\pi}\int_{-\pi}^{\pi} W(e^{j\omega})\, e^{j\omega k}\, d\omega. \qquad (14.1.12)$$

If such a signal is applied to a system with the transfer function $H(e^{j\omega})$, then the output will be

$$Y(e^{j\omega}) = H(e^{j\omega})\, W(e^{j\omega}). \qquad (14.1.13)$$

Equation (14.1.13) is the *Fourier-series transformation* of the discrete convolution (14.1.6).

EXAMPLE 14.1.2. Evaluate the transfer function for the system

$$y(n) = w(n) + 0.5w(n-1) + 0.2w(n-2)$$

by assuming that the input signal is $w(n) = e^{j\omega n}$.

Inserting the signal into the difference equation gives

$$y(n) = e^{j\omega n} + 0.5e^{j\omega(n-1)} + 0.2e^{j\omega(n-2)}$$
$$= e^{j\omega n}[1 + 0.5e^{-j\omega} + 0.2e^{-j2\omega}].$$

Comparing with (14.1.13), the transfer function is

$$H(e^{j\omega}) = 1 + 0.5e^{-j\omega} + 0.2e^{-j2\omega}$$
$$= (1 + 0.5\cos\omega + 0.2\cos 2\omega) - j(0.5\sin\omega + 0.2\sin 2\omega).$$

The transfer function is complex and we can evaluate its absolute value or phase as in the case of analog networks.

14.2. z-TRANSFORM

Consider an arbitrary sequence $w(k)$ with normalized sampling interval $T = 1$. If we define

$$z = e^{j\omega} \tag{14.2.1}$$

and insert this into Eq. (14.1.12), the latter changes into

$$W(z) = \sum_{k=-\infty}^{+\infty} w(k)z^{-k}. \tag{14.2.2}$$

This expression has been given the name *z-transform* [1-5]. Depending on the limits of the summation, we can have a *two-sided* z-transform, expressed by the above formula, or a *one-sided* z-transform, in which the lower limit is changed to $k = 0$. For signals starting at $k = 0$, the two-sided transform becomes a one-sided transform.

In order that (14.2.2) be meaningful, the sum must exist and rules governing convergence differ for the one- and two-sided transforms. We will not go into details of z-transform theory, because our aim is to introduce computer methods. Broadly speaking, when dealing with spectra, we use the two-sided transform. When dealing with time-domain response, we usually assume that the signal is zero for $k < 0$. This simplifies many considerations and corresponds to actual situations.

We will need one fundamental rule, the shift-property of the z-transform. Assume that $W(z)$ is defined by (14.2.2). We would like to know the z-transform of the signal $w(k - m)$. Inserting into (14.2.2) and defining $k - m = l$, we get

$$\sum_{k=-\infty}^{+\infty} w(k-m)z^{-k} = \sum_{l=-\infty}^{+\infty} w(l)z^{-m-l} = z^{-m} \sum_{l=-\infty}^{+\infty} w(l)z^{-l}$$
$$= z^{-m} W(z).$$

A delay of the signal by m units results in the multiplication of the z-transform by z^{-m}. This is usually expressed symbolically as follows

$$\begin{aligned} &\text{if:} && \mathcal{Z}[w(k)] = W(z) \\ &\text{then:} && \mathcal{Z}[w(k-m)] = z^{-m} W(z). \end{aligned} \tag{14.2.3}$$

EXAMPLE 14.2.1. Use the shift rule given by Eq. (14.2.3) and find the transfer function $H(z)$ for the difference equation

$$y(k) - y(k-1) + 0.5y(k-2) = 2w(k-1) - 2w(k-2).$$

Applying (14.2.3) to both variables gives

$$Y(z) - z^{-1}Y(z) + 0.5z^{-2}Y(z) = 2z^{-1}W(z) - 2z^{-2}W(z)$$

or

$$Y(z) = \frac{2z^{-1} - 2z^{-2}}{1 - z^{-1} + 0.5z^{-2}} W(z) = H(z)\,W(z).$$

The z-domain transfer function is

$$H(z) = \frac{2z^{-1} - 2z^{-2}}{1 - z^{-1} + 0.5z^{-2}} = \frac{2z - 2}{z^2 - z + 0.5}.$$

The frequency domain response can be calculated by selecting various values of ω and substituting $z = e^{j\omega}$. The result is complex and we can define absolute value and phase.

Some rules for z-transforms can be established by using the reader's knowledge of Laplace transforms. Let s be the complex frequency and assume analytic continuation by defining complex z as follows:

$$z = e^s.$$

If we now consider points on the imaginary axis of the s-domain, $s = j\omega$, they will be represented in the z-domain by $z = e^{j\omega}$, which is a unit circle with center at the origin of the z-plane. The imaginary axis of the s-domain folds onto the unit circle in the z-domain. What happens to the other points in the s-plane? Let the real part of s, $\text{Re}\, s = a < 0$. Then $z = e^{a+j\omega} = e^a e^{j\omega}$. As a is a negative number, the value $e^a < 1$ and the point lies inside the unit circle of the z-plane. We conclude that points in the left half plane of the s-domain will be represented by points inside the unit circle in the z-domain. Recalling that stable system transfer functions have their poles in the left half plane in the s-domain we conclude that the poles of the transfer function in the z-domain must be inside the unit circle in order to represent a stable system.

EXAMPLE 14.2.2. Determine whether the system function $H(z)$ of Example 14.2.1 represents a stable system.

The denominator is $z^2 - z + 0.5$. Its roots are $z_1, z_2 = 0.5 \pm j0.5$. As $|z_i| = \sqrt{0.5^2 + 0.5^2} = 0.707 < 1$, the system is stable.

Note that we may sometimes work with functions in terms of z^{-1}, as derived in Example 14.2.1. In such case the roots of the denominator in z^{-1} must be *outside* the unit circle in order to have a stable system.

14.3. FORMULATION OF DIGITAL NETWORK EQUATIONS

Let us now turn our attention to the representation of digital systems in the z-domain. We will consider digital networks composed of summers, multipliers, and simple delays, z^{-1}. An equivalent network is drawn for a given difference equation. This process could be called *synthesis* and is not unique; the same difference equation can be represented by several network topologies. As an example, consider the following difference equation:

$$y(k) = w(k) + aw(k-1) + bw(k-2) - cy(k-1) - dy(k-2). \quad (14.3.1)$$

It can be realized by the two digital networks shown in Fig. 14.3.1. In both cases, the transfer function is

$$H(z) = \frac{1 + az^{-1} + bz^{-2}}{1 + cz^{-1} + dz^{-2}}. \quad (14.3.2)$$

Clearly, some realizations will have superior performance compared to others, but we will not go into these questions. For analysis purposes and for the development of the methods, we will simply accept any given digital network.

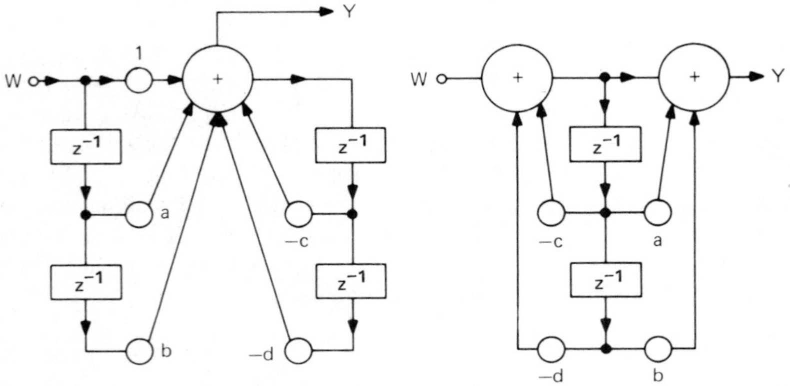

Fig. 14.3.1. Digital networks realizing Eq. (14.3.1).

Figure 14.3.1 is self-explanatory, but it does not help in finding a general method for the formulation of equations. To this end it is advantageous to introduce *flow graphs* and set up some rules:

1. Every multiplier or delay will be represented by an oriented line segment with either the multiplier constant or z^{-1} written next to it.
2. Every summer will be represented by a node. The nodes will be numbered consecutively and the value V_i will be associated with the ith node.

Applying these rules to the networks in Fig. 14.3.1 we obtain the flowgraphs shown in Fig. 14.3.2.

The value at the node, V_i, equals the sum of contributions due to edges *pointing into the node.* Edges leaving the node do not influence its value. Using this rule, we can write the following equations for the graph in Figure 14.3.2(b):

$$V_1 = W - cV_2 - dV_3$$

$$V_2 = z^{-1}V_1$$

$$V_3 = z^{-1}V_2$$

$$V_4 = V_1 + aV_2 + bV_3.$$

Since the values V_i are unknown and W represents the *source*, we transfer all the unknowns to the left side of the equations and rewrite in matrix form:

$$\begin{bmatrix} 1 & c & d & 0 \\ -z^{-1} & 1 & 0 & 0 \\ 0 & -z^{-1} & 1 & 0 \\ -1 & -a & -b & 1 \end{bmatrix} \begin{bmatrix} V_1 \\ V_2 \\ V_3 \\ V_4 \end{bmatrix} = \begin{bmatrix} W \\ 0 \\ 0 \\ 0 \end{bmatrix}. \tag{14.3.3}$$

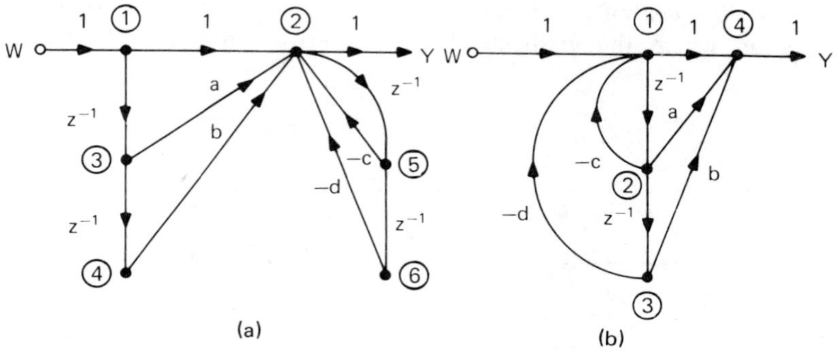

Fig. 14.3.2. Flow graphs for the networks in Fig. 14.3.1.

Study of this equation reveals the following rules for writing the system equations of a digital network:

1. Let an edge on the flow graph go from node i to node j and let it have the multiplier a. Then the value $(-a)$ is entered into the (j, i) position of the matrix. This rule also applies to the delays z^{-1}; see schematic representation in Fig. 14.3.3.
2. The system matrix has unit values on its diagonal.

At this point we can apply most of the frequency domain methods developed in the book. Let us denote the system as follows:

$$\mathbf{TV} = \mathbf{W}. \tag{14.3.4}$$

In addition, let us split the system matrix **T** into two matrices, one containing the multiplier constants and the unit entries and the other one containing entries which are multiplied by z^{-1}. We denote the matrices by **G** and **C**:

$$\mathbf{TV} \equiv (\mathbf{G} + z^{-1}\mathbf{C})\mathbf{V} = \mathbf{W}. \tag{14.3.5}$$

For the above example, the matrices are

$$\mathbf{G} = \begin{bmatrix} 1 & c & d & 0 \\ 0 & 1 & 0 & 0 \\ 0 & 0 & 1 & 0 \\ -1 & -a & -b & 1 \end{bmatrix}; \qquad \mathbf{C} = \begin{bmatrix} 0 & 0 & 0 & 0 \\ -1 & 0 & 0 & 0 \\ 0 & -1 & 0 & 0 \\ 0 & 0 & 0 & 0 \end{bmatrix}. \tag{14.3.6}$$

The following analyses are directly applicable:

1. *Frequency domain analysis.* Select ω, substitute $z^{-1} = e^{-j\omega}$, solve the system by **LU** decomposition.

2. *Sensitivity analysis.* Generation of sensitivities may be meaningful for optimization where the gradient of the objective function with respect to

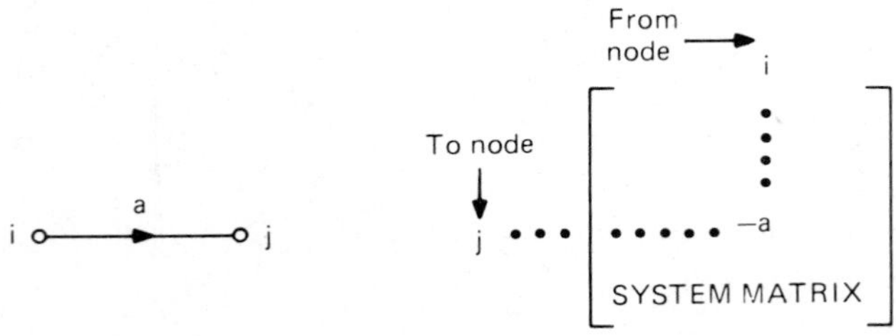

Fig. 14.3.3. Schematic way to enter a value into the system matrix.

multipliers is needed. Both methods of Chapter 6, i.e., the sensitivity network and the transpose system, can be applied directly. Differentiating (14.3.4) with respect to a parameter h gives

$$\begin{gathered}\frac{\partial \mathbf{T}}{\partial h}\mathbf{V} + \mathbf{T}\frac{\partial \mathbf{V}}{\partial h} = \mathbf{0} \\ \mathbf{T}\frac{\partial \mathbf{V}}{\partial h} = -\frac{\partial \mathbf{T}}{\partial h}\mathbf{V}.\end{gathered} \tag{14.3.7}$$

Assume that (14.3.4) has been solved by **LU** decomposition. The right-hand-side vector of (14.3.7) can be generated. Since the matrix **T** has already been decomposed only one additional forward and back substitution on (14.3.7) is required to obtain the sensitivities of *all* system variables with respect to *one* parameter.

In order to derive the transpose system, solve (14.3.7) formally:

$$\frac{\partial \mathbf{V}}{\partial h} = -\mathbf{T}^{-1}\frac{\partial \mathbf{T}}{\partial h}\mathbf{V}. \tag{14.3.8}$$

Let us now define an output function ϕ as a linear combination of the system variables **V**,

$$\phi = \mathbf{d}^t\mathbf{V} \tag{14.3.9}$$

where $\mathbf{d}^t$ is a constant vector. The derivative with respect to h is

$$\frac{\partial \phi}{\partial h} = -\mathbf{d}^t\mathbf{T}^{-1}\frac{\partial \mathbf{T}}{\partial h}\mathbf{V} = (\mathbf{V}^a)^t\frac{\partial \mathbf{T}}{\partial h}\mathbf{V} \tag{14.3.10}$$

where we defined

$$\mathbf{T}^t\mathbf{V}^a = -\mathbf{d}. \tag{14.3.11}$$

Solution of (14.3.11) requires only one additional forward and back substitution, as described in Chapter 6. Note that if h is a multiplier constant, $\partial\mathbf{T}/\partial h$ has only one nonzero entry.

3. *Symbolic analysis.* z^{-1} is a complex variable just as s was in the analog domain. If we select equidistant points on the unit circle and treat them as z_i^{-1}, all the steps given in Chapter 7 for the evaluation of the symbolic function in terms of s are applied without change. The methods explained in Chapter 8 are applied without change as well. Thus the network function can be generated with z^{-1} and the multiplier constants retained as variables.

4. *Poles and zeros and their sensitivities.* The methods of Chapters 7 and 6 apply without change.

Time domain calculations are simpler in digital networks. Since z^{-1} represents a delay, it is convenient to rewrite (14.3.5) in the following form:

$$\mathbf{GV} = -\mathbf{C}(z^{-1}\mathbf{V}) + \mathbf{W}$$

or

$$\mathbf{G}\mathbf{v}(n) = -\mathbf{C}\mathbf{v}(n-1) + \mathbf{w}(n). \tag{14.3.12}$$

Often the network structure is such that by suitable node renumbering **G** can be brought to lower triangular form.

14.4. SWITCHED-CAPACITOR NETWORKS

The use of active networks in the construction of low-frequency filters brought about a major reduction in network size because heavy and bulky inductors were replaced by small transistor elements, capacitors, and resistors. Another major change in the design philosophy of linear analog networks is currently in progress. The reason for it lies in the fact that in the popular MOS technology good quality capacitors and transistors are easy to fabricate but resistors are difficult to realize.

The breakthrough in the full integration of *analog* networks was achieved recently by means of a special simulation in which some capacitors are rapidly switched by means of transistor switches [6-8]. This rapid switching dissects the flow of the current into short impulses with the result that the switched capacitor simulates, roughly speaking, a resistor. To show this, consider Fig. 14.4.1. Switch 1 represents a short circuit during the first clock period, while switch 2 is a short circuit during the second. The average current I flowing

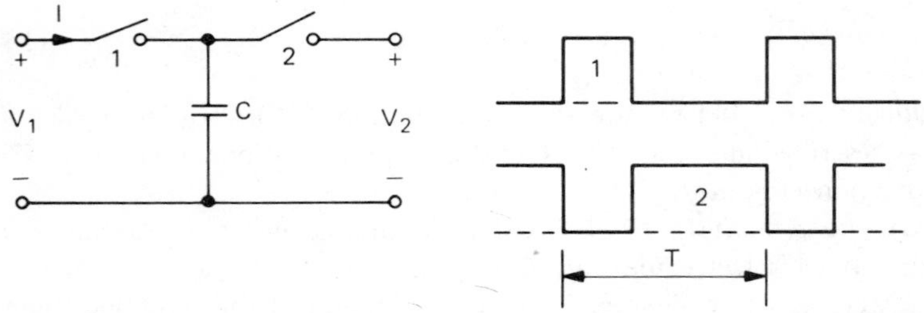

Fig. 14.4.1. Simulation of a resistor by a switched capacitor: (a) network; (b) two-phase clock sequence.

into the capacitor is given by

$$I = \frac{Q}{T} = \frac{C}{T}(V_1 - V_2) = G(V_1 - V_2)$$

where $G = C/T$ corresponds to a conductance and T is the clock period. Space limitations prevent us from giving the various synthesis techniques for switched-capacitor (SC) networks. For information, the reader is referred to the numerous papers which have appeared recently [9-14]. Here we will show that such networks can be represented as combinations of sampled and analog systems and that the linear analysis methods developed in this book still apply, although in considerably more complex form.

We will consider SC networks composed only of ideal elements: capacitors, switches, OPAMPs, VVTs, and voltage sources. An ideal switch has zero impedance when closed and an infinite impedance when open. An ideal VVT is assumed to have constant gain for all frequencies and an ideal OPAMP has infinite gain. In order to set up the equations for such networks, we use the charge-conservation law instead of the Kirchhoff current law: If a node is connected to capacitors only, the sum of charges on these capacitors is constant. As in Chapter 4, we need not write the equations at nodes connected to independent or dependent voltage sources, as they allow arbitrary charge transfer.

We will clarify the above statements by using the small example shown in Fig. 14.4.2. The switch in the network can be either in position 1 or 2. Starting with the moment of switching from 2 to 1, the new charge on the capacitor at node 2 must be equal to the old charge present at the time just before switching. Afterwards, the voltage depends on the source. Thus, for this node,

$$C_1[v_{1,2}(t) - v_{1,1}(t)] = C_1[v_{2,2} - v_{2,1}] \qquad t \in \text{phase 1}$$
$$\text{with} \quad v_{1,1}(t) = w(t).$$

The first subscript denotes the phase, the second the node of the network. The voltages appearing with argument (t) are *functions* of time while those without are *values* at the instants just *prior* to switching. Where required, the sampling time instant will be made explicit. Similarly, the transition from phase 1 to phase 2 requires

$$C_1[v_{2,2}(t) - v_{2,1}(t)] + C_2 v_{2,2}(t) = C_1[v_{1,2} - v_{1,1}] \qquad t \in \text{phase 2}$$
$$\text{with} \quad v_{2,1}(t) = w(t).$$

The equations can be written in matrix form:

Phase 1: $$\begin{bmatrix} -C_1 & C_1 \\ 1 & 0 \end{bmatrix} \begin{bmatrix} v_{1,1}(t) \\ v_{1,2}(t) \end{bmatrix} = \begin{bmatrix} -C_1 & C_1 \\ 0 & 0 \end{bmatrix} \begin{bmatrix} v_{2,1} \\ v_{2,2} \end{bmatrix} + \begin{bmatrix} 0 \\ 1 \end{bmatrix} w(t)$$

Phase 2: $$\begin{bmatrix} -C_1 & C_1 + C_2 \\ 1 & 0 \end{bmatrix} \begin{bmatrix} v_{2,1}(t) \\ v_{2,2}(t) \end{bmatrix} = \begin{bmatrix} -C_1 & C_1 \\ 0 & 0 \end{bmatrix} \begin{bmatrix} v_{1,1} \\ v_{1,2} \end{bmatrix} + \begin{bmatrix} 0 \\ 1 \end{bmatrix} w(t).$$

Let us denote the matrices on the left by $\mathbf{A}_1$, $\mathbf{A}_2$, the matrices on the right by $\mathbf{B}_1$, $\mathbf{B}_2$, and the vectors multiplying the input by $\mathbf{g}_1$, $\mathbf{g}_2$. The system is now written as

$$\mathbf{A}_1 \mathbf{v}_1(t) = \mathbf{B}_1 \mathbf{v}_2 + \mathbf{g}_1 w(t), \quad t \in I_1 \text{ (phase 1)}$$
$$\mathbf{A}_2 \mathbf{v}_2(t) = \mathbf{B}_2 \mathbf{v}_1 + \mathbf{g}_2 w(t), \quad t \in I_2 \text{ (phase 2)}.$$

General SC networks may have more than two phases. We will use N for the total number of phases and the subscript k for the kth phase. The various time slots and related definitions are shown in Fig. 14.4.3. In addition, let

$$\begin{aligned} \sigma_0 &= 0 \\ \sigma_N &= T. \end{aligned} \tag{14.4.1}$$

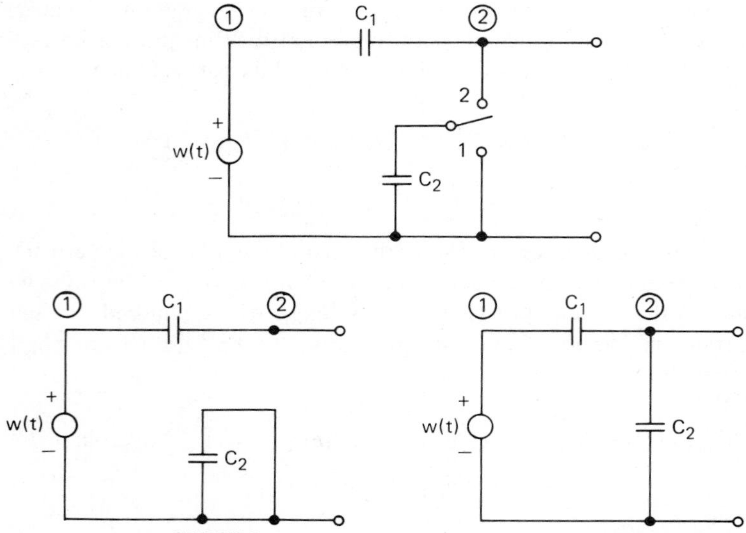

Fig. 14.4.2. A simple switched-capacitor network and its two phases.

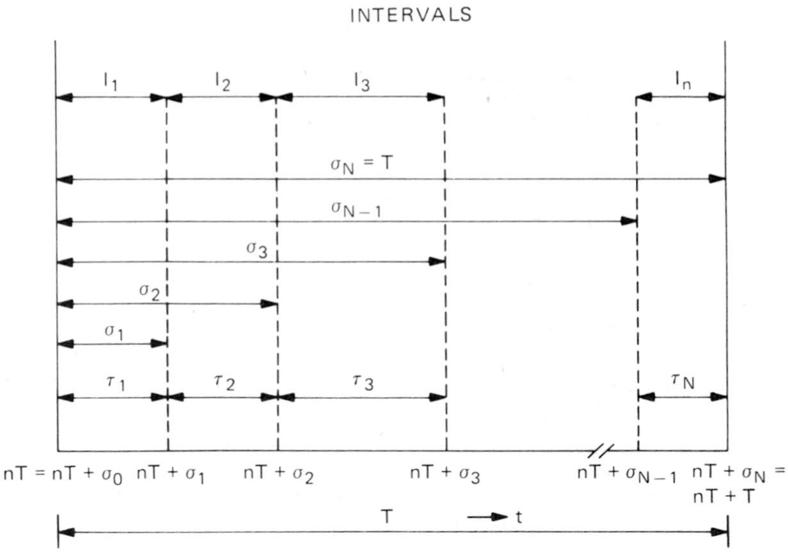

Fig. 14.4.3. Definitions for an N-phase switched-capacitor network.

For the kth phase we can write

$$\mathbf{A}_k \mathbf{v}_k(t) = \mathbf{B}_k \mathbf{v}_{k-1} + \mathbf{g}_k w(t), \qquad t \in I_k \tag{14.4.2}$$

with the understanding that whenever $k - 1 = 0$,

$$\mathbf{v}_0 = \mathbf{v}_N(nT). \tag{14.4.3}$$

The equations can be used for time domain solution. For frequency domain analysis, we modify (14.4.2) by simultaneously adding and subtracting $\mathbf{A}_k \mathbf{v}_k$ on the left side and $\mathbf{g}_k w(nT + \sigma_k) = \mathbf{g}_k w_k$ on the right side. This changes (14.4.2) into

$$\mathbf{A}_k \mathbf{y}_k(t) + \mathbf{A}_k \mathbf{v}_k = \mathbf{B}_k \mathbf{v}_{k-1} + \mathbf{g}_k r_k(t), \qquad t \in I_k \tag{14.4.4}$$

where we introduced the definitions

$$\left.\begin{aligned} \mathbf{y}_k(t) &= \mathbf{v}_k(t) - \mathbf{v}_k \\ r_k(t) &= w(t) - w_k \end{aligned}\right\} \quad t \in I_k. \tag{14.4.5}$$

The situation is sketched in Fig. 14.4.4. Note that *at the switching instants* $t = nT + \sigma_k$, both $\mathbf{y}_k(t)$ and $r_k(t)$ *are zero.* This enables us to partition (14.4.4)

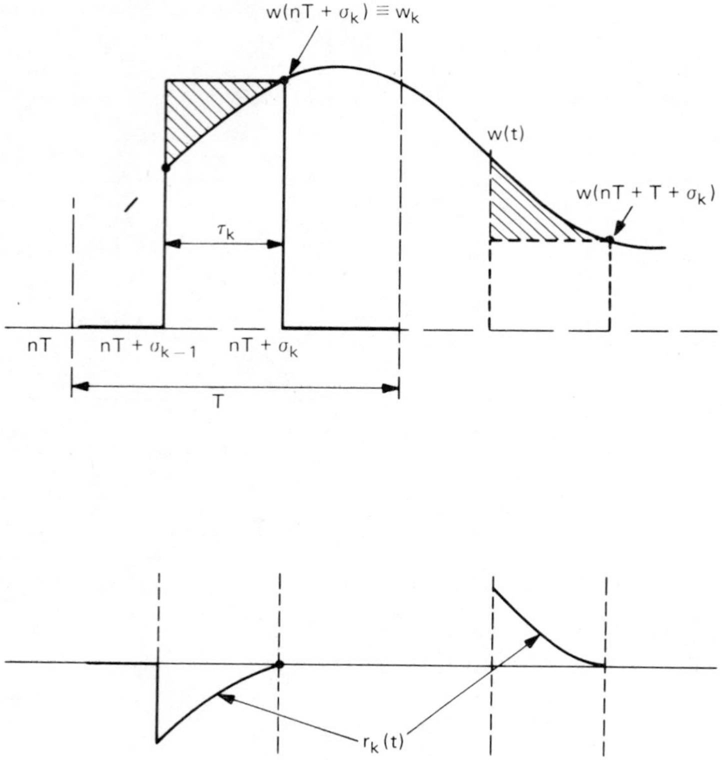

Fig. 14.4.4. Definition of $r_k(t)$. A similar picture applies for $\mathbf{y}_k(t)$.

into two sets, a discrete one valid at the switching instants only and an algebraic set valid elsewhere:

$$\mathbf{A}_k \mathbf{v}_k = \mathbf{B}_k \mathbf{v}_{k-1} + \mathbf{g}_k w_k \quad \text{(discrete)} \tag{14.4.6}$$

$$\mathbf{A}_k \mathbf{y}_k(t) = \mathbf{g}_k r_k(t) \quad \text{(algebraic)} \tag{14.4.7}$$

Defining

$$\mathbf{p}_k = \mathbf{A}_k^{-1} \mathbf{g}_k \tag{14.4.8}$$

(14.4.7) becomes

$$\mathbf{y}_k(t) = \mathbf{p}_k r_k(t) \tag{14.4.9}$$

Equations (14.4.6) and (14.4.9) represent two *decoupled* systems. If (14.4.6) is solved for the discrete time values $\mathbf{v}_k$, then using (14.4.5) we can write

$$\mathbf{v}_k(t) = \mathbf{v}_k + \mathbf{p}_k r_k(t). \tag{14.4.10}$$

The solution thus consists of two components:

(a) $\mathbf{v}_k$, the contribution of the discrete system (14.4.6).
(b) $\mathbf{p}_k r_k(t)$, the contribution due to *feed-through* system (14.4.9).

Independent solutions of (14.4.6) and (14.4.9) form the basis of frequency domain analysis of SC networks with continuous inputs.

14.5. FORMULATION OF MINIMAL-SIZE SC NETWORK EQUATIONS

Switching action in SC networks modifies the topology of the network and can result in a different number of nodes in each phase. Although switches can be incorporated into the modified nodal formulation so that the system matrix size remains invariant (see Section 4.4), such a choice invariably leads to a large set of equations. The approach recommended here reduces the set of equations in each phase to the smallest possible number. It is based on the two-graph method explained in Sections 4.7 and 4.8 and the reader should have working knowledge of the method before proceeding further. For easy reference, the subset of network elements usually encountered in SC networks and the way they enter the two-graph modified nodal formulation are given in Fig. 14.5.1. The two-graph representation results in contraction of some nodes. Further reduction in system size may occur due to the specific structure of the SC network. For instance, the voltage source may be disconnected from the network in some phases. In this case, the edge of the source is contracted on the voltage graph. In some phases, the output may be disconnected from the rest of the network; these situations can be detected topologically as well. In all such cases, the nodes are renumbered to follow a natural sequence and zero is reserved for ground.

The $\mathbf{A}_k$ matrices introduced in Section 14.4 are formed by considering the *I*- and *V*-graphs of the particular phase. The $\mathbf{B}_k$ matrices which represent the charges on the capacitors at the end of the previous phase are obtained by using the same rules but *taking the I-graph of that particular phase and the V-graph of the phase immediately preceeding it in time.*

EXAMPLE 14.5.1. Consider the SC network in Fig. 14.5.2(a). It has 7 nodes and 6 switches and operates under a two-phase clock. The nodes are numbered

ELEMENT	SYMBOL	I-GRAPH	V-GRAPH	MATRIX
VOLTAGE SOURCE	j $+$ I E j' $-$	$j_1 \equiv j_1'$	jv jv'	$\begin{bmatrix} jv & jv' \\ & \\ 1 & -1 \end{bmatrix}$ SOURCE VECTOR $\begin{bmatrix} \\ E \end{bmatrix}$
ADMITTANCE	j $+$ I y V j' $-$	j_1 j_1'	jv jv'	$\begin{array}{c} \\ j_1 \\ j_1' \end{array}\begin{bmatrix} jv & jv' \\ y & -y \\ -y & \cdot y \end{bmatrix}$
VVT	j k $+$ $+$ V μV j' $-$ $-$ k'	j_1 $k_1 \equiv k_1'$ j_1'	jv kv jv' kv'	$\begin{bmatrix} jv & jv' & kv & kv' \\ & & & \\ -\mu & \mu & 1 & -1 \end{bmatrix}$
OPERATIONAL AMPLIFIER	j k ∞ j' k'	j_1 $k_1 \equiv k_1'$ j_1'	kv $jv \equiv jv'$ kv'	——
UNITY GAIN BUFFER	j k 1 l	j_1' k_1	$jv \equiv kv$	——

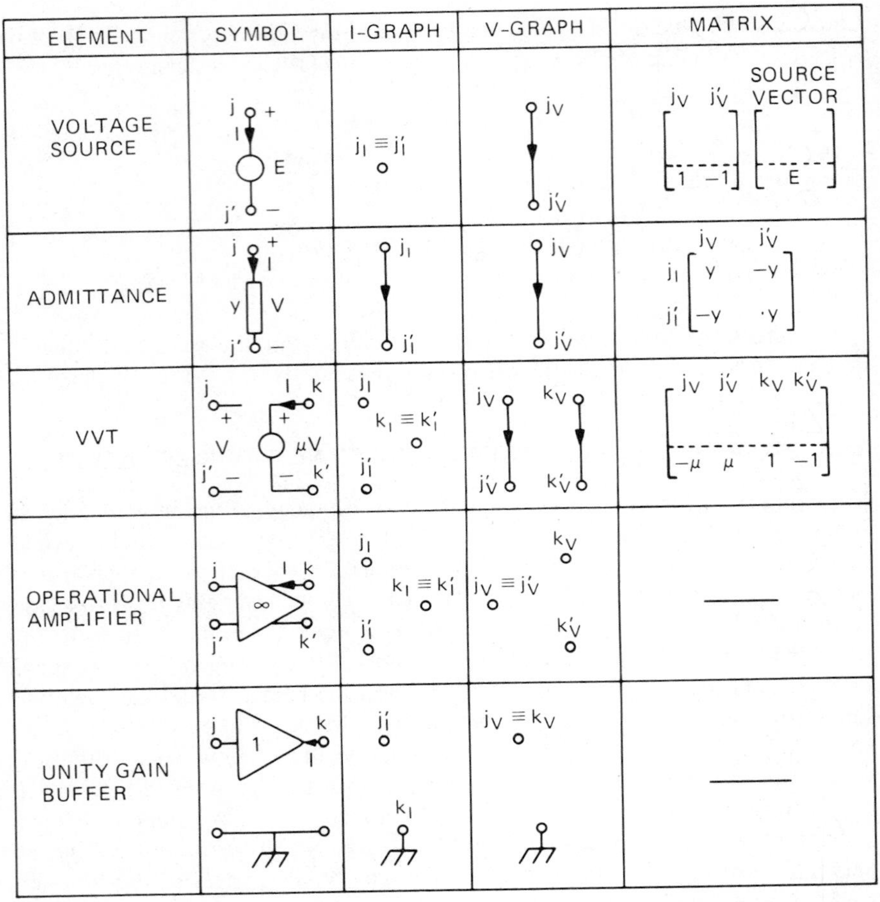

Fig. 14.5.1. Two-graph representation of the most important SC-elements and the way they enter the modified nodal two-graph formulation.

in circles, the numbers at the switches indicate the phase during which they are closed. Network configurations in the two phases are redrawn in Fig. 14.5.2(b, c). The initial data for the network are contained in a connectivity table (compare with Section 4.7):

	E	C_1	C_2	C_3	C_4	Op$_{in}$	Op$_{out}$
From:	1	2	4	5	6	0	7
To:	0	3	0	0	7	6	0

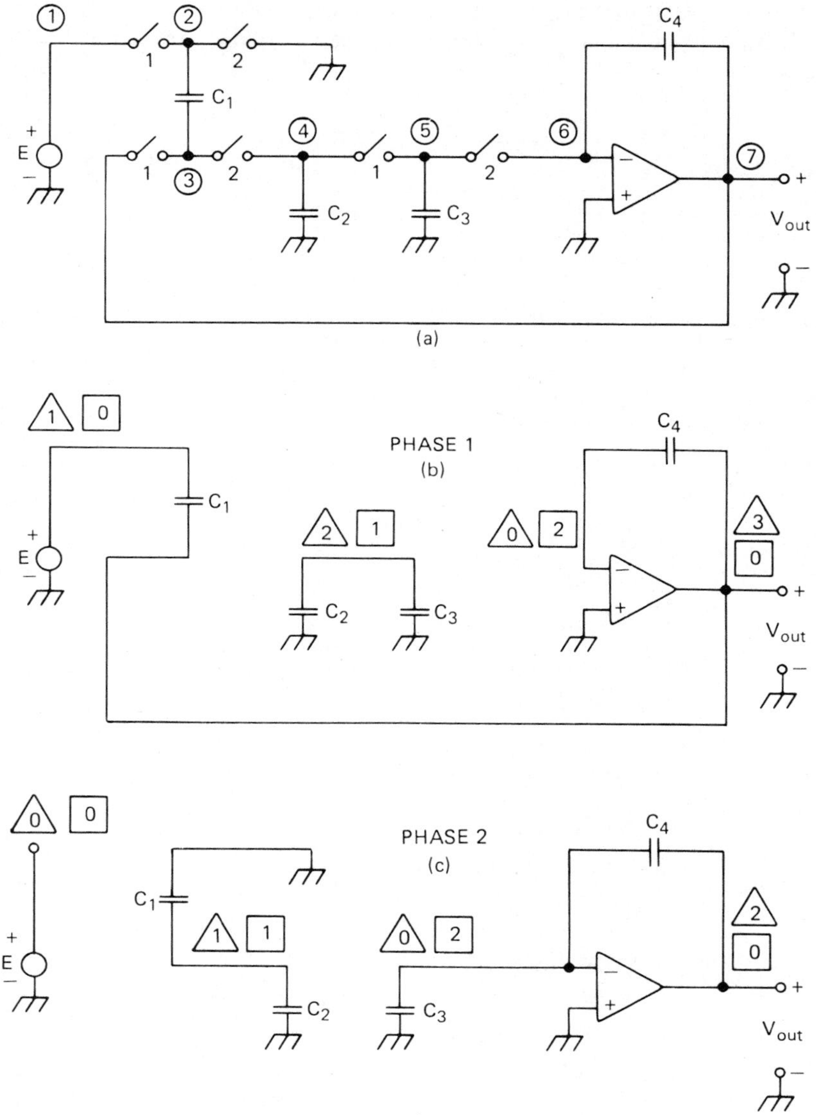

Fig. 14.5.2. A two-phase network and its configurations in the two phases.

Applying the rules given in Fig. 14.5.1, noting that the voltage source is disconnected in phase 2 and renumbering the nodes accordingly, we arrive at:

Phase 1:

	E	C_1	C_2	C_3	C_4	$\mathrm{Op_{in}}$	$\mathrm{Op_{out}}$	
From:	0	0	1	1	2	0	0	*I*-graph
To:	0	0	0	0	0	2	0	
From:	1	1	2	2	0	0	3	*V*-graph
To:	0	3	0	0	3	0	0	

Phase 2:

	E	C_1	C_2	C_3	C_4	$\mathrm{Op_{in}}$	$\mathrm{Op_{out}}$	
From:	0	0	1	2	2	0	0	*I*-graph
To:	0	1	0	0	0	2	0	
From:	0	0	1	0	0	0	2	*V*-graph
To:	0	1	0	0	2	0	0	

Using the rules of Section 4.8, the $\mathbf{A}_k$ matrices are

$$\mathbf{A}_1 = \begin{bmatrix} 0 & (C_2 + C_3) & 0 \\ 0 & 0 & -C_4 \\ \hdashline 1 & 0 & 0 \end{bmatrix}; \qquad \mathbf{A}_2 = \begin{bmatrix} (C_1 + C_2) & 0 \\ 0 & -C_4 \end{bmatrix}.$$

The $\mathbf{B}_k$ matrix must have the same number of rows as the $\mathbf{A}_k$ matrix and rows of zeros are appended at the bottom wherever needed. For the example,

$$\mathbf{B}_1 = \begin{bmatrix} C_2 & 0 \\ 0 & -C_4 \\ \hdashline 0 & 0 \end{bmatrix}; \qquad \mathbf{B}_2 = \begin{bmatrix} -C_1 & C_2 & C_1 \\ 0 & C_3 & -C_4 \end{bmatrix}.$$

The right-hand-side vectors $\mathbf{g}_k$ are

$$\mathbf{g}_1 = \begin{bmatrix} 0 \\ 0 \\ 1 \end{bmatrix}; \qquad \mathbf{g}_2 = \begin{bmatrix} 0 \\ 0 \end{bmatrix}.$$

14.6. FREQUENCY REPRESENTATION OF PERIODIC AND SAMPLED SIGNALS

For frequency domain analysis, Eq. (14.4.6) and (14.4.9) must be expressed by their Fourier transforms. The system is periodic with period T and each equa-

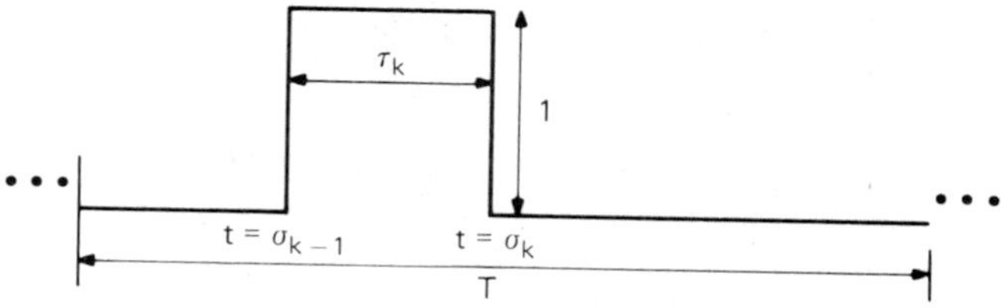

Fig. 14.6.1. Definition of the kth window function $\xi_k(t)$.

tion of the system is valid in one interval only. To take this fact into account, we use *window functions* $\xi_k(t)$ which are periodic with the same period T. The kth window function $\xi_k(t)$ is sketched in Fig. 14.6.1; it is nonzero in the interval from $(nT + \sigma_{k-1})$ to $(nT + \sigma_k)$ and its height is selected to be unity.

Spectral analysis of sampled functions is generally covered in communication theory and the appropriate expressions may be unknown to the reader. We therefore provide the relevant equations with some explanations in this section. Most of them can be found in [15].

1. A periodic function $f(t)$ of period T can be represented by the *Fourier series*

$$f(t) = \sum_{n=-\infty}^{+\infty} F_n e^{jn\omega_s t} \tag{14.6.1}$$

where

$$F_n = \frac{1}{T} \int_0^T f(t)\, e^{-jn\omega_s t}\, dt \tag{14.6.2}$$

and

$$\omega_s = \frac{2\pi}{T}. \tag{14.6.3}$$

2. The *Fourier transform* pair of a function $f(t)$ is given by

$$f(t) = \frac{1}{2\pi} \int_{-\infty}^{+\infty} F(\omega)\, e^{j\omega t}\, d\omega \tag{14.6.4}$$

and

$$F(\omega) = \int_{-\infty}^{+\infty} f(t)\, e^{-j\omega t}\, dt. \tag{14.6.5}$$

The Fourier transform of a periodic function with period T is

$$\mathfrak{F}[f(t)] = F(\omega) = 2\pi \sum_{n=-\infty}^{+\infty} F_n \delta(\omega - n\omega_s) \tag{14.6.6}$$

with F_n given by (14.6.2); $\delta(\omega)$ is a Dirac impulse. For notational simplicity, the limits on the summations will be dropped in the following.

EXAMPLE 14.6.1. Find the Fourier series coefficients and the Fourier transform of the impulse train $f(t) \equiv \delta_T(t) = \Sigma\, \delta(t - nT)$ shown in Fig. 14.6.2.

Using (14.6.2):

$$F_n = \frac{1}{T} \int_0^T \delta(t)\, e^{-jn\omega_s t}\, dt = \frac{1}{T}. \tag{14.6.7}$$

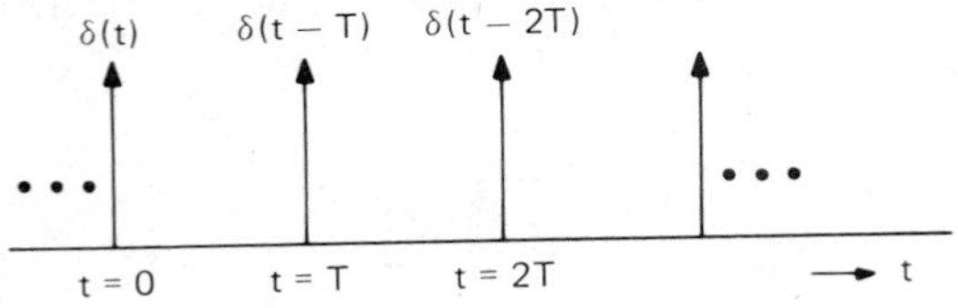

Fig. 14.6.2. Definition of the function $\delta_T(t)$.

Using (14.6.6):

$$\mathfrak{F}[\delta_T(t)] = \frac{2\pi}{T} \sum \delta(\omega - n\omega_s) = \omega_s \sum \delta(\omega - n\omega_s). \tag{14.6.8}$$

EXAMPLE 14.6.2. Find the Fourier series coefficients and the Fourier transform of the kth window function $f(t) = \xi_k(t)$ shown in Fig. 14.6.1.

Using (14.6.2)

$$\theta_{k,n} = \begin{cases} \tau_k / T, & \text{for } n = 0 \\ e^{-jn\omega_s \sigma_{k-1}} \dfrac{1 - e^{-jn\omega_s \tau_k}}{jn\omega_s T}, & \text{otherwise.} \end{cases} \tag{14.6.9}$$

Using (14.6.6)

$$\mathfrak{F}[\xi_k(t)] = 2\pi \sum \theta_{k,n}\, \delta(\omega - n\omega_s). \tag{14.6.10}$$

We will also need the Fourier transform of the product of a periodic function $f(t)$ and another arbitrary function $w(t)$:

$$g(t) = w(t) f(t). \tag{14.6.11}$$

The Fourier transform of the product of two time functions is the convolution of the respective transforms:

$$\mathfrak{F}[g(t)] = \mathfrak{F}[w(t) f(t)] = \frac{1}{2\pi} \int_{-\infty}^{+\infty} W(u) F(\omega - u)\, du$$

$$= \frac{1}{2\pi} \int_{-\infty}^{+\infty} W(u)\, 2\pi \left\{ \sum F_n \delta[(\omega - n\omega_s) - u] \right\} du$$

$$= \sum F_n W(\omega - n\omega_s). \tag{14.6.12}$$

EXAMPLE 14.6.3. Find the Fourier transform of the product $w(t)\, \xi_k(t)$ where $\xi_k(t)$ is the kth window function considered in Example 14.6.2. Denote $\mathfrak{F}[w(t)] = W(\omega)$.

Using (14.6.12)

$$\mathfrak{F}[w(t)\, \xi_k(t)] = \sum \theta_{k,n} W(\omega - n\omega_s) \tag{14.6.13}$$

where $\theta_{k,n}$ is defined by (14.6.9).

EXAMPLE 14.6.4. Consider the product $g(t) = w(t + \sigma)\, \delta_T(t)$ and find the Fourier transform by applying (a) formula (14.6.5) and (b) the convolution integral formula (14.6.12):

(a) $$\mathfrak{F}[g(t)] = \int_{-\infty}^{+\infty} w(t + \sigma) \left[\sum \delta(t - nT) \right] e^{-j\omega t}\, dt$$

$$= \sum w(nT + \sigma)\, e^{-jn\omega T}.$$

(b) By definition, $\mathfrak{F}[w(t)] = W(\omega)$. Using the shift property of the Fourier transform $\mathfrak{F}[w(t + \sigma)] = W(\omega)\, e^{j\omega\sigma}$ and inserting into the convolution integral formula (14.6.12), we can write

$$\mathfrak{F}[g(t)] = \frac{1}{2\pi} \int_{-\infty}^{+\infty} W(u)\, e^{ju\sigma} \left\{ \frac{2\pi}{T} \sum \delta[(\omega - n\omega_s) - u] \right\} du$$

$$= \frac{1}{T} \sum W(\omega - n\omega_s)\, e^{j(\omega - n\omega_s)\sigma}.$$

These two results give *Poisson's formula:*

$$\sum w(nT+\sigma)\, e^{-jn\omega T} = \frac{1}{T}\sum W(\omega - n\omega_s)\, e^{j(\omega - n\omega_s)\sigma}. \qquad (14.6.14)$$

EXAMPLE 14.6.5. Find the Fourier transform of the function shown in Fig. 14.6.3. It is represented by the train of pulses defined by the kth window function $\xi_k(t)$ but each having height $w(nT+\sigma_k)$.

Using (14.6.5) for one such pulse

$$F(\omega) = w(nT+\sigma_k)\int_{nT+\sigma_{k-1}}^{nT+\sigma_k} e^{-j\omega t}\, dt$$

$$= w(nT+\sigma_k)\, \frac{\exp\,[-j\omega(nT+\sigma_{k-1})] - \exp\,[-j\omega(nT+\sigma_k)]}{j\omega}.$$

For all pulses

$$\mathfrak{F}\left[\sum w(nT+\sigma_k)\,\xi_k(t)\right] = e^{-j\omega\sigma_{k-1}}\, \frac{1-e^{-j\omega\tau_k}}{j\omega} \sum w(nT+\sigma_k)\, e^{-jn\omega T}. \qquad (14.6.15)$$

Using Poisson's formula (14.6.14) we can write

$$\mathfrak{F}\left[\sum w(nT+\sigma_k)\,\xi_k(t)\right] = D_k(\omega)\sum W(\omega - n\omega_s)\exp\,[-j(\omega - n\omega_s)\sigma_k] \qquad (14.6.16)$$

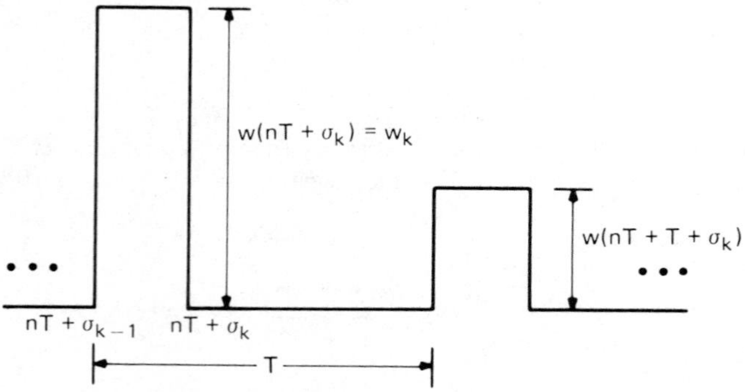

Fig. 14.6.3. A train of rectangular pulses having different heights.

where

$$D_k(\omega) = e^{-j\omega\sigma_{k-1}} \frac{1 - e^{-j\omega\tau_k}}{j\omega T}. \tag{14.6.17}$$

14.7. ANALYSIS OF THE DIGITAL SYSTEM

Solution of the digital system (14.4.6) is carried out by taking the z-transforms of the discrete time signals. Let us define

$$\begin{aligned} \sum \mathbf{v}_k(nT + \sigma_k)z^{-n} &= \mathbf{V}_k(z), \qquad k = 1, 2, \ldots, N - 1 \\ \sum \mathbf{v}_N(nT)z^{-n} &= \mathbf{V}_N(z) \end{aligned} \tag{14.7.1}$$

and

$$\begin{aligned} \sum w(nT + \sigma_k)z^{-n} &= W_k(z), \qquad k = 1, 2, \ldots, N - 1 \\ \sum w(nT)z^{-n} &= W_N(z). \end{aligned} \tag{14.7.2}$$

Also note that

$$\sum \mathbf{v}_N(nT + \sigma_N)z^{-n} = \sum \mathbf{v}_N(nT + T)z^{-n} = z\mathbf{V}_N(z) \tag{14.7.3}$$

and the same applies to $W_N(z)$. Using these definitions, the system (14.4.6) becomes

$$\begin{bmatrix} \mathbf{A}_1 & & & & -\mathbf{B}_1 \\ -\mathbf{B}_2 & \mathbf{A}_2 & & & \\ & -\mathbf{B}_3 & \mathbf{A}_3 & & \\ & & \ddots & \ddots & \\ & & & -\mathbf{B}_N & z\mathbf{A}_N \end{bmatrix} \begin{bmatrix} \mathbf{V}_1 \\ \mathbf{V}_2 \\ \mathbf{V}_3 \\ \vdots \\ \mathbf{V}_N \end{bmatrix} = \begin{bmatrix} \mathbf{g}_1 W_1(z) \\ \mathbf{g}_2 W_2(z) \\ \mathbf{g}_3 W_3(z) \\ \vdots \\ \mathbf{g}_N z W_N(z) \end{bmatrix} \tag{14.7.4}$$

or

$$\mathbf{M}(z)\mathbf{V}(z) = \mathbf{H}(z). \tag{14.7.5}$$

To obtain the response at any frequency ω substitute

$$z = e^{j\omega T}. \tag{14.7.6}$$

Application of Poisson's formula (14.6.14) to the right-hand side of (14.7.4) gives

$$W_k(e^{j\omega T}) = \sum w(nT + \sigma_k)\, e^{-j\omega nT} = \frac{1}{T} \sum W(\omega - n\omega_s) \exp\,[j(\omega - n\omega_s)\,\sigma_k]$$

$$W_N(e^{j\omega T}) = \frac{1}{T} \sum W(\omega - n\omega_s). \tag{14.7.7}$$

Here

$$\omega_s = 2\pi/T. \tag{14.7.8}$$

Let us now make the assumption that the input signal is a complex exponential of frequency ω_0:

$$w(t) = e^{j\omega_0 t}. \tag{14.7.9}$$

Then

$$W(\omega) = 2\pi\delta(\omega - \omega_0)$$

and

$$W(\omega - n\omega_s) = 2\pi\delta(\omega - \omega_0 - n\omega_s).$$

The system (14.7.4) has an infinite number of forcing terms on the right side. Consider the nth frequency

$$\omega = \omega_0 + n\omega_s \tag{14.7.10}$$

and note that

$$\exp\,[j(\omega_0 + n\omega_s)\,T] = e^{j\omega_0 T}.$$

The system matrix $\mathbf{M}$ is independent of n. The kth component of the right-hand side is

$$W_k(\exp\,[j(\omega_0 + n\omega_s)\,T]) = \frac{2\pi}{T}\, e^{j\omega_0 \sigma_k}, \tag{14.7.11}$$

independent of n as well, and

$$\mathbf{H}(e^{j\omega_0 T}) = \frac{2\pi}{T} \begin{bmatrix} \mathbf{g}_1 e^{j\omega_0 \sigma_1} \\ \mathbf{g}_2 e^{j\omega_0 \sigma_2} \\ \vdots \\ \mathbf{g}_N e^{j\omega_0 \sigma_N} \end{bmatrix}. \tag{14.7.12}$$

Solution of (14.7.4) is thus performed using ω_0 and the result is valid for *all frequencies* defined by (14.7.10). In the following we will not use the 2π originating from the Fourier transform and division by T is absorbed into the $D_{k,n}$ defined in (14.8.3). Therefore, for the digital system, we will use the right-hand-side vector

$$\mathbf{H} = \begin{bmatrix} g_1 e^{j\omega_0\sigma_1} \\ g_2 e^{j\omega_0\sigma_2} \\ \vdots \\ g_N e^{j\omega_0\sigma_N} \end{bmatrix}. \tag{14.7.13}$$

A special block substitution method for the solution of (14.7.4) will be given in Section 14.10.

14.8. SPECTRAL ANALYSIS OF SWITCHED-CAPACITOR NETWORKS

The total voltage in the kth phase is obtained from (14.4.1) as follows:

$$\mathbf{v}_k(t) = \mathbf{v}_k + \mathbf{p}_k r_k(t). \tag{14.8.1}$$

Since $\mathbf{v}_k(t)$ is defined in the kth phase *only*, this fact is taken into account through the kth window function $\xi_k(t)$ defined in Example 14.6.2. Applying the Fourier transform to (14.8.1) gives

$$\begin{aligned} \hat{\mathbf{V}}_k(\omega) &= \mathcal{F}[\mathbf{v}_k \xi_k(t)] + \mathbf{p}_k \mathcal{F}[r_k(t)\, \xi_k(t)] \\ &= D_k(\omega)\mathbf{V}_k + \mathbf{p}_k R_k(\omega). \end{aligned} \tag{14.8.2}$$

Here $\mathbf{V}_k$ is the kth phase vector obtained from the solution of (14.7.4) for $z = e^{j\omega_0 T}$ with the right hand side defined by (14.7.13). This solution represents components repeated at frequencies $\omega = \omega_0 + n\omega_s$, as discussed in Section 14.7. $D_k(\omega)$ was derived in (14.6.17) for all phases except the Nth. Since $\mathbf{V}_N$ was defined in (14.7.1) at the point $nT + \sigma_0 = nT$ and our derivation of (14.6.17) considered $nT + \sigma_N = nT + T$, this fact is taken into account by defining

$$D_{k,n} = \left.\frac{\exp[-j\omega\sigma_{k-1}] - \exp[-j\omega\sigma_k]}{j\omega T}\right|_{\omega=\omega_0+n\omega_s} \qquad k \neq N$$

$$D_{N,n} = e^{j\omega_0 T} \left.\frac{\exp[-j\omega\sigma_{N-1}] - \exp[-j\omega\sigma_N]}{j\omega T}\right|_{\omega=\omega_0+n\omega_s} \qquad k = N. \tag{14.8.3}$$

Here the first subscript on D denotes the phase and the second the frequency band. The spectrum of the scalar $R_k(\omega)$ is found by first substituting from (14.4.5):

$$R_k(\omega) = \mathcal{F}[w(t)\,\xi_k(t)] - \mathcal{F}[w_k \xi_k(t)].$$

The first component was derived in (14.6.13):

$$\mathcal{F}[w(t)\,\xi_k(t)] = \sum \theta_{k,n} W(\omega - n\omega_s).$$

The second component was derived in (14.6.16):

$$\mathcal{F}[w_k \xi_k(t)] = D_k(\omega) \sum W(\omega - n\omega_s) \exp\,[-j(\omega - n\omega_s)\,\sigma_k].$$

If we now consider a single frequency signal $z = e^{j\omega_0 T}$ and substitute $\omega = \omega_0 + n\omega_s$, the nth component of $R_k(\omega)$ will be

$$\begin{aligned} R_{k,n} &= \theta_{k,n} - D_{k,n} e^{j\omega_0 \sigma_k}, \qquad \text{for } k = 1, 2, \cdots, N-1 \\ R_{N,n} &= \theta_{N,n} - D_{N,n}. \end{aligned} \tag{14.8.4}$$

The nth harmonic component of (14.8.2) becomes

$$\hat{\mathbf{V}}_{k,n} = D_{k,n} \mathbf{V}_k + \mathbf{p}_k R_{k,n}. \tag{14.8.5}$$

At this point we refer the components of $\hat{\mathbf{V}}_{k,n}$ to the nodes of the original network (not the V-graph nodes) and the total spectrum at $\omega = \omega_0 + n\omega_s$ is

$$\mathbf{S}_n = \sum_{k=1}^{N} \hat{\mathbf{V}}_{k,n}. \tag{14.8.6}$$

The sequence of computational steps will be summarized in Section 14.10.

14.9. SINGLE OUTPUT AND ITS SENSITIVITY

The steps in Section 14.8 derived the spectrum for the nodal voltages of all nodes of the original network. This is seldom required; in most cases we are interested in a single output and, possibly, its sensitivity to network element or parameter changes.

Consider the spectrum of a single output defined as

$$\phi(\mathbf{S}_n) = \sum_{k=1}^{N} \mathbf{d}_k^t \hat{\mathbf{V}}_{k,n}. \tag{14.9.1}$$

Here $\mathbf{d}_k^t$ are the transposes of constant vectors similar to those defined in Chapter 6. Substituting (14.8.5) and defining

$$f_k = \mathbf{d}_k^t \mathbf{p}_k \tag{14.9.2}$$

the spectrum of the output becomes

$$\phi(\mathbf{S}_n) = \sum_{k=1}^{N} \mathbf{d}_k^t D_{k,n} \mathbf{V}_k + \sum_{k=1}^{N} f_k R_{k,n}. \tag{14.9.3}$$

We note that f_k are scalars independent of ω_0 and n and can be precomputed.

In order to replace the first summation in (14.9.3) by a simple vector product, multiply each $\mathbf{d}_k^t$ by the scalar $D_{k,n}$ and combine them into a single vector

$$\tilde{\mathbf{d}}_n^t = [D_{1,n}\mathbf{d}_1^t, D_{2,n}\mathbf{d}_2^t, \ldots, D_{N,n}\mathbf{d}_N^t]. \tag{14.9.4}$$

This modifies (14.9.3) into

$$\phi(\mathbf{S}_n) = \tilde{\mathbf{d}}_n^t \mathbf{V} + \sum_{k=1}^{N} f_k R_{k,n} \tag{14.9.5}$$

where $\mathbf{V}$ is the solution of the digital system (14.7.5) with $z = e^{j\omega_0 T}$,

$$\mathbf{V} = \mathbf{M}^{-1}\mathbf{H}. \tag{14.9.6}$$

Substituting into (14.9.5) gives

$$\phi(\mathbf{S}_n) = \underbrace{\tilde{\mathbf{d}}_n^t \mathbf{M}^{-1}}_{(\mathbf{V}_n^a)^t} \mathbf{H} + \sum_{k=1}^{N} f_k R_{k,n}. \tag{14.9.7}$$

Instead of solving (14.9.6), we find the vector $\mathbf{V}_n^a$ as the solution of the transpose system:

$$\mathbf{M}^t \mathbf{V}_n^a = \tilde{\mathbf{d}}_n \tag{14.9.8}$$

and the output is given by

$$\phi(\mathbf{S}_n) = (\mathbf{V}_n^a)^t \mathbf{H} + \sum_{k=1}^{N} f_k R_{k,n}. \tag{14.9.9}$$

A special sparse matrix solution of (14.9.8) is described in Section 14.10.

For sensitivity calculations, rewrite (14.9.9) by retaining explicitly all its components:

$$\phi(\mathbf{S}_n) = \tilde{\mathbf{d}}_n^t \mathbf{M}^{-1}\mathbf{H} + \sum_{k=1}^{N} \mathbf{d}_k^t \mathbf{A}_k^{-1} \mathbf{g}_k R_{k,n}$$

and differentiate with respect to some parameter h_j:

$$\frac{\partial \phi(\mathbf{S}_n)}{\partial h_j} = \tilde{\mathbf{d}}_n^t \frac{\partial \mathbf{M}^{-1}}{\partial h_j}\mathbf{H} + \sum_{k=1}^{N} \mathbf{d}_k^t \frac{\partial \mathbf{A}_k^{-1}}{\partial h_j} \mathbf{g}_k R_{k,n}. \tag{14.9.10}$$

We need a simple expression for the derivatives of the matrix inverses. Considering

$$\mathbf{A}^{-1}\mathbf{A} = \mathbf{1}$$

and differentiating with respect to h_j we get

$$\frac{\partial \mathbf{A}^{-1}}{\partial h_j} = -\mathbf{A}^{-1} \frac{\partial \mathbf{A}}{\partial h_j} \mathbf{A}^{-1}. \tag{14.9.11}$$

Using this formula in (14.9.10) gives

$$\frac{\partial \phi(\mathbf{S}_n)}{\partial h_j} = -\underbrace{\tilde{\mathbf{d}}_n^t \mathbf{M}^{-1}}_{(\mathbf{V}_n^a)^t} \frac{\partial \mathbf{M}}{\partial h_j} \underbrace{\mathbf{M}^{-1}\mathbf{H}}_{\mathbf{V}} - \sum_{k=1}^{N} \underbrace{\mathbf{d}_k^t \mathbf{A}_k^{-1}}_{(\mathbf{p}_k^a)^t} \frac{\partial \mathbf{A}_k}{\partial h_j} \underbrace{\mathbf{A}_k^{-1} \mathbf{g}_k}_{\mathbf{p}_k} R_{k,n}. \tag{14.9.12}$$

Here we introduced a new vector, $\mathbf{p}_k^a$, which is the solution of the system

$$\mathbf{A}_k^t \mathbf{p}_k^a = \mathbf{d}_k. \tag{14.9.13}$$

It is independent of ω_0 and n. In fact, for any given parameter h_j, the product

$$F_{k,j} = (\mathbf{p}_k^a)^t \frac{\partial \mathbf{A}_k}{\partial h_j} \mathbf{p}_k \tag{14.9.14}$$

is a scalar independent of ω_0 and n and can be precomputed. Finally,

$$\frac{\partial \phi(\mathbf{S}_n)}{\partial h_j} = -(\mathbf{V}_n^a)^t \frac{\partial \mathbf{M}}{\partial h_j} \mathbf{V} - \sum_{k=1}^{N} F_{k,j} R_{k,n}. \tag{14.9.15}$$

14.10. SOLUTION OF THE DIGITAL SYSTEM BY BLOCK SUBSTITUTION

All types of frequency domain analyses call for an efficient solution of the digital system (14.7.4) with the right-hand-side vector defined by (14.7.13). Because the frequency variable appears in the system matrix in the last partition only, it is possible to transfer a considerable part of the solution into the preprocessing stages of the algorithm [16].

Consider equation (14.7.4). We wish to reduce the system matrix to the upper-block triangular form by making all blocks below the main diagonal zero. This can be done by block elimination. Premultiply the first row by $\mathbf{B}_2\mathbf{A}_1^{-1}$ and add to the second row. A zero matrix is created in the (2, 1) position but position $(2, N)$ is filled by the product $-\mathbf{B}_2\mathbf{A}_1^{-1}\mathbf{B}_1$ and the product $\mathbf{B}_2\mathbf{A}_1^{-1}\mathbf{g}_1 W_1$ is added to the second row of the right-hand side. Next, premultiply the second row by $\mathbf{B}_3\mathbf{A}_2^{-1}$ and add to the third row. A zero block is created in the (3, 2) position but the $(3, N)$ position is now filled by the product $-\mathbf{B}_3\mathbf{A}_2^{-1}\mathbf{B}_2\mathbf{A}_1^{-1}\mathbf{B}_1$ and the third row of the right-hand side becomes $\mathbf{g}_3 W_3 + \mathbf{B}_3\mathbf{A}_2^{-1}\mathbf{g}_2 W_2 + \mathbf{B}_3\mathbf{A}_2^{-1}\mathbf{B}_2\mathbf{A}_1\mathbf{g}_1 W_1$. Proceeding similarly for all rows, the Nth row becomes

$$(z\mathbf{A}_N - \mathbf{E})\mathbf{V}_N = \sum_{k=1}^{N} \mathbf{g}_k^P W_k \tag{14.10.1}$$

where $\mathbf{E}$ is a real matrix

$$\mathbf{E} = \mathbf{B}_N\mathbf{A}_{N-1}^{-1}\mathbf{B}_{N-1}\mathbf{A}_{N-2}^{-1} \cdots \mathbf{B}_3\mathbf{A}_2^{-1}\mathbf{B}_2\mathbf{A}_1^{-1}\mathbf{B}_1 \tag{14.10.2}$$

and

$$\mathbf{g}_k^P = \mathbf{B}_N\mathbf{A}_{N-1}^{-1}\mathbf{B}_{N-1}\mathbf{A}_{N-2}^{-1} \cdots \mathbf{B}_{k+1}\mathbf{A}_k^{-1}\mathbf{g}_k; \qquad k = 1, 2, \ldots, (N-1) \tag{14.10.3}$$

with

$$\mathbf{g}_N^P = \mathbf{g}_N.$$

The superscript P stands for "processed." Since $\mathbf{E}$ and all $\mathbf{g}^P$ are independent of frequency, they can be *precomputed and stored*. Moreover, the "fills" in the Nth column are *not stored*. Once (14.10.1) has been solved, we go back to the *original* matrix equation (14.7.4) and solve, in sequence

$$\begin{aligned} \mathbf{A}_1\mathbf{V}_1 &= \mathbf{B}_1\mathbf{V}_N + \mathbf{g}_1 W_1 \\ \mathbf{A}_k\mathbf{V}_k &= \mathbf{B}_k\mathbf{V}_{k-1} + \mathbf{g}_k W_k; \qquad k = 2, 3, \ldots, N-1. \end{aligned} \tag{14.10.4}$$

The transpose system (14.9.8) can be solved efficiently using similar steps. Denote, for simplicity, $\mathbf{C}_k = \mathbf{A}_k^t$ and $\mathbf{D}_k = \mathbf{B}_k^t$. We need the solution of the following system

$$\begin{bmatrix} \mathbf{C}_1 & -\mathbf{D}_2 & & & & \\ & \mathbf{C}_2 & -\mathbf{D}_3 & & & \\ & & \mathbf{C}_3 & -\mathbf{D}_4 & & \\ & & & \ddots & \ddots & \\ & & & & \ddots & -\mathbf{D}_N \\ -\mathbf{D}_1 & & & & & z\mathbf{C}_N \end{bmatrix} \begin{bmatrix} \mathbf{V}_{1,n}^a \\ \mathbf{V}_{2,n}^a \\ \mathbf{V}_{3,n}^a \\ \vdots \\ \mathbf{V}_{N-1,n}^a \\ \mathbf{V}_{N,n}^a \end{bmatrix} = \begin{bmatrix} \mathbf{d}_1 & D_{1,n} \\ \mathbf{d}_2 & D_{2,n} \\ \mathbf{d}_3 & D_{3,n} \\ \vdots & \vdots \\ \mathbf{d}_{N-1} & D_{N-1,n} \\ \mathbf{d}_N & D_{N,n} \end{bmatrix} \tag{14.10.5}$$

As before, we wish to reduce this matrix to the upper block triangular form. To this end premultiply the first row by $\mathbf{D}_1\mathbf{C}_1^{-1}$ and add to the *last* row. A zero block is created in the $(N, 1)$ position but $-\mathbf{D}_1\mathbf{C}_1^{-1}\mathbf{D}_2$ appears in the $(N, 2)$ position. In addition, $\mathbf{D}_1\mathbf{C}_1^{-1}\mathbf{d}_1 D_{1,n}$ is added on the right side of the last row. In order to eliminate the "fill" in the $(N, 2)$ position, now premultiply the second row by $\mathbf{D}_1\mathbf{C}_1^{-1}\mathbf{D}_2\mathbf{C}_2^{-1}$ and add to the last row. This creates an entry $-\mathbf{D}_1\mathbf{C}_1^{-1}\mathbf{D}_2\mathbf{C}_2^{-1}\mathbf{D}_3$ in the $(N, 3)$ position, and adds $\mathbf{D}_1\mathbf{C}_1^{-1}\mathbf{D}_2\mathbf{C}_2^{-1}\mathbf{d}_2 D_{2,n}$ to the right-hand side. Proceeding similarly, we arrive at

$$(z\mathbf{A}_N^t - \mathbf{E}^t)\mathbf{V}_N^a = \sum_{k=1}^{N} \mathbf{d}_k^P D_{k,n} \tag{14.10.6}$$

where

$$\begin{aligned} \mathbf{d}_k^P &= \mathbf{B}_1^t(\mathbf{A}_1^t)^{-1}\mathbf{B}_2^t(\mathbf{A}_2^t)^{-1} \cdots \mathbf{B}_k^t(\mathbf{A}_k^t)^{-1}\mathbf{d}_k; \qquad k = 1, 2, \ldots, N-1 \\ \mathbf{d}_N^P &= \mathbf{d}_N \end{aligned} \tag{14.10.7}$$

and $\mathbf{E}^t$ is the transpose of the matrix $\mathbf{E}$ given by (14.10.2). The system matrix (14.10.6) is the transpose of the system matrix (14.10.1) and the decomposition need be done only once. The vectors $\mathbf{d}_k^P$ are precomputed and stored. As before, the fills are not generated and after solving (14.10.6) we return to the original transpose system (14.10.5) and solve:

$$\mathbf{A}_k^t\mathbf{V}_{k,n}^a = \mathbf{B}_{k+1}^t\mathbf{V}_{k+1}^a + \mathbf{d}_k D_{k,n}; \qquad k = N-1, N-2, \ldots, 1. \tag{14.10.8}$$

Computational steps taking advantage of all possible savings are now summarized:

A. Preprocessing independent of frequency and n.
   1. Formulate the matrices $\mathbf{A}_k$, $\mathbf{B}_k$ and the vectors $\mathbf{g}_k$ and $\mathbf{d}_k$.
   2. Copy $\mathbf{A}_N$ into an auxiliary matrix $\mathbf{Q}$.
   3. **LU** decompose all $\mathbf{A}_k$ matrices.
   4. Prepare vectors $\mathbf{p}_k$ using (14.4.8).
   5. Prepare matrix $\mathbf{E}$ using (14.10.2) and **LU** decomposed $\mathbf{A}_k$.
   6. Prepare vectors $\mathbf{g}_k^P$ using (14.10.3) and vectors $\mathbf{d}_k^P$ using (14.10.7).
   7. Calculate f_k using (14.9.2).
   8. Calculate $\mathbf{p}_k^a$ using (14.9.13).
   9. Calculate $F_{k,j}$ using (14.9.14).

   (Some of the above may not be needed for a given type of analysis.)

B. At given frequency ω_0 prepare the matrix $(e^{j\omega_0 T}\mathbf{Q} - \mathbf{E})$, equivalent to the system matrix in (14.10.1), and obtain its **LU** decomposition. Further steps depend on the type of analysis needed.

C. Spectrum analysis of Section 14.8. Solve (14.10.1) by forward and back substitution and find the remaining phases using (14.10.4). **LU**-decomposed $\mathbf{A}_k$ matrices are available from step A. For any selected n, calculate $D_{k,n}$, $R_{k,n}$, $\hat{\mathbf{V}}_{k,n}$ and $\mathbf{S}_n$ using equations of Section 14.8.

D. Single output and its sensitivity:
   1. Solve the transpose system (14.9.8) using the decomposition of step B and Eq. (14.10.6)-(14.10.8). Insert into (14.9.7).
   2. For sensitivity, solve (14.10.1) through (14.10.4) using the decomposition of step B. Insert into (14.9.15).

14.11. SAMPLE-HOLD INPUT AND SYMBOLIC ANALYSIS

Very often, the signal is not continuous but is sampled and held before it is applied to the SC network. Such situation is sketched in Fig. 14.11.1 and con-

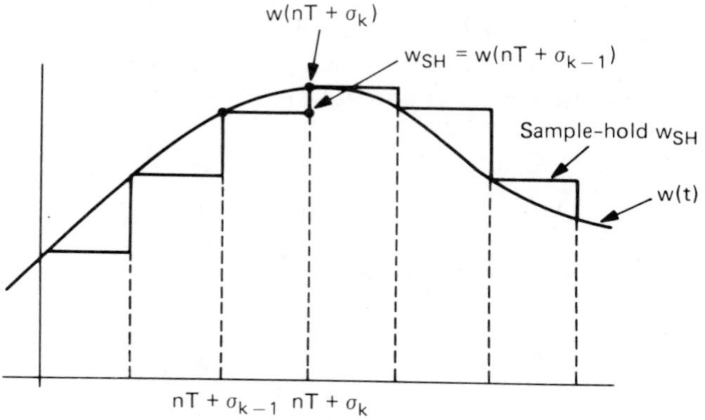

Fig. 14.11.1. Sample and hold input.

siderably simplifies the computational steps. Charges flow at the switching instants only and voltages remain constant in the intervals between. This changes equation (14.4.6) into

$$\mathbf{A}_k\mathbf{v}_k(nT+\sigma_k)=\mathbf{B}_k\mathbf{v}_{k-1}(nT+\sigma_{k-1})+\mathbf{g}_k w(nT+\sigma_{k-1}), \qquad t\in I_k \tag{14.11.1}$$

and makes

$$r_k(t)\equiv 0, \quad \text{for all } t.$$

The only system to be solved is the digital system. Tracing the steps in Section 14.7 we see that the only change occurs in the definition of the right-hand-side vector, which becomes

$$\mathbf{H}_{SH}(e^{j\omega_0 T})=\begin{bmatrix}\mathbf{g}_1\\ \mathbf{g}_2e^{j\omega_0\sigma_1}\\ \mathbf{g}_3e^{j\omega_0\sigma_2}\\ \vdots\\ \mathbf{g}_Ne^{j\omega_0\sigma_{N-1}}\end{bmatrix}. \tag{14.11.2}$$

Once the digital system has been solved, all the steps of previous sections remain valid except that all calculations associated with the feed-through are skipped; we do not calculate $\mathbf{p}_k$, f_k, $\mathbf{p}_k^a$, $F_{k,j}$, and $R_{k,n}$.

Symbolic analysis provides the transfer function of the digital network in terms of the variable z. Because the phases need not have equal time slots, it is necessary, in general, to provide the transfer functions from the source in any given clock phase to the output in all clock phases.

We will consider the case when unit excitation is applied in the kth clock period. The right-hand-side vector of (14.7.4) changes into

$$\mathbf{H}_k^{\text{symb}}=\begin{bmatrix}\mathbf{0}\\ \mathbf{0}\\ \vdots\\ \mathbf{g}_k\\ \vdots\\ \mathbf{0}\end{bmatrix}. \tag{14.11.3}$$

The transfer function to the output in the jth period will be

$$T_{k,j}(z) = \frac{N_{k,j}(z)}{D(z)} = \frac{\sum_{i=0}^{n_n} a_i z^i}{\sum_{i=0}^{n_m} b_i z^i} \tag{14.11.4}$$

where $D(z)$ is a common denominator of all such functions and both $N_{k,j}(z)$ and $D(z)$ are polynomials in z, having degrees n_n and n_m, respectively. Further steps are as explained in Chapter 7. The points z_i are selected on the unit circle. The denominator of the transfer function is equal to the following:

$$D(z_i) = \det \mathbf{M}(z_i) = \left[\prod_{k=1}^{N-1} \det \mathbf{A}_k\right] \cdot \det (z_i \mathbf{A}_N - \mathbf{E})$$

$$= \left[\prod_{k=1}^{N-1} \left\{\prod \text{diag. entries of } \mathbf{L}_k\right\}\right] \cdot \left\{\prod \text{diag. entries of } \mathbf{L}_N\right\}. \tag{14.11.5}$$

The factor in square brackets is obtained during preprocessing and only the second factor is computed at each new frequency z_i. We now apply forward and back block substitution and find the output in the jth phase. This generates the value $T_{k,j}(z_i)$ and, due to (14.11.4), the jth numerator value is obtained as

$$N_{k,j}(z_i) = D(z_i)\, T_{k,j}(z_i) \tag{14.11.6}$$

since $D(z_i)$ is already known from (14.11.5).

Assume next that we repeat the steps for $(n_0 + 1)$ distinct values of z_i, where $n_0 = \max\,[n_n, n_m]$. This will provide pairs of values $[z_i, D(z_i)]$ and $[z_i, N_{k,j}(z_i)]$ and the polynomials can be recovered in functional form by the discrete Fourier transform.

PROBLEMS

P.14.1. What are the stability properties of the following functions?

$$\frac{z+2}{8z^2 - 2z - 3}; \qquad \frac{1 - z^{-1} + z^{-2}}{2 + 5z^{-1} + 2z^{-2}}; \qquad \frac{2z^2 - 4}{2z^2 + z - 1}$$

P.14.2. Determine the transfer function of the following difference equation:

$$y(n) + y(n-1) = w(n); \qquad y(0) = 0.$$

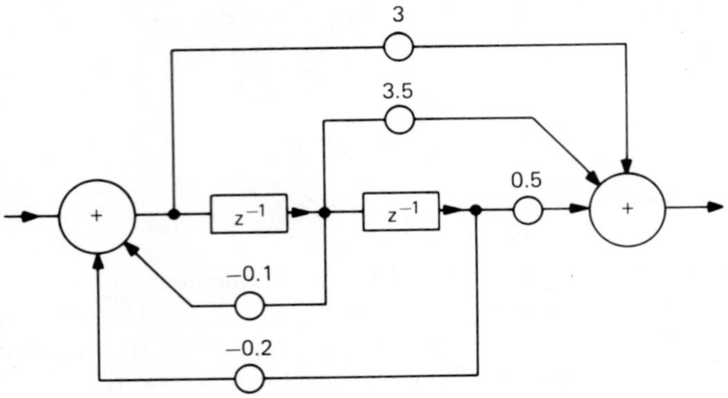

(a)

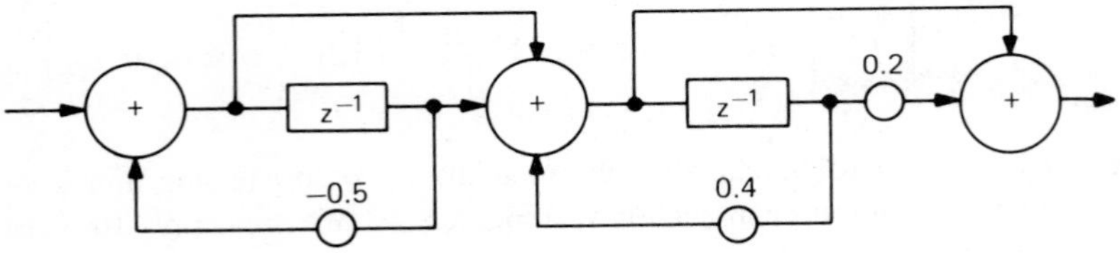

(b)

Fig. P.14.3.

P.14.3. What are the transfer functions of the digital networks shown in Fig. P.14.3?

P.14.4. Write the $\mathbf{A}_k$, $\mathbf{B}_k$ matrices and the $\mathbf{g}_k$, $\mathbf{d}_k$ vectors for the two-phase switched-capacitor networks in Fig. P.14.4.

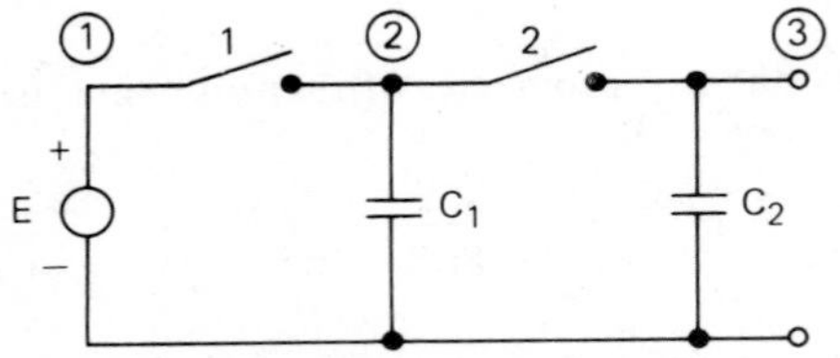

(a)

Fig. P.14.4.

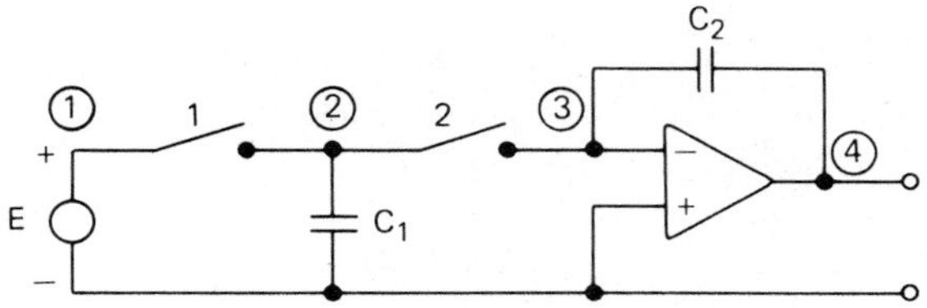

(b)

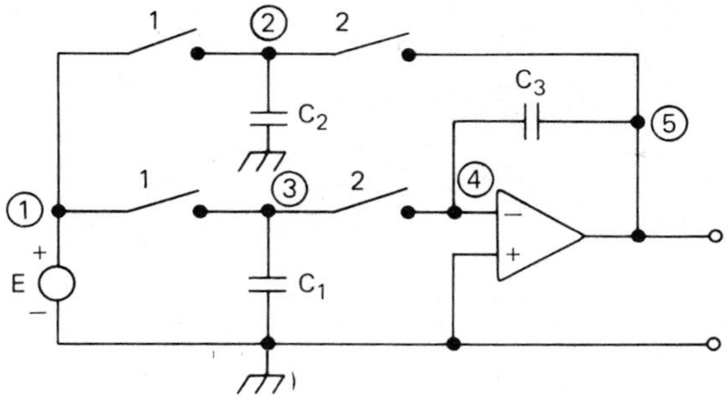

(c)

Fig. P.14.4. cont.

P.14.5. Find the z-domain transfer functions for the networks given in Problem P.14.4 by assuming that both clock periods are equal and the signal is sampled and held on the input.

P.14.6. Write the system matrix equations and derive the transfer functions for the digital networks in Fig. P.14.6.

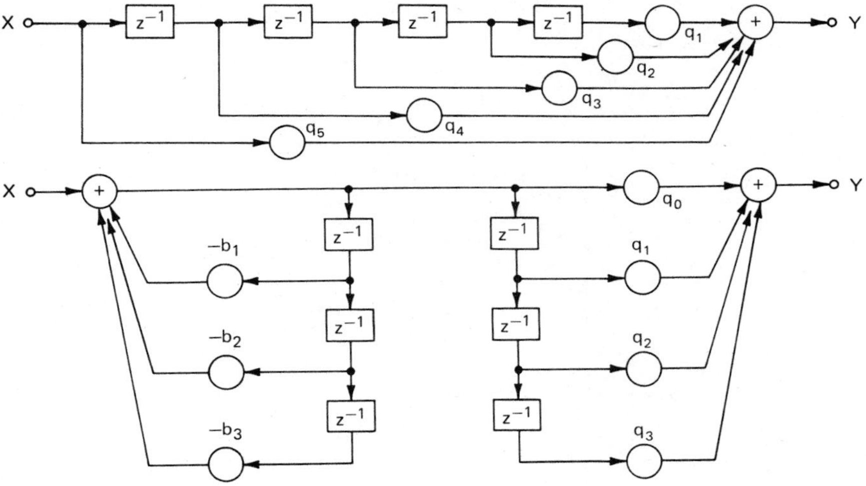

Fig. P.14.6.

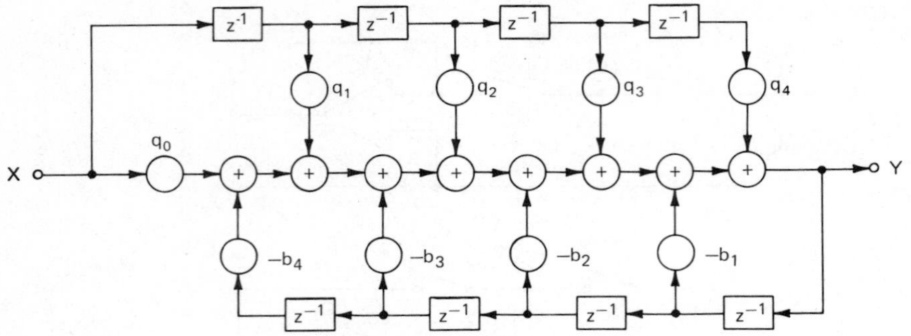

Fig. P.14.6. cont.

P.14.7. Using the two-graph method formulate the equations for the switched capacitor networks shown in Fig. P.14.7.

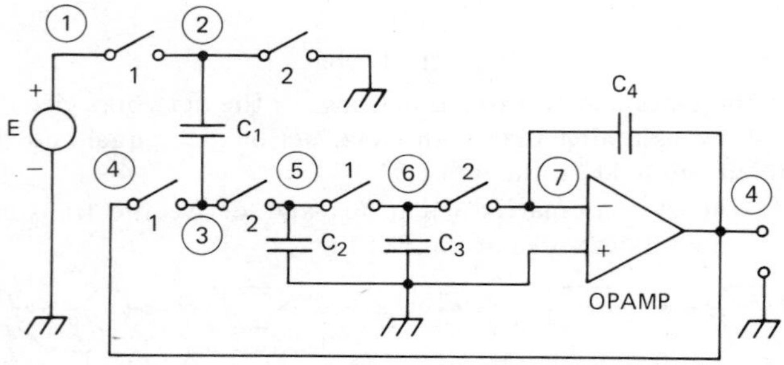

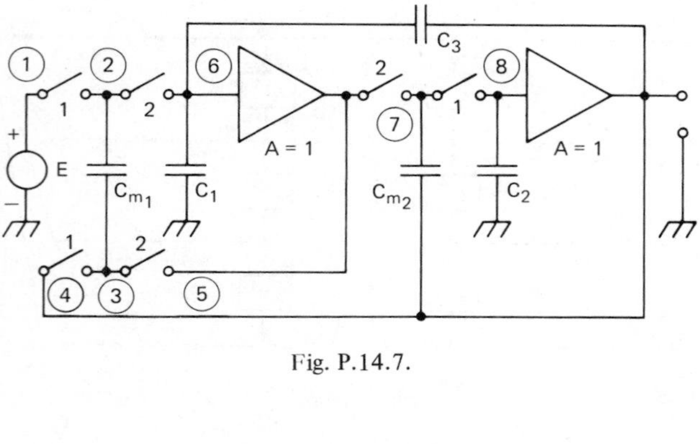

Fig. P.14.7.

REFERENCES

1. A. V. Oppenheim and R. W. Schafer: *Digital Signal Processing.* Prentice-Hall, Englewood Cliffs, NJ, 1975.
2. L. R. Rabiner and B. Gold: *Theory and Application of Digital Signal Processing.* Prentice-Hall, Englewood Cliffs, NJ, 1975.
3. A. Antoniou: *Digital Filters: Analysis and Design.* McGraw-Hill, New York, 1979.
4. R. E. Bogner and A. G. Constantinides: *Introduction to Digital Filtering.* J. Wiley & Sons, New York, 1975.
5. R. E. Crochiere and A. V. Oppenheim: Analysis of linear digital networks. *Proc. IEEE*, pp. 581–595, 1975.
6. B. J. Hosticka, R. W. Brodersen, and P. R. Gray: MOS sampled data recursive filters using switched-capacitor integrators. *IEEE Journal of Solid State Circuits*, Vol. SC-12, pp. 600–608, December 1977.
7. J. T. Caves, M. A. Copland, C. F. Rahim, and S. D. Rosenbaum: Sampled analog filtering using switched-capacitors as resistor equivalents. *IEEE Journal of Solid State Circuits*, Vol. SC-12, pp. 592–599, December 1977.
8. M. S. Ghausi and K. R. Laker: *Modern Filter Design: Active RC and Switched Capacitor.* Prentice-Hall, Englewood Cliffs, NJ, 1981.
9. C. F. Kurth and G. S. Moschytz: Nodal analysis of switched-capacitor networks. *IEEE Trans. on Circuits and Systems*, Vol. CAS-26, pp. 93–105, February 1979.
10. M. L. Liou and Y. L. Kuo: Exact analysis of switched-capacitor circuits with arbitrary inputs. *IEEE Trans. on Circuits and Systems*, Vol. CAS-26, pp. 213–223, April 1979.
11. Y. P. Tsividis: Analysis of switched-capacitor networks. *IEEE Trans. on Circuits and Systems*, Vol. CAS-26, pp. 935–947, November 1979.
12. J. Vandewalle, H. J. De Man, and J. Rabaey: Time, frequency and z-domain modified nodal analysis of switched-capacitor networks. *IEEE Trans. on Circuits and Systems*, Vol. CAS-28, pp. 186–195, March 1981.
13. *IEEE Trans. on Circuits and Systems*, Vol. CAS-27, June 1980. Special issue on integrated filters for communications.
14. *International Journal of Solid State Circuits.* Special issue on analog circuits, December 1977, 1978, 1979, 1980, 1981, 1982.
15. B. P. Lahti: *Signals, Systems and Communication.* J. Wiley & Sons, New York, 1965.
16. J. Vlach, K. Singhal, and M. Vlach: Analysis of switched capacitor networks. *IEEE International Symposium on Circuits and Systems*, pp. 9–12, 1982.

CHAPTER 15
Introduction to Optimization Theory

Optimization theory is used extensively in the design of networks. It is used to minimize or maximize a scalar function of several variables, eventually subject to additional constraints. The network designer need not have a thorough knowledge of the theory of optimization, but he is responsible for the preparation of the network function to be minimized and for providing the gradients required by most optimization routines.

In order to formulate such functions, the network designer must have at least some basic knowledge of optimization theory. He must be familiar with various technical terms used in this area and have information about the availability of various computer codes. This chapter is an attempt to provide such basic information.

The first section discusses the terminology. It is followed by a description of classical minimization theory and Lagrange multipliers are introduced for the solution of problems with equality constraints.

Most modern optimization algorithms are iterative. A basic algorithm, used in many available computer routines, is introduced in Section 15.3. Two steps in the basic algorithm are fundamental: the determination of a search direction and the search for the minimum in this direction. The search for a minimum in a specified direction is explained in Section 15.4 to an extent sufficient for most purposes. The determination of the search direction is the most difficult part of optimization theory. No attempt is made to cover this vast area, but some important methods are discussed and their advantages and disadvantages are pointed out. Finally, Section 15.7 covers constrained minimization, with emphasis being on a recent algorithm due to Powell that has proved very effective in practice. Applications are given in Chapter 17.

15.1. BASIC DEFINITIONS

The minimization problem is usually defined as follows:

$$\begin{array}{lll} \text{minimize the objective function:} & F = F(\mathbf{x}) & \\ \text{subject to equality constraints:} & e_i(\mathbf{x}) = 0, & i = 1, 2, \ldots, k_1 \\ \text{and inequality constraints:} & g_j(\mathbf{x}) \geqslant 0, & j = 1, 2, \ldots, k_2. \end{array} \tag{15.1.1}$$

The solution vector $\mathbf{x}^*$ must satisfy the above constraints. If there are no constraints, the problem is said to be *unconstrained*; otherwise it is *constrained.* The functions $e_i(\mathbf{x})$ and/or $g_j(\mathbf{x})$ may be either linear or nonlinear. A typical example of linear inequality constraints is the condition

$$x_i - l_i \geqslant 0 \tag{15.1.2}$$

which specifies that the variable x_i must be larger than a lower bound l_i. We could also restrict the range of x_i through an upper limit by the constraint

$$u_i - x_i \geqslant 0. \tag{15.1.3}$$

Constraints like these are often involved if the variables are values of network elements: we cannot realize negative elements and, eventually, we must restrict the values to lie within lower and upper bounds to obtain technically reasonable results.

The formulation of the objective function $F(\mathbf{x})$ requires insight into the problem at hand. As an example, the problem of finding a solution $\mathbf{x}^*$ of a set of m equations in n variables, $m \leqslant n$:

$$f_j(x_1, x_2, \ldots, x_n) = 0, \qquad j = 1, 2, \ldots, m$$

may be formulated as the minimization of a scalar function of the same variables:

$$F(\mathbf{x}) = \sum_{j=1}^{m} f_j^2(\mathbf{x}). \tag{15.1.4}$$

The minimum, for which $F(\mathbf{x}^*) = 0$, is obviously also the solution of the set of nonlinear equations.

Almost all modern minimization techniques are based on determining a sequence of vectors $\mathbf{x}^k$ such that

$$F(\mathbf{x}^0) > F(\mathbf{x}^1) > \cdots > F(\mathbf{x}^k). \tag{15.1.5}$$

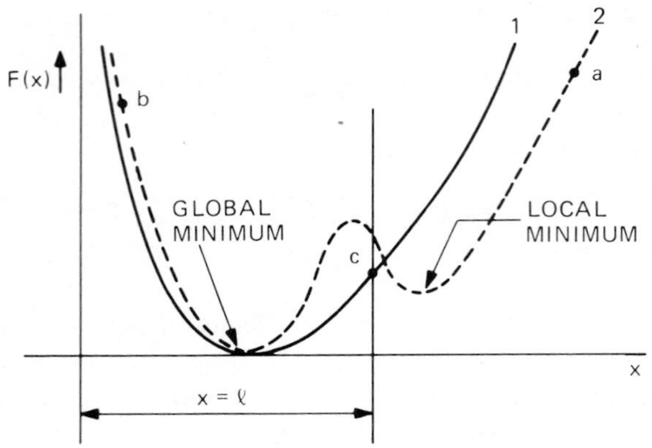

Fig. 15.1.1. Explanation of expressions used in optimization.

This sequence will converge to the minimum $\mathbf{x}^*$ if the function is *convex.* The minimum is then a *global minimum.* If the function is not convex, it may happen that we get only to a *local minimum.*

Without going into mathematical details of convexity we illustrate its implication on an example in a single variable. Figure 15.1.1 shows two curves. Let the steps described by (15.1.5) be performed on curve 1. No matter what point we start from, following a *downhill* direction will lead us to the global minimum. In this case our function is convex. On the other hand, starting on curve 2 at the point a and taking small steps in the downhill direction will lead us to the *local* minimum. Once this local minimum has been reached, small steps in either direction cannot find a new function value which is smaller than that at the local minimum. We need a large jump to get away from this minimum to land, say, at the point b, from which the downhill direction leads to the global minimum. We also note that the derivative is zero at each minimum.

In most cases we know nothing about the shape of the function, especially if there are many variables. It is very difficult (and probably useless) to try to establish the convexity of a given practical problem. It is much simpler to carry out the minimization several times, starting from various points and observing the point or points to which the algorithm converges. If the results differ, the problem has local minima. The concept of convexity is needed mainly for theoretical considerations and to establish proofs that a given method will converge.

We use the example of Fig. 15.1.1 to explain constrained minimization. The function is to be minimized under the additional condition $g(x) \equiv x - l \geqslant 0$. Starting on the right side of the curves and proceeding downhill will get us to the point c on curve 1 but only as far as the local minimum on curve 2. We say that the constraint is *active* in the first case and *inactive* in the second. The region where $g(x) \geqslant 0$ is the *feasible* region and any point on the curve is a *feasible point.* Points where $g(x) < 0$ are infeasible points.

To move downhill on a curve requires information about the direction. The direction can be established by exploratory moves (function evaluations) or can be deduced from the derivative of the function. In the case of functions of several variables the derivative information is contained in the ***gradient.***

The gradient of a function $F(\mathbf{x})$ of n variables is an n-vector

$$\nabla \mathbf{F} = \nabla \mathbf{F}(\mathbf{x}) = \begin{bmatrix} \frac{\partial F}{\partial x_1} & \frac{\partial F}{\partial x_2} & \cdots & \frac{\partial F}{\partial x_n} \end{bmatrix}^t . \tag{15.1.6}$$

It points in the direction of increasing function values and thus $-\nabla \mathbf{F}$ indicates the downhill direction.

If we consider another direction, $\mathbf{s}$, then the function will decrease in that direction if

$$-\mathbf{s}^t \nabla \mathbf{F} > 0. \tag{15.1.7}$$

Finally note that *minimization* or *maximization* are handled by the same computer routines since if $F(\mathbf{x})$ has a minimum at $\mathbf{x}^*$ then $-F(\mathbf{x})$ has a maximum at the same point.

15.2. CLASSICAL MINIMIZATION

Elementary calculus states that the maxima or minima of functions of a single variable are found by calculating the derivative, setting it equal to zero and solving for the point x^*. The same is true for functions of several variables, but now *all* the derivatives must be set equal to zero:

$$\nabla \mathbf{F}(\mathbf{x}) = \mathbf{0}.$$

This is a set of equations and their solution gives the optimum point $\mathbf{x}^*$.

EXAMPLE 15.2.1. Find the minimum of the function

$$F(\mathbf{x}) = (x_2 - x_1)^2 + (1 - x_1)^2$$

by setting the gradient equal to zero.

The gradient is

$$\nabla \mathbf{F}(\mathbf{x}) = \begin{bmatrix} 4x_1 - 2x_2 - 2 \\ 2x_2 - 2x_1 \end{bmatrix}.$$

and the solution vector is $\mathbf{x}^* = [1 \quad 1]^t$.

The simple problem in Example 15.2.1 lead to a system of linear equations. More complicated problems will lead to systems of nonlinear equations and iterative schemes would be required for their solution. The reader might try, for instance, the function $F(\mathbf{x}) = (x_2 - x_1^2)^2 + (1 - x_1)^2$ and apply the Newton-Raphson method for the solution.

The first method for constrained minimization was suggested by Lagrange. For the problem

$$\begin{aligned} &\text{minimize:} && F(\mathbf{x}) \\ &\text{subject to:} && e_j(\mathbf{x}) = 0, \qquad j = 1, 2, \ldots, k_1 \end{aligned}$$

a new function, called the *Lagrangian*,

$$L(\mathbf{x}, \boldsymbol{\lambda}) = F(\mathbf{x}) - \sum_{j=1}^{k_1} \lambda_j e_j(\mathbf{x}) \tag{15.2.1}$$

is formed. Here $\boldsymbol{\lambda} = [\lambda_1 \quad \lambda_2 \quad \cdots \quad \lambda_{k_1}]^t$ is a vector of additional variables called the *Lagrange multipliers*. In order to locate the optimum of the constrained problem, the derivatives of $L(\mathbf{x}, \boldsymbol{\lambda})$ with respect to $\mathbf{x}$ as well as $\boldsymbol{\lambda}$ are set to zero and the system of equations

$$\begin{aligned} \frac{\partial L}{\partial x_i} &= \frac{\partial F}{\partial x_i} - \sum_{j=1}^{k_1} \lambda_j \frac{\partial e_j(\mathbf{x})}{\partial x_i} = 0, \qquad i = 1, 2, \ldots, n \\ \frac{\partial L}{\partial \lambda_j} &= -e_j(\mathbf{x}) = 0, \qquad j = 1, 2, \ldots, k_1 \end{aligned} \tag{15.2.2}$$

is solved.

EXAMPLE 15.2.2. Find the minimum of

$$\begin{aligned} & && F(\mathbf{x}) = (x_2 - x_1)^2 + (1 - x_1)^2 \\ &\text{subject to:} && e(\mathbf{x}) = x_1 + x_2 - 4 = 0. \end{aligned}$$

Form

$$L(\mathbf{x}, \boldsymbol{\lambda}) = (x_2 - x_1)^2 + (1 - x_1)^2 - \lambda_1(x_1 + x_2 - 4).$$

Differentiating with respect to x_1, x_2, and λ_1, obtain

$$\frac{\partial L}{\partial x_1} = 4x_1 - 2x_2 - \lambda_1 - 2 = 0$$

$$\frac{\partial L}{\partial x_2} = -2x_1 + 2x_2 - \lambda_1 = 0$$

$$\frac{\partial L}{\partial \lambda_1} = -(x_1 + x_2 - 4) = 0$$

The solution of this linear system is $x_1 = \frac{9}{5}$, $x_2 = \frac{11}{5}$, $\lambda_1 = \frac{4}{5}$.

The method of Lagrange multipliers has mainly theoretical importance. Modern optimization methods rely on iterations in which a sequence (15.1.5) of intermediate solutions is found. The following sections outline the main features of such algorithms.

15.3. BASIC ITERATIVE ALGORITHM

Let the function of n variables $F(\mathbf{x})$ and an initial starting point

$$\mathbf{x}^0 = [x_1^0 \quad x_2^0 \quad \cdots \quad x_n^0]^t$$

be given. We wish to proceed from this point to other points such that

$$F(\mathbf{x}^0) > F(\mathbf{x}^1) > \cdots > F(\mathbf{x}^k). \tag{15.3.1}$$

To do so we define a direction in which we wish to proceed. A *direction* in an n-dimensional space is an n-vector $\mathbf{s} = [s_1 \quad s_2 \quad \cdots \quad s_n]^t$. Assume that we take a step of length d along this direction. For the kth iteration, the new point will be

$$\mathbf{x}^{k+1} = \mathbf{x}^k + d_k \mathbf{s}^k \tag{15.3.2}$$

where d_k is a real constant. The increment is defined as

$$\Delta \mathbf{x}^k = \mathbf{x}^{k+1} - \mathbf{x}^k = d_k \mathbf{s}^k. \tag{15.3.3}$$

To be effective, the search in the n-dimensional space must proceed in linearly independent directions. These directions can be collected in an $n \times n$ matrix

$$\mathbf{S} = [\mathbf{s}^0 \quad \mathbf{s}^1 \quad \cdots \quad \mathbf{s}^{n-1}]. \tag{15.3.4}$$

The matrix is updated according to some scheme. It is not practical to keep the matrix $\mathbf{S}$ unchanged but it will serve for an example.

EXAMPLE 15.3.1. Apply the minimization steps (15.3.1) through (15.3.4) to the function

$$F(\mathbf{x}) = x_1^2 + x_2^2 + 3x_3^2.$$

Let the matrix of directions be a unit matrix and let the starting point be $\mathbf{x}^0 = [1 \quad 2 \quad 1]^t$.

The function has an obvious global minimum for $x_1 = x_2 = x_3 = 0$. The matrix of directions is

$$\mathbf{S} = \begin{array}{c} \begin{matrix} \mathbf{s}^0 & \mathbf{s}^1 & \mathbf{s}^2 \end{matrix} \\ \begin{bmatrix} 1 & 0 & 0 \\ 0 & 1 & 0 \\ 0 & 0 & 1 \end{bmatrix} \end{array}.$$

The initial function value is $F(\mathbf{x}^0) = 8$. Take $\mathbf{s}^0$ as the first direction and a step length $d_0 = -0.5$ (so far the choice of d_0 is arbitrary). According to (15.3.2),

$$\mathbf{x}^1 = \begin{bmatrix} 1 \\ 2 \\ 1 \end{bmatrix} - 0.5 \begin{bmatrix} 1 \\ 0 \\ 0 \end{bmatrix} = \begin{bmatrix} 0.5 \\ 2 \\ 1 \end{bmatrix}.$$

The function value at $\mathbf{x}^1$ is $F(\mathbf{x}^1) = 7.25 < F(\mathbf{x}^0)$ and we accept this as the first successful result. Proceeding to the second direction $\mathbf{s}^1$ and taking, say, $d_1 = -1$, we get

$$\mathbf{x}^2 = \begin{bmatrix} 0.5 \\ 2 \\ 1 \end{bmatrix} - 1 \begin{bmatrix} 0 \\ 1 \\ 0 \end{bmatrix} = \begin{bmatrix} 0.5 \\ 1 \\ 1 \end{bmatrix}$$

and $F(\mathbf{x}^2) = 4.25$. We could continue with the third direction, then go back to the first one and repeat the procedure until we get to the minimum.

Several improvements are apparent at first glance. If we change our policy of accepting any solution which reduces the function value to trying to find a minimum in the given direction, the number of steps needed to get to the optimum point may be reduced. Thus *minimization along a line* will be needed. Secondly, we can use the derivatives of the function to get better directions. Finally, we can obtain second derivatives (or approximations to them) and get still more information about the best direction of search.

Equations (14.4.6) and (14.4.9) represent two *decoupled* systems. If (14.4.6) is solved for the discrete time values $\mathbf{v}_k$, then using (14.4.5) we can write

$$\mathbf{v}_k(t) = \mathbf{v}_k + \mathbf{p}_k r_k(t). \tag{14.4.10}$$

The solution thus consists of two components:

(a) $\mathbf{v}_k$, the contribution of the discrete system (14.4.6).
(b) $\mathbf{p}_k r_k(t)$, the contribution due to *feed-through* system (14.4.9).

Independent solutions of (14.4.6) and (14.4.9) form the basis of frequency domain analysis of SC networks with continuous inputs.

14.5. FORMULATION OF MINIMAL-SIZE SC NETWORK EQUATIONS

Switching action in SC networks modifies the topology of the network and can result in a different number of nodes in each phase. Although switches can be incorporated into the modified nodal formulation so that the system matrix size remains invariant (see Section 4.4), such a choice invariably leads to a large set of equations. The approach recommended here reduces the set of equations in each phase to the smallest possible number. It is based on the two-graph method explained in Sections 4.7 and 4.8 and the reader should have working knowledge of the method before proceeding further. For easy reference, the subset of network elements usually encountered in SC networks and the way they enter the two-graph modified nodal formulation are given in Fig. 14.5.1. The two-graph representation results in contraction of some nodes. Further reduction in system size may occur due to the specific structure of the SC network. For instance, the voltage source may be disconnected from the network in some phases. In this case, the edge of the source is contracted on the voltage graph. In some phases, the output may be disconnected from the rest of the network; these situations can be detected topologically as well. In all such cases, the nodes are renumbered to follow a natural sequence and zero is reserved for ground.

The $\mathbf{A}_k$ matrices introduced in Section 14.4 are formed by considering the *I*- and *V*-graphs of the particular phase. The $\mathbf{B}_k$ matrices which represent the charges on the capacitors at the end of the previous phase are obtained by using the same rules but *taking the I-graph of that particular phase and the V-graph of the phase immediately preceeding it in time.*

EXAMPLE 14.5.1. Consider the SC network in Fig. 14.5.2(a). It has 7 nodes and 6 switches and operates under a two-phase clock. The nodes are numbered

ELEMENT	SYMBOL	I-GRAPH	V-GRAPH	MATRIX
VOLTAGE SOURCE	j o + 1 $\bigcirc$ E j' o −	$j_I \equiv j'_I$ o	o j_V j'_V	SOURCE $\begin{array}{cc} j_V & j'_V \end{array}$ VECTOR $\begin{bmatrix} \\ \hline 1 & -1 \end{bmatrix} \begin{bmatrix} \\ \hline E \end{bmatrix}$
ADMITTANCE	j o + I y V j' o −	o j_I j'_I	o j_V j'_V	$\begin{array}{cc} j_V & j'_V \end{array}$ $\begin{array}{c} j_I \\ j'_I \end{array} \begin{bmatrix} y & -y \\ -y & \cdot y \end{bmatrix}$
VVT	j o + k $+$ V $\bigcirc$ μV j' − − k' o	j_I o $k_I \equiv k'_I$ o j'_I o	j_V o k_V o j'_V o k'_V o	$\begin{array}{cccc} j_V & j'_V & k_V & k'_V \end{array}$ $\begin{bmatrix} \\ \hline -\mu & \mu & 1 & -1 \end{bmatrix}$
OPERATIONAL AMPLIFIER	j o $\quad$ k ∞ j' $\quad k'$	j_I o $k_I \equiv k'_I$ o j'_I o	k_V o $j_V \equiv j'_V$ o k'_V o	———
UNITY GAIN BUFFER	j o $\triangleright$ k o 1 $\quad$ o $\quad$ o ⏚	j'_I o k_I o ⏚	$j_V \equiv k_V$ o ⏚	———

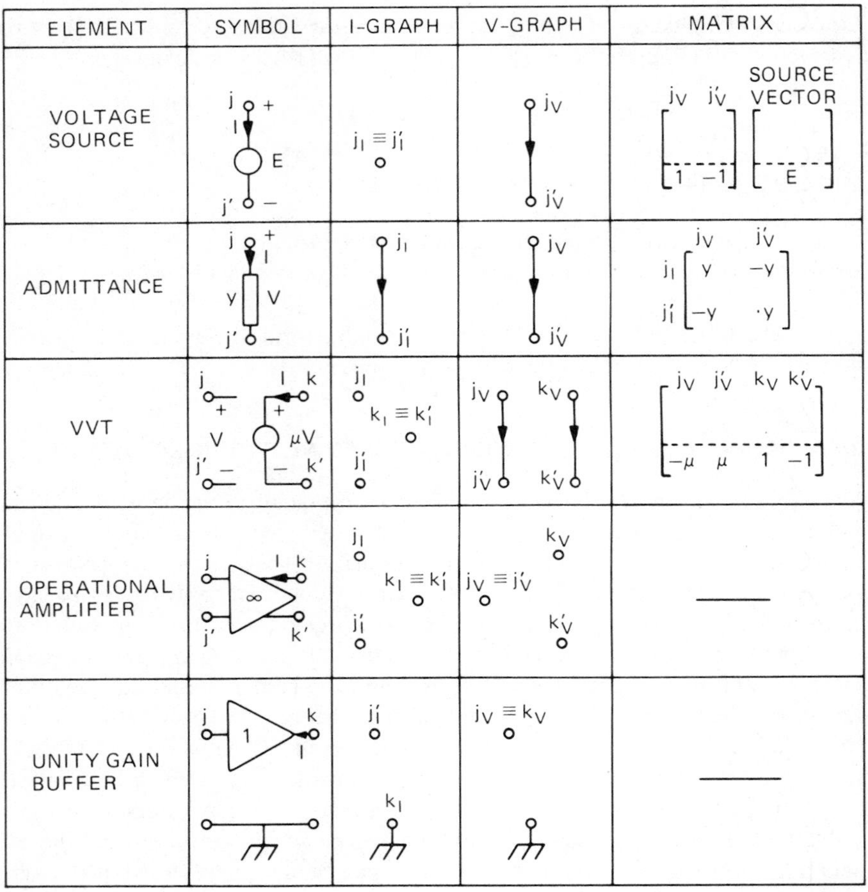

Fig. 14.5.1. Two-graph representation of the most important SC-elements and the way they enter the modified nodal two-graph formulation.

in circles, the numbers at the switches indicate the phase during which they are closed. Network configurations in the two phases are redrawn in Fig. 14.5.2(b, c). The initial data for the network are contained in a connectivity table (compare with Section 4.7):

	E	C_1	C_2	C_3	C_4	Op_{in}	Op_{out}
From:	1	2	4	5	6	0	7
To:	0	3	0	0	7	6	0

Methods which do not require derivatives of the function are called *direct search* methods and the simplest possible representative is the above example. We will not consider these methods here since, as we have shown in Chapter 6, *network theory provides the gradients very cheaply.* However, minimization in a particular direction will be needed and is explained in the next section.

If the gradient at a point is known, this information may speed up the minimization process. In fact, *steepest descent* methods are based on the assumption that the fastest decrease in the function will be achieved if we proceed along the negative of the direction of the gradient. However, these methods do not take advantage of information obtained at previous steps. If previous information is used in defining the next direction of search, one can hope for faster convergence. Such methods are summarized under the name of *conjugate gradient* techniques.

In some cases we use information about second derivatives. Usually, the second derivatives are simulated instead of being calculated directly. Such methods are known under the name *variable metric* techniques or, sometimes, *quasi-Newton* techniques. We summarize the material of this section by indicating a general algorithm which is valid for many iterative minimization methods. Differences appear in the selection of the search directions $\mathbf{s}^k$ and also in some details of the termination criteria.

1. Set $k = 0$ and select the starting point $\mathbf{x}^0$.
2. Calculate $F(\mathbf{x}^k)$ and $\nabla\mathbf{F}(\mathbf{x}^k)$ (if the method requires the gradient).
3. Determine the search direction $\mathbf{s}^k$.
4. Normalize the search vector to unit length.
5. In the direction $\mathbf{s}^k$, find a step length d_k such that either

$$F(\mathbf{x}^k + d_k\mathbf{s}^k) < F(\mathbf{x}^k)$$

   or $F(\mathbf{x}^k + d_k\mathbf{s}^k)$ is the minimum in the direction $\mathbf{s}^k$.
6. Obtain

$$\Delta\mathbf{x}^k = d_k\mathbf{s}^k$$
$$\mathbf{x}^{k+1} = \mathbf{x}^k + \Delta\mathbf{x}^k.$$

7. If $|F(\mathbf{x}^{k+1}) - F(\mathbf{x}^k)| < \epsilon_1$ and $||\Delta\mathbf{x}^k|| < \epsilon_2$, stop. Else set $k = k + 1$ and go to step 2.

Let it be mentioned that a vector $\mathbf{s}$ has a *norm*

$$||\mathbf{s}||^2 = \sum s_i^2. \tag{15.3.5}$$

If each entry of the vector is divided by its norm, the resulting vector is normalized to unit length.

15.4. SEARCH ALONG A LINE

The general optimization algorithm introduced in the last section required the determination of the step length d_k along the search direction $\mathbf{s}^k$. The possibility of selecting d_k to minimize the function F along the line $\mathbf{x}^k + d_k\mathbf{s}^k$ was mentioned. We will consider two possible ways of performing the line search. The first case does not require gradient information and interpolates a parabola by taking three distinct points along the line of search. In the second case we interpolate a cubic polynomial using function values and derivatives at two points.

We explain the search technique by defining the problem in a single real variable denoted by u and we let the function value be v. Consider Fig. 15.4.1. The first function value v_0 is the result of the previous minimization step and is known. We set the origin of the axes such that $u_0 = 0$. Select two (arbitrary) step sizes u_1 and u_2 and calculate the function values v_1, v_2. This provides three points $(0, v_0)$, (u_1, v_1), and (u_2, v_2) which are used to interpolate a parabola

$$v = Cu^2 + Bu + A.$$

Inserting the three points provides three equations for the unknowns A, B, C:

$$\begin{aligned} v_0 &= A \\ v_1 &= Cu_1^2 + Bu_1 + A \\ v_2 &= Cu_2^2 + Bu_2 + A. \end{aligned}$$

The solution is

$$\begin{aligned} C &= \frac{u_2(v_1 - v_0) - u_1(v_2 - v_0)}{u_1^2 u_2 - u_2^2 u_1} \\ B &= \frac{-u_2^2(v_1 - v_0) + u_1^2(v_2 - v_0)}{u_1^2 u_2 - u_2^2 u_1} \\ A &= v_0. \end{aligned}$$

The mininum of a parabola is found by setting $v' = 2Cu + B = 0$, provided $v'' > 0$. The distance to the minimum of the parabola is thus

$$d_{\min} = \frac{-B}{2C} = \frac{u_2^2(v_1 - v_0) - u_1^2(v_2 - v_0)}{2[u_2(v_1 - v_0) - u_1(v_2 - v_1)]} \tag{15.4.1}$$

provided $C > 0$.

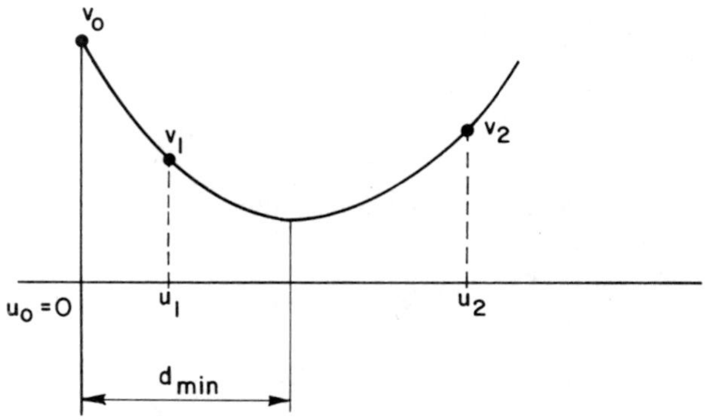

Fig. 15.4.1. Minimum of a parabola, obtained by means of three points.

EXAMPLE 15.4.1. Use the three-point search technique on the problem of Example 15.3.1. The initial point is $\mathbf{x}^0 = [1 \quad 2 \quad 1]^t$ and $F(\mathbf{x}^0) = 8$.

The first point is $u_0 = 0$, $v_0 = 8$. Select the distance $d_0 = -0.5$ along the direction $\mathbf{s}^0$. This was also done before, with $F(\mathbf{x}^0 - 0.5\mathbf{s}^0) = 7.25$. The second point has the coordinates $u_1 = -0.5$, $v_1 = 7.25$. We need another point with, say, $d = 0.5$, for which $F(\mathbf{x}^0 + 0.5\mathbf{s}^0) = 9.25$. The third point is $u_2 = 0.5$, $v_2 = 9.25$. Then

$$d_{\min} = \frac{0.25(7.25 - 8) - 0.25(9.25 - 8)}{2[0.5(7.25 - 8) + 0.5(9.25 - 8)]} = -1.$$

This distance is used to move from $\mathbf{x}^0$ to $\mathbf{x}^1$ by applying (15.3.2):

$$\mathbf{x}^1 = [1 \quad 2 \quad 1]^t + (-1)[1 \quad 0 \quad 0]^t = [0 \quad 2 \quad 1]^t, \quad \text{for which } F(\mathbf{x}^1) = 7.$$

Since our example is a quadratic function in three variables, the minimum in the direction $\mathbf{s}^0$ is obtained exactly. In more complicated cases the steps may be repeated again by calculating additional points until the true minimum has been found. Alternatively, we may search only for $F(\mathbf{x}^1) < F(\mathbf{x}^0)$ and proceed to the next direction.

If the gradients are easily available, then we consider the function value as well as the derivative. For the single-variable problem $u_0 = 0$, select u_1 and calculate v_0, v_0', v_1, and v_1'. This provides the necessary information for the interpolation of a cubic polynomial

$$v = Du^3 + Cu^2 + Bu + A. \tag{15.4.2}$$

Its derivative is

$$v' = 3Du^2 + 2Cu + B. \tag{15.4.3}$$

The two extremes are found by setting the derivative equal to zero:

$$u_{\text{extreme}} = \frac{-2C \pm \sqrt{4C^2 - 12BD}}{6D}. \tag{15.4.4}$$

To decide which sign must be taken for a minimum we note that the second derivative must be positive:

$$6Du + 2C > 0 \tag{15.4.5}$$

Inserting the extremes from (15.4.4) it can be shown that the positive sign corresponds to a minimum.

The coefficients A, B, C, D are still unknown, but we use (15.4.2) and (15.4.3):

$$\begin{aligned} v_0 &= A \\ v_0' &= B \\ v_1 &= Du_1^3 + Cu_1^2 + Bu_1 + A \\ v_1' &= 3Du_1^2 + 2Cu_1 + B. \end{aligned} \tag{15.4.6}$$

Since A, B are known already, insert into the last two equations and solve:

$$\begin{bmatrix} u_1^3 & u_1^2 \\ 3u_1^2 & 2u_1 \end{bmatrix} \begin{bmatrix} D \\ C \end{bmatrix} = \begin{bmatrix} v_1 - v_0' u_1 - v_0 \\ v_1' - v_0' \end{bmatrix}. \tag{15.4.7}$$

Then

$$d_{\min} = \frac{-C + \sqrt{C^2 - 3BD}}{3D}, \quad \text{if } D \neq 0. \tag{15.4.8}$$

If $D = 0$, the interpolated curve is only a parabola of second degree and the equations are modified appropriately.

EXAMPLE 15.4.2. Apply (15.4.8) to the problem of Example 15.4.1. The initial point is $\mathbf{x}^0 = [1 \quad 2 \quad 1]^t$, $\mathbf{s}^0 = [1 \quad 0 \quad 0]^t$, $F(\mathbf{x}^0) = 8$.

The gradient of the function is

$$\nabla \mathbf{F}(\mathbf{x}) = [2x_1 \quad 2x_2 \quad 6x_3]^t$$

and $\nabla \mathbf{F}(\mathbf{x}^0) = [2 \quad 4 \quad 6]^t$. Select an arbitrary step length, say $d_0 = -3$. Using (15.3.2), the point is obtained:

$$\mathbf{x}^0 - 3\mathbf{s}^0 = [1 \quad 2 \quad 1]^t - 3[1 \quad 0 \quad 0]^t = [-2 \quad 2 \quad 1]^t.$$

The function value is

$$F(\mathbf{x}^0 - 3\mathbf{s}^0) = 11$$

and the gradient is

$$\nabla \mathbf{F}(\mathbf{x}^0 - 3\mathbf{s}^0) = [-4 \quad 4 \quad 6]^t.$$

The derivatives in the search direction are calculated by means of the products $\mathbf{s}^t \nabla \mathbf{F}(\mathbf{x})$. Thus

$$(\mathbf{s}^0)^t \nabla \mathbf{F}(\mathbf{x}^0) = [1 \quad 0 \quad 0]\ [2 \quad 4 \quad 6]^t = 2$$

$$(\mathbf{s}^0)^t \nabla \mathbf{F}(\mathbf{x}^0 - 3\mathbf{s}^0) = [1 \quad 0 \quad 0]\ [-4 \quad 4 \quad 6]^t = -4.$$

We now identify the variables

$$u_0 = 0 \qquad u_1 = d_0 = -3$$

$$v_0 = F(\mathbf{x}^0) = 8 \qquad v_1 = F(\mathbf{x}^0 - 3\mathbf{s}^0) = 11$$

$$v_0' = (\mathbf{s}^0)^t \nabla \mathbf{F}(\mathbf{x}^0) = 2 \qquad v_1' = (\mathbf{s}^0)^t \nabla \mathbf{F}(\mathbf{x}^0 - 3\mathbf{s}^0) = -4.$$

Solution of (15.4.7) provides $D = 0$ and $C = 1$. The interpolated curve is only a parabola of second degree (as should be expected from the problem). Instead of (15.4.8) use the parabolic model with the result $d_{\min} = -1$, as before.

15.5. QUADRATIC FUNCTIONS IN SEVERAL VARIABLES

The choice of search directions is the most difficult part in the theory of minimization algorithms and many considerations must be taken into account. Usually, it is desirable that the algorithm require the user to provide only the first-order derivatives, since higher-order derivatives are often too expensive or too difficult to obtain. On the other hand, first derivatives do not contain sufficient information about the curvature of the function. For these reasons, many modern minimization algorithms approximate the second derivative information by means of special formulae. In order to be able to design such formulae, the properties of quadratic functions in n variables must be understood. This section derives the main properties and should help the reader understand the various specialized developments available in the literature.

A differentiable function $F(\mathbf{x})$ can be expanded into a Taylor series and the expansion truncated after the third term. This provides a quadratic approximation to the function:

$$F(\mathbf{x} + \Delta\mathbf{x}) = F(\mathbf{x}) + (\Delta\mathbf{x})^t\, \nabla\mathbf{F} + \tfrac{1}{2}\, (\Delta\mathbf{x})^t\, \mathbf{G}(\mathbf{x})\, \Delta\mathbf{x}. \qquad (15.5.1)$$

Here $\nabla \mathbf{F}$ is the gradient (15.1.6) and $\mathbf{G}(\mathbf{x})$ is a square symmetric matrix of second derivatives called the Hessian matrix:

$$\mathbf{G}(\mathbf{x}) = \begin{bmatrix} \frac{\partial^2 F}{\partial x_1 \partial x_1} & \frac{\partial^2 F}{\partial x_1 \partial x_2} & \cdots & \frac{\partial^2 F}{\partial x_1 \partial x_n} \\ \frac{\partial^2 F}{\partial x_2 \partial x_1} & \frac{\partial^2 F}{\partial x_2 \partial x_2} & \cdots & \frac{\partial^2 F}{\partial x_2 \partial x_n} \\ \vdots & \vdots & & \vdots \\ \frac{\partial^2 F}{\partial x_n \partial x_1} & \frac{\partial^2 F}{\partial x_n \partial x_2} & \cdots & \frac{\partial^2 F}{\partial x_n \partial x_n} \end{bmatrix}. \tag{15.5.2}$$

Before starting the study of quadratic functions we make an important observation valid for *any* differentiable function. Assume that we minimize $F(\mathbf{x})$ in a given direction $\mathbf{s}^k$ and reach its minimum at the point $\mathbf{x}^{k+1}$ in this direction. The gradient at this point must be orthogonal to the search direction:

$$(\mathbf{s}^k)^t \nabla \mathbf{F}^{k+1} = (\nabla \mathbf{F}^{k+1})^t \mathbf{s}^k = 0. \tag{15.5.3}$$

Assume for the moment that this is not true; in that case the gradient must have a component in the search direction, indicating that further downhill movement is still possible. Since this contradicts the assumption that we have reached the minimum, validity of (15.5.3) is confirmed. The situation is sketched in Fig. 15.5.1.

Returning to the quadratic function (15.5.1), assume that we reach a special point, $\hat{\mathbf{x}}$, at which the gradient is the null vector:

$$\nabla \mathbf{F}(\hat{\mathbf{x}}) = \mathbf{0}. \tag{15.5.4}$$

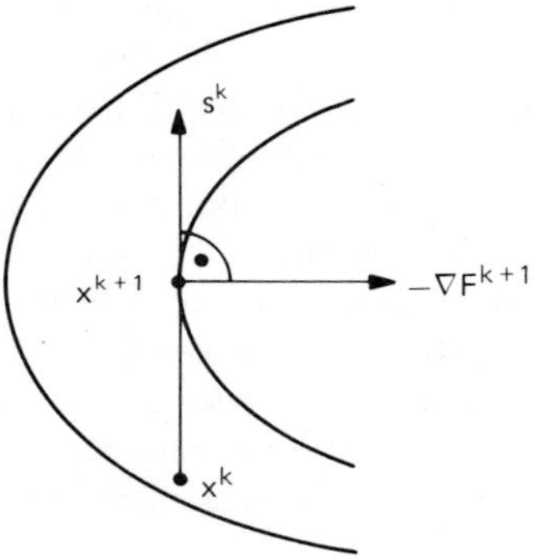

Fig. 15.5.1. Orthogonality of the search direction $\mathbf{s}^k$ and gradient at the minimum in that direction.

This simplifies (15.5.1) to

$$F(\hat{\mathbf{x}} + \Delta\mathbf{x}) = F(\hat{\mathbf{x}}) + \tfrac{1}{2}(\Delta\mathbf{x})^t\,\mathbf{G}(\hat{\mathbf{x}})\,\Delta\mathbf{x} \tag{15.5.5}$$

and the product $(\Delta\mathbf{x})^t\mathbf{G}\Delta\mathbf{x}$ determines the type of function we are dealing with. Three situations may occur. If the product is larger than zero for any choice of the vector $\Delta\mathbf{x}$, then the point must be a minimum (possibly local). If the product is smaller than zero for any $\Delta\mathbf{x}$, the point must be a maximum. If the choice of $\Delta\mathbf{x}$ can make the product either positive or negative, the point $\hat{\mathbf{x}}$ is a saddle point; the name originates from the shape of the two-dimensional surface. The three possibilities are determined by the properties of the matrix $\mathbf{G}$ and the following definitions are introduced for a general $n \times n$ matrix $\mathbf{G}$:

$$\text{Matrix } \mathbf{G} \text{ is } \left\{\begin{array}{l}\text{positive definite}\\ \text{negative definite}\\ \text{indefinite}\end{array}\right\} \text{ if } \left\{\begin{array}{l}\mathbf{s}^t\mathbf{G}\mathbf{s} > 0\\ \mathbf{s}^t\mathbf{G}\mathbf{s} < 0\\ \mathbf{s}^t\mathbf{G}\mathbf{s} \gtrless 0\end{array}\right. \tag{15.5.6}$$

for all nonzero $\mathbf{s}$.

Our further development will consider functions having minima and consequently positive definitness of the matrix will be of prime importance.

EXAMPLE 15.5.1. Show that the Hessian matrix of $F(\mathbf{x}) = (x_2 - x_1)^2 + (1 - x_1)^2$ (Example 15.2.1) is positive definite at the minimum $\mathbf{x}^* = [1 \quad 1]^t$.

The Hessian matrix is

$$\mathbf{G} = \begin{bmatrix} 4 & -2 \\ -2 & 2 \end{bmatrix}$$

and is, in this example, independent of $\mathbf{x}$. Select an arbitrary direction $\mathbf{s} = [s_1 \quad s_2]^t$. Then the product

$$\mathbf{s}^t\mathbf{G}\mathbf{s} = [s_1 \quad s_2]\begin{bmatrix} 4 & -2 \\ -2 & 2 \end{bmatrix}\begin{bmatrix} s_1 \\ s_2 \end{bmatrix} = 2[(s_1 - s_2)^2 + s_1^2] > 0$$

for any nonzero vector $\mathbf{s}$.

Equation (15.5.6) established special properties of the matrix $\mathbf{G}$ with respect to a vector. In the next step, we establish special properties of n vectors, $\mathbf{s}^i$, $i = 0, 1, \ldots, n-1$ with respect to an $n \times n$ *positive definite* matrix $\mathbf{G}$. If

$$(\mathbf{s}^i)^t\mathbf{G}\mathbf{s}^j = \begin{cases} 0, & \text{for } i \neq j \\ k_j > 0, & \text{for } i = j \end{cases} \tag{15.5.7}$$

then the vectors are said to be **G**-conjugate and are *linearly independent.* The independence can be established very simply. By definition, n vectors $\mathbf{s}^i$ are linearly independent if the condition

$$\sum_{j=0}^{n-1} a_j\mathbf{s}^j = \mathbf{0} \tag{15.5.8}$$

can be satisfied only by selecting *all* a_j identically equal to zero. To prove that this is true for **G**-conjugate vectors, premultiply (15.5.8) by $(\mathbf{s}^i)^t\mathbf{G}$. The sum must be equal to a_jk_j, as follows from (15.5.7). Since by definition $k_j > 0$, the constant a_j must be zero. Repeating for all $j = 0, 1, \ldots, n-1$, the linear independence is established.

G-conjugacy represents a wide class of vectors, as shown by the following simple example.

EXAMPLE 15.5.2. Use the Hessian matrix **G** from Example 15.5.1 and find

(a) the conjugate direction to $\mathbf{s}^0 = [1 \quad 0]^t$

(b) the conjugate direction to $\mathbf{s}^0 = [1 \quad -1]^t$.

To solve (a), form

$$\mathbf{G}\mathbf{s}^0 = \begin{bmatrix} 4 & -2 \\ -2 & 2 \end{bmatrix}\begin{bmatrix} 1 \\ 0 \end{bmatrix} = \begin{bmatrix} 4 \\ -2 \end{bmatrix}.$$

Defining the second vector as $\mathbf{s}^1 = [a_1 \quad a_2]^t$, we require

$$[a_1 \quad a_2]\ [4 \quad -2]^t = 0$$

or

$$a_2 = 2a_1.$$

The selection $\mathbf{s}^1 = [1 \quad 2]^t$ provides the solution.

Similarly for (b):

$$\mathbf{G}\mathbf{s}^0 = \begin{bmatrix} 4 & -2 \\ -2 & 2 \end{bmatrix}\begin{bmatrix} 1 \\ -1 \end{bmatrix} = \begin{bmatrix} 6 \\ -4 \end{bmatrix}.$$

Defining $\mathbf{s}^1 = [b_1 \quad b_2]^t$ we require $[b_1 \quad b_2]\ [6 \quad -4]^t = 6b_1 - 4b_2 = 0$, or $b_2 = 3b_1/2$. Selecting, for instance, $b_1 = 2$, the conjugate direction becomes

$\mathbf{s}^1 = [2 \quad 3]^t$. It is seen that **G**-conjugacy can be obtained starting with an arbitrary nonzero vector.

Further properties will be established on the general quadratic function

$$F(\mathbf{x}) = a + \mathbf{b}^t\mathbf{x} + \tfrac{1}{2}\,\mathbf{x}^t\mathbf{G}\mathbf{x} \tag{15.5.9}$$

having positive definite matrix **G**. The gradient is

$$\nabla\mathbf{F} = \mathbf{b} + \mathbf{G}\mathbf{x}. \tag{15.5.10}$$

Consider the gradients at two subsequent steps:

$$\nabla\mathbf{F}^k = \mathbf{b} + \mathbf{G}\mathbf{x}^k; \qquad \nabla\mathbf{F}^{k+1} = \mathbf{b} + \mathbf{G}\mathbf{x}^{k+1}.$$

Their difference is

$$\boldsymbol{\gamma}^k = \nabla\mathbf{F}^{k+1} - \nabla\mathbf{F}^k = \mathbf{G}(\mathbf{x}^{k+1} - \mathbf{x}^k). \tag{15.5.11}$$

Taking similarly the difference of two successive points:

$$\mathbf{x}^{k+1} - \mathbf{x}^k = \Delta\mathbf{x}^k = d_k\mathbf{s}^k \tag{15.5.12}$$

as was already given by (15.3.3), $\mathbf{s}^k$ being the kth search direction. Inserting into (15.5.11) we summarize:

$$\boldsymbol{\gamma}^k = \nabla\mathbf{F}^{k+1} - \nabla\mathbf{F}^k = \mathbf{G}(\mathbf{x}^{k+1} - \mathbf{x}^k) = \mathbf{G}\Delta\mathbf{x}^k = d_k\mathbf{G}\mathbf{s}^k. \tag{15.5.13}$$

In the following development we always assume that the distance d_k was selected such that the minimum in the direction $\mathbf{s}^k$ has been found, i.e., $d_k = d_{k\,\min}$. The assumption has the important implication that (15.5.3) is automatically satisfied.

Let us now select the following equality from (15.5.13):

$$\nabla\mathbf{F}^{k+1} = \nabla\mathbf{F}^k + d_k\mathbf{G}\mathbf{s}^k. \tag{15.5.14a}$$

Since the superscript indicates iteration, we can reuse the formula to obtain

$$\nabla\mathbf{F}^{k+1} = \nabla\mathbf{F}^{k-1} + d_{k-1}\mathbf{G}\mathbf{s}^{k-1} + d_k\mathbf{G}\mathbf{s}^k \tag{15.5.14b}$$

$$\nabla\mathbf{F}^{k+1} = \nabla\mathbf{F}^{k-2} + d_{k-2}\mathbf{G}\mathbf{s}^{k-2} + d_{k-1}\mathbf{G}\mathbf{s}^{k-1} + d_k\mathbf{G}\mathbf{s}^k \tag{15.5.14c}$$

$$\vdots$$

Consider (15.5.14a), transpose and postmultiply by $\mathbf{s}^{k-1}$ and note that $\mathbf{G}^t = \mathbf{G}$:

$$(\nabla\mathbf{F}^{k+1})^t\mathbf{s}^{k-1} = (\nabla\mathbf{F}^k)^t\mathbf{s}^{k-1} + d_k(\mathbf{s}^k)^t\mathbf{G}\mathbf{s}^{k-1}.$$

The first term on the right side is zero due to (15.5.3). If the vectors $\mathbf{s}^j$ are **G**-conjugate, the second term will be zero as well. Proceeding to (15.5.14b), transpose again and postmultiply by $\mathbf{s}^{k-2}$:

$$(\nabla\mathbf{F}^{k+1})^t\mathbf{s}^{k-2} = (\nabla\mathbf{F}^{k-1})^t\mathbf{s}^{k-2} + d_{k-1}(\mathbf{s}^{k-1})^t\,\mathbf{G}\mathbf{s}^{k-2} + d_k(\mathbf{s}^k)^t\,\mathbf{G}\mathbf{s}^{k-2}.$$

The same reasoning establishes that the right side is zero again. We can proceed further and establish the following general formula:

$$(\nabla\mathbf{F}^{k+1})^t\mathbf{s}^j = 0, \qquad j = 0, 1, 2, \ldots, k. \tag{15.5.15}$$

Now let $k + 1 = n$:

$$(\nabla\mathbf{F}^n)^t\mathbf{s}^j = 0, \qquad j = 0, 1, 2, \ldots, n-1. \tag{15.5.16}$$

Since the $\mathbf{s}^j$ directions are linearly independent and we have already used all of them, the gradient at the nth step must be zero:

$$\nabla\mathbf{F}^n = \mathbf{0}$$

and we conclude that the minimum of a quadratic positive definite function is reached by the above process in at most n iterations. This assumes perfect minimization in each direction.

The above development established some general rules which should be imposed on the minimization steps and on the selection of search directions, but no such directions have yet been determined. A wide number of possibilities exist, and some of them will be discussed next.

15.6. DESCENT METHODS FOR MINIMIZATION

This section will describe some of the well known methods used for unconstrained minimization. It starts from the simplest ones and goes to more sophisticated recently developed ones. An attempt is made to make the development clear and logical, but some of the details are omitted. When needed, special results are quoted without derivations or proofs.

A. Steepest Descent

This is the oldest and least effective method of minimization. The locally steepest descent is given by the negative of the gradient and used as search

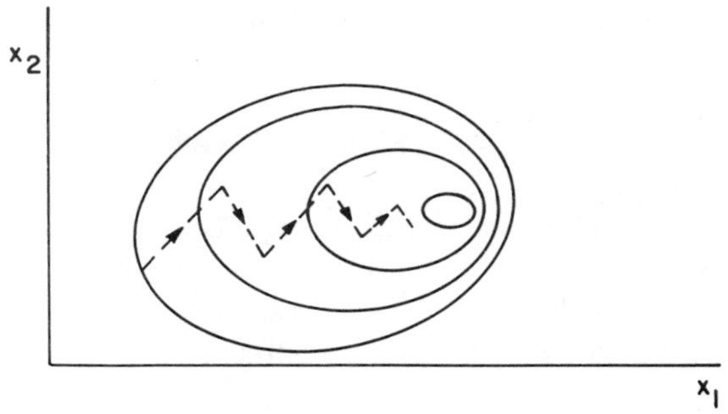

Fig. 15.6.1. Oscillating nature of the steepest descent search.

direction:

$$\mathbf{s}^k = -\nabla \mathbf{F}^k. \tag{15.6.1}$$

The method has the tendency to oscillate if the minimum is represented by an elongated valley, as sketched in Fig. 15.6.1 and thus convergence will be slow. Several modifications have been proposed to reduce the possibility of oscillations.

B. Conjugate Gradient Method

This method uses information from previous steps to define a new direction. It was developed for quadratic functions and can get to the minimum for these functions in n steps provided the function is minimized *exactly* along each search direction.

The quadratic function is defined by (15.5.1) but information about the second derivative is not used directly. The first search direction is taken as the steepest descent direction and the subsequent ones are linear combinations of the gradient at the given point and other previously defined search directions:

$$\begin{aligned}
\mathbf{s}^0 &= -\nabla \mathbf{F}^0 \\
\mathbf{s}^1 &= -\nabla \mathbf{F}^1 + K_{11}\mathbf{s}^0 \\
&\vdots \\
\mathbf{s}^k &= -\nabla \mathbf{F}^k + \sum_{i=1}^{k} K_{ik}\mathbf{s}^{i-1}, \qquad 1 \leqslant k \leqslant n-1.
\end{aligned} \tag{15.6.2}$$

Assuming perfect minimization in each search direction,

$$(\mathbf{s}^i)^t \nabla \mathbf{F}^{i+1} = 0, \qquad i = 0, 1, \ldots, n-1 \tag{15.6.3}$$

as follows from (15.5.3).

Since the first search direction is defined, the second one is found by satisfying **G**-conjugacy:

$$(\mathbf{s}^1)^t\mathbf{G}\mathbf{s}^0 = (-\nabla\mathbf{F}^1 + K_{11}\mathbf{s}^0)^t\mathbf{G}\mathbf{s}^0 = 0. \tag{15.6.4}$$

The constant K_{11} could be calculated from this expression *if the matrix* **G** *were known.* Since this is generally not the case, we wish to replace **G** in all expressions by function values and/or gradients at the respective points. To this end we use (15.5.13), written in the following form:

$$\mathbf{G}\mathbf{s}^0 = \frac{\nabla\mathbf{F}^1 - \nabla\mathbf{F}^0}{d_0}. \tag{15.6.5}$$

Substituting (15.6.5) into (15.6.4) and using (15.6.2) we get

$$[-\nabla\mathbf{F}^1 - K_{11}\nabla\mathbf{F}^0]^t \frac{\nabla\mathbf{F}^1 - \nabla\mathbf{F}^0}{d_0} = 0.$$

Invoking (15.6.3) and the fact that $\mathbf{s}^0 = -\nabla\mathbf{F}^0$ we get

$$\alpha_1 = K_{11} = \frac{[\nabla\mathbf{F}^1]^t\nabla\mathbf{F}^1}{[\nabla\mathbf{F}^0]^t\nabla\mathbf{F}^0}.$$

Applying the preceding steps for all directions, it is possible to show that

$$\alpha_k = K_{kk} = \frac{[\nabla\mathbf{F}^k]^t\nabla\mathbf{F}^k}{[\nabla\mathbf{F}^{k-1}]^t\nabla\mathbf{F}^{k-1}} \tag{15.6.6}$$

the remaining K_{ik} being zero. The iteration steps of the general algorithm given in Section 15.3 remain valid except for the third step, which is replaced by:

$$\text{Compute } \alpha_k \text{ from (15.6.6) and set } \mathbf{s}^k = -\nabla\mathbf{F}^k + \alpha_k\mathbf{s}^{k-1}. \tag{15.6.7}$$

If the sequence (15.6.6) and (15.6.7) is carried out on nonquadratic functions, only linear convergence is observed unless the search directions are reset periodically. This could be done after n steps: $\mathbf{s}^n = -\nabla\mathbf{F}^n$.

The algorithm is easy to program and requirements on storage are modest (only the previous search direction and previous gradient are needed). For this reason, it is often used for problems having large number of variables. The method is generally referred to as the conjugate gradient method of Fletcher and Reeves [1]. An improved version of the conjugate gradient method may be found in [2]. Though the storage requirements are somewhat larger, the performance on nonquadratic functions is superior. The search direction formula (15.6.7) is modified and the decisions on when and how to reset the search sequence are different. The computer code for the modified algorithm is available in [3] and [4].

C. The Newton Method

An iterative method based on a knowledge of second derivatives is generally referred to as the Newton method. Let the function $F(\mathbf{x})$ be expanded into Taylor series and truncated after the third term. This was done in (15.5.1). Rewrite in the following form:

$$F(\mathbf{x}^k + \Delta\mathbf{x}) - F(\mathbf{x}^k) = (\Delta\mathbf{x})^t \nabla\mathbf{F}^k + \tfrac{1}{2}(\Delta\mathbf{x})^t \mathbf{G}^k \Delta\mathbf{x}. \qquad (15.6.8)$$

We wish to *maximize* the difference on the left side. This can be done by differentiation of (15.6.8) with respect to $\Delta\mathbf{x}$ and by setting the result equal to zero:

$$\frac{\partial}{\partial \Delta\mathbf{x}}[F(\mathbf{x}^k + \Delta\mathbf{x}) - F(\mathbf{x}^k)] = \nabla\mathbf{F}^k + \mathbf{G}^k \Delta\mathbf{x} = \mathbf{0}$$

$$\mathbf{G}^k \Delta\mathbf{x} = -\nabla\mathbf{F}^k.$$

This equation is solved (possibly by **LU** decomposition) for $\Delta\mathbf{x}$. Formally, we can write

$$\Delta\mathbf{x} = -(\mathbf{G}^k)^{-1}\nabla\mathbf{F}^k = -\mathbf{H}^k\nabla\mathbf{F}^k$$

where $\mathbf{H} = \mathbf{G}^{-1}$ was used. The search direction is now set equal to this vector:

$$\mathbf{s}^k = \Delta\mathbf{x}^k = -\mathbf{H}^k\nabla\mathbf{F}^k \qquad (15.6.9)$$

and the general algorithm applied again.

Close to the minimum, the Hessian will be positive definite and in such case the full step size $d_k = 1$ may be used (i.e., no search in the direction $\mathbf{s}^k$ is needed). However, far from the minimum the Hessian may not even be positive definite. Moreover, calculation of the Hessian is usually very expensive. In order to avoid it, a whole class of methods has been developed. They are called *variable metric* or *quasi-Newton* methods.

D. Variable Metric Methods

Variable metric methods have been under development for a long time and have been summarized and generalized only recently. They are based on the *evaluation* of the gradients and *simulation* of the Hessian matrix or its inverse. The simulation is done by updating an initially positive definite matrix (usually an identity matrix) in a special way so as to preserve the positive definitness. Only when the minimum is reached, does this updated matrix simulate the Hessian (or its inverse). A detailed derivation of the formulae is beyond the scope of this text. In all the methods, the search direction is defined somewhat as in the Newton method:

$$\mathbf{s}^k = -\mathbf{H}^k \nabla \mathbf{F}^k. \tag{15.6.10}$$

At each iteration, the matrix $\mathbf{H}^k$ is updated by a special formula to provide $\mathbf{H}^{k+1}$. Many updating formulae are available in the literature and we give here a very general form [5]:

$$\mathbf{H}^{k+1} = \mathcal{F}(\alpha^k, \phi^k, \mathbf{H}^k, \Delta\mathbf{x}^k, \boldsymbol{\gamma}^k) \tag{15.6.11}$$

where

$$\mathcal{F}(\alpha, \phi, \mathbf{H}, \Delta\mathbf{x}, \boldsymbol{\gamma}) = \alpha\mathbf{H} + \left(1 + \alpha\phi \frac{\boldsymbol{\gamma}^t\mathbf{H}\boldsymbol{\gamma}}{(\Delta\mathbf{x})^t\boldsymbol{\gamma}}\right) \frac{(\Delta\mathbf{x})(\Delta\mathbf{x})^t}{(\Delta\mathbf{x})^t\boldsymbol{\gamma}} - \alpha \frac{1-\phi}{\boldsymbol{\gamma}^t\mathbf{H}\boldsymbol{\gamma}} \mathbf{H}\boldsymbol{\gamma}\boldsymbol{\gamma}^t\mathbf{H}$$

$$- \frac{\alpha\phi}{(\Delta\mathbf{x})^t\boldsymbol{\gamma}} [(\Delta\mathbf{x})\boldsymbol{\gamma}^t\mathbf{H} + \mathbf{H}\boldsymbol{\gamma}(\Delta\mathbf{x})^t]. \tag{15.6.12}$$

The formula is valid only if $(\Delta\mathbf{x})^t\boldsymbol{\gamma} \neq 0$ and $\boldsymbol{\gamma}^t\mathbf{H}\boldsymbol{\gamma} \neq 0$. Here α and ϕ are scalars and $\boldsymbol{\gamma}^k = \nabla\mathbf{F}^{k+1} - \nabla\mathbf{F}^k$, as introduced in (15.5.11).

Other well known formulae follow from (15.6.12) by selecting appropriate values of α and ϕ. For instance:

1. If $\alpha^k \equiv 1, \phi^k \equiv 0$:

$$\mathcal{F}(1, 0, \mathbf{H}, \Delta\mathbf{x}, \boldsymbol{\gamma}) = \mathbf{H} + \frac{\Delta\mathbf{x}(\Delta\mathbf{x})^t}{(\Delta\mathbf{x})^t\boldsymbol{\gamma}} - \frac{\mathbf{H}\boldsymbol{\gamma}\boldsymbol{\gamma}^t\mathbf{H}}{\boldsymbol{\gamma}^t\mathbf{H}\boldsymbol{\gamma}}. \tag{15.6.13}$$

This formula was derived by Davidon and Fletcher and Powell [6] and is called the DFP formula.

2. If $\alpha^k \equiv 1, \phi^k \equiv 1$:

$$\mathcal{F}(1, 1, \mathbf{H}, \Delta\mathbf{x}, \boldsymbol{\gamma}) = \mathbf{H} + \left(1 + \frac{\boldsymbol{\gamma}^t\mathbf{H}\boldsymbol{\gamma}}{(\Delta\mathbf{x})^t\boldsymbol{\gamma}}\right) \frac{\Delta\mathbf{x}(\Delta\mathbf{x})^t}{(\Delta\mathbf{x})^t\boldsymbol{\gamma}} - \frac{1}{(\Delta\mathbf{x})^t\boldsymbol{\gamma}} [(\Delta\mathbf{x})\boldsymbol{\gamma}^t\mathbf{H} + \mathbf{H}\boldsymbol{\gamma}(\Delta\mathbf{x})^t]. \tag{15.6.14}$$

This updating formula was developed independently by Broyden, Fletcher, Goldfarb, and Shanno around 1970 and is generally referred to as the BFGS formula.

Other simplifications exist as well. Modern routines are often based on a combination of (15.6.13) and (15.6.14). At each iteration, decision rules are given so that either of the formulae is selected for the update. The VA13A routine from the Harwell library (see [3] for address) is an efficient implementation of the above scheme.

15.7. CONSTRAINED MINIMIZATION

The general minimization problem was stated by Eq. (15.1.1) where both equality and inequality constraints have been introduced. Section 15.2 discussed the classical Lagrange solution to the problem with equality constraints. This section will deal with methods for constrained minimization having both types of constraints. The notation of Eq. (15.1.1) will be used.

One possibility is to transform the constrained problem into an unconstrained one and then use any of the available programs for unconstrained minimization. A widely known but *obsolete* way is to define a new function by introducing penalty coefficients. Two such methods will be mentioned:

(a) The *interior point* method forms a new function:

$$P(\mathbf{x}, r) = F(\mathbf{x}) + r \sum_{j=1}^{k_2} \frac{1}{g_j(\mathbf{x})} + \frac{1}{\sqrt{r}} \sum_{i=1}^{k_1} [e_i(\mathbf{x})]^2.$$

(b) The *exterior point* method forms the function

$$P(\mathbf{x}, r) = F(\mathbf{x}) + \frac{1}{r} \sum_{j=1}^{k_2} [\min (g_j(\mathbf{x}), 0)]^2 + \frac{1}{r} \sum_{i=1}^{k_1} [e_i(\mathbf{x})]^2.$$

In both cases the coefficient r is first chosen close to 1 and minimization is performed until the optimum is reached. In the next step, the value of r is reduced (say, by a factor of ten) and minimization performed again. Proceeding this way and reducing the coefficient r penalizes the combined function if the solution tends to violate the constraints. Ultimately, with very small r, the function is minimized and the constraints satisfied.

Both methods suffer from the fact that the problems become increasingly ill-conditioned as they get close to the solution. To avoid this ill-conditioning, modern methods are based on the Lagrange multiplier approach. The principle of these methods will be shown on problems with equality constraints; we will introduce the inequality constraints at the end of the section. The developments stress the basic understanding of the concepts rather than programming details.

Consider the following problem:

$$\begin{aligned}&\text{Minimize:} && F = F(\mathbf{x}) \\ &\text{subject to:} && e_i(\mathbf{x}) = 0, \qquad i = 1, 2, \ldots, k_1.\end{aligned} \tag{15.7.1}$$

Following the development in Section 15.2, form the Lagrangian function

$$L(\mathbf{x}, \boldsymbol{\lambda}) = F(\mathbf{x}) - \sum_i \lambda_i e_i(\mathbf{x}) = F(\mathbf{x}) - \boldsymbol{\lambda}^t \mathbf{e}(\mathbf{x}) \tag{15.7.2a}$$

$$= F(\mathbf{x}) - [\mathbf{e}(\mathbf{x})]^t \boldsymbol{\lambda} \tag{15.7.2b}$$

where

$$\begin{aligned}\mathbf{e} &= [e_1 \quad e_2 \quad \cdots \quad e_{k_1}]^t \\ \boldsymbol{\lambda} &= [\lambda_1 \quad \lambda_2 \quad \cdots \quad \lambda_{k_1}]^t.\end{aligned} \tag{15.7.3}$$

It is a matter of convenience which of the equations (15.7.2) is used. Differentiate (b) with respect to $\mathbf{x}$ and λ and set the derivatives equal to zero, as required at the minimum:

$$\begin{aligned}\frac{\partial L}{\partial \mathbf{x}} &= \nabla \mathbf{F} - \mathbf{N}(\mathbf{x})\,\boldsymbol{\lambda} = \mathbf{0} \\ \frac{\partial L}{\partial \boldsymbol{\lambda}} &= -\mathbf{e}(\mathbf{x}) \qquad\qquad = \mathbf{0}\end{aligned} \tag{15.7.4}$$

where

$$\mathbf{N} = [\nabla \mathbf{e}_1 \quad \nabla \mathbf{e}_2 \quad \cdots \quad \nabla \mathbf{e}_{k_1}] = \begin{bmatrix} \frac{\partial e_1}{\partial x_1} & \frac{\partial e_2}{\partial x_1} & \cdots & \frac{\partial e_{k_1}}{\partial x_1} \\ \frac{\partial e_1}{\partial x_2} & \frac{\partial e_2}{\partial x_2} & \cdots & \frac{\partial e_{k_1}}{\partial x_2} \\ \vdots & \vdots & & \vdots \\ \frac{\partial e_1}{\partial x_n} & \frac{\partial e_2}{\partial x_n} & \cdots & \frac{\partial e_{k_1}}{\partial x_n} \end{bmatrix} \tag{15.7.5}$$

was introduced. We can attempt to solve (15.7.4) by Newton–Raphson iteration. The Jacobian is needed:

$$\mathbf{M} = \begin{bmatrix} \mathbf{M}_1 & -\mathbf{N} \\ -\mathbf{N}^t & \mathbf{0} \end{bmatrix} \tag{15.7.6}$$

where the entries of $\mathbf{M}_1$ are

$$m_{jl} = \frac{\partial^2 F}{\partial x_j \partial x_l} - \sum_{i=1}^{k_1} \lambda_i \frac{\partial^2 e_i}{\partial x_j \partial x_l}. \tag{15.7.7}$$

Newton-Raphson iteration [compare with (12.1.9)] is performed on the following equation:

$$\mathbf{M}^k \begin{bmatrix} \Delta\mathbf{x}^k \\ \Delta\boldsymbol{\lambda}^k \end{bmatrix} = - \begin{bmatrix} \nabla\mathbf{F}^k - \mathbf{N}^k\boldsymbol{\lambda}^k \\ -\mathbf{e}^k \end{bmatrix}. \tag{15.7.8}$$

Cancellation in the first equation is possible; to show it, rewrite (15.7.8) as two equations but substitute $\Delta\boldsymbol{\lambda}^k = \boldsymbol{\lambda}^{k+1} - \boldsymbol{\lambda}^k$:

$$\mathbf{M}_1^k \Delta\mathbf{x}^k - \mathbf{N}^k(\boldsymbol{\lambda}^{k+1} - \boldsymbol{\lambda}^k) = -\nabla\mathbf{F}^k + \mathbf{N}^k\boldsymbol{\lambda}^k$$

$$-(\mathbf{N}^k)^t \Delta\mathbf{x}^k = \mathbf{e}^k$$

Canceling the terms $\mathbf{N}^k\boldsymbol{\lambda}^k$ in the first equation we arrive at a system

$$\begin{bmatrix} \mathbf{M}_1^k & -\mathbf{N}^k \\ -(\mathbf{N}^k)^t & \mathbf{0} \end{bmatrix} \begin{bmatrix} \Delta\mathbf{x}^k \\ \boldsymbol{\lambda}^{k+1} \end{bmatrix} = \begin{bmatrix} -\nabla\mathbf{F}^k \\ \mathbf{e}^k \end{bmatrix} \tag{15.7.9}$$

in which the changes in $\boldsymbol{\lambda}^{k+1}$ are influenced by the λ_i^k appearing in the m_{jl} terms of the matrix $\mathbf{M}_1$.

It can be shown that *precisely the same equations* can be obtained if we:

(a) expand $F(\mathbf{x}^k + \Delta\mathbf{x}^k)$ into a Taylor series and retain the first *three* terms, and

(b) expand each $e_j(\mathbf{x}^k + \Delta\mathbf{x}^k)$ into Taylor series and retain the first *two* terms.

The expansion of $F(\mathbf{x}^k + \Delta\mathbf{x}^k)$ was obtained in (15.5.1). Expansion of the equality constraints gives

$$\mathbf{e}(\mathbf{x}^k + \Delta\mathbf{x}^k) = \mathbf{e}(\mathbf{x}^k) + (\mathbf{N}^k)^t \Delta\mathbf{x}^k$$

and the simplified *quadratic problem* is defined as

$$\begin{aligned} &\text{Minimize:} && F(\mathbf{x}^k) + (\Delta\mathbf{x}^k)^t \nabla\mathbf{F}^k + \tfrac{1}{2}(\Delta\mathbf{x}^k)^t \mathbf{G}^k \Delta\mathbf{x}^k \\ &\text{subject to:} && (\mathbf{N}^k)^t \Delta\mathbf{x}^k + \mathbf{e}^k = \mathbf{0}. \end{aligned} \tag{15.7.10}$$

If we form the Lagrangian function (15.7.2) using the expression (15.7.10) and follow the same steps as before by differentiating with respect to $\Delta\mathbf{x}^k$, we will ultimately arrive at (15.7.9). In each iteration, the general formulation (15.7.1) can be replaced by the formulation (15.7.10).

Generally, the matrix $\mathbf{G}^k$ in (15.7.10) may not be positive definite. In order to secure a downhill move at each step, it is advisable, as in the case of unconstrained minimization, to replace it by a positive definite matrix, updated by means of the gradients of $F(\mathbf{x})$ and $\mathbf{e}(\mathbf{x})$. The formulae (15.6.13) or (15.6.14) can be used for this purpose.

Because Newton-Raphson iteration can experience convergence problems if the estimates are far from the solution, a *quadratic program* operating on (15.7.10) is used instead. This program returns $\Delta\mathbf{x}^k$ and $\boldsymbol{\lambda}^{k+1}$ and a new point is obtained by inserting into

$$\mathbf{x}^{k+1} = \mathbf{x}^k + \Delta\mathbf{x}^k. \tag{15.7.11}$$

After each step, the Lagrangian (15.7.2) is checked. The resultant step is accepted if a reduction in its value is obtained and a new iteration is started. If a reduction is not achieved, a search in the direction $\Delta\mathbf{x}^k$ is performed to obtain the minimum in this direction. Details about the quadratic program, about updating, and about the best method of search are beyond the scope of this book.

Due to the correspondence between the original problem and the quadratic approximation, the inequality constraints can be incorporated in the same way. Consider the following general problem:

$$\begin{aligned} &\text{Minimize:} && F(\mathbf{x}) && \\ &\text{subject to:} && e_i(\mathbf{x}) = \mathbf{0}, && i = 1, 2, \ldots, k_1 \\ &\text{and:} && g_j(\mathbf{x}) \geqslant \mathbf{0}, && j = 1, 2, \ldots, k_2. \end{aligned} \tag{15.7.12}$$

The Lagrangian is formed using two sets of Lagrange multipliers

$$L(\mathbf{x}, \boldsymbol{\lambda}, \boldsymbol{\mu}) = F(\mathbf{x}) - \boldsymbol{\lambda}^t\mathbf{e}(\mathbf{x}) - \boldsymbol{\mu}^t\mathbf{g}(\mathbf{x}) \tag{15.7.13}$$

and the problem approximated at each iteration by a quadratic program:

$$\begin{aligned} &\text{Minimize:} && F(\mathbf{x}^k) + (\Delta\mathbf{x}^k)^t\nabla\mathbf{F}^k + \tfrac{1}{2}(\Delta\mathbf{x}^k)^t\mathbf{G}^k\Delta\mathbf{x}^k \\ &\text{subject to:} && (\mathbf{N}_1^k)^t\Delta\mathbf{x}^k + \mathbf{e}^k = \mathbf{0} \\ & && (\mathbf{N}_2^k)^t\Delta\mathbf{x}^k + \mathbf{g}^k \geqslant \mathbf{0}. \end{aligned}$$

At each step, the coefficients μ_i must be maintained positive to satisfy the condition $g_j(\mathbf{x}) \geqslant 0$. Details of this technique are available in [7] while an efficient implementation is provided in the Harwell routine VF02A.

PROBLEMS

P.15.1. A *stationary point* of a function of a single variable x, $F(x)$, is the value x^* for which $F'(x^*) = 0$. The nature of the point is found by obtaining the second derivative:

$$F''(x^*) < 0, \qquad x^* \text{ is a maximum}$$
$$F''(x^*) > 0, \qquad x^* \text{ is a minimum}$$
$$F''(x^*) = 0, \qquad x^* \text{ is a saddle point.}$$

Find the stationary points and determine their nature for the functions given below. If several solutions exist, try at least two:

(a) $F(x) = x^{1/2} - ax$

(b) $F(x) = \dfrac{ax^2 + 1}{x - 1}$

(c) $F(x) = 1 - e^{-x} \sin x$

P.15.2. For the function

$$F(\Omega) = a \frac{1 + j\Omega}{1 + ja\Omega}$$

the phase angle is defined by

$$\phi = \tan^{-1} \Omega - \tan^{-1} a\Omega.$$

Assuming a = constant, find the value Ω^* for which ϕ is maximum.

P.15.3. Stationary points of functions of several variables are obtained by finding $\mathbf{x}^*$ such that $\nabla \mathbf{F}(\mathbf{x}^*) = \mathbf{0}$. Determine the stationary point of the function

$$F(x_1, x_2) = (3 - x_1 - x_2)^2 + (1 + x_1 + 2x_2 - x_1 x_2)^2$$

using Newton–Raphson iteration. Using (15.5.6) determine the type of stationary point.

P.15.4. Calculate the gradient and the Hessian matrix for the following functions:

(a) $F_1(\mathbf{x}) = 3x_1^2 - 2x_2 + x_3^2 - 2$

(b) $F_2(\mathbf{x}) = 2x_1 + 3x_2^2 x_3$

(c) $F_3(\mathbf{x}) = x_1 + x_1 x_2 + x_2 x_3$

P.15.5. Consider the function

$$F(x_1, x_2) = 2x_1^2 - x_1 x_2^2 + x_2^3.$$

It has two stationary points [0, 0] and [9, 6]. First find these points yourself, then determine which of them is a minimum. (*Hint:* Assume an unknown vector $\mathbf{s} = [s_1, s_2]$ and show that $\mathbf{s}^t\mathbf{H}\mathbf{s} > 0$ for any values of the s_1, s_2. [*Result:* The point [0, 0] is the minimum.])

P.15.6. Find the minimum of

$$x_1x_2 + x_1x_3 + x_2x_3$$

subject to

$$x_1 + 2x_2 + x_3 - 2 = 0.$$

[*Result:* $x_1 = 1, x_2 = 0, x_3, = 1, \lambda = 1.$]

P.15.7. Find the minimum of

$$F(x) = x_1^2 + x_1 + x_2^2 + 2x_2 + 5$$

subject to

$$x_1^2 + x_2^2 - 2 = 0.$$

P.15.8. Minimize

$$x_1^2 + x_2^2 - 14x_1 - 6x_2 - 7$$

subject to

$$3 - x_1 - x_2 = 0$$
$$2 - x_1 - 2x_2 = 0.$$

[*Result:* $x_1 = 4, x_2 = -1, \lambda_1 = 4, \lambda_2 = 2.$]

P.15.9. Sketch graphically the problem

$$F(\mathbf{x}) = (x_1 - 2)^2 + x_2^2$$

subject to

$$g_1(\mathbf{x}) = x_1 - x_2 + 3 \geqslant 0$$
$$g_2(\mathbf{x}) = -x_1^2 + x_2 - 0.5 \geqslant 0$$
$$x_1 \geqslant 0, \qquad x_2 \geqslant 0.$$

Note that $F(\mathbf{x})$ represents a circle having its center at (2, 0) and having a radius r. The first constraint represents values below the straight line $x_2 = x_1 - 3$, whereas the second constraint represents values inside the parabola having a minimum at (0, 0.5).

REFERENCES

1. R. Fletcher and C. M. Reeves: Function minimization by conjugate gradients. *Computer Journal*, pp. 149–154, 1964.
2. M. J. D. Powell: Restart procedures for the conjugate gradient method. *Mathematical Programming*, pp. 241–254, 1977.
3. VA14AD, routine from the Harwell library. Computer Science and Systems Division. ARE Harwell, Oxfordshire, OX11 ORA, England.
4. Subroutine ZXCGR from International Mathematical Statistical Library, IMSL, 7500 Bellaire Blvd., Houston, Texas, USA.
5. S. S. Oren and D. Leuenberger: Self-scaling variable metric algorithm. *Management Science*, pp. 845–874, 1974.
6. R. Fletcher and M. J. D. Powell: A rapidly convergent descent method for minimization. *Computer Journal*, pp. 163–168, 1963.
7. M. J. D. Powell: A fast algorithm for nonlinearly constrained optimization calculations. *Proceedings, Dundee Conference on Numerical Analysis*, Lecture Notes in Mathematics No. 630, Springer-Verlag, New York, 1977.

CHAPTER 16
Time Domain Sensitivities and Steady State

The concept of sensitivity of nonlinear networks in the time domain is much more complicated than in the frequency domain and the intuitive understanding developed for the frequency domain is largely lost in the complexity of the process. The time domain sensitivities can be plotted as functions of time but their main application is in generating gradients for objective functions in optimization problems.

The theoretical aspects of calculating the sensitivities are handled in the first two sections of this chapter. In addition to the usual parameters, a new set of parameters comes into the picture, namely the initial conditions. Section 16.1 develops a method in which the sensitivities are calculated simultaneously with the time domain solution; Section 16.2 formulates the problem by means of an objective function.

If the set of initial conditions is chosen such that after one period of the signal the network assumes the same initial conditions again, then we speak about the *steady state*. Sensitivities with respect to initial conditions can thus be utilized to reach the steady state solution faster than by means of direct integration till the initial transients have died out. Finding the steady state efficiently is still an open and important problem: it is a state in which many nonlinear networks are observed in the laboratory. Some methods have been proposed to simulate the steady state by means of a computer, and we will discuss three of them. The first two techniques, treated in Sections 16.3 and 16.4, could be called "classical" and are based on the theory of Sections 16.1 and 16.2. The third method represents a departure from previously published methods. It is based on the theory of extrapolation and is briefly described in Section 16.5. It is simple to program, does not require any derivatives, and gives excellent results.

16.1. SENSITIVITY NETWORKS

The reader may recall that we developed two methods for sensitivity calculations in the frequency domain: one of them obtained sensitivities of all network variables with respect to a single parameter [Eq. (6.1.4)] and the other provided sensitivity of an objective function with respect to all parameters [Eq. (6.1.8)]. This section develops the theory for the first method in the time domain. It is based on the time domain solution of a linearized but time varying *sensitivity network*. The system matrix of this network is independent of the parameters; only the right-hand side changes. This method has its merits and drawbacks. The advantages are that the sensitivity network is solved simultaneously with the time domain calculation of the original system and responses are available at each integration step for plotting or inspection. Further, the process can be stopped at any time instance. On the negative side, the problem grows with the number of parameters and memory requirements may become prohibitive.

To simplify derivations, we will assume in the following that all terminal equations for capacitors and inductors are defined by means of charges and fluxes, jointly denoted by the vector $\mathbf{q}$. The set of differential equations is linear and all nonlinearities are incorporated into the algebraic system. Under these conditions, the system equations can be partitioned into

$$\begin{aligned} \mathbf{q}' - \mathbf{E}\mathbf{x} = \mathbf{0}; \qquad & \mathbf{q}_0 = \mathbf{q}(0) \\ \mathbf{f}(\mathbf{q}, \mathbf{x}, \mathbf{w}, h, t) = \mathbf{0}. & \end{aligned} \tag{16.1.1}$$

Example 16.1.1 will illustrate this formulation. Here $\mathbf{q}_0$ represents the initial conditions, $\mathbf{E}$ is a matrix of zeros and ones, $\mathbf{x}$ represents the vector of node voltages and branch currents, and $\mathbf{w}$ is the vector of excitations. Vector $\mathbf{q}'$ consists of inductor voltages and capacitor currents. Finally, h represents the variable parameter. It is assumed that at $t = 0$ the initial conditions are consistent and (16.1.1) has a unique solution.

To start with, the initial conditions may not be known and the sensitivity of the initial conditions to parameter changes must be established. This is done by defining a simplified system in which $\mathbf{q}'$ is identically zero. Equation (16.1.1) reduces to

$$\begin{aligned} -\mathbf{E}\mathbf{x} = \mathbf{0} \\ \mathbf{f}(\mathbf{q}_0, \mathbf{x}_0, \mathbf{w}_0, h, 0) = \mathbf{0} \end{aligned} \tag{16.1.2}$$

and its solution provides the dc condition. It is found by obtaining the Jacobian and by defining the Newton-Raphson equation (12.1.9):

$$\begin{bmatrix} \mathbf{0} & -\mathbf{E} \\ \dfrac{\partial \mathbf{f}}{\partial \mathbf{q}} & \dfrac{\partial \mathbf{f}}{\partial \mathbf{x}} \end{bmatrix} \begin{bmatrix} \Delta \mathbf{q}_0 \\ \Delta \mathbf{x}_0 \end{bmatrix} = - \begin{bmatrix} -\mathbf{E}\mathbf{x} \\ \mathbf{f} \end{bmatrix}. \tag{16.1.3}$$

Iteration on (16.1.3) provides $\mathbf{q}_0$ and $\mathbf{x}_0$. At convergence, the Jacobian matrix is available in its factored form.

Sensitivity of the dc solution with respect to the parameter h is found by differentiating (16.1.2) with respect to h:

$$\begin{aligned} -\mathbf{E}\frac{\partial \mathbf{x}_0}{\partial h} &= \mathbf{0} \\ \frac{\partial \mathbf{f}}{\partial \mathbf{q}_0}\frac{\partial \mathbf{q}_0}{\partial h} + \frac{\partial \mathbf{f}}{\partial \mathbf{x}_0}\frac{\partial \mathbf{x}_0}{\partial h} + \frac{\partial \mathbf{f}}{\partial h} &= \mathbf{0}. \end{aligned} \tag{16.1.4}$$

Denote

$$\mathbf{y}_0 = \frac{\partial \mathbf{q}_0}{\partial h}; \qquad \mathbf{z}_0 = \frac{\partial \mathbf{x}_0}{\partial h}. \tag{16.1.5}$$

Then (16.1.4) becomes

$$\begin{bmatrix} \mathbf{0} & -\mathbf{E} \\ \dfrac{\partial \mathbf{f}}{\partial \mathbf{q}_0} & \dfrac{\partial \mathbf{f}}{\partial \mathbf{x}_0} \end{bmatrix} \begin{bmatrix} \mathbf{y}_0 \\ \mathbf{z}_0 \end{bmatrix} = \begin{bmatrix} \mathbf{0} \\ -\dfrac{\partial \mathbf{f}}{\partial h} \end{bmatrix}. \tag{16.1.6}$$

This is a linear algebraic system having the same system matrix as (16.1.3). The **LU** factors obtained there are reused to get $\mathbf{y}_0, \mathbf{z}_0$.

With these preliminary steps finished, we can now turn to the sensitivity of the original system (16.1.1) to the parameter h. Differentiating both the equations and the initial conditions with respect to h gives

$$\begin{aligned} \frac{\partial \mathbf{q}'}{\partial h} - \mathbf{E}\frac{\partial \mathbf{x}}{\partial h} &= \mathbf{0}; \qquad \frac{\partial \mathbf{q}_0}{\partial h} = \frac{\partial \mathbf{q}(0)}{\partial h} \\ \frac{\partial \mathbf{f}}{\partial \mathbf{q}}\frac{\partial \mathbf{q}}{\partial h} + \frac{\partial \mathbf{f}}{\partial \mathbf{x}}\frac{\partial \mathbf{x}}{\partial h} + \frac{\partial \mathbf{f}}{\partial h} &= \mathbf{0} \end{aligned} \tag{16.1.7}$$

where we assume that $\mathbf{w}$ is independent of h. Introducing new variables

$$\mathbf{y} = \frac{\partial \mathbf{q}}{\partial h}; \qquad \mathbf{z} = \frac{\partial \mathbf{x}}{\partial h} \tag{16.1.8}$$

and interchanging the order of differentiation with respect to t and h gives

$$\begin{gathered} \mathbf{y}' - \mathbf{E}\mathbf{z} = \mathbf{0}; \qquad \mathbf{y}_0 = \mathbf{y}(0) \\ \frac{\partial \mathbf{f}}{\partial \mathbf{q}} \mathbf{y} + \frac{\partial \mathbf{f}}{\partial \mathbf{x}} \mathbf{z} + \frac{\partial \mathbf{f}}{\partial h} = \mathbf{0}. \end{gathered} \tag{16.1.9}$$

At this point we have two algebraic-differential systems: the original one, (16.1.1), and the "sensitivity network" (16.1.9), which is linear and time varying. Both will be solved by the BDF formula. The corrector is taken from Chapter 13, Eq. (13.3.2), with Δt denoting the step size. Considering a formula of order k and letting $m = k - 1$

$$\mathbf{q}'_{n+k} = -\frac{1}{\Delta t} \sum_{i=0}^{m} a_i \mathbf{q}_{n+k-i} \tag{16.1.10}$$

and substituting into (16.1.1) we get

$$\begin{gathered} -\frac{a_0}{\Delta t} \mathbf{q}_{n+k} - \frac{1}{\Delta t} \sum_{i=1}^{m} a_i \mathbf{q}_{n+k-i} - \mathbf{E}\mathbf{x}_{n+k} = \mathbf{0} \\ \mathbf{f}(\mathbf{q}_{n+k}, \mathbf{x}_{n+k}, \mathbf{w}_{n+k}, h, t_{n+k}) = \mathbf{0}. \end{gathered}$$

The Newton-Raphson iteration equation requires the Jacobian and the right-hand side:

$$\begin{bmatrix} -\frac{a_0}{\Delta t} \mathbf{1} & -\mathbf{E} \\ \frac{\partial \mathbf{f}}{\partial \mathbf{q}} & \frac{\partial \mathbf{f}}{\partial \mathbf{x}} \end{bmatrix} \begin{bmatrix} \Delta \mathbf{q}_{n+k} \\ \Delta \mathbf{x}_{n+k} \end{bmatrix} = - \begin{bmatrix} -\frac{1}{\Delta t} \sum_{i=0}^{m} a_i \mathbf{q}_{n+k-i} - \mathbf{E}\mathbf{x}_{n+k} \\ \mathbf{f}(\mathbf{q}_{n+k}, \mathbf{x}_{n+k}, \mathbf{w}_{n+k}, h, t_{n+k}) \end{bmatrix} \tag{16.1.11}$$

The iteration provides $\mathbf{q}_{n+k}$ and $\mathbf{x}_{n+k}$ and at convergence the Jacobian matrix is available in its factored form.

The sensitivity network equations (16.1.9) are solved by the same BDF formula:

$$\mathbf{y}'_{n+k} = -\frac{1}{\Delta t} \sum_{i=0}^{m} a_i \mathbf{y}_{n+k-i}. \tag{16.1.12}$$

Since the system is linear, no iteration is needed and (16.1.9) takes the following form:

$$-\frac{a_0}{\Delta t}\mathbf{y}_{n+k} - \frac{1}{\Delta t}\sum_{i=1}^{m} a_i \mathbf{y}_{n+k-i} - \mathbf{E}\mathbf{z}_{n+k} = \mathbf{0}$$

$$\frac{\partial \mathbf{f}}{\partial \mathbf{q}}\mathbf{y}_{n+k} + \frac{\partial \mathbf{f}}{\partial \mathbf{x}}\mathbf{z}_{n+k} + \frac{\partial \mathbf{f}}{\partial h} = \mathbf{0}.$$

Transferring known quantities to the right-hand side and writing in matrix form we get

$$\begin{bmatrix} -\frac{a_0}{\Delta t}\mathbf{1} & -\mathbf{E} \\ \frac{\partial \mathbf{f}}{\partial \mathbf{q}} & \frac{\partial \mathbf{f}}{\partial \mathbf{x}} \end{bmatrix} \begin{bmatrix} \mathbf{y}_{n+k} \\ \mathbf{z}_{n+k} \end{bmatrix} = \begin{bmatrix} \frac{1}{\Delta t}\sum_{i=1}^{m} a_i \mathbf{y}_{n+k-i} \\ -\frac{\partial \mathbf{f}}{\partial h} \end{bmatrix}. \tag{16.1.13}$$

The matrix in (16.1.13) is the same as in (16.1.11), where it was available, at convergence, in its factored form. Solution of (16.1.13) represents only one forward and back substitution.

If the sensitivities with respect to several parameters are required, the right-hand side of (16.1.13) changes. A new right-hand-side vector must be prepared and the forward and back substitutions must be repeated for each case.

EXAMPLE 16.1.1. Write the equations for the network in Fig. 16.1.1 in the form of (16.1.1) and obtain the Jacobian matrix.

Let q_1 = charge on the capacitor and q_2 = flux on the inductor. Then $\mathbf{q} = [q_1 \quad q_2]^t$. The defining equations for the capacitor and inductor are

$$q_1 - Cv_C = q_1 - Cv_2 = 0$$

$$q_1' - i_C = 0$$

$$q_2 - Li_L = 0$$

$$q_2' - v_L = q_2' - v_1 + v_2 = 0.$$

Notice that the capacitor current now appears as a variable. The remaining algebraic equations are generated by applying the KCL at the two nodes:

$$i_L + i_D - j = i_L + (e^{kv_1} - 1) - j = 0$$

$$i_L - i_C - Gv_2 = 0.$$

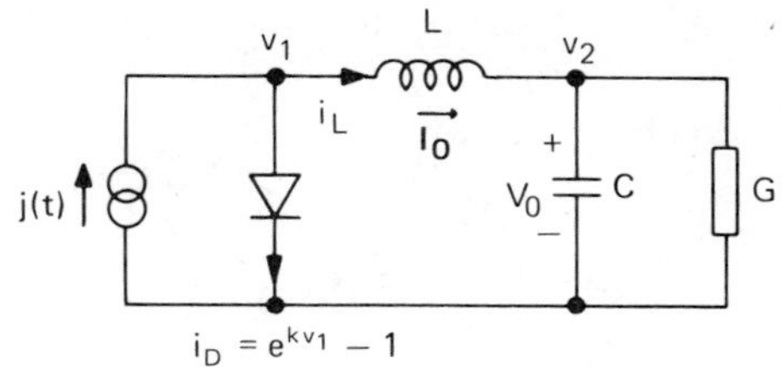

Fig. 16.1.1. Network for Example 16.1.1.

Collecting equations we have

$$\mathbf{q}' - \mathbf{Ex} \equiv \begin{bmatrix} q_1' \\ q_2' \end{bmatrix} - \begin{bmatrix} 0 & 0 & 1 & 0 \\ 1 & -1 & 0 & 0 \end{bmatrix} \begin{bmatrix} v_1 \\ v_2 \\ i_C \\ i_L \end{bmatrix} = \mathbf{0}; \qquad \mathbf{q}_0 = \begin{bmatrix} CV_0 \\ LI_0 \end{bmatrix}$$

and

$$\mathbf{f}(q_1, q_2, v_1, v_2, i_C, i_L) \equiv \begin{bmatrix} q_1 - Cv_2 \\ q_2 - Li_L \\ i_L + (e^{kv_1} - 1) - j \\ i_L - i_C - Gv_2 \end{bmatrix} = \mathbf{0}.$$

The Jacobian matrix in (16.1.11) has the following form:

$$\begin{array}{cc|cccc} q_1 & q_2 & v_1 & v_2 & i_C & i_L \\ -\dfrac{a_0}{\Delta t} & 0 & 0 & 0 & -1 & 0 \\ 0 & -\dfrac{a_0}{\Delta t} & -1 & 1 & 0 & 0 \\ \hline 1 & 0 & 0 & -C & 0 & 0 \\ 0 & 1 & 0 & 0 & 0 & -1 \\ 0 & 0 & ke^{kv_1} & 0 & 0 & 1 \\ 0 & 0 & 0 & -G & -1 & 1 \end{array}$$

16.2. SENSITIVITIES OF OJBECTIVE FUNCTIONS

An alternative method for time domain sensitivity computation of an objective function is considered in this section. The objective function is integrated over a *fixed* interval of time, t^*, and sensitivities with respect to *all* parameters can be obtained at this time point. However, they are not available within the interval 0 to t^*.

The objective function is defined by

$$\psi = \int_0^{t^*} \phi(\mathbf{q}', \mathbf{q}, \mathbf{x}, h)\, dt \tag{16.2.1}$$

in which $\mathbf{q}$ and $\mathbf{x}$ must satisfy the network algebraic-differential equations

$$\begin{aligned} \mathbf{q}' - \mathbf{E}\mathbf{x} &= \mathbf{0} \\ \mathbf{f}(\mathbf{q}, \mathbf{x}, \mathbf{w}, h, t) &= \mathbf{0} \end{aligned} \tag{16.2.2}$$

for any time t. Because (16.2.2) represents a constraint on (16.2.1), a Lagrangian

$$L = \phi + \boldsymbol{\lambda}^t(\mathbf{q}' - \mathbf{E}\mathbf{x}) + \boldsymbol{\mu}^t\mathbf{f} \tag{16.2.3}$$

is formed as in Section 15.2. Here $\boldsymbol{\lambda}(t)$ and $\boldsymbol{\mu}(t)$ are unknown functions of time. Use of (16.2.3) changes the objective function to

$$\psi = \int_0^{t^*} L\, dt = \int_0^{t^*} \{\phi(\mathbf{q}', \mathbf{q}, \mathbf{x}, h) + \boldsymbol{\lambda}^t(\mathbf{q}' - \mathbf{E}\mathbf{x}) + \boldsymbol{\mu}^t\mathbf{f}(\mathbf{q}, \mathbf{x}, \mathbf{w}, h, t)\}\, dt. \tag{16.2.4}$$

The first derivative with respect to a single parameter h is

$$\begin{aligned} \frac{\partial \psi}{\partial h} = &\int_0^{t^*} \left(\underbrace{\frac{\partial \phi}{\partial \mathbf{q}'} \frac{\partial \mathbf{q}'}{\partial h}} + \frac{\partial \phi}{\partial \mathbf{q}} \frac{\partial \mathbf{q}}{\partial h} + \frac{\partial \phi}{\partial \mathbf{x}} \frac{\partial \mathbf{x}}{\partial h} + \frac{\partial \phi}{\partial h} \right) dt \\ &+ \int_0^{t^*} \boldsymbol{\lambda}^t \left(\underbrace{\frac{\partial \mathbf{q}'}{\partial h}} - \mathbf{E} \frac{\partial \mathbf{x}}{\partial h} \right) dt \\ &+ \int_0^{t^*} \boldsymbol{\mu}^t \left(\frac{\partial \mathbf{f}}{\partial \mathbf{q}} \frac{\partial \mathbf{q}}{\partial h} + \frac{\partial \mathbf{f}}{\partial \mathbf{x}} \frac{\partial \mathbf{x}}{\partial h} + \frac{\partial \mathbf{f}}{\partial h} \right) dt. \end{aligned} \tag{16.2.5}$$

Equation (16.2.5) assumes that the excitation $\mathbf{w}$ is independent of h. Consider separately the terms underlined with braces and integrate by parts:

$$\int_0^{t^*} \left(\frac{\partial \phi}{\partial \mathbf{q}'} + \boldsymbol{\lambda}^t \right) \frac{\partial \mathbf{q}'}{\partial h}\, dt = \left(\frac{\partial \phi}{\partial \mathbf{q}'} + \boldsymbol{\lambda}^t \right) \frac{\partial \mathbf{q}}{\partial h} \Bigg|_0^{t^*} - \int_0^{t^*} \left[\frac{d}{dt} \left(\frac{\partial \phi}{\partial \mathbf{q}'} + \boldsymbol{\lambda}^t \right) \right] \frac{\partial \mathbf{q}}{\partial h}\, dt.$$

Inserting into (16.2.5) and rearranging terms gives

$$\frac{\partial \psi}{\partial h} = \left(\frac{\partial \phi}{\partial \mathbf{q}'} + \boldsymbol{\lambda}^t\right) \frac{\partial \mathbf{q}}{\partial h}\bigg|_0^{t^*} + \int_0^{t^*} \left[\frac{\partial \phi}{\partial \mathbf{q}} + \boldsymbol{\mu}^t \frac{\partial \mathbf{f}}{\partial \mathbf{q}} - \frac{d}{dt}\left(\frac{\partial \phi}{\partial \mathbf{q}'} + \boldsymbol{\lambda}^t\right)\right] \frac{\partial \mathbf{q}}{\partial h}\, dt$$

$$+ \int_0^{t^*} \left[\frac{\partial \phi}{\partial \mathbf{x}} - \boldsymbol{\lambda}^t \mathbf{E} + \boldsymbol{\mu}^t \frac{\partial \mathbf{f}}{\partial \mathbf{x}}\right] \frac{\partial \mathbf{x}}{\partial h}\, dt + \int_0^{t^*} \left(\frac{\partial \phi}{\partial h} + \boldsymbol{\mu}^t \frac{\partial \mathbf{f}}{\partial h}\right) dt. \tag{16.2.6}$$

Since arbitrary time functions $\boldsymbol{\lambda}$ and $\boldsymbol{\mu}$ were incorporated into (16.2.4), both these functions and their initial values can now be specified to simplify (16.2.6). We select them such that the first and second integrand in (16.2.6) are identically zero for all times. This specifies the "adjoint system"

$$\frac{\partial \phi}{\partial \mathbf{q}} + \boldsymbol{\mu}^t \frac{\partial \mathbf{f}}{\partial \mathbf{q}} - \frac{d}{dt}\left(\frac{\partial \phi}{\partial \mathbf{q}'} + \boldsymbol{\lambda}^t\right) = \mathbf{0}$$

$$\frac{\partial \phi}{\partial \mathbf{x}} - \boldsymbol{\lambda}^t \mathbf{E} + \boldsymbol{\mu}^t \frac{\partial \mathbf{f}}{\partial \mathbf{x}} = \mathbf{0}.$$

Transferring known (i.e., directly obtainable) quantities to the right side gives

$$\begin{aligned} -\frac{d}{dt}\boldsymbol{\lambda}^t + \boldsymbol{\mu}^t \frac{\partial \mathbf{f}}{\partial \mathbf{q}} &= \frac{d}{dt}\frac{\partial \phi}{\partial \mathbf{q}'} - \frac{\partial \phi}{\partial \mathbf{q}} \\ -\boldsymbol{\lambda}^t \mathbf{E} + \boldsymbol{\mu}^t \frac{\partial \mathbf{f}}{\partial \mathbf{x}} &= -\frac{\partial \phi}{\partial \mathbf{x}}. \end{aligned} \tag{16.2.7}$$

The initial values of $\boldsymbol{\lambda}$ (boundary conditions) have to be specified. Selecting the first term in (16.2.6) to be zero at $t = t^*$ provides

$$\boldsymbol{\lambda}^t(t^*) = -\frac{\partial \phi(t^*)}{\partial \mathbf{q}'}. \tag{16.2.8}$$

Equation (16.2.6) thus reduces to

$$\frac{\partial \psi}{\partial h} = -\left[\left(\frac{\partial \phi(0)}{\partial \mathbf{q}'} + \boldsymbol{\lambda}^t(0)\right) \frac{\partial \mathbf{q}(0)}{\partial h}\right] + \int_0^{t^*} \left(\frac{\partial \phi}{\partial h} + \boldsymbol{\mu}^t \frac{\partial \mathbf{f}}{\partial h}\right) dt. \tag{16.2.9}$$

This must be evaluated separately for each h. The adjoint system (16.2.7) is independent of h but its "initial" conditions are specified at time $t = t^*$ rather than at $t = 0$. The solution proceeds as follows:

1. Integrate the system (16.2.2) over the interval $(0, t^*)$ as described in Section 13.5 and store the resulting vectors $\mathbf{q}$, $\mathbf{x}$.
2. Integrate the adjoint system (16.2.7) backward starting at $t = t^*$ with the initial values specified by (16.2.8).
3. Simultaneously evaluate at each backward step the integral in (16.2.9).
4. When reaching $t = 0$, evaluate the first term in (16.2.9) to get the required sensitivity.

Note that in solving the adjoint system, the value $\mathbf{q}'$ at any step can be evaluated from stored values of $\mathbf{q}$ by the BDF formula.

16.3. STEADY STATE USING SENSITIVITY NETWORKS

In experimental work, networks are often observed in their steady state after the initial transients have died out. In computerized analysis, one can get to the steady state by integrating the system of equations over as many periods as required to eliminate the transients. Such an approach is probably the best for systems which reach the steady state in a few periods of the signal, but many practical networks are such that the transients die out only after hundreds of periods.

To avoid expensive integration, several methods have been proposed in the literature and we will discuss three of them. This section is based on the theory presented in Section 16.1 and was first used in [1].

Let the system of equations be the same as (16.1.1) with some initial condition $\mathbf{q}_0$:

$$\begin{aligned} \mathbf{q}' - \mathbf{E}\mathbf{x} = \mathbf{0}; \qquad \mathbf{q}_0 = \mathbf{q}(0) \\ \mathbf{f}(\mathbf{q}, \mathbf{x}, \mathbf{w}, t) = \mathbf{0}. \end{aligned} \tag{16.3.1}$$

Integrating over one period we obtain $\mathbf{q}(t^*)$. If the system is in steady state, $\mathbf{q}(t^*) = \mathbf{q}(0)$. If it is not, we note that $\mathbf{q}(t^*)$ is a function of $\mathbf{q}(0)$. After one period we can define an error vector

$$\boldsymbol{\epsilon}(\mathbf{q}_0) = \mathbf{q}(t^*, \mathbf{q}_0) - \mathbf{q}_0 \tag{16.3.2}$$

and we wish to reduce $\boldsymbol{\epsilon}$ to zero. Newton–Raphson iteration can be used, and the iterative equation becomes

$$\left[\frac{\partial \mathbf{q}(t^*, \mathbf{q}_0)}{\partial \mathbf{q}_0} - \mathbf{1}\right] \Delta \mathbf{q}_0 = -\boldsymbol{\epsilon}(\mathbf{q}_0). \tag{16.3.3}$$

The expression in square brackets represents the Jacobian to solve (16.3.2) for $\boldsymbol{\epsilon} = \mathbf{0}$. In this problem, the initial conditions become the parameters. Consider only one, the jth initial condition and differentiate (16.3.1) with respect to it:

$$\frac{\partial \mathbf{q}'}{\partial q_{0j}} - \mathbf{E}\frac{\partial \mathbf{x}}{\partial q_{0j}} = \mathbf{0}; \qquad \frac{\partial \mathbf{q}_0}{\partial q_{0j}} = \mathbf{e}_j$$

$$\frac{\partial \mathbf{f}}{\partial \mathbf{q}}\frac{\partial \mathbf{q}}{\partial q_{0j}} + \frac{\partial \mathbf{f}}{\partial \mathbf{x}}\frac{\partial \mathbf{x}}{\partial q_{0j}} = \mathbf{0}.$$

The vector of initial conditions simplifies to the jth unit vector $\mathbf{e}_j$. Defining

$$\mathbf{y}_j = \frac{\partial \mathbf{q}}{\partial q_{0j}}; \qquad \mathbf{z}_j = \frac{\partial \mathbf{x}}{\partial q_{0j}} \tag{16.3.4}$$

the sensitivity network system becomes

$$\begin{gathered} \mathbf{y}_j' - \mathbf{E}\mathbf{z}_j = \mathbf{0}; \qquad \mathbf{y}_{0j} = \mathbf{e}_j \\ \frac{\partial \mathbf{f}}{\partial \mathbf{q}}\mathbf{y}_j + \frac{\partial \mathbf{f}}{\partial \mathbf{x}}\mathbf{z}_j = \mathbf{0} \end{gathered} \tag{16.3.5}$$

and solution of (16.3.1) and (16.3.5) proceeds in the way explained in Section 16.1, using the BDF corrector formula.

Some problems may occur with this method. If not all the $\mathbf{q}$ are independent (loops of capacitors, cut sets of inductors), there will be Dirac impulses at $t = 0$. Their influence can be removed by considering the sensitivity network to be linear at $t = 0$ and by application of the initial value theorem of the Laplace transform. Alternatively, the method of Chapter 10, which is insensitive to such impulses, could be applied with very small step size ($\approx 10^{-10}$). Another problem associated with this method is the high storage requirements and the fact that the Jacobian matrix in (16.3.3) is generally dense, thus preventing application of sparse matrix methods.

An example will demonstrate generation of the sensitivity networks.

EXAMPLE 16.3.1. Indicate the method on the network shown in Fig. 16.1.1. The source $j(t)$ is assumed to be periodic. Since both the capacitor and inductor are linear, apply the simplest formulation method without introducing charges and fluxes.

The system equations are

$$\mathbf{f}(\mathbf{x}', \mathbf{x}, t) \equiv \begin{bmatrix} (e^{kv_1} - 1) + i_L - j(t) \\ C\dfrac{dv_2}{dt} + Gv_2 - i_L \\ v_1 - v_2 - L\dfrac{di_L}{dt} \end{bmatrix} = \mathbf{0}.$$

Define

$$\frac{\partial i_D}{\partial v_1} = ke^{kv_1} = g_D.$$

The sensitivity system for I_0 is

$$\frac{\partial \mathbf{f}}{\partial I_0} = \begin{bmatrix} g_D & 0 & 1 \\ 0 & G + C\dfrac{d}{dt} & -1 \\ 1 & -1 & -L\dfrac{d}{dt} \end{bmatrix} \begin{bmatrix} \partial v_1/\partial I_0 \\ \partial v_2/\partial I_0 \\ \partial i_L/\partial I_0 \end{bmatrix} = \mathbf{0}; \qquad \frac{\partial \mathbf{x}_0}{\partial I_0} = \begin{bmatrix} 0 \\ 0 \\ 1 \end{bmatrix}.$$

The sensitivity system for V_0 is

$$\frac{\partial \mathbf{f}}{\partial V_0} = \begin{bmatrix} g_D & 0 & 1 \\ 0 & G + C\dfrac{d}{dt} & -1 \\ 1 & -1 & -L\dfrac{d}{dt} \end{bmatrix} \begin{bmatrix} \partial v_1/\partial V_0 \\ \partial v_2/\partial V_0 \\ \partial i_L/\partial V_0 \end{bmatrix} = \mathbf{0}; \qquad \frac{\partial \mathbf{x}_0}{\partial V_0} = \begin{bmatrix} 0 \\ 1 \\ 0 \end{bmatrix}.$$

All three systems are integrated over the period of the driving signal. For the Newton–Raphson iteration the values i_L, v_C and their derivatives are retained.

16.4. STEADY STATE ON OBJECTIVE FUNCTION

The theory presented in Section 16.2 can be used for steady state analysis as well. Integration over one period of the signal provides the error function (16.3.2) but instead of using the Newton–Raphson algorithm, we form the following objective function [2]:

$$\psi(\mathbf{q}_0) = \tfrac{1}{2}\|\epsilon(\mathbf{q}_0)\|^2 = [\mathbf{q}(t^*) - \mathbf{q}_0]^t\,[\mathbf{q}(t^*) - \mathbf{q}_0] \tag{16.4.1}$$

which is minimized until $\psi = 0$. We will show that this is equivalent to

$$\psi = \psi(\mathbf{q}_0) = \int_0^{t^*} [\mathbf{q}(t) - \mathbf{q}_0]^t\,\mathbf{q}'(t)\,dt. \tag{16.4.2}$$

Indeed, performing the integration

$$\psi = \int_0^{t^*} \mathbf{q}^t\mathbf{q}'\,dt - \mathbf{q}_0^t \int_0^{t^*} \mathbf{q}'\,dt = \left(\tfrac{1}{2}\,\mathbf{q}^t\mathbf{q} - \mathbf{q}_0^t\mathbf{q}\right)\Big|_0^{t^*}$$

$$= \tfrac{1}{2}\,[\mathbf{q}(t^*) - \mathbf{q}_0]^t\,[\mathbf{q}(t^*) - \mathbf{q}_0].$$

Since (16.4.2) must be satisfied with constraints defined by

$$\begin{aligned} &\mathbf{q}' - \mathbf{E}\mathbf{x} = \mathbf{0}; \qquad \mathbf{q}_0 = \mathbf{q}(0) \\ &\mathbf{f}(\mathbf{q}, \mathbf{x}, \mathbf{w}, t) = \mathbf{0} \end{aligned} \tag{16.4.3}$$

we define the equivalent of (16.2.4):

$$\psi = \int_0^{t^*} [\phi + \boldsymbol{\lambda}^t(\mathbf{q}' - \mathbf{E}\mathbf{x}) + \boldsymbol{\mu}^t\mathbf{f}]\,dt \tag{16.4.4}$$

with

$$\phi = [\mathbf{q}(t) - \mathbf{q}_0]^t\mathbf{q}'(t). \tag{16.4.5}$$

Further steps follow those given in Section 16.2 by taking the initial conditions as parameters. The adjoint system (16.2.7) simplifies, because

$$\frac{\partial \phi}{\partial \mathbf{x}} = \mathbf{0}; \qquad \frac{\partial \phi}{\partial \mathbf{q}} = (\mathbf{q}')^t; \qquad \frac{d}{dt}\,\frac{\partial \phi}{\partial \mathbf{q}'} = \frac{d}{dt}\,[\mathbf{q}(t) - \mathbf{q}_0]^t = (\mathbf{q}')^t.$$

With these substitutions, (16.2.7) becomes

$$\begin{aligned} -\frac{d}{dt}\,\boldsymbol{\lambda}^t + \boldsymbol{\mu}^t\,\frac{\partial \mathbf{f}}{\partial \mathbf{q}} &= \mathbf{0} \\ -\boldsymbol{\lambda}^t\mathbf{E} + \boldsymbol{\mu}^t\,\frac{\partial \mathbf{f}}{\partial \mathbf{x}} &= \mathbf{0}. \end{aligned} \tag{16.4.6}$$

The boundary condition (16.2.8) becomes

$$\boldsymbol{\lambda}^t(t^*) = -\,[\mathbf{q}(t^*) - \mathbf{q}_0]^t. \tag{16.4.7}$$

Evaluation of (16.2.9) requires

$$\left.\frac{\partial \phi}{\partial \mathbf{q}'}\right|_{t=0} = [\mathbf{q}(t) - \mathbf{q}_0]^t\Big|_{t=0} = \mathbf{0}$$

$$\frac{\partial \mathbf{q}_0}{\partial q_{0j}} = \mathbf{e}_j$$

$$\frac{\partial \phi}{\partial q_{0j}} = \frac{\partial}{\partial q_{0j}} [\mathbf{q}(t) - \mathbf{q}_0]^t \mathbf{q}' = -\mathbf{e}_j^t \mathbf{q}'$$

$$\frac{\partial \mathbf{f}}{\partial q_{0j}} = \mathbf{0}.$$

Substituting into (16.2.9) gives

$$\begin{aligned}\frac{\partial \psi}{\partial q_{0j}} &= -[\{\mathbf{0} + \boldsymbol{\lambda}^t(0)\}\,\mathbf{e}_j] + \int_0^{t^*} (-\mathbf{e}_j^t \mathbf{q}')\,dt \\ &= -\boldsymbol{\lambda}^t(0)\,\mathbf{e}_j - \mathbf{e}_j^t[\mathbf{q}(t^*) - \mathbf{q}_0].\end{aligned}$$

Further simplification is possible by using (16.4.7). Then

$$\begin{aligned}\frac{\partial \psi}{\partial q_{0j}} &= -\boldsymbol{\lambda}^t(0)\,\mathbf{e}_j + \mathbf{e}_j^t \boldsymbol{\lambda}(t^*) \\ &= \lambda_j(t^*) - \lambda_j(0).\end{aligned}$$

16.5. STEADY STATE BY EXTRAPOLATION

The extrapolation method for steady state network solutions was proposed by Skelboe [3]. Its attractive features are quadratic convergence and the fact that it needs neither gradients nor Jacobians. If a general program for time domain solution of nonlinear networks is available, then only modest programming is required for its implementation. In this section we briefly describe its principles.

Let the network equations be given in any formulation and let an initial solution vector $\mathbf{x}_0$ be available. It can be either the dc solution or the result of integration of the network equations over one or more periods of the forcing signal. Proceeding over a number of periods of t^* obtain the solutions $\mathbf{x}_0, \mathbf{x}_1, \ldots, \mathbf{x}_k, \ldots$. In each case, the next solution $\mathbf{x}_{k+1}$ is obtained as some transformation of $\mathbf{x}_k$:

$$\mathbf{x}_{k+1} = \mathcal{F}(\mathbf{x}_k).$$

Consider also some other solution $\mathbf{y}_{k+1}$ starting from $\mathbf{y}_k$:

$$\mathbf{y}_{k+1} = \mathcal{F}(\mathbf{y}_k)$$

and form the difference

$$\mathbf{x}_{k+1} - \mathbf{y}_{k+1} = \mathcal{F}(\mathbf{x}_k) - \mathcal{F}(\mathbf{y}_k) = \mathcal{F}(\mathbf{y}_k + \mathbf{x}_k - \mathbf{y}_k) - \mathcal{F}(\mathbf{y}_k).$$

In the last expression we added and subtracted $\mathbf{y}_k$ to the argument. Next assume that the difference $\mathbf{x}_k - \mathbf{y}_k$ is small, expand $\mathcal{F}(\mathbf{y}_k + \mathbf{x}_k - \mathbf{y}_k)$ into a variational series about $\mathbf{y}_k$ and retain only the first two terms:

$$\begin{aligned}\mathbf{x}_{k+1} - \mathbf{y}_{k+1} &= \mathcal{F}(\mathbf{y}_k) + \mathcal{F}'(\mathbf{y}_k)(\mathbf{x}_k - \mathbf{y}_k) - \mathcal{F}(\mathbf{y}_k) \\ &= \mathcal{F}'(\mathbf{y}_k)(\mathbf{x}_k - \mathbf{y}_k).\end{aligned} \tag{16.5.1}$$

Now let $\mathbf{y}_k$ be the steady state solution, denoted for simplicity by $\mathbf{z}$. It follows that $\mathbf{y}_{k+1}$ must be $\mathbf{z}$ as well and (16.5.1) changes into

$$\mathbf{x}_{k+1} = \mathbf{z} + \mathbf{A}(\mathbf{x}_k - \mathbf{z}). \tag{16.5.2}$$

Here $\mathbf{A} = \mathcal{F}'(\mathbf{z})$ is a constant matrix and corresponds to the sensitivity of the solution at time t^* (the period) to changes in initial conditions. In Section 16.3, the equivalent of $\mathbf{A}$ was generated explicitly. Our objective now is to compute $\mathbf{z}$ without forming $\mathbf{A}$. Consider the sequence of $\mathbf{x}$ vectors generated by the recurrence relation (16.5.2) starting with $k = 0$:

$$\begin{aligned}\mathbf{x}_1 &= \mathbf{A}(\mathbf{x}_0 - \mathbf{z}) + \mathbf{z} \\ \mathbf{x}_2 &= \mathbf{A}(\mathbf{x}_1 - \mathbf{z}) + \mathbf{z} = \mathbf{A}^2(\mathbf{x}_0 - \mathbf{z}) + \mathbf{z} \\ &\vdots \\ \mathbf{x}_k &= \mathbf{A}^k(\mathbf{x}_0 - \mathbf{z}) + \mathbf{z}.\end{aligned} \tag{16.5.3}$$

The difference of two successive vectors is

$$\begin{aligned}\Delta\mathbf{x}_k = \mathbf{x}_{k+1} - \mathbf{x}_k &= \mathbf{A}^{k+1}(\mathbf{x}_0 - \mathbf{z}) - \mathbf{A}^k(\mathbf{x}_0 - \mathbf{z}) \\ &= (\mathbf{A} - \mathbf{1})\,\mathbf{A}^k(\mathbf{x}_0 - \mathbf{z}).\end{aligned} \tag{16.5.4}$$

For some $m < n$, the dimension of $\mathbf{x}$, the vectors $\Delta\mathbf{x}_k$ will become linearly dependent and nontrivial constants c_k exist such that

$$\sum_{k=0}^{m} c_k \Delta\mathbf{x}_k = \mathbf{0}. \tag{16.5.5}$$

The determination of the number m and the constants c_k will be considered later in this section. For the moment, assume that they are known. To obtain the extrapolation formula, return to (16.5.3), multiply each $\mathbf{x}_k$ by c_k and take the sum

$$\sum_{k=0}^{m} c_k \mathbf{x}_k = \sum_{k=0}^{m} c_k \mathbf{A}^k(\mathbf{x}_0 - \mathbf{z}) + \sum_{k=0}^{m} c_k \mathbf{z} \tag{16.5.6a}$$

$$= (\mathbf{A} - \mathbf{1})^{-1} \sum_{k=0}^{m} c_k(\mathbf{A} - \mathbf{1})\, \mathbf{A}^k(\mathbf{x}_0 - \mathbf{z}) + \mathbf{z} \sum_{k=0}^{m} c_k \tag{16.5.6b}$$

$$= (\mathbf{A} - \mathbf{1})^{-1} \sum_{k=0}^{m} c_k \Delta \mathbf{x}_k + \mathbf{z} \sum_{k=0}^{m} c_k \tag{16.5.6c}$$

$$= \mathbf{z} \sum_{k=0}^{m} c_k. \tag{16.5.6d}$$

In writing (16.5.6b) we assumed that none of the eigenvalues of $\mathbf{A}$ is equal to unity; (16.5.6c) follows from (16.5.4); and (16.5.6d) is obtained by use of (16.5.5). The steady state vector $\mathbf{z}$ can be obtained from (16.5.6d) as follows:

$$\mathbf{z} = \frac{\sum_{k=0}^{m} c_k \mathbf{x}_k}{\sum_{k=0}^{m} c_k}. \tag{16.5.7}$$

The disadvantage of (16.5.7) is the fact that the constants c_k were obtained from (16.5.5), for which the vectors of differences $\Delta \mathbf{x}_k$ had to be stored, whereas (16.5.7) requires storage of $\mathbf{x}_k$. To avoid such double storage, increments can be introduced into (16.5.7). Simple algebra leads to

$$\mathbf{z} = \mathbf{x}_m + \frac{\sum_{k=0}^{m-1} \left(\sum_{i=0}^{k} c_i \right) \Delta \mathbf{x}_k}{\sum_{k=0}^{m} c_k}. \tag{16.5.8}$$

In a nonlinear network, the system matrix $\mathbf{A}$ is not constant and several iterations may be necessary. The algorithm can be formulated as follows:

1. Obtain $\mathbf{x}_0$ by taking the dc operating point or by integrating over a few periods.
2. Integrate over two periods of the signal to obtain $\mathbf{x}_1, \mathbf{x}_2$. Calculate $\Delta\mathbf{x}_0$, $\Delta\mathbf{x}_1$ and set $m = 2$.
3. Integrate over one period t^* to get $\mathbf{x}_{m+1}$. Calculate $\Delta\mathbf{x}_m$.
4. "Solve" (16.5.5) by any suitable method (see below). For $m < n$, $\sum_{k=0}^{m} c_k \Delta\mathbf{x}_k$ may not be zero. If the error is sufficiently small, go to step 5. Else set $m = m + 1$ and go to step 3.
5. Calculate $\mathbf{z}$ using (16.5.8). Check whether steady state has been reached. If not, set $\mathbf{x}_0 = \mathbf{z}$ and go to step 2.

Consider next the solution of (16.5.5). Let us normalize the equation by choosing $c_m = -1$ and write it as follows:

$$\mathbf{B}_m \mathbf{c}_m = \Delta\mathbf{x}_m \qquad (16.5.9)$$

where

$$\mathbf{B}_m = [\Delta\mathbf{x}_0 \quad \Delta\mathbf{x}_1 \quad \cdots \quad \Delta\mathbf{x}_{m-1}]$$

is a matrix with n rows and m columns, $m \leqslant n$, and $\mathbf{c}_m$ is a vector

$$\mathbf{c}_m = [c_0 \quad c_1 \quad \cdots \quad c_{m-1}]^t.$$

As $\mathbf{B}_m$ is rectangular, an exact solution to (16.5.9) is often neither possible nor desirable. The aim is to find the smallest value of m and the corresponding vector $\mathbf{c}_m$ for which (16.5.9) is satisfied sufficiently well. To this end, define the residual vector

$$\mathbf{r}_m = \mathbf{B}_m \mathbf{c}_m - \Delta\mathbf{x}_m. \qquad (16.5.10)$$

The solution will be deemed acceptable when the size of $\mathbf{r}_m$ is small. Various measures of size exist and the Euclidean norm, $\|\mathbf{r}_m\|^2 = \sum_{i=1}^{n} r_i^2$, is the most convenient one in this application. We will define the error at step 4 of the algorithm above to be $\epsilon = \|\mathbf{r}_m\|^2$. At each step of 4, it now remains to solve (16.5.9) for $\mathbf{c}_m$ and determine ϵ.

In the mathematical and statistical literature this problem is called the *linear least squares problem* and is usually solved by *QR* decomposition. An excellent reference to such problems is [4], while computer codes may be found in [5].

EXAMPLE 16.5.1. The method described in this section was used to find the steady state of the network shown in Fig. 16.5.1. Figure 16.5.2 shows the

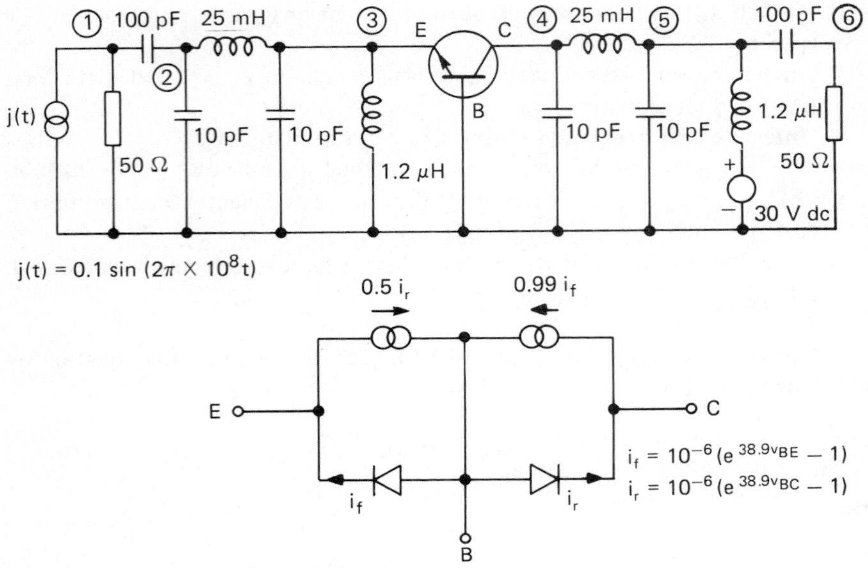

Fig. 16.5.1. Network for Example 16.5.1.

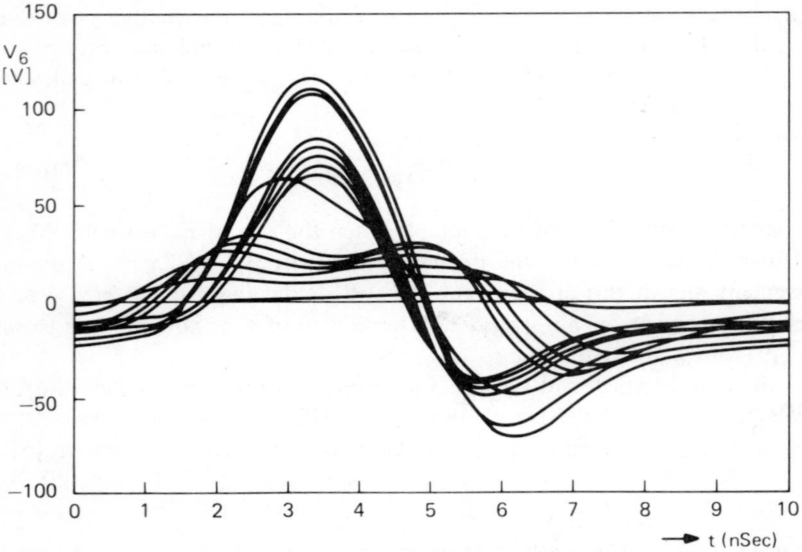

Fig. 16.5.2. Sequence of integrations and extrapolations on the network in Fig. 16.5.1.

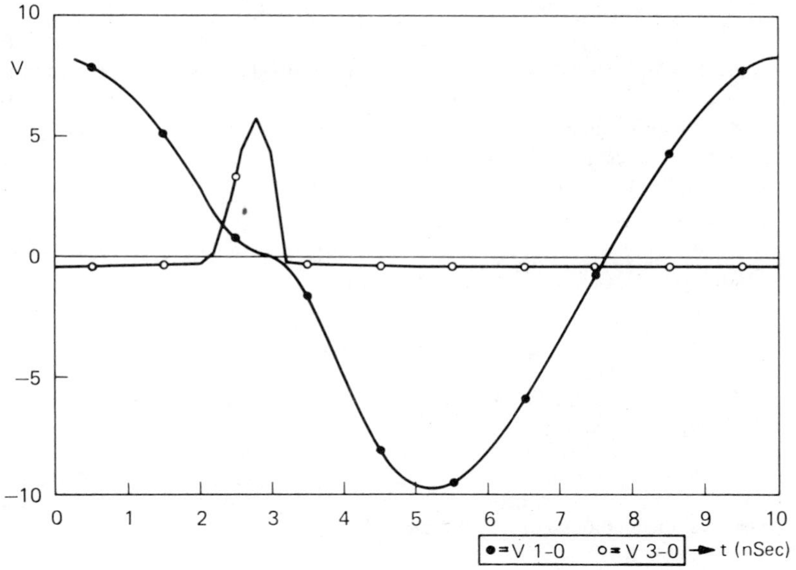

Fig. 16.5.3. Steady state responses at nodes 1 and 3.

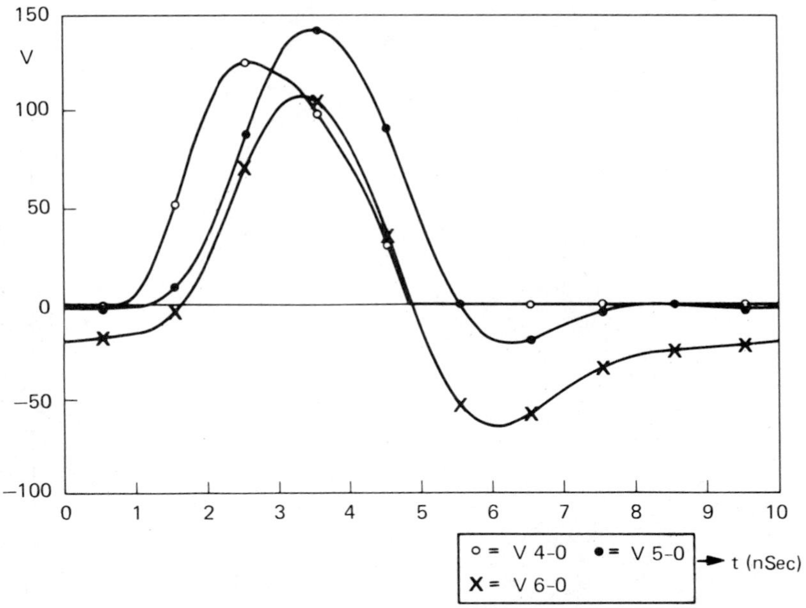

Fig. 16.5.4. Steady state responses at nodes 4, 5, and 6.

sequence of integrations as well as the extrapolation steps. The first seven lower curves represent integration over seven periods. Extrapolation was applied and integration continued over five additional periods when extrapolation was applied again. The group of upper curves represents another integration over several periods and one more extrapolation was needed before the steady state was reached. Figures 16.5.3 and 16.5.4 represent the steady state node voltage responses of the network.

REFERENCES

1. T. N. Trick, F. R. Colon, and S. P. Fan: Computation of capacitor voltage and inductor current sensitivities with respect to initial conditions for the steady state analysis of non-linear periodic circuits. *IEEE Transactions on Circuits and Systems*, Vol. CAS-22, pp. 391–396, May 1975.
2. S. W. Director and K. W. Current: Optimization of forced nonlinear periodic circuits. *IEEE Transactions on Circuits and Systems*, Vol. CAS-23, pp. 329–335, June 1976.
3. S. Skelboe: Computation of the periodic steady-state response of nonlinear networks by extrapolation methods. *IEEE Transactions on Circuits and Systems*, Vol. CAS-27, pp. 161–175, March 1980.
4. C. L. Lawson and R. J. Hanson: *Solving Least Squares Problems.* Prentice-Hall, Englewood Cliffs, NJ, 1974.
5. J. J. Dongarra, C. B. Moler, J. R. Bunch, and G. W. Stewart: *LINPACK Users Guide.* SIAM, Philadelphia, 1979.

CHAPTER 17
Design by Minimization

Minimization of objective functions is an important tool in the design of a network, especially in the final stages. It cannot be stressed strongly enough that *other available design tools should be used* to get as good an initial estimate as possible. The reader should realize that objective functions of complicated networks may have local minima and although optimization may proceed entirely satisfactorily, the result may be unacceptable because a local minimum has been found.

Often, a nominal design is available for a network with ideal elements. When the network is built, the actual response deviates from the desired response due, for example, to losses in inductors, nonideal frequency characteristics of the amplifiers, stray parasitics, and so on. The network response may be severely distorted and it may be necessary to use a sequence of minimizations, initially by assuming small deviations of the elements from their ideal properties and subsequently increasing the parasitic effects.

Four different minimization problems will be discussed on an informal basis, and no attempt is made to provide an exhaustive treatment. Section 17.1 describes the most common application in which the amplitude response of the network is matched to given specifications in the mean square sense. All equations are derived, from the objective function to the gradient. The theory used in this case is based on the development given in Chapter 6. Section 17.2 indicates another possibility in which specified complex values are matched by a network. This type of matching is useful, for instance, in representing the behavior of an antenna by a lumped *RLC* network or in the design of impedance matching networks.

Minimax optimization is described in Section 17.3. In this case the largest peaks of errors are reduced in magnitude while the smaller ones are allowed to grow. In most cases, such a design provides the widest safety margin and is desirable but usually difficult and expensive to obtain. Section 17.4 indicates how we could proceed if we wished to minimize sensitivities of active networks.

The minimization problems are given in the sequence of increasing complexity and examples show applications in all four sections.

A Monte Carlo verification analysis constitutes the last design step for networks that are to be mass produced. Here we simulate the actual production and field environment to make sure that the design is sufficiently reliable. This topic is considered in Section 17.5.

17.1. MEAN-SQUARE OBJECTIVE FUNCTIONS

In this section, we will define the mean-square objective function for matching of absolute values. The information given here should be sufficient to help the reader in defining similar objective functions for other purposes.

Before going into the details, let us repeat some steps from Chapter 6. Let the network be represented by the modified nodal system equations:

$$\mathbf{TX} = \mathbf{W}. \tag{17.1.1}$$

In the following derivations, we will consider a single frequency and a single parameter h to simplify notation. Differentiate (17.1.1) with respect to h:

$$\frac{\partial \mathbf{T}}{\partial h}\mathbf{X} + \mathbf{T}\frac{\partial \mathbf{X}}{\partial h} = \mathbf{0}.$$

This is valid when the vector $\mathbf{W}$ is independent of the parameter h, a typical situation in frequency domain design. The sensitivity vector becomes

$$\frac{\partial \mathbf{X}}{\partial h} = -\mathbf{T}^{-1}\frac{\partial \mathbf{T}}{\partial h}\mathbf{X}. \tag{17.1.2}$$

Consider next a network function composed of linear combinations of the entries of $\mathbf{X}$

$$\phi = \mathbf{d}^t\mathbf{X}. \tag{17.1.3}$$

The vector $\mathbf{d}$ will contain only one unit entry if the output is a nodal voltage or a branch current, or one positive and one negative unit entry if the output is the difference of two voltages. Since $\mathbf{d}$ is a constant vector,

$$\frac{\partial \phi}{\partial h} = \mathbf{d}^t\frac{\partial \mathbf{X}}{\partial h} \tag{17.1.4}$$

and inserting from (17.1.2)

$$\frac{\partial \phi}{\partial h} = -\mathbf{d}^t \mathbf{T}^{-1} \frac{\partial \mathbf{T}}{\partial h} \mathbf{X}. \tag{17.1.5}$$

At a given frequency and with given values of the parameters, the output is defined by (17.1.3). Assume that instead of $|\phi|$ we would like to have the value A. To this end define the error function

$$E = \tfrac{1}{2} [|\phi| - A]^2. \tag{17.1.6}$$

For a given frequency, the value of $|\phi|$ may be larger or smaller than A and the difference may be positive or negative. The square in (17.1.6) ensures that E will always be nonnegative. If we succeed in changing the element values such that E is forced to be zero, the objective has been reached. In most cases, we will not be able to reach zero, because the network may not be able to satisfy the required conditions over many frequencies. Nevertheless, minimization of (17.1.6) will reduce the value of E. We now derive the expressions for the gradient. Differentiating (17.1.6) with respect to h gives

$$\begin{aligned}\frac{\partial E}{\partial h} &= [|\phi| - A] \frac{\partial}{\partial h} [|\phi| - A] \\ &= [|\phi| - A] \frac{\partial |\phi|}{\partial h}.\end{aligned}$$

The formula for the derivative $\partial|\phi|/\partial h$ was derived in Section 6.5, Eq. (6.5.4). Its use gives

$$\frac{\partial E}{\partial h} = [|\phi| - A]|\phi| \operatorname{Re}\left[\frac{1}{\phi} \frac{\partial \phi}{\partial h}\right].$$

Place the absolute values inside the Re operator:

$$\frac{\partial E}{\partial h} = \operatorname{Re}\left\{\frac{[|\phi| - A]|\phi|}{\phi} \frac{\partial \phi}{\partial h}\right\}. \tag{17.1.7}$$

Substitute (17.1.5) in (17.1.7):

$$\frac{\partial E}{\partial h} = \operatorname{Re}\left\{\underbrace{- \frac{[|\phi| - A]|\phi|}{\phi} \mathbf{d}^t \mathbf{T}^{-1}}_{(\mathbf{X}^a)^t} \frac{\partial \mathbf{T}}{\partial h} \mathbf{X}\right\}. \tag{17.1.8}$$

At this point we recall how we introduced the adjoint system in Chapter 6. As indicated above, define

$$-\frac{[|\phi| - A]|\phi|}{\phi}\mathbf{d}^t\mathbf{T}^{-1} = (\mathbf{X}^a)^t$$

which is equivalent to solving the transpose system

$$\mathbf{T}^t\mathbf{X}^a = -\frac{[|\phi| - A]|\phi|}{\phi}\mathbf{d} \tag{17.1.9}$$

in which the nonzero entries of $\mathbf{d}$ are multiplied by the complex value $-[|\phi| - A]|\phi|/\phi$. Assume that both systems (17.1.1) and (17.1.9) have been solved and the vectors $\mathbf{X}$ and $\mathbf{X}^a$ are available *at the given frequency. Neither of these vectors depends on the variable parameter h* and for any h_i

$$\frac{\partial E}{\partial h_i} = \text{Re}\left\{(\mathbf{X}^a)^t\frac{\partial \mathbf{T}}{\partial h_i}\mathbf{X}\right\}. \tag{17.1.10}$$

The design will normally take m frequencies into consideration. The complete objective function will be

$$E = \sum_{j=1}^{m} w_jE_j = \tfrac{1}{2}\sum_{j=1}^{m} w_j[|\phi_j| - A_j]^2 \tag{17.1.11}$$

and the ith entry of its gradient will be

$$\frac{\partial E}{\partial h_i} = \sum_{j=1}^{m} w_j\frac{\partial E_j}{\partial h_i} = \sum_{j=1}^{m} w_j\,\text{Re}\left\{(\mathbf{X}_j^a)^t\frac{\partial \mathbf{T}_j}{\partial h_i}\mathbf{X}_j\right\} \tag{17.1.12}$$

where the subscript i includes all variable elements. The coefficient w_j is the weighting coefficient. Normally, it is set equal to 1. Should some frequency be more important than the others, a larger w_j may be selected for it. This will reduce the error at that particular frequency.

A simple but practical example demonstrates possible application. The amplifier shown in Fig. 17.1.1 is to work into a load having a 100 pF parasitic capacitance. We wish to design the amplifier to provide a gain of 40 with an improved passband.

The network is first designed as an RC amplifier with $R_L = 2000$ ohm and $L = 0$. An Ebers-Moll model was used to first find the operating point (the model equations are fairly complicated and are not given here). Using the

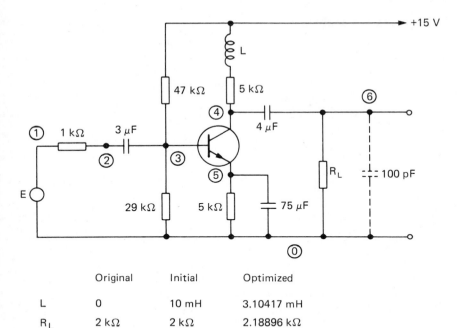

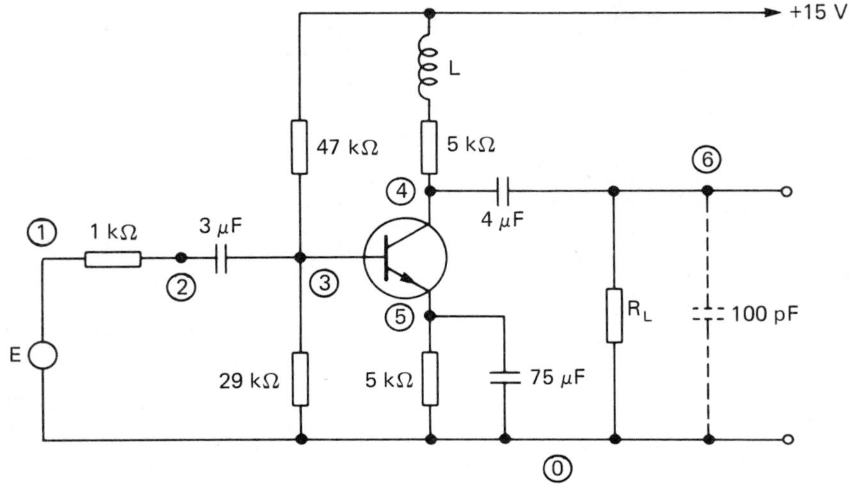

	Original	Initial	Optimized
L	0	10 mH	3.10417 mH
R_L	2 kΩ	2 kΩ	2.18896 kΩ

Fig. 17.1.1. Transistor amplifier design for maximum bandwidth. Optimized variables were L and R_L.

model values obtained for the operating point, the amplifier was analyzed; its frequency response is shown in Fig. 17.1.2 as curve ***a***. A gain of about 37 was achieved.

In the next step, the inductor was arbitrarily selected as $L = 10$ mH and the amplifier analyzed again. The response is shown as curve *b* and clearly indicates the peaking influence of the inductor. Finally, the network was optimized by allowing the resistor R_L and the inductor L to change. Final values, obtained by minimization, are $R_L = 2188.96$ ohm and $L = 3.10417$ mH. The amplitude response is shown as curve *c*. The gain 40 was achieved and the bandwidth increased.

17.2. MATCHING OF COMPLEX VALUES

The steps here will be similar to those explained in Section 17.1 except that the output ϕ should now match a complex number $C = C_{re} + jC_{im}$. Two possible formulations can be adopted in this design: either we can attempt to match separately the real and the imaginary parts, or we may attempt to match

$$E = |\phi - C|. \tag{17.2.1}$$

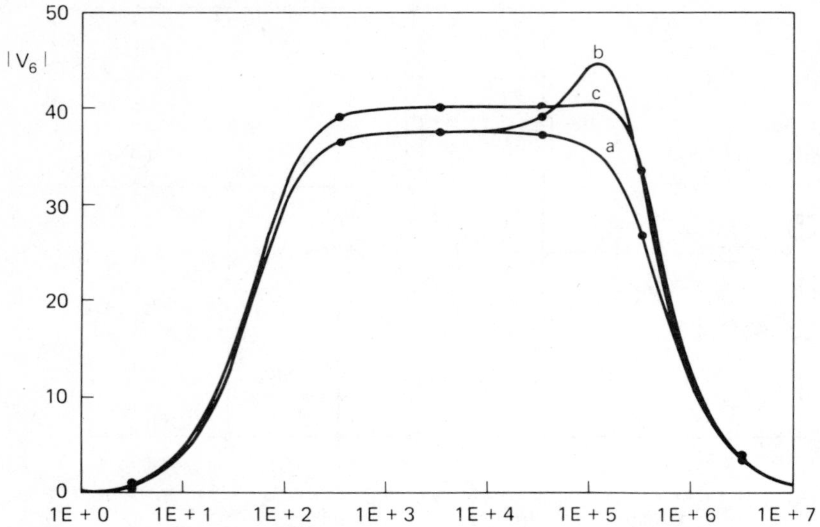

Fig. 17.1.2. Amplitude response of the network shown in Fig. 17.1.1 : (a) original design; (b) response with initial value $L = 10$ mH; (c) optimized response.

We will use this second possibility. Differentiating with respect to h gives

$$\frac{\partial E}{\partial h} = \frac{\partial}{\partial h} |\phi - C| = |\phi - C| \operatorname{Re} \left\{ \frac{1}{\phi - C} \frac{\partial \phi}{\partial h} \right\}$$

where formula (6.5.4) was applied. The absolute value can be placed under the Re operator and (17.1.5) substituted for $\partial\phi/\partial h$:

$$\frac{\partial E}{\partial h} = \operatorname{Re} \left\{ \underbrace{- \frac{|\phi - C|}{\phi - C} \mathbf{d}^t \mathbf{T}^{-1}}_{(\mathbf{X}^a)^t} \frac{\partial \mathbf{T}}{\partial h} \mathbf{X} \right\}. \tag{17.2.2}$$

Define the adjoint system as indicated above:

$$- \frac{|\phi - C|}{\phi - C} \mathbf{d}^t \mathbf{T}^{-1} = (\mathbf{X}^a)^t.$$

It is equivalent to solving the transpose system

$$\mathbf{T}^t\mathbf{X}^a = -\frac{|\phi - C|}{\phi - C}\,\mathbf{d}. \tag{17.2.3}$$

The nonzero entries of **d** are multiplied by the complex number $-|\phi - C|/(\phi - C)$. Assume that both systems (17.1.1) and (17.2.3) have been solved and that the vectors $\mathbf{X}$, $\mathbf{X}^a$ are available. As in the last section, they do not depend on the parameter but do depend on the frequency. The derivative with respect to any h_i is again given by (17.1.10). If m frequencies are taken into consideration, the objective function will be

$$E = \sum_{j=1}^{m} w_j E_j = \sum_{j=1}^{m} w_j |\phi_j - C_j| \tag{17.2.4}$$

and the ith entry of the gradient will be

$$\frac{\partial E}{\partial h_i} = \sum_{j=1}^{m} w_j \frac{\partial E_j}{\partial h_i} = \sum_{j=1}^{m} w_j \operatorname{Re}\left\{(\mathbf{X}^a)^t \frac{\partial \mathbf{T}_j}{\partial h_i}\mathbf{X}\right\} \tag{17.2.5}$$

with i running over all variable elements.

The above is illustrated by an impedance matching problem. Assume that we are interested in finding an RLC network which has the impedance values given in Table 17.2.1. To get the initial network configuration, assume that all the real parts of the specifications are equal to zero and only the imaginary parts are to be considered first. The imaginary part is zero approximately at 7 and 20 Hz and the peaks of the impedance occur at approximately 12 and 26 Hz. Using the theory of LC circuits we can assume that an ideal lossless impedance would have the following form:

$$Z_{LC} = \frac{[s^2 + (7 \times 2\pi)^2]\,[s^2 + (20 \times 2\pi)^2]}{s\,[s^2 + (12 \times 2\pi)^2]\,[s^2 + (26 \times 2\pi)^2]}\,.$$

The impedance is synthesized and an ideal network is obtained. It is shown in Fig. 17.2.1 with all resistors assumed to be removed. Next, without profound theoretical reason, assume that resistors as shown will provide the network losses. This initial network was subject to optimization and the result is given in Table 17.2.1. It can be seen that the network does represent, to some extent, the desired response. Large errors occur at 22 Hz (where the imaginary parts have different signs) and at the lower-frequency end of the band. These errors can be corrected by giving a better initial estimate and possibly a more complicated network. The polar plot in Figure 17.2.2 shows the impedance of the final result.

Table 17.2.1. Impedance Response to be Simulated by an *RLC* Network, and Response Obtained from Optimized Network.

Freq. Hz	Impedance Required		Impedance Resulting	
2	200	–520	21.5	–376
4	80	–190	81	–178
6	23	–48	59.5	–64.3
8	57	74	73	37.9
10	160	230	162	184.3
12	800	170	740	132
14	320	–340	237	–426.5
16	110	–250	73.7	–248.5
18	380	–120	47.2	–151.8
20	37	–27	50	–81.7
22	84	72	79.7	–12.2
24	230	124	184.3	58.9
26	390	–20	416	–82.4
28	220	–260	235.5	–326.3
30	65	–160	95.1	–282

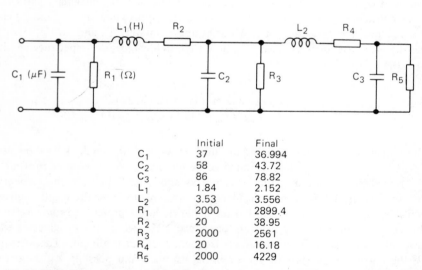

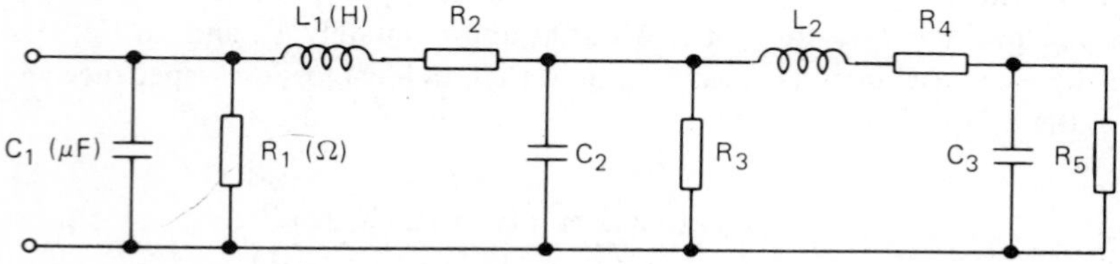

	Initial	Final
C_1	37	36.994
C_2	58	43.72
C_3	86	78.82
L_1	1.84	2.152
L_2	3.53	3.556
R_1	2000	2899.4
R_2	20	38.95
R_3	2000	2561
R_4	20	16.18
R_5	2000	4229

Fig. 17.2.1. Initial and optimized values of the network simulating data in Table 17.2.1.

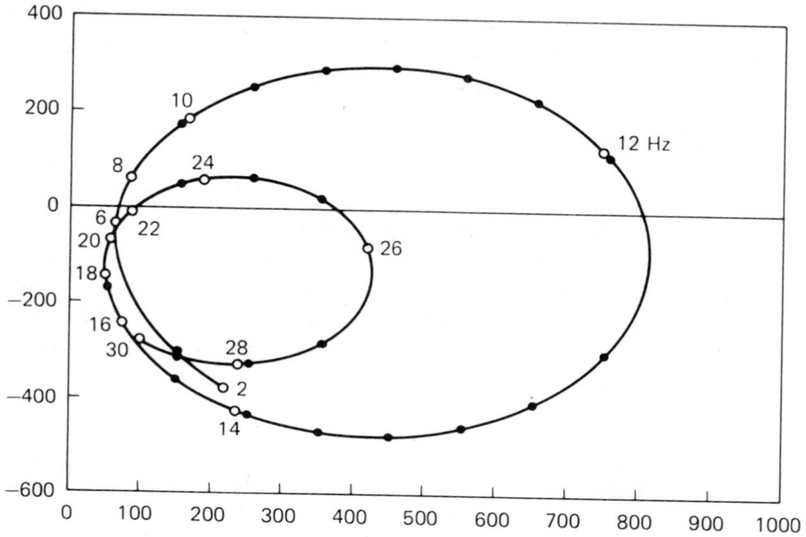

Fig. 17.2.2. Polar plot of the final input impedance.

17.3. MINIMAX SOLUTIONS

The minimization methods discussed in Sections 17.1 and 17.2 are mathematically simple and computationally fairly inexpensive, but the results may not always be the best solution to our problem. Since we are minimizing the sum of the squares of the errors (or their absolute values) and not each error individually, we cannot influence the peaks of the errors efficiently except in an indirect way by the choice of weight numbers. When the minimum of the sum is reached, the response will generally fluctuate about the desired solution and the peaks of errors will have different magnitudes. It is desirable to have a method which can further reduce the large error peaks by allowing the smaller ones to grow.

The mathematical formulation of the minimax problem is presented in terms of the network amplitude response. The variable network elements are denoted by the vector $\mathbf{h} = [h_1, h_2, \ldots, h_n]^t$ and the response is evaluated at m distinct frequencies f_j, $j = 1, 2, \ldots, m$. The error is given as follows:

$$E_j = |\phi_j(\mathbf{h})| - A_j \tag{17.3.1}$$

The maximum error over all frequency points is selected, $\max_j |E_j|$, and we wish to minimize it by changing the values of $\mathbf{h}$. We thus want to minimize $F(\mathbf{h}) =$

$\max_j |E_j|$. This can be expressed mathematically by $\min_{\mathbf{h}} \max_j |E_j(\mathbf{h})|$ and the name *minimax* used in the title of the section is based on this mathematical description. The general formulation of the problem is now

$$\text{minimize:} \qquad F(\mathbf{h}) = \max_j |E_j(\mathbf{h})| \tag{17.3.2}$$

subject to the usual equality and inequality constraints.

The direct solution of (17.3.2) can be attempted in many ways, almost all of them requiring considerable theoretical background and special coding. To avoid these complications we give a method [1] which makes use of a general program for constrained minimization. The number of variables is increased by one, h_{n+1}, and (17.3.2) redefined as

$$\begin{aligned} &\text{minimize:} && h_{n+1} \\ &\text{subject to:} && h_{n+1} - |E_j(\mathbf{h})| \geqslant 0;\ 1 \leqslant j \leqslant m \end{aligned} \tag{17.3.3}$$

and other possible constraints are appended. To start the iteration, all $|E_j|$ can be first evaluated at an initial estimate of $\mathbf{h}$ and the largest taken as the initial estimate of h_{n+1}.

The modification given by (17.3.3) works well if the number of active constraints is equal to $n + 1$ (regular problem) but may result in slow convergence if it is different [1]. An explanation of this property will be given by the following reasoning without mathematical details.

At some point in the computations, the routine for constrained minimization must solve the simplified quadratic problem as discussed in Section 15.7. The matrix of second derivatives is simulated by means of some updating formula which relies on the gradients of the minimized function and on the gradients of the constraints. If the problem is defined by (17.3.3), the size of the vector $\mathbf{h}$ has been increased to $n + 1$, but the problem does not have second derivatives with respect to h_{n+1}. Nevertheless, the updating formula will attempt to modify the matrix simulating second-order derivatives even for this variable and force the matrix to be positive definite. To prevent this from happening, it is advantageous to update the submatrix corresponding to n variables only and keep the entries in the $(n + 1)$st row and column equal to zero at all steps of the algorithm.

The modification discussed above was incorporated into the routine provided in [2] and results on a singular problem, taken from [1], are given.

EXAMPLE 17.3.1. Apply the algorithm (17.3.3) to

$$f(\mathbf{x}) = 0.505\,(x_1^2 + x_2^2) - 0.99\,x_1 x_2$$

using the starting point $\mathbf{x} = [2 \quad 4]^t$. The solution should be $\mathbf{x}^* = [0 \quad 0]^t$.

The vector $\mathbf{x}$ was augmented by one variable whose initial value was selected arbitrarily, $\mathbf{x}_a = [2 \quad 4 \quad 0]^t$. With no modification, the problem needed 12 iterations and 14 function calls to reach the values

$$\mathbf{x}^* = [-0.15 \times 10^{-7} \quad -0.136 \times 10^{-7} \quad -0.197 \times 10^{-12}]^t.$$

The same problem, run with the indicated modification, took only 7 iterations and 8 function calls. Next, the initial value of the augmented variable is changed to $x_3 = 10^4$ and the minimization is run again. Without the modification, many iterations are needed. With the modification, the result is reached again in 7 iterations and 8 function calls.

Application of minimax design will be demonstrated on the ninth-order filter discussed in Sections 4.10 and 6.7. The network is shown in Fig. 4.10.2, its element values are in Table 17.3.1 and its amplitude response with ideal OPAMPs is shown in Fig. 17.3.1 by curve *a*. In order to get a more realistic design, we now assume that all the OPAMPs will be approximated by the linear macromodel shown in Fig. 17.3.2. Performing the analysis we discover that the response deteriorated considerably, as shown in Fig. 17.3.1 by curve *b*. It now violates the specification on 0.03 db ripple in the pass-band.

Minimax optimization was applied by allowing the resistors with subscripts 1, 2, 6, 7, 11, 12, 16, 17 to change. The result is shown in Fig. 17.3.3. The requirements on the pass-band ripple are now satisfied, even though the run was terminated before a "true" minimax was reached. The final resistor values are given in Table 17.3.1. The response in the stop band was checked as well and is shown in Fig. 17.3.4 (the last peak at about 14 kHz is not shown in order to have a better picture around the frequency 4 kHz). Finally, stability of the filter was checked by calculating the poles and zeros by means of the QZ algo-

Table 17.3.1. Initial and Optimized Resistor Values of the Network Shown in Fig. 4.10.2.

Resistor, Ω	Initial Value	Final Value
1	5478	5507.41
2	2008	2005.02
6	4440	4460.17
7	5999	6002.61
11	3220	3233.23
12	5883	5879.67
16	3637	3652.10
17	1030	1016.02

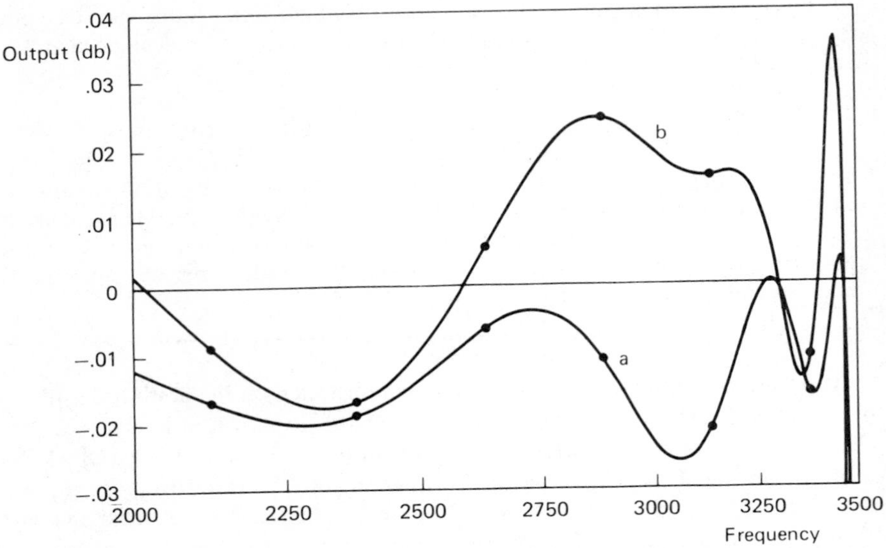

Fig. 17.3.1. Response of the filter in Fig. 4.10.2: (a) ideal OPAMPs; (b) deterioration of the response when the 741C linear macromodel is used.

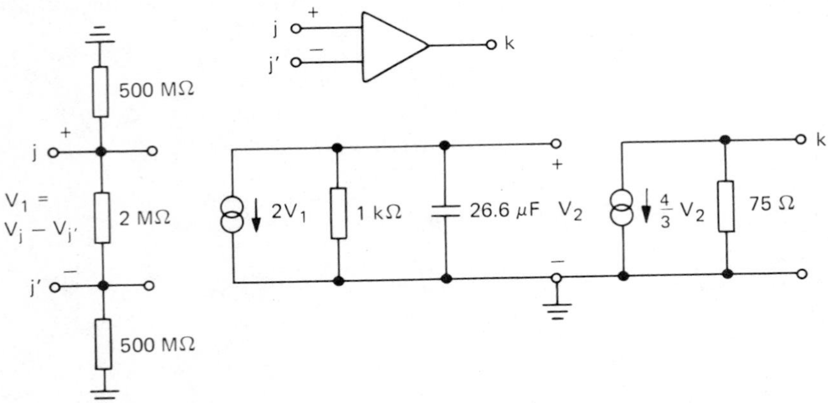

Fig. 17.3.2. Linear model of the 741C operational amplifier.

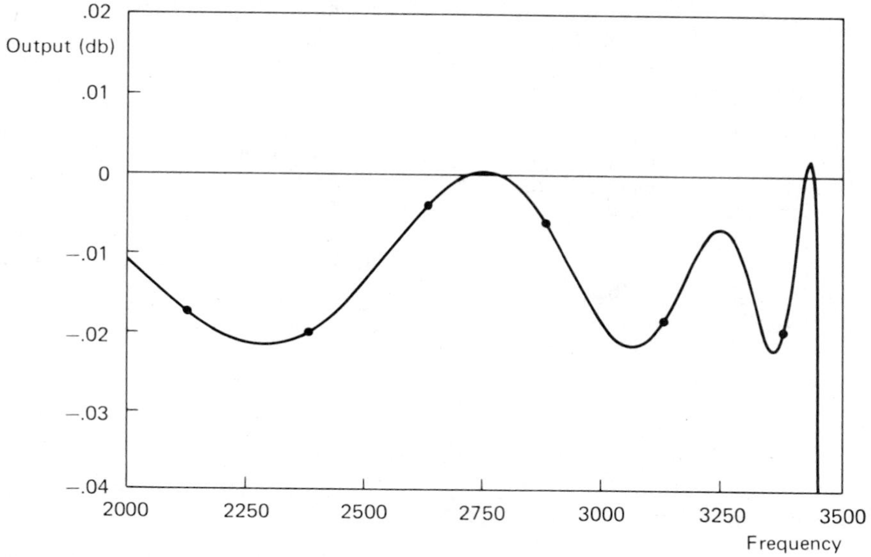

Fig. 17.3.3. Optimized pass-band response of the network in Fig. 4.10.2 with 741C linear macromodels.

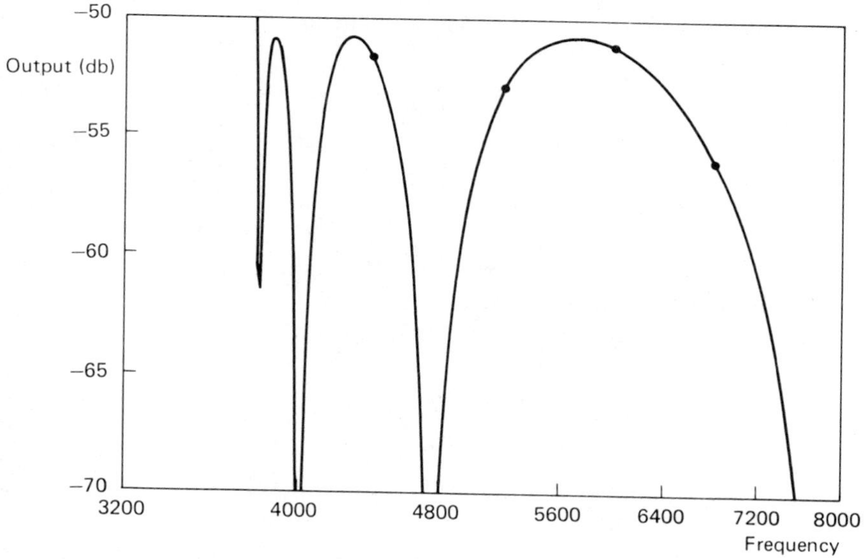

Fig. 17.3.4. Stop-band response of the network in Fig. 4.10.2 with 741C linear macromodels.

Table 17.3.2. Poles and Zeros of the Final Design of the Network in Fig. 4.10.2.

Poles		Zeros	
$-3.66792D+06$	$\pm 3.66872D+06$	$-3.63973D+06$	$\pm 3.64101D+06$
$-3.67557D+06$	$\pm 3.67532D+06$	$-3.64856D+06$	$\pm 3.64886D+06$
$-3.69491D+06$	$\pm 3.69453D+06$	$-3.69297D+06$	$\pm 3.69283D+06$
$-3.68697D+06$	$\pm 3.68649D+06$	$-3.68280D+06$	$\pm 3.68251D+06$
$-1.34054D+04$	0	$+5.02170D+00$	$\pm 4.88463D+04$
$-9.80250D+03$	$\pm 1.31409D+04$	$+1.64143D+00$	$\pm 2.98348D+04$
$-4.65777D+03$	$\pm 1.93524D+04$	$-3.22064D-02$	$\pm 2.51773D+04$
$-4.57567D+02$	$\pm 2.20955D+04$	$+2.52081D-01$	$\pm 2.38342D+04$
$-1.81201D+03$	$\pm 2.14668D+04$	—	—

rithm. They are given in Table 17.3.2. Since all poles are in the left half plane, the optimized filter is stable and the design is concluded.

17.4. MINIMIZATION OF SENSITIVITIES

In this section we will demonstrate the minimization of sensitivities on active networks with ideal elements and ideal operational amplifiers. The purpose of the section is to outline yet another application of constrained minimization. A full description of this technique is available in [3].

Assume that the network topology is given and some initial estimate of the element values selected. The resulting transfer function is

$$T(s) = \frac{\sum_{i=0}^{n_n} a_i s^i}{\sum_{i=0}^{n_d} b_i s^i} \tag{17.4.1}$$

where a_i, b_i are functions of all elements. This form can be obtained by the algorithm described in Chapters 7 and 8.

The initial estimate will not meet the specification which is given by

$$T^*(s) = \frac{\sum_{i=0}^{n_n} a_i^* s^i}{\sum_{i=0}^{n_d} b_i^* s^i}. \tag{17.4.2}$$

Here a_i^*, b_i^* are specified numbers. It is also tacitly assumed that the network is capable of meeting these specifications. The design will satisfy the requirement if

$$a_i - a_i^* = 0$$
$$b_i - b_i^* = 0. \tag{17.4.3}$$

Conditions (17.4.3) can be taken as equality constraints of the problem. In addition, inequality constraints on lower and upper bounds:

$$h_i - l_i \geqslant 0$$
$$u_i - h_i \geqslant 0 \tag{17.4.4}$$

have to be incorporated to prevent a wide spread of element values.

The objective function will be composed of normalized sensitivities, which can be accounted for in several ways. We can consider sensitivities of the transfer function, but then we will have to run evaluations over many frequencies. Equivalently, we can use the poles, p, and zeros, z, or the Q and ω_0 of the poles and zeros. The following description takes the pole and zero sensitivities into consideration. To simplify the notation, let us assume that we consider only second-order building blocks. Thus only one complex pole and one complex zero need to be taken and the objective function is defined as

$$F(\mathbf{h}) = \tfrac{1}{2}\, w_p \sum_{i=1}^{\text{elements}} \left|S_{h_i}^{\text{pole}}\right| + \tfrac{1}{2}\, w_z \sum_{i=1}^{\text{elements}} \left|S_{h_i}^{\text{zero}}\right|. \tag{17.4.5}$$

It is understood that $\mathcal{S}$ is substituted for S when the variable h_i represents $B = -1/A$ of the ideal OPAMP.

The algorithm described in Chapter 8 provides first- and second-order derivatives of the numerator N and denominator D. In the following discussion, only the denominator is considered since the formulae remain valid for the numerator and its zeros as well.

Both the pole p and the denominator D are functions of h_i, h_j and we can write

$$D[s(h_i, h_j), h_i, h_j]\big|_{s=p} = 0. \tag{17.4.6}$$

Differentiating with respect to h_i we get

$$\frac{\partial D}{\partial h_i} + \frac{\partial D}{\partial s}\frac{\partial s}{\partial h_i} = 0$$

from which

$$\frac{\partial p}{\partial h_i} = - \left. \frac{\partial D/\partial h_i}{\partial D/\partial s} \right|_{s=p} \tag{17.4.7}$$

This formula has already been derived in Chapter 6. Both D and $\partial D/\partial h$ are available from the algorithm of Chapter 8 and the derivative of D with respect to s is easily programed. Differentiating (17.4.6) with respect to h_j and keeping in mind that both D and s are function of h_i, h_j, we obtain the second derivative

$$\frac{\partial^2 p}{\partial h_i \partial h_j} = - \left. \frac{\dfrac{\partial^2 D}{\partial h_i \partial h_j} + \dfrac{\partial^2 D}{\partial s \partial h_i} \dfrac{\partial s}{\partial h_j} + \dfrac{\partial^2 D}{\partial s \partial h_j} \dfrac{\partial s}{\partial h_i} + \dfrac{\partial^2 D}{\partial s^2} \dfrac{\partial s}{\partial h_i} \dfrac{\partial s}{\partial h_j}}{\dfrac{\partial D}{\partial s}} \right|_{s=p} \tag{17.4.8}$$

All entries are either available from the algorithm or are easily calculated. Formulae (17.4.7) and (17.4.8) have to be further normalized but these details are omitted here; (17.4.7) is used in the objective function and (17.4.8) in the gradient.

The STAR network [4] shown in Fig. 17.4.1, will be considered as an example. Let the desired transfer function be

$$T(s) = K \frac{s^2 + 3.844628}{s^2 + 0.1\,s + 1} .$$

Using design equations published in [4] and selecting $G_1 = 25$, $G_3 = 75$ we obtain the "original network" given in Table 17.4.1. The "optimized network" is

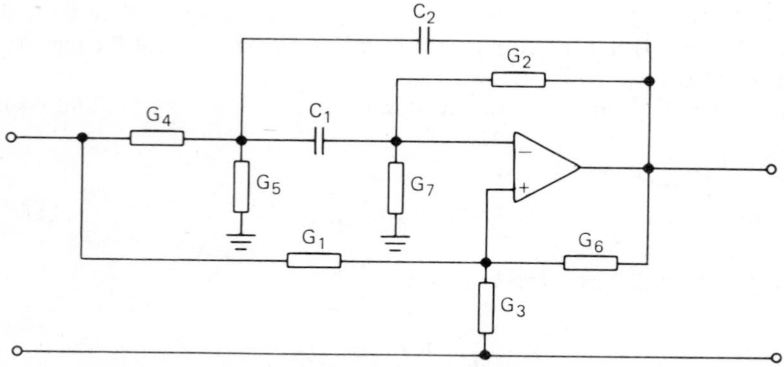

Fig. 17.4.1. STAR network.

Table 17.4.1. Element Values for the STAR Network.

	G_1	G_2	G_3	G_4	G_5	G_6	G_7	C_1	C_2
Original network	25.0	0.709	75.0	18.35	50.76	1	1.81	6.912	6.912
Optimized network	81.47	0.741	7.3	65	1.38	1	1.88	6.912	6.912

the result of minimization with $w_z = 2$ and $w_p = 1$. Considerable reduction in the variation of the zero was achieved.

To show that minimization indeed leads to networks having better overall properties than the original ones, a Monte Carlo simulation (to be considered in the next section) with 500 samples was performed. The resulting variations of the poles were about the same in both designs and are not shown. Variations of the zeros differ considerably. Fig. 17.4.2(a) shows the distribution of the

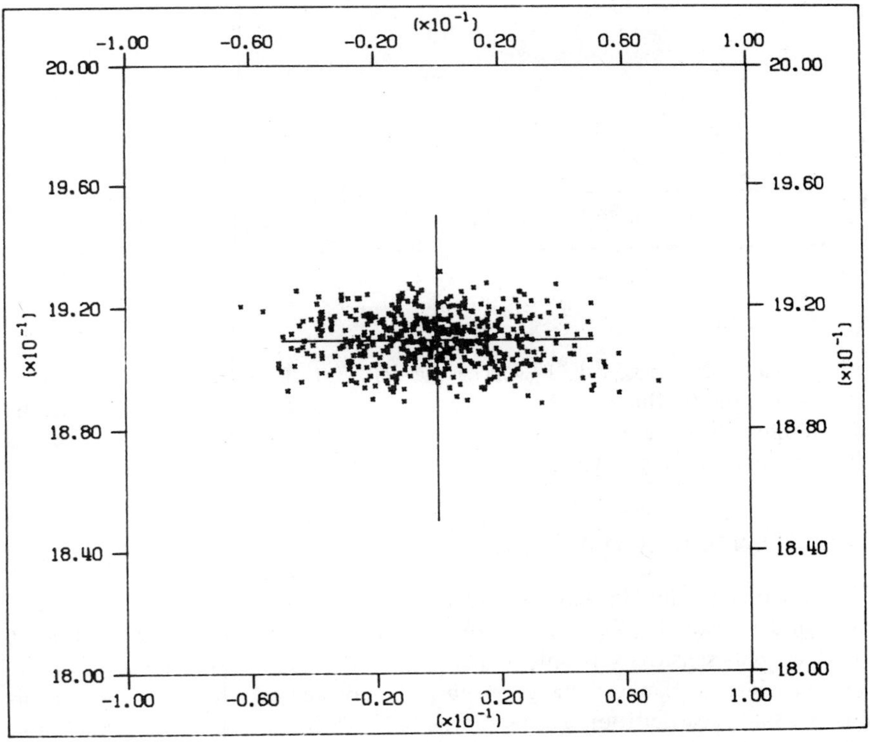

(a)

Fig. 17.4.2. Monte Carlo simulation of the STAR network with values given in Table 17.4.1.: (a) distribution of the zeros of the original network; (b) distribution of the zeros of the optimized network.

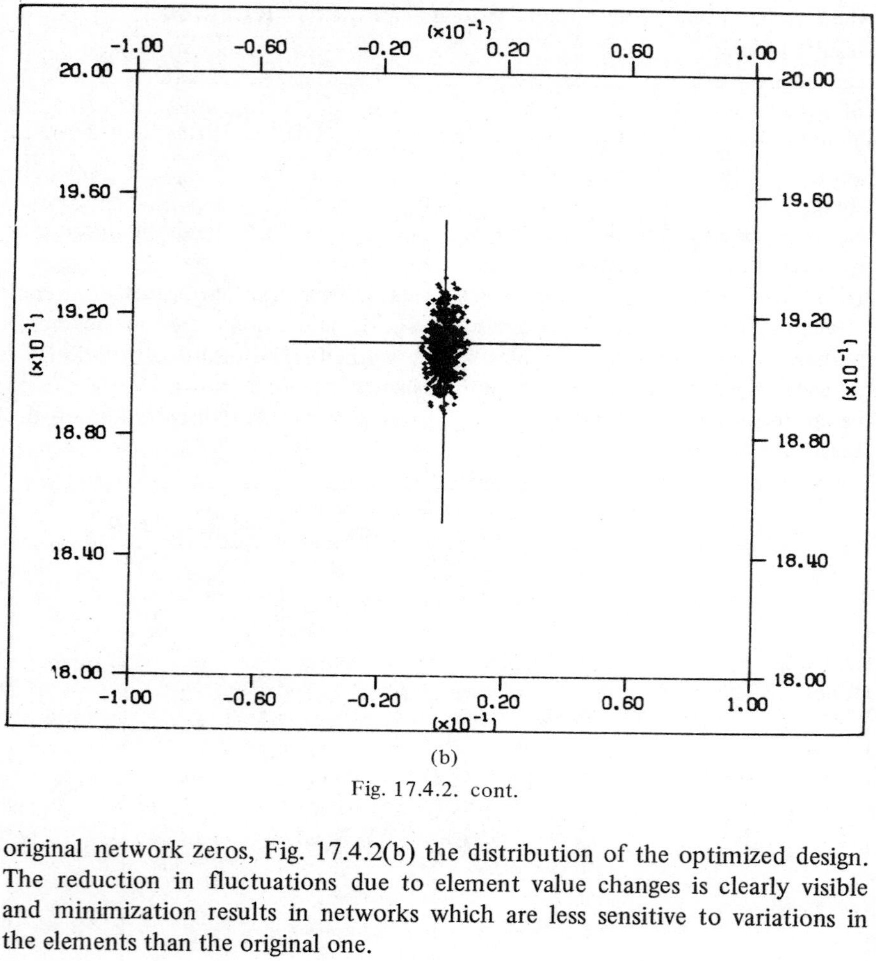

(b)

Fig. 17.4.2. cont.

original network zeros, Fig. 17.4.2(b) the distribution of the optimized design. The reduction in fluctuations due to element value changes is clearly visible and minimization results in networks which are less sensitive to variations in the elements than the original one.

17.5. MONTE CARLO ANALYSIS

The design steps thus far have provided us with a network that meets specifications and perhaps has been optimized such that it has low sensitivity. Recall, however, that sensitivity is only a first-order measure and may not be meaningful when large parameter changes need to be considered. A *Monte Carlo* analysis is usually carried out before the designs are put into volume production. Here one simulates the manufacturing and operating environment with factors like component tolerances, correlations, aging, temperature and humidity, etc. taken into account. A number of test circuits, typically 100 to 300, are "manufactured" on the computer, with the component values picked at random from their respective statistical distributions; the circuits are then analyzed and the results tabulated. If required, the influence of aging and environmental factors can also be simulated. A statistical analysis is then performed on the results of these computer experiments to determine the viability of the design under actual production and field conditions. Proper implementation of Monte Carlo code and the interpretation of the results requires knowledge of probability theory, the statistical disciplines of sampling and hypothesis testing, and statistical component modeling. Statistical circuit analysis and design is an area of current research interest, as can be seen from the many papers in recent issues of *IEEE Transactions on Circuits and Systems*, *IEEE Transactions on Computer Aided Design* and *IEE Proceedings* (*Part G*).

Space limitations prevent us from covering this area in depth; all we can do is provide an overview. Let us begin with some definitions. The function $f(x)$ is called the *probability density function* (pdf) if the probability of occurrence of a value $\tilde{x}$ such that $x \leqslant \tilde{x} < x + dx$ is $f(x)\,dx$. A related function is the *cumulative distribution function* (cdf) which is the integral of $f(x)$ from $-\infty$ to x,

$$F(x) = \int_{-\infty}^{x} f(x)\,dx = \text{prob}\,\{\tilde{x} < x\} \tag{17.5.1}$$

and gives the probability that the observed value will be below x. Probability functions have the following important properties:

1. $f(x) \geqslant 0$.
2. $F(\infty) = 1$. (17.5.2)
3. Prob $\{x_1 \leqslant \tilde{x} < x_2\} = F(x_2) - F(x_1)$.
4. The mean value μ, which is a measure of location, is given as follows:

$$\mu = \int_{-\infty}^{\infty} x f(x)\,dx \tag{17.5.3}$$

and the variance σ^2, which is a measure of spread about the mean, by

$$\sigma^2 = \int_{-\infty}^{\infty} (x - \mu)^2 f(x)\,dx. \tag{17.5.4}$$

The *normal* distribution plays an important role in all areas of statistical analysis and is defined as follows:

$$f(x) = \frac{1}{\sigma\sqrt{2\pi}} \exp\left[-\frac{1}{2}(x - \mu)^2/\sigma^2\right] \tag{17.5.5}$$

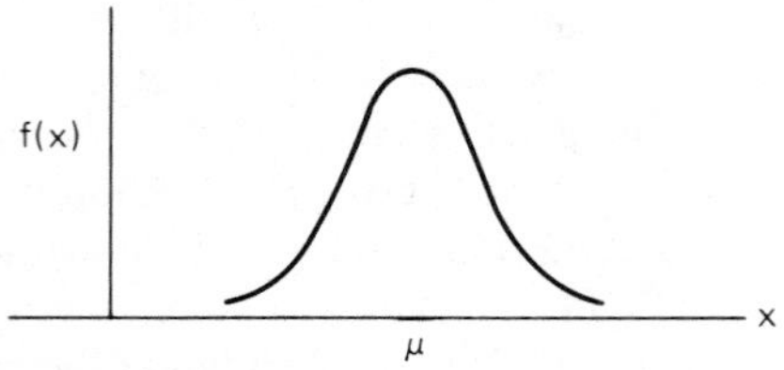

Fig. 17.5.1. A normal density with mean μ. Note that $F(\mu + i\sigma) - F(\mu - i\sigma)$ equals 0.683, 0.955, and 0.997 respectively for $i = 1, 2, 3$. Here σ is the standard deviation.

It has the form shown in Fig. 17.5.1. A *standard normal* distribution has zero mean and unit variance.

The manufacturing distributions of components, particularly in integrated circuits, have, in many cases, a form close to the normal. For discrete components manufacturers often *screen* the components and sell those that are closer to the mean values at higher prices. To better model the distribution of discrete components, the uniform, bimodal, and split triangular distributions shown in Fig. 17.5.2 are generally used.

When considering two or more components, the coupling between the component values also becomes important. The *correlation coefficient* relates a pair of random values. In the simplest case, generally valid in discrete realizations, the components are taken as *independently* distributed and have zero correlation. This assumption is not valid for semiconductor device model parameter values and for integrated circuit realizations. This is especially true for components manufactured on the same semiconductor wafer. Here a *multivariate normal* distribution is used to define the component densities.

Monte Carlo analysis requires that we pick the components from their densities. Subroutines to generate samples from standard normal and uniform distributions are available on most computer systems.

The uniform distribution can be used to generate values from most other distributions by using the ***inverse probability integral transformation***, which states that if r_i is a random number from the uniform distribution defined over

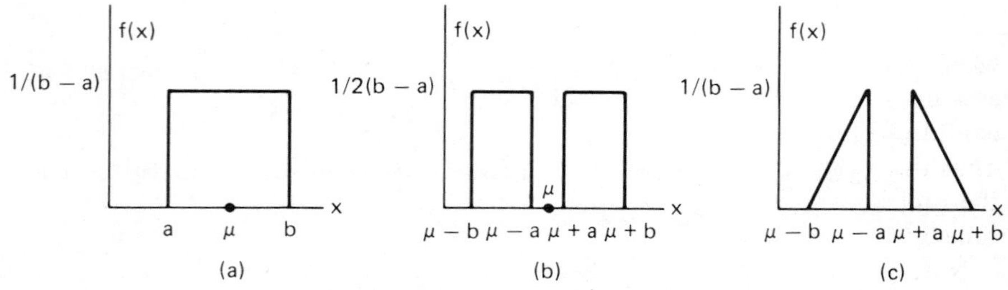

Fig. 17.5.2. Typical component tolerance distributions.

the range zero to one, and if x_i is such that

$$F(x_i) = r_i \tag{17.5.6}$$

then x_i will be a random number from a distribution with cdf $F(x)$. Equation (17.5.6) can be solved either analytically or graphically.

Once the desired number of circuits, say N, have been simulated, the resulting outputs, say $y_1, y_2, \ldots, y_N$, are analyzed statistically and presented to the user, typically in the form of histograms, mean values, standard errors, and confidence intervals.

A *histogram* resembles a pdf, though the area under it need not be unity. It provides an empirical estimate of the distribution function of the random variable. In order to construct a histogram, the range of y is divided into a set of discrete intervals, usually equal in width. We then determine the frequency of occurrence of the random variable within each interval and plot this information as a bar chart.

The sample mean value $\bar{y}$ and standard error s are computed as follows:

$$\bar{y} = \frac{1}{N} \sum_{i=1}^{N} y_i \tag{17.5.7}$$

and

$$s^2 = \frac{1}{N-1} \sum_{i=1}^{N} (y_i - \bar{y})^2 = \frac{1}{N-1} \left(\sum_{i=1}^{N} y_i^2 - N\bar{y} \right). \tag{17.5.8}$$

They are used to estimate the mean and variance, respectively, of the random variable. The distribution mean value μ_y is not equal to $\bar{y}$ because $\bar{y}$ is obtained by random sampling. The error between μ_y and $\bar{y}$ is also a random variable and, for N sufficiently large, a *confidence interval* of the following form can be constructed for it:

$$\text{Prob}\,\{|\mu_y - \bar{y}| \leqslant sU_{\alpha/2}/\sqrt{N}\} = 1 - \alpha \tag{17.5.9}$$

where $1 - \alpha$ is called the *confidence level* and the ordinate $U_{\alpha/2}$ is such that the area under the standard normal curve from $U_{\alpha/2}$ to ∞ is $\alpha/2$. Typically a 95% confidence level with corresponding $U_{\alpha/2} = 1.96$ is used in engineering practice. Thus the result of the experiment can be stated in words for this case as follows: the probability is 95% that the sample and actual mean values differ in magnitude by no more than $1.96\, s/\sqrt{N}$.

Note that the "error" decreases as $1/\sqrt{N}$ and we need four times as many samples to reduce the error by half. Many ingenious sampling techniques have been devised to reduce the number of samples required to obtain a sufficiently short confidence interval [5].

Most recent circuit analysis computer codes have Monte Carlo capability.

REFERENCES

1. R. K. Brayton, S. W. Director, G. D. Hachtel, and L. M. Vidigal: A new algorithm for statistical circuit design based on quasi-Newton methods and function splitting. *IEEE Transactions on Circuits and Systems*, Vol. CAS-26, pp. 784–794, September 1979.
2. Subroutine VF02AD, Computer Science and Systems Division, AERE, Harwell, Oxfordshire, OX11 0RA, England.
3. J. Vlach and K. Singhal: Sensitivity minimization of networks with operational amplifiers and parasitics. *IEEE Transactions on Circuits and Systems*, Vol. CAS-27, pp. 688–697, August 1980.
4. J. J. Friend, C. A. Harris, and D. Hilberman: STAR: An active biquadratic filter section. *IEEE Transactions on Circuits and Systems*, Vol. CAS-22, pp. 115–121, February 1975.
5. J. M. Hammersley and D. C. Handscomb: *Monte Carlo Methods.* Chapman and Hall, London, 1964.

APPENDIX A
Laplace Transforms

The Laplace transform of a signal that starts at $t = 0$ is defined by

$$V(s) = \int_{0-}^{\infty} v(t)\, e^{-st}\, dt \quad \text{or, symbolically,} \quad V(s) = \mathcal{L}[v(t)]. \tag{A.1}$$

The lower bound is understood to be $(0-)$ if $v(t)$ is discontinuous at $t = 0$ or if a Dirac impulse appears at $t = 0$. The inverse Laplace transform is given by

$$v(t) = \frac{1}{2\pi j} \int_{c-j\infty}^{c+j\infty} V(s)\, e^{st}\, ds \quad \text{or, symbolically,} \quad v(t) = \mathcal{L}^{-1}[V(s)]. \tag{A.2}$$

Let us review some of the basic properties of the Laplace transform.

1. Let $v_i(t)$ have the transform $V_i(s)$; then, applying (A.1), we have

$$\mathcal{L}[v_1(t) + v_2(t)] = \int_{0-}^{\infty} [v_1(t) + v_2(t)]\, e^{-st}\, dt = V_1(s) + V_2(s). \tag{A.3}$$

2. To determine $\mathcal{L}[v(kt)]$, write

$$\mathcal{L}[v(kt)] = \int_{0-}^{\infty} v(kt)\, e^{-st}\, dt.$$

Apply the transformation

$$kt = \tau; \qquad dt = d\tau/k.$$

Then

$$\mathcal{L}[v(kt)] = \frac{1}{k}\int_{0-}^{\infty} v(\tau)\, e^{-(s/k)\tau}\, d\tau = \frac{1}{k} V\left(\frac{s}{k}\right). \tag{A.4}$$

3. The formula for the transform of $v(t)$ delayed by an amount T is obtained by considering

$$\mathcal{L}[v(t-T)] = \int_{0}^{\infty} v(t-T)\, e^{-st}\, dt.$$

Changing the variable to $t - T = \tau$, we have

$$\mathcal{L}[v(t-T)] = \int_{-T}^{\infty} v(\tau)\, e^{-s(\tau+T)}\, d\tau.$$

By assumption, $v(t)$ starts at $t = 0$. The lower bound can therefore be changed to 0. The final formula is

$$\mathcal{L}[v(t-T)] = e^{-sT} V(s). \tag{A.5}$$

4. In a similar way one can derive

$$\mathcal{L}[e^{-qt}v(t)] = \int_{0-}^{\infty} e^{-qt}v(t)\, e^{-st}\, dt = \int_{0-}^{\infty} v(t)\, e^{-(s+q)t}\, dt = V(s+q). \tag{A.6}$$

5. Differentiation of the time function is reflected in the Laplace domain by

$$\mathcal{L}[v'(t)] = \int_{0-}^{\infty} v'(t)\, e^{-st}\, dt = v(t)\, e^{-st}\Big|_{0-}^{\infty} + s\int_{0-}^{\infty} v(t)\, e^{-st}\, dt = -v(0-) + sV(s). \tag{A.7}$$

6. If the function is differentiated several times, which we denote as $v^{(n)}(t) = d^n v(t)/dt^n$, it can be shown that

$$\mathcal{L}[v^{(n)}(t)] = s^n V(s) - \sum_{k=1}^{n} v^{(k-1)}(0-)\, s^{n-k}. \tag{A.8}$$

7. Integration of the time function is reflected in the Laplace domain by

$$\mathcal{L}\left[\int_{0-}^{t} v(x)\,dx\right] = \int_{0-}^{\infty}\left[\int_{0-}^{t} v(x)\,dx\right] e^{-st}\,dt$$

$$= \left[\frac{e^{-st}}{-s}\int_{0-}^{t} v(x)\,dx\right]\Bigg|_{0-}^{\infty} + \frac{1}{s}\int_{0-}^{\infty} v(t)\,e^{-st}\,dt.$$

Denote

$$\int_{0-}^{t} v(x)\,dx = v^{(-1)}(0-).$$

Then we have

$$\mathcal{L}\left[\int_{0-}^{t} v(x)\,dx\right] = \frac{1}{s}V(s) + \frac{1}{s}v^{(-1)}(0-). \tag{A.9}$$

8. Convolution of two time functions $v_1(t)$ and $v_2(t)$ is defined by the integrals

$$\int_{0-}^{t} v_1(t-\tau)\,v_2(\tau)\,d\tau \quad \text{or} \quad \int_{0-}^{t} v_2(t-\tau)\,v_1(\tau)\,d\tau.$$

For the first integral we have

$$\mathcal{L}\left[\int_{0-}^{t} v_1(t-\tau)\,v_2(\tau)\,d\tau\right] = \int_{0-}^{\infty}\left[\int_{0-}^{t} v_1(t-\tau)\,v_2(\tau)\,d\tau\right] e^{-st}\,dt.$$

Introduce a new variable $t - \tau = z$, $dt = dz$; then we have

$$\int_{-\tau}^{\infty}\left[\int_{0-}^{\infty} v_1(z)\,v_2(\tau)\,d\tau\right] e^{-(z+\tau)s}\,dz = \int_{0-}^{\infty} v_2(\tau)\,e^{-s\tau}\,d\tau \int_{-\tau}^{\infty} v_1(z)\,e^{-zs}\,dz.$$

Since $v_1(z)$ starts at $z = 0$, the lower limit may be changed and

$$\mathcal{L}\left[\int_{0-}^{t} v_1(t-\tau)\,v_2(\tau)\,d\tau\right] = \int_{0-}^{\infty} v_2(\tau)\,e^{-s\tau}\,d\tau \cdot \int_{0-}^{\infty} v_1(z)\,e^{-sz}\,dz = V_1(s)\,V_2(s). \tag{A.10}$$

The same result holds for the other form of the convolution integral given above.

9. Initial and final value theorems are derived using (A.7):

$$\int_{0-}^{\infty} v'(t)\, e^{-st}\, dt = sV(s) - v(0-).$$

Take the limit as $s \to 0$:

$$\lim_{s \to 0} \int_{0-}^{\infty} v'(t)\, e^{-st}\, dt = \lim_{s \to 0} [sV(s) - v(0-)].$$

On the left side, the integral changes to

$$\lim_{t \to \infty} [v(t) - v(0-)] = \lim_{s \to 0} [sV(s) - v(0-)].$$

Canceling $v(0-)$ on both sides results in the *final value theorem:*

$$\lim_{t \to \infty} v(t) = \lim_{s \to 0} sV(s). \tag{A.11}$$

Similarly, starting with (A.7) again, and setting the limit as $s \to \infty$, we have

$$\lim_{s \to \infty} \int_{0-}^{\infty} v'(t)\, e^{-st}\, dt = \lim_{s \to \infty} [sV(s) - v(0-)].$$

The integral becomes zero:

$$0 = \lim_{s \to \infty} [sV(s) - v(0-)]$$

and the *initial value theorem* is obtained:

$$\lim_{t \to 0-} v(t) = \lim_{s \to \infty} sV(s). \tag{A.12}$$

The above formulae are collected in Table A.1.

The inverse Laplace transform is usually found by means of *residue calculus.* If the function $V(s)$ is a rational function, it is first converted to simpler terms by means of partial fractions, described in Appendix B.

For a *simple pole*, the integration is based on the Cauchy integral formula:

$$\int_C \frac{f(s)}{s - p_0} = 2\pi j f(p_0). \tag{A.13}$$

The path C is closed counterclockwise around the pole p_0. The value $f(p_0)$ is called the *residue at the simple* pole p_0.

Table A.1. Operations with the Laplace Transform.

$v(t)$	$V(s)$
$av(t)$	$aV(s)$
$\frac{d}{dt} v(t)$	$sV(s) - v(0-)$
$\frac{d^n}{dt^n} v(t)$	$s^n V(s) - \sum_{i=1}^{n} s^{n-i} \frac{d^{(i-1)}}{dt^{i-1}} v(0-)$
$\int_{0-}^{t} v(z)\, dz$	$\frac{V(s)}{s} + \frac{v^{(-1)}(0-)}{s}$
	where $v^{(-1)}(0-) = \lim_{t \to 0-} \int_{-\infty}^{t} v(z)\, dz$
$v(t/a)$	$aV(as)$
$\int_{0-}^{t} v_1(t-z)\, v_2(z)\, dz$	$V_1(s)\, V_2(s)$
$v_1(t)\, v_2(t)$	$\frac{1}{2\pi j} \int_{c-j\infty}^{c+j\infty} V_1(u)\, V_2(s-u)\, du$
$\lim_{t \to 0-} v(t)$	$\lim_{s \to \infty} sV(s)$
$\lim_{t \to \infty} v(t)$	$\lim_{s \to 0} sV(s)$

If a function $F(s)$ is decomposed in many terms of the type (A.13), then

$$\int_C F(s)\, ds = 2\pi j \times (\text{sum of residues in the enclosed path}). \qquad \text{(A.14)}$$

Formulae (A.13) and (A.14) can be applied to the inversion of the Laplace integral (A.2) in which the path goes from $c - j\infty$ to $c + j\infty$ and c is chosen such that p_0 is to the left of the integration path. Close the path counterclockwise around p_0 by means of an infinitely large arc. Should the contribution to the integral along the arc be zero, the residue formula will give the correct result since the contribution to the integral will be along the straight path only. Conditions under which this method can be applied are found in books on Laplace transforms and are briefly discussed in Appendix C. Here it is sufficient to state that just about all practically encountered functions satisfy the requirement. The only commonly encountered function of s which would present problems is $V(s) = k$, the time response for which is the Dirac impulse $k\delta(t)$.

To invert, for instance,

$$V(s) = \frac{2s + 3}{(s + 1)(s + 2)} = \frac{1}{s + 1} + \frac{1}{s + 2}$$

we need

$$v(t) = \frac{1}{2\pi j} \int_{c-j\infty}^{c+j\infty} \left[\frac{e^{st}}{s + 1} + \frac{e^{st}}{s + 2} \right] ds.$$

Applying (A.13) and (A.14), the residues are e^{-t} and e^{-2t}, respectively, and

$$v(t) = \frac{2\pi j}{2\pi j} \left[\sum \text{residues} \right] = e^{-t} + e^{-2t}.$$

For multiple poles, the Cauchy formula is different:

$$\int_C \frac{f(s)}{(s - p_0)^{n+1}} \, ds = 2\pi j \left[\frac{1}{n!} f^{(n)}(p_0) \right]. \tag{A.15}$$

Here $f^{(n)}(p_0)$ is the nth derivative of $f(s)$ with respect to s with p_0 substituted after the differentiation. The value

$$\frac{1}{n!} f^{(n)}(p_0)$$

is called the *residue of the pole* $s = p_0$ *of multiplicity* $(n + 1)$; for instance:

$$\frac{1}{2\pi j} \int_C \frac{K e^{st}}{(s - p_0)^{n+1}} \, ds = \frac{2\pi j}{2\pi j} \left(\frac{K}{n!} \frac{d^n}{ds^n} e^{st} \right) \bigg|_{s = p_0} = K \frac{t^n e^{p_0 t}}{n!}.$$

APPENDIX B
Partial Fraction Decomposition of Rational Functions

Let the function be defined by

$$V(s) = \frac{\sum_{i=0}^{N} a_i s^i}{(s - p_1)^{m_1}(s - p_2)^{m_2} \cdots (s - p_k)^{m_k}} = \frac{N_N(s)}{D_M(s)} \tag{B.1}$$

with $M = m_1 + m_2 + \cdots + m_k$ = degree of the denominator, and with $N < M$. We wish to decompose (B.1) into simpler functions.

If all $m_i = 1$, the poles are simple and we can write

$$V(s) = \sum_{i=1}^{M} \frac{K_i}{s - p_i}. \tag{B.2}$$

K_i are called the *residues* of $V(s)$ and are calculated as follows:

$$K_i = [(s - p_i)\, V(s)]\big|_{s=p_i}. \tag{B.3}$$

This can be derived by first multiplying (B.2) by $(s - p_i)$

$$(s - p_i)\, V(s) = \frac{K_1(s - p_i)}{(s - p_1)} + \cdots + \frac{K_{i-1}(s - p_i)}{s - p_{i-1}} + K_i + \frac{K_{i+1}(s - p_i)}{s - p_{i+1}} + \cdots.$$

If $s = p_i$ is now inserted, all terms having $(s - p_i)$ in the numerator become zero and (B.3) results. For instance,

$$V(s) = \frac{(s+2)(s+4)}{(s+1)(s+3)(s+5)}$$

can be decomposed into partial fractions

$$V(s) = \frac{K_1}{s+1} + \frac{K_2}{s+3} + \frac{K_3}{s+5}$$

where, using (B.3),

$$K_1 = (s+1) \left. \frac{(s+2)(s+4)}{(s+1)(s+3)(s+5)} \right|_{s=-1} = \frac{1 \times 3}{2 \times 4} = \frac{3}{8}$$

$$K_2 = (s+3) \left. \frac{(s+2)(s+4)}{(s+1)(s+3)(s+5)} \right|_{s=-3} = \frac{(-1)\,1}{(-2)\,2} = \frac{1}{4}$$

$$K_3 = (s+5) \left. \frac{(s+2)(s+4)}{(s+1)(s+3)(s+5)} \right|_{s=-5} = \frac{(-3)(-1)}{(-4)(-2)} = \frac{3}{8}.$$

When some of the poles are multiple, another formula must be derived. This will be done using an example:

$$V(s) = \frac{N_N(s)}{D_M(s)} = \frac{N_N(s)}{(s-p_1)^3 (s-p_2)(s-p_3)}; \qquad N < M.$$

Assume that the decomposition has the following form:

$$V(s) = \frac{K_{31}}{(s-p_1)^3} + \frac{K_{21}}{(s-p_1)^2} + \frac{K_{11}}{(s-p_1)} + \frac{K_2}{(s-p_2)} + \frac{K_3}{(s-p_3)}.$$

It is advantageous to introduce two subscripts whenever $V(s)$ has multiple poles. Let the first subscript indicate the power of the term in the denominator and let the second subscript indicate the current index of the pole.

In order to determine K_{31}, multiply by $(s-p_1)^3$:

$$(s-p_1)^3\, V(s) = K_{31} + K_{21}(s-p_1) + K_{11}(s-p_1)^2 + \frac{K_2(s-p_1)^3}{s-p_2} + \frac{K_3(s-p_1)^3}{s-p_3}.$$

Inserting $s = p_1$ results in K_{31}. To obtain K_{21} differentiate first with respect to s:

$$\frac{d}{ds}\left[(s-p_1)^3\, V(s)\right] = K_{21} + 2K_{11}(s-p_1) + \left[\begin{matrix}\text{all remaining terms have} \\ (s-p_1) \text{ in the numerator}\end{matrix}\right].$$

Inserting $s = p_1$ again results in K_{21}. Another differentiation results in

$$\frac{d^2}{ds^2}[(s - p_1)^3 V(s)] = 2K_{11} + \begin{bmatrix}\text{all remaining terms have} \\ (s - p_1) \text{ in the numerator}\end{bmatrix}.$$

Inserting $s = p_1$, obtain

$$K_{11} = \frac{1}{2}\frac{d^2}{ds^2}[(s - p_1)^3 V(s)]\bigg|_{s=p_1}.$$

In general, we have

$$K_{ij} = \frac{1}{(m_j - i)!}\frac{d^{m_j - i}}{ds^{m_j - i}}[(s - p_j)^{m_j} V(s)]\bigg|_{s=p_j}, \qquad i = 1, 2, \ldots, m_j \tag{B.4}$$

and

$$V(s) = \sum_{j=1}^{k}\sum_{i=1}^{m_j}\frac{K_{ij}}{(s - p_j)^i}, \qquad k = \text{number of different poles.} \tag{B.5}$$

As an example, consider

$$V(s) = \frac{1}{(s - 1)^2 s^3}.$$

Choose the first pole to be $p_1 = 1$, the second one $p_2 = 0$. Then we have

$$p_1 = 1, \qquad j = 1, \qquad m_1 = 2$$
$$p_2 = 0, \qquad j = 2, \qquad m_2 = 3$$

and also

$$(s - 1)^2 V(s) = s^{-3}$$
$$s^3 V(s) = (s - 1)^{-2}.$$

Using (B.4) we get

$$K_{21} = \frac{1}{(2 - 2)!}[(s - 1)^2 V(s)] = s^{-3}\big|_{s=1} = 1$$

$$K_{11} = \frac{1}{(2 - 1)!}\frac{d}{ds}(s^{-3}) = -3s^{-4}\big|_{s=1} = -3$$

$$K_{32} = \frac{1}{(3-3)!}[s^3 V(s)] = (s-1)^{-2}\big|_{s=0} = 1$$

$$K_{22} = \frac{1}{(3-2)!}\frac{d}{ds}[(s-1)^{-2}] = -2(s-1)^{-3}\big|_{s=0} = 2$$

$$K_{12} = \frac{1}{(3-1)!}\frac{d^2}{ds^2}[(s-1)^{-2}] = \frac{1}{2}[6(s-1)^{-4}] = 3$$

and the decomposition (B.5) is

$$V(s) = \frac{1}{(s-1)^2} + \frac{-3}{s-1} + \frac{1}{s^3} + \frac{2}{s^2} + \frac{3}{s}\,.$$

Application of the Laplace transform to the decomposed rational function is straightforward. For simple poles use (A.13). The decomposition (B.2) is transformed into

$$v(t) = \sum_{i=1}^{M} K_i e^{p_i t}. \tag{B.6}$$

Table B.1. Laplace Transform Pairs of Some Functions.

$V(s)$	$v(t)$	Remark
1	$\delta(t)$	unit impulse
$1/s$	$u(t)$	unit step
$1/s^n$	$\dfrac{t^{n-1}}{(n-1)!}$	$0! = 1$ $n = 1, 2, \ldots$
$1/(s+a)$	e^{-at}	
$1/(s+a)^n$	$\dfrac{t^{n-1}e^{-at}}{(n-1)!}$	$n = 1, 2, \ldots$
$\omega/(s^2+\omega^2)$	$\sin \omega t$	
$s/(s^2+\omega^2)$	$\cos \omega t$	
$\dfrac{s+a}{(s+a)^2+\omega^2}$	$e^{-at}\cos \omega t$	
$\dfrac{\omega}{(s+a)^2+\omega^2}$	$e^{-at}\sin \omega t$	

If some poles are multiple, first apply (B.4) and obtain the decomposition (B.5). Use (A.15) to get the Laplace transform inverse in the form

$$v(t) = \sum_{j=1}^{k} \sum_{i=1}^{m_j} K_{ij} \frac{t^{i-1}}{(i-1)!} e^{p_j t}. \tag{B.7}$$

Pairs of Laplace transforms are available in numerous tables. Some of the more common pairs are collected in Table B.1.

APPENDIX C
Special Complex Integration of a Rational Function

The problem discussed in this appendix is needed in Chapter 10 for the numerical inversion of the Laplace transform. It involves the solution of

$$I \equiv \int_{c-j\infty}^{c+j\infty} V(s)\, ds \tag{C.1}$$

with

$$V(s) = \frac{\sum_{i=0}^{N} a_i s^i}{\sum_{i=0}^{M} b_i s^i}. \tag{C.2}$$

We wish to establish the condition under which the integral can be found by means of residue calculus as follows:

$$I = 2\pi j \times \text{(sum of the residues)}. \tag{C.3}$$

To apply formula (C.3) we close the path by a semicircle in the left half plane and let the radius grow without bound. If the contribution to the integral along this infinite semicircle is zero, then the whole integral will be given by the integration along the path indicated in (C.1) and the sum of residues will be the solution.

For the contribution I_1 along the semicircle introduce a new variable

$$s = Re^{j\phi}.$$

On the semicircle going from $+jR$ to $-jR$ in the left half plane R is constant, so that

$$ds = jRe^{j\phi}\, d\phi$$

and

$$I_1 = \int_{+\pi/2}^{-\pi/2} V(Re^{j\phi})\, jRe^{j\phi}\, d\phi.$$

For very large R, the terms with the highest powers dominate and we can simplify:

$$I_1 = \lim_{R\to\infty} \int_{+\pi/2}^{-\pi/2} \frac{a_N R^N e^{j\phi N}}{b_M R^M e^{j\phi M}}\, jRe^{j\phi}\, d\phi$$

$$= \lim_{R\to\infty} \frac{a_N}{b_M} \frac{j}{R^{M-N-1}} \int_{+\pi/2}^{-\pi/2} \exp\{j\phi(N+1-M)\}\, d\phi.$$

The last integral on the right is finite. In order to make the whole expression equal to zero, we must select M, N such that at least the first power of R remains in the denominator. This requires

$$M - N - 1 \geqslant 1$$

or

$$M \geqslant N + 2$$

and we can formulate a lemma:

> The integral of a rational function $V(s)$ along an infinite semicircle is zero whenever $V(s)$ has at least two more poles than zeros.

When integrating a rational function with $M \geqslant N + 2$ along the straight line parallel to the imaginary axis, the integral is equal to $2\pi j \times$ (sum of residues at poles to the left of the line) if the path is closed counterclockwise in the left half plane. If we close the integration path clockwise in the right half plane, the sum of the residues at poles appearing to the right of the line is taken but is multiplied by $-2\pi j$.

APPENDIX D
Program for Network Analysis

The program given in this appendix applies many of the theoretical and numerical methods discussed in the text. It is restricted to the analysis of linear analog and digital networks and is intended mainly for instructional purposes.

Three methods of formulating the network equations are used. One is the modified nodal formulation as described in Section 4.4. It is denoted in the program as MNT1. The second one, MNT2, is the two-graph modified nodal formulation, based on the theory developed in Section 4.8. These two formulations are for analog networks. Both have their merits. The first is straightforward, but the size of the matrix is large when there are many ideal elements; the second one leads to a much more compact set of equations. The third formulation is for digital network analysis. The matrices **G** and **C** (see Section 4.4) are printed whenever the matrix size is at most 10×10. The student can easily check his understanding of the formulations from the printout he obtains. The dimension of matrices that can be printed was restricted to avoid format problems. For various kinds of analyses, the system matrix **T** is given by $\mathbf{T} = \mathbf{G} + s\mathbf{C}$ for analog networks and by $\mathbf{T} = \mathbf{G} + z^{-1}\mathbf{C}$ for digital networks.

In published form, the program has the following restrictions:

1. Total number of elements $\leqslant 40$.
2. Total number of sources $\leqslant 10$.
3. Total number of outputs $\leqslant 10$.
4. Total size of the system matrix $\leqslant 25$.
5. At most 5 symbolic elements are allowed.
6. A maximum of 10 models may be defined for bipolar transistors, field effect transistors, and operational amplifiers.
7. Mixed analog/digital networks are not permitted.

The program includes extensive input error diagnostics. The formulation is table driven and easy to modify and extend. The solution of the system equations is performed by a "primitive" sparse solver which saves on operations but not on storage. Partial pivoting is performed to ensure numerical stability.

D.1. TYPES OF ANALYSIS

The program provides the following types of analysis: frequency domain with sensitivity calculations, time domain (analog networks only), symbolic analysis, and sensitivity analysis of poles, zeros, and their Q and ω.

A. Frequency Domain Analysis

For this analysis, $s = j\omega$ or $z^{-1} = e^{-j\omega}$ is substituted and the matrix equation $\mathbf{TX} = \mathbf{W}$ is solved by triangular decomposition followed by forward and back substitution. The output is calculated from the solution vector $\mathbf{X}$. Since this is a complex vector, the output can be either in the form of a complex number or as the amplitude in db and phase in degrees.

Sensitivities with respect to any element, including the inverted gain $B = -1/A$, $A \to \infty$, of the ideal operational amplifier is calculated by the steps covered in Chapter 6. This requires knowledge of the positions of the element values in the matrix $\mathbf{T}$, and such information is available from the formulation step. The transpose system is solved using the decomposition of $\mathbf{T}$. If the frequency response is desired in terms of real and imaginary parts, the sensitivities are also given in terms of real and imaginary parts. If the response is given in decibels differential sensitivity is found from Eqn. (6.5.7).

The program provides only linear frequency increments between the starting and final frequencies. The reader may wish to incorporate logarithmic frequency increments. Since the program is intended for instructional purposes, the frequency variable may be given either in Hz or in radians per second. The second option is somewhat more advantageous for school problems.

B. Poles, Zeros, Q and ω and Their Sensitivities

The network poles and zeros may be computed by two methods. With METHOD = 1 the program uses the polynomial interpolation technique followed by a call to a root-finding routine. METHOD = 2 uses the QZ algorithm. Codes for the root finding routine and QZ algorithm are not given; we have used standard IMSL routines available at Waterloo and the user may have to substitute other routines available on his system. In case of digital networks the variable z^{-1} is used in defining the polynomials and roots are also found in the z^{-1} domain. The Q and ω values are computed from the roots followed by the differential sensitivities of the roots, Q, and ω.

C. Symbolic Analysis

The theory explained in Chapters 7 and 8 is used for symbolic analysis. The program can provide the symbolic function either in terms of *variations* from nominal values (discussed in Chapter 8) or in terms of the element values themselves.

If there are no variable elements, the numerator and denominator polynomials are printed, followed by the root locations. If m variable elements are involved, 2^m polynomials are generated for the numerator and denominator. The polynomials correspond to coefficients associated with *element variations* (see Section 8.5) when IVAR = 1 and with the *elements* when IVAR $\neq$ 1.

The internal DIMENSION statements restrict the program to 5 symbolic variables and networks with numerator and denominator degrees $\leqslant 10$.

D. Time Domain Analysis

Programs for time domain analysis are usually based on numerical integration of differential equations. This is theoretically logical but a completely different set of routines is required for time domain than for frequency domain analysis. The numerical inversion of the Laplace transform, discussed in Chapter 10, can obtain time domain response for linear circuits by using frequency domain analysis routines. In order to keep the size of the program small, this method was used. The stepping algorithm of Section 10.4 is applied to two cases. If METHOD = 0, the Padé approximation with $M = 2$, $N = 0$ is taken. In this case only one triangular decomposition is needed and calculations are fast. However, a fairly small step size must be selected, since the method is equivalent to second-order integration. If METHOD = 1, the system matrix is decomposed repeatedly, 5 times for each step. This case is equivalent to order of integration 18, and fairly large steps can be taken. Initial conditions for the first step are taken from command cards IC, as explained later. No step-size control is built in, but two independent sources are available: the impulse source and the step source. Time domain analysis is possible only for *analog* networks.

D.2. INPUT DATA

Input to the program is supplied by *command cards* and *data cards*. Both have similar structure. The sequence of data input is:

TITLe card
followed by 80 character title

MODE1 card
followed by parameter values for built in linear models of bipolar and field effect transistors and operational amplifiers. Parameters for each model are given on one card. Up to 10 models can be defined.

NET card
followed by circuit description cards. Each element is given on one card. There may be up to 40 elements.

END card signals end of circuit description.

SENSitivity card if sensitivities are required.

[Analysis requests initiated by command cards AC, POLE, SYMB, and TIME. These may appear in any sequence.

[NEXT card indicates start of new network.

[STOP card indicates end of job.

The nodes, elements and the models should be assigned alphanumeric names with up to 3 characters. The ground node is labeled as either "0" or "GND."

A. Command Cards

TITLE

Title is optional. The first card is the command card, the second one can contain any text. The form of these cards is

TITL

↑1

arbitrary text.

MODEL

Parameters for the built in linear models for bipolar and field effect transistors and operational amplifiers may be specified. The model structures are shown in Figs. D.2.1, D.2.2, and D.2.3. Each model contains up to 8 parameters which are marked on the diagrams. Parameter values must be specified in mhos and farads. Model parameters are given as

MODE	$m \leqslant 10$ model names in (10A3) format

↑1 ↑11

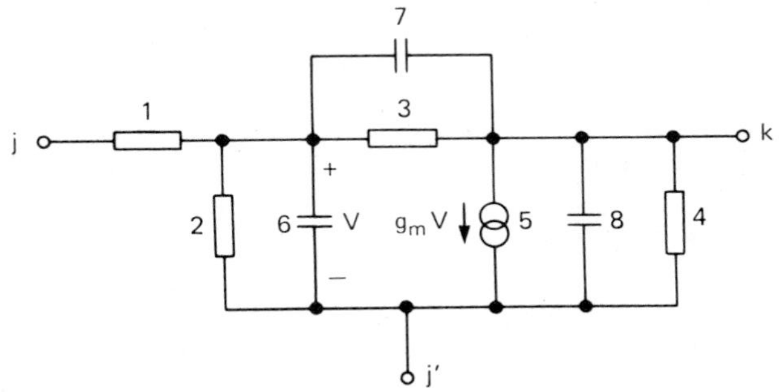

Fig. D.2.1. Built-in hybrid π model for element type TR (bipolar transistor).

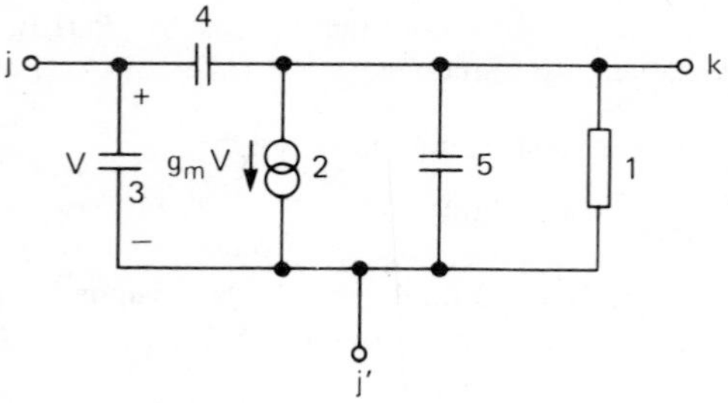

Fig. D.2.2. Built-in hybrid π model for element type FET (field effect transistor).

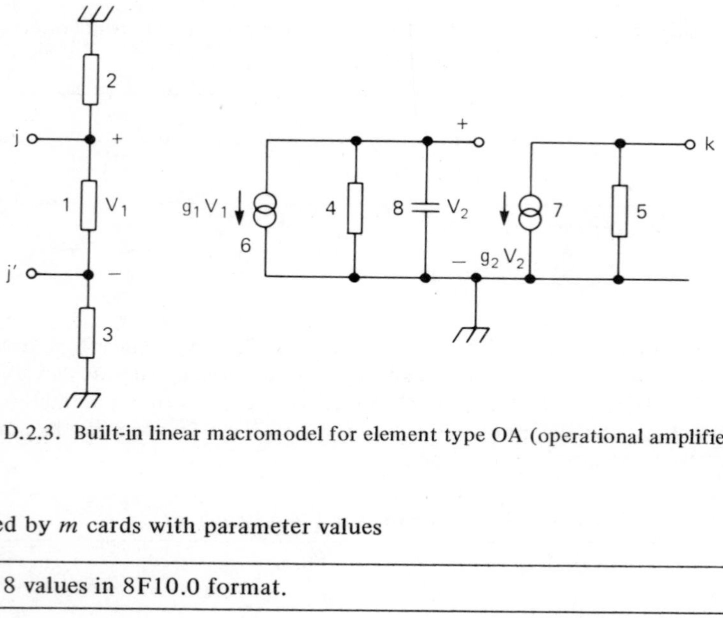

Fig. D.2.3. Built-in linear macromodel for element type OA (operational amplifier).

followed by *m* cards with parameter values

up to 8 values in 8F10.0 format.

TOPOLOGY

Topology is supplied by first giving the command card

NET	IFORM (I2)
↑1	↑5

IFORM = 1 provides modified nodal formulation described in Section 4.4
IFORM = 2 provides the two graph modified nodal formulation from Section 4.8
IFORM = 3 indicates a digital network.

The card NET is followed by cards containing element data and topology, see section on data cards below.

SENSITIVITY

Frequency domain sensitivities are initiated by the command card SENS, which must precede the card AC (if sensitivities are to be computed). Its form is

SENS	up to ten element names in (10A3) format
↑1	↑11

Output sensitivity is calculated with respect to specified elements. If there are many outputs only the first output (see data cards for output specification) is taken for sensitivity calculations.

FREQUENCY RESPONSE

The command card has the form

AC	LL,NEFREQ,MODE (3I2)	FSTART,FEND (2F10.0)
↑1	↑5	↑41

LL = 1	frequency is in Hz.
LL = 2	frequency in radians (useful for instructional purposes).
NFREQ⩽99	number of frequency intervals (NFREQ+1 = number of frequency points).
FSTART	initial frequency.
FEND	final frequency.
MODE = 0	result given in real and imaginary parts. Applies to sensitivities as well.
MODE = 1	result given in db and degrees. Applies to sensitivities as well

Note: inputs are given by the independent sources of the network, outputs are specified on data cards.

POLE–ZERO COMPUTATION

The command card has the form

POLE	MODE (I2)
↑1	↑5

MODE = 1	results in use of polynomial interpolation method.
MODE = 2	the QZ algorithm is used.

SYMBOLIC FUNCTION

The command card has the form

SYMB	IVAR (I2)	NVAR(1),NVAR(2) . . . NVAR(5) (5A3)
↑1	↑5	↑11

NVAR(I) names of elements which will be retained in the symbolic function in addition to the frequency variable. Maximum number is 5. If none is specified, the symbolic function with the frequency variable s (or z^{-1}) is obtained.

IVAR = 1 Symbolic function is generated in terms of element *perturbations.* This is equivalent to obtaining derivatives of the numerator and denominator with respect to the elements.

IDER ≠ 1 Symbolic function with elements kept as symbols is printed. *Comment:* If there are more than one input and/or output, only the first input and first output are taken for this analysis.

TRANSIENT RESPONSE

The following sequence of cards must be given:

TRAN

IC	four variables (4A3) corresponding to element names	four initial conditions on these elements (4F10.0)
	↑11	

TIME	METHOD,IRESP (2I2)	H,TEND (2F10.0)
↑1	↑5	↑41

IC cards are optional. They indicate initial voltages across the capacitors or initial currents through the inductors. The reference directions are shown in Fig. D.2.4, j being the first and j' being the second node specified on the card. Any number of IC cards may be given.

Time domain solution is found by numerical inversion of the Laplace transform as described in Section 10.4. No error control is provided.

METHOD = 0 uses Padé approximation $M = 2, N = 0$. Small steps must be selected.

METHOD = 1 uses $M = 10, N = 8$. Moderately large steps can be taken.

IRESP = 0 The source is a Dirac impulse.

IRESP = 1 The source is a step function.

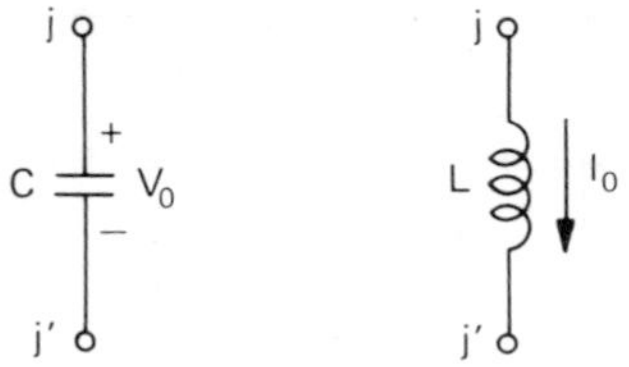

Fig. D.2.4. Positive directions of the initial conditions on C and L with respect to the first (j) and second (j') node read in the data.

H	step size.
TEND	endtime of calculations.

B. Data Cards

Element values and their connection in the network are given by cards of the form

code	NAME, J, JP, K, KP, MO (6A3)	Value (F10.0)
↑1	↑11	↑41

The codes are given in Fig. D.2.5 and are self-explanatory. Resistors should normally be given as type R or as conductance G. If given as R, the value is converted into $G = 1/R$ and handled as a conductance (if resistor value $\neq 0$). Should there be a *special reason*, the resistor may be given by the RZ type. In this case the current through the resistor is available as one of the solution variables. The size of the system matrix grows by one for each such resistor.

The elements A (for "Ammeter") and V (for "Voltmeter") indicate outputs. The ammeter acts as a short circuit and the current through it is available as a solution. The voltmeter gives the voltage between the nodes to which it is connected. Each connection of the ammeter increases the size of the system matrix by 1.

The element IOA is an ideal operational amplifier. Sensitivity with respect to B and use of B as a symbolic variable is possible in the MNT = 1 formulation.

Some elements have their currents available in the solution. They are shown in Figs. 4.4.1 and 4.8.2, depending on which formulation is requested. Similarly, voltages across some elements are directly available as well. For such elements, A and V should not be given. The outputs are printed by the program when MO=YES is set for that particular element (see Fig. D.2.5). In case of transistor or operational amplifier models, MO indicates model name.

The integers, J, JP, K, KP correspond to j, j', k, k' in Figs. 4.4.1 and 4.8.2.

The limitations on the number of elements, inputs and outputs and on the size of the system matrix were given in the introduction to this appendix.

	Code	j	j'	k	k'	If MO=YES, the following is printed	Value	Remark
Analog	G	*	*			voltage across G	*	
	C	*	*			voltage across C	*	
	VCT	*	*	*	*	controlling voltage	*	
	CCT	*	*	*	*	controlling current	*	
	VVT	*	*	*	*	controlling voltage	*	
	J	*	*			voltage across J	*	
	E	*	*			current through E	*	current available as output *only* if MNT1 formulation used.
	IOA	*	*	*	*	—	—	
	L	*	*			current through L	*	
	R	*	*			voltage across G	*	changed into G
	RZ	*	*			current through RZ	*	
	CVT	*	*	*	*	controlling current	*	
	A	*	*			—	—	current is an output
	V	*	*			—	—	voltage is an output
	TR	*	*	*			—	Linear models force MNT1 formulation. For node numbers see Figs. D.2.1–D.2.4.
	FET	*	*	*		MO indicates Model number	—	
	OA	*	*	*			—	
Digital	IN	*					*	input node
	OUT	*					—	output node
	MUL	*	*				*	multiplier from j to j'
	DEL	*	*				—	delay from j to j'

Fig. D.2.5. Elements incorporated into the program; * indicates entries provided by the user.

D.3. USE OF THE PROGRAM

The network shown in Fig. D.3.1 will be used to demonstrate the use of the program. For better understanding, various expressions are also derived theoretically. Initial voltage across one capacitor is given in order to demonstrate the use of initial conditions in the time domain analysis.

The output voltage of the network is

$$V_{out} = \frac{\mu G_1 G_2 E_{in}}{D} + \frac{\mu (G_1 + G_2 + sC_1) C_2 V_0}{D}$$

where

$$D = s^2 C_1 C_2 + s[C_1 G_2 (1 - \mu) + C_2 (G_1 + G_2)] + G_1 G_2 .$$

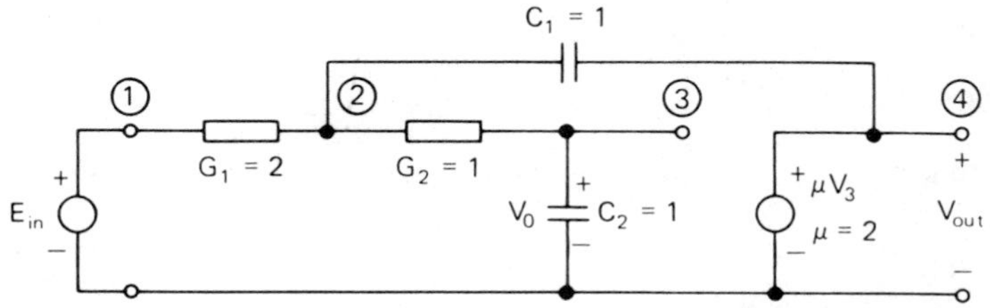

Fig. D.3.1. Example solved by the program. Initial voltage $V_0 = 1$ is used for impulse response but not for the step response.

The second term expresses the influence of the initial voltage across the capacitor and will be used in the time domain analysis only.

A. Frequency Domain Analysis

The results are indicated for $f = 1$ Hz and $V_0 = 0$. Then $s = 2\pi j$ and the transfer function is

$$T(2\pi j) = \frac{4}{-4\pi^2 + 4\pi j + 2} = -0.09594 - j0.03217.$$

Sensitivity of the output with respect to G_1 is obtained theoretically by first keeping G_1 as the variable in the transfer function

$$T(s, G_1) = \frac{2G_1}{s^2 + sG_1 + G_1}$$

and then by differentiating with respect to G_1. The result is

$$\frac{\partial T(s, G_1)}{\partial G_1} = \frac{2s^2}{(s^2 + 2s + 2)^2}$$

and for $f = 1$ Hz:

$$\frac{\partial T(2\pi j, G_1)}{\partial G_1} = -0.04032 - j0.03046$$

which is the result obtained numerically by the program. Frequency response can also be given in radians per second and the output obtained as magnitude (in db) and phase (in degrees). In this case

$$T(j1) = \frac{4 - j8}{5}$$

from which

$$\alpha(1) = 5.051 \qquad \text{(db)}$$

$$\phi(1) = -63.43 \qquad \text{(degrees)}.$$

Sensitivity of the magnitude and phase are calculated using Eqs. (6.5.7) and (6.5.5). For the variable G_1

$$D_{G_1}^{T(j1)} = \frac{\partial T(j1, G_1)}{\partial G_1} = \frac{6 + 8j}{25}.$$

Obtain the ratio

$$\frac{D_{G_1}^{T(j1)}}{T(j1)} = \frac{6 + 8j}{25} \times \frac{5}{4 - 8j} = \frac{-1 + 2j}{10}.$$

Thus $\partial\alpha(1)/\partial G_1 = -0.1$ (in Neper) and $\partial\phi(1)/\partial G_1 = 0.2$ (in radians). To convert the result to db, multiply $\partial\alpha(1)/\partial G_1$ by 8.686. To get the sensitivity in degrees, multiply $\partial\phi(1)/\partial G_1$ by 57.29578. The results -0.8686 and 11.46 are printed.

B. Poles and Zeros

The analysis is based on the polynomials obtained by the symbolic analysis, and requires a polynomial root-finding routine which is not supplied with the program. Any standard routine can be used.

In the example, the denominator poles are the roots of $s^2 + 2s + 2$; they are $-1 \pm j1$. Q and ω_0 values are defined by the expressions (6.5.22) and (6.5.23) Numerically, they are $Q = 0.707$ and $\omega_0 = 1.41$.

The sensitivities of the poles and zeros are calculated by Eqns. (6.5.20) and (6.5.13), those of ω_0 and Q by (6.5.27) and (6.5.26), respectively. For the given example, we find the sensitivities with respect to G_1. Keeping the denominator as a function of s and G_1, $D = s^2 + sG_1 + G_1$. The roots are

$$\text{poles} = -\frac{G_1}{2} \pm j\left(G_1 - \frac{G_1^2}{4}\right)^{1/2}$$

and

$$\omega_0 = \left(\frac{G_1^2}{4} + G_1 - \frac{G_1^2}{4}\right)^{1/2} = \sqrt{G_1}$$

$$Q = \omega_0/G_1 = 1/\sqrt{G_1}.$$

The sensitivity of the pole is

$$\frac{d}{dG_1}\,(\text{pole}) = -\frac{1}{2} + j\,\frac{1}{2}\left(G_1 - \frac{G_1^2}{4}\right)^{-1/2}\left(1 - \frac{2G_1}{4}\right) = -\frac{1}{2}.$$

The sensitivities of ω_0 and Q are

$$\frac{d\omega_0}{dG_1} = \frac{1}{2}\,(G_1)^{-1/2} = 0.354; \qquad \frac{dQ}{dG_1} = -\frac{1}{2}\,(G_1)^{-3/2} = -0.177.$$

These results are printed.

Round-off errors can introduce superflous roots. These are automatically suppressed by the program. POLE/ZERO analysis should be used with *normalized* networks.

C. Symbolic Analysis

Three types of symbolic analysis are shown on the sample output. If all elements are given their nominal values, the transfer function is

$$T(s) = \frac{V_{\text{out}}}{E_{\text{in}}} = \frac{4}{s^2 + 2s + 2}.$$

Calculation of the derivatives of the numerator and denominator is demonstrated on the same function by assuming that the gain μ is the variable element. Then

$$T(s, \mu) = \frac{2\mu}{(s^2 + 4s + 2) - \mu s}.$$

The zeroth order derivatives are $N(s) = 4$ and $D(s) = s^2 + 2s + 2$. The derivatives with respect to μ are

$$\frac{\partial N}{\partial \mu} = 2; \qquad \frac{\partial D}{\partial \mu} = -s$$

and the values are printed by the program.

As another type of symbolic analysis, let us keep the two conductors G_1, G_2 as variables. Then

$$T(s, G_1, G_2) = \frac{N(s, G_1, G_2)}{D(s, G_1, G_2)}$$

with

$$N(s, G_1, G_2) = (0 + 0s + 0s^2) + (0 + 0s + 0s^2)\,G_1 + (0 + 0s + 0s^2)\,G_2 + (2 + 0s + 0s^2)\,G_1 G_2$$

and

$$D(s, G_1, G_2) = (0 + 0s + 1s^2) + (0 + 1s + 0s^2)\,G_1 + (0 + 0s + 0s^2)\,G_2 + (1 + 0s + 0s^2)\,G_1 G_2 .$$

The polynomials given in the brackets are printed on the output.

Comment: SYMBOLIC ANALYSIS SHOULD BE APPLIED TO NORMALIZED NETWORKS.

D. Transient Response

The transient response is first indicated for unit step input and for $V_0 = 0$. In this case

$$V_{out} = \frac{4}{s(s^2 + 2s + 2)} = \frac{2}{s} + \frac{-1 - j}{s + 1 + j} + \frac{-1 + j}{s + 1 - j}$$

and

$$v(t) = \mathcal{L}^{-1}[V_{out}] = 2 - 2e^{-t}[\cos t + \sin t].$$

For instance,

$$v(0.5) = 0.353866; \qquad v(1) = 0.983348.$$

The second time domain example uses initial voltage $V_0 = 1$ across the capacitor C_2 and an impulse at the input. Now

$$V_{out} = \frac{4}{s^2 + 2s + 2} + \frac{2s + 6}{s^2 + 2s + 2} = \frac{2s + 10}{s^2 + 2s + 2} .$$

The partial fraction decomposition is

$$V_{out} = \frac{1 + 4j}{s + 1 + j} + \frac{1 - 4j}{s + 1 - j}$$

and

$$v(t) = \mathcal{L}^{-1}[V_{out}] = 2e^{-t}(\cos t + 4 \sin t).$$

For instance, $v(0.1) = 2.523298$, $v(1) = 2.874011$.

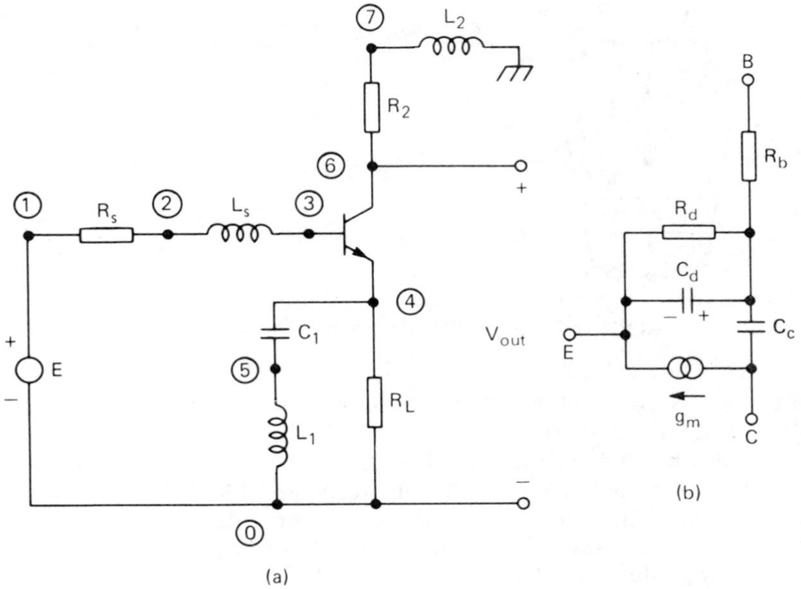

Fig. D.3.2. Sample network (a) with transistor model (b).

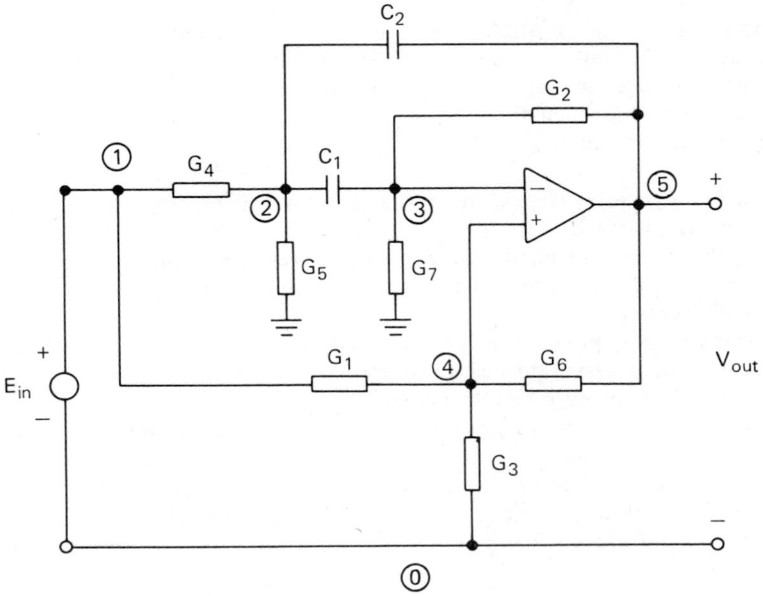

Fig. D.3.3. STAR network with ideal operational amplifier.

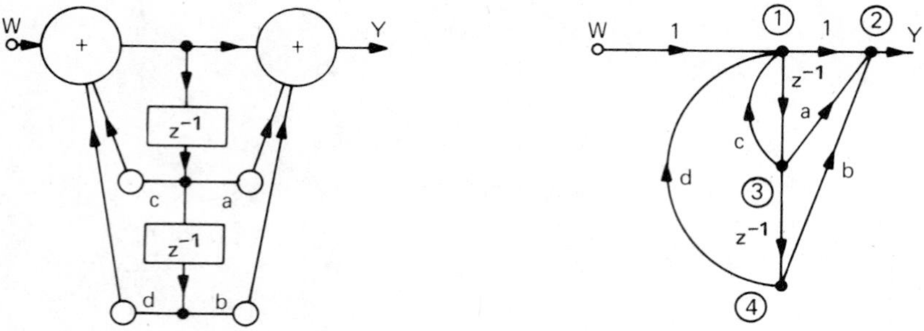

Fig. D.3.4. Sample digital network and associated graph.

In this analysis we used the 0/2 Padé approximation and the program gave the results 2.52025 and 2.86260.

Three other networks are shown in Figs. D.3.2–D.3.4. They represent a simple single transistor amplifier for which a hybrid π model is used, a filter with an ideal operational amplifier and a digital circuit. Input data for the networks in Figs. D.3.1–D.3.4 are shown in Fig. D.3.5. Fig. D.3.6 contains an edited version of the output produced by the program.

D.4. EXTENSIONS OF THE PROGRAM

The program discussed in this appendix is intended for educational purposes and its application is limited. However, basic formulation techniques and the data structure have been set up with possible extensions in mind. The theory for such extensions has been treated adequately in the various chapters. Some of the possible improvements are considered below.

1. In order to solve large circuits, the sparse matrix algorithm in Appendix E would replace **LU**.
2. In the present form, the program computes sensitivities with respect to element values. The other possibilities discussed in Chapter 6 can be implemented.
3. The program provides sensitivities and can therefore form the basis for linear circuit design through optimization.
4. Monte Carlo analysis can be included.
5. Analysis of nonlinear networks. The solution routines must be converted into real arithmetic.
6. Time domain solution by numerical integration could be incorporated, possibly with control of order of integration and step size. The theory was covered in Chapters 9 and 13.

INPUT DATA

```
TITL
NETWORK OF FIGURE D.3.1
NET  2
E          EIN   1   0                       1.
G          G1    1   2                       2.
G          G2    2   3                       1.
C          C1    2   4                       1.
C          C2    3   0                       1.
VVT        MU    3   0   4   0               2.
V          VOU   4   0
END
SENS       G1  C2
AC    1  2  0                                0.        2.
AC    2  2  1                                0.        2.
POLE  2
SYMB  0
SYMB  1    MU
SYMB  0    G1  G2
TRAN
TIME  1  1                                   .25       2.
TRAN
IC         C2                                1.
TIME  0  0                                   .1        1.
NEXT
TITL
NETWORK OF FIGURE D.3.2
MODE       Q1
50.        2000.      0.         0.          150.      50.       1.        0.
NET   2
E          E     1   0                       1.
R          RS    1   2                       .02
L          LS    2   3                       .001
TR         TRA   3   4   6   Q1
C          C1    4   5                       15.
L          L1    5   0                       .06
R          RL    4   0                       .2
R          R2    6   7                       .15
L          L2    7   0                       .1
V          VOU   4   0
END
POLE  1
NEXT
TITL
NETWORK OF FIGURE D.3.3
NET   1
E          EIN   1   0                       1.
G          G4    1   2                       18.3547
G          G5    2   0                       50.7603
C          C1    2   3                       6.9115
C          C2    2   5                       6.9115
G          G7    3   0                       1.80974
G          G2    3   5                       .709248
G          G1    1   4                       25.
G          G3    4   0                       75.
G          G6    4   5                       1.
IOA        OA    3   4   5
V          VOU   5   0
END
SENS       OA
POLE  1
NEXT
TITL
NETWORK OF FIGURE D.3.4
NET   2
IN         W     1                           1.
OUT        Y     2
MUL              1   2                       1.
MUL        A     3   2                       2.
MUL        B     4   2                       3.
more...
MUL        C     3   1                       -.1
MUL        D     4   1                       -.5
DEL              1   3
DEL              3   4
END
POLE  1
SYMB  1    A  B  C  D
STOP
```

Fig. D.3.5. Input data for the networks in Figs. D.3.1–D.3.4.

SOLUTIONS

```
NETWORK OF FIGURE D.3.1
Circuit description
Type Name Node1 Node2 Node3 Node4 Model/Output          Value
E    EIN    1     0                                     1.00000
G    G1     1     2                                     2.00000
G    G2     2     3                                     1.00000
C    C1     2     4                                     1.00000
C    C2     3     0                                     1.00000
VVT  MU     3     0     4     0                         2.00000
V    VOU    4     0                                     .0
2 Graph Formulation method
New ground node is numbered  5
The voltage graph has  4 nodes and the current graph  2 nodes
    User node      V-Graph node          I-Graph node
        1               1                     5
        2               2                     1
        3               3                     2
        4               4                     5
Equation number  3 corresponds to element EIN
Equation number  4 corresponds to element MU
Values in matrix G
  -2.00    3.00  -1.00    0.0
   0.0    -1.00   1.00    0.0
   1.00    0.0    0.0     0.0
   0.0     0.0    2.00   -1.00
Values in matrix C
   0.0     1.00   0.0    -1.00
   0.0     0.0    1.00    0.0
   0.0     0.0    0.0     0.0
   0.0     0.0    0.0     0.0
Transpose of RHS vector
   0.0     0.0    1.00    0.0
NETWORK OF FIGURE D.3.1
AC analysis
Frequency in cycles per second
             Outputs at elements
    F                    VOU
             Differential sensitivity of first output with respect to
                         G1                           C2
                 Re               Im            Re             Im
             --------------------         --------------------
 .0        Res   2.000D+00   0.0
           Sen  -1.110D-16   0.0           0.0            0.0
 1.00      Res  -9.594D-02  -3.217D-02
           Sen  -4.032D-02  -3.046D-02     1.097D-01      2.242D-02
 2.00      Res  -2.501D-02  -4.031D-03
           Sen  -1.202D-02  -3.979D-03     2.594D-02      2.218D-03
NETWORK OF FIGURE D.3.1
AC analysis
Outputs and sensitivities in db and degrees
Frequency in radians
             Outputs at elements
    W                    VOU
             Differential sensitivity of first output with respect to
                         G1                           C2
                Mag            Phase            Mag            Phase
             --------------------         --------------------
 .0        Res   6.021D+00   0.0
           Sen  -4.822D-16   0.0           0.0            0.0
 1.00      Res   5.051D+00  -6.343D+01
           Sen  -8.686D-01   1.146D+01    -8.686D+00     -5.730D+01
 2.00      Res  -9.691D-01  -1.166D+02
           Sen   1.737D+00   2.292D+01    -1.390D+01     -1.146D+01
NETWORK OF FIGURE D.3.1
Pole zero analysis
QZ algorithm for Zeros (see chapter 7)
  I           ALPHA(I)                        BETA(I)
        ----------------------
  1     2.23607          .0                   .0
more...
```

Fig. D.3.6. Program output corresponding to the data in Fig. D.3.5.

```
   2    -1.54919          .0                    .0
   3    -.353549          .612373               .224275D-05
   4    -.577346         -1.00001               .366242D-05
   5     1.41421          .0                    .448547D-05
QZ algorithm for Poles (see chapter 7)
   I             ALPHA(I)                       BETA(I)
        -----------------------
   1     2.23607          .0                    .0
   2    -1.37840          .0                    .0
   3     .424795          .424795               .424795
   4     .763763         -.763763               .763763
The network function gain =           4.00000
Poles, Q and omega values
   I             Pole(I)                        Q(I)             Omega(I)
        -----------------------
   1    -1.00000         -1.00000              .707107           1.41421
   2    -1.00000          1.00000              .707107           1.41421
Pole, Q and omega differential sensitivities
Pole no    var           Pole-sens                  Q-sens            W-sens
                      ----------------------
   2        G1       -.500           -.255D-15           -.177              .354
            C2       -.500           -1.50               -.707             -.707
NETWORK OF FIGURE D.3.1
Symbolic analysis
Network function coeffecients
        Power        Numerator                      Denominator
        of s
           0     -4.00000000D+00               -2.00000000D+00
           1      0.0                          -2.00000000D+00
           2      0.0                          -1.00000000D+00
The network function gain =           4.00000
Poles, Q and omega values
   I             Pole(I)                        Q(I)             Omega(I)
        -----------------------
   1    -1.00000          1.00000              .707107           1.41421
   2    -1.00000         -1.00000              .707107           1.41421
NETWORK OF FIGURE D.3.1
Symbolic analysis
Symbolic function in terms of variations
Variable               Power       Numerator                         Denominator
Elements               of s
                          0       -4.000000D+00                    -2.000000D+00
                          1        0.0                             -2.000000D+00
                          2        0.0                             -1.000000D+00
MU                        0       -2.000000D+00                     0.0
                          1        0.0                              1.000000D+00
NETWORK OF FIGURE D.3.1
Symbolic analysis
Symbolic function in terms of variable elements
Variable               Power       Numerator                         Denominator
Elements               of s
                          2        0.0                             -1.000000D+00
G1                        1        0.0                             -1.000000D+00
G1   G2                   0       -2.000000D+00                    -1.000000D+00
NETWORK OF FIGURE D.3.1
Time domain analysis
8/10 approximation  Step      Response
  Time           VOU
 2.500D-01   1.05464D-01
 5.000D-01   3.53866D-01
    .            .
    .            .
 2.000D+00   1.86652D+00
NETWORK OF FIGURE D.3.1
Time domain analysis
Initial conditions
Element        Init. Condn.
 C2             1.00D+00
0/2  approximation  Impulse  Response
  Time           VOU
more...
```

Fig. D.3.6. (*Continued*)

```
   1.000D-01   2.52025D+00
   2.000D-01   2.90038D+00
      .            .
      .            .
   1.000D+00   2.86260D+00
NETWORK OF FIGURE D.3.2
Device models
Model name    Parameter values
   Q1                50.00            2000.              .0                 .0
                     150.0            50.00             1.000               .0
NETWORK OF FIGURE D.3.2
Circuit description
Type Name Node1 Node2 Node3 Node4 Model/Output            Value
E     E      1      0                                     1.00000
R     RS     1      2                                     .200000E-01
L     LS     2      3                                     .100000E-02
TR    TRA    3      4      6             Q1               .0
C     C1     4      5                                     15.0000
L     L1     5      0                                     .600000E-01
R     RL     4      0                                     .200000
R     R2     6      7                                     .150000
L     L2     7      0                                     .100000
V     VOU    4      0                                     .0
1 Graph Formulation method
User defined node = internal node number
  1 =   1         2 =   2         3 =   3         4 =   4         6 =   5
  5 =   6         7 =   7
Equation and variable  8 correspond to element E
Equation and variable  9 correspond to element LS
Equation and variable 10 correspond to element TRA
Equation and variable 11 correspond to element L1
Equation and variable 12 correspond to element L2
NETWORK OF FIGURE D.3.2
Pole zero analysis
Network function coeffecients
          Power        Numerator                    Denominator
          of s
            0      3.58333350D+07               4.25833354D+07
            1      6.20833337D+06               2.93158344D+07
            2      3.59583352D+07               4.71561272D+07
            3      5.67083327D+06               1.06220006D+07
            4      3.33750085D+06               4.20880521D+06
            5      7.50000198D+04               1.08687527D+05
            6      0.0                          3.75000073D+02
The network function gain =            200.000
Zeros, Q and omega values
   I             Zero(I)                        Q(I)             Omega(I)
          -----------------------
   1      -.433811D-15     1.05409          .121492D+16        1.05409
   2      -.433811D-15    -1.05409          .121492D+16        1.05409
   3      -.750000         3.07205          2.10819            3.16228
   4      -.750000        -3.07205          2.10819            3.16228
   5      -43.0000          .0              .500000            43.0000
Poles, Q and omega values
   I             Pole(I)                        Q(I)             Omega(I)
          -----------------------
   1      -.262461         1.02332          2.01258            1.05644
   2      -.262461        -1.02332          2.01258            1.05644
   3      -.921761         2.96850          1.68607            3.10831
   4      -.921761        -2.96850          1.68607            3.10831
   5      -43.0938          .0              .500000            43.0938
   6      -244.371          .0              .500000            244.371
NETWORK OF FIGURE D.3.3
Circuit description
Type Name Node1 Node2 Node3 Node4 Model/Output            Value
E     EIN    1      0                                     1.00000
G     G4     1      2                                     18.3547
G     G5     2      0                                     50.7603
C     C1     2      3                                     6.91150
C     C2     2      5                                     6.91150
more...
```

Fig. D.3.6. (*Continued*)

```
G     G7        3      0                                                    1.80974
G     G2        3      5                                                    .709248
G     G1        1      4                                                    25.0000
G     G3        4      0                                                    75.0000
G     G6        4      5                                                    1.00000
IOA   OA        3      4      5                                             .0
V     VOU       5      0                                                    .0
1 Graph Formulation method
User defined node = internal node number
  1 =  1        2 =  2        3 =  3        5 =  4                 4 =  5
Equation and variable  6 correspond to element EIN
Equation and variable  7 correspond to element OA
Values in matrix G
 43.35  -18.35    0.0     0.0   -25.00    1.00    0.0
-18.35   69.12    0.0     0.0     0.0     0.0     0.0
  0.0     0.0     2.52   -0.71    0.0     0.0     0.0
  0.0     0.0    -0.71    1.71   -1.00    0.0     1.00
-25.00    0.0     0.0    -1.00  101.00    0.0     0.0
  1.00    0.0     0.0     0.0     0.0     0.0     0.0
  0.0     0.0     1.00    0.0    -1.00    0.0     0.0
Values in matrix C
  0.0     0.0     0.0     0.0     0.0     0.0     0.0
  0.0    13.82   -6.91   -6.91    0.0     0.0     0.0
  0.0    -6.91    6.91    0.0     0.0     0.0     0.0
  0.0    -6.91    0.0     6.91    0.0     0.0     0.0
  0.0     0.0     0.0     0.0     0.0     0.0     0.0
  0.0     0.0     0.0     0.0     0.0     0.0     0.0
  0.0     0.0     0.0     0.0     0.0     0.0     0.0
Transpose of RHS vector
  0.0     0.0     0.0     0.0     0.0     1.00    0.0
NETWORK OF FIGURE D.3.3
Pole zero analysis
Network function coeffecients
        Power        Numerator                       Denominator
        of s
          0      4.35249686D+03                4.77688779D+03
          1     -5.15523617D-03                4.77689120D+02
          2      1.19422080D+03                4.77688319D+03
The network function gain =              .250000
Zeros, Q and omega values
    I            Zero(I)                         Q(I)              Omega(I)
         ----------------------
    1      .215841D-05     1.90909             -442245.           1.90909
    2      .215841D-05    -1.90909             -442245.           1.90909
Poles, Q and omega values
    I            Pole(I)                         Q(I)              Omega(I)
         ----------------------
    1     -.500001D-01     .998750              9.99999           1.00000
    2     -.500001D-01    -.998750              9.99999           1.00000
Zero, Q and omega differential sensitivities
Zero no    var          Zero-sens                      Q-sens              W-sens
                   ----------------------
    1      OA        .0              .0                  .0                  .0
Pole, Q and omega differential sensitivities
Pole no    var          Pole-sens                      Q-sens              W-sens
                   ----------------------
    1      OA       -5.37           1.07               -.106D+04            1.34
NETWORK OF FIGURE D.3.4
Circuit description
Type Name Node1 Node2 Node3 Node4 Model/Output                  Value
IN    W     1                                                  1.00000
OUT   Y     2                                                  .0
MUL         1     2                                            1.00000
MUL   A     3     2                                            2.00000
MUL   B     4     2                                            3.00000
MUL   C     3     1                                            -.100000
MUL   D     4     1                                            -.500000
DEL         1     3                                            .0
DEL         3     4                                            .0
Digital Formulation method
more...
```

Fig. D.3.6. (*Continued*)

```
User defined node = internal node number
  1 =  1       2 =  2        3 =  3        4 =  4
Values in matrix G
  1.00     0.0      0.10    0.50
 -1.00     1.00    -2.00   -3.00
  0.0      0.0      1.00    0.0
  0.0      0.0      0.0     1.00
Values in matrix C
  0.0      0.0      0.0     0.0
  0.0      0.0      0.0     0.0
 -1.00     0.0      0.0     0.0
  0.0      0.0     -1.00    0.0
Transpose of RHS vector
  1.00     0.0      0.0     0.0
NETWORK OF FIGURE D.3.4
Pole zero analysis
Network function coeffecients
        Power       Numerator                       Denominator
        of 1/z
            0      1.00000000D+00               1.00000000D+00
            1      2.00000000D+00               1.00000024D-01
            2      3.00000000D+00               5.00000000D-01
The network function gain =               6.00000
Zeros in the 1/z domain
    I              Zero(I)
        -----------------------
    1   -.333333           .471405
    2   -.333333          -.471405
Poles in the 1/z domain
    I              Pole(I)
        -----------------------
    1   -.100000           1.41067
    2   -.100000          -1.41067
NETWORK OF FIGURE D.3.4
Symbolic analysis
Symbolic function in terms of variations
Variable                   Power        Numerator                  Denominator
Elements                   of 1/z
                              0         1.000000D+00               1.000000D+00
                              1         2.000000D+00               1.000000D-01
                              2         3.000000D+00               5.000000D-01
A                             1         1.000000D+00               0.0
    B                         2         1.000000D+00               0.0
        C                     1         0.0                       -1.000000D+00
            D                 2         0.0                       -1.000000D+00
```

Fig. D.3.6. (*Continued*)

LISTING OF THE PROGRAM

```
C**MAIN*************************************************************
      REAL*8 TITLE(10),V1,V2
      REAL ANAL(10)
      INTEGER    NN(10),ISENS(10),BLANK/'    '/
      DATA ANAL/'TITL','NET','AC','SYMB','TRAN','STOP','SENS','POLE',
     $'NEXT','MODE'/,TITLE/' ',' ',' ',' ',' ',' ',' ',' ',' ',' '/
      COMMON /$$3/ VMODEL(8,10),IMODEL(10),$TMD(4,21),$IS(3),$JT(3),$JG
     $(3),MODMAX
      CALL ALLOW (256,0,0)
   10 INET = 0
      DO 20 I=1,10
   20 IMODEL(I) = BLANK
   30 READ (5,190) CODE,I1,I2,I3,NN,V1,V2
      DO 40 I=1,10
          IF (CODE.EQ.ANAL(I)) GO TO 60
   40 CONTINUE
      WRITE (6,200) CODE
   50 STOP
   60 GO TO (70,80,90,100,110,50,120,130,10,140), I
   70 READ (5,210) TITLE
      GO TO 30
   80 WRITE (6,220) TITLE
      CALL NET (I1,IER)
      IF (IER.NE.0) GO TO 30
      NSENS = 0
      INET = 1
      GO TO 30
   90 WRITE (6,230) TITLE
      IF (INET.EQ.0) GO TO 170
      CALL AC (I1,I2,I3,V1,V2,NSENS,ISENS)
      GO TO 30
  100 WRITE (6,240) TITLE
      IF (INET.EQ.0) GO TO 170
      CALL SVALID (NN,NN,5,NSYM)
      CALL SYMBOL (I1,NSYM,NN)
      GO TO 30
  110 WRITE (6,250) TITLE
      IF (INET.EQ.0) GO TO 170
      CALL TRAN
      GO TO 30
  120 IF (INET.EQ.0) GO TO 170
      CALL SVALID (NN,ISENS,10,NSENS)
      GO TO 30
  130 WRITE (6,260) TITLE
      IF (INET.EQ.0) GO TO 170
      CALL POLE (I1,NSENS,ISENS)
      GO TO 30
  140 MODMAX = 0
      DO 150 K=1,10
          IF (NN(K).EQ.BLANK) GO TO 160
          MODMAX = K
          IMODEL(K) = NN(K)
  150 READ (5,180) (VMODEL(I,K),I=1,8)
  160 WRITE (6,280) TITLE,(NN(K),(VMODEL(I,K),I=1,8),K=1,MODMAX)
      GO TO 30
  170 WRITE (6,270)
      STOP
  180 FORMAT (8F10.0)
  190 FORMAT (A4,3I2,10A3,2F10.0)
  200 FORMAT (' *** INVALID COMMAND ***   ',A4)
  210 FORMAT (10A8)
  220 FORMAT (//1X,10A8//' Circuit description'/)
  230 FORMAT (//1X,10A8//' AC analysis'/)
  240 FORMAT (//1X,10A8//' Symbolic analysis'/)
  250 FORMAT (//1X,10A8//' Time domain analysis'/)
  260 FORMAT (//1X,10A8//' Pole zero analysis'/)
  270 FORMAT (' *** NO CIRCUIT DEFINED ***')
  280 FORMAT (//1X,10A8//' Device models'/' Model name',T15,'Parameter',
     $' values'/(4X,A4,T15,4G15.4/T15,4G15.4))
      END
more...
```

Fig. D.4.1. Listing of the program for the analysis of linear analog and digital networks.

```
C**BLOCK DATA*********************************************************
      BLOCK DATA
C*TABLES FOR FORMULATION, ERROR CONDITION DETECTION AND TRANSISTOR
C*AND OPERATIONAL AMPLIFIER MODELS.
C*COMMON BLOCK $$0 IS GENERAL FORMULATION TABLE
C*COMMON BLOCK $$1 IS FOR 1 GRAPH MNT FORMULATION
C*COMMON BLOCK $$2 IS FOR 2 GRAPH MNT FORMULATION
C*COMMON BLOCK $$3 STORES MODEL PARAMETERS AND IMBEDS THEM INTO MNT
C*COMMON BLOCK $$4 DEFINES DIMENSIONAL CONSTANTS
C*COMMON BLOCK $$5 CONTAINS FORMULATION MATRICES AND VECTORS
C*COMMON BLOCK $$6 CONTAINS CIRCUIT DATA
      IMPLICIT INTEGER ($)
      COMPLEX*16 Y,RHS,RHST,X,XT
      REAL*8 G,C,B
      COMMON /$$0/ $T1(21,6)
      COMMON /$$1/ $M1(21,5),$T1G(4,21),$T1U(4,11)
      COMMON /$$2/ $M2(14,7),$T2R(14),$T2C(14),$T2G(8,14),$T2U(4,3),$T2S
     $(3,3)
      COMMON /$$3/ VMODEL(8,10),IMODEL(10),$TMD(4,21),$IS(3),$JT(3),$JG
     $(3),MODMAX
      COMMON /$$4/ NELMAX,NMAX,NNMAX,NMMAX,MAXIN,MAXOU,MAXSY
      COMMON /$$5/ Y(25,25),RHS(25),RHST(25),X(26),XT(26),G(26,26),C(26,
     $26),B(26)
      COMMON /$$6/ VALUE(40),NEMT(10,40),NAMES(50),IOUT(10),IN(10),NOUT,
     $NIN,IFORM,NEL,NODES,N,NLAST,NORDR
      DATA $T1/'G  ','C  ','VCT','CCT','VVT','J  ','E  ','IOA',
     $         'L  ','R  ','RZ ','CVT','A  ','V  ','TR ','FET',
     $         'OA ','IN ','OUT','MUL','DEL'                        ,
     $         1   , 1   , 1   , 1   , 1   , 1   , 1   , 1   ,
     $         1   , 1   , 1   , 1   , 1   , 1   , 1   , 1   ,
     $         1   , 0   , 0   , 0   , 0                          ,
     $         0   , 0   , 0   , 0   , 0   , 1   , 1   , 0   ,
     $         0   , 0   , 0   , 0   , 0   , 0   , 0   , 0   ,
     $         0   , 1   , 0   , 0   , 0                          ,
     $         0   , 0   , 0   , 0   , 0   , 0   , 0   , 0   ,
     $         0   , 0   , 0   , 0   , 1   , 1   , 0   , 0   ,
     $         0   , 0   , 1   , 0   , 0                          ,
     $         2   , 1   , 2   , 2   , 2   , 3   , 3   , 6   ,
     $         1   , 2   , 2   , 2   , 4   , 4   , 5   , 5   ,
     $         5   , 3   , 4   , 2   , 1                          ,
     $         2   , 2   , 4   , 4   , 4   , 2   , 2   , 3   ,
     $         2   , 2   , 2   , 4   , 2   , 2   , 3   , 3   ,
     $         3   , 1   , 1   , 2   , 2                          /
      DATA $M1/ 1   , 1   , 1   , 1   , 1   , 1   , 1   , 0   ,
     $         1   , 1   , 1   , 1   , 0   , 0   , 2   , 2   ,
     $         2   , 1   , 0   , 0   , 0                          ,
     $         1   , 1   , 1   , 1   , 1   , 0   , 0   , 1   ,
     $         1   , 1   , 1   , 1   , 0   , 0   , 0   , 0   ,
     $         0   , 0   , 0   , 1   , 0                          ,
     $         0   , 0   , 0   , 3   , 10  , 0   , 8   , 7   ,
     $         1   , 0   , 1   , 3   , 3   , 0   , 0   , 0   ,
     $         0   , 0   , 0   , 0   , 0                          ,
     $         0   , 0   , 0   , 2   , 2   , 0   , 2   , 2   ,
     $         2   , 0   , 2   , 4   , 2   , 0   , 0   , 0   ,
     $         0   , 0   , 0   , 0   , 0                          ,
     $         0   , 0   , 0   , 1   , 1   , 0   , 1   , 1   ,
     $         1   , 0   , 1   , 2   , 1   , 0   , 1   , 0   ,
     $         1   , 0   , 0   , 0   , 0                          /
      DATA $M2/ 1   , 1   , 1   , 1   , 1   , 1   , 0   , 0   ,
     $         1   , 1   , 1   , 1   , 0   , 0                    ,
     $         1   , 1   , 1   , 1   , 1   , 0   , 0   , 0   ,
     $         1   , 1   , 1   , 1   , 0   , 0                    ,
     $         0   , 0   , 0   , 2   , 3   , 0   , 3   , 0   ,
     $         1   , 0   , 1   , 1   , 2   , 0                    ,
     $         0   , 0   , 0   , 1   , 1   , 0   , 1   , 0   ,
     $         2   , 0   , 2   , 2   , 1   , 0                    ,
     $         0   , 0   , 0   , 0   , 0   , 0   , 0   ,-1   ,
     $         1   , 0   , 1   , 0   , 0   , 0                    ,
     $         0   , 0   , 0   , 1   , 2   , 0   , 3   , 1   ,
     $         0   , 0   , 0   , 1   , 1   , 0                    ,
more...
```

Fig. D.4.1. (*Continued*)

```
     $             0    , 0    , 0    , 1    , 1    , 0    , 1    , 2    ,
     $             0    , 0    , 0    , 2    , 1    , 0                   /
      DATA $T1G/    1,2,1,2,    1,2,1,2,    3,4,1,2,    3,4,6,5,
     $              6,5,1,2,    2,1,1,2,    6,5,6,5,    6,5,3,4,
     $              5,6,6,5,    1,2,1,2,    5,6,6,5,    5,7,6,5,
     $              5,5,6,5,    5,5,1,2,    0,0,0,0,    0,0,0,0,
     $              0,0,0,0,    1,5,5,5,    5,5,1,5,    5,2,1,5,
     $              5,2,1,5/
      DATA $T1U/    1,2,6,5,    6,5,1,2,    7,8,1,2,    1,2,7,8,
     $              6,5,3,4,    3,4,6,5,    3,4,5,6,    5,6,1,2,
     $              1,2,5,6,    5,6,4,3,    3,4,5,6/
      DATA $T2R/ 0,0,0,0,1,0,1,0,1,0,1,1,0,0/
      DATA $T2C/ 0,0,0,1,0,0,0,0,1,0,1,1,1,0/
      DATA $T2G/9 ,9 ,9 ,9 ,1 ,2 ,5 ,6 ,   9 ,9 ,9 ,9 ,1 ,2 ,5 ,6 ,
     $          9 ,9 ,9 ,9 ,3 ,4 ,5 ,6 ,   9 ,9 ,1 ,2 ,3 ,4 ,11,9 ,
     $          8 ,7 ,9 ,9 ,10,9 ,5 ,6 ,   9 ,9 ,9 ,9 ,2 ,1 ,5 ,6 ,
     $          5 ,6 ,9 ,9 ,10,9 ,9 ,9 ,   9 ,9 ,9 ,9 ,9 ,9 ,9 ,9 ,
     $          5 ,6 ,1 ,2 ,9 ,10,11,9 ,   9 ,9 ,9 ,9 ,1 ,2 ,5 ,6 ,
     $          5 ,6 ,1 ,2 ,9 ,10,11,9 ,   7 ,8 ,1 ,2 ,9 ,10,11,9 ,
     $          9 ,9 ,1 ,2 ,9 ,9 ,11,9 ,   9 ,9 ,9 ,9 ,9 ,9 ,5 ,6 /
      DATA $T2U/    6,5,1,2,    3,4,7,8,    5,6,1,2/
      DATA $T2S/   1,1,2,       2,3,4,      2,1,2/
      DATA $TMD/    1,4,1,4,    4,2,4,2,    3,4,3,4,    3,2,3,2,
     $              3,2,4,2,    4,2,4,2,    4,3,4,3,    3,2,3,2,
     $              3,2,3,2,    3,2,1,2,    1,2,1,2,    1,3,1,3,
     $              3,2,3,2,    1,2,1,2,    1,6,1,6,    2,6,2,6,
     $              4,6,4,6,    3,6,3,6,    4,6,1,2,    3,6,4,6,
     $              4,6,4,6/
      DATA $IS/ 1, 9, 14/ , $JT/ 8, 13, 21/ , $JG/ 5, 10, 20/
      DATA NELMAX/40/,NMAX/25/,NNMAX/50/,NMMAX/50/
      DATA MAXIN/10/,MAXOU/10/,MAXSY/5/
      END
C**NET...READ THE NETWORK DATA*****************************************
      SUBROUTINE NET (IFRM,IER)
      IMPLICIT INTEGER ($)
      COMPLEX*16 Y,RHS,RHST,X,XT
      REAL*8  G,C,B,FORM(3)/' 1 Graph',' 2 Graph',' Digital'/
      INTEGER  ICOUNT(21),I10/'R'/,IEND/'END'/,CODE,NN(4)
      INTEGER  GND(5)/'GND',' ','0  ',' 0 ','  0'/,YES/'YES'/
      COMMON /$$0/ $T1(21,6)
      COMMON /$$1/ $M1(21,5),$T1G(4,21),$T1U(4,11)
      COMMON /$$2/ $M2(14,7),$T2R(14),$T2C(14),$T2G(8,14),$T2U(4,3),$T2
     $(3,3)
      COMMON /$$3/ VMODEL(8,10),IMODEL(10),$TMD(4,21),$IS(3),$JT(3),$JG
     $(3),MODMAX
      COMMON /$$4/ NELMAX,NMAX,NNMAX,NMMAX,MAXIN,MAXOU,MAXSY
      COMMON /$$5/ Y(25,25),RHS(25),RHST(25),X(26),XT(26),G(26,26),C(26
     $26),B(26)
      COMMON /$$6/ VALUE(40),NEMT(10,40),NAMES(50),IOUT(10),IN(10),NOUT
     $NIN,IFORM,NEL,NODES,N,NLAST,NORDR
      IER = 0
      NORDR = 0
      NAMES(1) = GND(1)
      NODES = 1
      NIN = 0
      NOUT = 0
      MM = NELMAX+1
      DO 10 I=1,21
   10 ICOUNT(I) = 0
      WRITE (6,410)
      DO 180 I=1,MM
         READ (5,460) CODE,NAME,NN,MO,VALU
         IF (CODE.EQ.IEND) GO TO 190
         WRITE (6,470) CODE,NAME,NN,MO,VALU
         DO 20 J=1,21
            IF (CODE.EQ.$T1(J,1)) GO TO 30
   20    CONTINUE
         WRITE (6,360)
         IER = 1
         GO TO 180
more...
```

Fig. D.4.1. (*Continued*)

```
   30        NEMT(10,I) = NAME
             ICOUNT(J) = ICOUNT(J)+1
             LL = $T1(J,6)
             IF (LL.EQ.4) GO TO 50
             LP1 = LL+1
             DO 40 K=LP1,4
   40        NN(K) = 0
   50        DO 80 K=1,LL
                  NK = NN(K)
                  DO 60 L=2,5
   60             IF(NK.EQ.GND(L))NK = GND(1)
                  DO 70 M=1,NODES
                       IF (NK.EQ.NAMES(M)) GO TO 80
   70             CONTINUE
                  NODES = NODES+1
                  NAMES(NODES) = NK
                  M = NODES
   80        NN(K) = M-1
             DO 90 K=1,4
   90        NEMT(K+1,I) = NN(K)
             IF (CODE.NE.I10) GO TO 110
             IF (VALU.NE.0.) GO TO 100
             J = 11
             GO TO 110
  100        VALU = 1./VALU
             J = 1
  110        NEMT(1,I) = J
             VALUE(I) = VALU
             IF ($T1(J,3).EQ.0) GO TO 120
             NIN = NIN+1
             IN(NIN) = I
             GO TO 180
  120        IF ($T1(J,5).NE.5) GO TO 150
             DO 130 L=1,MODMAX
                  IF (MO.EQ.IMODEL(L)) GO TO 140
  130        CONTINUE
             WRITE (6,370)
             IER = 1
  140        NEMT(6,I) = L
             GO TO 180
  150        IF ($T1(J,5).NE.6) GO TO 160
             IF(VALU.NE.0)NORDER = NORDER+1
             GO TO 180
  160        IF ($T1(J,4).EQ.1) GO TO 170
             IF (MO.NE.YES) GO TO 180
             IF ((IFRM.EQ.1.OR.IFRM.EQ.3).AND.$M1(J,1).EQ.1) GO TO 170
             IF (IFRM.EQ.2.AND.$M2(J,1).EQ.1) GO TO 170
             IER = 1
             WRITE (6,380)
             GO TO 180
  170        NOUT = NOUT+1
             IOUT(NOUT) = I
  180   CONTINUE
        IER = 1
        WRITE (6,350)
  190   NEL = I-1
        IF (NOUT.NE.0) GO TO 200
        IER = 1
        WRITE (6,390)
  200   IF (NIN.NE.0) GO TO 210
        IER = 1
        WRITE (6,400)
  210   IC1 = 0
        IC2 = 0
        IC3 = 0
        DO 220 I=1,14
  220   IC1 = IC1+ICOUNT(I)
        DO 230 I=15,17
  230   IC2 = IC2+ICOUNT(I)
        DO 240 I=18,21
more...
```

Fig. D.4.1. (*Continued*)

```
  240 IC3 = IC3+ICOUNT(I)
      IC4 = IC1+IC2
      IF (IC3*IC4.EQ.0) GO TO 250
      IER = 1
      WRITE (6,480)
  250 IF (IER.EQ.1) RETURN
      IFORM = IFRM
      IF(IC2.NE.0)IFORM = 1
      IF(IC3.NE.0)IFORM = 3
      IF(IFORM.NE.1)NORDR = 0
      NORDR = NORDR+ICOUNT(2)+ICOUNT(9)+ICOUNT(21)+2*(ICOUNT(15)+ICOUNT
     $(16))+ICOUNT(17)
      NLAST = 0
      GO TO (260,280,300), IFORM
  260 DO 270 I=1,17
  270 NLAST = NLAST+ICOUNT(I)*$M1(I,5)
      GO TO 300
  280 DO 290 I=1,14
  290 NLAST = NLAST+ICOUNT(I)*$M2(I,5)
  300 NODES = NODES-1
      N = NODES+NLAST
      NLAST = N+1
      NN1 = NLAST
      IF(IFORM.EQ.2)NN1 = NODES+1
      DO 310 I=1,NEL
          DO 310 J=2,5
  310 IF(NEMT(J,I).EQ.0)NEMT(J,I) = NN1
      WRITE (6,340) FORM(IFORM)
      IF (IFORM.EQ.1.OR.IFORM.EQ.3) CALL MNT1
      IF (IFORM.EQ.2) CALL MNT2
      CALL FORMGC
      IF (N.GT.10) RETURN
      WRITE (6,420)
      DO 320 I=1,N
  320 WRITE (6,430) (G(I,J),J=1,N)
      WRITE (6,440)
      DO 330 I=1,N
  330 WRITE (6,430) (C(I,J),J=1,N)
      WRITE (6,450) (B(I),I=1,N)
      RETURN
  340 FORMAT (/A8,' Formulation method')
  350 FORMAT (' ** NUMBER OF ELEMENTS EXCEEDS MAXIMUM ALLOWED')
  360 FORMAT (' ** INVALID DATA CODE')
  370 FORMAT (' ** MODEL NOT DEFINED')
  380 FORMAT (' ** INVALID OUTPUT REQUEST')
  390 FORMAT (' ** NETWORK HAS NO OUTPUTS')
  400 FORMAT (' ** NETWORK HAS NO INPUTS')
  410 FORMAT (T2,'Type',T7,'Name',T12,'Node1 Node2 Node3 Node4 Model/Out
     $put         Value')
  420 FORMAT (' Values in matrix G')
  430 FORMAT (10F7.2)
  440 FORMAT (' Values in matrix C')
  450 FORMAT (' Transpose of RHS vector'/(10F7.2))
  460 FORMAT (A4,6X,6A3,12X,F10.0)
  470 FORMAT (1X,A4,T7,A4,T11,4A6,A9,T51,G15.6)
  480 FORMAT (' ** NETWORK CONTAINS ANALOG AND DIGITAL ELEMENTS')
      END
C**MNT1...1 GRAPH MODIFIED NODAL TABLEAU FORMULATION******************
      SUBROUTINE MNT1
      IMPLICIT INTEGER ($)
      INTEGER ITMP(7)
      COMMON /$$0/ $T1(21,6)
      COMMON /$$1/ $M1(21,5),$T1G(4,21),$T1U(4,11)
      COMMON /$$3/ VMODEL(8,10),IMODEL(10),$TMD(4,21),$IS(3),$JT(3),$JG
     $(3),MODMAX
      COMMON /$$4/ NELMAX,NMAX,NNMAX,NMMAX,MAXIN,MAXOU,MAXSY
      COMMON /$$6/ VALUE(40),NEMT(10,40),NAMES(50),IOUT(10),IN(10),NOUT,
     $NIN,IFORM,NEL,NODES,N,NLAST,NORDR
      WRITE (6,70) (NAMES(I+1),I,I=1,NODES)
      ITMP(5) = NLAST
more...
```

Fig. D.4.1. (*Continued*)

```
      ITMP(6) = NODES
      ITMP(7) = NODES+1
      DO 60 I=1,NEL
          J = NEMT(1,I)
          DO 10 K=1,4
   10     ITMP(K) = NEMT(K+1,I)
          IF ($M1(J,5).EQ.0) GO TO 20
          ITMP(6) = ITMP(6)+1
          ITMP(7) = ITMP(7)+1
          WRITE (6,80) ITMP(6),NEMT(10,I)
   20     IF ($T1(J,5).NE.5) GO TO 30
          NEMT(5,I) = ITMP(6)
          NEMT(7,I) = NLAST
          GO TO 50
   30     DO 40 K=1,4
   40     NEMT(K+5,I) = ITMP($T1G(K,J))
          IF (J.NE.12) GO TO 50
          ITMP(6) = ITMP(6)+1
          WRITE (6,80) ITMP(6),NEMT(10,I)
          ITMP(7) = ITMP(7)+1
   50     CONTINUE
   60 CONTINUE
      RETURN
   70 FORMAT (' User defined node = internal node number'/5(1X,A3,' = ',
     $I2,4X))
   80 FORMAT (' Equation and variable',I3,' correspond to element ',A3)
      END
C**MNT2...2-GRAPH MIXED NODAL TABLEAU FORMULATION***********************
      SUBROUTINE MNT2
      IMPLICIT INTEGER ($)
      INTEGER NN(11),NM(4),NODEV(30,2),NEWN(30,2)
      EQUIVALENCE (I1,NN(1)), (I2,NN(2)), (I3,NN(3)), (I4,NN(4)), (J1,NM
     $(1)), (J2,NM(2)), (J3,NM(3)), (J4,NM(4))
      COMMON /$$0/ $T1(21,6)
      COMMON /$$2/ $M2(14,7),$T2R(14),$T2C(14),$T2G(8,14),$T2U(4,3),$T2S
     $(3,3)
      COMMON /$$6/ VALUE(40),NEMT(10,40),NAMES(50),IOUT(10),IN(10),NOUT,
     $NIN,IFORM,NEL,NODES,N,NLAST,NORDR
C*FORM I AND V GRAPHS, RENUMBER NODES, FIND MNT SIZE (NLAST-1)
      NN(9) = NLAST
      NODES1 = NODES+1
      DO 10 I=1,NODES1
          NODEV(I,1) = I
   10 NODEV(I,2) = I
      DO 30 I=1,NEL
          K = NEMT(1,I)
          L = $M2(K,7)
          IF (L.EQ.0) GO TO 30
          M = $M2(K,6)-1
          DO 20 MM=1,L
   20     CALL SHORT (NEMT(1+$T2S(2,MM+M),I),NEMT(1+$T2S(3,MM+M),I),
     $    NODEV(1,$T2S(1,MM+M)),NODES1)
   30 CONTINUE
      CALL NEWNOD (NODEV(1,1),NEWN(1,1),NODES1,NN(11),NLAST)
      CALL NEWNOD (NODEV(1,2),NEWN(1,2),NODES1,NN(10),NLAST)
      WRITE (6,70) NLAST,NN(11),NN(10),(NAMES(I+1),NEWN(I,1),NEWN(I,2),I
     $=1,NODES)
C*ENTER ELEMENTS INTO MNT
      DO 60 I=1,NEL
          DO 40 J=1,4
              K = NEMT(J+1,I)
              NN(J) = NEWN(K,2)
   40     NN(J+4) = NEWN(K,1)
          K = NEMT(1,I)
          NN(10) = NN(10)+$T2R(K)
          NN(11) = NN(11)+$T2C(K)
          IF ($T2R(K).NE.0) WRITE (6,80) NN(10),NEMT(10,I)
          IF ($T2C(K).NE.0) WRITE (6,90) NN(11),NEMT(10,I)
          DO 50 J=1,8
   50     NEMT(J+1,I) = NN($T2G(J,K))
more...
```

Fig. D.4.1. (*Continued*)

```
   60 CONTINUE
      N = NN(10)
      RETURN
   70 FORMAT (' New ground node is numbered ',I2/' The voltage graph',
     $' has ',I2,' nodes and the current graph ',I2,' nodes '/5X,
     $'User node',T20,'V-Graph node',T40,'I-Graph node'/(9X,A3,T25,I3,
     $T45,I3))
   80 FORMAT (' Equation number ',I2,' corresponds to element ',A3)
   90 FORMAT (' Variable number ',I2,' corresponds to element ',A3)
      END
C**SHORT...CALLED ONLY FROM MNT2...SHORT NODES I AND J
      SUBROUTINE SHORT (I,J,NV,NODES1)
      INTEGER NV(NODES1)
      IF (NV(I).EQ.NV(J)) RETURN
      IF (NV(I).LT.0) GO TO 10
      IF(NV(J).GT.0)NV(J) = -J
      NV(I) = NV(J)
      RETURN
   10 IF (NV(J).LT.0) GO TO 20
      NV(J) = NV(I)
      RETURN
   20 K = NV(I)
      L = NV(J)
      DO 30 M=1,NODES1
   30 IF(NV(M).EQ.K)NV(M) = L
      RETURN
      END
C**NEWNOD...CALLED ONLY FROM MNT2...FIND NEW NODE NUMBERS
      SUBROUTINE NEWNOD (NV,NEW,NODES1,NNEW,NLAST)
      INTEGER NV(NODES1),NEW(NODES1)
      N = NODES1-1
      I = NV(NODES1)
      DO 10 K=1,NODES1
           IF (NV(K).NE.I) GO TO 10
           NV(K) = 0
           NEW(K) = NLAST
   10 CONTINUE
      NNEW = 0
      DO 50 K=1,N
           IF (NV(K)) 20,50,40
   20      NNEW = NNEW+1
           I = NV(K)
           DO 30 L=K,N
                IF (NV(L).NE.I) GO TO 30
                NV(L) = 0
                NEW(L) = NNEW
   30      CONTINUE
           GO TO 50
   40      NNEW = NNEW+1
           NEW(K) = NNEW
   50 CONTINUE
      RETURN
      END
C**FORMGC...FORM MATRICES G, C AND VECTOR B*****************************
      SUBROUTINE FORMGC
      IMPLICIT INTEGER ($)
      COMPLEX*16 Y,RHS,RHST,X,XT
      REAL*8 G,C,B,V
      INTEGER ITMP(4)
      COMMON /$$0/ $T1(21,6)
      COMMON /$$1/ $M1(21,5),$T1G(4,21),$T1U(4,11)
      COMMON /$$2/ $M2(14,7),$T2R(14),$T2C(14),$T2G(8,14),$T2U(4,3),$T2S
     $(3,3)
      COMMON /$$3/ VMODEL(8,10),IMODEL(10),$TMD(4,21),$IS(3),$JT(3),$JG
     $(3),MODMAX
      COMMON /$$4/ NELMAX,NMAX,NNMAX,NMMAX,MAXIN,MAXOU,MAXSY
      COMMON /$$5/ Y(25,25),RHS(25),RHST(25),X(26),XT(26),G(26,26),C(26,
     $26),B(26)
      COMMON /$$6/ VALUE(40),NEMT(10,40),NAMES(50),IOUT(10),IN(10),NOUT,
     $NIN,IFORM,NEL,NODES,N,NLAST,NORDR
more...
```

Fig. D.4.1. (*Continued*)

```
      DO 10 J=1,NLAST
         B(J) = 0.
         DO 10 I=1,NLAST
            C(I,J) = 0.
   10 G(I,J) = 0.
      DO 160 I=1,NEL
         J = NEMT(1,I)
         V = VALUE(I)
         K = $T1(J,5)
         GO TO (20,30,40,90,50,80), K
   20    IF(IFORM.EQ.3.AND.V.EQ.0.DO)V = 1.DO
         CALL SETM (C,NEMT(6,I),V,4)
         GO TO 90
   30    CALL SETM (G,NEMT(6,I),V,4)
         GO TO 90
   40    CALL SETM (B,NEMT(6,I),V,2)
         GO TO 90
C*TRANSISTOR MODEL
   50    L = J-14
         IV = NEMT(6,I)
         L1 = $IS(L)
         L2 = $JT(L)
         L3 = $JG(L)
         DO 70 M=L1,L2
            DO 60 KK=1,4
   60       ITMP(KK) = NEMT($TMD(KK,M)+1,I)
            V = VMODEL(M+1-L1,IV)
            IF (M.LE.L3) CALL SETM (G,ITMP,V,4)
            IF (M.GT.L3) CALL SETM (C,ITMP,V,4)
   70    CONTINUE
         GO TO 160
   80    IF (IFORM.EQ.2.OR.V.EQ.0.) GO TO 90
         CALL SETM (C,NEMT(6,I),V,4)
   90    GO TO (100,130,160), IFORM
  100    L = $M1(J,4)
         IF (L.EQ.0) GO TO 160
         L1 = $M1(J,3)-1
         DO 120 LL=1,L
            DO 110 KK=1,4
  110       ITMP(KK) = NEMT(1+$T1U(KK,L1+LL),I)
  120    CALL SETM (G,ITMP,1.DO,4)
         GO TO 160
  130    L = $M2(J,4)
         IF (L.EQ.0) GO TO 160
         L1 = $M2(J,3)-1
         DO 150 LL=1,L
            DO 140 KK=1,4
  140       ITMP(KK) = NEMT(1+$T2U(KK,L1+LL),I)
  150    CALL SETM (G,ITMP,1.DO,4)
  160 CONTINUE
      IF (IFORM.NE.3) RETURN
      DO 170 I=1,NLAST
  170 G(I,I) = G(I,I)+1.DO
      RETURN
      END
C**SETM...ENTER VALUES...CALLED ONLY FROM FORMGC
      SUBROUTINE SETM (A,K,V,I)
      REAL*8 A(26,1),V
      INTEGER K(1),M(4)
      EQUIVALENCE (M(1),I1), (M(2),I2), (M(3),J1), (M(4),J2)
      DO 10 L=1,4
   10 M(L) = K(L)
      IF (I.EQ.2) GO TO 20
      A(I1,J1) = A(I1,J1)+V
      A(I2,J2) = A(I2,J2)+V
      A(I1,J2) = A(I1,J2)-V
      A(I2,J1) = A(I2,J1)-V
      RETURN
   20 A(I1,1) = A(I1,1)+V
      A(I2,1) = A(I2,1)-V
more...
```

Fig. D.4.1. (*Continued*)

```
      RETURN
      END
C**SVALID--CHECK FOR VALIDITY OF SENSITIVITY OR SYMBOLIC REQUEST*******
      SUBROUTINE SVALID (N1,N2,M1,M2)
      IMPLICIT INTEGER ($)
      INTEGER    N1(M1),N2(1),BLANK/' '/
      COMMON /$$0/ $T1(21,6)
      COMMON /$$1/ $M1(21,5),$T1G(4,21),$T1U(4,11)
      COMMON /$$2/ $M2(14,7),$T2R(14),$T2C(14),$T2G(8,14),$T2U(4,3),$T2S
     $(3,3)
      COMMON /$$4/ NELMAX,NMAX,NNMAX,NMMAX,MAXIN,MAXOU,MAXSY
      COMMON /$$6/ VALUE(40),NEMT(10,40),NAMES(50),IOUT(10),IN(10),NOUT,
     $NIN,IFORM,NEL,NODES,N,NLAST,NORDR
      M2 = 0
      DO 70 I=1,M1
          K = N1(I)
          IF (K.EQ.BLANK) RETURN
          DO 10 L=1,NEL
              IF (K.EQ.NEMT(10,L)) GO TO 20
   10     CONTINUE
          WRITE (6,90) K
          GO TO 70
   20     M = NEMT(1,L)
          GO TO (30,40,30), IFORM
   30     IF ($M1(M,2).EQ.0) GO TO 60
          GO TO 50
   40     IF ($M2(M,2).EQ.0) GO TO 60
   50     M2 = M2+1
          N2(M2) = L
          GO TO 70
   60     WRITE (6,80) $T1(M,1)
   70 CONTINUE
      RETURN
   80 FORMAT (' ** INVALID SENSITIVITY OR SYMBOLIC REQUEST',' FOR ELEMEN
     $T TYPE ',A4)
   90 FORMAT (' ** ELEMENT NAME',A5,' UNDEFINED')
      END
C**AC...FREQUENCY DOMAIN ANALYSIS AND SENSITIVITY**********************
      SUBROUTINE AC (LL,NFREQ,MODE,FSTART,FEND,NSENS,ISENS)
      IMPLICIT REAL*8 (A-H,O-Z),INTEGER($)
      COMPLEX*16 Y,RHS,RHST,X,XT,DET,COUT(10),CSENS(10),S,CDEXP,AAC,BBC,
     $ADJ
      REAL*8 G,C,B,AA(2),BB(2)
      REAL VALUE
      INTEGER ISENS(10),IFR(2)
      EQUIVALENCE (AAC,AA(1)), (BBC,BB(1))
      DATA IFR/'F','W'/,IBLANK/' '/,PI2/6.283185307179586D0/,DEGR/57.
     $29577951308232D0/
      COMMON /$$0/ $T1(21,6)
      COMMON /$$5/ Y(25,25),RHS(25),RHST(25),X(26),XT(26),G(26,26),C(26,
     $26),B(26)
      COMMON /$$6/ VALUE(40),NEMT(10,40),NAMES(50),IOUT(10),IN(10),NOUT,
     $NIN,IFORM,NEL,NODES,N,NLAST,NORDR
      IF (MODE.EQ.1) WRITE (6,150)
      IF (LL.EQ.1) WRITE (6,110)
      IF (LL.EQ.2) WRITE (6,120)
      IPR = MIN0(4,MAX0(NSENS,NOUT))
      WRITE (6,160) IFR(LL),(NEMT(10,IOUT(I)),I=1,NOUT)
      IF (NSENS.NE.0) WRITE (6,170) (NEMT(10,ISENS(I)),I=1,NSENS)
      IF (MODE.EQ.0) WRITE (6,130) (IBLANK,I=1,IPR)
      IF (MODE.NE.0) WRITE (6,140) (IBLANK,I=1,IPR)
      WRITE (6,200) (IBLANK,I=1,IPR)
      PIZ = 1.D0
      IF(LL.EQ.1)PIZ = PI2
      NP01 = NFREQ+1
      DELF = (FEND-FSTART)/NFREQ
      DO 10 J=1,N
   10 RHS(J) = B(J)
      X(NLAST) = (0.D0,0.D0)
      IF (NSENS.EQ.0) GO TO 30
more...
```

Fig. D.4.1. (*Continued*)

```
      XT(NLAST) = (0.D0,0.D0)
      DO 20 J=1,N
   20 RHST(J) = (0.D0,0.D0)
      K = IOUT(1)
      K1 = NEMT(9,K)
      K2 = NEMT(8,K)
      ADJ = (1.D0,0.D0)
   30 DO 100 I=1,NPO1
         F = FSTART+(I-1)*DELF
         W = F*PIZ
         S = DCMPLX(0.D0,W)
         IF(IFORM.EQ.3)S = CDEXP(-S)
         CALL FORMY (S)
         CALL LU (Y,N,RHS,X,DET,1,0)
         CALL LU (Y,N,RHS,X,DET,3,0)
         DO 40 J=1,NOUT
            K = IOUT(J)
   40    COUT(J) = X(NEMT(8,K))-X(NEMT(9,K))
         IF (MODE.EQ.0) GO TO 60
         ADJ = 1.D0/COUT(1)
         DO 50 J=1,NOUT
            AAC = COUT(J)
            BB(1) = 20.D0*DLOG10(CDABS(AAC))
            BB(2) = DATAN2(AA(2),AA(1))*DEGR
   50    COUT(J) = BBC
   60    WRITE (6,180) F,(COUT(J),J=1,NOUT)
         IF (NSENS.EQ.0) GO TO 100
C*COMPUTE SENSITIVITIES
         RHST(K1) = ADJ
         RHST(K2) = -ADJ
         CALL LU (Y,N,RHST,XT,DET,4,0)
         DO 70 J=1,NSENS
            K = ISENS(J)
            CSENS(J) = (XT(NEMT(6,K))-XT(NEMT(7,K)))*(X(NEMT(8,K))-X
     $      (NEMT(9,K)))
            K = NEMT(1,K)
   70    IF(K.EQ.2.OR.K.EQ.9)CSENS(J) = CSENS(J)*S
         IF (MODE.EQ.0) GO TO 90
         DO 80 J=1,NSENS
            AAC = CSENS(J)
            AA(1) = AA(1)*8.685889638065037D0
            AA(2) = AA(2)*DEGR
   80    CSENS(J) = AAC
   90    WRITE (6,190) (CSENS(J),J=1,NSENS)
  100 CONTINUE
      RETURN
  110 FORMAT (' Frequency in cycles per second')
  120 FORMAT (' Frequency in radians ')
  130 FORMAT (T20,4(A1,'Re',10X,'Im',9X))
  140 FORMAT (T18,4(A1,'Mag',9X,'Phase',6X))
  150 FORMAT (' Outputs and sensitivities in db and degrees')
  160 FORMAT (/T15,'Outputs at elements'/A9,(T7,4A24))
  170 FORMAT (T15,'Differential sensitivity of first output with ',
     $'respect to'/(T7,4A24))
  180 FORMAT (/G10.3,' Resp',(T15,1P8D12.3))
  190 FORMAT (T11,' Sens',(T15,1P8D12.3))
  200 FORMAT (T17,4(A1,20('-'),3X))
      END
C**FORMY...SERVICE ROUTINE TO FORM Y=G+S*C******************************
      SUBROUTINE FORMY (S)
      IMPLICIT INTEGER ($)
      COMPLEX*16 Y,RHS,RHST,X,XT,S
      REAL*8 G,C,B
      REAL VALUE
      COMMON /$$5/ Y(25,25),RHS(25),RHST(25),X(26),XT(26),G(26,26),C(26,
     $26),B(26)
      COMMON /$$6/ VALUE(40),NEMT(10,40),NAMES(50),IOUT(10),IN(10),NOUT,
     $NIN,IFORM,NEL,NODES,N,NLAST,NORDR
      DO 10 J=1,N
         DO 10 I=1,N
more...
```

Fig. D.4.1. (*Continued*)

```
   10 Y(I,J) = G(I,J)+S*C(I,J)
      RETURN
      END
C**SYMBOL...SYMBOLIC ANALYSIS WITH UPTO 5 VARIABLES 10TH ORDER**********
      SUBROUTINE SYMBOL (IVAR,NSYM,NVAR)
      IMPLICIT REAL*8 (A-H,O-Z),INTEGER($)
      COMPLEX*16 Y,RHS,RHST,X,XT,S(11),CO(11),F(6,6,6),XA(26),AA,BB,
     $DETMAT,BC(6,32),AC(6,32),BA(25),NGRAD(32),DGRAD(32),PROD(32),COEFF
     $(11),DCONJG
      REAL*8 G,C,B,VAR(5)
      REAL VALUE
      INTEGER NVAR(1),NL(6),NK(6),IPOWER(12),KVAR(6),ISC(10),IOU(10)
      COMMON /$$5/ Y(25,25),RHS(25),RHST(25),X(26),XT(26),G(26,26),C(26,
     $26),B(26)
      COMMON /$$6/ VALUE(40),NEMT(10,40),NAMES(50),IOUT(10),IN(10),NOUT,
     $NIN,IFORM,NEL,NODES,N,NLAST,NORDR
      INTEGER    IPW(3)/'s','s','1/z'/,BLANK/' '/
      IF (NSYM.EQ.0) GO TO 230
      XA(NLAST) = (0.D0,0.D0)
      NP1 = NORDR+1
      DO 10 J=1,NP1
   10 IPOWER(J) = J-1
      NS1 = NSYM+1
      DO 20 I=1,6
   20 KVAR(I) = BLANK
      DO 30 II=1,NSYM
           I = NS1-II
           ISC(II) = NVAR(I)
           IOU(II) = NVAR(I)
           VAR(II) = VALUE(NVAR(I))
   30 KVAR(II) = NEMT(10,NVAR(II))
      NCOL = 2**NSYM
      ISC(NS1) = IN(1)
      IOU(NS1) = IOUT(1)
      K1 = NP1/2+1
      CALL COORD (S,NP1)
      DO 40 JJ=1,N
   40 BA(JJ) = (0.D0,0.D0)
C*PERFORM ANALYSIS AT DIFFERENT POINTS
      DO 160 IFR=1,K1
           CALL FORMY (S(IFR))
           CALL LU (Y,N,BA,XA,DETMAT,1,0)
           CALL LU (Y,N,BA,XA,DETMAT,2,0)
C*FIND MATRIX F
           DO 50 IK=1,NS1
                KL = ISC(IK)
                AA = (1.D0,0.D0)
                IF(NEMT(1,KL).EQ.2.OR.NEMT(1,KL).EQ.9)AA = AA*S(IFR)
                BA(NEMT(6,KL)) = AA
                BA(NEMT(7,KL)) = -AA
                CALL LU (Y,N,BA,XA,AA,3,0)
                BA(NEMT(6,KL)) = (0.D0,0.D0)
                BA(NEMT(7,KL)) = (0.D0,0.D0)
                DO 50 L=1,NS1
                     KL = IOU(L)
   50      F(L,IK,1) = XA(NEMT(8,KL))-XA(NEMT(9,KL))
C*FIND DERIVATIVES AT THIS FREQUENCY
           NGRAD(1) = F(NS1,NS1,1)*DETMAT
           DGRAD(1) = DETMAT
           II = 1
           PROD(1) = DETMAT
           L = 1
           NK(NS1) = 1
           DO 60 I=1,NSYM
   60      NK(I) = 0
   70      NK(L) = 1
           DO 80 NN=L,NSYM
                IF (NK(NN+1).EQ.1) GO TO 90
   80      CONTINUE
   90      II = II+1
more...
```

Fig. D.4.1. (*Continued*)

```
           IB = NS1-NN
           IP = NS1-L
           IS = IP+1
           AA = F(IP,IP,IB)
           PROD(IS) = PROD(IB)*AA
           DGRAD(II) = PROD(IS)
           NGRAD(II) = PROD(IB)*(AA*F(NS1,NS1,IB)-F(NS1,IP,IB)*F(IP,NS1,
     $     IB))
           IF(CDABS(AA).GE.1.D-14)AA = 1.D0/AA
           DO 100 J=IS,NS1
                BB = AA*F(IP,J,IB)
                DO 100 I=IS,NS1
  100      F(I,J,IS) = F(I,J,IB)-F(I,IP,IB)*BB
           DO 110 L=1,NSYM
                IF (NK(L).EQ.0) GO TO 70
  110      NK(L) = 0
           IF (IVAR.EQ.1) GO TO 140
C*SOLVE TRIANGULAR SYSTEM
           K2 = 1
           DO 130 I=1,NSYM
                PI = VAR(NS1-I)
                IF (PI.EQ.0.D0) GO TO 130
                K3 = 2*K2
                DO 120 K11=1,NCOL,K3
                     K4 = K11+K2-1
                     DO 120 K=K11,K4
                          NGRAD(K) = NGRAD(K)-PI*NGRAD(K+K2)
  120           DGRAD(K) = DGRAD(K)-PI*DGRAD(K+K2)
  130      K2 = 2*K2
  140      DO 150 I=1,NCOL
                AC(IFR,I) = DGRAD(I)
  150      BC(IFR,I) = NGRAD(I)
  160 CONTINUE
C*USE DFT TO FIND COEFFICIENTS
      IF (IVAR.EQ.1) WRITE (6,240)
      IF (IVAR.NE.1) WRITE (6,250)
      WRITE (6,260) NEMT(10,ISC(NS1)),NEMT(10,IOU(NS1)),IPW(IFORM)
      II = 1
      L = 1
      DO 170 I=1,6
           NL(I) = NS1
  170 NK(I) = NS1
      NK(NS1) = NS1+1
  180 DO 190 J=1,K1
           BB = AC(J,II)
           AA = BC(J,II)
           IF(J.NE.1)CO(NP1+2-J) = DCONJG(AA)+(0.D0,1.D0)*DCONJG(BB)
  190 CO(J) = AA+(0.D0,1.D0)*BB
      CALL DFTC (S,COEFF,CO,NP1)
      CALL SCREEN (COEFF,NP1,1.D-10)
      NST = NP1
      NEN = 0
      DO 200 J=1,NP1
           IF (CDABS(COEFF(J)).EQ.0.D0) GO TO 200
           NST = MIN0(NST,J)
           NEN = MAX0(NEN,J)
  200 CONTINUE
      IF (NST.LE.NEN) WRITE (6,270) (KVAR(NL(J)),J=1,5),(IPOWER(J),COEFF
     $(J),J=NST,NEN)
      NK(L) = L
      II = 1+II
      IF (II.GT.NCOL) RETURN
      DO 210 J=1,NSYM
  210 NL(J) = NK(J)
      DO 220 L=1,NSYM
           IF (NK(L).EQ.NS1) GO TO 180
  220 NK(L) = NS1
      GO TO 180
  230 CALL POLE (1,0,IPOWER)
      RETURN
more...
```

Fig. D.4.1. (*Continued*)

```
  240 FORMAT (/' Symbolic function in terms of variations'/)
  250 FORMAT (/' Symbolic function in terms of variable elements'/)
  260 FORMAT (/' Input at ',A4,',    Output at ',A4//' Variable',T24,
     $'Power',T35,'Numerator',T60,'Denominator'/' Elements',T24,'of ',A3
     $//)
  270 FORMAT (/1X,5A4,(T25,I3,T30,1PD17.6,T55,1PD17.6))
      END
C**POLE**FIND POLES,ZEROS,Q,OMEGA AND THEIR SENSITIVITIES***************
C*EXTERNAL ROUTINES: ZRPOLY AND EIGZF FROM IMSL
      SUBROUTINE POLE (MODE,NSENS,ISENS)
      IMPLICIT REAL*8 (A-H,O-Z),INTEGER($)
      COMPLEX*16 Y,RHS,RHST,X,XT,S1(11),DET,AA,BB,DCONJG,CSENS(10),COEFF
     $(11),ROOTS(26,2),CO(11),DE
      REAL*8  G,C,B,AI(11,2),CMAG(10),WK(26),EPS/1D-5/,EPS1/1D5/,
     $        QSENS(10),OMEGAS(10),QROOT(10),OMEGAR(10),Z(1),BETA(26),GP
     $(2)
      REAL  VALUE,POLEZ(2)/'Zero','Pole'/
      INTEGER   ISENS(10),IPOWER(11),NDEG(2),IPW(3)/'s','s','1/z'/
      COMMON /$$5/ Y(25,25),RHS(25),RHST(25),X(26),XT(26),G(26,26),C(26,
     $26),B(26)
      COMMON /$$6/ VALUE(40),NEMT(10,40),NAMES(50),IOUT(10),IN(10),NOUT,
     $NIN,IFORM,NEL,NODES,N,NLAST,NORDR
      X(NLAST) = (0.D0,0.D0)
      DO 10 I=1,N
   10 RHS(I) = B(I)
      K = IOUT(1)
      K3 = NEMT(8,K)
      K4 = NEMT(9,K)
         IF (MODE.NE.1) GO TO 90
C*EVALUATE NUMERATOR/DENOMINATOR COEFFECIENTS BY INTERPOLATION
      NP1 = NORDR+1
      DO 20 I=1,NP1
   20 IPOWER(I) = I-1
      K1 = NP1/2+1
      CALL COORD (S1,NP1)
      DO 30 IFR=1,K1
         CALL FORMY (S1(IFR))
         CALL LU (Y,N,RHS,X,DET,1,0)
         CALL LU (Y,N,RHS,X,DET,2,0)
         CALL LU (Y,N,RHS,X,DET,3,0)
         AA = DET*(X(K3)-X(K4))
         IF(IFR.NE.1)CO(NP1+2-IFR) = DCONJG(AA)+(0.D0,1.D0)*DCONJG(DET)
   30 CO(IFR) = AA+(0.D0,1.D0)*DET
      CALL DFTC (S1,COEFF,CO,NP1)
      CMAX = 0.D0
      DO 40 I=1,NP1
   40 CMAX = DMAX1(CMAX,CDABS(COEFF(I)))
      CALL SCREEN (COEFF,NP1,CMAX*1.D-12)
      WRITE (6,320) IPW(IFORM),(IPOWER(I),COEFF(I),I=1,NP1)
C*EVALUATE POLES AND ZEROS
      NP2 = NP1+1
      DO 50 I=1,NP1
         AI(NP2-I,1) = DREAL(COEFF(I))
   50 AI(NP2-I,2) = DIMAG(COEFF(I))
      DO 80 K=1,2
         DO 60 I=1,NP1
            IF (AI(I,K).NE.0.D0) GO TO 70
   60    CONTINUE
   70    NDEG(K) = NP1-I
         IF (I.NE.NP1) CALL ZRPOLY (AI(I,K),NDEG(K),ROOTS(1,K),IER)
   80 GP(K) = AI(I,K)
      GO TO 140
C*USE QZ ALGORITHM TO FIND THE ROOTS
   90 NP1 = N+1
      DO 100 I=1,N
         C(I,NP1) = 0.D0
         C(NP1,I) = 0.D0
         G(I,NP1) = B(I)
  100 G(NP1,I) = 0.D0
      C(NP1,NP1) = 0.D0
more...
```

Fig. D.4.1. (*Continued*)

```
      G(NP1,K3) = -1.D0
      G(NP1,K4) = 1.D0
      G(NP1,NP1) = 0.D0
      NN = NP1
      DO 130 K=1,2
           CALL EIGZF (G,26,C,26,NN,0,ROOTS(1,K),BETA,Z,1,WK,IER)
           WRITE (6,300) POLEZ(K),(I,ROOTS(I,K),BETA(I),I=1,NN)
           CALL FORMGC
           DE = 1.D0
           NFIN = 0
           DO 120 I=1,NN
                IF (DABS(BETA(I)).LE.EPS) GO TO 110
                NFIN = NFIN+1
                ROOTS(NFIN,K) = -ROOTS(I,K)/BETA(I)
                DE = DE*BETA(I)
                GO TO 120
  110           DE = DE*ROOTS(I,K)
  120      CONTINUE
           NN = N
           NDEG(K) = NFIN
  130 GP(K) = DE
  140 GAIN = GP(1)/GP(2)
      WRITE (6,310) GAIN
      DO 160 KK=1,2
           NPZ = NDEG(KK)
           IF (NPZ.EQ.0) GO TO 160
           IF (IFORM.NE.3) WRITE (6,270) POLEZ(KK),POLEZ(KK)
           IF (IFORM.EQ.3) WRITE (6,280) POLEZ(KK),POLEZ(KK)
           DO 150 I=1,NPZ
                WR = CDABS(ROOTS(I,KK))
                QR = 1.D75
                IF(DABS(DREAL(ROOTS(I,KK))).NE.0.D0)QR = -.5D0*WR/DREAL
     $          (ROOTS(I,KK))
                IF (IFORM.NE.3) WRITE (6,290) I,ROOTS(I,KK),QR,WR
  150      IF (IFORM.EQ.3) WRITE (6,290) I,ROOTS(I,KK)
  160 CONTINUE
      IF (NSENS.EQ.0) RETURN
C*COMPUTE SENSITIVITIES
      XT(NLAST) = (0.D0,0.D0)
      DO 170 I=1,N
  170 RHST(I) = (0.D0,0.D0)
      RHST(K4) = (1.D0,0.D0)
      RHST(K3) = (-1.D0,0.D0)
      DO 220 KK=1,2
           NPZ = NDEG(KK)
           IF (NPZ.EQ.0) GO TO 220
           IF (IFORM.NE.3) WRITE (6,230) POLEZ(KK),POLEZ(KK),POLEZ(KK)
           IF (IFORM.EQ.3) WRITE (6,240) POLEZ(KK),POLEZ(KK),POLEZ(KK)
           DO 210 I=1,NPZ
                AA = ROOTS(I,KK)
                R = CDABS(AA)
                IF (R.LT.EPS.OR.R.GT.EPS1) GO TO 210
                IF (DIMAG(AA).LT.-EPS) GO TO 210
                CALL FORMY (AA)
                CALL LU (Y,N,RHS,X,DET,1,KK-1)
                CALL LU (Y,N,RHS,X,DET,2*(KK-1)+3,0)
                CALL LU (Y,N,RHST,XT,DET,2*(KK-1)+4,0)
                BB = (0.D0,0.D0)
                DO 190 II=1,N
                     DET = (0.D0,0.D0)
                     DO 180 JJ=1,N
  180                DET = DET+C(II,JJ)*X(JJ)
  190           BB = BB-DET*XT(II)
                QK = 1.D75
                IF(DREAL(AA).NE.0.D0)QK = -R/DREAL(AA)*.5D0
                DO 200 J=1,NSENS
                     K = ISENS(J)
                     CSENS(J) = (XT(NEMT(6,K))-XT(NEMT(7,K)))*(X(NEMT(8,K))
     $               -X(NEMT(9,K)))/BB
                     IF(CDABS(CSENS(J)).LE.EPS)CSENS(J) = (0.D0,0.D0)
more...
```

Fig. D.4.1. (*Continued*)

```
                 K = NEMT(1,K)
                 IF(K.EQ.2.OR.K.EQ.9)CSENS(J) = CSENS(J)*AA
                 DET = CSENS(J)*DCONJG(AA)
                 QSENS(J) = 1.D75
                 IF(DREAL(AA).NE.0.D0)QSENS(J) = -.5D0*DIMAG(AA)/DREAL
     $           (AA)**2/R*DIMAG(DET)
  200          OMEGAS(J) = DREAL(DET)/R
               IF (IFORM.NE.3) WRITE (6,250) I,(NEMT(10,ISENS(J)),CSENS(J
     $         ),QSENS(J),OMEGAS(J),J=1,NSENS)
               IF (IFORM.EQ.3) WRITE (6,260) I,(NEMT(10,ISENS(J)),CSENS(J
     $         ),J=1,NSENS)
  210       CONTINUE
  220 CONTINUE
      RETURN
  230 FORMAT (/1X,A4,', Q and omega differential sensitivities'/1X,A4,
     $' no',T12,'var',T25,A4,'-sens',T49,'Q-sens',T64,'W-sens'/19X,22
     $('-'))
  240 FORMAT (/1X,A4,' differential sensitivities'/1X,A4,' no',T12,'var'
     $,T25,A4,'-sens'/19X,22('-'))
  250 FORMAT (I5,(T12,A3,1X,2G13.3,2X,2G15.3))
  260 FORMAT (I5,(T12,A3,1X,2G13.3))
  270 FORMAT (/1X,A4,'s, Q and omega values'/T5,'I',T17,A4,'(I)',T45,
     $'Q(I)',T59,'Omega(I)'/8X,23('-'))
  280 FORMAT (1X,A4,'s in the 1/z domain'/T5,'I',T17,A4,'(I)'/8X,23('-')
     $)
  290 FORMAT (I5,2G15.6,T40,G15.6,T55,G15.6)
  300 FORMAT (/' QZ algorithm for ',A4,'s (see chapter 7)'/T5,'I',T17,
     $'ALPHA(I)',T45,'BETA(I)'/8X,23('-')/(I5,2G15.6,5X,G15.6))
  310 FORMAT (/' The network function gain =',G20.6)
  320 FORMAT (/' Network function coeffecients'//T9,'Power',T20,
     $'Numerator',T45,'Denominator'/T9,'of ',A4//(T10,I3,T15,1PD17.8,T40
     $,1PD17.8))
      END
C**SCREEN**ZERO OUT SMALL COEFFECIENTS. USED IN POLE AND SYMBOL
      SUBROUTINE SCREEN (C,N,EPS)
      REAL*8 C(1),EPS,DABS
      NN = 2*N
      DO 10 I=1,NN
   10 IF(DABS(C(I)).LT.EPS)C(I) = 0.D0
      RETURN
      END
C**COORD...CALLED FROM SYMBOL & POLE...FINDS POINTS ON UNIT CIRCLE
      SUBROUTINE COORD (X,NP1)
C*SUBROUTINE COORD  CALCULATES THE COORDINATES OF NP1 POINTS X(I)
C*UNIFORMLY DISTRIBUTED ON THE UNIT CIRCLE
      IMPLICIT REAL*8 (A-H,O-Z)
      COMPLEX*16 CDEXP,X(NP1),DCMPLX
      Z = 6.283185307179586D0/DFLOAT(NP1)
      DO 10 I=1,NP1
   10 X(I) = CDEXP(DCMPLX(0.D0,Z*DFLOAT(I-1)))
      RETURN
      END
C**DFTC...CALLED FROM SYMBOL & POLE...DFT TO FIND COEFFICIENTS
      SUBROUTINE DFTC (X,A,F,NP1)
C*SUBROUTINE DFTC CALCULATES THE COMPLEX DISCRETE FOURIER TRANSFORM
C*COEFFICIENTS A(I) FROM GIVEN COMPLEX FUNCTION VALUES F(I).
C*IT REQUIRES COMPLEX COORDINATES X(I) OF POINTS UNIFORMLY DISTRI-
C*BUTED ON THE UNIT CIRCLE. THE POINTS ARE SUPPLIED BY THE SUBROU-
C*TINE COORD. NP1 IS THE NUMBER OF POINTS X(I)
      COMPLEX*16 SUM,X(NP1),F(NP1),A(NP1)
      NP2 = NP1+1
      DO 20 LL=1,NP1
           SUM = (0.D0,0.D0)
           J = NP2-LL
           DO 10 I=1,NP1
   10      SUM = SUM+F(I)*X(1+MOD(J*(I-1),NP1))
   20 A(LL) = SUM/NP1
      RETURN
      END
C**TRAN...TRANSIENT ANALYSIS BY NUMERICAL INVERSION OF LAPLACE TRANSFORM
more...
```

Fig. D.4.1. (*Continued*)

```
      SUBROUTINE TRAN
      IMPLICIT REAL*8 (A-H,O-Z),INTEGER($)
      COMPLEX*16 Y,RHS,RHST,XX,XT,S,KP(6),Z(6),DZ,CSOL(26)
      REAL*8 G,C,B,X(26),XO(26),SOLN(10),IC(4),RES(2)
      REAL VALUE
      INTEGER    NN(4),IMDT(2),BLANK/' '/
      EQUIVALENCE (DZ,DZ1), (IC(1),H), (IC(2),TEND)
      DATA Z/(1.D0,1.D0),(11.83009373916819D0,1.593753005885813D0),(11.
     $22085377939519D0,4.792964167565669D0),(9.933383722175002D0,8.
     $033106334266296D0),(7.781146264464616D0,11.36889164904993D0),(4.
     $234522494797D0,14.95704378128156D0)/,KP/(0.D0,-2.D0),(16286.
     $62368050479D0,-139074.7115516051D0),(-28178.11171305162D0,74357.
     $58237274176D0),(14629.74025233142D0,-19181.80818501836D0),(-2870.
     $418161032078D0,1674.109484084304D0),(132.1659412474876D0,17.
     $47674798877164D0)/,INIT/'IC'/,ITIM/'TIME'/,RES/'Impulse','Step'/,
     $IMDT/'0/2','8/10'/
      COMMON /$$5/ Y(25,25),RHS(25),RHST(25),XX(26),XT(26),G(26,26),C(26
     $,26),B(26)
      COMMON /$$6/ VALUE(40),NEMT(10,40),NAMES(50),IOUT(10),IN(10),NOUT,
     $NIN,IFORM,NEL,NODES,N,NLAST,NORDR
      INITO = 0
      IO = 0
      TIME = 0.D0
      DO 10 I=1,NLAST
   10 XO(I) = 0.D0
      X(NLAST) = (0.D0,0.D0)
   20 READ (5,240) ICODE,METHOD,IRESP,NN,IC
      IF (ICODE.EQ.ITIM) GO TO 80
      IF (ICODE.NE.INIT) GO TO 70
C*INITIAL CONDITIONS
      IF (INITO.EQ.0) WRITE (6,220)
      DO 60 I=1,4
          K = NN(I)
          IF (K.EQ.BLANK) GO TO 60
          DO 30 LL=1,NEL
              IF (K.EQ.NEMT(10,LL)) GO TO 40
   30     CONTINUE
          WRITE (6,200) K
          GO TO 60
   40     L = NEMT(1,LL)
          IF (L.EQ.2.OR.L.EQ.9) GO TO 50
          WRITE (6,210) K
          GO TO 60
   50     WRITE (6,230) K,IC(I)
          K = LL
          V = VALUE(K)*IC(I)
          IF(L.EQ.9)XO(NEMT(6,K)) = -V
          IF (L.NE.2) GO TO 60
          XO(NEMT(6,K)) = XO(NEMT(6,K))+V
          XO(NEMT(7,K)) = XO(NEMT(7,K))-V
   60 CONTINUE
      INITO = 1
      GO TO 20
   70 WRITE (6,250) ICODE
      STOP
   80 IF (IRESP.NE.0) GO TO 100
      DO 90 I=1,N
   90 XO(I) = XO(I)+B(I)
  100 N1 = 1
      N2 = 1
      WRITE (6,260) IMDT(METHOD+1),RES(IRESP+1),(NEMT(10,IOUT(I)),I=1,
     $NOUT)
      IF (METHOD.EQ.0) GO TO 110
      N1 = 2
      N2 = 6
  110 IF (TIME.GT.TEND) RETURN
      IF (IO.EQ.0) GO TO 140
      DO 130 I=1,N
          SUM = 0.D0
          DO 120 J=1,N
more...
```

Fig. D.4.1. (*Continued*)

```
  120       SUM = SUM+X(J)*C(I,J)
  130 X0(I) = SUM
  140 DO 150 I=1,N
  150 X(I) = 0.D0
      DO 180 I=N1,N2
          S = Z(I)/H
          DO 160 J=1,N
              RHS(J) = X0(J)
  160     IF(IRESP.EQ.1)RHS(J) = B(J)/S+X0(J)
          IF (METHOD.EQ.0.AND.I0.NE.0) GO TO 170
          CALL FORMY (S)
          CALL LU (Y,N,RHS,CSOL,DZ,1,0)
  170     CALL LU (Y,N,RHS,CSOL,DZ,3,0)
          S = KP(I)/H
          DO 180 J=1,N
              DZ = S*CSOL(J)
  180 X(J) = X(J)-DZ1
      I0 = 1
      DO 190 J=1,NOUT
  190 SOLN(J) = X(NEMT(8,IOUT(J)))-X(NEMT(9,IOUT(J)))
      TIME = TIME+H
      WRITE (6,270) TIME,(SOLN(J),J=1,NOUT)
      GO TO 110
  200 FORMAT (' ** INVALID ELEMENT NAME ',A4)
  210 FORMAT (' ** INVALID ELEMENT TYPE FOR INITIAL CONDITIONS ',A4)
  220 FORMAT (/' Initial conditions'/' Element',T15,'Init. Condn.')
  230 FORMAT (1X,A5,T15,1PD11.2)
  240 FORMAT (A4,2I2,2X,4A3,18X,4F10.0)
  250 FORMAT (' ***COMMAND ERROR IN TRAN*** ',A4)
  260 FORMAT (/A5,' approximation',A10,' Response'/'    Time',(T9,5A13))
  270 FORMAT (1PD12.3,(T13,1P5D13.5))
      END
C**LU DECOMPOSITION AND SOLUTION ROUTINE*******************************
      SUBROUTINE LU (Y,N,B,X,DET,JOB,IPOL)
C*Y IS N X N MATRIX OF ABSOLUTE DIMENSION 25
C*JOB 1  FACTOR Y INTO LU WITH PARTIAL PIVOTING
C*    2  FIND THE DETERMINANT AND SET IN DET
C*    3  SOLVE Y.X = B USING FACTORS OF Y
C*    4  SOLVE Y'X = B USING FACTORS OF Y
C*    5  SOLVE U.X = E(N). REQUIRED IN POLE SENSITIVITY
C*    6  SOLVE L'X = E(N). REQUIRED IN POLE SENSITIVITY
C*       HERE E(N) IS THE N'TH UNIT VECTOR
C*ROUTINE USES A PRIMITIVE FORM OF SPARSE PROCESSING TO REDUCE
C*COMPUTATIONS. THE 'MAGNITUDE' IS TAKEN AS ABS(REAL)+ABS(IMAG)
C*DURING THE SEARCH FOR THE PIVOT. IPZ = 1 WHEN FACTORING AT POLE
      COMPLEX*16 Y(25,25),B(N),X(N),TC,TC1,DET
      REAL*8  T(2),TR,TI,P,P0,PMAX,PR,ZEROM/1.D-14/
      INTEGER NZ(25,25),NU(25),PVT(25)
      EQUIVALENCE (TC,T(1),TR), (T(2),TI)
      NM1 = N-1
      IF (JOB.LE.4) GO TO 20
      DO 10 K=1,NM1
   10 X(K) = (0.D0,0.D0)
      X(N) = (1.D0,0.D0)
   20 GO TO (30,120,140,210,180,250), JOB
   30 DO 100 K=1,NM1
          KP1 = K+1
C*LOCATE NONZEROS IN COL K & FIND MAX
          NR = K-1
          P0 = 0.D0
          NRMAX = 0
          DO 40 I=K,N
              TC = Y(I,K)
              P = DABS(TR)+DABS(TI)
              IF (P.EQ.0.D0) GO TO 40
              NR = NR+1
              NZ(NR,K) = I
              IF (P0.GE.P) GO TO 40
              P0 = P
              NRMAX = NR
more...
```

Fig. D.4.1. (*Continued*)

```
   40      CONTINUE
           IF (NRMAX.EQ.0) GO TO 110
           PVT(K) = NZ(NRMAX,K)
           IF(NZ(K,K).NE.K)NZ(NRMAX,K) = NZ(K,K)
           NZ(K,K) = NR
           IF (PO.LE.ZEROM) WRITE (6,290) PO,K
C*INTERCHANGE ROWS FROM PIVOT COLUMN ON IF REQUIRED
           KPVT = PVT(K)
           IF (KPVT.EQ.K) GO TO 60
           DO 50 J=K,N
              TC = Y(K,J)
              Y(K,J) = Y(KPVT,J)
   50      Y(KPVT,J) = TC
C*FIND SPARSE REPRESENTATION OF PIVOT ROW
   60      NC = K
           TC1 = 1.D0/Y(K,K)
           Y(K,K) = TC1
           DO 70 J=KP1,N
              TC = Y(K,J)
              P = DABS(TR)+DABS(TI)
              IF (P.EQ.0.D0) GO TO 70
              Y(K,J) = TC*TC1
              NC = NC+1
              NZ(K,NC) = J
   70      CONTINUE
           NU(K) = NC
           IF (NC.EQ.K.OR.NR.EQ.K) GO TO 90
C*PERFORM PIVOT STEP
           DO 80 JJ=KP1,NC
              J = NZ(K,JJ)
              TC = Y(K,J)
              DO 80 II=KP1,NR
                 I = NZ(II,K)
   80      Y(I,J) = Y(I,J)-Y(I,K)*TC
   90      CONTINUE
  100 CONTINUE
      TC = Y(N,N)
      P = DABS(TR)+DABS(TI)
      IF (P.LE.ZEROM.AND.IPOL.EQ.0) WRITE (6,290) P,N
      Y(N,N) = 1.D0/Y(N,N)
      RETURN
  110 WRITE (6,300) K
      RETURN
C*FIND DETERMINANT
  120 PR = 1.D0
      DET = Y(N,N)
      DO 130 K=1,NM1
         IF(PVT(K).NE.K)PR = -PR
  130 DET = DET*Y(K,K)
      DET = PR/DET
      RETURN
C*FORWARD SOLUTION
  140 DO 150 K=1,N
  150 X(K) = B(K)
      DO 170 K=1,NM1
         KPVT = PVT(K)
         TC = X(KPVT)
         IF(KPVT.NE.K)X(KPVT) = X(K)
         P = DABS(TR)+DABS(TI)
         IF (P.EQ.0.D0) GO TO 170
         TC = TC*Y(K,K)
         NR = NZ(K,K)
         IF (NR.EQ.K) GO TO 170
         KP1 = K+1
         DO 160 II=KP1,NR
            I = NZ(II,K)
  160    X(I) = X(I)-Y(I,K)*TC
  170 X(K) = TC
      X(N) = X(N)*Y(N,N)
C*BACK SUBSTITUTION
more...
```

Fig. D.4.1. (*Continued*)

```
  180 DO 200 KK=1,NM1
          K = N-KK
          NC = NU(K)
          IF (NC.EQ.K) GO TO 200
          KP1 = K+1
          TC = X(K)
          DO 190 JJ=KP1,NC
              J = NZ(K,JJ)
  190         TC = TC-Y(K,J)*X(J)
          X(K) = TC
  200 CONTINUE
      RETURN
C*TRANSPOSE FORWARD SOLUTION
  210 DO 220 K=1,N
  220 X(K) = B(K)
      DO 240 K=1,NM1
          TC = X(K)
          P = DABS(TR)+DABS(TI)
          IF (P.EQ.0.D0) GO TO 240
          NC = NU(K)
          IF (NC.EQ.K) GO TO 240
          KP1 = K+1
          DO 230 JJ=KP1,NC
              J = NZ(K,JJ)
  230         X(J) = X(J)-TC*Y(K,J)
  240 CONTINUE
C*TRANSPOSE BACK SOLVE
      X(N) = X(N)*Y(N,N)
  250 DO 280 KK=1,NM1
          K = N-KK
          NR = NZ(K,K)
          TC = X(K)
          IF (NR.EQ.K) GO TO 270
          KP1 = K+1
          DO 260 II=KP1,NR
              I = NZ(II,K)
  260         TC = TC-Y(I,K)*X(I)
  270         KPVT = PVT(K)
          X(K) = X(KPVT)
  280 X(KPVT) = TC*Y(K,K)
      RETURN
  290 FORMAT (' ***RESULTS UNRELIABLE*** PIVOT=',G15.4,' AT STEP',I3)
  300 FORMAT (' ***SINGULAR MATRIX*** ALL ZERO PIVOTS IN COL ',I3)
      END
```

Fig. D.4.1. (*Continued*)

APPENDIX E
Sparse Matrix Solver

The program in this appendix solves systems of equations that are large, sparse, structurally symmetric and require no pivoting for numerical stability. It contains routines to handle data stored as linked lists, a minimum local fill-in ordering routine, a symbolic factorization routine, and routines for numeric factorization and solution. Interface routines are provided for user convenience. The symbolic factorization routine SFACT and the numeric factorization routine NFACT are based on the Yale sparse code developed by Eisenstat et al. while the rest depend on theory given in Section 2.10.

The user interacts with the package through three interface routines whose function and arguments are as follows:

(a) INTF1(IJA,NZA,N,W,IW,IWMAX,JUMAX,IER)

On input: IJA(1,K),IJA(2,K),K=1,2. . .NZA contain the location (I,J) of the Kth nonzero in the matrix.

N is the dimension of the matrix.

W is an integer work vector of dimension IW. Note that IW must be larger than 8N+2(NZA)+1.

On output: W(1),W(2). . .W(IWMAX) contain internal pointer information and should not be changed by the user.

JUMAX contains the size of the upper triangle of the factored matrix.

IER is an error indicator which is set to 1 if the routine fails due to insufficient work space. Remedy is to increase dimension of W and try again.

The routine determines the new equation and variable sequence and performs a symbolic factorization to determine the structure of the upper triangle of the factored matrix. It is called once for a given matrix structure.

Comment: In network applications IER=1 is very unusual. It can arise in finite element solution of two and three dimensional transistor models. For very large problems (say over 1000 nodes) a minimum degree preprocessor and logic based on cliques in graphs should be added to the ordering routine.

(b) INTF2(A,W,DUL,IER)

On input: A(1), . . . ,A(NZA) contain the nonzeros of A with row/column indices as defined in IJA (see INTF1 description).

W is the integer work vector produced by INTF1.

DUL is a real work vector of minimum dimension N+2(JUMAX) where JUMAX was found by INTF1.

On output: DUL contains the factors of A.

IER is an error indicator which is set to 1 if a very small pivot is found on the diagonal.

This routine is called each time the values in A are changed.

(c) INTF3(DUL,B,W,X,R)

On input: DUL is the vector as produced by INTF2.

B is of dimension N and contains the right-hand side.

W is the integer work vector produced by INTF1.

R is an N-dimensional real work vector.

On output: X, a real vector of dimension N, contains the solution.

This routine is called when the right-hand side is changed.

Comment: B and X may be the same variable in the calling program. In such case the right-hand-side vector is destroyed.

EXAMPLE E.1. The same problem provided in the program code consists of the two dimensional resistive grid shown in Fig. E.1. The sample main problem handles grids with up to 100 total nodes. A test was run on a 10 × 10 grid, i.e., 100 total nodes. The total CPU time

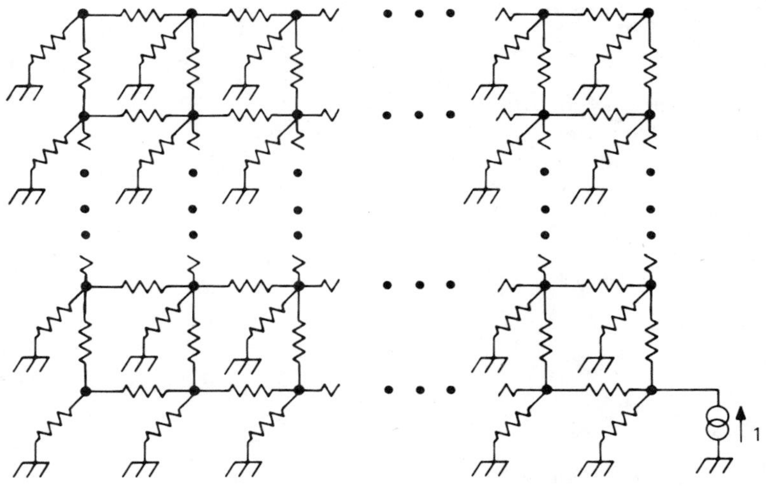

Fig. E.1. Sample test problem in sparse matrix solver. Network has NX nodes in *x*-orientation and NY nodes in *y* orientation. All resistors have unit value.

was 0.4 sec on an IBM4341 computer. Of this, 50% was spent in the ordering routines, 20% each in the symbolic and numeric factorizations, and 4% in the solution routines. There were 460 nonzeros in the admittance matrix and 1146 in its factors. There was thus a nearly threefold growth in the off-diagonal nonzeros. This is a particularly severe test problem for the ordering routine; such large growth in nonzeros occurs seldom in typical networks. The factorization required 4000 operations and the solution 698. These should be compared with the 333 thousand and 10 thousand operations which would be required by a dense solver.

Our production version of this package contains enhancements that speed up the ordering by a factor of 2, provides for the case when only a few entries of the solution are required and has options for generating interpretive and machine codes.

```
C*SPARSE PACKAGE TEST PROBLEM GENERATOR
C*TWO DIMENSIONAL RESISTIVE GRID WITH (NX,NY) NODES IN X AND Y
C*DIRECTIONS. EACH NODE IS CONNECTED TO AT MOST FOUR OTHER NODES
C*ADJACENT TO IT AND THE GROUND PLANE BY RESISTORS OF UNIT VALUE.
C*UNIT EXCITATION IS APPLIED TO NODE (NX,NY). IN THE ADMITTANCE MATRIX,
C*INTERNAL NODES HAVE VALUE 5, BOUNDARY NODES HAVE VALUE 4 AND CORNER
C*NODES HAVE VALUE 3 ON THE DIAGONAL. OFF DIAGONAL ENTRIES ARE ALL -1.
C*NUMBER OF NODES IS NX*NY AND NUMBER OF NONZEROS OFF THE DIAGONAL IS
C*4*NX*NY-2*(NX+NY). NX AND NY ARE .LE. 10 IN TEST PROGRAMME
C*
      REAL A(460),B(100),R(100),X(100),DUL(1200)
      INTEGER  IJA(2,460),W(2000),IW/2000/
   10 READ (5,*) NX,NY
      IF (NX.EQ.0) STOP
      N = NX*NY
      DO 20 L=1,N
        A(L) = 5.
        IJA(1,L) = L
   20 IJA(2,L) = L
      K = N-NY
      DO 30 I=1,NY
        A(I) = 4
   30 A(K+I) = 4.
      K = 1
      L = N+1
      DO 40 J=1,NX
        A(K) = 4.
        A(L-K) = 4.
   40 K = K+NY
      A(1) = 3.
      A(NY) = 3.
      A(N) = 3.
      A(N-NY+1) = 3.
C*DIAGONAL ENTRIES ARE NOW SET
      NZA = 5*N-2*(NX+NY)
      NP1 = N+1
      DO 50 L=NP1,NZA
   50 A(L) = -1.
      M = N+1
      NY1 = NY-1
      DO 60 J=1,NX
        L = 1+(J-1)*NY
        DO 60 I=1,NY1
          IJA(1,M) = L
          IJA(2,M+1) = L
          L = L+1
          IJA(2,M) = L
          IJA(1,M+1) = L
   60 M = M+2
      NX1 = NX-1
      DO 70 J=1,NX1
        L = 1+(J-1)*NY
        DO 70 I=1,NY
          IJA(1,M) = L
          IJA(2,M+1) = L
          IJA(2,M) = L+NY
          IJA(1,M+1) = L+NY
          L = L+1
   70 M = M+2
C*MATRIX IS NOW SET
      DO 80 I=1,N
   80 B(I) = 0.
      B(N) = 1.
      WRITE (6,140) NX,NY,N,NZA
      CALL INTF1 (IJA,NZA,N,W,IW,IWMAX,JUM,IER)
      IF (IER.EQ.1) GO TO 10
      NZR = N+2*JUM
      WRITE (6,120) NZR
      CALL INTF2 (A,W,DUL,IER)
      IF (IER.EQ.1) GO TO 10
more...
```

```
      CALL INTF3 (DUL,B,W,X,R)
C*SULUTION IS NOW STORED IN VECTOR X. PERFORM VERIFICATION
      DO 90 I=1,N
   90 R(I) = 0.
      DO 100 II=1,NZA
         I = IJA(1,II)
         J = IJA(2,II)
  100 R(I) = R(I)+A(II)*X(J)
      SUM = 0.
      DO 110 I=1,N
  110 SUM = SUM+(B(I)-R(I))**2
      WRITE (6,130) SUM
      GO TO 10
  120 FORMAT (' FACTORED MATRIX HAS',I5,' NONZEROS')
  130 FORMAT (' RESIDUAL SUM OF SQUARES =',G20.6)
  140 FORMAT (' GRID HAS',I5,' NODES IN X AND',I5,' NODES IN Y DIRECTION
     $ '/' MATRIX HAS DIMENSION',I5,' AND',I5,' INITIAL NONZEROS')
      END
C**INTF1*****************************************************************
      SUBROUTINE INTF1 (IJA,NZA,N,W,IW,IWMAX,JUMAX,IER)
C*THIS ROUTINE IS THE INTERFACE TO THE ORDERING AND SYMBOLIC
C*FACTORIZATION ROUTINES
C*ON INPUT
C*    N=DIMENSION OF THE MATRIX
C*    NZA=NUMBER OF NONZEROS IN THE MATRIX
C*    IJA=MATRIX OF DIMENSION 2,NZA. IT CONTAINS THE (I,J) INDICES OF
C*         THE NONZEROS
C*    W=AN INTEGER WORK VECTOR OF DIMENSION IW WHICH IS AT LEAST
C*      8*N+2*NZA+1
C*ON OUTPUT
C*    THE FIRST IWMAX ENTRIES OF W CONTAIN INTERNAL POINTER INFORMATION
C*    AND SHOULD NOT BE CHANGED BY USER. JUMAX IS THE NUMBER OF ENTRIES
C*    IN THE UPPER TRIANGULAR MATRIX U.
C*
      INTEGER IJA(2,NZA),W(IW),SMAX,FILLS,Z,P,V,S,U
      COMMON/S$P$/NZ,NA,JUM,KA,IU,JU,I1,I2,I3,I4
      SMAX = (IW-8*N-1)/2
      IF (SMAX.LT.NZA) GO TO 10
      NZ = NZA
      NA = N
      LAST = 1
      NEXT = LAST+N+1
      FILLS = NEXT+2*N
      IT1 = FILLS+N
      LT1 = IT1+N
      LT2 = LT1+N
      Z = LT2+N
      P = Z+N
      V = P+SMAX
      CALL LIST (W(P),W(V),SMAX,IJA,NZA,S,N)
      NZRO = (S-1-N)/2
      CALL FILL (W(P),W(V),W(FILLS),W(Z),W(NEXT),W(LAST),N)
      CALL ORDER (W(P),W(V),W(NEXT),W(LAST),W(FILLS),W(IT1),W(LT1),W(LT2
     $),W(Z),N,S,IFILL,IER)
      IF (IER.NE.0) GO TO 10
      KA = N+1
      IU = KA+NZA
      JU = IU+N
      JUM = NZRO+IFILL
      JUMAX = JUM
      I1 = JU+JUM
      I2 = I1+N
      IWMAX = I2+N-1
      IF (IWMAX.GT.IW) GO TO 10
      CALL SFACT (IJA,NZA,W(1),W(KA),N,W(IU),W(JU),W(I1),W(I2),W(I2),W
     $(I2))
      IER = 0
      RETURN
   10 WRITE (6,20)
      IER = 1
more...
```

```
      RETURN
   20 FORMAT (' ** INSUFFICIENT SPACE IN ARRAY W **')
      END
C**INTF2***************************************************************
      SUBROUTINE INTF2 (A,W,DUL,IER)
C*INTERFACE ROUTINE TO PERFORM NUMERIC FACTORIZATION
C*ON INPUT
C*     A CONTAINS THE NONZEROS IN THE MATRIX
C*     W IS THE WORK VECTOR AS GENERATED FROM INTF1
C*ON OUTPUT
C*     DUL OF MINIMUM DIMENSION N+2*JUMAX CONTAINS THE DECOMPOSITION
C*     IER=1 IN CASE FACTORIZATION FAILS DUE TO SMALL PIVOT
C*
      REAL A(1),DUL(1)
      INTEGER W(1),U
      COMMON/S$P$/NZA,N,JUM,KA,IU,JU,IL,JL,U,L
      IDUL = N+2*JUM
      DO 10 I=1,IDUL
   10 DUL(I) = 0.
      DO 20 I=1,NZA
        K = W(N+I)
   20 DUL(K) = DUL(K)+A(I)
      U = N+1
      L = U+JUM
      CALL NFACT (W(IU),W(JU),N,DUL(1),DUL(U),DUL(L),W(IL),W(IL),W(JL),
     $IER)
      RETURN
      END
C**INTF3***************************************************************
      SUBROUTINE INTF3 (DUL,B,W,X,R)
C*INTERFACE ROUTINE FOR SOLUTION
C*ON INPUT
C*     DUL IS THE DECOMPOSITION AS PRODUCED BY INTF2
C*     B IS THE RIGHT HAND SIDE VECTOR
C*     W IS THE WORK VECTOR AS PRODUCED BY INTF1
C*     R IS A REAL WORK VECTOR OF DIMENSION N
C*ON OUTPUT
C*     X CONTAINS THE SOLUTION
C*
      REAL DUL(1),B(1),X(1),R(1)
      INTEGER W(1),U
      COMMON/S$P$/NZA,N,JUM,KA,IU,JU,IL,JL,U,L
      DO 10 I=1,N
   10 R(W(I)) = B(I)
      CALL NSOLV (DUL(1),DUL(U),DUL(L),W(IU),W(JU),N,R)
      DO 20 I=1,N
   20 X(I) = R(W(I))
      RETURN
      END
C**LIST****************************************************************
      SUBROUTINE LIST (P,V,SMAX,IJA,NZA,S,N)
C*PREPARE INITIAL LINKED LIST IN P AND V FROM INFORMATION IN IJA
      INTEGER P(1),V(1),SMAX,S,IJA(2,NZA),Q
      DO 10 I=1,N
        P(I) = I
   10 V(I) = 0
      S = N+1
C*CREATE I,J ENTRY IN UPPER TRIANGLE AFTER CHECKING FOR DUPLICATION
      DO 40 KK=1,NZA
        I = IJA(1,KK)
        J = IJA(2,KK)
        IF (I.EQ.J) GO TO 40
        L = MIN0(I,J)
        M = MAX0(I,J)
        K = L
   20   Q = K
        K = P(K)
        IF (V(K)-M) 30,40,20
   30   P(S) = K
        P(Q) = S
```

more...

```
         V(S) = M
         V(L) = V(L)+1
         S = S+1
   40 CONTINUE
C*FILL IN THE LOWER TRIANGLE AND FORM LINKS ON FREE SPACE
      NM1 = N-1
      DO 60 II=1,NM1
         I = N-II
         L = I
   50    L = P(L)
         IF (L.EQ.I) GO TO 60
         J = V(L)
         V(J) = V(J)+1
         P(S) = P(J)
         P(J) = S
         V(S) = I
         S = S+1
         GO TO 50
   60 CONTINUE
      DO 70 I=S,SMAX
   70 P(I) = I+1
      P(SMAX) = 0
      RETURN
      END
C**FILL*****************************************************************
      SUBROUTINE FILL (P,V,FILLS,Z,NEXT,LAST,N)
C*COMPUTE INITIAL FILLS AND ORDER THROUGH LINKED LISTS LAST,NEXT
      INTEGER P(1),V(1),FILLS(N),NEXT(1),LAST(1),SUM,SUM1,VL,F
      LOGICAL Z(N)
      NP1 = N+1
      NM1 = N-1
      DO 10 I=1,N
         Z(I) = .TRUE.
         NEXT(I+N) = NP1
   10 FILLS(I) = V(I)*(V(I)-1)/2
      DO 80 M=1,NM1
         IF (FILLS(M).EQ.0) GO TO 80
         L = M
         IND = 0
   20    L = P(L)
         IF (L.EQ.M) GO TO 30
         VL = V(L)
         IF (VL.LT.M) GO TO 20
         IND = IND+1
         NEXT(IND) = VL
         GO TO 20
   30    IF (IND.LE.1) GO TO 80
         DO 40 I=2,IND
   40    Z(NEXT(I)) = .FALSE.
         IND1 = IND-1
         SUM = 0
         DO 70 II=1,IND1
            I = NEXT(II)
            SUM1 = 0
            L = I
   50       L = P(L)
            IF (L.EQ.I) GO TO 60
            VL = V(L)
            IF (Z(VL)) GO TO 50
            SUM1 = SUM1+1
            FILLS(VL) = FILLS(VL)-1
            GO TO 50
   60       FILLS(I) = FILLS(I)-SUM1
            SUM = SUM+SUM1
   70    Z(NEXT(II+1)) = .TRUE.
         FILLS(M) = FILLS(M)-SUM
   80 CONTINUE
      DO 90 KK=1,N
         K = NP1-KK
         F = FILLS(K)
more...
```

```
        F = MIN0(F,NM1)+NP1
        LAST(K) = F
        NEXT(K) = NEXT(F)
        NEXT(F) = K
   90 LAST(NEXT(K)) = K
      RETURN
      END
C**ORDER***********************************************************
      SUBROUTINE ORDER (P,V,NEXT,LAST,FILLS,IT1,LT1,LT2,Z,N,S,IFILL,IER)
C*MINIMUM LOCAL FILL-IN REORDERING ROUTINE FOR STRUCTURALLY SYMMETRIC
C*MATRICES STORED AS LINKED LISTS P AND V. FILLS CONTAINS INITIAL
C*FILL-IN INFORMATION AND IS UPDATED AT EACH STEP. ON OUTPUT, THE
C*FIRST N ENTRIES OF ARRAY LAST CONTAIN THE COMPLEMENT TO THE
C*PERMUTATION VECTOR.
      INTEGER P(1),V(1),NEXT(1),LAST(1),IT1(N),FILLS(N),S
     $,PVT,P1,POINT,VL,ROW,COL,F,SUM,SUM1
      LOGICAL Z(N),LT1(N),LT2(N)
      IFILL = 0
      NP1 = N+1
      NM1 = N-1
      NP2 = 2*N
      NP3 = NP2-1
      LABEL = 0
      NEND = 0
      POINT = NP1
      DO 10 I=1,N
        LT1(I) = .FALSE.
        LT2(I) = .FALSE.
   10 Z(I) = .FALSE.
C*FIND THE NEXT PIVOT
   20 IF (POINT.EQ.NP2) GO TO 50
   30 DO 40 M=POINT,NP3
        IF (NEXT(M).NE.NP1) GO TO 80
   40 CONTINUE
   50 P1 = NEXT(NP2)
   60 PVT = P1
      F = FILLS(PVT)
   70 P1 = NEXT(P1)
      IF (P1.EQ.NP1) GO TO 90
      IF (FILLS(P1)-F) 60,70,70
   80 PVT = NEXT(M)
      POINT = M
C*PROCESS PIVOT ROW
   90 INDEX = 0
      IF (V(PVT).EQ.0) GO TO 120
      L = PVT
  100 L = P(L)
      IF (L.EQ.PVT) GO TO 120
      VL = V(L)
      IF (Z(VL)) GO TO 100
      IF (V(VL).NE.NM1-LABEL) GO TO 110
      CALL DELROW (P,VL,S,NEXT,LAST,N-NEND,Z)
      NEND = NEND+1
      GO TO 100
  110 INDEX = INDEX+1
      IT1(INDEX) = VL
      V(VL) = V(VL)-1
      GO TO 100
  120 LABEL = LABEL+1
      CALL DELROW (P,PVT,S,NEXT,LAST,LABEL,Z)
      IF (LABEL+NEND.EQ.N) RETURN
      IF (INDEX.EQ.0) GO TO 30
      F = FILLS(PVT)
      IFILL = IFILL+F
      INDEX1 = INDEX
      IF (F.EQ.0) GO TO 260
C*DETERMINE FILL-INS AND ADJUST FILL
      INDEX2 = INDEX-1
      DO 130 M=1,INDEX
  130 LT1(IT1(M)) = .TRUE.
more...
```

```
      DO 230 M=1,INDEX2
         ROW = IT1(M)
C*PROCESS ROW
         L = ROW
  140    I = L
  150    L = P(I)
         IF (L.EQ.ROW) GO TO 170
         IF (Z(V(L))) GO TO 160
         LT2(V(L)) = .TRUE.
         GO TO 140
  160    P(I) = P(L)
         P(L) = S
         S = L
         GO TO 150
  170    M1 = M+1
         SUM = 0
         DO 200 M4=M1,INDEX
           COL = IT1(M4)
           IF (LT2(COL)) GO TO 200
C*FILL AT (ROW,COL)
           F = F-1
           SUM1 = NEND
           L = COL
  180      L = P(L)
           IF (L.EQ.COL) GO TO 190
           VL = V(L)
           IF (.NOT.LT2(VL)) GO TO 180
           FILLS(VL) = FILLS(VL)-1
           SUM1 = SUM1+1
           IF (LT1(VL)) GO TO 180
           LT1(VL) = .TRUE.
           INDEX1 = INDEX1+1
           IT1(INDEX1) = VL
           GO TO 180
  190      SUM = SUM+V(ROW)-SUM1
           FILLS(COL) = FILLS(COL)+V(COL)-SUM1
           CALL INSERT (P,V,ROW,COL,S,IER)
           IF (IER.NE.0) GO TO 280
           LT2(COL) = .TRUE.
  200    CONTINUE
C*RESET ROW
         L = ROW
  210    L = P(L)
         IF (L.EQ.ROW) GO TO 220
         LT2(V(L)) = .FALSE.
         GO TO 210
  220    FILLS(ROW) = FILLS(ROW)+SUM
         IF (F.EQ.0) GO TO 240
  230 CONTINUE
  240 DO 250 M=1,INDEX1
  250 LT1(IT1(M)) = .TRUE.
C*ADJUST FILLS LINKED LIST
  260 KT=NEND+INDEX-1
      DO 270 M=1,INDEX1
        M1 = IT1(M)
        IF(M.LE.INDEX)FILLS(M1) = FILLS(M1)-V(M1)+KT
        NEXT(LAST(M1)) = NEXT(M1)
        LAST(NEXT(M1)) = LAST(M1)
        F = MIN0(FILLS(M1),NM1)+NP1
        LAST(M1) = F
        NEXT(M1) = NEXT(F)
        NEXT(F) = M1
        LAST(NEXT(M1)) = M1
  270 POINT = MIN0(POINT,F)
      GO TO 20
  280 WRITE (6,290) LABEL
      RETURN
  290 FORMAT (' ***INSUFFICIENT FREE SPACE AT PIVOT STEP***',I5)
      END
C**DELROW************************************************************
more...
```

```
      SUBROUTINE DELROW (P,I,S,NEXT,LAST,LABEL,Z)
C*DELETE ROW I FROM THE LINKED LIST
      INTEGER P(1),S,T,NEXT(1),LAST(1)
      LOGICAL Z(1)
      T = P(I)
      P(I) = S
      S = T
      NEXT(LAST(I)) = NEXT(I)
      LAST(NEXT(I)) = LAST(I)
      LAST(I) = LABEL
      Z(I) = .TRUE.
      RETURN
      END
C**INSERT**********************************************************
      SUBROUTINE INSERT (P,V,I,J,S,IER)
C*INSERT A NEW ENTRY AT (I,J)
C*IER=1 IF THERE IS NO MORE SPACE IN FREE LIST
      INTEGER P(1),V(1),S,T
      IER = 1
      T = P(S)
      IF (T.EQ.0) RETURN
      P(S) = P(I)
      V(S) = J
      P(I) = S
      S = P(T)
      IF (S.EQ.0) RETURN
      P(T) = P(J)
      P(J) = T
      V(T) = I
      V(I) = V(I)+1
      V(J) = V(J)+1
      IER = 0
      RETURN
      END
C**SFACT***********************************************************
      SUBROUTINE SFACT (IJA,NZA,ORDERC,KA,N,IU,JU,JL,IL,Q,Z)
C*SYMBOLIC FACTORIZATION ROUTINE DETERMINES STRUCTURE OF U AND PUTS
C*NEW LOCATIONS OF A INTO ARRAY KA. ARRAYS IL, Q AND Z CAN BE THE
C*SAME IN THE CALLING PROGRAMME.
      INTEGER IJA(2,NZA),KA(1),ORDERC(N),IU(N),JU(1),JL(N),IL(N),Q(N),QM
     $,VJ
      LOGICAL Z(N),NULROW
      NP1 = N+1
      NM1 = N-1
      JP = 1
      DO 10 K=1,N
        IU(K) = 0
        JL(K) = 0
   10 Z(K) = .FALSE.
      N3 = 2*NZA
C*LINK NONZEROS OF A THROUGH KA
      DO 30 M=1,NZA
        I1 = IJA(1,M)
        J1 = IJA(2,M)
        IF (I1.EQ.J1) GO TO 20
        I = MIN0(ORDERC(I1),ORDERC(J1))+1
        KA(M) = IU(I)
        IU(I) = M
        GO TO 30
   20   KA(M) = ORDERC(I1)
   30 CONTINUE
      IU(1) = 1
C*MAIN LOOP
      DO 180 K=1,NM1
        JS = JP
        M = IU(K+1)
   40   IF (M.EQ.0) GO TO 60
        VJ = MAX0(ORDERC(IJA(2,M)),ORDERC(IJA(1,M)))
        IF (Z(VJ)) GO TO 50
        Z(VJ) = .TRUE.
more...
```

```
      JU(JP) = VJ
      JP = JP+1
 50   M = KA(M)
      GO TO 40
 60   I = K
 70   I = JL(I)
      IF (I.EQ.0) GO TO 90
      JMIN = IL(I)+1
      IL(I) = JMIN
      JMAX = IU(I+1)-1
      IF (JMIN.GT.JMAX) GO TO 70
      DO 80 J=JMIN,JMAX
        VJ = JU(J)
        IF (Z(VJ)) GO TO 80
        Z(VJ) = .TRUE.
        JU(JP) = VJ
        JP = JP+1
 80   CONTINUE
      GO TO 70
C*WE NOW HAVE ROW K OF U
 90   JE = JP-1
      IF (JS.GT.JE) GO TO 170
C*ORDER COLUMN INDICES BY LINKING THROUGH Q. REPLACE FOR LARGE N
      Q(K) = NP1
      DO 110 J=JS,JE
        VJ = JU(J)
        QM = K
 100    M = QM
        QM = Q(QM)
        IF (QM.LT.VJ) GO TO 100
        Q(M) = VJ
 110  Q(VJ) = QM
      I = K
      DO 120 J=JS,JE
        I = Q(I)
 120  JU(J) = I
      DO 130 J=JS,JE
 130  Q(JU(J)) = J
      M = IU(K+1)
 140  IF (M.EQ.0) GO TO 150
C*LOCATE ENTRIES OF A IN D-U-L
      I1 = ORDERC(IJA(1,M))
      J1 = ORDERC(IJA(2,M))
      J = MAX0(I1,J1)
      MM = Q(J)+N
      IF(I1.GT.J1)MM = -MM
      MT = M
      M = KA(M)
      KA(MT) = MM
      GO TO 140
 150  DO 160 J=JS,JE
 160  Z(JU(J)) = .FALSE.
      IF (JS.EQ.JE) GO TO 170
      I = JU(JS)
      JL(K) = JL(I)
      JL(I) = K
      IL(K) = JS
 170  IU(K+1) = JP
 180 CONTINUE
     JP = JP-1
     DO 190 I=1,NZA
 190 IF(KA(I).LT.0)KA(I) = -KA(I)+JP
     RETURN
     END
C**NFACT***************************************************************
     SUBROUTINE NFACT (IU,JU,N,D,U,L,IND,IL,JL,IER)
C*NUMERIC FACTORIZATION OF STRUCTURALLY SYMMETRIC MATRIX
C*IND AND IL CAN BE THE SAME VECTOR IN THE CALLING PROGRAMME.
     REAL D(N),L(1),U(1),LKI,EPS/1.E-6/
     INTEGER IU(N),JU(1),IND(N),IL(N),JL(N)
more...
```

```
      LOGICAL NULROW
      DO 10 K=1,N
   10 JL(K) = 0
      DO 80 K=1,N
        IF (K.EQ.N) GO TO 30
        IF (NULROW(K,IU,JS,JE)) GO TO 30
        DO 20 J=JS,JE
   20   IND(JU(J)) = J
   30   NXTI = JL(K)
        DK = D(K)
   40   I = NXTI
        IF (I.EQ.0) GO TO 60
        NXTI = JL(I)
        ILI = IL(I)
        UKI = U(ILI)
        LKI = L(ILI)
        DK = DK-UKI*LKI
        JMIN = ILI+1
        JMAX = IU(I+1)-1
        IF (JMIN.GT.JMAX) GO TO 40
        DO 50 J=JMIN,JMAX
          JJ = IND(JU(J))
          U(JJ) = U(JJ)-U(J)*LKI
   50   L(JJ) = L(JJ)-L(J)*UKI
        IL(I) = JMIN
        J = JU(JMIN)
        JL(I) = JL(J)
        JL(J) = I
        GO TO 40
   60   IF (ABS(DK).LT.EPS) GO TO 90
        DK = 1./DK
        D(K) = DK
        IF (K.EQ.N) GO TO 80
        IF (JS.GT.JE) GO TO 80
        DO 70 J=JS,JE
   70   U(J) = U(J)*DK
        IL(K) = JS
        I = JU(JS)
        JL(K) = JL(I)
        JL(I) = K
   80 CONTINUE
      IER = 0
      RETURN
   90 WRITE (6,100) K
      IER = 1
      RETURN
  100 FORMAT (' *** ZERO PIVOT AT STEP',I5)
      END
C**NSOLV*****************************************************************
      SUBROUTINE NSOLV (D,U,L,IU,JU,N,X)
C*NUMERIC FORWARD AND BACK SUBSTITUTION ROUTINE
      REAL D(N),L(1),U(1),X(N),T
      INTEGER IU(N),JU(1)
      LOGICAL NULROW
C*FORWARD SUBSTITUTION
      NM1 = N-1
      DO 20 I=1,NM1
        IF (X(I).EQ.0.) GO TO 20
        IF (NULROW(I,IU,JS,JE)) GO TO 20
        T = X(I)*D(I)
        X(I) = T
        DO 10 J=JS,JE
   10   X(JU(J)) = X(JU(J))-T*L(J)
   20 CONTINUE
      X(N) = X(N)*D(N)
C*BACK SUBSTITUTION
      DO 40 II=1,NM1
        I = N-II
        IF (NULROW(I,IU,JS,JE)) GO TO 40
        T = X(I)
more...
```

```
         DO 30 J=JS,JE
   30    T = T-X(JU(J))*U(J)
         X(I) = T
   40 CONTINUE
      RETURN
      END
C**NULROW*****************************************************************
      LOGICAL FUNCTION NULROW(K,IU,JS,JE)
      INTEGER IU(1)
      JS = IU(K)
      JE = IU(K+1)-1
      NULROW = JS.GT.JE
      RETURN
      END
```

Sample output for NX=10, NY=10 follows ......

```
 GRID HAS   10 NODES IN X AND   10 NODES IN Y DIRECTION
 MATRIX HAS DIMENSION  100 AND  460 INITIAL NONZEROS
 FACTORED MATRIX HAS 1146 NONZEROS
 RESIDUAL SUM OF SQUARES =        0.235031E-11
```

APPENDIX F
Selected Mathematical Topics

F.1. VECTOR SPACES

The totality of vectors that can be constructed by scalar multiplication and vector addition from the vectors in a given set is called a *vector space*. A set of vectors that is capable of generating the totality of vectors by these operations is said to *span* the space. If the set consists of the least number of vectors that span the space, it is called a *basis* for the space. The number of vectors in the basis is called the *dimensionality* of the space. Thus n basis vectors generate an n-dimensional space. Any subset of r basis vectors forms the basis of an r-dimensional *subspace*. A necessary and sufficient condition that a set of n vectors be confined to a subspace is that the set be *linearly dependent*, i.e., there exist coefficients c_i, not all zero, such that

$$\sum_{i=1}^{n} c_i \mathbf{x}_i = \mathbf{0}$$

Otherwise the set is *linearly independent*. Any r linearly independent vectors can serve as a basis of the subspace.

F.2. MATRICES AND SETS OF EQUATIONS

In matrix algebra, relations and operations are defined for rectangular arrays of numbers called *matrices*. We assume that the reader is familiar with the elementary concepts of matrix addition, multiplication, transposition, inversion etc. We will only provide a quick review of material that is often glossed over in a first course on linear algebra.

The vector space generated by the rows of a matrix $\mathbf{A}$ is called the *row space* and that by the columns, the *column space*. The dimensionality of these two spaces is the same and is called the *rank of* $\mathbf{A}$. The sufficient condition that a system of n nonhomogenous linear equations in n unknowns

$$\mathbf{Ax} = \mathbf{b}$$

have a unique solution

$$\mathbf{x} = \mathbf{A}^{-1}\mathbf{b}$$

is that $\mathbf{A}$ be *nonsingular*, i.e., rank $[\mathbf{A}] = n$. This condition, however, is not necessary. When the rank of $\mathbf{A}$ is $r < n$, the system has a solution if it satisfies the *consistency condition*

$$\text{rank } [\mathbf{A}|\mathbf{b}] = \text{rank } [\mathbf{A}].$$

Thus the system is consistent if and only if $\mathbf{b}$ is subject to the same linear dependencies as the rows of $\mathbf{A}$. If the equations are permuted such that the first r are linearly independent, then in partitioned form

$$\begin{array}{c} r \\ n-r \end{array}\overset{\begin{array}{cc} r & n-r \end{array}}{\begin{bmatrix} \mathbf{A}_{11} & \mathbf{A}_{12} \\ \mathbf{A}_{21} & \mathbf{A}_{22} \end{bmatrix}} \begin{bmatrix} \mathbf{x}_1 \\ \mathbf{x}_2 \end{bmatrix} = \begin{bmatrix} \mathbf{b}_1 \\ \mathbf{b}_2 \end{bmatrix}$$

and the consistency condition implies

$$\mathbf{x}_1 = \mathbf{A}_{11}^{-1}\mathbf{b}_1 - \mathbf{A}_{11}^{-1}\mathbf{A}_{12}\mathbf{x}_2.$$

Thus if the equations are consistent, we get a solution in the sense that any values arbitrarily assigned to $\mathbf{x}_2$ uniquely determine $\mathbf{x}_1$. Because $\mathbf{x}_2$ is arbitrary, there is an infinity of solutions, each corresponding to a point in the $(n - r)$ dimensional space of $\mathbf{x}_2$. This space is called the *solution space.*

F.3. DETERMINANTS

The *determinant* of an $n \times n$ matrix $\mathbf{A}$, $|\mathbf{A}|$, is defined by the Laplace expansion

$$|\mathbf{A}| = \sum (-1)^k a_{1\alpha} a_{2\beta} \ldots a_{n\nu}$$

where $\alpha, \beta, \ldots, \nu$ represent one of the permutations of the natural numbers 1 through n. The total number of terms in the sum is $n!$. The number k which determines the sign of each term in the expansion is either zero or one, according as the permutation is *odd* or *even.* A permutation is odd if the number of pairs of integers which are out of natural order is odd; else it is called even. Thus 1432 is an odd permutation as 32, 43 and 42 are out of natural order. On the other hand, the permutation 1342 is even because two pairs 42 and 32 are out of natural order. As each of the numbers $1, 2, \ldots, n$ appears only once as a row subscript and once as a column subscript, any term of the expansion contains only one element from each row and column of **A**. The Laplace expansion above can be generalized to partitioned matrices where each submatrix is square. In such case the $a_{1\alpha}$, $a_{2\beta}$ etc. become the determinants of the individual submatrices.

The determinant of an $r \times r$ submatrix of a larger matrix **A** is called a *minor* of order r. The rank of **A** is also the order of the largest submatrix with nonzero minor. Thus if $|\mathbf{A}| \neq 0$ for a square matrix, then **A** is of full rank or, as is usually said, nonsingular. Rank determination is a difficult numerical task and methods based on orthogonal transformations are needed [1].

F.4. NORMS

The concept of *distance* is generalized in the case of vectors through the use of *norms.* The norm of a vector **x**, $\|\mathbf{x}\|$, is a real nonnegative number such that

$$\|\mathbf{x}\| = 0 \quad \text{if and only if} \quad \mathbf{x} = \mathbf{0}$$

$$\|c\mathbf{x}\| = |c|\,\|\mathbf{x}\| \quad \text{for all scalars } c \text{ and vectors } \mathbf{x}$$

$$\|\mathbf{x}_1 + \mathbf{x}_2\| \leqslant \|\mathbf{x}_1\| + \|\mathbf{x}_2\| \quad \text{for all } \mathbf{x}_1 \text{ and } \mathbf{x}_2.$$

There exist many norms for vectors. Three of the commonly used ones are

$$\|\mathbf{x}\|_1 = \sum |x_i|$$
$$\|x\|_2 = \sqrt{\sum |x_i|^2}$$
$$\|x\|_\infty = \max_i |x_i|.$$

The general properties of norms are such that it usually does not make much difference which particular norm is used in the development. Once an appropriate vector norm is selected the *induced matrix norm* is defined as

$$\|\mathbf{A}\| = \max_{\|\mathbf{x}\|=1} \|\mathbf{A}\mathbf{x}\|.$$

Corresponding to the three vector norms considered above we have the matrix norms:

$$\|\mathbf{A}\|_1 = \max_j \sum_i |a_{ij}|$$

$$\|\mathbf{A}\|_2 = (\text{maximum eigenvalue of } \mathbf{A}^*\mathbf{A})^{1/2}$$

$$\|\mathbf{A}\|_\infty = \max_i \sum_j |a_{ij}|$$

where * denotes transpose conjugate. The positive square roots of the eigenvalues of $\mathbf{A}^*\mathbf{A}$ are called the *singular values* of **A** and the 2-norm is often known as the *spectral norm.*

The matrix norm satisfies the following relations

$$\|c\mathbf{A}\| = |c|\,\|\mathbf{A}\|$$

$$\|\mathbf{A}\mathbf{x}\| \leqslant \|\mathbf{A}\|\,\|\mathbf{x}\|$$

$$\|\mathbf{A}\mathbf{B}\| \leqslant \|\mathbf{A}\|\,\|\mathbf{B}\|$$

$$\|\mathbf{A} + \mathbf{B}\| \leqslant \|\mathbf{A}\| + \|\mathbf{B}\|.$$

F.5. ERRORS IN SOLUTION

Use of a digital computer with its associated finite arithmetic precision inevitably leads to some errors in the numerical solution of sets of equations. Generally, these errors are small and their effect is ignored. However, there can be cases, as with a singular matrix, where caution must be exercised. A detailed error analysis can be found in [2], here we provide some simple bounds. Consider first the perturbation $\Delta\mathbf{x}$ in $\mathbf{x}$ due to a variation $\Delta\mathbf{b}$ in $\mathbf{b}$

$$\mathbf{A}(\mathbf{x} + \Delta\mathbf{x}) = \mathbf{b} + \Delta\mathbf{b}$$

or

$$\mathbf{A}\Delta\mathbf{x} = \Delta\mathbf{b}$$

$$\Delta\mathbf{x} = \mathbf{A}^{-1}\Delta\mathbf{b}$$

$$\|\Delta\mathbf{x}\| \leqslant \|\mathbf{A}^{-1}\|\,\|\Delta\mathbf{b}\|.$$

Also from $\mathbf{A}\mathbf{x} = \mathbf{b}$

$$\|\mathbf{A}\|\,\|\mathbf{x}\| \geqslant \|\mathbf{b}\|$$

and dividing, we get the bound on the *relative perturbation*

$$\frac{\|\Delta\mathbf{x}\|}{\|\mathbf{x}\|} \leqslant \|\mathbf{A}\|\,\|\mathbf{A}^{-1}\|\,\frac{\|\Delta\mathbf{b}\|}{\|\mathbf{b}\|}.$$

The quantity $K(\mathbf{A}) = \|\mathbf{A}\|\,\|\mathbf{A}^{-1}\|$ is called the *condition number* of $\mathbf{A}$ and in any norm $K(\mathbf{A}) \geqslant 1$. It measures the relative amplification produced in the solution vector due to perturbations in the right hand side. Large values of $K(\mathbf{A})$ imply that even small changes in $\mathbf{b}$, as may be produced by truncation on the computer, can lead to vastly different solutions.

Let us now consider the effect of changes in the coefficient matrix $\mathbf{A}$. These changes could be due to truncation when storing the initial matrix or roundoff during factorization. Wilkinson [2] has shown that these effects lead to a solution vector $\hat{\mathbf{x}}$ which satisfies

$$(\mathbf{A} + \epsilon)\,\hat{\mathbf{x}} = \mathbf{b}. \qquad \text{(F.1)}$$

If the exact solution of $\mathbf{Ax} = \mathbf{b}$ is denoted by $\mathbf{x}$, then two measures of error are:

$$\mathbf{r} = \mathbf{b} - \mathbf{A}\hat{\mathbf{x}}$$

and

$$\mathbf{e} = \mathbf{x} - \hat{\mathbf{x}}$$

where $\mathbf{r}$ is the *residual* and $\mathbf{e}$ the *solution error.* We now obtain bounds for $\mathbf{r}$ and $\mathbf{e}$. From (F.1)

$$\boldsymbol{\epsilon}\hat{\mathbf{x}} = \mathbf{b} - \mathbf{A}\hat{\mathbf{x}} = \mathbf{r}$$

or

$$\|\mathbf{r}\| \leqslant \|\boldsymbol{\epsilon}\| \, \|\hat{\mathbf{x}}\|$$

or

$$\frac{\|\mathbf{r}\|}{\|\mathbf{A}\| \, \|\hat{\mathbf{x}}\|} \leqslant \frac{\|\boldsymbol{\epsilon}\|}{\|\mathbf{A}\|}$$

where the quantity on the left is normalized with respect to the size of $\mathbf{A}$ and $\hat{\mathbf{x}}$ and is called the *relative residual.* Wilkinson has shown that in Gaussian elimination with partial pivoting

$$\frac{\|\boldsymbol{\epsilon}\|}{\|\mathbf{A}\|} = \phi\beta^{-t}$$

where t digits in base β arithmetic are used and ϕ rarely exceeds β. For IBM 360 and 370 systems $\beta = 16$ and $t = 6$ or 14, depending on whether single or double precision arithmetic is being used. This leads to corresponding values of approximately 10^{-6} and 2×10^{-16} for $\|\boldsymbol{\epsilon}\|/\|\mathbf{A}\|$. Thus with partial pivoting the *residual will always be small!* Now from

$$\mathbf{Ae} = \mathbf{A}(\mathbf{x} - \hat{\mathbf{x}}) = \mathbf{b} - \mathbf{A}\hat{\mathbf{x}} = \mathbf{r}$$

$$\mathbf{e} = \mathbf{A}^{-1}\mathbf{r}$$

$$\|\mathbf{e}\| \leqslant \|\mathbf{A}^{-1}\| \, \|\mathbf{r}\| \leqslant \|\mathbf{A}^{-1}\| \, \|\boldsymbol{\epsilon}\| \, \|\hat{\mathbf{x}}\|$$

or

$$\frac{\|\mathbf{e}\|}{\|\hat{\mathbf{x}}\|} \leqslant \|\mathbf{A}^{-1}\| \, \|\mathbf{A}\| \frac{\|\boldsymbol{\epsilon}\|}{\|\mathbf{A}\|} = K(\mathbf{A}) \frac{\|\boldsymbol{\epsilon}\|}{\|\mathbf{A}\|}$$

and, depending on $K(\mathbf{A})$, the relative solution error can be very large. For example, if $K(\mathbf{A}) = 10^7$, then in single precision on an IBM machine the errors will be larger than the solution.

Computing $K(\mathbf{A})$ is expensive, as $\mathbf{A}^{-1}$ must be found. However, a method for estimating good lower bounds on $K(\mathbf{A})$ has been proposed in [3]. It requires the solution of two additional systems of equations once **A** has been factored and costs approximately $3n^2$ operations. As this cost is relatively small compared with the $n^3/3$ required for the factorization, the technique has been incorporated into recent production codes [1]. A condition number estimation method for sparse matrices is also available in [4].

If an estimate of the condition number is not available, a rule of thumb is that the matrix is ill-conditioned if small pivot elements are encountered during the factorization. Unfortunately, the converse is *not* true.

F.6. MULTIVARIABLE CALCULUS

In optimization problems and in the solution of systems of nonlinear equations, we have considered the influence of simultaneous changes in many variables on scalar and vector functions. Formally, this requires a *multivariate Taylor expansion* which is best represented through *tensors.* However, as for the most part, we are interested in small variations in the variables, higher order terms can be ignored and the results expressed in more familiar vector-matrix notation.

Let us start with the Taylor expansion of a scalar function f with respect to variation Δx in the scalar variable x

$$\begin{aligned} f(x + \Delta x) &= f(x) + \Delta x \frac{df}{dx} + \frac{1}{2} \Delta x^2 \frac{d^2 f}{dx^2} + \cdots \\ &= \sum_{i=0}^{\infty} \frac{1}{i!} (\Delta x)^i \frac{d^i f}{dx^i}. \end{aligned}$$

Typically, only the first two or three terms are retained in the expansion. Generalizing to a scalar function of vector variables $\mathbf{x}$

$$\begin{aligned} f(\mathbf{x} + \Delta \mathbf{x}) &= f(\mathbf{x}) + \sum \frac{\partial f}{\partial x_i} \Delta x_i + \frac{1}{2} \sum_i \sum_j \frac{\partial^2 f}{\partial x_i \partial x_j} \Delta x_i \Delta x_j + \cdots \\ &= f(\mathbf{x}) + \frac{\partial f}{\partial \mathbf{x}} \Delta \mathbf{x} + \frac{1}{2} (\Delta \mathbf{x})^t \frac{\partial^2 f}{\partial \mathbf{x}^2} (\Delta \mathbf{x}) + \cdots . \end{aligned}$$

Here $\partial f / \partial \mathbf{x}$ is the row vector

$$\left[\frac{\partial f}{\partial x_1}, \frac{\partial f}{\partial x_2}, \ldots, \frac{\partial f}{\partial x_n} \right]$$

and $(\partial^2 f / \partial \mathbf{x}^2)$ is the Hessian matrix with entries $[\partial^2 f / \partial x_i \partial x_j]$. Terms beyond the third must either be left as summations or written in terms of tensors (which can be visualized as higher-dimensional arrays).

The expansion of an m-dimensional vector function $\mathbf{f}$ of n independent variables $\mathbf{x}$ is obtained by considering $\mathbf{f}$ component by component

$$f_1(\mathbf{x} + \Delta\mathbf{x}) = f_1(\mathbf{x}) + \frac{\partial f_1}{\partial \mathbf{x}} \Delta\mathbf{x} + \cdots$$

$$f_2(\mathbf{x} + \Delta\mathbf{x}) = f_2(\mathbf{x}) + \frac{\partial f_2}{\partial \mathbf{x}} \Delta\mathbf{x} + \cdots$$

$$\vdots$$

$$f_m(\mathbf{x} + \Delta\mathbf{x}) = f_m(\mathbf{x}) + \frac{\partial f_m}{\partial \mathbf{x}} \Delta\mathbf{x} + \cdots$$

or, more compactly,

$$\mathbf{f}(\mathbf{x} + \Delta\mathbf{x}) = \mathbf{f}(\mathbf{x}) + \frac{\partial \mathbf{f}}{\partial \mathbf{x}} \Delta\mathbf{x} + \cdots$$

where $\partial\mathbf{f}/\partial\mathbf{x}$ is an $m \times n$ matrix with entries $[\partial f_i/\partial x_j]$. Higher order terms in the expansion involve products of the Δx_j and cannot be expressed as vectors or matrices. Generally, $m = n$ and $\partial\mathbf{f}/\partial\mathbf{x}$ is a square matrix.

REFERENCES

1. J. J. Dongarra, J. R. Bunch, C. B. Moler, and G. W. Stewart: *LINPACK User's Guide.* SIAM Philadelphia, 1979.
2. J. W. Wilkinson: *The Algebraic Eigenvalue Problem.* Oxford University Press, 1965.
3. A. K. Cline, C. B. Moler, G. W. Stewart, and J. W. Wilkinson: An estimate for the condition number of a matrix. *SIAM J. Numerical Analysis*, pp. 368–375, 1979.
4. R. G. Grimes and J. G. Lewis: Condition number estimation for sparse matrices. *SIAM J. Scientific and Statistical Computing*, pp. 384–388, 1981.

Bibliography

This general bibliography provides mostly the titles of books, references to articles being restricted to those with special importance. The reader might wish to check some special issues of journals relevant to the material in this book:

Special Issues of *IEEE Transactions of Circuits and Systems:*

Nonlinear Circuits and Systems	November 1980
Integrated Filters for Communications	June 1980
Automatic Analog Fault Diagnosis	July 1979
Computational Methods	September 1979
Large-Scale Networks and Systems	December 1976
Computer Aided Design	November 1973
Large-Scale Networks	May 1973
Computer-Aided Circuit Design	January 1971

Special Issues of *IEEE Journal of Solid-State Circuits*

Linear Circuits	February 1971
Computer-Aided Circuit Analysis and Device Modeling	August 1971
Linear Integrated Circuits	December 1968

Special Issues of *Proceedings of the IEEE*

Computer-Aided Design	October 1981
Computers in Design	January 1972
Computer-Aided Design	November 1967

IEEE Press book on *Computer Aided Filter Design.*

COMPUTER AIDED DESIGN

Calahan, D. A.: *Computer Aided Network Design*. McGraw-Hill, New York, 1972.

Chua, L. O., and Lin, P. M.: *Computer Aided Analysis of Electronic Circuits: Algorithms and Computational Techniques*. Prentice-Hall, Englewood Cliffs, NJ, 1975.

Director, S. W. (editor): *Computer-Aided Circuit Design*. Dowden, Hutchinson & Ross, Stroudsburg, Pennsylvania, 1973.

Ho, C. W., Zein, D. A., Ruehli, A. E., and Brennan, P. A.: An algorithm for dc solutions in an experimental general purpose interactive circuit design program. *IEEE Transactions on Circuits and Systems*, Vol. CAS-24, pp. 416–422, August 1977.

Kaplan, G.: Computer-aided design. *IEEE Spectrum*, pp. 40–47, October 1979.

Kuo, F. F., and Magnuson, W. G.: *Computer Oriented Circuit Design*. Prentice-Hall, Englewood Cliffs, NJ, 1969.

McCalla, W. J., and Pederson, D. O.: Elements of computer-aided circuit analysis. *IEEE Transactions on Circuit Theory*, Vol. CT-18, No. 1, pp. 14–26, Jan. 1971.

Weeks, W. T., Jimenez, A. J., Mahoney, G. W., Mehta, D., Qassemzadeh, H., and Scott, T. R.: Algorithms for ASTAP–A network-analysis program. *IEEE Transactions on Circuit Theory*, Vol. CT-20, No. 6, pp. 628–634, Nov. 1973.

NETWORK ANALYSIS

Books dealing with the general subject of network analysis are too numerous to be listed here. A short selection is given:

Budak, A.: *Circuit Theory Fundamentals and Applications*. Prentice-Hall, Englewood Cliffs, NJ, 1978.

Chan, S. P., Chan, S. Y., and Chan, S. G.: *Analysis of Linear Networks and Systems: A Matrix-oriented Approach with Computer Applications*. Addison-Wesley, Reading, Mass., 1972.

Cruz, J. B., Jr., and Van Valkenburg, M. E.: *Introductory Signals and Circuits*. Blaisdell, Waltham, Mass., 1967.

Desoer, C. A., and Kuh, E. S.: *Basic Circuit Theory*. McGraw-Hill, New York, 1969.

Huelsman, L. P.: *Basic Circuit Theory with Digital Computations*. Prentice-Hall, Englewood Cliffs, NJ, 1972.

Johnson, D. E., Hilburn, J. L., and Johnson, J. R.: *Basic Electric Circuit Analysis*. Prentice-Hall, Englewood Cliffs, NJ, 1978.

Kim, W. H., and Meadows, H. E., Jr.: *Modern Network Analysis*. Wiley, New York, 1971.

Kinariwala, B., Kuo, F. F., and Tsao, N.: *Linear Circuits and Computation*. Wiley, New York, 1973.

Leon, B. J., and Wintz, P. A.: *Basic Linear Networks for Electrical and Electronics Engineers*. Holt, Rinehart and Winston, New York, 1970.

Murdoch, J. B.: *Network Theory*. McGraw-Hill, New York, 1970.

Roe, P. H. O'N.: *Networks and Systems*. Addison Wesley, Reading, Mass., 1966.

Trick, T. N.: *Introduction to Circuit Analysis*. Wiley, New York, 1977.

Some more advanced books dealing with the general subject of networks, linear systems and related computations are:

Director, S. W.: *Circuit Theory: A Computational Approach*. Wiley, New York, 1975.

Kailath, T.: *Linear Systems*. Prentice-Hall, Englewood Cliffs, NJ, 1980.

Schwarz, R. J., and Friedland, B.: *Linear Systems*. McGraw-Hill, New York, 1965.

Wing, O.: *Circuit Theroy with Computer Methods*. Holt, Rinehart & Winston, New York, 1972.

Zadeh, L. A., and Desoer, C. A.: *Linear System Theory*. McGraw-Hill, New York, 1963.

Papers

Branin, F. H., Jr., Hogsett, G. R., Lunde, R. L., and Kugel, L. E.: ECAP-II-A new electronic circuit analysis progran, *IEEE Journal of Solid-State Circuits*, Vol. SC-6, No. 4, pp. 146–166, August 1971.

Branin, F. H.: A unifying approach to the classical methods of formulating network equations. *IEEE Symp. on Circuits and Systems*, San Francisco, pp. 750–754, 1974.

MATHEMATICAL AND NUMERICAL METHODS

Acton, F. S.: *Numerical Methods that Work*. Harper & Row, New York, 1970.

Arden, B. W., and Astill, K. N.: *Numerical Algorithms: Origins and Applications*. Addison-Wesley, Reading, Mass., 1970.

Atkinson, K. E.: *An Introduction to Numerical Analysis*. Wiley, New York, 1978.

Dahlquist, G., and Björck, A.: *Numerical Methods*. Prentice-Hall, Englewood Cliffs, NJ, 1974.

Daniels, R. W.: *An Introduction to Numerical Methods and Optimization Techniques*. North-Holland, Amsterdam, 1978.

Dodes, I. A.: *Numerical Analysis for Computer Science*. North-Holland, Amsterdam, 1978.

Faddeeva, V. N.: *Computational Methods of Linear Algebra*. Dover, New York, 1959.

Forsythe, G. S., Malcolm M. A., and Moler, C. B.: *Computer Methods for Mathematical Computations*. Prentice-Hall, Englewood Cliffs, NJ, 1974.

Forsythe, G. S., and Moler, C. B.: *Computer Solution of Linear Algebraic Equations*. Prentice-Hall, Englewood Cliffs, NJ, 1967.

Johnston, R. L.: *Numerical Methods: A Software Approach*. Wiley, New York, 1982.

Kreyszig, E.: *Advanced Engineering Mathematics*, third edition. Wiley, New York, 1972.

Ralston, A., and Rabinowitz, P.: *A First Course in Numerical Analysis*. McGraw-Hill, New York, 1978.

Ralston, A., and Wilf, H. S. (editors): *Mathematical Methods for Digital Computers*, Vols. 1, 2 and 3. Wiley, New York, 1967–77.

Stiefel, E. L.: *An Introduction to Numerical Mathematics*. Academic Press, New York, 1963.

Young, D. M., and Gregory, R. T.: *A Survey of Numerical Mathematics*. Addison-Wesley, Reading, Mass., 1972.

Wilkinson, J. H.: *The Algebraic Eigenvalue Problem*. Clarendon, Oxford, 1965.

Papers

Davison, E. J.: On the calculation of zeros of a linear constant system. *IEEE Transactions on Circuit Theory*, Vol. CT-18, No. 1, pp. 183–184, Jan. 1971.

Guidorzi, R. P.: On the algorithms for computing the zeros of large systems. *IEEE Transactions on Automatic Control*, Vol. AC-17, No. 5, pp. 731–732, Oct. 1972.

Jenkins, M. A.: Algorithm 493. Zeros of a real polynomial. *ACM Transactions on Mathematical Software*, Vol. 1, No. 2, pp. 178–189, June 1975.

Müller, D. E.: A method for solving algebraic equations using an automatic computer. *Math. Tables Aids Comput.*, Vol. 10, pp. 208–215, 1956.

Wilkinson, J. H.: The evaluation of the zeros of ill-conditioned polynomials. Part 1, 2. *Numerische Mathematik*, Vol. 1, pp. 150–166 and pp. 167–180, 1959.

SPARSE MATRIX TECHNIQUES

Barker, V. A. (editor): *Sparse Matrix Techniques*. Springer-Verlag, New York, 1977.

Brameller, A. A., and Norman N.: *Sparsity: Its Practical Application to Systems Analysis*. Pitman, London, 1976.

Bunch, J. R., and Rose, D. J. (editors): *Sparse Matrix Computations*. Academic Press, New York, 1976.

Duff, I. S. (editor): *Sparse Matrices and their Uses*. Academic Press, London, 1981.

Reid, J. K. (editor): *Large Sparse Sets of Linear Equations*. Academic Press, New York, 1971.

Rose, D. J., and Willoughby, R. A. (editors): *Sparse Matrices and Their Applications*. Plenum Press, New York, 1972.

Willoughby, R. (editor): *Proceedings of the Symposium on Sparse Matrices and their Applications*. Yorktown Heights, N.Y., IBM Report RA1(#11707), 1969.

Papers

Bennet, J. M.: Triangular factors of modified matrices. *Numerische Mathematik*, Vol. 7, pp. 217–221, 1965.

Berry, R. D.: An optimal ordering of electronic circuit equations for a sparse matrix solution. *IEEE Transactions on Circuit Theory*, Vol. CT-18, No. 1, pp. 40–50, Jan. 1971.

Duff, I. S.: A survey of sparse matrix research. *Proc. IEEE*, Vol. 65, No. 4, pp. 500–535, April 1977. (Contains extensive bibliography on sparse matrix methods and applications.)

Erisman, A. M., and Spies, G. E.: Exploiting problem characteristics in the sparse matrix approach to frequency domain analysis. *IEEE Transactions on Circuit Theory*, Vol. CT-19, No. 3, pp. 260–264, May 1972.

Gustavson, F. G., Liniger, W., and Willoughby, R.: Symbolic generation of an optimal Crout algorithm for sparse systems of linear equations. *JACM,* Vol. 17, pp. 87–109, Jan. 1970.

Hachtel, G. D., Brayton, R. K., and Gustavson, F. G.: The sparse tableau approach to network analysis and design. *IEEE Transactions on Circuit Theory*, Vol. CT-18, No. 1, pp. 101–113, Jan. 1971.

Hajj, I. N.: Sparsity considerations in network solution by tearing. *IEEE Transactions on Circuits and Systems*, Vol. CAS-27, pp. 357–366, May 1980.

Markowitz, H. M.: The elimination form of the inverse and its application to linear programming. *Management Sci.*, Vol. 3, pp. 255–269, 1957.

Sato, N., and Tinney, W. F.: Techniques exploiting the sparsity of the network admittance matrix. *IEEE Transactions on Power Apparatus and Systems*, pp. 944–950, December 1963.

Pooch, U. W., and Nieder, A.: A survey of indexing techniques for sparse matrices. *Computing Surveys*, Vol. 5, No. 2, pp. 109–133, June 1973.

Tinney, W. F., and Meyer, W. S.: Solution of large sparse systems by ordered triangular factorization. *IEEE Transactions on Automatic Control*, Vol. AC-18, pp. 333–346, August 1973. (Nice tutorial introduction.)

Tinney, W. F., and Walker, J. W.: Direct solutions of sparse network equations by optimally ordered triangular factorization. *Proc. IEEE*, Vol. 55, pp. 1801–1809, Nov. 1967.

GRAPH THEORY AND STATE VARIABLES

Deo, N.: *Graph Theory with Applications to Engineering and Computer Science*. Prentice-Hall, Englewood Cliffs, NJ, 1974.

DeRusso, P. M., Roy, R. J., and Close, C. M.: *State Variables for Engineers*. Wiley, New York, 1965.

Harary, F.: *Graph Theory*. Addison-Wesley, Reading, Mass., 1969.

Kim, W. H., and Chien, R. T.: *Topological Analysis and Synthesis of Communication Networks*. Columbia Univ. Press, New York, 1962.

Mayeda, W.: *Graph Theory*. Wiley-Interscience, New York, 1972.

Rohrer, R. A.: *Circuit Theory: An Introduction to the State Variable Approach*. McGraw-Hill, New York, 1970.

Seshu, S., and Reed, M. B.: *Linear Graphs and Electrical Networks*. Addison-Wesley, Reading, Mass., 1961.

Wilson, R. J., and Beineke, L. W. (editors): *Applications of Graph Theory.* Academic Press, New York, 1979.

Paper

Bryant, P. R.: The order of complexity of electrical networks. Monograph No. 335 E, June 1959, Part C, *Proceeding of the Institution of Electrical Engineers*, London.

NETWORK SENSITIVITY

Brayton, R., Spence, R.: *Sensitivity and Optimization.* Elsevier, Amsterdam, 1980.

Bruton, L. R.: *RC-Active Circuits: Theory and Design.* Prentice-Hall, Englewood Cliffs, NJ, 1980.

Daryanani, G.: *Principles of Active Network Synthesis and Design.* Wiley, New York, 1976.

Geher, L.: *Theory of Network Tolerances.* Akademiai Kiado, Budapest, 1971.

Heinlein, W., and Holmes, H.: *Active Filters for Integrated Circuits.* Prentice-Hall, Englewood Cliffs, NJ, 1974.

Huelsman, L. P., and Allen, P. E.: *Introduction to the Theory and Design of Active Filters.* McGraw-Hill, New York, 1980.

Mitra, S. K.: *Analysis and Synthesis of Linear Active Networks.* Wiley, New York, 1969.

Sedra, A. S. and Brackett, P. O.: *Filter Theory and Design: Active and Passive.* Matrix Publishers, Portland, Oregon, 1978.

Tomovic, R., and Vukobratovic, M.: *General Senstivity Theory.* American Elsevier Publishing Co., New York, 1972.

Papers

Bordejwijk, J. L.: Inter-reciprocity applied to electrical networks. *Appl. Sci. Res.*, Vol. 6, pp. 1–74, 1956.

Branin, F. H. Jr.: Network sensitivity and noise analysis simplified. *IEEE Transactions on Circuit Theory*, Vol. CT-20, No. 3, pp. 285–288, May 1973.

Desoer, C. A.: Teaching adjoint networks to juniors. *IEEE Transactions on Education*, Vol. E-16, No. 1, pp. 10–14, Feb. 1973.

Director S. W.: LU factorization in network sensitivity computations. *IEEE Transactions on Circuit Theory*, Vol. CT-18, No. 1, pp. 184–185, Jan. 1971.

Director, S. W., and Rohrer, R. A.: Automated network design: The frequency domain case. *IEEE Transactions on Circuit Theory*, Vol. CT-16, pp. 330–337, Aug. 1969.

Director, S. W., and Wayne, D. A.: Computational efficiency in the determination of Thévenin and Norton equivalents. *IEEE Transactions on Circuit Theory*, Vol. CT-19, pp. 96–98, January 1972.

Eslami, M., and Marleau, R. S.: Theory of sensitivity as applied to circuit theory—the state of the art. *21st Midwest Symposium on Circuits and Systems*, Iowa State Univ., Ames, pp. 1–16, 1978. (Contains many references.)

Hayes, L. L., and Temes, G. C.: An efficient numerical method for the computation of zero and pole sensitivities. *Int. J. Electronics*, Vol. 33, pp. 21–31, 1972.

Penfield, P., Jr., Spence, R., and Duinker, S.: A generalized form of Tellegen's theorem. *IEEE Transactions on Circuit Theory*, Vol. CT-17, No. 3, pp 302–305, Aug. 1970.

Rohrer, R. A., Nagel, L., Meyer, R., and Weber, L.: Computationally efficient electronic-circuit noise calculations. *IEEE J. Solid State Circuits*, Vol. SC-6, pp. 204–213, 1971.

Temes, G. C., Ebers, R. M., and Gadenz, R. N.: Some applications of the adjoint network concept in frequency domain analysis and optimization. *Computer-Aided Design*, pp. 129–134, April 1972.

LARGE CHANGE SENSITIVITY AND SYMBOLIC ANALYSIS

Alderson, G. E., and Lin, P. M.: Computer generation of symbolic network functions; a new theory and implementation. *IEEE Transactions on Circuit Theory*, Vol. CT-20, No. 1, pp. 48–56, Jan. 1973.

Haley, S. B.: Large change response sensitivity of linear networks. *IEEE Transactions on Circuits and Systems*, Vol. CAS-27, pp. 305–310, April 1980.

Katzenelson, J.: Symbolic analysis of linear networks–A survey. NATO Advanced Study Institute on Network and Signal Theory, Bournemouth, U. K., Sept. 1972.

Kaufman, I.: On poles and zeros of linear systems. *IEEE Transactions on Circuit Theory*, Vol. CT-20, No. 2, pp. 93–101, March 1973.

Kurth, C. F.: A simple calculation of the determinant polynomial of general networks. *IEEE Transactions on Circuit Theory*, Vol. CT-14, pp. 234–236, 1967.

Lin, P. M.: A survey of applications of symbolic network functions. *IEEE Transactions on Circuit Theory*, Vol. CT-20, No. 6, pp. 732–737, Nov. 1973.

Sandberg, I. W., and So, H. C.: A two-sets-of-eigenvalues approach to the computer analysis of linear systems. *IEEE Transactions on Circuit Theory*, Vol. CT-16, No. 4, pp. 509–517, Nov. 1969.

Singhal, K., and Vlach, J.: Symbolic analysis of analog and digital circuits. *IEEE Transactions on Circuits and Systems*, Vol. CAS-24, No. 11, pp. 598–609, November 1977.

Singhal, K., Vlach, J., and Bryant, P. R.: Efficient computation of large change multiparameter sensitivity. *Circuit Theory and Applications*, Vol. 1, pp. 237–247, 1973.

Troop, W. J., and Peskin, E.: The transfer function and sensitivity of a network with n variable elements. *IEEE Transactions on Circuit Theory*, Vol. CT-16, No. 2, pp. 242–244, May 1969.

Wehrhahn, R.: A new approach in the computation of poles and zeros in large networks. *IEEE Transactions on Circuit and Systems*, Vol. CAS-26, pp. 700–707, September 1979.

DISCRETE AND FAST FOURIER TRANSFORM

Brigham, E. O.: *The Fast Fourier Transform.* Prentice-Hall, Englewood Cliffs, NJ, 1974.

Papers

Bergland, G. D.: A guided tour of the fast Fourier transform. *IEEE Spectrum*, pp. 41–52, July 1969.

Cooley, J. W., Lewis, P. A. W., and Welch, P. D.: The fast Fourier transform algorithm: programming considerations in the calculation of sine, cosine and Laplace transforms. *Journal of Sound and Vibration*, Vol. 12, No. 3, pp. 315–337, 1970.

Cooley, J. W., and Tukey, J. W.: An algorithm for the machine calculation of complex Fourier series. *Math. of Computation*, Vol. 19, pp. 297–301, 1965.

Singhal, K., and Vlach, J.: Interpolation using the fast Fourier transform. *Proc. IEEE*, Vol. 60, p. 1558, Dec. 1972.

Singhal, K., and Vlach, J.: Accuracy and speed of real and complex interpolation. *Computing*, Vol. 11, pp. 147–158, 1973.

LAPLACE TRANSFORM AND ITS NUMERICAL INVERSION

Laplace transform theory can be found in most books on network analysis.

Bellman, R., Kalaba, R. E., and Lockett, J. A.: *Numerical Inversion of the Laplace Transform.* American Elsevier, New York, 1966.

Kreyszig, E.: *Advanced Engineering Mathematics.* Wiley, New York, 1972.

Krylov, V. I., and Skoblya, N. S.: *Handbook of Numerical Inversion of Laplace Transforms.* Israel Program for Scientific Translations, Jerusalem, 1969.

Lepage, W. R.: *Complex Variables and the Laplace Transform for Engineers.* McGraw-Hill, New York, 1961.

Spiegel, M. R.: *Theory and Problems of Laplace Transforms.* Schaum's Outline Series, McGraw-Hill, New York, 1965.

Strum, R. D., and Ward, J. R.: *Laplace Transform Solution for Differential Equations: A Programmed Text.* Prentice-Hall, Englewood Cliffs, NJ, 1968.

Thomson, W. T.: *Laplace Transformation.* Prentice-Hall, Englewood Cliffs, NJ, 1960.

Williams, J.: *Laplace Transforms.* George Allen & Unwin, London, 1973.

Papers

Piessens, R.: A new numerical method for the inversion of the Laplace transform. *J. Inst. Math. Applic.*, Vol. 10, pp. 185–192, 1972.

Singhal, K., Vlach, J., and Nakhla, M.: Absolutely stable, high order method for time domain solution of networks. *Archiv für Elektronik und Ubertragungstechnik (Electronics and Communication)*, Vol. 30, pp. 157–166, April 1976.

Singhal, K., and Vlach, J.: Computation of time domain response by numerical inversion of the Laplace transform. *Journal of the Franklin Institute*, Vol. 299, No. 2, pp. 109–126, February 1975.

Vlach, J.: Numerical method for transient responses of linear networks with lumped, distributed or mixed parameters. *Journal of the Franklin Institute*, Vol. 288, No. 2, pp. 99–113, Aug. 1969.

Wing, O.: An efficient method of numerical inversion of Laplace transforms. *Computing*, Vol. 2, pp. 153–156, 1967.

ELECTRON DEVICES AND NETWORKS WITH ELECTRON DEVICES

Altman, L.: *Large Scale Integration.* McGraw-Hill, New York, 1976.

Bar-Lev, A.: *Semiconductors and Electronic Devices.* Prentice-Hall, Englewood Cliffs, NJ, 1979.

Browne, B. T., and Miller, J. J. H. (editors): *Numerical Analysis of Semiconductor Devices.* Boole Press, Dublin, 1979.

Chirlian, P. M.: *Analysis and Design of Integrated Electronic Circuits.* Harper & Row, New York, 1981.

Cobbold, R. S. C.: *Theory and Applications of Field-Effect Transistors.* Wiley, New York, 1970.

Cowles, L. G.: *Transistor Circuit Design.* Prentice-Hall, Englewood Cliffs, NJ, 1972.

Gray, P. R., and Myer, R. G.: *Analysis and Design of Analog Integrated Circuits.* Wiley, New York, 1977.

Herskowitz, G. J., and Schilling, R. B.: *Semiconductor Device Modeling for Computer-Aided Design.* McGraw-Hill, New York, 1972.

Logan, J.: Modelling for circuit and system design, *Proc. IEEE*, Vol. 60, No. 1, pp. 78–85, Jan. 1972.

Malvino, A. P.: *Transistor Circuit Approximations.* McGraw-Hill, New York, 1973.

Manasse, F. K.: *Semiconductor Electronics Design.* Prentice-Hall, Englewood Cliffs, NJ, 1977.

Mead, C., and Conway, L.: *Introduction to VLSI Systems.* Addison-Wesley, Reading, Mass., 1980.

Millman, J.: *Microelectronics: Digital and Analog Circuits and Systems.* McGraw-Hill, New York, 1979.

Milnes, A. G.: *Semiconductor Devices and Integrated Electronics.* Van Nostrand Reinhold, New York, 1980.

Navon, D. H.: *Electronic Materials and Devices.* Houghton Mifflin Co., Boston, 1975.

Roberge, J. K.: *Operational Amplifiers: Theory and Practice.* Wiley, New York, 1975.

Streetman, B. G.: *Solid State Electronic Devices.* Prentice-Hall, Englewood Cliffs, NJ, 1980.

Yang, E. S.: *Fundamentals of Semiconductor Devices.* McGraw-Hill, New York, 1978.

Information on electron devices and their modeling can be found in *IEEE Transactions on Electron Devices.* Application of electron devices to circuits is available in *IEEE Journal of Solid State Circuits* and also in some special issues or in articles in *IEEE Transactions on Circuits and Systems.*

DIFFERENTIAL EQUATIONS AND THEIR NUMERICAL SOLUTION

Arnold, V. I.: *Ordinary Differential Equations.* MIT Press, Cambridge, Mass., 1973.

Bellman, R., and Cooke, K. L.: *Modern Elementary Differential Equations.* Addison-Wesley, Reading, Mass., 1971.

Birkhoff, G., and Rota, G. C.: *Ordinary Differential Equations.* Blaisdell, Waltham, Mass., 1969.

Buck, C. R., and Buck, E. F.: *Introduction to Differential Equations.* Houghton Mifflin, Boston, 1976.

Collatz, L.: *The Numerical Treatment of Differential Equations.* Springer-Verlag, New York, 1966.

Cronin-Scanlon, J. S.: *Differential Equations: Introduction and Qualitative Theory.* Marcel Dekker, New York, 1980.

Fried, I.: *Numerical Solution of Differential Equations.* Academic Press, New York, 1979.

Gear, C. W.: *Numerical Initial Value Problems in Ordinary Differential Equations.* Prentice-Hall, Englewood Cliffs, NJ, 1971.

Henrici, P.: *Discrete Variable Methods for Ordinary Differential Equations.* Wiley, New York, 1962.

Shampine, L. F., and Gordon, M. K.: *Computer Solution of Ordinary Differential Equations: The Initial Value Problem.* W. H. Freeman, San Francisco, 1975.

Papers

Brayton, R. K., Gustavson, F. G., and Hachtel, G. D.: A new efficent algorithm for solving differential-algebraic systems using implicit backward differentiation formulas. *Proc. IEEE*, Vol. 60, No. 1, pp. 98–107, Jan. 1972.

Calahan, D. A.: Numerical considerations for implementation of a nonlinear transient circuit analysis program. *IEEE Transactions on Circuit Theory*, Vol. CT-18, No. 1, pp. 66–73, Jan. 1971.

Dahlquist, G. G.: A special stability problem for linear multistep methods. *BIT*, Vol. 3, pp. 27–43, 1963.

Gear, C. W.: Simultaneous numerical solution of differential-algebraic equations. *IEEE Transactions on Circuit Theory*, Vol. CT-18, No. 1, pp. 89–95, Jan. 1971.

Genin, Y.: A new approach to the synthesis of stiffly stable linear multistep formulas. *IEEE Transactions on Circuit Theory*, Vol. CT-20, No. 4, pp. 352–360, July 1973.

Hajj, I. N., and Skelboe, S.: Time domain analysis of nonlinear systems with finite number of continuous derivatives. *IEEE Transactions on Circuits and Systems*, Vol. CAS-26, pp. 297–303, May 1979.

Skelboe, S.: The control of order and steplength for backward differentiation methods. *BIT*, Vol. 17, pp. 91–107, 1977.

Van Bokhoven, W. M. G.: Linear implicit differentiation formulas of variable step and order. *IEEE Transactions on Circuits and Systems*, Vol. CAS-22, pp. 109–115, February 1975.

OPTIMIZATION

Adby, P. R. D., and Michael, A. H.: *Introduction to Optimization Methods*. Chapman and Hall, London, 1974.

Bazaraa, M.: *Foundations of Optimization*. Springer-Verlag, New York, 1976.

Beale, E. M. L., Balinski, M. L., and Hellerman, E.: *Computational Practice in Mathematical Programming*. North-Holland, Amsterdam, 1975.

Bradley, S. P., Hax, A. C., and Magnanti, T. L.: *Applied Mathematical Programming*. Addison-Wesley, Reading, Mass., 1977.

Brent, R. P.: *Algorithms for Minimization without Derivatives*. Prentice-Hall, Englewood Cliffs, NJ, 1972.

Demkilanov, V. F., and Malozemov, V. N.: *Introduction to Minimax*. Wiley, New York, 1974.

Fiacco, A. V., and McCormick, G. P.: *Nonlinear Programming: Sequential Unconstrained Minimization Techniques*. Wiley, New York, 1968.

Gill, P. E., and Murray, W. (editors): *Numerical Methods for Constrained Optimization*. Academic Press, New York, 1974.

Himmelblau, D. M.: *Applied Nonlinear Programming*. McGraw-Hill, New York, 1972.

Jacoby, S. L. S., Kowalik, J. S., and Pizzo, J. T.: *Iterative Methods of Nonlinear Optimization Problems*. Prentice-Hall, Englewood Cliffs, NJ, 1972.

Krabs, W.: *Optimization and Approximation*. Wiley, New York, 1979.

Luneberger, D. G.: *Introduction to Linear and Nonlinear Programming*. Addison-Wesley, Reading, Mass., 1973.

Polak, E.: *Computational Methods in Optimization: A Unified Approach*. Academic Press, New York, 1971.

Zangwill, W. I.: *Nonlinear Programming: A Unified Approach*. Prentice-Hall, Englewood Cliffs, NJ, 1969.

Papers

Director, S. W.: Survey of circuit oriented optimization techniques. *IEEE Transactions on Circuit Theory*, Vol. CT-18, No. 1, pp. 3–10, Jan. 1971.

Fletcher, R.: A new approach to variable metric algorithms. *Computer Journal*, Vol. 13, No. 3, pp. 317–322, Aug. 1970.

Fletcher, R., and Powell, M. J. D.: A rapidly convergent descent method for minimization. *Computer Journal*, Vol. 6, No. 2, pp. 163–168, July 1963.

Fletcher, R., and Reeves, C. M.: Function minimization by conjugate gradients. *Computer Journal*, Vol. 7, No. 2, pp. 149–154, July 1964.

Gill, P. E., and Murray, W.: The computation of Lagrange-multiplier estimates for constrained minimization. *Mathematical Programming*, pp. 32–60, 1979.

TOLERANCING AND MONTE CARLO METHODS

Becker, P. W., and Jensen, F.: *Design of Systems and Circuits for Maximum Reliability or Maximum Production Yield*. McGraw-Hill, New York, 1977.

Geher, K.: *Theory of Network Tolerances*. Akademiai Kiado, Budapest, 1971.

Hammersley, J. M., and Handscomb, D. C.: *Monte Carlo Methods*. Methuen & Co., London, 1964.

Karafin, B.: *The General Component Tolerance Assignment Problem in Electrical Networks*. Ph. D. Thesis, Univ. of Pennsylvania, 1974.

Meyer, H. A. (editor): *Symposium on Monte Carlo Methods.* J. Wiley & Sons, New York, 1956.

Tahim, K. S., and Spence, R.: A radial exploration approach to manufacturing yield estimation and design centering. *IEEE Transactions on Circuits and Systems*, Vol. CAS-26, pp. 768–774, September 1979.

For tolerance design see the special issue of *Bell System Technical Journal* April 1971 and *IEEE Proceedings, Part G, Electronic Circuits and Systems*, August 1982.

Index